A Publication of the SSRC Cambridge Group
for the History of Population and Social Structure

Family forms in historic Europe

Family forms in historic Europe

Edited by

RICHARD WALL

in collaboration with

JEAN ROBIN

and

PETER LASLETT

of the SSRC Cambridge Group for the

History of Population and Social Structure

CAMBRIDGE UNIVERSITY PRESS

Cambridge

New York   London   New Rochelle

Melbourne   Sydney

Published by the Press Syndicate of the University of Cambridge
The Pitt Building, Trumpington Street, Cambridge CB2 1RP
32 East 57th Street, New York, NY 10022, USA
296 Beaconsfield Parade, Middle Park, Melbourne 3206, Australia

First published 1983

Printed in Great Britain at the
University Press, Cambridge

Library of Congress catalogue card number: 82-4376

British Library cataloguing in publication data
Wall, Richard
Family forms in historic Europe.
1. Europe – Population – History
I. Title   II. Laslett, Peter   III. Robin, Jean
304.6'094   HB3581
ISBN 0 521 24547 8

WV

Contents

Contributors

Andorka, Rudolf *Sociologist, Central Statistical Office, Budapest, Hungary*

Czap, Peter, Jr *Professor of History, Amherst College, Amherst, Mass., U.S.A.*

Danhieux, Luc *Archivist, Rijksarchief, Bruges, Belgium*

Faragó, Tamás *Historian, Library of the Central Statistical Office, Budapest, Hungary*

Fauve-Chamoux, Antoinette *Maître-assistant in the Ecole des Hauts Etudes en Sciences Sociales, Paris, France*

Gaunt, David *Lecturer in History, Department of History, University of Umeå, Sweden*

Hajnal, J. *Professor of Statistics, London School of Economics, University of London, England*

Hammer, Carl I., Jr *Consultant, Corporate Planning, Westinghouse Electric Corporation, Pittsburgh, Pa., U.S.A.*

Kochanowicz, Jacek *Assistant Professor in Economic History, Faculty of Economics, University of Warsaw, Poland*

Laslett, Peter *Reader in Politics and History of Social Structure, and Fellow of Trinity College, University of Cambridge, England*

Mitterauer, Michael *Professor, Institut für Wirtschafts- und Sozialgeschichte, University of Vienna, Austria*

Palli, H. *Senior Research Fellow in the Institute of History, Estonian Academy of Science, Tallinn, Estonia, U.S.S.R.*

Plakans, Andrejs *Professor of History, Iowa State University, Ames, Iowa. U.S.A.*

Robin, Jean *Research Assistant, SSRC Cambridge Group for the History of Population and Social Structure, and Fellow of Lucy Cavendish College, Cambridge, England*

Schmidtbauer, P. *Research Assistant, Institut für Wirtschafts- und Sozialgeschichte, University of Vienna, Austria*

Sieder, Reinhard *Research Assistant, Institut für Wirtschafts- und Sozialgeschichte, University of Vienna, Austria*

Wall, Richard *Senior Research Officer, SSRC Cambridge Group for the History of Population and Social Structure, Cambridge, England*

Preface

The discipline of family history has grown so rapidly in recent years that inevitably it has come to suffer from a certain lack of comparability and methodology. The earliest studies in the present generation of writing were on the grand scale, outlines of family systems applying to half or more of the European continent. Later the thematic approach, descriptions of families within economic, cultural, or legal systems, and the local study came to be favoured. Family history lends itself particularly well to the latter, since it is easier at this level to set out the social, economic, and cultural influences on family patterns. Nevertheless, other approaches retain their validity, not only to guard us against the atypical case study but to focus attention on key concepts such as the family as work group, concepts which are all too easily lost sight of when sifting through the detail of a particular community study.

The individual contributions to the present volume reflect this division in the literature, some being particular, some general or thematic; indeed, they have been selected to illustrate both the range of approach to, and the variations in, European social structure of past times. Inevitably, a work of this sort could not go forward without a great deal of collaboration among the various contributors, and I am grateful to them and to others for responding so fully to points that have been raised during the editorial process. Our debts in this direction are acknowledged at the appropriate place in each chapter. The major burden, however, has been borne by the staff of the SSRC Cambridge Group, past and present, and here I would like to record my appreciation of the editorial and secretarial assistance of Karla Oosterveen, Doreen Togher, Les Pepper, and Amanda Tanner and the advice of my fellow editors, Peter Laslett and Jean Robin. On Karla Oosterveen initially and then on Jean Robin have fallen some of the most burdensome tasks of reference checking and table standardization.

SSRC Cambridge Group   RICHARD WALL
June 1982

1

Introduction

RICHARD WALL

Our initial approach to the subject of the household and family took its cue from prevailing expectations about the shape of the family in the past. It was almost inevitable that the discussion should focus on whether families were larger or smaller then than now, and in particular whether households were more or less likely to contain relatives beyond the immediate nuclear core of head, spouse, and unmarried child. Even so, *Household and family in past time*, when published in 1972,[1] contained within it a great deal more than a simple statement about the predominance of the nuclear family in pre-industrial society, although the information on children, servants, and marital status is often by-passed by those eager to denounce, or defend, its major theme.

In the present volume it is our intention to look in more detail at all the constituent parts of the household and to place the household within the broad economic and social context. There is much more attention paid than was possible in 1972 to the life cycle of the household and to the influence of occupation on its structure. The questions that we have set ourselves include the following: What structure of the household is implied by a given inheritance pattern or work pattern? If we know the occupation or age of the head of the household, how much can legitimately be inferred about the overall composition of the household? In fact, as the study of Bruges in 1814 shows (see chapter 14 below), the occupation of the household head was a good guide to the number of servants and relatives within, and even inmates attached to, the household. The age of the household head, however, was a less successful predictor of household composition, and neither age nor occupation matched the influence exerted by the sex of the head.

Elsewhere in the volume the emphasis is on regional variations in

---

[1] P. Laslett and Wall (eds.), *Household and family* (1972).

1

household structure, in Austria or England for example. Urban–rural differences also come in for particular attention. All this tends to blur the distinction between western Europe and the 'rest', so clearly drawn by Peter Laslett in 1977.[2] We will have to consider below whether there is any useful sense in which even the Flemish farmers and labourers can be said to share common characteristics with their counterparts across the North Sea. Antoinette Fauve-Chamoux in her study of early-nineteenth-century Rheims in chapter 15 raises the issue as to whether there may not have been a distinctly urban familial form, in which the characteristic, if not the numerically dominant, element was the broken or denuded family and the solitary individual rather than the conjugal family.

Nevertheless, it is still possible to identify major differences between the household systems of eastern and western Europe, systems which it has long been suspected lie at opposite ends of the spectrum. John Hajnal in chapter 2 picks out nuclear-family households and life-cycle servants (young men and women who lived in the households of their masters) as characteristic features of western households and contrasts these with the multifamily households and the absence of life-cycle servants in the east, moving indeed well outside the frontiers of Europe to make clear the unique nature of north-west Europe. In the last section of this introduction we will set out some further characteristics that might be added to Hajnal's list. We need to do more than that, however, for it is not enough to establish the differences between east and west. We must try to explain them. Inevitably we have to face the question of why the households of enserfed Russia were so complex. Was it due to the power of the landlord? Or the reaction of the peasant family to the demands made on it? Or indeed some older custom of communal living that conditioned both the demands of the landlord and the response of the peasant?

A particularly fruitful approach to such questions is through detailed case studies of individual communities, in which the shape of the household can be explored in relation to well-documented estate management practice. This is the line taken by Peter Czap in his study of the divisions of serf households on the Mishino estate on the fringe of the Black Earth region of Russia (see chapter 3), by Jacek Kochanowicz in documenting the use of labour on farms in Poland (chapter 4), and by Andrejs Plakans in describing serfs of the Baltic provinces (chapter 5). All these contributions give prominence to the ability of the landlord to

---

[2] P. Laslett, *Family life and illicit love* (1977a): ch. 1.

regulate the flow of people into and out of households. Yet all equally suggest that there was some peasant autonomy, some meeting of interests between peasant and lord – and equally there can be no doubt that the household systems are far from being identical. There are parallels to be found in Carl Hammer's account of the management of the estates of Abbot Sigifrid at Lauterbach in Bavaria (chapter 7), although the lists he uses were drawn up a millennium earlier than those used for Russia and Poland.

Where peasants could pass land freely to their descendants or could move freely from one rented farm to another, the relationship between land and the household may be expected to have been different but, it has been thought, no less strong. As an example of such a western-type community, we have selected a number of villages in West Flanders (chapter 12) and shown that in this instance the ownership of property had little impact on the shape of the household, despite a close link between owning property and age at marriage or incidence of marriage. In the west, it would appear, the shape of the household was much more a matter of personal attributes in that it was the occupation and sex of the household head that played the role that land took in the east.

An inherent drawback to the presentation of detailed case studies is that it is impossible in the available space to provide evidence of their typicality. This is as true of the West Flanders study as of the others. It remains an open question whether we would have found a different pattern in another group of Flemish villages, or, alternatively, the same pattern in a Walloon community where different inheritance customs would lead us to expect other relationships between land ownership and the family and the household.

The constraint of space has also led us deliberately to focus on the major differences between the household patterns of eastern and western Europe. Consequently, a number of interesting areas within 'historic Europe' have had to be omitted or referred to only in passing: Ireland, Prussia, and the Rhineland for example, and Mediterranean Europe. In time it is hoped that other studies will be forthcoming, using the methodology pioneered here, to fill these gaps and check upon the typicality of the results presented in this volume.

Another drawback inherent in the case-study approach is that it is very easy to lose oneself in a morass of detail and small numbers when comparing one study with another. This is never more so than when trying to treat the household as a dynamic and not a static unit. Nor have the critics of the static view yet been able to devise a satisfactory methodology,[3] usually being content to analyse household structure in relation to the age of the household head in the hope that the experience of any one age group at one point in time will represent the experience of all other age groups either earlier or later. In other words, it is assumed that each cohort will experience similar household patterns. Two contributors to the present volume side-step this problem by monitoring the same household from census to census but come up with two distinct methodologies. In chapter 10, Reinhard Sieder and Michael Mitterauer take the individual farm or property as the base unit and trace the comings and goings and succession strategies over periods as long, sometimes, as fifty years. Then in a more modest study, Luc Danhieux, using four censuses, follows households, the sequence breaking when a new owner or tenant arrives who is unrelated to the previous possessor (see chapter 13).

This difference in methodology hides a more fundamental disagreement as to whether the household is the right unit of analysis for understanding how society works, or whether the focus should be on property, considered as fixed family capital, and how people use it and pass it on to their descendants. The latter is an approach that has worked well with Austrian data before the mid-nineteenth century, but it is not easy to adapt it to circumstances in which property is sold to strangers, divided, converted into moveables, and dissipated. On the other hand, the alternative 'household focus' soon runs into trouble, for a household, like a property, has a certain 'life', and a rather short one at that. When is the life of a household to be said to begin and to end? If one begins with the marriage of a young couple and ends with the death or remarriage of the surviving partner, one immediately creates the conjugal family as the linchpin of the entire group. This may be satisfactory for north-west Europe alone, and perhaps not universally even there. Clearly, the methodology of analysing change over time deserves some of the attention that has been lavished on the household as a static unit.

In addition to the chapters of case studies, we have included in the present volume some more thematic essays. Peter Laslett, for example, examines the notion of the household as a work group and finds it wanting (chapter 17). David Gaunt looks at attitudes towards the elderly enshrined in law and custom (chapter 8). This takes us well beyond the household as a unit of study, and it is important that we should make this move. The household is not the whole family system.[4] The

---

[3] One notable exception is the study by van de Walle of the Belgian community of La Hulpe: 'Household dynamics in a Belgian village' (1976).

[4] Yet we have sometimes been accused of believing they are equivalents despite protestations to the contrary in P. Laslett and Wall (eds.) (1972): 1.

next two sections of this introduction will therefore be devoted to this theme. First, we will take a basic building block of society, the household, and assess its function as a consumption unit and how this relates to other entities such as 'family', 'work', and peer groups with which it may have competing and differing loyalties; and housing, which provides a framework and perhaps an identity for its actions. By the term 'consumption unit' is meant the provisioning of a fund on which all members of the household may draw. It is recognized, nevertheless, that freedom of individuals to do this may in practice be limited, either by custom which gives greater power to the household head or to the husband;[5] or by contract, servants, for example, being paid a stipulated amount for their work. Second, we will examine the various support channels that link family to family, particularly those which connect parents to their married children. We aim to see to what extent families supported themselves from their own resources and how far the nuclear-family household (or for that matter the extended-family or multiple-family household) succeeded in being truly independent. For this purpose we have chosen to use the family budgets collected by the great nineteenth-century theorist of the family, Frederick Le Play. Le Play's ideas are often cited, and more often misunderstood, but his detailed investigations into the family histories and living conditions of European workers seem rarely to be read. Nor, to the best of our knowledge, has any such series of histories been subject to systematic analysis as opposed to the selection of the chance quotation to support a particular and often predetermined point of view. The simple scheme of analysis that we propose for showing ties between an individual family and its relatives, its employers, and others will, we hope, be picked up and used with other biographies.

In the third section of the introduction we return to the question of household structure and the problem of its measurement. One of the great successes of *Household and family in past time* could be said to be the table on households by kin composition. It is the table most often replicated even by those who maintain a formal antipathy to household studies *per se*. Unfortunately, all too often it is left as the only comment on the household and therefore, quite rightly, has run into criticism for

[5] Although de Maroussem, following in the footsteps of Le Play, cites an instance where in practice the power to direct the affairs of a complex household community lay with one of the women. See his account of sharecroppers in Charente, *Ouvriers des deux mondes*, 2nd ser., 3 (1892). In other cases power was divided, a master directing the work of the men and a mistress the work of the women, as in the study of the Nivernais farmers by de Cheverry in *Ouvriers des deux mondes*, 1st ser., 5 (1885).

providing an undue emphasis on the kin component in the household.[6] Accordingly we have proposed below (see p. 41) to count the number of adults per household. This, we argue, will be a more satisfactory summary measure of household composition in that it provides a more accurate reflection on the function of the household as an economic unit.

Nevertheless, we reserve our position on two counts. First, no summary measure on its own can provide an adequate picture of the household: in other words, the household needs to be looked at in all its various aspects.[7] Second, the kin component of the household is interesting in its own right, even when it forms as small a proportion of the household as it did in pre-industrial England. Given the financial and moral support channelled through kin,[8] it is important to see precisely who amongst a group of relatives was received into the individual's household, and under what circumstances. The final section of the introduction will therefore be devoted to kin, beginning with an assessment of the extent to which east–west differences in the frequency of taking kin into the household reported on elsewhere in this volume are still reflected in the latest round of census statistics (broadly *c.* 1970). We then move on to consider whether, when the kin component of the household is small, as in north-west Europe both present and past, this necessarily implies other common features and, finally, to reflect more generally on the nature of the differences in the household systems of eastern and western Europe and their underlying causes.

I. Family, household, and society

Whereas the word 'family' can take on a number of different meanings (either limited to the people to whom one is related and with whom one lives, or expanded to cover parents, offspring, even all acknowledged

---

[6] Persuasively argued by Mitterauer, 'Familiengrösse – Familientypen – Familienzyklus' (1975a). The original title of our table 'Structures of households' (P. Laslett and Wall (eds.) (1972): 31) is perhaps at fault, and we have amended it to read 'Households by kin composition' in the revised and extended series of household analysis tables to which further reference is made below (see p. 36).

[7] For example, the single summary measure of the number of adults per household, proposed above, will be affected by the social context: in England, lodgers and inmates would be excluded, while in Hungary all who contributed to or drew from a common budget would be considered household members, whether lodgers or not.

[8] There are many studies of such support, some at the individual level, e.g. Macfarlane, *The family life of Ralph Josselin* (1970); others at the community level, e.g. R. M. Smith, 'Kin and neighbours' (1979b) and Levine and Wrightson, *Poverty and piety in an English village* (1979): ch. 4, and cf. below, sect. II. 'Kin' is used loosely in this introduction as a synonym for relatives of the household head other than spouse or offspring.

kin and affines), the household represents something very specific: the co-resident domestic group. It marks out the living space of a group of people that is private to them in that other people may not enter it without their permission. Much more tangible than the family, it was inevitable that the household should become the focus of attention in the reconstruction of family systems of past times, because the intangibles, the bonds between people who did not live with each other and who were not tied to the rest of the community or to some superior power, went largely unrecorded.

In narrowing the focus to fall on the household, it might appear that the door has been arbitrarily closed on the network of relationships that exist beyond it linking it to its neighbours. This is not the case, however, for the decision to study the household involves assumptions about its value as a unit of analysis. In attributing a variety of functions to the household we are in effect saying that they are not being carried out elsewhere. It follows that the household cannot be understood in isolation from the rest of the society of which it formed a part.

Assumptions about the household may either be explicit or implicit. In *Household and family in past time* the household was defined in terms of residence (sleeping together) and in terms of consumption (at least one main meal together). It was implicitly assumed that in order to eat together, all working members of the household would pool their income, except for the servants who shared the household in the residential sense but had no 'right' to its communal income. On the base of common participation, further ties are likely to arise: loyalties of household members to each other and to a recognized head, the feeling for the privacy of the household, and the process of socialization under which those reared in a household will reproduce a similar household in their own adulthood when circumstances permit. In a specific context, temporal or spatial, the household may also function as a unit of production and afford shelter to those members of the community unable to subsist on their own resources. In so far as there is a conventional picture of the development of the household over time, personal relationships among household members are deemed to be strengthened by the very process which has brought the household to shed its broader functions of shelter and production.[9] In practice, though, it is impossible, except in very rare instances, to say that a particular house-

[9] By way of example see B. Laslett, 'Family membership past and present' (1978): 486. Barbara Laslett agrees that the modern household provides shelter but argues that it differs from the form of shelter under discussion here. The former is shelter in the form of a retreat by each individual into his own home rather than the extension of the household to take care of the elderly and the orphaned.

hold had any, let alone all, of these characteristics detailed above. Admittedly, in the censuses, and before that in the unofficial listings of inhabitants, there appear blocks of names that look like households. The better listings and censuses refer to the sorts of people we would expect to find in households: parents, children, relatives, a few non-relatives (not identified as inmates), and servants. But in exactly what sense were these groups of people households?

Even in the present day it is possible to produce examples of living arrangements where it is difficult to sustain the concept of the household. The current practice of the takers of the British census is to rely on the consumption of one main meal in common, which leads to any group of people who share a living room but eat serially rather than communally, or take their meals outside of the house, being classed as so many separate households rather than as one. In this particular case, the idea of the household as a consumption unit and as a living unit, representing an arena for interpersonal contact, are pulling in different directions. Nor would such a group of persons necessarily recognize one of their number as constituting a distinct household head.

For the most part, such problems can be considered minor in the late twentieth century, relevant to such a small section of society that it scarcely disturbs the number of households by size and type whatever decision is adopted. It is quite a different matter in nineteenth-century England, when, particularly in towns, a multiplicity of subletting created a world of boarders and lodgers, some virtually independent, some not so independent, of the principal household. Using a definition of household close to that of the present day, the census authorities of the time were clearly desirous of classifying all lodgers as separate households, but would appear to have met considerable resistance from the enumerators and perhaps from householders (responsible from 1841 for filling in their own schedules), who tended to incorporate lodgers into their own households. While their interest in the family lasted, the census authorities attempted various adjustments to the published figures to allow for these 'mistakes'.[10]

If we take as a working definition of a household one that would have been acceptable to the residents of those households, then we are led inexorably away from a definition of the household on the basis of common consumption towards a definition that is based on the occupa-

[10] *Census of Great Britain 1851*, Appendix to Report, table 13: c–ci; *Census of Great Britain 1861*, Appendix to Report, tables 34–7; 94–5. I have written in greater detail about definitions of the household in British censuses in Wall, 'Regional and temporal variation in the structure of the British household since 1851' (1982a).

tion of distinct living space over which the household had independent, day-to-day control. Lodgers in England, whether or not they were catered for separately, did not hold the same control over their living space as did households. Therefore they were not households, and our usual approach is to treat lodgers as attached to, though not full members of, their 'landlord's' household.

But this does not mean that a change on these lines would be universally applicable. Hajnal, for example, in chapter 2 argues for a consistent definition of a household as a consumption unit. A similar approach is taken by Andorka and Faragó in chapter 9, who claim that in Hungary both the census officials and the villagers agreed that those who shared their meals in common constituted a single *'familia'*, even if they lived separately. The common budget therefore becomes their preferred definition for a household. Cotters would be excluded from, and servants included in, the households, in conformity with how the feudal system is believed to have operated. But when evidence is lacking they have to make the working assumption that any non-relative (including any non-related servant) of the household head who had a family of his own (spouse or children) constituted a separate 'household', but that a non-relative without a family did not. In either case it is likely that both sorts of non-relative contributed to some of the production and shared some of the resources of the principal household.

The definition of a household, therefore, varies from place to place just as its structure does (see p. 21). As the definition adopted affects the structure we observe, this makes the analysis of the structure of the household a very difficult matter indeed. The comparative analysis of the household gives rise to greater problems than comparative demography, because there is more room for argument than over what constitutes a birth, a death, or even a marriage.

In certain contexts, units which seem unambiguously households might suffer from some of the limitations on their independence that one would associate with the lodging groups discussed above. The classic case is where several households occupied a tenement building in which there was a resident concierge.[11] The concierge represented the interests of the landlord, collected the rents, and let the rooms and, through the exercise of this power, came to control not only the public section of the building, such as the stairs, but some of the activities of the individual household members. Particularly when the tenants were working class, the concierge might be found refusing entry or depar-

[11] The following account relies heavily on the description of the Paris carpenter by Le Play and Focillon in *Ouvriers des deux mondes*, 1st ser., 1 (1857): 67.

tures after a certain hour, turning visitors out before midnight, and suppressing the noise of the children. However, there was no doubt in the mind of contemporary observers that these groups constituted households.

In yet other instances, the concept of the household as we have outlined it might seem altogether inappropriate. The study by Fél and Hofer of the village of Átány on the Hungarian Great Plain has become well known and is worth looking at again.[12] In this one village the family took on a variety of forms in which a house, housekeeping, or work might alternatively be communal or divided between father and son or brother and brother, giving rise to the following combinations as set out in table 1.1.

The impression of variety, however, is in an important sense illusory. The peasants, asked for their opinion on the type of living arrangements, distinguished only between those cases where the sons had scattered, moving out of the paternal farm altogether, and those where they had remained. Information on precise living arrangements and the degree of division could be, and was, obtained by Fél and Hofer but did not impinge on the consciousness of the inhabitants. In this case, the concept of the household was irrelevant not because the household could take on a variety of forms, but because the peasants defined their families in a way that played down the importance of co-residence.

The division of work and property between father and son is only one of the lines of demarcation running through Átány society. The farm buildings were usually situated at some little distance from the houses, and the men often slept on the farm. As the details on the individual families show, neither the nature of the work nor the distance involved necessarily prevented the men from living at home. Therefore, one has to consider the work patterns as a result of a preference by the community, or at least the male section of it, for this type of arrangement. The segregation of the domestic group paralleled that which the community displayed in public through the seating arrangements in church. But it would be an error to try and see the group of males around the *kert* (farmyard) as a rival to the 'house'. It is true that the *kert* was the living place of the men and the centre of economic activity, but the house alone was the place for family celebrations and social gatherings. The mistake is to try and interpret loyalty in purely economic terms. If we do this, then the groups fragment, showing a variety of loyalties to farm and house, differing according to the age and sex of the individual,

[12] Fél and Hofer, *Proper peasants* (1969): 80, 92, 103. See also Andorka and Faragó, ch. 9 below, for further references to this study.

Table 1.1. *House, household, and work group in Átány, Hungary, in 1960*

Family type[a]	House-keeping, communal	House, communal	Farm work, communal	House-keeping, separate	House, separate	Farm work, separate
1	X	X	X			
2		X	X	X		
3			X	X	X	
4		X		X		X[b]
5				X	X	X[b]
6				X	X	X

[a] Categories reflecting whether housekeeping, house, and farm work were communal or separate.
[b] In these cases there was individual ownership of the livestock, but the farm work was undertaken collectively.
Source: Fél and Hofer (1969): 111.

whereas in reality the overriding loyalty of the inhabitants, male as well as female, was to 'home' as a social institution.

This is not to deny the existence of other loyalties, to work groups or individual consumption units, but to point out their subsidiary nature. Let us take a different example, the peasant family of Lavedan in Hautes-Pyrénées as described by Le Play in 1857.[13] This classic *famille souche*, as Le Play saw it, contained within it a number of sub-elements. In particular, two individuals, well into middle age at the time of Le Play's inquiry, had been granted the right to graze their own sheep with the common herd and keep the profit for their own purposes, in return for ceding their legal rights to a share in the inheritance. Such profits could be considerable; for those who wished to marry they could buy dowries, or trousseaux. On the other hand, all such activities, although important to the individual, were subordinate to the main enterprise of running the peasant family farm, and it is not clear how great a subsidiary importance should be attached to them. Perhaps even those concerned might not have been able to agree about this. In the Átány study, it was noted that if the men had their work groups (in this case based on the extended family's communal farm), married women's loyalties were to their immediate nuclear families, nor could any property they might hold be integrated into the family property. A woman struggling to secure the maximum resources for her daughter's trousseau ultimately succeeded in a permanent division of the 'house community'.

Some scholars have been prepared to argue that the household need

[13] *Ouvriers des deux mondes*, 1st ser., 1 (1857): 152.

not be a residential group. For example, the mere fact of an aged parent's existence has been considered sufficient to keep alive the claims of his 'household', regardless of where or how he was living. The argument here is that he was physically, but not socially, alone because of the general recognition that he had both financial and moral claims on others, claims that might, if necessity arose, result in the reconstruction of his household.[14] However, we would suggest that to argue in this way is to confuse the household with the bonds that exist between all households, which are stronger in some cases than in others. Le Play and the followers of his method never went so far. They included some non-residents in the household who returned their earnings to a common fund or who were, exceptionally, maintained at the charge of their families. However, the old parents in their own house supported by the contributions of their daughters and sons-in-law, and the son, aided by his father and with his own establishment within his father's home, are firmly treated as separate households.[15] To our mind the inclusion in the household of any non-residents is likely to give rise to problems with the concept of 'household', which implies at least a certain measure of co-residence as well as dependence on a common budget.

This sort of issue is relevant to a number of contributions to the present volume. For example, do parents who retire to the *Altenteil* (the old persons' part) in certain regions of Austria remain within the household of the heir? And is it the same if, on the other hand, the *Altenteil* is occupied by persons who are unrelated to the present owner of the farm? Sieder and Mitterauer argue forcefully in chapter 10 that both types of person deserve to be seen as equal members of the farm community from which they derive their means of subsistence. The question of whether they lived separately or not (some took their meals in common and others did not) is for them irrelevant.

Let us consider this line of reasoning in the light of English experience, using, in the best tradition of Le Play, one particular example. A farmer retires and hands his farm to his son, receiving an annuity in exchange. He then moves to another settlement. How different is this situation from the Austrian one described above? The answer is: hardly at all except that the place of residence is not the farmstead of the heir but in another community altogether. It follows, therefore, that if the

[14] J. Davis, *People of the Mediterranean* (1977): 174–5, citing Lineton on depopulation in southern Greece.
[15] *Ouvriers des deux mondes*, 1st ser., 2 (1858), makers of steel tools in Doubs; 1st ser., 1 (1857), Paris quarrymen; 1st ser., 4 (1862), vine-grower in Lower Bourgogne; Le Play, *Les ouvriers européens*, 2nd edn (1877–9): vol. II, peasants, stevedores, and boatbuilders on the *abrok* system, Oka, Central Russia.

focus is on the number of persons dependent on a particular economic enterprise, then it is logical to include both retired farmers within the larger group. On the other hand, if the attempt is made to identify the household, the group of people who live together, who have a common budget (as opposed to money set aside for their needs), it is not clear whether the retired farmer in Austria, like his English counterpart, has his own household. The Austrian retirement system, the *Altenteil*, represents a perception by the contemporary community of a certain degree of separateness of interests. Other evidence pointing strongly in this direction is the taking of meals separately, and in certain areas the use of quite separate buildings. It would seem, however, that none of these arrangements amount to the 'separateness' accorded to the household on the English model.

It is not an easy matter, therefore, to categorize households and families, even when the community under investigation can be visited. The boundaries of household and family are so fluid that it becomes difficult to ascribe distinct functions to them, and these problems multiply if we start to talk of regional or national family patterns rather than this or that individual household or village. Nevertheless, from the mass of details, the essential elements of different family systems can be identified. Any society has to find solutions for a number of basic problems, such as the mechanism for transferring wealth between generations, how to care for the elderly and the infirm, and the degree of independence that can be allowed to the individual family or household. If the problems are the same, the solutions, however, are not. Some of these we will now consider.

II. Connections among households

The English model is one in which the majority of married couples are required to establish their own households at the time of their marriage. Yet there is no reason to think that English parents are any less eager than other parents to leave their wealth to their offspring rather than to strangers, or that their progeny are more reluctant than others to accept this largesse. To see how this could work out in a specific context let us take the village of Elmdon in Essex, recently studied by Jean Robin.[16] The older generation at first sight had little to leave the younger. After all, most of the inhabitants did not own the property in which they lived, and their right to reside there was often conditional on their working for

[16] Robin, *Elmdon* (1980): esp. 68, 128, 175–6, 186–7.

the principal landowner or his tenant farmers. Nevertheless, certain families were able to establish at least one descendant in the village over several generations. The 'inheritance', always subject to the discretion of the landlord, may have been no more than the opportunity to work and live in the same village as the previous generation, but its importance should not be underestimated merely because it did not come in the form of family property. In accordance with the principle that married offspring should, wherever possible, have their own households, the continuance of the family line in the same village was achieved without making necessary the formation of multiple-family households containing married couples from successive generations. For this there were two main reasons. First, for those with strong village associations, there were a number of employment opportunities even in a society as small as Elmdon's (population 520 in 1861). The heir waiting to succeed to the tenant farm might run a shop; a blacksmith's son, a public house; and so on. Second, those for whom there was no economic niche in the village could look for opportunities in neighbouring villages or further afield. This migration often turned out to be permanent for those individuals, although their descendants might return to Elmdon.

Successive generations could readily be financially independent in a diversified economy. This seems likely in nineteenth-century England,[17] but what then of the situation in other societies or indeed in England in former times? In fact Elmdoners had actually lost one of the mechanisms that had helped to make this possible. Young and unmarried Elmdon men were no longer accepted into farmers' households as resident farm servants. In former centuries this had both given them the opportunity to accumulate savings for their marriage and own household and relieved the parents of the burden of their keep. Only the many Elmdon women moving away to domestic service continued to make savings in this way. Service on its own, however, is not a sufficient guarantee of independence on marriage, as savings are often absorbed by the process of establishing a new household. We have, therefore, to look both for the existence of opportunities in service before marriage and some prospect of independent employment after marriage. Our own starting point will be the case of England between the sixteenth and nineteenth centuries.

[17] Even so, there are exceptions where rents were high, savings had not been accumulated, and it was necessary for married women to take on full-time work outside the home. All these conditions were met in the English textile town of Preston, Lancs. in the middle of the nineteenth century. See Anderson, *Family structure in nineteenth century Lancashire* (1971).

The presence of large numbers of servants in pre-industrial English society was first noted by Peter Laslett over a decade ago.[18] The majority of servants were young (between the ages of 15 and 29), and there was no doubt that they would in due course be founding households of their own. At about the same time the first reconstitution study, based on the parish registers of the Devon parish of Colyton, established that marriage for both sexes ordinarily took place in the middle to late 20s.[19] These results have since been confirmed for more than a dozen other reconstitutions selected to represent the widest possible variety of economies.[20] Delayed marriage gave individuals up to a decade of working life as unmarried adults, during which savings could be accumulated for eventual marriage. More important still, the postponement of marriage by women curtailed the period of fecundity spent in marriage, making it more likely that the new household could support from its own resources the number of children which the couple were likely to have. The link between marriage and economic independence is suggested also by the fact that between the sixteenth and early nineteenth centuries the marriage rate in England paralleled, with a 30-year lag, the trend in the level of real wages.[21]

Prior to the sixteenth century, although there are no lists of inhabitants or parish registers to function as guides, the situation in essentials would appear to be the same. The proportions of married men amongst the poll-tax payers in 1377 are so low as to be incompatible with a mean age at first marriage for men of below 25 years.[22] The position in regard to women is less clear because of the underenumeration of unmarried females in the taxation returns, but, having taken this fact into consideration, it seems more likely that the mean age at marriage lay in the middle to late 20s than in the late teens. There are also many references in English medieval sources to the presence of servants. The poll-tax return for Rutland in 1381 reveals that 20% of households contained servants, which is equivalent to the level established for the sixteenth, seventeenth, and eighteenth centuries.[23] Further, without claiming that the medieval economy of England was as diverse as it was to be in the seventeenth century, it is clear that there were opportunities of non-agricultural employment and of hired labour which gave individuals a

---

[18] P. Laslett, 'Size and structure of the household in England over three centuries' (1969): 219.
[19] Wrigley, 'Family limitation in pre-industrial England' (1966).
[20] R. M. Smith, 'Population and its geography in England 1500–1730' (1978).
[21] Wrigley and Schofield, *The population history of England 1541–1871* (1981): fig. 10.9.
[22] R. M. Smith, 'Origins of the "European marriage pattern" in England' (1979a): 83.
[23] *Ibid.* 100.

possibility of forming households without having first obtained access to land.[24]

In respect of both age at marriage for women and economic opportunities, English society, even in the Middle Ages, presents a sharp contrast with much of eastern and southern Europe. Family reconstitution studies of parishes in the south of France, Spain, Tuscany, Sicily, and Malta indicate marriage ages for women in the range 18–20 years.[25] It is also clear that nearly all women married, whereas in England a sizeable, though variable, proportion remained permanently celibate. Marriage in southern and eastern Europe, moreover, was for many unconnected with the need to establish an independent household. By the age of 25, 50% of men in fifteenth-century rural Tuscany had married. Only 17% of them, however, had become heads of households.[26] The fact that the majority were still dependants of others (principally their fathers) can be clearly linked with the absence of a developed labour market which would enable them to hire their services to other farmers. In practice, almost all the labour was provided by members of the farmers' own families. It follows that the age and incidence of marriage are unlikely to have been linked with movements in the real wage, and there is some evidence from Tuscany that such linkage did not occur.[27]

For Russian serfs this sort of pattern took an extreme form, because of the burdens imposed on the peasant family from above, together with the limitations on individual mobility. This is clear from Peter Czap's account for the population of the Mishino estates in the early nineteenth century (chapter 3, below). On these estates, men as well as women married early, complex households contained not only married sons of the head but also married grandsons, and very few of the serfs moved off the estate. But wherever one finds signs of a diversified social structure, then the pattern begins to break down.

It can be shown that when people marry at a later age, there are fewer complex households and more households containing only parents and their unmarried children. This was the situation not just in England but in much of north-west Europe. In northern France and the rural communities of West Flanders that I have studied (chapter 12) marriage was late, many remained permanently celibate, and there was a considerable movement out of the parental household prior to marriage by persons of both sexes taking up employment as servants in other

[24] *Ibid.* 102.
[25] R. M. Smith, 'The people of Tuscany and their families' (1981a): 111.
[26] *Ibid.* 120.
[27] *Ibid.* 113–14.

households.[28] In a number of these communities, the standard of living of the cottagers and day labourers was without doubt appreciably lower than that of the English labourer. Nevertheless, even the poorest were able to make the necessary savings to establish independent households on marriage. This point is made expressly by J. Arrivabene in a report on the conditions of the labouring population in the commune of Gaesbeck in Brabant in the year 1830.[29] The creation of new families was financed by the use of savings accumulated by both marriage partners while in service with the farmers. Nor had they to wait for the inheritance or sale of any parental property, for houses could be let, or even be newly built, on land bought or rented with part of their savings.

Younger married couples and their means of support

We must be careful, however, not to create the impression that even in north-west Europe new households were formed and maintained solely on the proceeds of savings and earnings, or that these were without importance in eastern Europe or Russia. There are a variety of forms of dependency on parents, of which co-residence with the parental generation is only one. Nor were parents by any means the only external source of support on which a household might call. At first sight it might seem a hopeless task to try and reconstruct those channels of support, and it is fortunate that, particularly in the nineteenth century, a number of social investigators put on record the detailed budgets of individual families.

Those budgets that we have chosen to use were collected by Le Play and his collaborators in connection with their own pursuit of European family types. Whatever else might be held against Le Play, he was certainly thorough. The detail recorded on individual families is impressive, and a real attempt seems to have been made to select families from a number of diverse situations. The reports following the Le Play model have the advantage of combining an albeit brief history of the family with a detailed budget, designed to establish what proportion of the family's resources came from its own property and what proportion was received for work performed on its own account or for others. The disadvantages of the reports are the well-known ones, noted by Le Play himself, namely the difficulty of establishing what is really representative of the community in question when only one family is to be selected; and the further difficulty of ensuring that the co-operation of

---

[28] For northern France see Dupâquier, *La population rurale du bassin parisien* (1979): 211, 299–301, 307.

[29] Arrivabene, *Sur la condition des laboureurs et des ouvriers belges* (1843): 55–6.

the family could be obtained.[30] In some cases the family put on a public image for the investigator, appearing more respectable, more purposeful, and certainly more ambitious for the future than was probably the case. In other instances the whole report is coloured by the view of the investigator himself that this was a 'good' or 'bad' family. It is interesting that although the name of Le Play is associated with approval of the stem-family household, a number of other family forms where the level of kin support was high are classified as 'bad' in his studies and those of his colleagues.

If used with care, however, Le Play's material can show how important to the married child was the support of parents and others. It indicates a much greater range of variation than is apparent from a study limited to the number and type of persons resident in households. In part this is simply the result of shifting the focus from the community to the individual family. There would be few scholars nowadays who would be prepared to follow Le Play in seeing the whole of the society reflected in the behaviour of the chosen family. Rather, it would be argued that it is necessary to know where these families lived, their class positions, and their positions in relation to their kin, precisely because it is essential to guard against overgeneralizing about societies. This is not to deny, of course, that there are hints in the behaviour of individual families of the working of the society of which they form a part.

Le Play and the stem family

There are many misconceptions of Le Play's notions of the stem family which a study of the family biographies helps to dispel. Le Play's own classificatory system (table 1.2) is a mixture of the family systems with which his name is associated ('patriarchal' and 'stem') and the geographical.[31] Despite a rigorous definition of what constituted a household, he defined his family systems in a way which took little account of residence patterns.[32] His 'patriarchal' or 'stem' systems often

[30] See the introduction to *Ouvriers des deux mondes*, 1st ser., 4 (1862): 17–18, repeating *Les ouvriers européens*. Le Play's desire to find a representative household was somewhat at odds with his belief that 'complete' households were more illuminating. Households consisting of solitaries and of the no-family type (cf. n. 33 below) are therefore underrepresented in the collection of budgets.

[31] In addition to the areas specifically identified by Le Play, it is interesting to note that the number of French examples amongst his three western 'systems' (see table 1.2) ranges from 5 out of 11 (west: stem or patriarchal) to 8 of 12 (west: unsettled) and 11 of 13 (west: disorganized).

[32] A fact that is often overlooked. See for example Parish and Schwartz, 'Household complexity in nineteenth century France' (1972): 154, 158; Mitterauer and Sieder, *Vom Patriarchat zur Partnerschaft* (1977): 48; and our own statements about Le Play in P. Laslett and Wall (eds.) (1972): 16–21.

Table 1.2. *The family systems of Le Play and households by kin structure:*
a cross-classification

Family system (Le Play)[a]	Household type (Hammel–Laslett)[b] at time of Le Play's investigation					
	Solitary	No family	Simple	Extended	Multiple	Total
1. East: patriarchal	0	0	4	1	4	9
2. North: stem	0	0	8	1	0	9
3. West: stem or patriarchal	1	0	9	0	2	12
4. West: unstable: unsettled population	0	0	12	0	1	13
5. West: unstable: disorganized population	0	0	11	3	0	14
TOTAL	1	0	44	5	7	57

[a] According to the titles and subtitles of Le Play (1877–9): vols. II–VI.
[b] Laslett and Wall (eds.) (1972): 28–32. The extended-family households all involve an extension upwards from the conjugal family unit except for one lateral extension in family system 5. The multiple-family households in most cases are formed by the addition of secondary conjugal family units of a generation younger than that of the head, but there are instances of laterally linked units in family system 1 and of upwardly linked units in family system 4.

indicate no more that that real power lay with the current household head, i.e. with the older generation. A married couple living in England, self-supporting, with their eldest son in Australia, would still be seen by Le Play as 'stem', because the head of the household in England had full power to dispose of his wealth as he saw fit. Conversely, two related married couples living together, with the headship in the younger generation, or households which had the occasional relative attached to them could, quite consistently with his classificatory system, be included in the categories Le Play reserved for the most disorganized sections of the population, where headship carried little authority.

It is quite different with the Laslett classification scheme for household structure, which is based on the structure of the residential group at one point in time.[33] From table 1.2 it is immediately clear that under

[33] Laslett's classificatory system is explained in full in P. Laslett and Wall (eds.) (1972): 28–31. Its base is the conjugal family unit, the simple-family households of table 1.2 (married couple or parents(s) plus unmarried child(ren)). With other relatives present, not forming a conjugal family unit in their own right, the household is said to be 'extended', and the household becomes 'multiple' if two or more related conjugal family units are present. The other household types allow for persons living alone ('solitaries') and co-resident relatives and non-relatives not forming a conjugal family unit ('no family').

all Le Play's family systems a majority, or close to it, of the households correspond to the Laslett simple type.

We should consider here two further points. First, while the structure of the household is measured by Laslett at one point in time, Le Play was able to look at the household over time. Yet following his households back in time adds but few more multiple households to the total already recorded for the patriarchal areas. Second, there is Le Play's habit of selecting a particular family and then describing and classifying families in general, regardless of whether his chosen family conformed to what he saw as the dominant type. This is what causes at least one of the aberrations in table 1.2, the solitary individual within the family system which he labelled 'West: patriarchal or stem'.

In table 1.3 we look at the location of Le Play's selected families in a little more detail. As the intention is to examine the financial circumstances of young married couples, a small number of the biographies have had to be excluded (see table notes). However, to the biographies with the requisite detail in *Les ouvriers européens* we have added other, and generally fuller, biographies from the occasional publication *Les ouvriers des deux mondes*, which Le Play helped to found and which continued to appear long after his death. This yields a total of 132 families, which might not seem much for half a century of effort until one recalls the level of detail that was required for the inclusion of a study. The distribution by country is decidedly uneven. France, as one might expect, is well represented. On the other hand, eastern Europe is covered only sketchily, and so is Scandinavia. The latter studies and those on the German families, some by Le Play himself, are below average quality, lapsing into generalities which leave it uncertain how the particular family was formed and maintained. Le Play and his followers even occasionally strayed outside Europe, although usually only to where there was an established French connection, to Algeria and Morocco, to Cambodia and to French Canada, in a tradition of national anthropology that has continued to the present day. Even the man interviewed in California was French.[34] These cases, however, where they involve families, have been included for the sake of completeness in our analysis.

It should be borne in mind, therefore, that *Les ouvriers des deux mondes* and *Les ouvriers européens* provide a selection of families and not a complete cross-section of the population. As a selection, however, they appear satisfactory. Certainly it is suggestive that Le Play found mul-

---

[34] *Ouvriers des deux mondes*, 1st ser., 3 (1859).

Table 1.3. *The households of* 'Les ouvriers des deux mondes' *and* 'Les ouvriers européens': *location and structure*

Location[a]	Household type[b]			
	Simple	Extended	Multiple	Total
England	6	1	0	7
Netherlands	2	0	0	2
Belgium	8	0	0	8
France, North[c]	28	2	1	31
Paris	17	3	0	20
South	10	4	5	19
Spain	3	0	0	3
Italy	4	3	2	9
Scandinavia	2	0	1	3
Switzerland	3	0	0	3
Germany (east and west)	6	0	0	6
Austria	1	0	0	1
Czechoslovakia	1	0	0	1
Hungary	0	1	0	1
Yugoslavia	1	0	0	1
Bulgaria	1	0	0	1
U.S.S.R.	3	0	4	7
North Africa	0	0	3	3
Syria	0	0	1	1
Réunion Is.	1	0	0	1
China and Cambodia	1	0	1	2
Canada and United States	1	1	0	2
TOTAL	99	15	18	132

[a] Within the national frontiers of 1981.
[b] Cf. P. Laslett and Wall (eds.) (1972): 28–32.
[c] Departments north of 47° N.
Sources: Ouvriers des deux mondes, 1st ser., vols. 1–5, 2nd ser., vols. 1–5 (1857–99); Le Play (1877–9): vols. II, IV, V; 1st edn (1855). As this table was prepared in conjunction with the study of crisis finance (table 1.4 below), 4 households which lacked a conjugal pair and 6 households described in insufficient detail have been omitted.

tiple-family households in southern, but not northern, France, in North Africa, Russia, and in parts of Italy, that is in just those areas where more extensive research at the level of the community has confirmed their presence or where the existence of the multiple-family household seems likely.[35] Extended households, on the other hand, occurred sporadically. The one surprise in view of present-day patterns (see below) must be Spain: no extended or multiple households among the three

[35] Cf. for France, Parish and Schwartz (1972) and P. Laslett (1977a): ch. 1; for Russia, Czap, ch. 3 below; and for Italy, P. Laslett, ch. 17 below.

families selected. It may be that there was considerable variation in household types within the Iberian peninsula, or perhaps simply that Le Play was for once 'unlucky' with his choice of families.

Unfortunately, neither the Le Play nor the Laslett classification scheme meets our present purpose of showing the channels of support between families. Focusing initially on the financial problems of young married couples, we can, however, use the family biographies to identify four such channels which could supplement the young couple's own resources: channels involving parents, other relatives, employers, and 'others'. In practice, the last category comprises a miscellaneous group of people: some charitable individuals, but also institutions or the community in general, as in many of the Russian examples. Nevertheless, a number of general points need to be noted to avoid any possible misunderstanding. First, the emphasis is on financial and not moral support. The fact that in particular cases substantial aid might have been received from the parental generation does not mean that the relationship was close and harmonious or that regular contact had been maintained. Second, while some households may have been able to call on more than one type of support, others may have been more circumscribed. For example, not all couples may have had parents alive at the time of their marriage. In principle there is no reason why the classification scheme should not be extended to show the number receiving parental aid as a proportion of those with parents alive at the time of the support. The complication is not necessary for our present purpose, however, which is simply to record the support mechanisms actually used by all households. Third, there are obvious problems in deciding what should constitute a significant measure of support. Almost all households succeeded in making some savings during the course of their existence, just as almost all households received some financial support from kin. For the poorer families, the help, even if spasmodic and amounting to a small proportion of what it received from other sources, might still save them from starvation or the poor-house.

Nevertheless, to take account of all this would simply obliterate what are undoubtedly major differences in the level of support derived from various quarters. We must therefore try to quantify 'major support'. This is harder than the task Le Play faced of valuing the work performed and property held by each family, but the definition we have used is one where a close reading of the family's history suggests that the standard of living for the family at the time of the investigation would have been markedly different in the absence of that support. The extent to which a family capitalized on its good fortune is irrelevant. A legacy used to buy a business that failed or that was dissipated in the nearest alehouse has as much value in terms of the support received as a legacy used to move a family slowly but permanently into a different social class. There will always be room, though, for argument about a certain number of cases. Most difficulty has been encountered with the 'other support' category, as it is less easy to define from the family biographies when it was critical to the family's well-being. Finally, the emphasis is deliberately on families at moments of difficulty and not on the factors that enabled them to balance their normal budgets. Difficulties were fairly general immediately on marriage when the new family had to be assured of some economic future, whether established as an independent household or not. But other crisis points, widowhood, for example, or a period of unemployment or the death of an adult family member, occurred fairly frequently and were reported on by Le Play and his followers. Only in the case of marriage, however, are the crisis points common to enough families to be represented as a distinct category in table 1.4.

We can begin our consideration of this table by recording how regularly households relied on their own resources. In such cases they were not always living alone, that is independently of relatives. Living with a relative was, however, the exception (cf. the discussion of table 1.3 above), and it was usual for the family to constitute at the same time both a household and an economic unit.

On the other hand, in more than half of the families investigated, the family of a married child also received additional support from parents or parents-in-law, either at the time of marriage or later. Nor were the instances of such support confined to southern or eastern Europe or non-European areas. For example, a London cow-keeper was lent money by his father-in-law to establish his business, a Paris weaver obtained money, part dowry, and part loan, from his father to finance his marriage in 1845, while an Aisne peasant used his wife's dowry and borrowed to buy a house.[36] It is worth emphasizing that support could be proffered without obliging the married child to live with either of the sets of parents. In certain cases the opportunity for the creation of a joint household existed but was not taken. There is the steelworker from Doubs who reconstructed his house so that his elder son could occupy the second storey but operate as a separate household. Similarly the worker in the Nevers earthenware manufactory let part of his house to his daughter and her husband. This again was a separate household, although another daughter, still living in the parental household, was

---

[36] *Ouvriers des deux mondes*, 1st ser., 1 (1857); 4 (1862).

Table 1.4. *Young married couples: crisis finance by country of residence*

Location	Total	Own resources[a] on marriage	Parents of husband or wife	Other relative	Employer	Other
			Support on marriage[a] or later from			
England	7	7	3	1	0	1
Netherlands	2	2	1	0	1	2
Belgium	8	5	4	1	2	2
France, North	31	14	21	1	9	5
Paris	20	15	8	9	3	6
South	19	10	16	5	3	2
Spain	3	3	0	0	1	2
Italy	9	5	6	3	2	3
Scandinavia	3	0	1	0	2	1
Switzerland	3	2	1	0	0	0
Germany	6	4	3	1	4	1
Eastern Europe	5	1	3	0	3	2
U.S.S.R.	7	2	7	4	6	2
North Africa	3	2	2	1	0	0
Syria	1	0	1	1	0	0
Réunion Is.	1	1	0	0	1	0
China and Cambodia	2	1	1	0	0	1
Canada and United States	2	1	1	0	0	0
TOTAL	132	75	79	27	37	30

[a] The categories are not mutually exclusive.
Sources: See table 1.3.

employed by her sister. Co-operation was desirable; co-residence was not.

Apart from parents, more distant relatives occasionally stepped in to help a new household. The uncle of his wife provided capital for a Paris water-carrier's first business venture after his marriage. Again in Paris, a carpenter picked up a legacy on the death of his unmarried sister. Such instances, however, were rare. Rather more common for the families represented in table 1.4 was help from employers. This involved a number of quite different arrangements, from the provision of subsidized housing associated with a particular job[37] to the payment of the costs of training a man for an occupation and loans to cover the cost of setting up a new household. For the present we would make two points

[37] Robin (1980): 192 documents an extension to this policy. In nineteenth-century Elmdon the widows of labourers were permitted by the major landowner to continue in their tied cottages which had been allocated to the workers on his estate.

only. First, we would draw attention to the employer as a source of aid to families, aid that helped to maintain independent households, if at a low standard of living. Second, we would offer a comment on the sharp contrast that is often drawn between the responsibilities of the employer for his servants and the cessation of the responsibility when wage labour is used. Thus it is argued that individuals, ceasing to be servants, became freer to form their households when and as they wished and that eventually the whole of society became freer of familial control (cf. Schmidtbauer, chapter 11 below, for an argument on these lines). The experiences of these particular families suggest that we should be wary of drawing the contrast too rigidly. Employers went on modifying the familial patterns of individuals in the period when the labour force had ceased to be contained within their own households.

If we now look at the way in which support channels varied in frequency across Europe, we find that in England, in the Low Countries, in Spain, and in the German and Swiss examples, and in Paris, couples were meeting at least part of the cost of their new home from their own resources. Elsewhere, this was less common, although some examples of it can be found in almost all societies. In this regard, it is particularly interesting that, in contrast to what has been observed in terms of the composition of the household, there is no discernible difference, once Paris is excluded, between the pattern in northern and southern France.

The question of parental support on marriage or after it (column 3 of table 1.4) is not quite the mirror image of the use of 'own resources'. However, parental support is certainly less in evidence in the examples from England, the Low Countries, Spain, Germany, and Switzerland and in Paris than it is elsewhere in Europe. Identification of other patterns in the sets of figures is difficult because of the small number of families at issue when the cases are divided according to country, but we might note the absence of employer support in all the English examples and the importance of 'other relatives' in Paris. These relatives counter-balanced the absence of parental support and might perhaps be seen as a distinctively Parisian phenomenon of the nineteenth century brought about by sections of the population having to adapt to urban living while their parents remained in remote rural areas.

With this in mind we can go on to examine the nature of the support (own resources or parental) against Le Play's own categorization of family types. This information is set out in table 1.5, for which we have had to return to the smaller number of families as described in *Les ouvriers européens*. It emerges that even within the populations classed by Le Play as unstable and disorganized, some families had received critical

Table 1.5. *Young married couples: crisis finance and family system*

Le Play's family system[a]	Cases in observation[a]	Own resources on marriage[b]	Support of parents of husband or wife on or after marriage[b]
1. East: patriarchal	8	2	8
2. North: stem	9	6	4
3. West: stem or patriarchal	11	7	6
4. West: unstable: unsettled population	12	6	4
5. West: unstable: disorganized population	13	9	3
TOTAL	53	30	25

[a] According to the titles and subtitles of Le Play (1877–9): vols. II–VI, but omitting 4 case studies lacking sufficient detail.
[b] The categories in the last two columns are not mutually exclusive.

financial support from their parents and that, conversely, within the patriarchal east, there were a number of families for whom their own savings were important. Nevertheless, the overall pattern, particularly in regard to parental support, is clear. Such support was ubiquitous throughout the family system called 'East: patriarchal' by Le Play. It was recorded for about half the families attributed to the 'North: stem' and 'West: patriarchal or stem' systems but on no more than a third of the occasions in the unstable west. This confirms the east–west differences in family patterns and the variation within western Europe noted by Le Play but links them to the ways in which families acted as new economic units at the moment of formation.

For the final table of the series, table 1.6, it is appropriate, therefore, to look at all support channels in relation to the social position of the young couple, using the occupation of the husband as the primary indicator of social position. There are insufficient cases, unfortunately, to provide a cross-tabulation of social position by the national groupings. The pattern that emerges, however, is a fairly clear one and implies that much of the national variation considered above was economic and perhaps social in origin. For example, those most likely to have received parental support were, not surprisingly, those families identified by Le Play as 'peasants', closely followed by fishermen and smallholders.[38] For other social groups different support channels were of above-average import-

[38] Apart, that is, from the serfs whose family patterns are described below in sect. IV.

Table 1.6. *Young married couples: crisis finance by social position*

			Support on marriage or later[b] from			
Social position[a] of couple	Total	Own resources[b] on marriage	Parents of husband or wife	Other relative	Employer	Non-relative
Peasant	17	6	16	7	0	2
Sharecropper	8	3	5	1	4	1
Market gardener Smallholder	10	7	8	1	2	2
Fisherman	6	4	5	2	0	2
Commerce	3	2	2	1	0	0
Craftsman	41	28	23	6	13	11
Factory worker Smelter	11	5	5	1	6	2
Miner, quarrier	14	10	4	0	4	1
Labourer	7	5	2	2	1	4
Services Administration	10	4	4	4	2	4
Serf	5	1	5	2	5	1
TOTAL	132	75	79	27	37	30

[a] Social position is usually defined here on the basis of the husband's occupation, except in the case of the serfs and those owning small amounts of land. With these exceptions in mind, the term 'social position' is preferred to 'occupational group'.
[b] The categories are not mutually exclusive.
Sources: See table 1.3.

ance: employers for sharecroppers and factory workers; other non-relatives for those employed in services and for labourers.[39] The differences between smallholders and labourers seem particularly revealing. The smallholder, like the peasant but unlike the labourer, was regularly a receiver of parental support.[40] Yet, as the detailed biographies show, the smallholder was in most cases also a labourer or had been one.[41] However, labourer and smallholder were similar in one respect: in that it was more likely that they would use their own

[39] Some of this support could be considered as part of the wage but paid in kind. However, there is an impact on family patterns that would not occur if the 'worker' was simply in receipt of a money wage.
[40] Cf. Wall, 'Real property, marriage and children' (1982b) for an illustration of the differences in the composition of the households of labourers with and without real property in the much-studied parish of Colyton in Devon.
[41] Particularly true of vine-growers. See the account of vine workers' households in Charente-Inférior (now Charente-Maritime) in *Ouvriers des deux mondes*, 1st ser., 3 (1861); in lower Bourgogne, 1st ser., 4 (1862); and in Alsace, 2nd ser., 3 (1892).

resources at the time of their marriage than either the peasant or sharecropper.

To push the argument much further at this stage would be unwise because of the small number of cases. On the other hand, we do maintain that the issue of support channels as we have defined them offers a valuable insight into the workings of the social system, for the ties between employer and employee as well as between relatives. Future work will, we hope, be able to confirm what at present can only be a suggestion in the figures in the tables: that the poorest social group, the labourers, was the most likely to have to call on the support of non-relatives.

However, although we have analysed the frequency of support from own resources and from parents and others according to the socio-economic status of the recipient, we should be wary of overstressing the interrelationship. Le Play himself commented on the English families that public opinion expected the family to be independent; in other words the independence of the family was a value in its own right.[42] But only a society with many opportunities could have provided the means to this independence. We cannot be sure that Le Play was correct in this opinion, but it would tie in very well with what we have discovered about the number of young adults in England in a position to form their own households (cf. section III below). The significance of the argument lies in the fact that a family's use of 'own resources' no longer appears as an economically determined variable, but as one of the values of society, influenced by the social context no doubt, but exerting its own independent influence on family patterns.

Care of the elderly

So far we have been looking at families at an early period in their life cycle. We have shown how young adults benefited from parental resources. What we have not seen is how parents fared after the parental wealth, or a share of it, had been handed over to their children. Here we may again refer to the studies of individual families made by Le Play and others who followed his methods.

There are two problems to which we ought to refer. First, the focus here is on parents of the people interviewed, and there is less information available on their situation than on that of the interviewees. Second, parents may be able to live independently at one time but not at

---

[42] Le Play (1855): 210.

another, with independence becoming impossible in extreme old age or on widowhood. If, however, one were to make a general statement about the period when the two generations overlapped, one conclusion would be inescapable. Parents were in the majority of cases able to maintain a financial as well as a residential independence from their children (table 1.7).[43] Financial independence was secured by continued employment, often on a part-time basis, or from savings made during an earlier period of life.

In table 1.7 we have assessed whether parents were independent or dependent according to the location of the family,[44] the social status of the parents, and whether they were the parents of the husband or of the wife studied in *Les ouvriers européens* or *Les ouvriers des deux mondes*. One would expect little difference between the financial position of the husband's and wife's parents. Table 1.7 suggests such a difference, but in fact it is produced by the lack of information on the wives' fathers within the 'patriarchal family system' most of whom would have been heading their own households with dependent offspring. Once allowance is made for this factor, there is little difference in the number of wives' parents as opposed to husbands' parents identified as 'independent'.

In regard to national patterns, the areas where the elderly maintained a dominance over their adult offspring, that is to say Russia, southern France, parts of Italy, and North Africa, are clearly identifiable. These of course are the prime areas of multiple-family households (cf. table 1.3). Italy and southern France are, however, different from the other two, in that the elderly could also fall into a dependent situation. Otherwise, it is difficult on the basis of this number of cases to make out any distinct national pattern; the common expectation across most of Europe seems to have been for a third of the older generation to be 'dependent'. It should be emphasized again, however, that by no means all the instances of dependence necessitated co-residence (table 1.7, column 4). The final section of this table looks at the frequency of dependency by the social position of the parent, but again, perhaps because of the small numbers, no distinctive pattern emerges. Dependence could be the fate of the peasant as well as of the miner and the labourer, but does seem to have been a rather more frequent occurrence for those social groups representing the poorer elements in society. Smallholders, craftsmen,

---

[43] Parents in receipt of a pension or annuity were in practice no more than semi-dependent and should be excluded from the calculation, leaving less than a third of all the parents fully dependent.

[44] Ideally, the parents of couples interviewed in Paris should have been reallocated according to their region of origin, but this has not been attempted because in some cases the parents themselves had spent part of their lives in Paris.

Table 1.7. *The older generation: independence and dependence*

	Independent		Dependent				
			Pension/annuity representing a proportion of offspring's resources	Direct support by offspring generation			
	Household head; offspring dependent	Supported from own resources		Within household of study family[a]	Sibling[a]	Study family	Total
Husband's parent(s)	13	24	6	7	3	8	61
Wife's parent(s)	2	20	7	6	3	6	44
TOTAL	15	44	13	13	6	14	105
Location							
England	0	3	0	0	0	1	4
Netherlands	0	0	0	1	0	0	1
Belgium	0	5	1	1	0	1	8
France, North	0	15	3	5	1	3	27
Paris	0	9	2	3	1	1	16
South	4	4	4	0	3	3	18
Italy	4	1	1	2	1	1	10
Scandinavia	0	0	0	0	0	0	1
Switzerland	0	2	0	0	0	0	2
Germany	0	1	0	1	0	0	2
Austria	0	2	0	0	0	0	2
Hungary	0	0	0	0	0	1	1
Bulgaria	0	0	0	0	0	1	1
U.S.S.R.	4	0	0	0	0	0	4
North Africa	2	0	0	0	0	0	2

							TOTAL
Réunion Is.	0	1	0	0	0	0	1
China and Cambodia	1	1	1	0	0	0	3
Canada and United States	0	0	1	1	0	0	2
TOTAL	15	44	13	6	13	14	105
Social position of parent[b]							
Peasant	7	2	6	0	0	3	18
Sharecropper	4	0	1	0	1	0	6
Market gardener ⎫ Smallholder ⎬	0	12	1	1	3	1	18
Fisherman	0	2	0	1	0	1	4
Commerce	1	4	1	0	0	1	7
Craftsman	0	10	2	0	5	0	17
Factory worker ⎫ Smelter ⎬	0	1	0	0	1	1	3
Miner, quarrier	0	1	1	2	1	1	6
Labourer	0	1	0	1	0	1	3
Services/administration	0	5	1	0	2	0	8
Serf	3	0	0	0	0	0	3
Unknown	0	6	0	1	0	5	12
TOTAL	15	44	13	6	13	14	105

[a] 'Study family' indicates the family visited by Le Play or his adherents and 'Sibling' the wife's husband's brother or sister. In most cases of sibling support it seems that the parent resided with the sibling.

[b] The social position of the parent is not always clear, and in some cases the parent changed occupation late in life. The aim has been to classify the parent according to the social position occupied during the larger part of adult life, but even so the category 'Smallholder' is probably overrepresented at the expense of others.

Sources: As for table 1.3, although many more families had to be excluded because of insufficient information concerning the parental generation.

and those with lesser service or administrative functions or enjoying the proceeds of a small commerce, were the most likely to be supporting themselves from their own resources.

The potential for intergenerational conflict was greatest when parents and children were competitors for resources. This was true of the stem families that Le Play admired so much and may also fit families whose economic future was uncertain or whose resources were only sufficient to maintain the family for part of the year. A suggestion that these patterns may have been very widespread indeed comes from David Gaunt's account of attitudes towards the elderly in chapter 8. The difficulty is that the sources Gaunt used do not readily yield hard evidence about what was actually happening to elderly relatives. In some cases it is unclear whether the stories originated with the parents or with the children. Whether it was the child or the parent who felt he had been cheated out of his rights to a proper livelihood depended on who told the story. Other stories appear apocryphal. There is a case like this in the material collected by Le Play and his followers.[45] The interviewer was obviously told of the dispossession of elderly parents by their offspring, but the family investigated had a mother-in-law acting in support of her son-in-law's household so that her daughter could work. At the same time other examples can be found where the handover between generations went far from smoothly because offspring were dissatisfied with their share of parental wealth or could not be given a fair share. There were even cases of heirs declining to take over parental responsibilities because of 'better' opportunities elsewhere. Elaborate arrangements for retirement, the spelling out of respective rights, can be either a sign of the underlying tension or an attempt to forestall it. Undoubtedly, examination of this sort of record can tell us a lot about intergenerational relationships, particularly when set alongside details of living arrangements and, where we can find them, family biographies.

Similarly, we have to compare the actual process of passing on the headship of the household with the inheritance customs of the region (cf. Danhieux, and Sieder and Mitterauer below). It is clear that there was a great deal more variation in the successorship to households than custom might suggest. In part this was the result of demographic accidents which left certain families without direct heirs, providing opportunities for their secondary heirs and the heirs of other families to add to their holdings. Another relevant factor is that, just as with household

---

[45] See M. Callage on the Aisne peasant in *Ouvriers des deux mondes*, 1st ser., 4 (1862): 69.

forms, inheritance customs are not necessarily shared by the entire population. Cuesenier makes a useful distinction between the legal rules of inheritance and actual practice, when the rules are either ignored or an appropriate selection of the rules made that meet the testator's personal wishes.[46] The point I would emphasize about such arrangements is that conflict is likely to be aroused whenever there is more than one potential heir, since all are at liberty to refer to rules or customs which suit their own interests. These divisions seriously weaken Davis's argument that societies can be said to be following rules rather than maximizing individual interests if 'rights' are created when the rules are broken.[47]

There is one further issue that ought to be considered here. In the fullest study yet published of a nineteenth-century English community, Michael Anderson has drawn attention to the mutual benefits both the old and young drew from the pattern of co-residence in the same household.[48] For the old, there was the prospect of companionship, care if ill, and a useful function after the end of working life. For the married child, the benefits included economies over rent, the modification of expenditure patterns, the postponement of saving to set up a separate household, and help with both the finding of a house and with household responsibilities. The last was particularly important, as in the community Anderson studied (Preston) the livelihood of the household depended on married women working out of the home.

It is not easy to find evidence of such reciprocity in the studies conducted by Le Play and his colleagues. This is because parent and child were in very different situations. Wealth rested primarily in the parental generation; need, in the child generation. Hence aid was more often channelled down the generational line than up (compare tables 1.6 and 1.7). When parents could not save or had not saved sufficient to maintain themselves in old age, then and only then might they become dependent on their children. This would appear to have been the case in Preston in the mid-nineteenth century, but we would be unwise to see this as a natural consequence of industrialization. In the family of the Doubs steelworker already cited, it was clearly the son who was in the dependent situation.[49]

What perhaps we should be looking for is not direct, but delayed or latent reciprocity, that is that the children would not repay their parents

---

[46] Cited by J. Davis (1977): 194.
[47] J. Davis (1977): 206f.
[48] Anderson (1971): 141.
[49] See above and n. 15.

but would in turn act out the parental behaviour in regard to the next generation. The family of the Aisne peasant interviewed by M. Callage in 1861 provides a case in point.[50] Early in the marriage the mother of the wife had helped to care for the children so that the wife could work. Later, when these children had grown up and married, daughter and granddaughter generations combined to help with major household chores such as the washing. The reciprocity is latent because there seems to be no economic advantage to one partner in a particular arrangement. They may be building up credit, perhaps unconsciously, in case they in turn may need assistance in due course. Another way of putting it would be to say that the individual is socialized into certain types of behaviour through the medium of the familial system.

However, bonds between generations can as easily be overstressed as tensions. For every case where intergenerational aid was proffered we can find another where expectations were not fulfilled. A study conducted by one of Le Play's colleagues involves the classic case of the mother-in-law who turned over her house to her daughter's husband and was then forbidden to speak when in his presence.[51] Some families were impervious to their good standing in the community or the ideals of Le Play. Economic opportunities, whether presented to them by their parents or arising from a fluid economic system, gave them the power to break the conventional standards of 'good behaviour'.

III. Measurement of the family and household

As was pointed out earlier, the sources available to the historian only rarely allow social systems to be described in their totality. If one is working primarily from a list of inhabitants, the nature of the groups into which the inhabitants have been divided has to be obtained from the way in which the persons are described – 'child', 'servant', 'foster child', 'inmate', and so on. It is assumed that the blocks of names represent residential groups of some sort. A few listmakers are known to have gone round from house to house taking a note of the population, and even in a village of upwards of 100 inhabitants there is scarcely any other way in which the population could have been enumerated. The greatest difficulty with census-type documents, however, is not in fact the way in which the population was enumerated but the basis on which individuals were credited to particular residential groups. Some

[50] See n. 45 above.
[51] L. A. Toussaint on the vine-grower of Charente-Inférior in *Ouvriers des deux mondes*, 1st ser., 3 (1861).

censuses are ideal (i.e. descriptions of where people should be), while others are real (descriptions of where people actually were on census night). Having worked through numbers of pre-industrial census-type documents, it is our impression that almost all of these were ideal. Only with the coming of official census-taking and the issuing of schedules for householders to complete, which happened in England from the middle of the nineteenth century, is there an attempt to record where people were actually staying on a particular night. Even so, some householders were confused as to who should be entered on the census form, giving rise to double counting when individuals appeared in their own house-holds and as relatives or visitors elsewhere. The movement from 'ideal' to 'real' in census-taking may account for some, though perhaps not all, of the often cited rise in the proportion of households with relatives in England between the eighteenth and nineteenth centuries.

This is by no means the only difficulty that has to be faced when using the census to throw light on the household. There is the problem of whom to include and whom to exclude from the household and the problem of how the composition of the household should then be recorded. The first issue has already been given some consideration in *Household and family in past time.* The household was there defined, and we shall define it here again, to include spouse, child, relative, and servant of the head. Other residents such as unrelated boarders, visitors, and inmates were excluded but were said to live within the houseful, which was left deliberately suspensive in character to allow for a greater or lesser connection of inmates to the household in different societies (see for example the quite complex situation in Bruges, chapter 14 below). The instances that were given above of households dependent on others though quite separate in residential terms complicate the situation further. The standard solution would be to follow the norms of the society, to take as a household that which the society itself would have taken as a household, providing, of course, that that can be determined. However, as we have seen, a society may not have a norm to which one can refer. Certain groups in the population may conceive of the situation quite differently, women stressing the immediate fam-ily; men, perhaps, the production group, as in Átány in Hungary (see above, pp. 10–11).

Once a decision has been taken about the delimitation of the bound-ary of the household, the second problem to which we alluded asserts itself: how to measure the composition of the household. Of the many tables in *Household and family in past time,* the one that has proved most useful, and most widely used, is that devoted to the structure of the household. It was, however, never claimed that on its own this table would suffice to reveal the nature of the household, let alone the family system of which the household forms a part. No one table, even a set of tables, could possibly do this, but we have spent much time in Cambridge constructing a set of tables that we believe captures the differences between households. An earlier version of this set was included in *Household and family in past time*, and a revised set has now been worked out for two settlements at opposite ends of Europe: Krasnoe Sobakino, a village on the Mishino estate in Greater Russia (see also chapter 3), and Elmdon in Essex. One specimen table for each place and a list of the others are to be found in Laslett's chapter 17 below.

It should be pointed out, however, that in many cases a large number of the tables cannot be filled in because the censuses do not contain the necessary information. This is the case even with the above-average lists like the one of Mishino. In addition we are well aware that the time taken to complete a full set of tables is considerable, imposing heavy burdens on the researcher, for whom detailed examination of the households may well be part of a wider study of the social structure. In practice, therefore, a summary table such as the one on household structure, which can be quickly completed, will continue to be widely used, and it is important to realize that this particular table does not in fact give an overall view of the household. What it represents is a classification of the households in terms of kin structure and as such could be criticized for giving an undue place to the kin element in the household through using various combinations of kin as the defining characteristic. Kin, however, may have had a variety of roles in the household. They may also have had the same role as non-related persons such as servants or inmates whose presence or absence does not affect this particular classification of the household.

It is naturally easier to draw attention to the limitations of a particular table than to find a suitable replacement. Scholars working on contemporary censuses make considerable use of headship rates, i.e. the proportion of persons of a particular age group, sex, and marital status who head their own households, but surprisingly little use has been made of them in connection with historical data.[52] Figs. 1.1 to 1.3 therefore set out the first substantial information on headship rates in pre-industrial Europe.[53]

---

[52] There is, however, a table on headship rates in P. Laslett and Wall (eds.) (1972): 79.
[53] To avoid unnecessary detail, the marital status variable has not been introduced into figs. 1.1–3. This information is, in any case, not available for all the communities in question.

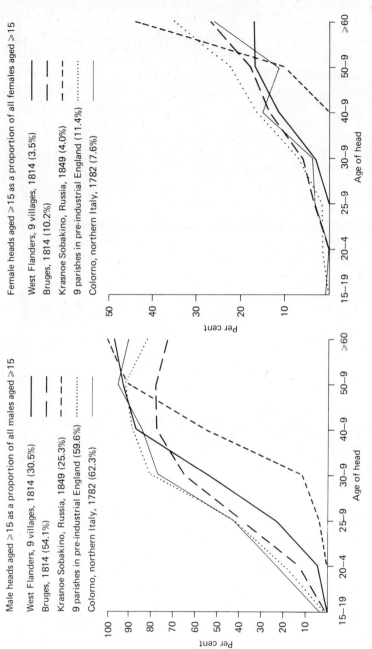

Male heads aged ≥15 as a proportion of all males aged ≥15

West Flanders, 9 villages, 1814 (30.5%) ———
Bruges, 1814 (54.1%) — — —
Krasnoe Sobakino, Russia, 1849 (25.3%) – – –
9 parishes in pre-industrial England (59.6%) ·········
Colorno, northern Italy, 1782 (62.3%) ————

Female heads aged ≥15 as a proportion of all females aged ≥15

West Flanders, 9 villages, 1814 (3.5%) ———
Bruges, 1814 (10.2%) — — —
Krasnoe Sobakino, Russia, 1849 (4.0%) – – –
9 parishes in pre-industrial England (11.4%) ·········
Colorno, northern Italy, 1782 (7.6%) ————

Fig. 1.1. Headship rates, western Europe and Krasnoe Sobakino, Russia. Note that in figs. 1.1–3 the age groups are in five-year blocks until age 30 and that the rates for males and females are drawn to different scales.

37

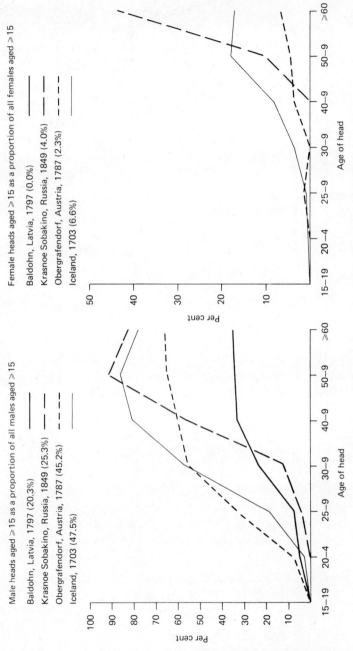

Male heads aged >15 as a proportion of all males aged >15

Baldohn, Latvia, 1797 (20.3%)

Krasnoe Sobakino, Russia, 1849 (25.3%)

Obergrafendorf, Austria, 1787 (45.2%)

Iceland, 1703 (47.5%)

Female heads aged >15 as a proportion of all females aged >15

Baldohn, Latvia, 1797 (0.0%)

Krasnoe Sobakino, Russia, 1849 (4.0%)

Obergrafendorf, Austria, 1787 (2.3%)

Iceland, 1703 (6.6%)

Fig. 1.2. Headship rates, central and eastern Europe and Iceland.

38

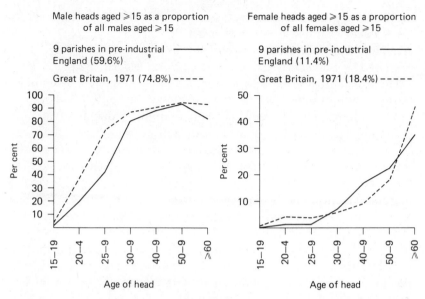

Fig. 1.3. Headship rates, pre-industrial England and Great Britain, 1971.

Headship rates for males were high in pre-industrial England, higher, though similar in distribution between age groups, than they were in the Flemish communities that have been studied for the purposes of this volume (cf. chapters 12 and 14 below), and quite distinct from the Russian experience. Only 1 in 10 of men in their 30s in Krasnoe Sobakino headed their own household. Eight out of 10 in their 30s were household heads in pre-industrial England. A second major difference concerns the 60+ age group. In western Europe their headship rate fell slightly from earlier levels, indicating that some men did renounce headship in old age. In Krasnoe Sobakino this did not happen, reflecting the greater authority exercised by the old, a facet of Russian society which, as we have seen, was emphasized by Le Play. In this case a simple measure such as the headship rate bears out what Le Play was able to observe of the power structure within the family.

Female headship rates (the chances of a woman heading a household) are more difficult to interpret. They reflect not simply the desire or ability of a woman to establish her own household and the factors associated with this such as the proportion of women never marrying, but also the frequency of widowhood and opportunities for, and prohibitions surrounding, remarriage. Nevertheless, we can see from fig. 1.1 that where the male headship rate is high, so too is the female headship rate.[54] This is so in the case of pre-industrial England, while in the Russian example the female headship rate rises sharply, like the male, in old age, showing that authority, at least nominally, came to be exercised by the elderly woman as well as the elderly man.

The Russian patterns, both for males and females, were also unlike those of communities that we have examined in central and eastern Europe (cf. fig. 1.2), where the presence of numbers of married lifetime (as opposed to life-cycle) servants resulted in a curious flat profile to the headship rate. What we must not do is fall into the trap of jumping to the conclusion that the Russian or the English pattern was unique, despite the attraction of emphasizing the individuality of the English.[55] On the present evidence, the Russian pattern may be unique; the English one clearly is not. From Colorno in northern Italy in 1782 we have headship rates that were similar, and indeed in the case of males even exceeded the English ones; but then, Colorno was on the Lombardy plain, an area of rich farms and day labourers.[56] It is not therefore too surprising that the English and Colorno household patterns should in certain key respects resemble each other. We would not, however, go further and argue that a high headship rate must necessarily indicate either relative prosperity or an area of capitalist farming with day labourers. Regard as always has to be paid to the social and economic conditions of the community under study.[57]

Finally, fig. 1.3 offers a point of comparison with headship rates for the present day, using England as a case study. Given the great changes that have occurred in English society within the last 200 years, there is remarkably little difference between the modern and the pre-industrial headship rate. Certainly they are closer than the 'historic' English and Russian examples, and in some respects they are closer than the 'historic' English and Flemish headship rates. Yet there has been some change. By 1971 a higher proportion of men were household heads, and this is particularly marked for men in their 20s for two reasons. First, men are marrying earlier on average than they did in the past, and, second, a higher proportion of men are leaving home prior to marriage. The latter trend indicates that the relationship between marriage and household formation is now less close than was the case in England in

[54] The female headship rates and the proportion of women living alone are set out in more detail in Wall, 'Woman alone in English society' (1981).
[55] Cf. Macfarlane, *The origins of English individualism* (1978).
[56] See U. Guérin in *Ouvriers des deux mondes*, 2nd ser., 2 (1890): 430.
[57] Cf. the analysis by the United Nations of headship rates in the contemporary developed and developing world: United Nations, *The determinants and consequences of population trends*, I (1973): 348.

earlier centuries. For women, the shape of the headship rate has altered, with more women nowadays heading households both in early adulthood and in old age. This trend, however, has been partly balanced by rather fewer women heading households in middle age. These trends, we would argue, are associated with new economic opportunities (for some women);[58] with the postponement of widowhood into old age; and with the ever-widening gap to the advantage of women between the life expectancy of the male and the female.

There is a serious weakness, though, in relying solely on the headship rate in that nothing is said about the position of those who do not head households. We now suggest, therefore, that a count of the number of adults of prime working age per household should be set alongside the headship rate. This immediately presents us with the problem of how one should define 'prime working age', and it will be seen below that we have included only men and women between the ages of 20 and 59. This is not to deny the contribution of other age groups to the working power of the household, particularly of those aged between 15 and 19 or of those over 60 to work, either directly or by freeing others for this purpose. However, the age span 20–59 provides the best approximation of 'prime working age', identifying those individuals who in the vast majority of cases were mentally and physically capable of running their own households. We can see from the information given above on headship rates how close various societies came to achieving this potential, while others fell far short of it.[59] Table 1.8 extends the picture by revealing how adults were distributed among households. The analysis is almost entirely at community, rather than national, level. This is inevitable given the newness of the undertaking and necessitates some caution in generalizing on the basis of the findings.

The conclusions that it does seem safe to draw on the basis of table 1.8 are the following. First, it was generally true that a household (even including the head) would more likely contain at least one woman than it would one man of 'prime working age'. Second, there was a clear difference between England and the rest in the number of households without males and females of prime working age. Third, the Baltic and

[58] The possibility that the 'welfare state' helps to maintain households that might otherwise collapse and be absorbed by other households or institutions also needs to be considered. On the other hand, this should not be seen as a totally new departure. The Poor Law, even at times the New Poor Law of the nineteenth century, did not send all those in need of support to the nearest workhouse; see Thomson, 'Provision for the elderly in England' (1980).

[59] Figs. 1.1–3 cover all age groups from 15 years onwards 'at risk' to be heads of households, rather than those aged 20–59, in order to be comparative with other data.

Table 1.8. *Number and proportion of households with given number of adult members of prime working age*

Country	Place	Date	Total house-holds (no.)	Proportion of households with males 20–59			Proportion of households with females 20–59		
Selected communities[a]				None (%)	1 (%)	≥2 (%)	None (%)	1 (%)	≥2 (%)
England	Ealing	1599	85	25	55	20	13	59	28
	Clayworth	1851	136	28	59	13	21	62	17
	Elmdon	1861	115	24	71	5	18	72	10
Belgium	Lampernisse	1814	66	20	48	32	2	68	30
France	Longuenesse	1778	66	12	62	26	8	71	21
Austria	Obergrafendorf	1787	290	12	60	28	6	57	37
Serbia	Belgrade	1733–4	106	16	51	33	9	71	20
Latvia	Baldohn	1797	104	0	2	98	0	7	93
Russia	Krasnoe Sobakino	1849	44	0	11	89	0	16	84
Japan	Nishinomiya	1713	132	11	42	47	16	50	34

[a] Further information on the structure of the household in Ealing, Clayworth, Longuenesse, Belgrade, and Nishinomiya is to be found in P. Laslett and Wall (eds.) (1972): chs. 1, 15, 19, and P. Laslett (1977a): chs. 1, 2. Lampernisse is studied in detail by Danhieux, ch. 13 below. Krasnoe Sobakino forms part of the Mishino estate investigated by Czap, ch. 3 below.

Russian populations have far and away more households containing two or more males and two or more females between the ages of 20 and 59. To interpret these findings, we need again to bear in mind not only the economic but also the social and cultural factors that might influence the household. That households would more rarely lack an adult woman than an adult man can scarcely be surprising, given the domestic responsibilities that fall to women in the vast majority of societies. Indeed, the expectation was that it would be ubiquitous across the range of societies represented in table 1.8. However, Nishinomiya did not conform, and it would be interesting to look at other Japanese communities of the Tokugawa period to see how common this pattern was and whether it was related to other known features of their culture such as the adoption of sons or even female infanticide.[60]

As to our second conclusion, the number of households without males and females of prime working age can obviously be a function of the age structure of the population. If there was a high proportion of

[60] See the ideographs of households in Nishinomiya in P. Laslett and Wall (eds.) (1972): 534f, and for infanticide, T. C. Smith, *Nakahara* (1977): 64–7 and Hanley and Yamamura, *Economic and demographic change in pre-industrial Japan* (1977): 238–41.

elderly people in the population, then, other things being equal, one would expect a higher proportion of households containing only elderly people. The point must, though, be pursued further. Even if England had more households without adults of prime working age because a higher proportion of its population was over the age of 60 (and this has yet to be established), it would still have to be explained how households consisting of elderly people on their own supported themselves. A critical factor here seems to have been the acceptance of a communal responsibility for the basic economic welfare of elderly people in their own households, with transfers of wealth formalized through a local taxation system operated under the Poor Laws.

Finally, the much larger number of households in the Russian and Latvian examples with two or more adults of both sexes might seem to be the inevitable consequence of estate management practices when the management of land spilled over into the management of people. We will be questioning this assumption in the final section of this introduction. In the meantime, we might note that although land was allocated to Russian serfs on the basis of the number of working units (i.e. married couples) a household could muster, a finer analysis of the household than that of table 1.8 shows that more serf households in Krasnoe Sobakino contained four or more females of prime working age than contained an equivalent group of males. This may seem a strange outcome when the household is supposed to function as a work group, but any surplus women in the adult population had to be allocated to some household. In any case, in a society where only the estate owner had servants, the number of women in the household could confer the status on the household head, and do the work, that servants did elsewhere.[61]

With the Latvian population, there might even be some suspicion that the groups of people identified in the lists were not in fact households, but workers of a particular parcel of land and their dependants. However, for some cases at least, Andrejs Plakans is able to show (chapter 5 below) that on some occasions the larger group of people shared a house and ate together, that is they did constitute a household as conventionally defined.

To carry the analysis beyond the preliminary points that have been made here requires more data at the level of the community and, where possible, at the level of the individual household. We may take two

---

[61] See the descriptions of Bachkir families in Russia east of the Urals, and of peasants, stevedores, and boatbuilders in Oka, Central Russia in Le Play (1877–9): vol. II; and of Corsican families in *Ouvriers des deux mondes*, 2nd ser., 2 (1890).

examples, the first English and the second Austrian. It can be seen from table 1.8 that households with two or more males or females of prime working age were somewhat unusual in England. Of the communities included in this table, the lowest proportions were recorded for the Essex village of Elmdon in 1861. Fortunately we have the opportunity, thanks to the work of Jean Robin, to look at those households which did contain two or more adults and assess what the factors were that caused such households to break the norms of the society. Indeed, we can go on to ask whether there were norms to which people attempted and were expected to conform, or whether the unusual households were simply those subject to a chance occurrence that might affect most at some stage of their history.[62] The examination of Elmdon households with two or more men or women of prime working age suggests that such households fell into three principal categories. A few were recent (and temporary) formations caused, probably, by a bereavement in the family. Second, some of the households with two or more females of prime working age reflected the presence of servants. However, the majority of households containing two or more adults, whether those adults were male or female, were produced by grown-up children staying on in the parental home until marriage. Who precisely stayed on was strongly influenced by the social class of the parent, the sex of the child, and the number and sex of other siblings still at home. In Elmdon, daughters stayed with their parents when there was no son of equivalent age at home;[63] the sons who stayed were principally the sons of agricultural labourers. None of the categories implies any breaking of social norms, although it would be unwise on the basis of the present evidence to declare this an impossibility.

The Austrian example is interesting because it provides the first extended analysis of the proportion of households according to the number of adults of prime working age. In all, data similar to those of table 1.8 are available for 87 communities, encompassing villages, market towns, and major cities such as Vienna and Salzburg. This allows Obergrafendorf, a solitary example from Austria in table 1.8, to be placed in some sort of perspective.[64] For example, the variation in the proportion of households containing two or more males of prime work-

[62] This analysis was carried out by Jean Robin and is based on her own work on Elmdon (using parish registers as well as census material), and I am most grateful for her assistance.

[63] Cf. Wall, 'The age at leaving home' (1978) for other English communities showing differences in residence patterns of offspring according to the age and sex of the offspring and the marital status and occupation of the parents.

[64] This analysis was undertaken by Dr J. Ehmer of the Institüt für Wirtschafts und Sozialgeschichte in the University of Vienna, and I am grateful to him for allowing me to

ing age was very considerable, ranging from 75% in St Lorenzen in Carinthia in 1757 to 6% in Koppl, Salzburg in 1805. Obergrafendorf with 28% of its households containing at least two males of prime working age comes towards the lower end of the distribution.[65] Much more work needs to be done both on the nature of the local economies and on other aspects of the household before we can offer a definitive interpretation of these patterns.

Yet even a simple ranking of the communities according to the number of households with two or more males or females of prime working age, or without any, has been illuminating. Thus there were two sorts of settlement where the proportion of households without any male of prime working age was well above average:[66] first, a number of market towns and, second, places which had experienced a crisis of major proportions, notably two communities enumerated in the aftermath of the two European wars of the twentieth century.[67] It is less easy to find features common to those communities where the proportion of households lacking males of prime working age was well below average (bottom 10% of the distribution), since they included areas of mining and industry and both wealthy and poverty-stricken agricultural communities. The areas of large and rich farms and the mining and industrial communities (but not the poor agricultural areas) also reappear in a group of communities where the proportion of households with two or more males and two or more females of prime working age was well above average. Summary measures of the household, therefore, have their limitations, encouraging the unwary researcher to put communities into a single category when the economic context suggests that the unexamined inner structure of households might be quite dissimilar. Nevertheless, it remains our contention that the results presented in this section demonstrate that a count of the number of adults per household, especially when used in conjunction with economic data, will prove a valuable indicator of household types: an indicator, moreover, which is free of any ideological bias that might attach to comparisons of kin or servants in different cultures.

cite his preliminary findings. A complete print-out of the results is available for consultation in the library of the SSRC Cambridge Group.

[65] A ranking of the 87 communities in terms of the proportion of households with two males of prime working age leaves Obergrafendorf in 65th position.

[66] Based on the top 10% of the distribution when the communities are placed in rank order from most to least households lacking males of prime working age.

[67] It might be argued that communities enumerated after 1900 or 1914 should not form part of the series, but the vast majority were enumerated earlier, i.e. 10, pre-1750; 25, 1750–94; 22, 1800–49; 27, 1850–99. Schmidtbauer (see below, note to table 1.11) has effectively used a subset of this material.

IV. The kin component of the household over time

For a fuller understanding of how the household functions, a count of
the number of adults per household has to be supplemented by some
consideration of who these people were, their relationship to each other
and to the head of the household. Of the various elements within the
household, the one which has probably attracted the most attention is
that of kin, the relatives of the head by blood or marriage, excluding
spouse, offspring, and stepchildren. Households have been declared to
be extended' when they contain such a relative, 'nuclear' when they do
not. Indeed whole family systems have been described in terms of their
presence or absence. Kinship forms one of the pillars of John Hajnal's
description of north-west European household patterns (chapter 2,
below) and of Peter Laslett's 'western family', but there are many other
examples.[68]

In view of this attention it is somewhat surprising to find that no
attempt has yet been made to discover whether the north-west European household system, in which the vast majority of households did
not contain relatives, and an eastern and southern European one in
which there were many households with relatives have persisted to the
present day. This omission we will now correct, and this will lead us to
consider the validity of generalizations about a 'north-west European
household pattern' both for Europe today and in the past. It is obviously
a generalization, and some variation within the 'system' is permissible,
but how significant is this variation? Is there any danger of taking for
one unified system what are in reality a number of quite distinct behavioural patterns, the presence of which can only be detected by
detailed examination of the small minority of households in western
Europe that did contain relatives other than spouse and offspring?

To assemble information on the kin structure of the contemporary
European household seems at first sight a straightforward task. After all,

[68] P. Laslett (1977a): ch. 1. Laslett's 'western' and Hajnal's 'north-western' relate to
approximately the same area. The household classification system first developed for
Household and family in past time has been used in a number of studies of widely diverse
areas. But most of the other classification schemes that have been devised are also
kin-based, as is clear from the files of the *Journal of Family History*. See for example R. J.
Smith, 'The domestic cycle in selected commoner families in urban Japan' (1978),
Berkner and Shaffer, 'The joint family in the Nivernais' (1978), and Hammel, 'Household structure in fourteenth-century Macedonia' (1980). Schmidtbauer, 'Households
and household forms of Viennese Jews' (1980) is more thorough but has a multiplexity
of categories, and the only major exception that has arisen concerns studies of North
American communities where the principal categorization of households as 'isolated
nuclear', 'primary augmented', and 'sub-nuclear' conflates kin and boarders. See
Chudacoff, 'Newlyweds and family extension' (1978).

censuses are held at regular intervals in almost all European countries; most publish data on household and family structure; and the United Nations and other interested organizations issue guidelines on how the census should be conducted, the definitions of family and household that ought to be applied, and the form of tabulations and the level of detail that ought to result. Yet in practice it has proved difficult to muster comparative data on the kin component of the European household. Table 1.9, in which this information is presented, is replete with various measures of the kin component and the different definitions that underpin them, and this means that we shall only take the figures as approximations. We are therefore in the strange position of being able to describe the 'historic' European household, albeit in a restricted number of places, with rather more certainty than we can European households of today.

The problem with the contemporary data has arisen because individual countries, in defiance sometimes of the spirit and sometimes of the letter of the United Nations guidelines, have failed to agree on what should constitute the 'resident' population, or a 'household' or a 'family', let alone agree on a definition of 'a related person' or the level of detail in a table. In part these disagreements stem from the fact that while all can agree on what a 'birth' or 'death' means (and in most cases a 'marriage') and provide comparative statistics about them, notions of 'household' and 'family' are so closely linked with the culture of a particular nation that the respective census offices feel obliged to plough their own definitional furrow. This affects the comparative analysis we are trying to undertake in a number of ways. For example, a greater propensity to reclassify the inmates of institutions by their household of usual residence (as in Germany) against a more 'real' definition of the institutional population (as in France) will, relative to the French figures, depress the proportion of households with kin in Germany if the majority of these persons are credited to one-person households.[69] On the other hand, the use of the 'housing' concept of the household (all persons in a dwelling considered to form a household), as in France, Switzerland, and Sweden, in place of the 'housekeeping unit' concept of the household will reduce the number of identified households, and particularly of one-person households, because 'lodgers' who cater for

[69] The age structure of the institutional population in conjunction with the household patterns of West Germany makes this likely. If those in institutions had, relative to the population outside institutions, a greater propensity to be kin, then the opposite would apply, i.e. an 'exaggeration' of the number of households with kin. This example is based on my reading of Le Bras, *Child and family* (1979): 131–3.

Table 1.9. *Europe c. 1970: proportion of households containing relatives*

	Date	≥Two-family households[a] as proportion of all households (%)	One-family households with relatives as proportion of one-family households (%)	All family households with relatives as proportion of all households (%)	Households with relatives as proportion of all households (%)
Western Europe					
England	1971	1	4	5	8
Scotland	1971	1	6	6	9
Wales	1971	2	6	9	11
Northern Ireland	1971	4	—	—	—
Eire	1971	4	—	—	—
Netherlands	1971	1	4	4	5
Belgium	1970	2	5	5	—
France	1975	1	—	—	—
Luxembourg	1970	—	—	14	15
Switzerland	1970	—	—	5	7
West Germany	1977	2	3	4	5
Iceland and Scandinavia					
Iceland	1960	5	—	—	—
Norway	1970	3	—	5	7
Sweden	1970	1	—	—	—
Denmark	1970	7	—	—	3
Finland	1970	—	7[b]	7[b]	—
Southern Europe					
Portugal	1970	8	7	13	—
Spain	1970	6	—	—	—
Italy	1971	—	—	—	17
Yugoslavia	1971	12	11	18	19
Central and eastern Europe					
Austria	1971	4	8	9	10
Hungary	1970	6	17	18	—
Czechoslovakia	1970	4	—	—	—
German D.R.	1971	1	—	—	—
Poland	1970	5	10[c]	12[c]	12[c]
U.S.S.R.	1970	4	20	23	—

[a] Not all of these households necessarily contain related families, although where the evidence is available only a very small minority consist of unrelated families.
[b] 10% and 9% respectively if a further category of households with relatives and/or non-relatives is included.
[c] 14%, 15%, and 18% respectively if a further category of households with relatives and/or non-relatives is included.
Definitions: Every attempt has been made to exclude figures which are not directly comparable, although, because of the differences in defining household, family, and relatives, all the figures are to be understood as approximations. In most cases there is an undercount of the true number of households with relatives, defining relatives as all persons related to the household head other than spouse or offspring. Most uncertainty

surrounds the figure for France because of the limiting definition of family (parent(s) and child(ren) under age 25) and for Sweden, while the proportion of households with relatives in Luxembourg and of two-family households in Denmark seems suspiciously high. However, in Luxembourg grandchildren appear to be included in the count of relatives, whereas in certain other countries, West Germany and the United Kingdom, for example, when their parents are not resident they are regarded as offspring in the relevant tabulations.

Sources: This table has been compiled from information supplied by the census or statistical bureaus of the respective countries. The numbers from which these proportions have been derived are, for the most part, found in the appropriate 'household' or 'family' volumes of each of the national censuses. Exceptionally, in the case of Denmark, some of the material was unpublished. In addition I have had occasion to refer to the following publications: Le Bras (1979); *United Nations demographic yearbook* (1976): table 42; C. M. Van't Klooster-van Wingerden, *Huishoudenssamenstelling en Samenlevingsvormen* (1979); German Democratic Republic, *Statistisches Jahrbuch 1974 der Deutschen Demokratischen Republik* (1974): tables 18, 23. I would also like to thank for their assistance and advice H. Palli, B. Benson, C. M. Van't Klooster-van Wingerden, A. Wrightson, J. Kochanowicz, R. Andorka, E. Hammel, P. Plas, K. Mehlan, P. Schmidtbauer, and R. Beacham.

themselves will not be considered as forming households.[70] Finally, the definition of 'family' and of the related persons themselves can inflate or depress the number of kin recorded for one country in relation to those recorded for another.[71] Grandchildren, in particular, are rarely comprehensively recorded, particularly if they are present in a household but their parents are not.

In most cases, therefore, the figures in table 1.9 are not only approximations but are also minimal figures.[72] The proportion of households with relatives is almost everywhere somewhat greater than is suggested here.

Imperfections in the way the data have been tabulated make it necessary to proffer four different measures of households with kin in table 1.9. In essentials the system of tabulating households with relatives approximates to the Laslett classificatory scheme as outlined in *Household and family in past time* (see n. 33 above). Thus there is the same sort of division between households with two and those with only one family unit (married couple or parent-and-child group). To produce a

[70] The terms and definitions referred to here are from Le Bras (1979): 75–8, who provides the best brief guide to these issues though still raising more questions than he resolves.

[71] For example, there will be fewer two-family households if, as in France, families are limited to parent(s) and unmarried child(ren) under the age of 25, while elsewhere no age bar is applied.

[72] All the figures included in table 1.9 have been scrutinized in relation to the definitions of household, family, and kin that applied in each country. Where there is reason to suspect the validity of a particular figure, reference to this has been made in the table notes. However, I would not wish to claim that all serious biases have been identified, let alone eliminated, since the definitional notes which accompany the census volumes on the household are often obscure, are rarely fully translated into English even when table headings are in English, and can scarcely hope to suffice for such a major exercise in comparative analysis as that undertaken here.

figure for the overall proportion of households with relatives, it is
necessary to add the proportion of family households with relatives as
represented in column 4 of table 1.9 to those no-family households
which contain relatives.[73] When this overall figure is missing from table
1.9, it is because the appropriate census office has not continued the
count of relatives through all the categories of household. Often, to put a
limit on the number of subcategories of household, it is the no-family
households that are not completely described. Even more unfortunate is
the fact that the count of relatives has sometimes been abandoned
altogether in certain countries where the number of households with
relatives is now very low.

We have, therefore, to be cautious in framing conclusions about the
shape of the contemporary European household, and for the present we
will be content with the following two observations. First, whatever
may have been the position earlier, it was not Britain that in 1971 had
the lowest proportion of households containing relatives, for there were
a number of other countries – Denmark, West Germany, the Netherlands, Switzerland, and Norway – with proportions lower than the
English ones. Second, there is evidence that there is still quite considerable variation across Europe in the proportion of households containing kin. This is a matter of some surprise, for data from a number of
countries confirm the substantial decline in this type of household
during the post-Second World War period. In Switzerland, the proportion of persons identified as the kin of the household head has fallen
from 5.0% in 1960 to 3.2% in 1970.[74] In Finland the decline has been
from 3.6% in 1960 to 2.7% in 1970 and in England between 1947 and
1970 from 11.5% to 4.7%.[75]

Yet this similiarity in the trend has not removed the differences
between European nations in the frequency of living with relatives, at
least not yet. Table 1.9 demonstrates that there are many more households with relatives in the countries of eastern and southern Europe
than in western Europe. Even within western Europe, moreover, there

[73] Column 3 of table 1.9 ('One-family households with relatives as a proportion of
one-family households') has been included to give some idea of the proportion of
households with relatives that would also contain children. Cf. the socialization hypothesis in P. Laslett (1977a): 35–6.
[74] Le Bras (1979): 14. In 1930, kin constituted only 4.3% of the population, revealing how
mistaken it would be to project into the past a linear decline in households containing
kin.
[75] The proportions for Finland include only grandchildren or parents of the household
head; see Le Bras (1979): 167. The two figures for England are from Gray, 'The British
household' (1947) and R. Barnes and Durant, 'Pilot work on the General Household
Survey' (1970). Both are derived from samples, but for other data on English households, broadly confirming the trend, see Wall (1982a).

is some variation, as may be seen if one sets the figures for Luxembourg and the admittedly crude ones on Ireland (both north and south) alongside those for some of the Scandinavian countries.

It would be very tempting to propose at this stage the general statement that the further east or south one goes in Europe, the more likely it is that the households will be complex, that is to say to contain relatives. The evidence seems to be there at the level of the nation, although the countries that constitute the British Isles would stand as an exception to such a trend, but the general statement can easily be shown not to hold at a regional level. We cite below the case of Hungary (fig. 1.4), although there are other nations to which we might equally well refer – Italy for example.

Apart from any differences in the proportion of households with relatives, both the number and type of relative incorporated into the household also vary from one country to another. This level of detail on the household is available for far fewer countries but is sufficient to reveal that such variation occurs even when there is little absolute difference between the two countries in the proportion of households containing relatives. This is so with Austria and England in 1971 (10% and 8% of households respectively containing relatives). In Austria, however, there are 18 relatives per 100 households, whereas in England, where the household head is less likely to have his parents co-resident, there are only 11 relatives per 100 households.

What we have to ask ourselves is how it is that these differences have persisted despite the recent Europe-wide trend towards smaller and less complex households. One possibility, which the present study is well equipped to assess, is whether there is a long-standing tendency in different countries to form a particular type of household; a cultural norm, perhaps, long outlasting the economic and social forces to which it owed its origin. It emerges that there is little evidence of such norms in regard to the kin component of the household (compare tables 1.10 and 1.11). In Austria, for example, sections of which one might well expect to exhibit 'traditional' behaviour patterns, there has been a considerable change between the 'historic' period and the present. Indeed, there is a much closer similarity in England between households in the seventeenth century and in 1971 than there is between 'old' and 'new' Austria. Yet even for England we can produce evidence of quite a different structure to the kin group during the intervening period (cf. Wall, chapter 16 below).

It could perhaps be argued that, first, the aspect on which to focus is the frequency with which households contained relatives, rather than

Table 1.10. *Composition of the kin group within the household: contemporary data, number of relatives per 100 households*[a]

Relationship to household head	England 1970	Belgium 1970	Switzerland 1970	Austria 1971	Finland 1970
Parent(s)[b]	3	5	3	8	5
Siblings[b]	2	3	—	—	—
Son/daughter-in-law	2	—	—	—	—
Nephew/niece	—	—	—	—	—
Grandchild	2	—	—	—	3
Other relative	2	—	7	10	—
TOTAL	11	—	9	18	—

[a] Calculated to the nearest whole number, and hence the sum of the individual items and the column totals may not agree. Blanks in the columns indicate that the relevant information was unavailable. In certain cases this means that the count of relatives is incomplete, in which case the total line has also been left blank.
[b] Includes in-laws.
Sources:
Le Bras (1979).
England: R. Barnes and Durant (1970).
Austria: Findl and Helczmanovszki, *The population of Austria* (1977): table 38.

the particular type or even the number of kin in the household, and, second, that this commitment to kin would be more likely to be in evidence at regional than at national level, where a number of divergent local patterns may be obscured through a self-cancelling effect. Certain types of familial patterns are known to have persisted over long periods of time. Peter Laslett, for example, in his intensive survey of illegitimacy, has found whole regions which have maintained a tradition of a higher or lower incidence of base-born children over several centuries and economic transformations.[76] We shall now attempt to see whether there is any evidence for a similar tradition in regard to the composition of the household. For this purpose we have chosen three countries to serve as case studies, namely Hungary, Britain, and France,[77] and have plotted

[76] P. Laslett, Oosterveen, and Smith (eds.), *Bastardy and its comparative history* (1980): 29–48.
[77] For the 1970s we have abstracted information from the respective national census publications on the household. The analysis of the Hungarian data was generously undertaken by R. Andorka of the Central Statistical Office in Budapest. Andorka with Faragó is also the source of household patterns in Hungary in 1828 (see ch. 9 below). Their map (fig. 9.2) covers Hungary within its traditional boundaries, and so much of this as is related to present-day Hungary is shown in fig. 1.4a. Some slight adjustment to areas where there were above-average proportions of sons (and/or sons-in-law) might be necessary if the basic data (not available in Cambridge) were reworked to reflect the smaller area in observation. Figures for France in 1858 have been calculated from

Table 1.11. *Composition of the kin group within the household: historical data, number of relatives per 100 households[a]*

Relationship to household head[b]	England 1650– 1749	Iceland 1703	Geneva 1720	Norway 1801	Austria 1632– 1919
Parent(s)[c]	2	11	4	15	5
Siblings[c]	2	18	6	9	7
Son/daughter-in-law	1	0	1	1	—
Nephew/niece	1	2	4	—	—
Grandchild	3	1	1	4	4
Other relative	2	0	1	3	8
TOTAL	11	33	18	32	23
N (households)	2,675	8,150	3,034	163,564	17,770

[a] Calculated to be the nearest whole number, and hence the column totals and the sum of the individual cells may disagree.
[b] Where cells are left blank, persons with this relationship have not been separately distinguished and are subsumed in the category 'Other relative'.
[c] Includes in-laws.
Sources:
England: manuscript analyses held at the SSRC Cambridge Group.
Iceland: Statistical Bureau of Iceland, *Manntalid 1703* (1960): table VIII.
Geneva: recalculated excluding married sons and daughters from Perrenoud, *La population genève* (1979): 136.
Norway: calculated from information supplied by S. Dyrvik of the University of Bergen.
Austria: calculated from Schmidtbauer, 'Daten zur historischen Demographie und Familienstruktur' (1977). The 40 local censuses for which the relevant information has been tabulated (total households and composition of the kin group) range in date from 1637 to 1919, but the vast majority are eighteenth-century (17) or nineteenth-century (16). Only 2 are later than 1900.

present and past interregional variations in the proportion of households with relatives.[78]

In 1970, the areas of Hungary with complex households were located in the west and north of that country. There is almost no match with 1828, where, according to Andorka and Faragó's data, the areas of

Mendels, 'La composition du ménage paysan' (1978): 800–1. The information on Britain in 1851 represents a preliminary analysis of the households in the random sample of districts throughout the country initially assembled with much labour by Michael Anderson of the University of Edinburgh.

[78] Differences in the way in which the household has been analysed and occasional imperfections in the available data cannot but render these comparisons crude ones. For example, it may be questioned whether the calculation of the proportion of households with relatives in Britain in 1851 in place of the mean number of relatives per household would have yielded a different regional pattern. Until Michael Anderson's sample tapes can be more fully exploited we cannot exclude this as a possibility, but there was such a

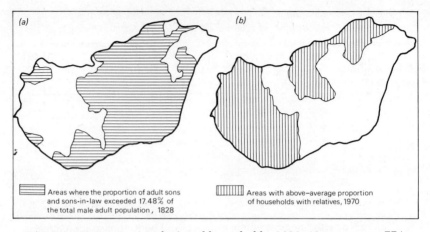

Fig. 1.4a. Hungary: complexity of households, 1828. (*Source:* see n. 77.)

Fig. 1.4b. Hungary: complexity of households, 1970. (*Source:* see n. 77.)

complex households, as calculated from the variation in the proportion of adult sons and sons-in-law in the total population, were predominantly in central and southern Hungary (fig. 1.4). Clearly there is little carry-over of regional patterns here.

For Britain, the position seems the same. At first, the 1971 pattern of more complex households in the west and fewer complex households in the east, shown in fig. 1.5a, looks like a type of cultural heritage. There is after all no obvious economic factor to suggest why the south-west, industrial south Wales, rural mid-Wales, Merseyside, Cumbria, and indeed western Scotland might participate in a common household pattern.[79] Yet this pattern was not in existence in its entirety even 20 years earlier (see fig. 1.5b), while in 1851, though we have to rely for the present on the admittedly crude measure of the mean number of relatives per household, the regional pattern was altogether different (see fig. 1.5c). The clue to the origin of these regional patterns therefore most probably lies with the economic structure generated during the course of the late nineteenth and early twentieth centuries.[80]

wide range between regions in the number of kin that it seems unlikely that the alternative calculation would seriously alter the regional pattern shown in fig 1.5c. There are similar problems in the case of Hungary, as the comparison is of the proportion of households with relatives (1971) in relation to adult sons and sons-in-law in the population (1828), with the latter probably subject to the influence of fertility levels as well as to the frequency of one particular type of complex household.

[79] Fig. 1.5 shows only variations by region. Variations in household types between subdivisions of economic planning regions are set out in Wall (1982a).

[80] This cannot be more than a hypothesis at this stage. Censuses after 1851 remain unanalysed apart from the occasional community study and from 1891 are closed under

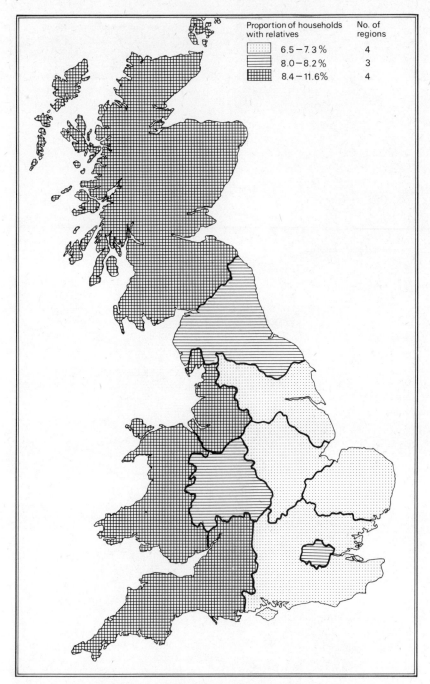

Proportion of households | No. of
with relatives | regions
6.5 – 7.3 % | 4
8.0 – 8.2 % | 3
8.4 – 11.6 % | 4

Fig. 1.5a. Distribution of complex households by economic planning regions (definition of 1971), Great Britain, 1971. (*Source:* Wall (1982a).)

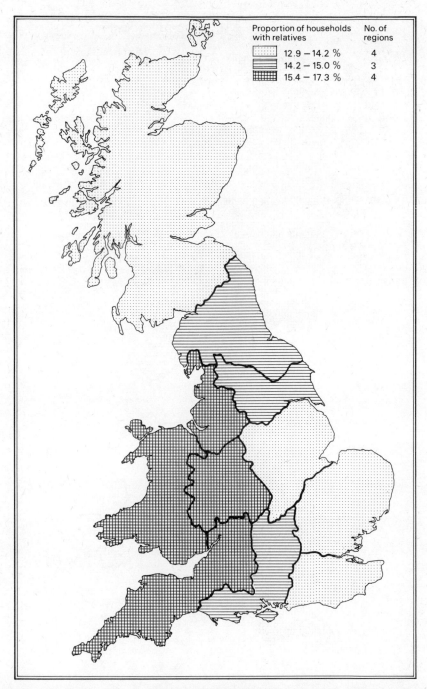

Fig. 1.5b. Distribution of complex households by standard regions, Great Britain, 1951. (*Source:* Wall (1982a).)

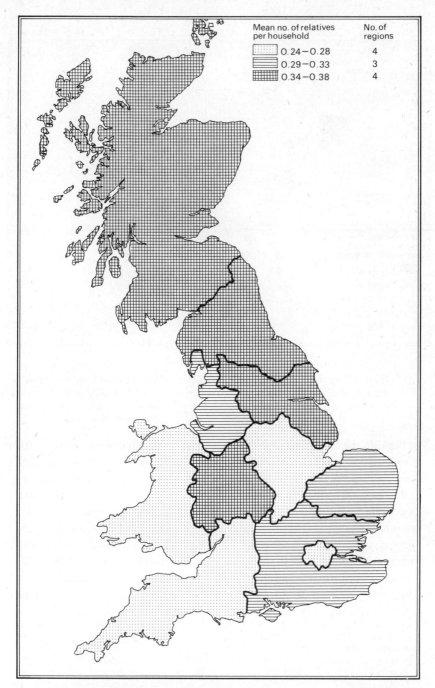

Fig. 1.5c. Distribution of complex households by economic planning region (definition of 1971), Great Britain, 1851. (*Source:* Wall (1982a).)

Richard Wall

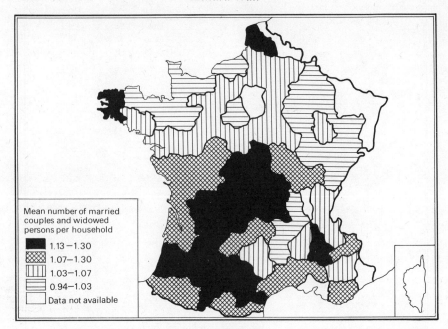

Fig. 1.6a. Distribution of complex households by department, France, 1856.
(*Source:* Calculated from Mendels (1978): 800–1. Some of the categories
overlap, and the departments have been placed within them according to
their position in the hierarchy determined from other information given
by Mendels on the number of adult members of the family.)

Finally, we may turn to France, and there we discover a north–south
divide in 1975 not unlike that of the mid-nineteenth century (see figs.
1.6a and b). We are certainly not the first to find more complex households in southern than in northern France. Laslett and Flandrin have
been able to illustrate it for periods anterior to the nineteenth century.[81]
Mendels has linked it to inheritance practices in the middle of the
nineteenth century, and more recently Todd and Le Bras, in a very
speculative work, have seen it as underpinning other regional differences from the level of suicide to the power of the church and voting
allegiances right up to the 1970s.[82] This may be to carry the importance

the 100-year rule. Nor is there any thorough analysis of households in any of the census
volumes (indeed, none at all between 1861 and 1951). Even the census of 1971 lacks a
tabulation of household type by occupation of the household head at regional level.
However, the national-level tabulation shows own-account farmers and industrial
workers as most likely and agricultural workers as least likely to have relatives in their
households. The regional distribution of these occupations might help to explain what
would otherwise be a very puzzling regional pattern in households with kin.

[81] P. Laslett (1977a): 25; Flandrin, *Families in former times* (1979): 70–4.
[82] Mendels (1978); Le Bras and Todd, *L'invention de la France* (1981): 38–40, 44, 52.

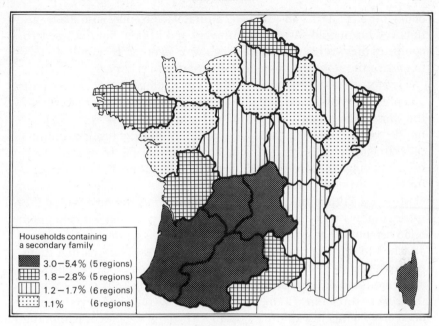

Households containing
a secondary family

▓ 3.0−5.4% (5 regions)
▦ 1.8−2.8% (5 regions)
▥ 1.2−1.7% (6 regions)
▦ 1.1% (6 regions)

Fig. 1.6b. Distribution of complex households by region, France, 1975. (*Sources:* Institut National de la Statistique et des Etudes Economiques, *Census of France, 1975*: regional vols., table D 23; for Corsica, Observatoire Economique d'Ajaccio, *Economie corse* (1979): table D 23.)

of the family too far. The evidence to support the authors' claims is weak in that only a minority of households conform to the type identified with a particular region. On the other hand, a preference for a particular type of household, albeit as a minority phenomenon, that can be detected in 1856 and again in 1975 merits careful attention. Given the social and economic change of the intervening 120 years, the pattern has clearly outlasted any economic and social factors which might have provided the rationale for its existence. Indeed the most recent census figures (1975) show that the greater preference for complex households in southern France is exercised not only by those with more traditional occupations, that is those with agricultural employment, but also by those residents of the rural areas with non-agricultural employment and even by the inhabitants of the towns. For France, therefore, there is some evidence of a long-lasting association of a particular household pattern with a particular region, induced by factors that seem not to be in any immediate sense 'economic' but which are usually referred to as 'cultural'; that is to say an unexplained preference for a particular

behavioural pattern. Of course, cultural factors may also have influenced household patterns in Hungary and Britain, but in these two
countries they were not strong enough *vis-à-vis* other, economic, factors
to ensure the stability of regional differences over time.[83]

It is a pity that we cannot as yet make more comparisons between past
and present. We have no way of knowing whether the kin group within
the Norwegian or Icelandic household is the same now as in the past,
nor do we have information for a sufficient number of historic communities in Finland or Belgium to produce a 'national' figure against which
we could judge the kin group of the present day. There is, however, one
further point to be made on the basis of the data in table 1.11 above.
North-west Europe has been aptly categorized as the area where the
nuclear family predominated, that is where few households contained
relatives, but it has not always been clear what significance should be
attached to this fact. It does not mean, as table 1.11 shows, that there
existed a unified system in terms of the number and type of kin present
in the household. In Iceland in 1703 and Norway in 1801, for example,
there were three times as many kin as there were in late-seventeenth-
and early-eighteenth-century England. The largest element within the
group of kin were the grandchildren of the head in England and the
head's parents in Norway, while the siblings of the head predominated
in the other areas represented in table 1.11.

The information provided by this table modifies in two important
ways Peter Laslett's delineation of the western European family.[84] First,
it raises anew the question of whether the Scandinavian household fits
the western European model (little information on Scandinavia was
available when Laslett wrote in 1977). Second, it demonstrates considerable diversity across north-west Europe in the range and type of kin
incorporated into the household. This has only become clear now
because so many of the earlier studies had to be conducted at village
level, where a large amount of the variation could be imputed to chance
influences. Admittedly, in placing any significance on kin within the
household one should not forget that these kin represented only a
fraction of the number of kin appertaining to each individual, to aid and
be aided, but given the importance of such support (see above, section
II), particularly between parents and married children, it seems
plausible to argue that the type of kin within the household will provide
a useful pointer to the nature of the family system.

[83] Nor is the absence of a cultural norm to be inferred from the fact that its adoption confers
    an economic advantage on the participants; cf. J. Davis (1977): 206f, 222.
[84] P. Laslett (1977a): 29.

However, any system is an abstraction: an ideal type that necessarily ignores the variations that exist in the real world. Often an examination of the *structure* of that variation can illuminate the relationships between the family system and other aspects of the economic and social context. In a single country, Norway, for instance, it is possible to identify a significant variation in the shape of the composition of the kin group according to the occupation of the household head.[85] The overriding characteristic, the supplanting of the old by the young (extension upwards in household), went right across Norwegian society in 1801. It was the farmers, however, who exhibited this *par excellence*, while the 'modern' element in Norwegian society, the merchants, administrators, and shopkeepers, made relatively greater use of more distant kin. Industrial workers had a pattern somewhat intermediate between the two, although with generally small numbers of total kin. Some of the variation may be imputed to differences in wealth. Some households could simply afford to support more kin than others. For example, farmers had more kin co-resident than crofters, and merchants more than shopkeepers, but only a small part of the variation is to be explained in this way. Much more appears to have arisen from the economic circumstances of the receiving households requiring the services, and providing the opportunities, for different sets of people. From a study of the variation in the kin group within the household according to the occupation of the head and the other family members, particularly at the level of the individual community, we come as close as we can to an understanding of the actual function of kin in particular households.

The lack of significant variation among occupational groups, as in societies in which serfdom was common, can be equally illuminating in drawing attention to the strength of cultural factors. In Russian serf populations, for example, generally only the old had an opportunity to head a household, and women had a low status, taking over many of the functions of servants in western Europe. In a recent paper Mitterauer and Kagan have found some differences between Russian household structure and that of central Europe.[86] For example, Russian household

---

[85] Based on information supplied by S. Dyrvik of the University of Bergen, derived in turn from recent tabulations of the 1801 census by the Central Bureau of Statistics in Oslo. Further analysis in Cambridge involved the calculation for each occupational group of the mean number of parents and 'other kin' per household.

[86] For Russia relying on an analysis of households in Jaroslavl, 250 km north-east of Moscow, and Czap's material on Mishino (see ch. 3 below). See Mitterauer and Kagan, 'Russian family structures from a central European point of view' (1980). In drawing the contrast between central European and Russian households the authors are careful to point out that households were not invariant across Greater Russia and that in

heads were less inclined to remarry, and there were more widower- than widow-headed households, all this stemming from the much greater emphasis in Russia on the patrilineal principle. Some of these differences are no doubt more critical than others, but what is really at issue are the factors that produce such different households in Russia. The key, clearly, does not rest with the occupational structure nor with the absence of individual wealth. Mitterauer and Kagan not only find that the rural serfs of the nobility, both so-called 'farmers' and house servants, had complex households, but that this was also true of factory serfs and, to a lesser extent, of town craftsmen.[87] The obvious factor uniting the bulk of the population was serfdom itself. Could complex households be the means by which the serf owner exerted his power over a subject population, guaranteed labour for his estates and produc- tion in his factories? Could they at the same time provide the means by which the serfs could ensure that they met these obligations?

However, serfdom could take many forms (see the chapters by Kochanowicz, Plakans, and Palli below). In parts of Austria the lord of the manor was no less concerned to ensure that his farmsteads were in capable hands, an interest that frequently led to the retirement of the older generation and their ejection to the *Altenteil*. How was it, there- fore, that in Russia the serf owner was able to exert effective control through the medium of the older generation of peasants? It seems most unlikely that the serf owner was brought to act in this way because the peasantry (or critical sections of it) saw some particular advantage to itself in these arrangements (though these advantages may have been there). More tempting is the argument that the different types of serf- dom reflect differences at some time in the past in the balance of two key resources: people and land. By the nineteenth century, however, com- plex households were to be found in sparsely and densely populated regions, and a more plausible explanation, at least for the eighteenth and nineteenth centuries, is that there existed certain long-standing norms of behaviour to which all sections of society bowed as they accepted them implicitly. These norms, though, were a somewhat strange mixture. They involved acceptance and respect for those in authority, coupled with a conceptualization of rights and duties, not only to the serf owner but also to other family members through the formation of dowries, as being a communal rather than an individual

particular households were smaller, fewer households were complex, and marriage came later for both men and women in Jaroslavl than in Mishino. See also R. E. F. Smith, *Peasant farming in Muscovy* (1977) for a radically different account of Russian household structure.

[87] Mitterauer and Kagan (1980).

responsibility. Such norms would change very slowly, their origin lying well back in Russia's past, since in the nineteenth century a similar family system could be found operating in the area east of the Urals where serfdom was unknown.[88] Conceivably it was because of such norms that when the serf owner relaxed interest in his estate and when the serfs were finally freed, other communal organizations so easily moved into the power vacuum that had been created.

In tracing the evolution of the household over time we have tried to move beyond a simple description of patterns and trends to an appreciation of why the pattern took one form rather than another, was modified when change was unexpected, or remained static when change was anticipated. Often our interpretation has been couched in economic terms, as in the case of the variation in the composition of the kin group with the occupation of the household head in the Norwegian census of 1801. Moreover, the different occupational complexion of British regions probably underlay the regional differences in household composition noted for 1971. Yet, particularly when it came to interpreting the pattern of household composition across Europe, it has not been easy to find convincing 'economic' explanations. Hence we have argued above for cultural factors influencing a minority to form one type of household in southern France and another type in the north.

It is not easy to prove that there are norms to which households may be expected to conform, the more so when one is not in a position of being able to interview the people concerned. Frederick Le Play considered the norm in England to be the independence of each family, a norm that may have been desired but, as we know, was not so regularly achieved (cf. tables 1.5 and 1.7 and discussion above). The headship rates for pre-industrial England, however, show that as many as 60% of all the males over the age of 15 headed their own households (see fig. 1.1). The context for this was both a norm (a preference for a particular type of household) and a set of economic circumstances that enabled people to translate the preference into reality. The critical factors were, for the young, the demand for non-familial labour and, for the elderly, the existence of non-familial support in times of crisis. The situation is, therefore, inevitably complex and an examination of the household in all its aspects central to an understanding of social, economic, and demographic history.

[88] Le Play (1877–9): vol. II, describing the Bachkirs, semi-nomadic shepherds.

2

Two kinds of pre-industrial household formation system

J. HAJNAL

I. Introduction

A similar discovery about household size has been made in the last few decades about widely different societies, namely parts of Europe in pre-industrial times, India, and China. It was until recently widely believed that in pre-industrial Europe, as well as in India and China, large households used to be the norm. The discovery that the average household size was of the order of only five persons therefore came as a surprise.

The traditional household formation systems of India and China are similar (at least in the aspects dealt with in this chapter). But the household formation systems of north-west Europe in the seventeenth and eighteenth centuries were very different (though they yielded households of roughly the same size). The aim of this chapter is to compare and contrast the two kinds of household formation system in quantitative terms. The term 'household formation system' has been used to indicate that the intention is to compare modes of behaviour which result in the formation of households of various kinds as well as to compare the results of that behaviour. A household formation system is defined by household formation rules, as described in section II.

Enough data have now been accumulated by historians to support strongly, in spite of gaps in the evidence, the conclusion that (as was implied in the previous paragraph) the household formation systems of all populations in pre-industrial north-west Europe shared certain com-

This paper was written during a stay at the Office of Population Research, Princeton University (supported by the Mellon Foundation) and at Rockefeller University (supported by the Ford Foundation). Without the help of many people at both institutions (especially the extraordinary amount of assistance given by the library staff at the Office of Population Research) the chapter could not have been written. I wish especially to record my gratitude to Joel E. Cohen, whose initiative and warm support made possible my period of work in the United States.

mon features which distinguished them from India, China, and many other pre-industrial populations.

The term 'north-west Europe' as used here covers the Scandinavian countries (including Iceland, but excluding Finland), the British Isles, the Low Countries, the German-speaking area, and northern France. This area showed the European pattern of late marriage, as much evidence now confirms, back into the seventeenth century. The data on household composition in this area show, among other characteristics to be described, a high proportion of 'servants' (see section VI) and very small numbers of households comprising more than one married couple. The late age at marriage and household composition are clearly related and reflect the distinguishing features of the pre-industrial north-west European household formation systems, as explained in section II below.

The term 'pre-industrial north-west Europe' denotes north-west Europe in the seventeenth and eighteenth centuries.[1]

No attempt will be made in this chapter to discuss household composition in southern Europe or in Finland and the Baltic countries during those centuries (even though these areas are also mostly areas of late marriage by the end of the nineteenth century).[2] The reason for singling out north-west Europe in this way is twofold; namely lack of data for the other areas mentioned and evidence which suggests that in the seventeenth and eighteenth centuries household formation systems in at least some parts of these regions did not have the distinguishing north-west European features. There is evidence that in the eighteenth century and earlier the first marriage of women in parts of southern France and Italy occurred at a younger age.[3] There is also evidence that the composition of households did not everywhere in southern France and Italy display the north-west European characteristic. In Finland and the Baltic countries also there is evidence from the eighteenth century of both earlier marriage and household composition patterns departing from the pre-industrial north-west European norms. There are also large areas (for example the Iberian peninsula) from which no household data for the relevant period appear to have been published. It may well be that the distinguishing features of north-west European house-

[1] The adjective 'pre-industrial' has, however, usually been omitted; i.e. the terms 'north-west Europe' and 'north-west European' will refer to north-west Europe in the seventeenth and eighteenth centuries unless otherwise stated.
[2] See Hajnal, 'European marriage patterns' (1965). The present chapter may be regarded as a sequel to that paper.
[3] R. M. Smith, 'Origins of the "European marriage pattern" in Europe' (1979a) reviews this evidence.

hold formation systems were to be found in the seventeenth and eighteenth centuries among populations outside north-west Europe as we have defined that region. We must wait for further research to decide this question. By the end of the nineteenth century the European pattern of late marriage certainly extended beyond the boundaries of north-west Europe.

North-west European populations in the seventeenth and eighteenth centuries were both demographically and economically 'traditional' societies. They had a 'young' age structure (and, of course, the age structure has a very great effect on household size and composition). North-west Europe was at that time largely pre-industrial in the sense that populations almost everywhere were mainly rural. 'Productive' economic activities (farming, fishing, crafts) were mainly carried out in and by households and not in enterprises or workplaces specialized for the purpose (plantations, factories, offices, etc.). It does not follow that all households functioned as productive enterprises. For the purposes of this chapter households are 'housekeeping units', as is explained below. Many households were not economically 'productive'.

This chapter attempts to contrast the household formation systems of pre-industrial north-west Europe with the household formation systems of a number of other populations which also showed these pre-modern demographic and economic characteristics. In particular all the populations treated in this paper had a 'young' age composition (with 44% or more of the population under 20 years of age). They were all populations of high fertility compared with the levels of fertility found in Europe today. All of them also had much higher mortality rates than those of modern Europe. All of them were predominantly rural, and the 'productive' economic activities of these rural populations were mainly carried out in and by households (sometimes in some populations with two or more households combining for farming or other 'productive' purposes). However, many households in most of the populations discussed were not economically 'productive'.

The household formation systems of the populations outside north-west Europe dealt with in sections IV and V shared certain common characteristics (as described in section II below). Household formation systems sharing these characteristics will be called 'joint household systems'. The different kinds of data which are available for different populations have largely dictated the comparisons with north-west Europe which it has been possible to make.

For comparisons of household structure between very different societies, it is desirable to be explicit about what is meant by 'house-

hold'. The intention has been to use data which treat each 'housekeeping unit' as a separate household. The matter is dealt with in greater
detail in the appendix to this chapter.

In some populations there is a substantial difference in household size
and structure between urban and rural areas. The aim of this chapter is
to describe household formation in the rural areas. So far as possible,
data for rural areas have been used. Where the urban population constituted only a small proportion of the total population, data for the total
population will reflect the behaviour of the rural component. This is
mostly the case with the populations covered in this chapter.

The emphasis has been placed as far as possible upon large-scale data
covering populations of say 5,000 or more people, rather than upon
data from individual communities, which are often used in discussions
of demographic and other statistical data for past centuries. The household composition data for small communities displayed substantial
variation (both variation between different communities and variation
over time in the same community) even when vital rates and household
formation rules were identical and unchanged.[4]

This chapter, like all work dealing with historical household data,
owes a great deal to the work of the Cambridge Group for the History of
Population and Social Structure. In particular the volume *Household and
family in past time* put the historical study of households on a new factual
basis. The theme of the present paper bears an obvious affinity to
chapter 1 of Peter Laslett's book *Family life and illicit love in earlier
generations*, but I have tried to put emphasis on other kinds of data and
other types of questions than those dealt with in the two works just
mentioned.[5]

II. Household formation rules

By a 'joint household' we mean a household comprising two or more
related married couples. (A 'simple household', correspondingly, is one
which contains only one married couple or none at all.) The north-west
European household formation systems operated in such a manner as to
produce very few joint households. The majority of persons, even of
those who survived to middle age, were never members of a joint
household.

[4] Information on the 'random variation' in household characteristics to be expected in
small populations may be found in Wachter with Hammel and Laslett, *Statistical studies of
historical social structure* (1978).
[5] My debt to the Cambridge Group goes far beyond the reading of their publications. I
have benefited greatly from many discussions with Peter Laslett and other members of
the Group (especially Richard Smith and Richard Wall).

The joint household systems did not normally produce a situation where the majority of households were joint at any one time, though there have been joint household systems which have operated in that way. However, under a joint household system, the majority of people were members of a joint household at some stage in their lives.

The two kinds of household formation systems being compared can each be characterized by three rules of normal household formation behaviour, as follows.

1. *Formation rules common to north-west European simple household systems*
   a. Late marriage for both sexes (mean ages at first marriage[6] are, say, over 26 for men and over about 23 for women).
   b. After marriage a couple are in charge of their own household (the husband is head of household).
   c. Young people before marriage often circulate between households as servants.

2. *Formation rules common to joint household systems*
   a'. Earlier marriage for men and rather early marriage for women (mean ages at first marriage are under about 26 for men and under 21 for women).
   b'. A young married couple often start life together in a household of which an older couple are in charge[7] (usually the household of which the young husband has been a member).
   c'. Households with several married couples may split to form two or more households, each containing one or more couples.

These rules have been stated here in general qualitative terms. There was much variation, within both kinds of formation system, between different areas, and also probably over time, in the way in which the same rule was carried out, for example in the age at which changes specified in the rules took place. (This is illustrated by the discussion below of the splitting rule (2c').) Moreover, the two sets of rules are not complete in that they would not suffice to determine the movement of individuals between households. It is not possible for everyone to remain until death in the household into which he or she was born unless moved by marriage, entry into service, or the splitting of households.

[6] Mean ages at first marriage are intended to refer to the mean ages at first marriage which would be experienced by a cohort passing through life. Usually, only other types of indices of mean age at marriage will be available. (The singulate mean age at marriage (SMAM) will be somewhat higher than the mean age at marriage of a cohort.)

[7] There is no accepted term for the couple who are jointly in charge of a household; it might be useful to adopt the term 'housekeepers', quoted by Richard Wall from a history of the parish of Corfe Castle in England (see Wall, 'Mean household size in England' (1972): 166).

J. Hajnal

Additional movements not governed by the rules stated must occur. But the rules listed suffice to determine the features with which this paper is concerned.

The rules require some explanation.

The north-west European rule 1b, that a married couple are in charge of their own household, implies that upon marriage, either a new household was created or one spouse joined the other in a household in which there had been no married couple, or that if they took over a farm run by the parents of one of them, the parents retired when the young people married. The custom whereby one of the sons marries and takes over the farm on the retirement of his father has often been regarded as one of the essential characteristics of a 'stem family system' (at least on some definitions of that contentious term). A stem family system with this characteristic is compatible with the general north-west European household formation rules, and such systems are indeed widely found in pre-industrial north-west Europe. Such a stem family system is compatible with our north-west European rules, because the son, whether or not his retired parents live separately from the young married couple, becomes head of his own household on marriage. On the other hand, the kind of stem family system in which the old household head does not retire when his heir marries falls into neither of the two major kinds of system we are discussing. The young couple are subordinate to the parents, so rule 1b of the north-west European simple household systems is not followed. In fact this kind of stem family system did not occur in seventeenth- or eighteenth-century north-west Europe. (The very small numbers of households in pre-industrial north-west Europe where married children are recorded as members of households headed by the parents of one of them seem to refer to temporary circumstances.)

No kind of stem family system can be classified as a joint household system in our sense. In a stem family system only one heir on marriage remains in the parents' household, while under the joint household systems (rule 2b') all sons of the household normally bring their brides into the household.

It is the third rule for each of the two kinds of system (i.e. 1c and 2c') which will probably appear most surprising. The argument here is that in each case the rule was essential to the operation of the household formation systems in question.

The circulation of servants in north-west European systems is dealt with further in section VI below. Servants are found in substantial numbers concentrated at young adult ages throughout pre-industrial north-west Europe. It seems highly probable that the circulation of servants made possible the late age at marriage, for service provided a function for young unmarried adults. Because of the institution of service, young men and women were able to move away from farms and villages where their labour could not be effectively used. On the other hand, the availability of servants provided an adjustable labour supply to those farm or craft households where the number of family members available for work was too small.

The formation rules listed above (1a, 1b and 1c), which were common to all north-west Europe, had no tendency to create very large households. Very large households did occur in north-west Europe because some wealthy and important householders employed very many servants, but such large households were not the inevitable result of the common north-west European household formation rules. Rules 2a′ and 2b′ for joint household systems, however, will produce some enormous households unless splitting occurs. Even under conditions of high mortality, some men will have several sons surviving to adulthood. (It must be remembered that the variance of the total number of children born to men is much larger than for women. Men who marry a number of times continue to father children till an age well past the limits of the female reproductive period.) If a man has a number of surviving sons who bring their brides into the household, and if some of the sons have several surviving sons in their turn, a very large household will result. A joint household system, therefore, needs the splitting rule (2c′). The descriptive literature concerning joint household systems contains references to the splitting of households in all societies where the joint household systems operated.[8]

The practices in regard to the splitting of households have a crucial effect on the size and composition of households under a joint household system. If young couples tend to split away even before the husband's father has died, and if brothers surviving their father's death tend to split not many years later, households under a joint household system will be comparatively small. If, however, not only brothers, but also the children of brothers, tend to stay together, much larger households will result. This matter will be further dealt with in section V below.

Needless to say, there is much variation within each of the two basic kinds of system. But it is hoped that the data quoted below will not only show that the basic distinction is a valid one, but give a useful

---

[8] For some references see Wheaton, 'Family and kinship' (1975): 619. See also Czap, ch. 3 below, pp. 135–41.

quantitative picture of the operation of the two kinds of system and their varieties (a quantitative picture with a number of surprising features).

The formation and composition of households are clearly linked to many aspects of the general functioning of a society. It would be interesting to explore whether wider systematic differences exist between the north-west European system and joint household systems in general, but such an inquiry would not only exceed the competence of the author, but also lengthen the chapter beyond reasonable limits.

The institution of service in north-west Europe may have made possible not only late marriage, but also adjustment to changing conditions of the age at marriage. When conditions were unfavourable for setting up new households, it was possible for the unmarried to remain in service longer, moving to the farms and localities where their labour was most useful.

Finally, it should be explicitly stated that there are other kinds of household formation system besides the two considered here (for example, as has already been mentioned, the kind of stem family in which a single heir in each household remains in the household with his spouse after marriage, while the old head does not retire). Moreover, there are populations to which it would not be appropriate to apply the household concept used in this chapter.

It also needs to be emphasized that the study of households is still in its infancy in comparison with the study of such topics as fertility or mortality. What is said here is, therefore, tentative in many ways. The methods of classification and analysis to be used in the interpretation and comparison of household data from different societies are likely to undergo much modification and refinement in the future. It remains to be seen, in particular, whether the category of joint household formation systems as used in this paper, i.e. household formation systems for which rules 2a', 2b', and 2c' hold, is a useful one. Joint household systems in this sense have occurred under a variety of very different conditions widely separated in time and space. It may turn out, when statistical data on households for many other populations have been analysed in addition to those whose household data have so far been studied, that it is not fruitful to group together all the populations exhibiting those household formation rules which for the purposes of this paper are the defining characteristics of joint household systems.

III. Household composition in north-west Europe – and in rural Denmark in particular

Unfortunately, there are no data for large populations tracing the movements of individuals between households as they pass through life. Instead we can infer the consequences of household formation behaviour from censuses and similar data which show the distribution over households of all individuals in a population at a particular time. We can thus verify indirectly that the household formation rules stated were in fact in operation. A particularly useful form of analysis is provided by classifications of populations by relationship to the head of household. Such classifications display characteristic differences between the north-west European systems and joint household systems. We may summarize these as follows: (1) Populations following joint household systems have much higher proportions of joint households, as one would expect; however, they do not, on that account, necessarily have larger households on average. (2) Households under the two kinds of formation systems are made up of different sorts of individuals. In joint household systems almost all household members are relatives of the head. There are substantial numbers of such relatives in addition to the wives and children of the household head. (3) In north-west Europe, on the other hand, the composition of households is different. The numbers of such other relatives (i.e. other than wives and children of the head) are small; instead we find substantial numbers of servants and also some other persons called 'lodgers' (or some equivalent term), who may be related to the head of the household or may not (e.g. they may be farm labourers). Some of these persons (e.g. farm labourers' families living on a part of the farm but doing their own cooking) should probably be counted as separate households.[9]

We shall proceed by considering in detail one population illustrative of each of the two kinds of household formation system. Data for other populations will then be more briefly reviewed. The present section considers data for rural Denmark as representing north-west Europe.

There were official Danish censuses in 1787 and 1801. The data are of exceptionally high quality for the eighteenth century and suitable for our purposes in various ways (for example, marital status was explicitly recorded at the original enumeration; it does not need to be indirectly inferred when the data are reanalysed, e.g. by presuming that a man and woman are married if they are listed in succession at the beginning of

[9] The way such subsidiary units are recorded in the original enumerations, and how they ought to be treated, are problems which are discussed in the appendix to this chapter.

the household).[10] Not only is the original Danish census material of high quality, but it has been carefully retabulated from the original documents by H. C. Johansen of Odense University.[11] His painstaking analysis underlies much of what follows.

Professor Johansen has analysed not the whole Danish population, but a sample of 26 rural parishes (with a total population of some 7,000 persons) whose population, as he shows, resembles the whole Danish rural population in a great variety of characteristics. We may confidently take his figures as a picture of the rural Danish population as a whole. Some 80% of the population of Denmark lived in rural parishes.

Table 2.1 shows how the rural population in Denmark at the end of the eighteenth century was distributed by relation to the head of the household. The table shows the numbers in each relationship category per 100 households.[12]

Children, it should be noted, are defined in this kind of tabulation by relationship to the head, not by being under a certain age. No doubt the category included not only the biological children of the head, but others who would have an analogous position in the household, e.g. children of the wife by a former husband, or even children of a remarried wife's former husband by his first wife. The category 'servants' will be further discussed below.

Table 2.1 represents the position at the end of the eighteenth century. However, we can go back in time by one and a half centuries and add a comparative set of figures for rural parishes in the Danish islands of Moen in 1645. They result from an enumeration carried out for tax purposes by the local clergymen, and the surviving listings were analysed with exemplary care early in the twentieth century by E. P. Mackeprang.[13] Table 2.2 compares Mackeprang's data with the position at the end of the eighteenth century. ('Other relatives' and 'Others' have had to be combined in one category.) In this case, it is not clear from the original listing just what persons constitute a separate house-

[10] Thus, for example, the Danish data show how many married servants there were; but it is not possible to obtain this information from listings where, for a servant, only his relation to the household head, i.e. the fact that he is a servant, is recorded, but not his marital status.

[11] See H. C. Johansen, *Befolkningsudvikling og familiestruktur* (1975): ch. 10. I owe thanks to Professor Johansen for supplying additional materials and answering questions about his data. I am grateful to Ulla Larsen for helping with Danish text.

[12] The numbers in the table result from dividing the numbers of persons in each category by the total number of households and multiplying by 100. This calculation was done separately for 1787 and 1801, and the results were then added and divided by 2. The 1787 and 1801 figures are very similar. Differences between them are discussed in the appendix.

[13] Mackeprang, 'Et brudstykke af en folketelling' (1907).

Table 2.1. *Rural Denmark – average for 1787 and 1801: persons per 100 households by relationship to head*

	Married heads and wives	Other heads	Children	Other relatives	Servants	Others	Total
Males	88	5	99	8	50	5	255
Females	88	7	96	15	40	9	255
Both sexes	176	12	195	23	90	14	510

Note: The data relate to a sample of 26 rural parishes.
Source: Computed from H. C. Johansen (1975): 148.

Table 2.2. *Rural Denmark, 1645 (island of Moen) and 1787/1801 (26 parishes): persons (both sexes) per 100 households by relationship to head*

	Married men and wives	Other heads	Children	Servants	Others	Total
Moen (1645)	175	12	249	62	25	523
26 parishes (1797/1801)	176	12	195	90	37	510

Source: 1645 data computed from Mackeprang (1907): 258, using Mackeprang's estimate (p. 260) of the number of independent households among labourers (*husmaend* in Danish).

hold, and the figure for average household size depends, in part, on a guess of the number of households made by Mackeprang.

The only substantial differences between the Moen data and the later Danish parish sample lie in the larger number of children in Moen in 1645, compensated for, in part, by a smaller number of servants.[14]

The categories distinguished in table 2.2 are categories of household membership which were taken for granted in the seventeenth and eighteenth centuries in north-west Europe, but, as we shall see, were different from those appropriate in joint household systems. In the very first work ever written on demography, John Graunt[15] wrote that 'I imagined . . . there were about eight persons in a family,[16] one with

[14] The difference may be slightly exaggerated by the figures as given. There were, in 1787 and 1801, grandchildren, children of other relatives, lodgers, etc. who were not included among 'children'. Their counterparts in 1645 may, however, have been classified as children.
[15] Graunt, *Natural and political observations on the Bills of Mortality* (1662): 60.
[16] He uses the term 'family', as was universal usage at the time, for what today would be called a household.

another, *viz.* the man and his wife, three children, and three servants, or lodgers.' (His numbers for children and servants or lodgers are somewhat high, a natural illusion for various reasons.) It is noteworthy, in the light of the comparisons to be made with joint household systems, that he assumes that relatives other than children can be ignored and that servants (or lodgers) are present in the households in substantial numbers, though they are not permanent members by virtue of relationship.

In the Danish data in table 2.1, the 'Other relatives' amounted to under 5% of the population, which is a clear indication that there could have been few joint households.

The data enable us to study directly the way in which the married were distributed among households.

The proportions of married men by relationship to the head in 1787 and 1801 (the proportions are based on 2,606 married men for both censuses combined) are shown in the accompanying list.

	%
Heads	93.4
Sons of heads	0.7
Fathers of heads	1.9
Relatives other than fathers or sons	0.1
Servants	2.0
Others	1.9
Total	100.0

Most of the couples who were not in charge of their own household were, as H. C. Johansen points out, old people or very recently married (servants, labourers). Married servants did not live with their wives in their masters' households. Johansen suggests that they went home periodically to their wives from their masters' houses.

It is likely that some of the retired married parents and some of the other married men (who were often labourers) formed independent housekeeping units of their own, and were not fully integrated in the household to which they were allocated at the census (this matter is discussed in the appendix). It thus seems that the number of households with two related married couples must have formed well under 4% of all households.

It is clear, therefore, that the great majority of married men became heads of their own households upon marriage (see also section V below).

It hardly needs emphasis that Denmark was a country of late marriage for both sexes, with mean ages at first marriage of some 30 to 31 years for men and 26 to 28 years for women in the population to which our tables relate.[17]

The remaining north-west European household formation rule (namely the circulation of young people as servants) shows its effects in the numbers of servants in table 2.1 and 2.2. It will be treated in detail in section VI below.

There are data from other parts of north-west Europe similar to those which have just been reviewed for Denmark, namely classifications of the population by relationship to the head of household. Such data have been published for areas or communities in Austria, Belgium, England, Germany, Iceland, and Norway. (It is hoped to publish a brief review of this material elsewhere.) The features illustrated by the Danish rural population, which contrast with what is found under joint household systems, apply throughout north-west Europe. Few households comprise more than one married couple. Households consist largely of heads and wives, their children, and servants. The number in other categories than these, such as lodgers or retired parents, is in some cases rather larger than in the Danish data, and the mean number of persons per household is also greater. In such cases, some of these additional elements probably constituted separate households (on the definition of a household as a consumption unit).[18] The size of households and their composition were in these cases probably, in reality, closer to the Danish situation than the data appear to show at first sight.

Another kind of data which confirms our conclusions regarding north-west European household systems consists of classifications of households by types, defined in terms of the relationship among the individuals they contain (i.e., nuclear households, extended family households, etc.). The classification system for households worked out by the Cambridge Group has been applied by historians to a large number of communities, and this evidence has been assembled by Peter Laslett.[19] There is a slight point of terminology which arises in relating that evidence to the argument of this paper. Households which comprise more than one married couple do not form a separate category in the classification scheme of the Cambridge Group. The category 'multiple-family households' in that classification includes all households which comprise two or more conjugal family units connected by kinship

---

[17] H. C. Johansen (1975): 85.
[18] This matter is discussed in the appendix.
[19] P. Laslett, *Family life and illicit love* (1977a): tables 1.1 and 1.2. Table 1.5 containing data on 'other' relatives is also relevant.

or by marriage. Most conjugal family units will comprise a married couple, but other groups, such as a widow and her child, also constitute conjugal family units. The category 'multiple-family households' thus includes not only all joint households, but in addition some households containing only one married couple. The fact that the number of multiple-family households in all north-west European communities so far · studied is so small is thus strong evidence that the proportion of joint households must have been small (say less than 6%).[20]

IV. India (and China)

The Danish household composition data have been presented for the purpose of contrasting these with the situation in a society with a joint household system. Our example is India. We shall show that, while households are no larger than in pre-industrial north-west Europe, there is a substantial proportion of joint households. Data will be presented showing the frequency of the various types of joint household.

The Indian censuses are too well known to require description here. In 1951 and 1961 tabulations regarding households were obtained from samples of the census schedules. The tabulations on households were different at the two censuses, the sampling was different, and the quality of the data varied among parts of that enormous country.[21]

India in 1951 is not quite an ideal comparison for our purposes. It is, of course, a joint household system of enormous importance in that it affects so large a population. In 1951, India was still an overwhelmingly rural country of small villages (over 80% of the population were classified as rural), and yet it must be presumed that 'modern' influences had, to some slight unknown extent, affected the traditional household formation system. The composition of Indian households in 1951 is presented in table 2.3.

Comparison of tables 2.1 and 2.3 shows that the average number of persons per household was about the same (about five in each case). The number of heads and their wives and the numbers of children per

[20] Of course the evidence, especially for the seventeenth century, is patchy for much of north-west Europe. It seems to me to be conceivable that evidence will come to light showing that there were areas with a somewhat larger proportion of retired parents than 6% living in fully integrated households with married children. Even then, the number of joint households would be much smaller than under the joint household system.

[21] The information about households to be found in the Indian censuses up to and including 1961 is surveyed in K. Dandekar and Unde, *Size and composition of households* (n.d.).

Table 2.3. *Rural India, 1951:*
persons per 100 households by relationship to head

	Married heads and wives	Other heads	Children	Other relatives	Unrelated	Total
Males	71	19	110	48	3	251
Females	71	10	81	74	3	239
Both sexes	142	29	191	122	6	490

Source: Census of India (1951), I, *India*, Part I.A, *Demographic tables*: table C I (ii).

household were also about the same. It is to be noted, however, that whereas in Denmark there were about the same number of children of both sexes, in India there were far more sons than daughters. The daughters had moved out of their original household on marriage and become daughters-in-law; i.e. they are included under 'Other relatives' in table 2.3.

A basic difference between north-west European and Indian household composition is that in north-west Europe, servants (and to a smaller extent some other categories of 'unrelated' individuals) take the place of most of the 'other relatives' in Indian households. Indian households consist almost entirely of related persons with only very few household members (well under 2%) unrelated to the head.

As will be noted below, some of the servants were probably related to the head of household, but unlike 'relatives' such as daughters-in-law in India, they did not have permanent household membership by virtue of the relationship.

It is well known that India satisfies the characteristic of joint household systems by which both sexes marry early. For our purposes, it is not marriage as recorded in Indian censuses that is relevant (which in European terms is more like an irreversible betrothal). We must take as 'marriage' movement of the bride into the husband's household, which takes place later than the formal marriage. Even so, the 'effective' marriage in this sense occurred for both men and women at a much earlier age, on average, than marriage in north-west Europe.

In Denmark, as we have seen, married people were almost all in charge of their own households. This was not so in rural India; only some 64% of married men in 1951 were heads of households.[22] Conse-

---

[22] This figure is not given directly in the census. The census gives the number of male heads and a single total for the female heads and wives of heads combined. From these figures,

quently, in a substantial number of households two or more married couples lived together. The number and types of joint households (in terms of the relationship between the married men living in them) will depend in part upon the extent to which couples survive and the circumstances under which couples living together decide to split.

There is some information on the numbers and types of joint households in India. In the 1961 census household composition analyses, the numbers of married sons and other married relations of the head were obtained.

Some 67% of married men in 1961 were heads of households; 22% were sons of their head of household, and 11% were related to the head in other ways. For every 100 households there were 24 married sons and 12 married men related to the head in other ways. The majority of joint households were therefore formed by married sons living with their fathers. But there were also substantial numbers of married brothers and married couples related in other ways living together. Nevertheless, splitting occurred at an early enough stage to allow the average size of household to remain of the order of five.[23]

A more detailed picture of the frequencies of various types of joint household in India is available from a survey carried out in the state of Maharashtra in 1947–51 (table 2.4). The sample comprised some 12,000 households selected from about 74 villages.[24] At any one time, the great majority of households (some 77%) contained no married couple, or only one. However, it can be inferred that many couples at some stage form part of a joint household, and while the father–son type is the most frequent, other combinations occur in numbers which are not negligible.

Table 2.4 also shows the distribution of the households of Nepal in 1976 by numbers of couples. These data come from a sample household survey taken as part of the World Fertility Survey. The results are

taken in conjunction with the total number of households (i.e. the total number of heads), it is possible to deduce the number of married male heads. This number can be compared with the total number of married men. This sequence of steps is complicated by the fact that household data on the one hand, and marital status data on the other, were obtained from different samples of the census schedules.

[23] The mean number of persons per household was slightly larger at the 1961 census, namely about 5.2, than in 1951.

[24] No details of the sampling methods or other survey procedures are given in the report (cited under table 2.4). However, in various characteristics (distribution of households by size, number of couples per household, etc.) the results conform to the census. They are taken as representative of conditions elsewhere in India in K. Dandekar and Unde (n.d.): 58. The comparison with Nepal given in table 2.4 also suggests that the results of the survey give the right orders of magnitude. In 1961, 70% of married men in rural Maharashtra were reported as household heads, just a little higher than for all India.

Table 2.4. *Proportions of households with different numbers of married couples in varying relationships*

	India (Maharashtra) 1947–51 (%)	Nepal 1976 (%)
No couple	19	17
One couple	58	63
Two couples		
Father and son	10 ⎫	
Two brothers	5 ⎬16	15
Other relatives	1 ⎭	
Three couples	5	3
More than three couples	2	1
TOTAL	100	99
No. of households in sample	12,030	5,537

Sources: V. M. Dandekar and Pethe, 'Size and composition of rural families' (1960); Kabir, *The demographic characteristics of household populations* (1980).

remarkably similar to those of the Maharashtra survey. Over 90% of the Nepalese are reported as Hindus, and Nepal displays a marriage pattern of Indian type.[25] The Nepalese rural population, according to the survey, constitutes over 97% of the total Nepalese population. The mean number of persons per household was 5.2.

Finally, we present some household composition data for traditional China. Because of the enormous significance of China, it seems worthwhile to present a few figures even though they are subject to a number of uncertainties in interpretation and regarding their representativeness. The data come from the China Land Utilization of 1929–31.[26]

Demographic data were collected and analysed for over 100 rural localities spread over 16 provinces with a total population of over 202,000. These data have recently been subjected at the Princeton

[25] Nepal resembles India in that (1) marriage occurs very early (the mean age at first marriage for Nepalese women was 16 years, according to the World Fertility Survey data), (2) marriage is virtually universal (98% of Nepalese women were reported as having been married among those aged 30–4 and in older age groups), and (3) there is frequently a substantial delay between marriage and the onset of cohabitation. See Goldman, Coale, and Weinstein, 'The quality of data in the Nepal fertility survey' (1979).
[26] The survey is described in Buck (ed.), *Land utilization in China* (1937). (See esp. ch. XIII, by F. W. Notestein.) For comments on the representativeness and quality of the data, the following should be consulted: Taeuber, 'The families of Chinese farmers' (1970) and Barclay *et al.*, 'A reassessment of the demography of traditional China' (1976).

Office of Population Research to modern methods of analysis developed for dealing with imperfect data.[27]

This analysis reveals a population of early marriage for both sexes (mean ages at first marriage are 21.3 years for men and 17.5 years for women)[28] and of high birth and death rates (each estimated at 41 per 1,000). In the survey, the household was defined as consisting of 'all persons living and eating together, including non-relatives such as *hired labourers*' (my italics). In spite of the words in italics, the number of non-relatives enumerated was very small, as table 2.5, constructed on the same lines as tables 2.1 and 2.3, shows.

Apart from the data for the whole survey, table 2.5 also gives figures for two of the seven regions into which the data was divided for analysis. These regions are the extremes, i.e. those which have respectively the largest and the smallest numbers of persons per household.[29]

In comparison with north-west European data, the Chinese figures present many of the same features as the Indian ones, namely the presence of substantial numbers of relatives and very small numbers of unrelated individuals. It is especially conspicuous (though not shown in the table) that there were virtually no women unrelated to the head of the household. Such few unrelated household members as there were, were men. In the whole survey there were about 12 times as many unrelated males as females. The absence of unrelated persons from traditional Chinese households, as well as some of the other features found in table 2.5, can be documented from Chinese populations which were under Japanese rule, with the result that statistical data were collected by the Japanese administration.[30]

V. The age at becoming head

Within any one population, joint households are, on average, larger than simple households. Yet, again on average, households under a joint household formation system are not necessarily larger than were households under the north-west European simple household systems. Nor is the distribution by size distinctly different under the two kinds of

[27] Barclay *et al.* (1976).
[28] These figures are SMAMs, implying that the average ages at first marriage would be even lower (since the SMAM, in effect, assumes that there is no mortality within the age range where marriage occurs).
[29] The 'south' comprised six localities with a total population of 11,107 in Kwantung and Fukien. The 'south-eastern hills' comprised four localities with a total population of 7,680 in Kiangsi and Chekiang.
[30] See in particular Barclay, *Colonial development and population in Taiwan* (1954).

Table 2.5. *Survey of rural Chinese communities 1929–31:*
persons of both sexes per 100 households by relationship to head

	Heads and wives	Children	Other relatives	Unrelated	Total
Whole survey	190	238	94	8	530
'South'	190	250	142	1	583
'South-eastern hills'	191	205	68	6	470

Source: Taeuber (1970).

Table 2.6. *Distribution of households by size*
(proportions of households in each size group)

	No. of persons					Average no. of persons per household
	1–3	4–6	7–9	10+	Total	
100 English communities						
1574–1821	36	42	17	5	100	4.8
Rural India 1951	34	43	17	6	100	4.9
Denmark 1787						
(26 rural parishes)	30	43	21	6	100	5.2
Taiwan 1915	30	42	18	10	100	5.3
Norway 1801						
(3 areas)	21	46	24	9	100	5.7

Sources: P. Laslett and Wall (eds.), *Household and family* (1972): 83; *Census of India* (1951), I, I.A: table C I (ii); H. C. Johansen (1975); Barclay (1954); Drake, *Population and Society in Norway* (1969).

household formation system, as table 2.6 shows.[31] North-west European data have been underlined.

This seems paradoxical. Indeed, a number of papers using mathematical models have been devoted to showing how much larger households would be, on average, if married children joined the households of their parents (as is the case under the joint household systems) than if they formed independent households at marriage (as was the case in north-west Europe). These models assume 'other things equal' – in particular the same age at marriage.[32] As the two kinds of household

[31] The population of Taiwan was a population of Chinese culture and followed a joint household system.

[32] See, for example, Burch, 'Some demographic determinants of average household size' (1970).

formation system in fact operated, the north-west European ones could create households as large, on average, as under joint household systems.

One way to gain insight into the situation is to compare certain kinds of movements between households under the two kinds of formation system. Suppose, for example, that a girl aged 17 from household X becomes a servant in household Y under a north-west European system; and consider for comparison under a joint household system a girl aged 17 from household X^* who is married and joins her husband in household Y^*, which is headed by his married father. The number of persons in household X could be the same as in X^*, and the number of persons in household Y could be the same as in Y^*. Then the effect of the movement between households on the distribution of households by size is exactly the same in the two cases. Yet in one case, but not in the other, a joint household has been created.

Another way of shedding light on the apparent paradox is to consider the age at which men become household heads. The ways in which household headship is attained constitute an important difference between the two kinds of household formation system.

The reason why the age at which headship is attained is relevant to the size of households may be seen most easily if simplifying assumptions are made. Assume that (1) all household heads are men; (2) every man becomes a head of household if he survives long enough; (3) once a man is a household head, he remains a household head. The number of heads of household is, of course, equal to the number of households. Then we know that:[33]

$$\text{Mean number of persons per household} =$$
$$\frac{\text{total population}}{\text{no. of households}} = \frac{\text{total population}}{\text{no. of heads}}$$

If men become heads of household later in life, there will, at any one time, be fewer household heads and thus fewer households. Hence, the mean size of household will be greater.[34]

It is not easy to find data which show how entry into household

---

[33] Here, as throughout this chapter, it is assumed that every person is allocated to one household and that the institutional population can be neglected.

[34] It would be tempting to conclude that under our simplifying assumptions we should have:
No. of heads = total male population aged above the mean age of accession to headship. This relationship will, however, not hold exactly in general, not even in a stationary population, though it will be correct in a stationary population where there is no mortality over the age range where accession to headship occurs.

headship varies with age under our two kinds of household formation system. Under north-west European systems men mostly became heads of household at first marriage; entry into headship was thus concentrated into a comparatively narrow age group. This may be shown by the kind of data given in table 2.7 for the Danish rural population in 1801.

The first and last columns of table 2.7, which are graphically presented in fig. 2.1, show that both marriage and the attainment of

Table 2.7. *Relation between entry into marriage and into headship:*
Danish rural parishes, 1801 (males)

	Proportion of all males in age group who are		
Age group	Ever-married (%)	Heads of household (%)	Ever-married heads of household (%)
18–22	2	2	2
23–7	23	19	18
28–32	56	52	51
33–7	74	74	72
38–42	90	90	88
43–7	91	90	88
48–52	94	90	90
53–7	95	93	91
58–62	96	88	88

Source: Data received from Professor H. C. Johansen.

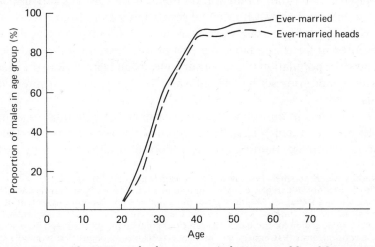

Fig. 2.1. Denmark, 1801, males by age, marital status, and headship position.

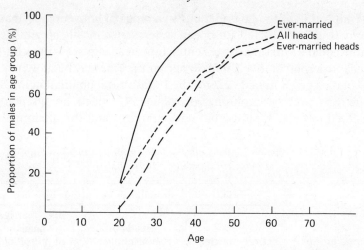

Fig. 2.2. Pisa, 1427–30: males by age, marital status, and headship position.

headship were very largely concentrated in the 24–40 age group. All three columns of table 2.7 show very similar figures. (Only two columns are represented in fig. 2.1. If all three columns were shown there, the resulting three curves would not appear clearly separate.)

The only comparable set of data for a joint household system known to me comes from a population not so far discussed, that of fifteenth-century Tuscany (Italy) whose rich records (compiled in connection with taxation) have been analysed in magnificent detail by Herlihy and Klapisch.[35] The rural population of fifteenth-century Tuscany displays all the marks of a joint household formation system in our sense.

Table 2.8, which exactly parallels table 2.7 and is graphically represented in fig. 2.2, relates to a part of this Tuscan rural population, namely the population of the countryside around Pisa.[36] Here the mean number of persons per household was 4.7. (The data cover some 3,900 households.)

Under the joint household system, marriage is not, in most cases, the point of time at which headship is attained. Two other routes to headship predominate, namely (1) succession to headship when the head

[35] Herlihy and Klapisch-Zuber, *Les Toscans et leurs familles* (1978).
[36] The figures for this part of the Tuscan rural population were given in an earlier article by Klapisch and Demonet, 'A uno vino e uno pane' (1972). The full publication of the whole material in the book by Herlihy and Klapisch-Zuber in 1978 does not contain the corresponding data for the whole Tuscan rural population, but the graph on p. 490 of the book suggests that figures for the whole Tuscan rural population would be very similar to those of our table 2.8.

Table 2.8. *Relation between entry into marriage and into headship: countryside around Pisa (Tuscany), 1427–30 (males)*

| Age group | Proportion of all males in age group who are | | |
	Ever-married (%)	Heads of household (%)	Ever-married heads of household (%)
18–22	15	14	3
23–7	53	30	16
28–32	74	45	36
33–7	85	57	48
38–42	93	70	67
43–7	96	74	72
48–52	95	84	81
53–7	93	86	82
58–62	95	90	87

Source: Klapisch and Demonet (1972).

dies; (2) becoming head of one of the households formed by splitting a larger one. These processes are spread out over a much wider age span than marriage.

In Pisa, as table 2.8 shows, there was no relationship between marriage and headship. Of the young married, only a small proportion were heads, with this proportion slowly growing up to men in their 60s. The mean age at entry to headship in the Pisan rural population was probably of the same order of magnitude as in the Danish rural population, i.e. in the region of 30 years of age.

It is of interest to note that the distribution of households by the number of married couples in the household is not in fifteenth-century Tuscany so very different from twentieth-century India. A rough comparison between the data given above in table 2.4 for the Indian state of Maharashtra and the fifteenth-century Tuscan population is shown in table 2.9. (This table refers to the whole Tuscan population, not just the rural part.)

In spite of some lack of comparability in the two classifications of households by type from which table 2.9 has been constructed, the broad similarity between the two distributions seems beyond doubt.[37] It

[37] The classification used for the Tuscan data by Herlihy and Klapisch-Zuber (1978) is fortunately detailed. It largely follows the Cambridge Group classification which was mentioned at the end of section III above, i.e. the classification is in terms of the number and type of conjugal family units in the household, rather than in terms of the number

Table 2.9. *Proportion of households by number of couples in household*

	India (Maharashtra) 1947–51 (%)	Tuscany 1427 (%)
No couple	19	23
1 couple	58	58
2 couples: father and son	10 ⎫	11 ⎫
2 brothers	5 ⎬16	4 ⎬15
other relatives	1 ⎭	
3 or more couples	7	4
TOTAL	100	100

Sources: V. M. Dandekar and Pethe (1960); Herlihy and Klapisch-Zuber (1978): 482.

is very striking how similar a result has been produced by two joint household formation systems in two such widely different cultures.

There seems to be only one population subject to a joint household system for which a direct analysis has been made of the frequency of the two modes of attaining headship which have just been mentioned, namely succession and splitting. Peter Czap has studied populations of Russian serfs on two estates in the first half of the nineteenth century.[38] He was able to utilize successive enumerations of sufficient detail to distinguish between the two modes of accession to headship. Before quoting his data on this point, we first give a brief description of the household formation system of the serf population. Households were much larger than in the populations so far considered. The mean number of persons per household was over nine. From Peter Czap's careful description of the operation of these households, it is clear that they really were integrated households, in spite of their size.

of couples. The figures in table 2.9 have been produced by combining suitable categories from the Tuscan data, as follows:

Name of group in table 2.9	*Corresponding categories in table 77 on p. 482 of Herlihy and Klapisch-Zuber (1978)*
No couple	All of 1 and 2 plus 3c and 3d
1 couple	3a and 3b plus all of 4
2 couples: father and son	5a ('verticaux à deux noyaux')
2 couples: 2 brothers	5c ('horizontaux à deux noyaux')
3 or more couples	5b ('verticaux à trois noyaux ou plus') plus 5d ('horizontaux à trois noyaux ou plus')

[38] See ch. 3 below. Professor Czap also very kindly made available to me a paper entitled 'The perennial multiple family household, Mishino, Russia, 1782–1858', now published in the *Journal of Family History* (1982), and helped me with a number of queries.

Some household composition data for the serfs on one estate are presented in table 2.10,[39] which follows the pattern of tables 2.1 and 2.3. It will be seen that the figures for heads and their wives and children in table 2.10 are broadly of the same magnitude as in other populations covered in this paper.[40] It is the large numbers of 'Other relatives' which make the serf households so big. In the serf households there were very few, if any, persons unrelated to the head. (The category 'Others' in table 2.10 comprises persons whose relationship to the head could not be determined.)

Indeed, it can be shown, since Czap gives a breakdown of household members by category of relationship, that in the serf households the great majority of members were not only related to the head, but were fairly closely related. Some 85% of household members (other than heads) were wives of heads, children of heads or the spouses of children, grandchildren, or nephews or nieces. The remaining 15% included many whose relationship was only slightly more remote, such as great-grandchildren.

The number of married men per household was high in the serf population (on average about two married men per household),[41] and much higher than in the other joint household systems covered by this paper. A related index is the proportion of joint households, which was also much higher than in other joint household populations. Of the serf households, some 75% were joint[42] at any one time, compared with some 15% to 30% in other joint household systems (as shown, for

[39] As can be seen from the note under table 2.10, that table is based on rather smaller numbers of households and of persons than the other tables in this chapter. However, Czap has analysed eight enumerations between 1814 and 1858 for the serf population of Mishino estate. This cumulative body of evidence makes it clear that the picture given in table 2.10, as well as the other facts (age at marriage, number of married men per household, proportion of joint households) quoted in the text, are not the result of random fluctuations associated with small sample size. Some changes over time can be deduced from the sequence of eight enumerations, but these changes are not discussed in this chapter.

[40] The figures for heads and children in table 2.10, while of the same broad orders of magnitude as elsewhere, do present some special features. The number of married heads is smaller and the number of 'Other heads' (i.e. in this case widowed heads) is larger than elsewhere presumably because headship was on average entered into much later in life than elsewhere. The great predominance of sons over daughters among the children of the heads reflects the very young ages at marriage in the serf population, i.e. daughters became daughters-in-law (and hence 'Other relatives' for the purposes of table 2.10) early on in life.

[41] Czap utilizes the classification scheme of the Cambridge Group (see end of section III above) and hence gives data not on the numbers of married men per household, but on the number of conjugal family units per household, i.e. a slightly higher figure.

[42] Czap, utilizing the classification scheme of the Cambridge Group, gives not the proportion of joint households, but the proportion of multiple households (i.e. the households containing more than one conjugal family unit), which is slightly larger.

Table 2.10. *Russian serfs (Mishino estate in Riazan province), 1814:*
persons per 100 households by relationship to head

	Married heads and wives	Other heads	Children	Other relatives	Others	Total
Males	62	23	130	207	10	432
Females	62	15	79	313	14	483
Both sexes	124	38	209	520	24	915

Note: The data relate to 1,173 persons in 128 households.
Source: Computed from Czap, table 3.11 below.

example, in tables 2.4 and 2.9). Because these joint households were larger than simple households, the great majority of the serf population at any one time were members of joint households. Most serfs were members of a joint household either all their lives or for most of their lives.

What, in terms of household formation behaviour, were the causes of large household size, large numbers of married men per household, and a very high proportion of joint households? The mean age at first marriage was under 20 for both sexes. The fact that both men and women became parents so young meant that they survived their sons' marriages by a longer period than in populations where marriage occurs at later ages; this tends to create more households comprising married sons, living under the headship of their father, than would occur with later marriage. There was also a tendency to delay the splitting of households far beyond the point at which it would have occurred in other joint household systems. Married brothers, and also cousins, stayed together in the same household in much larger numbers than in other joint household systems.

We now return to the age at attaining headship. Czap found that in the period 1782–1858 there were 343 cases on the Mishino estate where headship was attained by succession (at ages ranging from 12 to 92) and 112 cases where it was attained by splitting (at ages ranging from 18 to 77). When fission occurred among the Russian serfs, the new daughter households were usually also joint households. In both cases (succession and splitting), the mean age of the new head was 46. This mean age of 46 contrasts with somewhere around 30 which the data for the fifteenth-century Tuscan population showed and which may be presumed to be the right order of magnitude for most joint household systems. Of course, under the serf system, a far higher proportion of men died without ever becoming heads than under other household formation systems.

Most of Peter Czap's work so far has been devoted to the peasants of one estate, Mishino in Riazan province, and it is his data for this estate on which our description of serf households has been based. However, Czap has also analysed four enumerations for an estate in another province, Tver. In the 1816 enumeration for that estate he found that the mean household size was 9.1 and that some 75% of all households were joint.[43] It must be presumed that the striking household formation system revealed by Czap's detailed study of the Mishino estate was shared by other serf populations. Indeed, it seems likely that something like the Mishino household formation system prevailed among populations numbering millions. Average household size can be calculated from aggregate data on population and numbers of households which were compiled and published in the 1850s and early 1860s by an organ of the Tsarist administration, the Imperial Central Statistical Committee. From these data Czap shows that the large mean household sizes (of eight or more persons per household) prevailed over substantial parts of Russia in the 1850s, though there were also regions where average household size was rather lower (between six and seven persons per household).

There is, however, evidence suggesting that there may also have been populations outside Russia with household formation systems similar to those of the serfs studied by Czap. The censuses taken at the end of the eighteenth century, in the territory then under the Hungarian crown, covered Croatia, where mean household size was as large as among the serfs studied by Czap and the number of married men per household was also of the same order of magnitude. Data from these censuses have been published by the Hungarian Statistical Office. Table 2.11 summarizes the 1787 count.

The brief summary in table 2.11 shows how Croatia stands apart. There are counties within Croatia which were more extreme than Croatia as a whole: Pozsega (population 64,000) recorded a mean number of persons per household of 10.2 with an average of 2.0 married men per household. In Zagreb (population 150,000) the corresponding figures were 10.6 and 2.3. The Croatian population comprised large

---

[43] The Tver province estate whose enumerations Czap has analysed contained far fewer households and persons than the Mishino estate, to which most of his work has been devoted. He has also analysed three more enumerations of this estate (for 1834, 1850, and 1856), in addition to the 1816 enumeration. The 1816 enumeration covered 46 households. Given the small numbers of households covered, it is difficult to be sure of firm conclusions.

Table 2.11. *Territory of Hungary: census of 1787*

	Population (000)	Persons per household	Married men per household
Hungary proper	6,085	5.22	1.05
Transylvania	1,372	5.03	1.03
Croatia	617	8.33	1.70
61 'free royal cities'	485	4.45	0.84
TOTAL	8,559	5.28	1.06

Source: Hungary, Library of the Central Statistical Office and Archives Section of the Education Ministry, *Az elsö magyarországi népszámlálás (1784–1787)* (The first Hungarian census 1784–1787) (1960).

numbers of serfs (Czap suggests that households would have been smaller among his serfs if they had been free to form more separate households, as they indeed did when serfdom was abolished). A Slav tradition shared with the Russians may be relevant to the interpretation of this phenomenon.

In Hungary proper, the figures for different counties on size of household and married men per household suggest that in some places joint household formation systems may have been in operation that more resembled those of other populations considered in this chapter. Detailed analyses of listings of inhabitants for three villages for years between 1792 and 1816 confirm this picture in combination with family reconstitution materials. They show early marriage (the average age at first marriage was under 24 for men and under 19 for women), an absence of unrelated household members, and substantial numbers of joint households (though as in India and other joint household populations, the joint households constituted a minority of all households).[44]

VI. The circulation of servants

Many of the words describing relationships within a household have much the same meaning across different societies and across the centuries (with no doubt as to what are equivalent words in different

[44] Andorka, 'Peasant family structure' (1976a). I have also used a mimeographed paper kindly given to me by Dr Andorka entitled 'Micro-demographic researches in Hungary (family reconstitution and types of household structure)'.

There is a wealth of surviving documents from eighteenth- and early-nineteenth-century Hungary which are relevant to the study of household composition. Much work on these materials has been done by Hungarian scholars. I have not had the opportunity of studying most of this work, but I felt justified in including the points mentioned in the text.

languages). For example 'children of the head' is probably very much the same category in all the societies considered in this paper.

Servants are a characteristic and on average substantial component of rural pre-industrial north-west European households;[45] but unlike the word 'child', the term 'servant' and its equivalents in other European languages are apt to be misunderstood. The term refers to an institution which, so far as is known, was uniquely European[46] and has disappeared.

The servants who are recorded[47] as household members in the data for pre-industrial Europe were in the main not servants in the now customary meaning of the term, i.e. people ministering to the personal comforts of the more prosperous section of the population. They participated in the productive tasks of the households in which they lived, i.e. mainly in farming or craft activities. It must be remembered that at the time 'production' was largely carried on in households and that in such households there was no sharp division between activities now classed as 'production' and those classed as 'consumption'. Servants lived as integrated members of the household; in particular they usually participated in meals.

The number of servants does not by itself bring out the significance of the circulation of servants between households in pre-industrial Europe. For example, table 2.1 showed that in Denmark at the end of the eighteenth century there were on average 90 servants per 100 households, so that 17.6% of the total population were servants. But the servants were concentrated at adolescent and young adult ages, as table 2.12 shows. This table also shows that in rural Denmark in 1787/1801 well over 50% of those who survived past adolescence were in service at some point in their lives. Now, the proportion of servants in the Danish population at that period was higher than in many other parts of north-west Europe. But it was always true that a very substan-

---

[45] See tables 2.1 and 2.2. There is much additional evidence. P. Laslett (1977a): table 1.6 contains a summary of historical materials relating to the proportion of servants in the populations of various communities. Sogner, *Folkevekst og flytting* (1979) and Berkner, 'The stem family' (1972a) also contain additional data. The presence of farm servants as a substantial part of the agricultural labour force can still be traced in nineteenth-century censuses in north-west European countries; see e.g. Knodel and Maynes, 'Urban and rural marriage patterns' (1976).

[46] The institution of service in the European sense was, of course, shared by European populations overseas.

[47] This chapter is concerned with the meaning of the word 'servant' only as applied to persons recorded as servants in this way. There has been some controversy about the meaning of 'servant' in seventeenth-century English. This matter is discussed in Ann Kussmaul's book *Servants in husbandry* (1981): appendix I. I am grateful to Dr Kussmaul for sending me a typescript of her book in advance of publication.

94   *J. Hajnal*

Table 2.12. *Servants as a proportion of total population
in each age–sex group: Danish rural parishes,
1787 and 1801*

Age group	Males (%)	Females (%)
5–9	4	4
10–14	36	26
15–19	52	50
20–4	56	51
25–9	43	28
30–4	23	13
35–9	14	6
40–4	6	5
45–9	6	4
50–4	5	3
55–9	5	2

Source: H. C. Johansen (1975): table 10.18. Values have
been averaged for 1787 and 1801 from data given only
as integers. In the original table the age groups are given
as 6–10, 11–15, 16–20, etc., but in terms of 'ages at last
birthday' the data are for the age groups 5–9, 10–14,
15–19, etc. (private communication from H. C. Johansen).

Table 2.13. *Servants as a proportion of total population in each age–sex group*

	Iceland, 1729 (3 counties)		Norway, 1801 (3 areas)	9 Flemish villages, 1814		6 English communities, 1599–1796	
	Males (%)	Females (%)	Both sexes (%)	Males (%)	Females (%)	Males (%)	Females (%)
10–14	21	20	10	14	5	5	4
15–19	33	34	32	38	31	35	27
20–4	39	44	33	48	36	30	40
25–9	34	32	19	35	25	15	15
30–9	12	24	8	23	6	6	7
40–9	9	17	3	8	2	2	2

Sources:
Iceland: Hansen, *Population census 1729* (1975).
Norway: Drake (1969).
Flemish villages: private communication from Richard Wall (see also ch. 12 below).
English communities: P. Laslett (1977a): table 1.7.

tial proportion of young men and women experienced service at some point in their lives. Table 2.13 summarizes some data (similar to those of table 2.12) which are available for other populations.[48]

Servants, as has already been mentioned, were almost entirely unmarried, especially female servants. 'All masters discourage the marrying of their male servants and admit not by any means the marrying of the female who are then supposed altogether to be incapacitated for their service.' So wrote David Hume in his essay entitled *Of the populousness of ancient nations* (first published in 1752). A variety of data bear out his words. Service was in general a stage for young people between leaving home and marriage, i.e. a stage in the life cycle.[49] Servants in pre-industrial north-west Europe were, in a phrase coined by Peter Laslett, 'life-cycle servants'. Servants often moved repeatedly between households; they were members of their master's household not by any permanent right, but by virtue of a contract usually fixed for a limited period.

It was not only the poor and landless whose children went into service. Those who operated their own farms and even large farmers sent their children into service elsewhere, sometimes replacing them with hired servants in their own households.[50] Under certain conditions a high proportion of all servants were the children of farmers, though of course the children of those with little or no land (here called labourers) were more likely to go into service than farmers' children, since they did not have the option of employment on their parents' farm. This matter was first documented in the pioneering study by Mackeprang (1907) of the 1645 data for the Danish island of Moen (see table 2.2 above).

The basic data for Mackeprang's simple calculation are shown in table 2.14. Mackeprang assumed that the total of unmarried young people at each age was divided between farmers' and labourers' children in the same ratio as at 0–4, i.e. some 18% of the total in each age group would have been labourers' children. Thus of the total of 557 persons aged 10–14 some 103 would have been labourers' children. Since there were

[48] Mitterauer, 'Zur Familienstruktur' (1973): 205 notes that in two seventeenth-century Austrian villages more than 50% of young people between 18 and 20 were in service. It should be remembered that the proportion of young people who experienced service at some point in their lives must have exceeded (perhaps sometimes considerably) the highest proportion of servants in any one age group, for some who were servants at a younger age would have left service before reaching the age at which the proportion was at its maximum. Others may have entered service for the first time after the age of the maximum proportion.

[49] Concerning the ages at which young people left home see Wall, 'The age at leaving home' (1978).

[50] These facts are documented in Kussmaul (1981), ch. 5. Children of craftsmen and tradesmen in England also became farm servants.

Table 2.14. *Danish island of Moen, 1645:*
numbers of unmarried young people at home and in service

Age group	Farmers' children at home	Labourers' children at home	Servants	Total
0–4	478	108	0	586
5–9	458	97	20	575
10–14	368	66	123	557
15–19	175	6	165	346
20–4	93	8	110	211
TOTAL	1,572	285	418	2,275

Source: Mackeprang (1907): 263.

66 labourers' children in that age group living at home, there would have been 37 in service. One then reaches the picture given in table 2.15.

This method of calculation involves several questionable assumptions. In essence it assumes that rates of migration out of the area and rates of mortality and marriage at each age are roughly the same for the children of farmers and of labourers, and that there is no appreciable immigration of servants into the area. However, the general picture can hardly be in doubt. Because labourers formed only a small minority of the population, most servants must have been the children of farmers. A similar situation obtained in Iceland and probably obtained elsewhere in Europe.[51]

There was a great increase in the proportion of the landless population in Denmark (and indeed elsewhere)[52] during the seventeenth and eighteenth centuries. In the 1801 sample of Danish rural parishes some 50% of the newborn were labourers' children, as compared with 18% on the island of Moen in 1645. Under the circumstances of Denmark in 1801 a much higher proportion of servants must have been drawn from among the children of labourers.

To summarize, the characteristics of the institution of service in the rural populations of pre-industrial north-west Europe may be subsumed under the following headings. (1) Servants were numerous, apparently always constituting at least 6%, and usually over 10%, of the

---

[51] Kramer, *Bauern und Bürger* (1957): 155 says of servants in a part of Germany: 'Mostly (*grösstenteils*) they were the sons and daughters of farmers, later-born children who could not inherit the parental farm and who for that reason entered service till the opportunity of a favourable marriage arose.'

[52] See e.g. Sogner (1979); Berkner (1972a): 409.

Table 2.15. *Danish island of Moen, 1645:*
estimated distribution of servants by the social class of their parents

Age group	Number of servants who were children of		Proportion who were servants among unmarried children of	
	Farmers (no.)	Labourers (no.)	Farmers (%)	Labourers (%)
5–9	11	9	2	8
10–14	86	37	19	36
15–19	107	58	38	91
20–4	79	31	46	80
TOTAL	283	135		

Source: Calculated from previous table as described. (The figures differ very slightly from Mackeprang's own results.)

total population. (2) Almost all servants were unmarried and most of them were young (usually between 10 and 30 years of age). (3) A substantial proportion of young people of both sexes were servants at some stage in their lives. (4) Most servants were not primarily engaged in domestic tasks, but were part of the work-force of their master's farm or craft enterprise. (5) Servants lived as integrated members of their master's household. (6) Most servants were members of their master's household by contract for a limited period. (7) There was no assumption that a servant, as a result only of being in service, would necessarily be socially inferior to her or his master. Most servants eventually married and ceased being servants. Their social class before service (i.e. usually the class of their parents) and their social class after service could be the same as their master's (and in some north-west European populations at some periods this was not infrequently the case).

Servants (or persons whose designation can be translated by that word) are of course found outside Europe. But elsewhere, and in particular in societies following a joint household system, the servants represent different kinds of phenomena both in function and in scale from the north-west European variety. Nowhere in data for agricultural joint household populations is there any suggestion of service as it was in north-west Europe where a high proportion of men and women spent some portion of their lives circulating among households in that condition. Purely domestic servants (often especially numerous in cities) or household heads whose occupation is 'servant' are clearly different from north-west European rural servants. So is the 'estate servant caste', a distinct population on the Russian estates whose serf populations are studied by Peter Czap (see chapter 3 below). Types of 'servant' in another joint household system, namely traditional China, are described by J. L. Watson.[53] It is clear that these kinds of 'service' (e.g. hereditary domestic servants constituting rather less than 2% of the population and not living in the master's household) bore no resemblance in scale or function to the north-west European variety. In these and other instances, the groups designated 'servants' do not have several of the features which, as described in the last paragraph, characterized service in pre-industrial north-west Europe.

It would be impossible in a society where women married very early for them to spend time as servants in the north-west European sense and on the north-west European scale.

Another argument which supports the conclusion that the north-west European type of service did not exist in the joint household systems is based on the very small numbers of individuals 'unrelated' to the head found therein. The number of such persons in the data for joint household systems is much less (usually under 2% of the total population) than the number of servants in pre-industrial north-west Europe.

It may be objected to this argument that some servants were relatives of the head. It is indeed even true that some servants were close relatives. Ann Kussmaul has pointed out that kinship affected servant hiring in two ways: 'Servants found places with their own kin; masters found servants through theirs.' Servants were probably more likely to be related to their master than to other members of the communities in which they lived. It is possible, moreover, that the hiring of relatives as servants was much more widespread in some parts of north-west Europe than in others. Nevertheless, the great majority of servants were probably either unrelated to their masters or much less closely related than household members in joint household systems.[54] In any case, servants were present in the household on a temporary basis under contract; they did not have a permanent right to household membership by virtue of their relationship.

The circulation of servants between households seems to have been an essential feature of north-west European household systems. The

[53] 'Transactions in people' (1980).
[54] The identity of surname between master and servant has been used as an indicator of relationship. The proportion of cases of master–servant surname identity ought, however, to be compared with the proportion of identical surnames among randomly selected pairs of individuals in the same population. Only then can valid inferences be made about the role which relationship played in placing servants with particular masters. For more direct information on servants related to their masters see Wall, ch. 12 below.

connection between late marriage and the existence of life-cycle service has already been pointed out. Another reason for regarding life-cycle service as an essential ingredient of north-west European household systems is that the other north-west European formation rules (rules 1a and 1b of section II above) would frequently have resulted in households consisting of a couple and their very young children, i.e. a unit without sufficient people capable of doing the work needed to run the farm. The possibility of hiring servants overcame this problem.[55]

The north-west European systems, like the joint household systems, were workable under conditions very close to subsistence level, as in Iceland. Probably they could exist under such conditions only because of the institution of life-cycle service.

APPENDIX
The definition of a household

What is a household? If one wishes to make meaningful statistical comparisons of household size and composition between cultures and across centuries, it is necessary to use a household concept which is appropriate to all the societies being compared, and to be able to suppose that the statistical data used are the result of enumeration of recording procedures where the chosen concept has been at least roughly applied.

One important restriction on the concept, for the purposes of the present chapter, arises from the fact that it must be possible to allocate every person (or virtually every person)[56] in the population of an area uniquely to one household. Given this constraint and the nature of the available data, there seems in effect no choice. A household, for our purposes, must be defined as a housekeeping or consumption unit. A definition of this type is used in the majority of modern censuses. The essential characteristic of a household in this sense has often been taken to be the eating of meals together by all members of the household, or the sharing of meals deriving from a common stock of food. (When shared consumption is taken as the defining characteristic of a house-

---

[55] The hiring of day labourers was another possibility. But the system worked in areas where there were very few labourers, e.g. one of the Norwegian areas (Heroy) studied in Drake (1969). Perhaps the presence of labourers was not always an essential part of household formation systems of the north-west European type. However, it is suggested that no systems of this type could have functioned without the institution of service.

[56] In the populations dealt with here, institutional households are not of sufficient importance to affect in any appreciable way any of the quantities with which we are concerned.

hold, it is in general tacitly assumed that spouses and, more particularly, parents and their young children are in the great majority of cases in the same household. This assumption holds true for the populations dealt with in this chapter.)

The notion that a household comprises all those who share their food with one another has clearly been current among many peoples over many centuries and is embodied in such descriptions of a household (or 'family')[57] as comprising those eating from a common pot or sharing the same wine and bread. Economic dependence on the household head is, under pre-industrial conditions, a closely related notion. The people's own notion of who constituted members of one household must have had a great influence on the process of compiling censuses, administrative records, etc. where individuals were to be listed by household.[58]

The definition of a household as consisting of those depending on one head and sharing the same stock of food is already explicitly formulated in the instructions for the censuses carried out in Austria–Hungary towards the end of the eighteenth century. These censuses covered large populations of diverse nationalities, cultures, and patterns of household formation. The essence of the definition used in these Austro–Hungarian censuses was as follows: 'All these should be counted in one household, and accordingly entered on the same household schedule, who do not cook for themselves but are nourished under one master or mistress on the same table and bread, whether they be married or not.' Where more than one married couple share the same table and bread, they are thus counted in the same household, as are living-in servants or others who do not cook for themselves.[59] By this definition it was possible to have more than one household in the same house or to have one household sharing several dwellings. In the territories under the Hungarian crown enumerated in 1784–7, the numbers of households per house were as follows:

---

[57] In past centuries, the term 'family' and its equivalents in other languages were commonly used to denote what is now called a household. In referring to texts from past centuries below, I have felt free to use 'household' where 'family' occurs in the original.

[58] The phrase *'a uno vino e uno pane'* became the title of a celebrated article on households as recorded in the taxation records of medieval Tuscany. See Klapisch and Demonet (1972).

[59] The German version of this definition, as used in Austria in 1777, is quoted in Mitterauer (1973): 177. The Hungarian version, as used at the censuses of the territories under the Hungarian crown in 1784–7, is given in Hungary, Library of the Central Statistical Office, *Az első magyarországi népszámlálás* (1960): 8. The two versions are virtually identical. Mitterauer argues that in Austria there was a development from a commonly accepted larger concept of the household in the seventeenth century (the notion of *'das ganze Haus'*) to the narrower housekeeping unit concept in the eighteenth century.

Hungary	1.24
Transylvania	1.12
Croatia	0.96
61 'free royal cities'	1.59

Thus in Croatia, where households contained an average of 1.7 married couples, there were more houses than households. At the other extreme, the sharing of a house by several households was most common in the cities.

The effects of different definitions and of inconsistencies in their application in the enumerations are probably greater in north-west Europe than in other populations with which this chapter is concerned. One reason is that in the joint household systems households consist almost entirely of members who have a permanent right to belong by virtue of relationship (including adoptive relationship). Such a household is a fully integrated unit, leaving little room for doubt who its members are. In north-west Europe, on the other hand, there were frequently to be found living in the same farm, house, or group of buildings groups of individuals not sharing fully in one integrated household. In such cases the subsidiary group (usually the smaller one) could be, and was by contemporaries, treated variously either as a separate household or as part of the main household. One such sort of group were the retired persons, in particular parents who had handed over their farm to the heir in return for a contract guaranteeing an allowance. This category was fairly frequent in some areas of north-west Europe. The extent to which a retired couple or widowed retired person, possibly with children or servants on their own, lived apart and led an independent existence in terms of meals, etc. must have varied.[60]

Labourers with their families living on the farm for which they worked constituted another sort of subsidiary group whose relationship to a larger household could be problematic. The Danish scholar E. P. Mackeprang noted in 1907 in his exemplary analysis of the 1645 census of the island of Moen that *husmaend* (labourers) were sometimes enumerated with the farm household and sometimes on their own, with inconsistent enumeration practices among the parishes of the island.[61]

[60] Mitterauer (1973): 302 quotes a study of Austrian contracts of retirement which exemplify a wide range of possibilities, from complete integration of the retired with the household to whom they handed over, to substantial separation of the retired couple by removal to a house of their own. H. C. Johansen (1975): 145, for Denmark in 1787 and 1801 together, gives a figure of 46 retired people living as part of a larger household, as compared with 32 living independently.

[61] Mackeprang (1907): 258. Mackeprang's estimate of the number of *husmaend* with independent households was used in table 2.2 above.

General terms such as 'lodgers' and equivalent terms in other languages often cover subsidiary groups whose integration with the main
household may be questionable.

Interesting light on the possible effect of different definitions of a
household in instructions to census-takers is shed by a comparison
between the Danish censuses of 1787 and 1801. At the 1787 census it
was specified that 'farmers with their households should be counted
separately and labourers with their households separately'. In 1801
there was an additional instruction that 'if several households live in a
house or farm, then every household should be counted separately,
together with the persons belonging to it'.

Johansen analyses the allocation of individuals to households at the
two censuses in some detail, and concludes that the 1801 addition to the
instructions resulted, in particular, in the separate identification of
households of labourers living on farms.[62] He believes that in the 1787
census the number of households distinguished was some 2–3% too
low. Changes in definition also affected the number of retired people
classed as living independently.

A most illuminating discussion of the differing treatment of households in many different listings of the inhabitants of one area was given
half a century ago by the Swiss scholar W. Schnyder in his book *Die
Bevölkerung der Stadt und Landschaft Zürich vom 14.–17. Jahrhundert*
(1925). His work related to listings of the population of Zürich and the
substantial region surrounding it which was subject to the government
of the city. The listings were drawn up over a period of some four
centuries. The earliest tax listings, which date from the fourteenth
century, gave for each house only the names of those persons of both
sexes who were liable to a property tax. In 1408 the tax lists for some
parts of the area began to include other family members, servants, and
lodgers. In 1467 households living in the same house were distinguished, a space being left after each household. The picture of household composition given by 1467 tax lists was, however, apparently very
different from the standard north-west European pattern of later centuries. Households in the 1467 lists, Schnyder says, often included
parents together with their married children and their families, brothers
and their married children, and lodgers with their families. (Schnyder's
remarks about the 1467 tax lists raise the intriguing question whether
the inhabitants of the area around Zürich in the Middle Ages lived in

[62] H. C. Johansen (1975): 144–5. For a discussion of the treatment of subsidiary groups in
households at the Danish census of 1769 see Elklit, 'Household structure in Denmark
1769 – *ca.* 1890' (1978).

joint households like the people of medieval Tuscany. The Zürich archives may contain material for the kind of comprehensive study accomplished for medieval Tuscany by Herlihy and Klapisch-Zuber.)

In the seventeenth century the Zürich authorities imposed on all clergymen the obligation to compile at intervals of three years lists of all the households 'entrusted to their care'. The lists were to include information on the age of all persons and on their competence in 'prayer, catechism, and singing of psalms'. No guidance was given for the way in which these lists were to be drawn up. In the event the clergymen tended to follow one of two simple and consistent procedures. Either they lumped together all inhabitants of one house in the manner of the early tax lists, or they treated each couple and their children as separate households, while others, such as widows and widowers and lodgers, were treated as separate households if they had children or servants (single individuals were treated as part of the household to which they were attached). In 1649/50 households enumerated according to this second procedure comprised 5.1 persons on average. (This figure is for the population of the countryside around Zürich, some 100,000 persons in all.)

Large numbers of listings of inhabitants drawn up to record religious practices seem to have survived in the archives of European countries. They derive from the tradition in the Roman Catholic church by which the parish priest was supposed to prepare, and revise regularly, a list of his parishioners, noting who had been confirmed, attended communion, etc. This regular check on religious practice was instituted later than the registration of baptisms and marriages, but in 1614 the promulgation of the Rituale Romanum under Pope Paul V formalized a long-standing tradition and laid down procedures for the priest to follow in maintaining a register of souls (*Liber status animarum*) along with registers of marriages, baptisms and burials.

The crucial feature, from the point of view of the present chapter, was that the register was to be kept by households, presumably for the same practical reasons that censuses and surveys enumerate people by households. However, no definition was laid down of what constitutes a household. The Rituale Romanum of 1614 prescribed that the *Liber status animarum* be kept in the following manner: 'Each household is to be separately noted, with a space left between each one and the following one; the name, surname and age are to be listed of each individual who is of the household or lives in it temporarily.'[63] There follow

---

[63] I have broken up the sentence in translation for clarity. The original is as follows:
'Familia quaequae distincte in libro notetur, intervallo relicto ab unaquaque ad alteram

instructions for the notations recording conformity to the various religious obligations. This Catholic tradition continued to have effect after the reformation in Protestant countries, as has already been seen in the case of Zürich, and listings were compiled by clergymen there on similar principles.[64]

For most of the older European listings of individuals by households, whether they be general government censuses, administrative documents, taxation registers, confession books, or whatever, there is no explicit definition of what was to be taken to constitute a household. Sometimes there is uncertainty about just which of the persons listed the original compiler of the documents intended to include in one household. But where the categories of persons mentioned (such as retired people or farm workers) who are likely to have formed separate housekeeping units are present in substantial numbers without forming their own households, we may suspect that some of the 'households' are larger units than they would be on the basis of a strict housekeeping unit definition. The larger average household sizes recorded in north-west Europe generally occur where the numbers of persons in such subsidiary groups are large (as in Norway in 1801).

subsequentem, in quo singillatim scribantur nomen, cognomen, aetas singulorum, qui ex familia sunt, vel tanquam advenae in ea vivunt' (quoted in Mols, *Introduction à la démographic historique des villes d'Europe* (1954–6): III, 37).

[64] See e.g. P. Laslett (1977a): 54ff; Utterström, 'Two essays on population' (1965): 533–4; Mols (1954–6): I, 75–102.

3

'A large family: the peasant's greatest wealth': serf households in Mishino, Russia, 1814–1858

PETER CZAP, Jr

Introduction

'Nowhere is a large family a greater blessing than among the Russian peasants. Sons always mean additional shares of land for the head of the family . . . In western Europe a large family is an immense burden and nuisance for the lower classes; in Russia a large family represents the peasant's greatest wealth.'[1] So observed the German political economist August von Haxthausen of the peasantry of the central provinces of European Russia in the 1840s. Publication of the journal of his travels is credited with awakening the interest of educated Russian society in the peasantry, and leaving with Russian intellectuals the suggestion that Russia retained features of the traditional society that had disappeared in western Europe. Haxthausen attributed the large and complex households of central Russia to a unique cultural configuration and a peculiar Russian need for 'secure family ties'.[2] Frederick Le Play, travelling in the province of Orenburg in 1853, was also struck by the large size and complexity of serf households, which he attributed to the implacable authority of the peasant family patriarch.[3]

These descriptions of the peasant family by two eminent western European observers, while arresting the attention of Russians and non-Russians alike, were not, however, the first to be written. One of the earliest published descriptions of serf peasant households appeared in

The author wishes to thank the International Research and Exchanges Board (IREX), the National Science Foundation (SOC 75–06555), and the National Institutes of Health (HD 10798) for support and assistance. Grateful acknowledgement is also due to the officers and staffs of the Central State Archive of Ancient Acts (TsGADA) in Moscow and the State Archive of Riazan Oblast (GARO) for their assistance in making available the documentation used in this work.

[1] Haxthausen, *Studies on the interior of Russia* (1972): 82.

[2] *Ibid*. 67.

[3] Le Play, *Les ouvriers Européens* (1877–9): II, 66–7.

Russia in 1829. It signalled growing awareness by gentry landlords that to improve rural estates something must be known about their basic units of labour and taxation – the serf family/household.[4] This and other early descriptions refer to a certain proportion of peasants living in 'family communes' of 30 to 40 individuals under the rule of a stern patriarch. None of these accounts provides a statistical basis for generalization, and all are at best impressionistic. At worst they may be nothing more than the wishful thinking of seigneurs, who favoured 'strong households' (*krepkie semii*) among their peasants.[5]

The Russian peasant household became an object of more systematic study after the abolition of serfdom in 1861. However, by this time the interest of investigators had moved away from the size and composition of the household and towards customs governing the marriage and succession of its members; the place of women in peasant society; and the collapse of the patriarchal family as a factor in reducing the peasantry to misery.[6] It was axiomatic for virtually all these later social investigators that under serfdom peasants had lived in large, cohesive patriarchal households, although there is doubt about what, if any, empirical basis existed for their assumption. There appeared to be more certainty, based on statistics gathered by the *zemstva*, organs of local self-government introduced in the 1860s, that mean household size among peasants was declining steadily as the nineteenth century wore on, the consequence, it was alleged, of the growth of individualism, the collapse of traditional family ideology, and the increase in the rate of household divisions.[7]

These alleged divergences in the character of pre- and post-emancipation peasant households were challenged by a *zemstvo* statistician writing in 1905, who argued that changes of definition and methods of enumeration invalidated the hypothesis that peasant households before and after the emancipation differed significantly.[8] A classic study published by Fenomenov in 1925 of a village in the province of Novgorod gave considerable attention to family history and argued the case for strong continuity in the peasant household throughout the nineteenth century.[9] Interpolating from the observation that in the period 1923–5 not one of the 88 households making up the village

[4] Kosven, *Semeinaia obshchina i patronimiia* (1963): 15.

[5] *Ibid.* 86.

[6] See for example Efimenko, *Issledovaniia narodnoi zhizni* (1884).

[7] Skvortsov, 'Itogi krestianskogo khoziaistva po zemskim statisticheskim issledovaniiam' (1892): 75.

[8] Chernenkov, *Kharakteristika krestianskogo khoziaistva* (1905): 61–2.

[9] Fenomenov, *Sovremennaia derevnia* (1925).

contained two married brothers, the author concludes that 'the separation of married brothers . . . is a continuous phenomenon'.[10] He suggests that while mean household size shifted only slightly in the decades after emancipation, more significant changes might have occurred in the internal make-up of the family household.

In the years since Fenomenov's work appeared nothing has been published, in the Soviet Union or elsewhere, which systematically confronts the conflicting impressions and assertions about the character and the history of the Russian peasant household in the nineteenth century. The conventional wisdom that Russian serfs lived preponderantly in large, complex patriarchal households, the basic cell of rural life, remains unproven for European Russia as a whole or any of its regions.[11]

In what follows I will test this conventional wisdom through the analysis of eight successive enumerations of a population of proprietary serfs carried out during the last five decades of serfdom in Russia. There are no known studies with which the findings adduced in this essay can be directly compared. I am concerned therefore to stress the preliminary nature of the conclusions offered here. Regional variations in demographic behaviour for similar categories of population have been noted in a country the size of Belgium. Unquestionably, therefore, local differences will emerge as further studies similar to this one are undertaken for various regions of Russia. The data for such studies are promising, and only after a number have been completed will it be possible to construct a typology of Russian national demographic structures and behaviour.

Location

The data employed for this study have been drawn from the province of Riazan in an area approximately 170 kilometres south-east of Moscow (see fig. 3.1). Here the central black-earth belt begins to give way to the forests and the thinner soils of the north. Natural conditions favoured agriculture, which dominated the region's economy. Rye was the principal crop. In 1858 Riazan was the seventh most densely settled province of the Empire. The region was originally opened to settlement in

[10] *Ibid.* I, 168.
[11] The work of A. Plakans on the Baltic region of the Russian Empire concerns a non-Russian population for which personal bondage ended in 1817. See his 'Peasant farmsteads and households in the Baltic littoral' (1975a). Another study dealing with the same general region is Palli, 'Historical demography of Estonia in the 17th–18th centuries and computers' (1971). See also chs. 5 and 6 below.

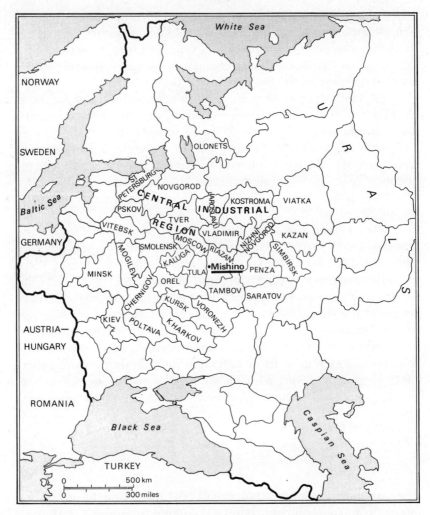

Fig. 3.1. Provinces of central European Russia.

the early seventeenth century as a buffer zone between Moscow and the
Tatars, who still mounted desultory raids against the older population
centres to the north. By the end of the eighteenth century in-migration
ceased to be a significant factor in the region's population growth. The
area's population has always been predominantly Great Russian.
Peasants made up nine-tenths of the population of the province.
Approximately 65% were proprietary serfs; state peasants, servile agri-

culturalists living on state-owned land, accounted for the bulk of the remaining peasantry.[12]

Discovery of rich source materials of extraordinarily high quality for an estate located in the southern half of the administrative district of Mikhailovskii in the province of Riazan is responsible for the location of this investigation. Whatever general hypotheses can be constructed based upon the study of an agricultural estate from this region will be considered below.

The estate of Mishino consisted of four villages, in two of which parish churches were located. It was a larger than average proprietary estate, carefully managed and prosperous.[13] In 1800 the majority of peasants settled in the villages of Mishino performed labour services (*barshchina*) for their seigneur, Prince Nikolai Sergeevich Gagarin, a magnate and government office-holder who owned approximately 27,000 serfs on various estates at the time of his death in 1842. Between 1830 and 1849, the seigneurial obligations of the peasants of Mishino were gradually converted to quit rent (*obrok*), with only incidental labour services remaining.[14]

The estate administration, consisting of an overseer (*upravliaiushii*) and several assistants (*prikazshchik, kontorshchik, pisar*), was centred in the village of Mishino, which also contained a parish church and an infrequently used manor house (*gospodskii dom*). Records indicate a water mill, several windmills, fish ponds, orchards and gardens, and a stud located among the four villages making up the estate. The economic mainstay of the estate was the production of rye, oats, and buckwheat in that order of importance. The production of small amounts of other commodities rendered the estate largely self-sufficient in foodstuffs. Cattle raising was an important part of the seigneurial economy.

In addition to their agricultural labour, a number of peasants engaged in trade or were artisans. One-third of the households contained one or more members engaged in some kind of non-agricultural work. Carpenter and cooper were the most frequently listed crafts and the inventory included blacksmith, bricklayer, felt-maker, miller, pitch-boiler, sawyer, stonecutter, stove-maker, tailor, wheelwright, etc. Trade was carried on by the peasants in charcoal, bast, rope, harnesses, and pitch. The fleeting presence of non-peasants in the villages is marked in

[12] Troinitskii, *Krepostnoe naselenie v Rossii po 10-i narodnoi perepisi* (1861): 49. For a discussion of the various categories of peasant in Russia see Blum, *The end of the old order in rural Europe* (1978): 43.

[13] Kovalchenko, *Krestiane i krepostnoe khoziaistvo Riazanskoi i Tambovskoi gubernii v pervoi polovine xix veka* (1959): 127–36.

[14] *Ibid.* 180.

records of the estate, which carry notations about grain dealers, merchants, and occasional government officials inquiring about anomalies
appearing in reports compiled by the estate administration on behalf of
the central government.

Character of the data

Thanks to the tireless efforts and bureaucratic habits of numerous
zealous officials, clerks, and scribes, civil and ecclesiastical, data for the
study of the Russian population are abundant and in some instances
remarkable. While the subject deserves an essay of its own, only the two
types of data drawn upon for this essay will be characterized here.

Soul revisions (*revizskie skazki*), enumerations ordered by the central
government of the personally taxable population of the Russian Empire,
were carried out 10 times between 1720 and 1858: in 1720, 1746, 1763,
1782, 1795, 1811, 1816, 1834, 1850, 1858.[15] With each male 'soul' a
unit of taxation, the revisions served primarily a fiscal purpose. However, they also served a legal purpose, to state the civil status (*sostoianie*)
of each individual enumerated – vital in a society with hereditary serfs
and a system of defined estates (*soslovie*). Payment of the capitation tax
imparted a social stigma and thus defined the non-privileged orders of
Russian society.

Questions included in the revisions varied somewhat over time, but
from the fourth through the tenth, the revisions enumerated the total
taxable population, male and female, giving the following information:
given name, patronymic, family name (if there was one); sex; age;
status in household; estate (i.e. 'peasant', 'townsman', etc.); official
place of residence.[16] In the nineteenth century, landowners or their
agents carried out the revision and submitted the results to local officials
of the government, a practice that virtually assured the uneven quality
of individual revisions.[17] A system of double-entry book-keeping
employed for the male population insured that every male alive at the
time of a revision would appear in a minimum of two revisions, for the
last time in the revision following his death, with the date of death
noted. If male peasants were given up to the army, were sold, or became
fugitives, this information along with a date was noted in order legally to
remove their names from the rolls. Soul revisions showed no trace of the
lives of peasants who lived out their years completely in an interval
between revisions.

[15] Blum (1978): 66.   [16] Females were excluded from the sixth revision (1811).
[17] Den, *Naselenie Rossii po piatoi revizii* (1902): I, 99–100.

In addition to the soul revisions, many seigneurs ordered periodic enumerations of the serfs on their estates. The origin of the resulting household registers (*podvornie opisi* or *vedomosti*) has been traced to the eighteenth century and efforts of the Russian Free Economic Society to foster rational estate management. Treatises, which included detailed sample tables and graphs, urged the registration of serfs and their material resources as the first step toward improving seigneurial economies.[18] Naturally, the detail and the quality of such registers vary enormously from landowner to landowner. For the estate of Mishino registers were compiled almost annually between 1814 and 1842, although not all have survived. After the death of Nikolai Sergeevich Gagarin in 1842 estate management seemed to falter, but the registrations continued, although somewhat irregularly, until the eve of emancipation. In addition to duplicating information contained in the soul revisions, the household registers of Mishino provided information about the peasants' horses, cattle and pigs, grain reserves, labour dues and arrears, crafts and trades, the condition of dwellings and outbuildings, physical handicaps and deportment, as the extract from the 1822 register for the village of Slobodka shows (see the appendix at the end of this chapter).

The data for this essay are drawn from eight listings of the population of the estate of Mishino between 1814 and 1858. Three are soul revisions: 1834, 1850, 1858.[19] The remaining five are household registers: 1814, 1822, 1825, 1831, 1843.[20] Both types of listing consist of names of individuals arranged in numbered blocks. Each block referred to a '*dvor*' (household) or to a '*sem'ia*' (family) and represented a *de jure* residential group. Evidence such as petitions, contracts, records of dues and arrears, work rosters listing the names of serfs, and disciplinary records indicates that individuals whose names appear together in blocks were also members of *de facto* co-residential groups who shared – not always without conflict – common premises and an interest in a single domestic economy.

A number of Russian and Soviet scholars have criticized the soul revisions as inadequate sources for the reconstruction of the history of the whole Russian population, and this may be true.[21] For purposes of

---

18 Struve, *Krepostnoe khoziaistvo* (1913): 213–28.
19 U.S.S.R., Tsentralnyi Gosudarstvennyi Arkhiv Drevnikh Aktov, Moscow (hereafter TsGADA), Fond 1262, Gagarina, opis 2, d. 260 (1834); d. 406 (1850); Gosudarstvennyi Arkhiv Riazanskoi Oblasti, Riazan (GARO), Fond 129, opis 1–58, d. 56 (1858).
20 TsGADA, Fond 1262, opis 2, d. 48 (1814); d. 119 (1822); d. 189 (1825); d. 234 (1831); d. 336 (1843).
21 Den (1902): I, 13–16; Kabuzan, 'Materialy revizii kak istochnik po istorii naseleniia Rossii XVIII-pervoi poloviny XIX v. 1718–1858 gg.' (1959).

microanalysis, however, especially when revisions can be used in connection with complementary listings, they are less problematic. With positive test results for reliability, the universe of the revisions and household registers can be taken as a given, recognizing that it is only a small part of a greater universe whose full dimensions for the present we do not know.

The eight listings referred to above have yielded 10,868 entries, representing the entire population of the estate for the years selected. Each entry includes an individual's complete name, age, sex, and family relationship, together with household, village, and censal identifiers. This data base has been subjected to computer analysis to classify households and produce the distributions and generate the statistics adduced here.

The peasant household

The first problem in describing Russian serf households is to understand just what is being described. The Russian term *'dvor'* had two complementary meanings in the nineteenth century. First, it referred to a distinct, usually enclosed, space which encompassed all the structures and appurtenances of a single economy: dwelling, barns, sheds, threshing floor, haycocks, gardens – in short a farmstead. Second, it described a group of individuals, or perhaps more accurately a collective, whose members were connected by a unity of material interests and usually (but not exclusively) by ties of kinship, and residing in a single farmstead. The unit excluded from membership hired workers and servants, i.e. all those who may have worked about the farmstead but who did not contribute their earnings to and did not draw upon the common purse (*ottsovskii koshel*).[22] *'Dvor'* was also used, rather ambiguously, as a synonym for the following words: *dom* (home); *izba*, *dym* (peasant dwelling); *sem'ia* (family); and *tiaglo* (a unit of human labour).[23] It is in all these senses combined that the word *'dvor'* will be used in this essay – a physical entity, and also a domestic group which was simultaneously a dwelling and reproduction unit, a production and consumption unit.

Russian peasant farmsteads were constructed according to well-defined conventions, with regional variations dictated by weather conditions and available building materials. In the province of Riazan a farmstead was usually square in shape, its limits formed by the walls of

---

[22] Veletskii, *Zemskaia statistika* (1899): II, 666.
[23] Dal, *Tolkovyi slovar* (1956): I, 422–3.

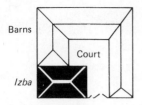 

Fig. 3.2. *Dvor.*

the dwelling and outbuildings, which enclosed an inner court.[24] The entire complex was set on a parcel of land, an acre or more, called the *usadba*, which in addition to the farmstead included space for a kitchen garden, fruit trees, and summer enclosures for domestic animals. Construction of the dwellings and more substantial outbuildings was of hewn, unpainted logs, and the roofs were of straw.

The dwelling (*izba*) sided on the street and in its simplest form consisted of a single room dominated by a large earthenware stove (the shaded area in fig. 3.3) which was used for cooking and heating. An *izba* of this type varied in size from 15 to 34 square metres, with as much as a quarter of this space given over to the stove.[25] Different corners of the room were used for cooking, dining, entertaining guests, and sleeping. More elaborate dwellings included open or enclosed porches and unheated storage areas. Some farmsteads contained two dwellings (*izby*), semi-detached structures which shared a common enclosed passageway.[26] The second dwelling space was sometimes an unheated summer residence (*letnaia izba*), also referred to as 'white' or 'clean' (*chistaia izba*). Such additions to living space, used perhaps for storage in the winter and for living only in warm weather, were something of a luxury and possible only for better-off peasants. Occasionally, however, large households, unable to divide, were forced to add dwelling space within the *dvor*. In these cases the second *izba* would be the conventional heated type. Available as a year-round living space, this type was called 'warm' (*teplaia*) or 'black' (*chernaia*), referring to the fact that peasant huts on the whole were chimneyless, with smoke from the stove filtering through the thatched roof.[27]

The typical village layout in the province of Riazan was linear, its farmsteads standing close together along the bank of a lake, stream, or

[24] Aleksandrov (ed.), *Russkie: istoriko-etnograficheskii atlas: karty* (1967): 33.
[25] *Ibid.* 26. See also Semenov, *Rossiia: polnoe geograficheskoe opisanie nashogo otechestva* (1902): II, 174–5.
[26] Aleksandrov (ed.) (1967): 27.
[27] Blomkvist and Gantskaia, 'Tipy russkogo krestianskogo zhilishcha serediny XIX – nachala XX v.' (1967): 136.

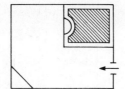

Fig. 3.3. *Izba.*

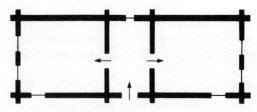

Fig. 3.4. Two *izby.*

road. The arable surrounded the village. A plan for the village of Krasnoe Sobakino confirms this typical lay-out for at least one village from
the estate of Mishino.[28]

Population

The serfs of Mishino are an example of a nearly closed, but not necessarily immobile, population. Between 1814 and 1858 permanent out-
migration among males was confined largely to military recruits, who
served in the army for 25 years. In addition, occasional solitaries and
orphans, when they were not relocated among the villages of Mishino,
were transferred to one or another Gagarin estate. The listings also refer
to fugitives, but they number no more than six in 40 years. Because
women appeared on a list only if they were present – unlike males,
whose names were 'cleared' after their disappearance with a notation
about their recruitment, transfer, or death – it is not possible to speak
about their movements with the same certainty. Women disappearing
from the lists are assumed to have married off the estate, died, or
perhaps been transferred to work in a cloth mill Gagarin built in 1817 on
an estate elsewhere in Riazan province. However, the rate of female
endogamy within the estate was over 90%, so the number of women
who disappeared and cannot be accounted for directly or indirectly is
low.

[28] TsGADA, Fond 1262, op. 2, d. 369 (1845).

The in-migration of males, with only one major exception, was virtually non-existent. In 1825 Prince Gagarin purchased from another nobleman 13 serf families, consisting of 77 individuals, and settled them all in the village of Krasnoe Sobakino.[29] Included in this number were 5 serfs who had died between the 1816 revision and the transfer of ownership in 1825 and remained on the prince's rolls until they were removed in the 1834 revision – 'dead souls' like those immortalized in Gogol's great novel. Finally, there was a small but steady flow of females marrying into the estate, coming most likely from other estates belonging to the prince. In the main the circulation of the population of Mishino between 1814 and 1858 was confined to the four villages of the estate.

Some of the male population could be expected to be temporarily absent from the estate at any given time, more in winter than in summer. On the order or with the permission of the estate administration, peasants could leave their homes for periods of weeks or months. They hauled the lord's grain to market, delivered produce to or fetched manufactured goods from Moscow, or travelled about the countryside as itinerant craftsmen. The names of such travellers always appeared in the soul revisions, which were lists of official inscription. Yet in Mishino the difference between *de jure* and *de facto* residence was not great. Moscow, at a distance of 170 kilometres, did not exert a strong attraction for peasants seeking additional earnings. The Riazan region itself did not offer many alternatives to agriculture. Even after the peasants' obligations had been largely transformed into quit rent, most peasants remained on the estate to till the land.

The serfs of Mishino were of two types – *krestiane* (peasants or agricultural serfs) and *dvorovye liudi* (household people). Agricultural serfs, who constituted the overwhelming majority of the estate's population, lived in family groups in their own farmsteads. In addition to their obligations to their lord, they had to maintain themselves, their animals, and their equipment, including their dwellings and outbuildings. The peasants of each village were organized in a *mir* – the traditional Russian agrarian commune which bore collective responsibility for the lord's obligations and the annual soul tax levied by the central government and collected by the lord.

Household people were personal servants of the lord and received all or most of their subsistence from the lord. In Mishino the household people appear to have been a separate caste, rarely marrying their daughters to the sons of agricultural serfs or taking in brides from them.

[29] TsGADA, Fond 1262, op. 2, d. 260 (1834).

No detailed plan for the village of Mishino, where most of the household people lived, has yet been found. But other estate records suggest that the household people lived apart from the agricultural serfs, clustered around the manor house. The solitaries among the household people may have lived in dormitory-like accommodation.

With the manor house of Mishino almost never visited by the lord, the household people living on the estate were assigned tasks connected with supervising and maintaining the seigneurial economy. Household people filled the offices of steward (*prikazshchik*), foreman (*smotritel*), clerk (*kontorshchik*), and scribe (*pisar*). The estate steward was also described as 'architect'. The estate's gardeners, driver, stableman, and stockyard man were likewise household people.

Seigneurial control over the domestic lives of household people was extensive. Petitions from household people have been found begging permission of the lord to marry. No similar appeals made by agricultural serfs have been found, although the latter occasionally called upon the lord to help in facilitating a match. Individual household people were liable to be transferred from Mishino without their immediate families, a fate that rarely if ever befell a Mishino agricultural serf in the first half of the nineteenth century as far as we can determine.

It is evident from this brief discussion of household people that their social and economic roles differed from those of the agricultural serfs. They were separately enumerated in both the soul revisions and the household registers. Although the majority of household people were organized into families, doubt persists about the precise living arrangements of some of them. For these reasons the household people of Mishino are excluded from detailed examination throughout the remainder of this essay, although their aggregate numbers and sex distribution appear in table 3.2 below. All discussion and general conclusions hereafter refer to agricultural serfs.

The total population of Mishino grew, by fits and starts, from approximately 1,263[30] in 1814 to 1,632 in 1858. The number of agricultural peasants increased from 1,173 to 1,522, while that of household people went from 94 in 1817 to 110 in 1858. In many ways the years were difficult ones for the peasants of Mishino, as for the Russian peasantry as a whole. The years 1812–15 and 1853–6 saw Russia forced to defend itself against foreign invasion. A militia was raised during these crises to fight alongside the standing army, and the increase in the military levy is reflected in the abnormal sex ratio for the enumeration of 1814. The

[30] In the absence of an enumeration of household people for 1814 an estimate of 90 is being used here. The number for the nearest enumeration, 1817, is 94.

Table 3.1. *Agricultural peasants, Mishino estate*

Village	1814 M	1814 F	1822 M	1822 F	1825 M	1825 F	1831 M	1831 F	1834 M	1834 F	1843 M	1843 F	1849 M	1849 F	1850 M	1850 F	1858 M	1858 F
Mishino	109	125	120	124	139	141	145	135	138	143	134	120	146	143	144	136	157	160
Slobodka	160	171	174	167	176	178	182	177	178	176	180	179	170	163	175	172	183	189
Lokna	143	152	143	154	156	153	154	165	155	169	137	145	136	149	136	165	154	150
Krasnoe Sobakino	142	171	165	150	180	176	233	234	218	221	247	251	250	266	260	275	263	266
Total by sex	554	619	602	595	651	648	714	711	689	709	698	695	702	721	715	748	757	765
Total population	1,173		1,197		1,299		1,425		1,398		1,393		1,423		1,463		1,522	
Sex ratio	89.4		101.1		100.4		100.4		97.1		100.4		97.3		95.5		98.9	

Table 3.2. *Household people, Mishino estate*

Village	1817 M	1817 F	1834 M	1834 F	1850 M	1850 F	1858 M	1858 F
Mishino	36	38	39	56	45	55	45	53
Krasnoe Sobakino	9	11	8	8	7	7	6	6
Total by sex	45	49	47	64	52	62	51	59
Total population	94		111		114		110	
Sex ratio	91.8		73.4		83.8		86.4	

soul revision of 1858 indicates that a total of 46 recruits were taken from Mishino between 1850 and 1858 – 36 into the standing army and 10 into the militia – more than 6% of the male population. In addition to war, epidemics and poor harvests afflicted the population during this period, especially after 1830. Cholera was endemic in the Russian Empire through the nineteenth century, and major epidemics occurred in 1830, 1831, 1847, 1848, 1849, 1853, and 1855.[31] Between 1830 and 1858, 12 years were marked by poor harvests, while in 8 years the harvest was recorded as above average.[32] The combined effect on Mishino of cholera in 1830 and 1831 and a poor harvest in 1833 can be seen in the decline of the peasant population between the 1831 and 1834 enumerations. But for the cholera and poor harvests, the population of Mishino could have been expected to grow at the same rate in the 1830s

[31] Onitskanskii, *O rasprostranenii kholery v Rossii* (1911): 1–2.
[32] Pokrovsky, 'Influence des récoltes et des prix du blé sur le mouvement naturel de la population de la Russie' (1899): 179–80; Kovalchenko (1959): 37–41.

and 1840s as it had in the 1820s. However, even in 1849 the population had not fully recovered to its level of 1831.

The total population of the Russian Empire increased by approximately 65% between 1815 and 1858, from roughly 45 million to 74 million. While all other categories of the population grew steadily throughout this period, proprietary serfs experienced an absolute loss of numbers between 1835 and 1858 of approximately 1.6%, from almost 22 million to slightly more than 21 million. Whether this loss came about through changes in the legal status of some serfs or from a decline in their rate of natu·al increase or from some other cause is not clear.[33] Whatever the cause of the aggregate loss, the phenomenon was not replicated among the agricultural serfs of Mishino. The population of Mishino grew at an average annual rate of 1.1% between 1814 and 1834, but between 1834 and 1858 the average annual increase fell to 0.3%.

Age structure

The age structure of Mishino agricultural serfs did not change dramatically between 1814 and 1858. Perhaps more significant, the dependent proportion of the population, defined as those below the age of 15 and above the age of 59, remained relatively steady within the range 42% to 46%.

Marriage

Among the important factors contributing to the household size and composition of the agricultural serfs of Mishino was the particular marriage pattern that prevailed among them. Peasant nuptiality has been treated at length elsewhere, but a brief discussion of its salient features is in order here.[34] The dynamics of Russian peasant nuptiality are by no means fully understood, but the data for Mishino make it clear that they worked to produce a consistent pattern of early and nearly universal marriage for both sexes. The results are illustrated in table 3.4. In broad comparative terms the pattern is not an exceptional one – Hajnal would define it as an example of a robust 'non-European' marriage pattern.[35] Viewed in a European context, however, it represents an

[33] Robinson, *Rural Russia under the old regime* (1967): 62. The most recent discussion of this phenomenon by a Soviet scholar, which indicates that further study is needed, is Perkovskii, 'Krizis demograficheskogo vosproizvodstva krepostnogo krestianstva Rosii v pervoi polovine XIX stoletiia' (1977): 167–90.
[34] Czap, 'Marriage and the peasant joint family in Russia' (1978).
[35] Hajnal, 'European marriage patterns' (1965): 101–43.

Table 3.3. *Peasant population by age*

Age	1814 (%)	1822 (%)	1825 (%)	1831 (%)	1834 (%)	1843 (%)	1850 (%)	1858 (%)
0–14	39.4	38.5	39.5	38.6	37.6	36.8	38.2	42.1
15–59	57.5	57.8	56.1	56.7	57.1	59.2	57.9	53.8
60+	3.1	3.7	4.4	4.7	5.3	4.0	3.9	4.1

Table 3.4. *Agricultural peasants: proportions ever married*

Age group Males	1814 (%)	1822 (%)	1825 (%)	1831 (%)	1834 (%)	1843 (%)	1850 (%)	1858 (%)
15–19	54.7	53.1	45.7	30.1	19.2	22.2	22.6	43.2
20–4	94.7	92.0	92.3	83.8	85.7	84.0	82.5	95.1
25–9	96.4	100.0	100.0	100.0	95.8	96.7	98.1	98.0
SMAM[a]	17.0	17.7	18.0	19.3	19.7	19.5	18.9	18.0
Females								
15–19	34.4	26.2	23.0	23.3	30.7	23.8	23.6	62.9
20–4	90.3	93.7	91.2	84.2	86.8	92.9	87.1	100.0
25–9	97.6	94.5	95.1	96.4	91.3	95.8	94.1	96.3
SMAM[a]	18.5	18.8	18.7	19.5	18.9	19.0	19.0	16.6
Proportion of older wives	43.7	41.1	44.7	42.5	46.4	40.4	37.0	32.9
Sex ratio	89.5	101.2	100.5	100.4	97.3	100.4	97.4	98.9

[a] The singulate mean age at marriage (SMAM) is a figure arrived at by a calculation which simulates the marriage experience of a single cohort of the population spread over all the years when marriage is likely to take place. See n. 36.

extreme case, with certain peculiar features which warrant special attention. A unique feature of the Russian peasant marriage pattern, as the singulate mean age at marriage (SMAM) suggests, is the small age difference between spouses.[36] This is uncharacteristic in a marriage pattern in which women consistently married on average below the age of 20. A comparison of spouses' ages appearing in the Mishino listings shows a minimum of 33% and a maximum of 46% of wives older than their husbands. Since in compiling this statistic no attempt was made to identify second or third marriages, which for males invariably involved a younger woman, the proportion of men ever married to an older

[36] Hajnal, 'Age at marriage and proportions marrying' (1953): 111–36.

woman is undoubtedly somewhat higher. In circumstances where the peasant arable was periodically redistributed to take account of changes in the household labour force, the probable reason for the high proportion of older wives lay in the advantage that accrued to a household which could import an able-bodied worker. The advantage could be hastened if a match were concluded between a 15-year-old groom and an 18-year-old bride. Any economic disadvantage the bride's household might suffer was compensated by a bride price. Furthermore, peasant wisdom held that a good match must not be passed up lightly, for the longer a young woman remained unmarried the greater the chance she would be dishonoured and bring shame on her family.[37] In 1834 32.6% (N = 133) of all wives were reported to be one to three years older than their spouses; 11.5% (N = 47), four to six years older; and 1.9% (N = 8), seven to nine years older. The mean difference in age between all spouses was 0.0.

In addition to the expected role taken by parents in the marriage of their offspring, in Mishino, as in many proprietary estates, the peasant community and the seigneur or his agents also took part in shaping nuptial behaviour.[38] An order (*prikaz*) written in December 1817, which informed the overseer of Mishino of the opening of a cloth mill on the Gagarin estate of Petrovskaia in Riazan province, is one dramatic example of seigneurial interference in the nuptial process. The order indicated a need at the mill for young female operators who would be drawn from among unmarried females 15 years and older and young widows living on Mishino and other Gagarin estates in the province. The estate administration was instructed to compile a special register of all females falling into the germane categories and to convene a meeting of their parents to explain the situation. Parents were given the option of arranging marriages for their daughters before the arrival in Mishino of an agent of the prince or risk the loss of their daughters to the mill in Petrovskaia. An annotated copy of the special register, dated February 1818, documents the impact on the peasant community of the prince's order.[39] Two 16-year-olds, two 17-year-olds, and an 18-year-old were shown to have wed since the issuing of the order. Parents of a majority of the remaining young women appearing on the list made firm promises to have their daughters wed by the end of the first week after Easter. A number of women appearing on the register were indicated by

[37] Mironov, 'Traditsionnoe demografischeskoe povedenie krestian v XIX–nachale XX' (1977): 90.
[38] Aleksandrov, *Selskaia obshchina v Rossii (XVII – nachalo XIX v.)* (1976): 304–8.
[39] TsGADA, Fond 1262, op. 2, d. 74 (1817), 11: 150–1.

the overseer as unsuitable for marriage by reason of physical handicaps, and six 15-year-olds and one 16-year-old were indicated as 'immature' (*malorosla*).

The rapid remarriage of widows and widowers indicated by the data, while it may have been in the interests of the immediate parties concerned, was also a matter of interest to the peasant commune and the seigneur. To facilitate remarriage, it was frequently necessary in Mishino for households to break up and recombine, processes which could take place only with the consent of the commune or the estate administration.

The peasants of Mishino were considerably less free than the individuals living in most societies studied by historical demographers to respond spontaneously to the variables which normally affect the timing and extent of nuptiality – availability of mates and feasibility and desirability of marriage. Having made this observation, it must be pointed out that the constraints notwithstanding, the marriage behaviour of the Mishino peasants was neither monolithic nor unchanging. The results in table 3.4 indicate a steady rise in the SMAM for both males and females into the 1850s. At this stage of research it is too early to say whether this rise was a local phenomenon or reflected a tendency among the peasantry as a whole.

There is less question that the marked decrease in the SMAM for 1858 was part of a broader tendency. Aggregate data, reflecting the demographic behaviour of the Orthodox population of the whole Empire indicates an increase in the rate of marriage occurring at this time: from an annual average rate of 9/1,000 for the years 1851–5 to 11/1,000 for the years 1856–60. The crude birth rate of the Orthodox population was affected by the increase in the rate of marriage. The average annual crude birth rate of 50/1,000 for 1851–5 increased to 53/1,000 for 1856–62.[40]

It remains problematic why a trend towards later marriage which lasted nearly 50 years was reversed at the end of the decade of the 1850s and why an already high birth rate surged even higher. However, to speculate on these questions is interesting. The year 1856 coincided with the end of the Crimean War and, perhaps more important, with the spread of the news that the government would soon abolish serfdom – which it did in 1861. Along with the general diffuse euphoria caused by news of the impending emancipation of the serfs, peasants may have perceived opportunities and threats arising from abolition – opportunities and threats which moved them to modify their nuptial behaviour.

[40] Pokrovsky (1899): 187.

Statistics for Mishino, which appear consistent with aggregate data concerning marriage for the Orthodox population as a whole, could be interpreted as evidence that agricultural serfs, anticipating a land division with the abolition of serfdom, embraced a nuptiality and fertility strategy designed to take advantage of the peculiar system of land partibility that existed among them.

Household size

It became commonplace at the end of the eighteenth and beginning of the nineteenth century for Russian seigneurs to issue instructions forbidding, or at the least controlling, household fission among their peasants. Whether these orders were an attempt to halt the erosion of a family system based on the prevalence of large, complex households or to encourage the growth of such a system has yet to be demonstrated empirically. Semevskii, among others, strongly argues for the first proposition.[41]

Prince Gagarin was one of those serf owners who attempted to control his peasants' domestic arrangements. His 'instruction' concerning household divisions, if one was ever issued, has not been found. But the reports of his overseer carry references to the prince's 'firm wish' that peasant households in Mishino be allowed to divide only for urgent reasons. The prince's direct interest in this question is reflected by his order that a special register be compiled at the end of 1816 summarizing household divisions among the peasants of Mishino for the preceding four years. His concern to preserve households that could suitably be described as 'economically viable' (*tiaglosposobnyi*), along with the peasants' natural inclination to regard their own domestic arrangements at least in part from an economic point of view, combined to produce a family system in Mishino unlike any found by investigators of western societies. Employing the variables that are conventionally used to characterize household forms – size, relational composition, generational depth – the parameters for the peasant households of Mishino compare most closely with those reported for rural households in Latvia and Hungary in the eighteenth and nineteenth centuries, albeit on the side of somewhat larger, more complex units.[42]

Household size is the first variable in which households in Mishino deviate from the western standard. At the upper limit of their range, households in the period 1814–58 fluctuated between a maximum size

[41] Semevskii, *Krestiane v tsarstvovanie Imperatritsy Ekateriny II* (1903): I, 320–1.
[42] P. Laslett, *Family life and illicit love* (1977a): 22–3.

Table 3.5. *Household size*

	1814	1822	1825	1831	1834	1843	1850	1858
Number of households	128	130	134	152	164	172	166	169
Total population	1,173	1,197	1,299	1,425	1,398	1,393	1,463	1,522
Range	1–20	1–18	2–22	2–21	1–20	1–18	1–24	2–25
Mean	9.1	9.2	9.7	9.3	8.5	8.0	8.8	9.0
(Standard deviation)	(3.831)	(3.659)	(4.024)	(3.510)	(3.641)	(3.577)	(4.083)	(3.981)
Median	9	9	9	9	9	8	9	8
Mode	7/12	8	7	8	8	7	6	7
Mean experienced household size[a]	10.7	10.6	11.3	10.6	10.1	9.6	10.7	10.7
% population in households size 9 or larger	70.8	68.0	71.6	68.1	57.3	56.6	66.7	66.2
% population in households size 15 or larger	18.1	17.6	19.6	15.0	14.0	13.6	18.8	13.3

[a] 'Mean experienced household size' is household size considered from the perspective of any individual chosen at random. For a discussion of this concept see Halpern, 'Town and countryside in Serbia' (1972): 409.

of 18 and 25, although households of 20 persons or more were rare. Households of 1 or 2 persons were equally rare and invariably a fleeting phenomenon – households of this small size captured in one listing failing to appear in the next.

Mean household size fluctuated between 8.0 and 9.7, but the much steadier median size of 9 (8 in two listings) is a more accurate indication of the relative stability in household size over the whole period. The mean size of conjugal family units and the mean number of conjugal family units per household also remained steady (see table 3.7).

Although household size changed little in the aggregate, noticeable changes were taking place in the frequencies of households at particular sizes. Between 1814 and 1858 there is a small but noticeable decline in the proportion of households containing 15 or more individuals and a corresponding decrease in the number of persons living in such households. The decline in the proportion of the largest households correlated obversely with an increase in the proportion of households with 5 and 6 persons.

The average number of conjugal family units (CFUs) per household

Table 3.6. *Proportions of households and residents by household size*

Year	Household size	
	5–6 (%)	15 and over (%)
1814		
Households	11.6	10.1
Population	7.1	18.1
1822		
Households	14.6	9.9
Population	8.5	17.6
1825		
Households	12.6	11.1
Population	7.5	19.6
1831		
Households	9.8	8.5
Population	5.7	15.0
1834		
Households	23.0	7.2
Population	14.8	14.3
1843		
Households	19.1	6.9
Population	14.8	13.6
1850		
Households	19.8	9.6
Population	12.7	18.7
1858		
Households	17.1	6.4
Population	10.8	13.3

Table 3.7. *Conjugal family units*

	1814	1822	1825	1831	1834	1843	1850	1858
Number of households	128	130	134	152	164	172	166	169
Number of CFUs	322	308	327	393	369	373	382	371
Mean no. of CFUs/household	2.5	2.4	2.4	2.3	2.1	2.1	2.0	2.1
Mean CFU size	3.7	3.6	3.8	3.8	3.7	3.6	3.9	3.7
Mean experienced CFU	4.2	4.4	4.5	4.4	4.4	4.1	4.4	4.3

was 2.2 over the whole period; the range, 0 to 7. In 1814, 79% of all the households in Mishino included 2 or more CFUs; in 1858, 73%. In Mishino, therefore, mean household size of 9.0 translated into approximately 75% complex households.

As an example of a household with 9 persons, let us consider the

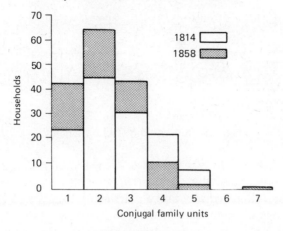

Fig. 3.5. Households by number of conjugal family units, 1814 and 1858.

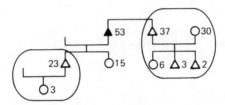

Fig. 3.6. Household of Dimitri Fedorov.

Fig. 3.7. Household of Sergei Vasilev.

household of Dmitri Fedorov. A widower aged 53, he headed a farmstead composed of married brother and sister-in-law and their children
and his own unmarried daughter, widowed son, and granddaughter.

A household of 6 persons was that of Sergei Vasilev, widower, aged
54. The other members of his family were his married son and daughter-
in-law and their unmarried children. On average between 1814 and
1858, 26% of the population of Mishino lived in households of 6 or
fewer persons. The most singular feature of household size in Mishino,
however, was that on average 65% of the population lived in households of 9 or more persons. An example of a household at the upper

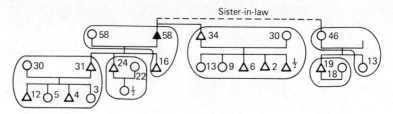

Fig. 3.8. Household of Tikhon Ignatev.

limit of the size range was that of 58-year-old Tikhon Ignatev, composed of his wife and their 2 married sons plus 5 unmarried grandchildren, an unmarried son, and a married brother with 5 children. In addition the household contained Tikhon's widowed sister-in-law, her married son, and her unmarried daughter.

Household type

Given the consistent median household size of 9 in Mishino, it would be reasonable to expect at all times a high proportion of complex households among the domestic groups composing the estate. The system of classification adopted here, with minor modification, is the typology elaborated by Laslett in 1972 in *Household and Family in Past Time*. Table 3.8 summarizes the distribution of households by type and year for approximately 40 years.

All households (categories 1, 2c, and 6 excepted) are composed of individuals who can be demonstrated to have kin or affinal relationship to the household head and participate in or be dependent on a single domestic economy. Category 6, 'Partially unclassifiable', contains the households, of whatever type otherwise, which include one or more members with no determinable kin or affinal link with the household head. The majority of individuals with indeterminate relationships to a household head are widows and widowers, occasionally with unmarried children. The present purpose of category 6, in some ways an unsatisfying rubric, is to underscore the intense kin basis for the households of Mishino. Progress so far in a turnover study of the eight censuses used here suggests that the number of partially unclassifiable households can be reduced as kin links not overtly stated become apparent, and that the consequences of reducing the number of households now located in category 6 will be to increase the number in categories 4 and 5 – extended- and multiple-family households.

A look behind the numbers included in table 3.8 will reveal some of the dynamics of household formation in Mishino. Category 1, 'Solitaries', contains a small, almost insignificant, number of households over the entire period under scrutiny. There was no accommodation in Mishino for able-bodied males or females to live alone, and ageing widows or widowers ending their days alone in a hut at the end of the village were also unknown. Provision was made, usually but not always, for kin to provide shelter for the aged and likewise the orphaned young. The 'No family' category similarly accounted for an insignificant number of households, whose members were quickly accommodated in other ways.

The proportion of 'Simple-family households' was small by comparison with western societies but nevertheless formed a significant proportion of the domestic groups in Mishino. Here simple families were typically not composed of a newly married couple with or without children. The formation generally was linked to other phases of the family life cycle. The ages of the heads of the 10 simple households which appear in the 1814 listing were 68, 56, 53, 47, 38, 36, 32, 24, 23, and unknown (a soldier's wife and her 13-year-old daughter). Of these 10 simple households only 2 appeared as simple households in a listing for 1811. Six of the 10 were newly formed between 1811 and 1814, 3 as a consequence of the hiving off of a married brother from each of 3 households consisting in 1811 of 4 married brothers and their offspring. One arose from the hiving off of a married brother from a household consisting of 3 married brothers and their offspring. Another simple household formed when one of two married brothers sharing a household died and the widow remarried and left with her offspring. Two of the remaining 4 simple households were formed as a consequence of the death of a parent and the recruitment of a brother. The history of the remaining 2 simple households in 1814, each headed by a soldier's wife, could not be fully reconstructed from data now available.

The formation of simple households between 1811 and 1814 falls into a pattern which is typical for the entire period under examination – and atypical of the process as it has been documented for western societies. Conspicuously absent from this category in Mishino are households consisting of newly married couples or couples with very young children. The married brothers establishing simple households referred to above were 38, 36, 32, and 24 in 1814, only one married less than 12 years. The process of hiving which produced 4 of the 10 simple households did not result in the complete fission of any of the affected households. Indeed, not one of the households losing a married brother was left with less than two co-residing married brothers. If we subtract

Table 3.8. *Households by type*

Household types	1814 No.	1814 %	1822 No.	1822 %	1825 No.	1825 %	1831 No.	1831 %	1834 No.	1834 %	1843 No.	1843 %	1850 No.	1850 %	1858 No.	1858 %
Solitaries																
1a. Widowed solitaries	1	0.7	0	0.0	0	0.0	0	0.0	0	0.0	0	0.0	0	0.0	0	0.0
1b. Single, or of unknown marital status	0	0.0	1	0.7	0	0.0	0	0.0	2	1.2	4	2.3	2	1.2	0	0.0
Subtotal	1	0.7	1	0.7	0	0.0	0	0.0	2	1.2	4	2.3	2	1.2	0	0.0
No family																
2a. Co-resident siblings	0	0.0	0	0.0	0	0.0	0	0.0	0	0.0	0	0.0	0	0.0	0	0.0
2b. Co-resident relations of other kinds	0	0.0	0	0.0	0	0.0	1	0.6	2	1.2	2	1.1	7	4.2	2	1.1
2c. Persons not evidently related	0	0.0	0	0.0	0	0.0	0	0.0	0	0.0	0	0.0	0	0.0	0	0.0
Subtotal	0	0.0	0	0.0	0	0.0	1	0.6	2	1.2	2	1.1	7	4.2	2	1.1
Simple-family households																
3a. Married couples alone	1	0.7	1	0.7	3	2.2	0	0.0	0	0.0	1	0.5	1	0.6	5	2.9
3b. Married couples with child(ren)	7	5.4	7	5.3	7	5.2	15	9.8	19	11.5	13	7.5	18	10.8	15	8.8
3c. Widowers with child(ren)	0	0.0	0	0.0	0	0.0	0	0.0	0	0.0	2	1.1	1	0.6	0	0.0
3d. Widows with child(ren)	2	1.5	1	0.7	2	1.4	0	0.0	1	0.6	3	1.7	3	1.8	1	0.5
Subtotal	10	7.6	9	6.7	12	8.8	15	9.8	20	12.1	19	10.8	23	13.8	21	12.2
Extended-family households																
4a. Extended upwards	10	7.8	5	3.8	3	2.2	7	4.6	14	8.5	6	3.4	5	3.0	10	5.9
4b. Extended downwards	3	2.3	3	2.3	2	1.4	2	1.3	1	0.6	2	1.1	3	1.2	3	1.7
4c. Extended laterally	0	0.0	1	0.7	2	1.4	2	1.3	4	2.4	2	1.1	0	0.0	4	2.3
4d. Combinations of 4a–4c	1	0.7	5	3.8	3	2.2	3	1.9	5	3.0	2	1.1	4	2.4	3	1.7
Subtotal	14	10.8	14	10.6	10	7.2	14	9.1	24	14.5	12	6.7	11	6.6	20	11.6

Multiple-family households

	N	%	N	%	N	%	N	%	N	%	N	%	N	%	N	%
Multiple-family households																
5a. Secondary units up	0	0.0	1	0.7	0	0.0	0	0.0	3	1.8	2	1.1	9	5.4	3	1.7
5b. Secondary units down	49	38.2	60	46.1	66	49.2	72	47.3	52	31.7	62	36.0	49	29.5	65	38.4
5c. Secondary units lateral	22	17.1	19	14.6	21	15.6	19	12.5	29	17.6	40	23.2	26	15.6	26	15.3
5d. Other multiple-family households	24	18.7	25	19.2	23	17.1	22	14.4	23	14.0	20	11.6	26	15.6	21	12.4
Subtotal	95	74.0	105	80.6	110	81.9	113	74.2	107	65.1	124	71.9	110	66.1	115	67.8
6. Partially unclassifiable households	8	6.2	1	0.7	2	1.4	9	5.9	9	5.4	11	6.3	13	7.8	11	6.5
Total households	128	100.0[a]	130	100.0[a]	134	100.0	152	100.0	164	100.0	172	100.0	166	100.0	169	100.0

[a] Because numbers following the decimal point have not been rounded up, the actual totals in this and succeeding tables do not always reach 100%.

129

from table 3.8 for 1814 the households in categories 1 and 3, it becomes apparent that 91% of all households in Mishino consisted in part of kin beyond the nuclear family.

Extended-family households, numbering 14 in 1814, included 6 stem families, e.g. a widowed representative of the parental generation living with one married son, or daughter and son-in-law, and their unmarried children. The remaining 8 extended households included other extensions, such as an uncle, grandparent, or mother-in-law. Whether the stem families encountered in 4a and again in 5b were the result of conscious planning or whether they took shape as the result of random demographic events cannot be answered with certainty until a systematic turnover study of the Mishino population is completed. However, it would appear that the system of land partibility commonly practised by Russian peasants, periodic redistribution of arable to reflect changes in unit work-force, would have made the calculated formation of stem families, from a purely economic point of view, counterproductive.[43]

It is in category 5 – 'Multiple-family households' – that one looks to find the classic peasant patriarchal family of Russian literature and folklore. Of 49 households in 1814 disposed downward, 40 were pure patrilines, i.e. households with one couple from the parental generation together with their married children, grandchildren, and great-grandchildren. Another 5 were patrilines with additional elements, for example, married nephews. The remaining 4 multiple-family households disposed downward were units whose basic structure rested on an uncle–nephew link.

Among the 22 multiple-family households disposed laterally, 9 were pure *frérèches*, 5 were *frérèches* with upward extension, and 8 were households consisting of cousins living together with their wives and children. Category 5d contains, in general, the largest and most complex households in Mishino, two or more married brothers with their children and grandchildren, and other variations. Households like these, with secondary units disposed laterally and down, represented 18.7% (N = 24) of the households in Mishino in 1814.

Were these large domestic groups, which occasionally reached a size of 20 or more persons, households according to our earlier definition? Whereas the population appearing in the 1814 listing is divided into numbered households (*dvory*), the census provides no further information about living arrangements. The listing for 1843, however, informs us that 17 of the 172 households appearing in the list were settled in farmsteads containing two peasant dwellings (*izby*), the typical floor

[43] Aleksandrov (1976): 219–20.

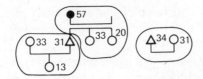

Fig. 3.9. Household occupying two *izby*.

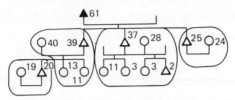

Fig. 3.10. Household of Mikhei Kassianov, occupying two *izby*.

plan for which was shown in fig. 3.4. It is reasonable that we should raise the question whether the presence of two dwellings in a farmstead should carry any implications for household classification. The size range of households with two *izby* was 5 to 18 persons, and the mean was 11 persons. The latter number is in contrast with a mean household size of 8 for all 172 households in the listing. The mean number of conjugal family units per household with two *izby* was 3.0, compared with 2.1 for all households. Sixteen of the households with two *izby* were exclusively kin-based. The exception looked like fig. 3.9. The 34-year-old heading his own conjugal family unit is indicated in the listing as 'accepted' or 'adopted into the household' (*priniatyi vo dvor*), in other words, made an integral member of the domestic economy based on the farmstead plus the share of arable. Every member of the *dvor*, kin, affine, or adoptive member, shared equally in the right to succeed to the common property of the household. As the term '*dvor*' was used interchangeably with the word for family, we can ask whether adoption into the *dvor* implied initiation into the intimacy of the family circle as well as integration into the domestic economy.

The 1843 listing provides no hint whatever as to how premises which included two *izby* were occupied. We can only speculate how members of the household of 61-year-old Mikhei Kassianov used their premises, which included two *izby*, for sleeping, cooking and eating and the reception of guests, and storage.

It is problematic what clarity could be lent to this discussion by the creation of an additional analytical category to cover the case of households with two *izby*. The term 'houseful', suggested for use where the nature and force of integrative factors linking individuals sharing the same physical premises are not precisely known, does not seem appropriate here. We know, in fact, a good deal about these links. The presence of two *izby* on a small number of farmsteads, rather than suggesting the need for an additional analytical category, stresses the importance for the peasants of Mishino of existing physical premises in determining residence patterns. The peasants were not free to establish new farmsteads as their population grew nor to divide households at their pleasure. The serfs of Mishino moved from one set of premises to another only with the agreement of the head of their household, their community, and their seigneur or his agents. Unable to move about freely, the peasants, when resources were available to them, added on to their premises to create the phenomenon we are discussing.

Generational composition

Despite a mean life expectancy at birth no greater than 31 years for males and 33 for females,[44] households of three or more generations represented a majority of all households for the entire period under examination. This was the result of large household size, the short interval between generations, and the peculiar features of the family process common to Mishino peasants.

Just as we do not find newly married couples living apart from their parents or other representatives of the parental generation, we also do not find a significant proportion of the elderly living apart from their children or kin of the offspring generation. Those peasants about to start families and those who had completed theirs lived together in large households, headed usually by representatives of the older generations. This residence pattern was the pre-condition for the large percentage of three- and four-generational households.

The early age at marriage reduced the time interval between generations on average to a little over 20 years. Using an adaptation of the Hajnal formula for calculating SMAM, it was possible to calculate the singulate mean age of mother at first birth, which for Mishino in 1814 was 21.3. Observation of the data shows that it was possible for peasants and their offspring fortunate enough to elude accident, recruitment, and death, to become parents at age 18–20, grandparents at age 38–40, and great-grandparents at age 55. The household of Ivan Mikhailov, aged 65 in 1814, illustrates the pattern.

[44] Kuczynski, *The balance of births and deaths* (1931): II, 9. The ages cited above were the life expectancies calculated for the years 1896–7.

Table 3.9. *Generational span*

		1814	1822	1825	1831	1834	1843	1850	1858
1 generation	No.	3	3	5	1	4	8	5	6
	%	2.3	2.3	3.7	0.6	2.4	4.6	3.0	3.6
2 generations	No.	41	45	35	39	50	73	54	47
	%	32.0	34.6	26.1	25.6	30.4	42.3	32.5	27.8
3 generations	No.	72	77	88	93	95	84	99	109
	%	56.3	59.1	65.6	61.1	57.8	48.8	59.6	64.5
4 generations	No.	12	5	6	19	15	7	8	7
	%	9.4	3.7	4.3	12.4	9.0	4.0	4.8	4.1
Subtotal: 3 and 4 generations	No.	84	82	94	112	110	91	107	116
	%	65.7	62.8	69.9	73.5	66.8	52.8	64.4	68.6
Indeterminate	No.	0	0	0	0	0	0	0	0
	%	0.0	0.0	0.0	0.0	0.0	0.0	0.0	0.0

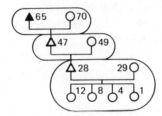

Fig. 3.11. Household of Ivan Mikhailov.

In terms of cross-cultural comparisons, the proportion of households in Mishino with three or more generations, on average 65%, is greater than any that has so far come to light.[45]

Relational composition

In 1814 fewer than 4% (7 out of 192) of the children of Mishino aged 0–5 lived in simple households.[46] The great majority lived in households which included kin other than members of their immediate family. The norm for the majority of all unmarried members of the community was to grow up in a welter of cousins, uncles, and aunts. A larger number of unmarried offspring in households were grandchildren than children of the head.

'Other unmarried relatives' consisted for the most part of 70 nieces

[45] P. Laslett (1977a): 23.
[46] For cross-cultural comparison see *ibid.* 36.

Table 3.10. *Unmarried relatives of heads of household, 1831*
(number of households = 152)

Unmarried persons	No.	%
Children of head	218	31.5
Grandchildren of head	280	40.5
Great-grandchildren of head	24	3.4
Other unmarried relatives of head of all ages	154	22.3
Orphans	4	0.5
Illegitimate	2	0.2
Indeterminate	8	1.1
TOTAL	690	100.0

and nephews, 56 great-nieces and -nephews, and unmarried brothers, sisters, and cousins of the head.

If we examine the frequency of kin terms irrespective of marital status, it becomes evident that the most important kin links tying together the family system of the Mishino peasants were the relationships of household heads with one or more sons and grandsons (see table 3.11). In 1814, when the estate contained 128 households, 80 were headed by married males, 28 by widowers, 1 by an unmarried male, and 19 by widows or soldiers' wives. In the listing, 'son' was the relation of the head appearing most frequently: sons represented 15.9% (N = 167) of the total population excluding heads of households. The proportion of the entire population, excluding household heads, represented by direct offspring of the head (sons and daughters) was 25.6%. 'Grandson' was next in frequency after 'son'.

Daughters-in-law were more numerous in the list of relatives than either daughters or wives, underscoring the modal character of the multiple family in the Mishino family system. The large number of nephews, nieces, and sisters-in-law is consistent with the significant lateral disposition among multiple-family households and lateral extension in the extended households. The virtual absence in all the listings of 'father' and 'mother' of the head is explained by the tendency for family patriarchs to remain household heads until their deaths, to be succeeded by their widows.[47] The convention has been adopted throughout this study to accept the first name to appear in each household block as the head of household. There is ample qualitative evidence to support the

[47] The positive relationship between age of head and size of household, as would be expected, is exceedingly strong. For the listing of 1843, the chi square, with 221 degrees of freedom, is 96%.

Table 3.11. *Kin and affines of household heads[a] by category and sex for Mishino estate, Riazan province, 1814 (total population 1,173; households 128)*

	Males			Females		
	No.	%[b]			No.	%[b]
Son	167	15.9	Daughter-in-law		110	10.5
Grandson	114	10.9	Daughter		101	9.6
Nephew	68	6.5	Granddaughter		94	8.9
Brother	40	3.8	Wife		80	7.6
			Niece		61	5.8
			Sister-in-law		50	4.7
Other[c]	43	4.1	Other[d]		86	8.2
Indeterminate	13	1.2	Indeterminate		18	1.7
TOTAL	445	42.4	TOTAL		600	57.4

[a] Includes 80 married males, 28 widowers, 1 unmarried male, and 19 widowed females.
[b] Percentage of 1,045 (= total population less 128, the number of household heads).
[c] Includes great-grandsons, grandnephews, cousins, and sons-in-law.
[d] Includes great-granddaughters, grandnieces, granddaughters-in-law, spouses of various male kin, and affines.

notion that a widowed female head of household (*bolshachikha*) was an accepted cultural norm.

Family life process

The view of the peasant household adduced thus far has been cross-sectional and static. The need to consider the family as process as well has been cogently argued in the work of Goody and Fortes.[48] The work of Berkner and Hareven has demonstrated the value of the concept of the domestic life cycle or 'life course' in illuminating systematic change in the family.[49] In Mishino the flow of births and deaths, and the exchange of household members through marriage and to a lesser extent adoption, constantly changed the size and composition of households and simultaneously marked stages in their evolution. The centrifugal forces which conventionally seem to strain the coherence of large households in most societies studied to date (disputes between brothers, mother-in-law/daughter-in-law strife, and miscellaneous, diffuse animosities), or various moments of passage such as the death of the head or the marriage of the eldest or youngest son which resulted in house-

[48] Goody (ed.), *The development cycle in domestic groups* (1958), esp. Fortes's introduction.
[49] Berkner, 'The stem family' (1972a); Hareven, 'Cycles, courses and cohorts' (1978a).

hold fission, met strong countervailing forces in the circumstances of life
in Mishino. The authority of the seigneur to inhibit household fission
wherever possible could not be resisted, at least not directly. The peasant
commune, which bore corporate responsibility for the performance of
peasant labour services and the payment of quit rent, also looked upon
requests for household division with a sceptical eye. Finally, the household head, who could usually, but not always under all circumstances,
depend on the community to uphold his authority, could prevent
members of his household from hiving off.

For the investigation of individual and domestic group life processes
in Mishino, we are fortunate to have a special register, drawn up in
1816, containing information about all household divisions which
occurred on the estate in the preceding four years.[50] Between 1812 and
1816, 9 households, out of approximately 130 on the estate, underwent
partial or complete fission. Each case is documented in the register with
information about the composition of the families/households before
and after fission and factors leading to the changes. As it is used here,
fission refers to the removal of one or more conjugal family units from
the household of orientation. With the exception of brides, a single
individual rarely moved to another household and never established
one of his own. According to the register, two households experienced
partial fission as a 'consequence of marriage', i.e. bachelors married out
of their households to enter those of their wives. In each case the groom,
moving into a small household, took with him a widowed parent and
unmarried siblings. Also in each case, the abandoned unit, although
reduced in size, remained a multiple-family household, one consisting
of three conjugal family units, the other of two. Each household taking
in a groom and his family, respectively a simple- and an extended-
family household, became a multiple-family unit.

'Constant fighting' was the explanation given to six of the nine
household fissions in Mishino between 1812 and 1816. In these instances division served to relieve potentially disruptive social pressures.
The case of a 57-year-old widower living with his granddaughter who
was joined by his married nephew, whose family included three unmarried children, illustrates a different purpose served by household division. Here the process of fission/fusion transformed a marginal household into one more closely approaching a size and generational composition typical of the estate. Finally, two of the nine fissions were
carried out 'wilfully' (*samovolno*), meaning presumably against the will

---

[50] TsGADA, Fond 1262, opis 2, d. 63 (1816).

Table 3.12. *List of households which divided between 1812 and 1816*

1812–15		Mean household size	1816			Mean household size
Simple	0	0	0.0	Simple	4	3, 7, 5, 6	5.2
Extended	0	0	0.0	Extended	4	7[a], 4, 6, 6	5.7
Multiple	9	15, 7, 22, 15, 14, 16, 17, 11, 18	15.0	Multiple	10	10, 16, 11, 8[a], 12, 6[a], 9, 7, 12, 12	10.3

[a] This household is the product of both fission and fusion, as discussed in the text.

of the heads of the affected households but tolerated by the community and the overseer.

Four simple households resulted from the nine fissions/fusions. The ages of the heads of these simple-family households were 42, 40, 36, and 36 years. The ages in 1816 of the remaining new heads of households were 56, 55, 54, 44, 43, and 35 years. Caution should be exercised in using the experience of 1812–16 as a model for the pattern of household divisions in Mishino for the entire period of this study, but one of the demographic characteristics of this early period that can be demonstrated throughout is a high age for household heads. Median age for all household heads for the years 1814–34 was 50–4 years. For 1843–58 it was 45–9 years. Only 5% of household heads in 1814 were below the age of 35; in 1858 the proportion had risen to 13.5%. These figures suggest an easing of the conditions leading to headship but not a fundamental change in the overall circumstances. Although marriage and parenthood came early to the peasants of Mishino, household headship, in most societies one of the important indicators of full social maturity, came late. The family system being described here was hostile to the free formation of new households and thus denied to many males, perhaps a majority of those who survived to marry, the opportunity to become household heads.

The events recorded in the 1816 register of household divisions further suggest that when household fissions occurred they seldom completely reduced complex households to their component parts, i.e. to a number of households equal to the number of conjugal family units which made up the original unit (or one household less, presuming that parents would continue to reside with one married son). Rather, the process of fission recorded in the 1816 register is piecemeal, linked to none of the conventional moments of passage. It seemed to occur when a farmstead fell vacant or when its occupants ceased to be 'able'; when domestic strife threatened a household's economic viability; or when the physical premises could no longer be modified to accommodate the members of the unit.

It is hard to discern in circumstances like these a cyclic rhythm in the developmental path followed by the households of Mishino. But before rejecting a cyclic pattern outright, the possibility of the presence of such a modality should be carefully explored. This can be done by attempting to fit to the circumstances of household development in Mishino the domestic group life cycle propounded by Fortes.[51] Fortes posits three developmental stages in the life of the family: (1) expansion – which lasts from the marriage of two people until the completion of their family of procreation; (2) dispersion or fission – which begins with the marriage of the eldest child; (3) replacement – which begins with the marriage of the youngest child, who remains with the parents, and ends with the death of the original marital pair. If a further proposition can be added – that a household can exist in two or all three stages simul-taneously – the Fortes model may provide a useful way of viewing the development of Mishino peasant households.

The first phase is controlled by the wife's (or wives') fertility. The early age at marriage in Mishino meant that the first stage could last for 20 to 25 years. Since marriage of the eldest son did not usually lead to any hiving off of members from the parental household, the first and second stages of the cycle overlapped. The condition where all three stages overlapped could be found in a three- or four-generational household. Marriage, however, reduced the size of one household, usually the bride's, and established a new reproducing couple in the household of the groom. But the time of marriage was not the moment at which a household divided, distributed common property, and established new households. Birth, death, and recruitment must therefore be given consideration as significant events in the developmental cycle of the peasant household.

Overlapping stages in the domestic group life cycle based on the Fortes model can be illustrated by the history of the household of Timofei Grigoriev, aged 44. In 1814 the household combined the expan-sion and dispersion stages (fig. 3.12). Headship passed in 1822 to Timofei's brother, Makar Grigoriev, aged 43 in that year. The household

---

[51] Fortes, 'Introduction' (1958): 2.

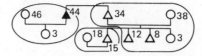

Fig. 3.12. Household of Timofei Grigoriev, 1814.

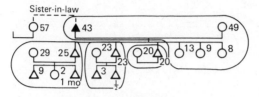

Fig. 3.13. Household of Makar Grigoriev, 1822.

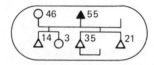

Fig. 3.14. Household of Evdokim Makarov, 1858.

then was at its apogee, consisting of 17 members, and combined all three stages of the developmental life cycle (fig. 3.13). In 1837 Makar was succeeded by his middle son Evdokim Makarov, aged 23 in 1822, the eldest son, Petr, having died in 1830 at age 33. Petr's widow married out of the household in 1831, taking her young children with her. One of Petr's sons, Pavel Petrov, returned to the household of his birth some time before 1843 and settled in as a nephew of the head. Pavel died in 1843, and his childless widow married out of the household. In 1843 the younger brother of Evdokim Makarov, Fedor Makarov, died at the age of 48. Thereafter the household proceeded to contract steadily as widowed sisters-in-law, nieces, and nephews of the head married out to join other households. In 1858 Evdokim Makarov headed a household which included children by his first and second wives and stood in the expansion and dispersion phases of the developmental cycle (fig. 3.14). The original household of Timofei Grigoriev, over a period of 40 years, was in turn multiple, extended, and simple, and passed through all three developmental stages without once experiencing a complete household fission.

A household whose demographic experience was different and which continued to grow steadily over 40 years was that of Fedot Denisov, aged 37. In 1814 the household was in the midst of its expansion stage

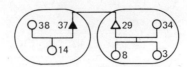

Fig. 3.15. Household of Fedot Denisov, 1814.

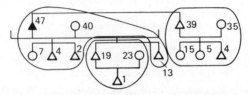

Fig. 3.16. Household of Fedot Denisov, 1825.

(fig. 3.15). Fedot lost his wife and remarried before 1816, bringing in addition to his new wife her two young male children, aged 10 and 3, the latter indicated as illegitimate. Fedot's brother Kharlam, aged 29 in 1814, added a surviving child to his family in 1821. By 1825 the older of Fedot's stepsons had married and fathered a son. Fedot continued to produce children of his own with his second wife, the last surviving one born in 1829 when Fedot was 50 and his wife 43 years old. The household in 1825 stood in the expansion and dispersion stages (fig. 3.16). By 1831 Fedot's second stepson, aged 13 in 1825, was married and living in the household with his wife. Fedot's brother, Kharlam, aged 39 in 1825, also continued to live in the household – producing and losing children. In 1831 two of Kharlam's children, aged 10 and 9, lived in the household. The household numbered 15. By 1834 Fedot was four times a grandfather, thanks to his stepsons, and the household numbered 17 persons. Between 1834 and 1843 Kharlam Denisov, with his wife and two children, left the household headed by Fedot and moved into a household headed by the husband of Kharlam's eldest daughter. That household, including Kharlam's grandchildren by his eldest daughter, numbered 10 persons. In the meantime Fedot's eldest son by his second marriage married and remained in his father's household. In 1843 Fedot Denisov was 66 years old (see fig. 3.17). When Fedot died in 1852 at the age of 75, he presided over a household of 21 persons which reflected simultaneously various developmental stages of the domestic group life cycle. The members of his household were prolific and fortunate to have escaped the full force of the harsh social and demographic forces which maintained the majority of households at a smaller size. In

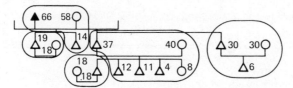

Fig. 3.17. Household of Fedot Denisov, 1843.

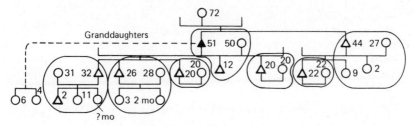

Fig. 3.18. Household of Alexander Danilov, 1858.

1858 the household, now headed by Fedot's older stepson, Alexander Danilov, numbered 25 persons living in 7 conjugal families (fig. 3.18).

The use of Fortes's model, while it provides the basis for an additional possible household typology, does not allow an outside observer of family process in Mishino to predict with any reliability when household divisions might take place or how extensive they might be. Pending completion of a turnover study of the entire population which may reveal patterns not now discernible, we are led to conclude that the concept 'cycle' is not appropriate to a description of the developmental process of Mishino households. Instead, what we find is a family system characterized by an overwhelming proportion of 'perennial households', households for which one can determine no beginning or end in a continuous sequence of generations.[52]

Population turnover

Closely related to the problem of the domestic group life process is the question of population turnover. Examination of the data for Mishino has not proceeded far enough for a complete statement on the question, but a partial picture of population turnover can be constructed from the results of an examination of the male population of Krasnoe Sobakino, one of the four villages composing the estate of Mishino.

In 1814 the village consisted of 28 households and a male population

[52] Mitterauer and Sieder, 'The developmental process of domestic groups' (1979).

Table 3.13. *Male population turnover, Krasnoe Sobakino, 1814–34 (1814 N = 135 males)*

Persisting		83 (61.4%)
Of those persisting:		
Remained in household of origin	61 (45.1%)	
Were located in different household	22 (16.1%)	
Disappearing		52 (38.5%)
Of those disappearing:		
Died	42 (31.1%)	
Recruited	6 (4.4%)	
Migrated	4 (2.9%)	
	135 (100.0%)	

of 135. The mean number of males per household was 4.8. Over a period of 20 years, from 1814 until 1834, 83 (61.4%) of the original male population survived in the village of Krasnoe; 42 (31.1%) had died; 6 (4.4%) had entered the army; and 4 (2.9%) had migrated from the village. Of the latter 4, 3 lived elsewhere in the Mishino estate and 1 had been transferred to a Gagarin estate in Tambov province.

During the same period 2 households disappeared and 6 households experienced fission, leading to a net increase of 4 households in 1834.[53] Fifteen males moved from one Krasnoe household to another as a consequence of household fissions, and an additional 3 males changed from their households of origin for other reasons. Add to this number the 4 males who moved away from the village to live elsewhere in Mishino and Tambov, and a total of 22 males (16.1%) of the original 135 is reached who found themselves in 1834 established outside their households of origin. Put another way, 61 (73.4%) of all surviving males were still attached to their households of origin after 20 years.

A survey of the turnover of household headship confirms the strong father/son link suggested by the kin structure analysis above. The heads of 5 of 6 new households appear as 'brother' in their households of origin, suggesting that the status 'uncle' of the head was one to avoid whenever possible, since each would have occupied this role in 1834 had he been unable to form a household of his own. Therefore, the moment when that point of transition occurs in the lives of household members and in the life process of peasant households may be one of particular significance in the evolution of Russian peasant domestic

[53] In 1825 Gagarin purchased a number of serf families from another seigneur and settled them in Krasnoe Sobakino. These immigrants have been excluded from the results discussed here.

Table 3.14. *Household succession, Krasnoe Sobakino, 1814–34*

Households which persisted					New households Relationship of head to head of household of origin		
	Succeeded by						
Head survived	Son	Grand- son	Brother	Nephew	Brother	Nephew	
9	11	2	1	3	5	1	= 32 (1834)

groups. The listing for 1814, which has been examined for kin links with the household head, revealed only one uncle of a head in 128 households. Conversely the number of nephews and grandnephews of the head is significant – 15.2% of the male population excluding male heads of household. It would appear, therefore, that if the head of a complex household is survived by a brother but succeeded by a son the chances are high that a significant restructuring of the household will occur. If, however, succession goes to the brother, chances are high that younger males in the household, i.e. sons and nephews of the new head, will remain in place.

Although the numbers used in this partial turnover study are small, it seems reasonable to speculate that as many as half of the male peasants living in Mishino in the first decades of the nineteenth century could expect to pass their entire lives not only within their village of origin, but also within their household of birth. Whether this remained true for the last decade before the emancipation of the serfs, when the proportion of simple households rose, is less certain. The life experience of females, the great majority of whom left their households of birth by the age of 20, was of course greatly different.

Additional influences on the family system

Most of the foregoing has been descriptive. For a fuller explanation of the origins of the family system described here and the forces which sustained it, further analysis of the Mishino data will be necessary. In addition to demographic imperatives and the internal organization of the estate, economic factors no doubt also influenced the family system which prevailed in Mishino. Economic data for the individual households in Mishino exist, but have not yet been systematically correlated with the demographic data. It is nevertheless possible to make limited, if perhaps obvious, observations about the distribution of material resources among the households of Mishino. Larger households seemed to possess larger numbers of work and dairy animals, pigs and beehives; that is, they displayed the outward signs of prosperity. Until further work is done, however, it cannot be asserted whether this prosperity was the cause or the consequence of household size. In a study based on late-nineteenth-century data, Shanin found a strong relationship between household size and prosperity on the one hand and identifiable stages in the Russian peasant family life cycle on the other.[54] Perennial households of the type noted above did not appear to figure significantly in Shanin's sample. The Russian peasants studied by Shanin were no longer serfs. Whether the relationship he found evolved in the decades after emancipation or had roots in the serf past can eventually be determined.

Extrinsic social factors like war, the transfer of property to a new seigneur, or rumours concerning emancipation would also seem to affect the family system.

Finally, values, customs, and traditions – the peasants' and the seigneurs' – must also have exerted strong influence on the processes of household development. These may be the most difficult to document. 'Peasant culture' (*krestianskii byt*) in the era of serfdom, with its own standards of correct behaviour, is still to be described, and the points of contact and conflict between this cluster of beliefs and the culture of the landlords remain to be charted.

Conclusions

Analysis of the Mishino revisions and household lists leaves the overwhelming impression of a stable family system, preserving its fundamental characteristics over a period of 40 years. The large, multigenerational families/households prevalent in Mishino appear to be like those encountered in the world of Russian folklore and literature. Individual members were susceptible to early death and conjugal family units to sudden dissolution, but the larger entities which contained them were remarkably durable and offered refuge and continuity to survivors, young and old. It is difficult to conceive how any peasant born in Mishino would not have passed a significant part of his life, certainly his earliest years, in crowded physical proximity with kin other than members of his biological family. Whether the family system which prevailed in Mishino realized a peasant ideal or whether it was a burden to him we do not know. Certainly partial responsibility for it must go to

[54] Shanin, *The awkward class* (1972).

the peasant community (*obshchestvo*) and the seigneur. Until an individual became a head of household, he was perforce responsible, as a worker and as a member of a household, to three levels of authority – the household head, the community, and the seigneur. Not until he succeeded to headship – on average in his late 30s or early 40s – could he partially change that situation.

Where the demographic regime was harsh – as it was in Mishino – large family size was an important element in household stability. From a landlord's perspective, one reproducing couple in a farmstead signified a precarious economic unit, for precisely such households were the most likely to become extinct. Tolstoi represented one landlord's response to this situation in the First Epilogue to *War and Peace*, where he wrote of Count Nikolai Rostov: 'He kept the peasant families together in the largest groups possible and would not allow them to split into separate households.' In a historical period almost exactly congruent with the fictional time of Tolstoi's masterpiece, Prince Nikolai Sergeevich Gagarin achieved an enviable degree of stability among his households in Mishino – persistence of over 90% in the 20-year period 1814 to 1834 – employing the same general principle.[55] This leads to the question whether wide significance for Russian society can be attached to the analysis adduced in this essay. Or was the experience of Prince Gagarin with Mishino an isolated phenomenon, and the behaviour of Tolstoi's Rostov merely the reflection of a social myth? Put another way, does the family system which flourished in Mishino at least until the eve of emancipation point to the existence throughout Russia of a well-established eastern European family type, and if so what were its regional peculiarities and their geographic distribution in the first half of the nineteenth century?

Although our analysis of the Mishino data has not been exhaustive, and the data admittedly represent a small sample of the whole Russian population, a preliminary answer to the question can be attempted. In contrast to the western European family type,[56] an eastern European type can be posited. It should include a large proportion of multiple-family households, with a significant number consisting of three or more generations; the units should be relatively large, with mean household size significantly greater than 5.0, and contain an average 2.0 conjugal family units. Near-universal early marriage and childbearing would be additional features of the eastern European family type.

[55] This finding is based on the analysis of data for the village of Krasnoe Sobakino, 1814–34.
[56] P. Laslett (1977a): 12–49.

Aggregate statistics published by the Imperial Central Statistical Committee in the late 1850s and early 1860s have long suggested the existence in Russia of a distinctive family system, but this remained until now, rightfully, problematic. Results from the analysis of the Mishino data offer insight into the possible significance of these statistics. The findings of our analysis give us an empirical definition of the term '*dvor*', the peasant household, as well as expectations about the composition of peasant households falling within the range of mean size 7 to 8. If, from what has been demonstrated here, mean household size among Russian agricultural peasants can be taken as a rough token for the underlying family system, the aggregate data collected in the mid-nineteenth century strongly point to the premise that the family system found in Mishino, with allowance for regional variation, was neither unique nor specific to a sharply limited territory.

Concerning the area immediately surrounding Mishino, mean household size for the southern half of Mikhailovskii district, where Mishino was located, was 9.3 in 1859 (population 58,418).[57] Mean household size for Riazan province as a whole (population 1,368,599) was 8.8. These figures closely fit the mean household size of 9.0 calculated for Mishino in 1858. The figures for Mikhailovskii and Riazan province include not only proprietary serfs (about 65% of the total population), but also state peasants (about 25% of the total population) as well as residents of towns and cities. If mean household size signified roughly the same thing for the preponderantly peasant population of Riazan province as a whole as it did for the inhabitants of Mishino, i.e. an average of two conjugal family units per household, then a family system dominated by complex households was almost certainly generic for both proprietary serfs and state peasants throughout the province.

In Orel province (see fig. 3.1), located in the black-earth belt to the south-west of Riazan, mean household size in 1866, five years after the emancipation, was 9.1 (population 1,474,610).[58] In less densely settled Saratov province to the south-east of Riazan, mean household size in 1859 was 8.0 (population 1,578,774).[59] In Tver province, located in the Central Industrial Region and contiguous with the north-western

[57] Russia, Central Statistical Committee, *Spiski naselennykh mest Rossiiskoi imperii, sostavlennye i izdavaemye Tsentralnym statisticheskim komitetom Ministerstva vnutrennikh del. Riazanskaia guberniia*, vyp. 35 (1862): XIII. Volumes in this series, prepared by the Central Statistical Committee, present aggregate data which include population by sex and the number of households (*dvory*) by village, town, or city.
[58] *Spiski naselennykh mest . . . Orlovskaia guberniia*, vyp. 29 (1871): XXXVI.
[59] *Spiski naselennykh mest . . . Saratovskaia guberniia*, vyp. 38 (1862): XXXII.

Table 3.15. *Household size, Sukhovarova estate, Tver province*

	1816	1834	1850	1856
Number of households	46	54	54	56
Total population	420	461	454	464
Range	3–21	4–15	3–16	1–18
Mean	9.1	8.5	8.4	8.2
Median	8	8	8	8
Mode	8	6	8/11	11

Table 3.16. *Household type, Sukhovarova estate, Tver province*

	1816		1834		1850		1856	
	No.	%	No.	%	No.	%	No.	%
Solitaries	0	0.0	0	0.0	0	0.0	1	1.7
No family	0	0.0	1	1.8	0	0.0	2	3.5
Simple family	5	10.8	2	3.7	4	7.4	4	7.1
Extended family	3	6.5	4	7.4	4	7.4	2	3.5
Multiple family	35	76.0	43	79.6	38	70.3	37	66.0
Partially unclassifiable	3	6.5	4	7.4	8	14.8	10	17.8
Total households	46	100.0	54	100.0	54	100.0	56	100.0

boundary of Moscow province, mean household size in 1859 was 7.3 (population 1,334,180).[60]

From Tver province, in addition to the aggregate data from the Central Statistical Committee, we have collected and analysed four consecutive revisions for the proprietary estate of Sukhovarova in Zubtsovskii district, property of the family of Kvashnin-Samarin.[61] The information summarized in tables 3.15, 3.16, and 3.17 leaves no doubt that all the criteria for the posited eastern European family type were met in the domestic circumstances of the agricultural serfs of Sukhovarova – mean household size of 8.2 in 1856; 66% multiple-family households and 48% three- and four-generational households. The data demonstrate that a mean household size of approximately 8.0 in Russia suggests that the predominant family form will not be simple, but complex to one degree or another.

Certainly the peasants of Mishino presented a more robust example of

[60] *Spiski naselennykh mest . . . Tverskaia guberniia*, vyp. 43 (1862): XXXI.
[61] U.S.S.R., Gosudarstvennaia Biblioteka SSSR im. V. I. Lenina, Moscow, Rukopisnyi Otdel, Fond 123, k. 5, ed. khr. 188, 192, 196, 198.

the posited eastern European family type than the peasants of Sukhovarova. But it was anticipated that in an attempt to plot the distribution
of this family type, regional differences in household size and therefore
complexity and generationality would be encountered. Semevskii discussed this phenomenon for the late eighteenth century. He found
differences in mean household size, not always predictable, among
different categories of peasants in the same province, e.g. proprietary
serfs (subdivided into those performing corvée and those paying quit
rent), state peasants, economic peasants (formerly owned by church
institutions), and others.[62] He also noted regional variation, finding the
. smallest average households, 2.8 male souls per household, in provinces
of the Central Industrial Region (Moscow, Tver, Iaroslavl etc.) and the
largest, 4.3 male souls per household, in the black-earth belt where
corvée was widespread. He attributed these differences to the greater
availability of non-agricultural work in the industrial region centred on
Moscow and a corresponding weakening of control by seigneurs over
the domestic behaviour of their more mobile serfs. A striking feature of
Semevskii's findings to which he fails to draw attention, and which is
borne out by later particular and general data from Riazan province, is
the higher degree of uniformity among mean household sizes of
peasants of different categories within a region than among peasants of
the same categories across regions. State peasants were generally regarded as less harshly exploited and freer to arrange their domestic lives
than proprietary serfs, and serfs paying quit rent correspondingly freer
than those performing labour services. Yet mean household size for the
province of Riazan as a whole, where 25% of the population consisted
of state peasants, differs by only 0.2 persons per household from households of proprietary serfs in Mishino. But on this point we are working
with fragmentary evidence.

More significant, perhaps, is the fact that in the mid-nineteenth
century, mean household size for the Central Industrial Region as a
whole was lower than that for the more southerly agricultural region:
Vladimir, 6.9;[63] Iaroslavl, 6.8;[64] and Kostroma, 6.2.[65] These figures are so
low that they suggest the presence of a socio-demographic frontier. If
this finding is confirmed by microanalysis – using sample data for all
categories of peasantry in a region – it would suggest that not only legal
status, economic conditions, and the means of social control, but also

[62] Semevskii (1903): I, 320.
[63] *Spiski naselennykh mest . . . Vladimirskaia guberniia*, vyp. 6 (1863): XXXI.
[64] *Spiski naselennykh mest . . . Iaroslavlkaia guberniia*, vyp. 50 (1865): XXXIII.
[65] *Spiski naselennykh mest . . . Kostromskaia guberniia*, vyp. 18 (1877): XXXV.

Table 3.17. *Generational span, Sukhovarova estate, Tver province*

	1816		1834		1850		1856	
1 generation	1	2.1	0	0.0	0	0.0	2	3.5
2 generations	17	36.9	21	38.8	29	53.7	27	48.2
3 generations	27	58.6	30	55.5	24	44.4	25	44.6
4 generations	1	2.1	3	5.5	1	1.8	2	3.5
Indeterminate	0	0.0	0	0.0	0	0.0	0	0.0
Total households	46	100.0	54	100.0	54	100.0	56	100.0

cultural and ecological factors played a role in determining variations in the family system in different parts of the country.

Although the family system reflected in the earliest listing for Mishino used here, 1814, was fundamentally intact in 1858, it was not stagnant and showed measurable changes over 40 years. The difference between the relatively elastic birth rate of the peasants and the relatively inelastic rate of household formation narrowed. This was reflected in the near doubling of the proportion of simple households, from 7.6% in 1814 to 12.2% in 1858. The proportion of extended families remained almost unchanged, but the proportion of multiple-family households declined from 80% in 1822 to 67.8% in 1858. While the mean household size remained remarkably steady over the span of 40 years, the proportion of individuals living in households at the higher end of the scale, 15 and more persons, declined steadily from 18.1% in 1814 to 13.3% in 1858. The rules concerning household fission and the establishment of separate farmsteads seemed to be changing.

The reasons for these changes are not obvious. They occurred in a period, according to Struve, which witnessed the final collapse of the moral viability of serfdom.[66] This could have been accompanied by a general lessening of seigneurial will to dominate the peasants' personal lives as completely as earlier. The Soviet historian I. D. Kovalchenko saw the same years as ones of increased exploitation and economic differentiation for the serf population.[67] Either or both of these considerations could have exercised an influence on the peasants' family system. However, in Mishino itself the period 1814–49 saw the conversion of the peasants' seigneurial obligations from labour services to quit rent. Also, on the death of Nikolai Sergeevich Gagarin in 1842, Mishino passed into the hands of his son Lev Nikolaievich, whose management of the estate was not marked by the same concern for detail as his

[66] Struve (1913): 154.
[67] Kovalchenko (1959): 219–20.

father's. These local effects alone may be sufficient to explain the changes summarized in the preceding paragraph.

Although the descriptive statistics presented in these pages do not completely illuminate the family system of the peasants of Mishino, nor give a satisfactory explanation for it, they do offer a clear point of departure for further study. With the prevalence of the joint family established for Mishino and Sukhovarova (in Tver province), one must ask to what degree it reflected the peasants' need for 'secure family ties' as Haxthausen speculated, or other peasant cultural impulses, and how much it rested upon preferences of the landlords. Evidence of the seigneurs' wishes is fairly abundant and seemingly unambiguous; at the present time, unfortunately, the same cannot be said about evidence of the peasants' wishes. If this essay has achieved nothing more, it has shown that demographic sources of high quality and great interest are available for Russia which invite further study of the questions left unanswered here.

Censuses and household inventories have verified that a family type like the one posited above, distinguished by large unit size and considerable complexity, existed in Mishino and Sukhovarova. Aggregate statistics read in light of the analysis of these listings suggest that the same family type was widespread in large parts of Russia. The evidence to prove or refute this proposition is available. Russia may indeed be the classic area in modern times in which a large society exhibited predominantly big and complex households, in contrast with western Europe and particularly England. Furthermore, it may be a society where family ideology and family experience overlapped to a great degree – also in contrast to the societies of western Europe. That experience, which displayed a greater magnitude of vertical and horizontal proliferation of kin-linked household members than any that has been empirically verified as yet, may warrant rethinking some of the more highly generalized theories of family structure, which preclude on various grounds the possibility of a social actuality like the one found to have existed in Mishino.

APPENDIX

Peasants in the village of Slobodka, 28 April 1822

| | | | Household | | | | | Horses | | Property | | | | |
		Age	Male Workers	Male Non-workers	Female Workers	Female Non-workers	Total	Work	Non-work	Cows	Sheep	Pigs	Bees	
1	Ivan Andreev – widowed	72		1										Good behaviour
	His children													
	Mikhail – widowed	47	1											
	Maksim	37	1					4	1	1	7	2	—	Cooper and stonecutter
	Mikhail's children													
	Zakhar	18	1											
	Makhail	15		1										
	Nikita	11		1										
	Daughter Aksin'ia	10				1								
	Maksim's wife Matrena	37			1									
	Their son Varlamm	17		1										
	Zakhar's wife Nadezhda Il'ina	21			2	1	10							
2	…		3	4										

Source: TsGada, Fond 1262, opis 2, d. 119.

151

4

The peasant family as an economic unit in the Polish feudal economy of the eighteenth century

JACEK KOCHANOWICZ

The interaction of economic and demographic factors in peasant family life

The Polish economy of the eighteenth century was basically agrarian, the peasant family farm being the dominant unit of production. However, we have only a limited knowledge of its functions. Earlier studies have concentrated on those aspects which can be most easily found in the sources, that is the distribution of land among the villagers, the obligations connected with the holding of land, the size of holdings, and the amount of production, though this was usually confined to the production of corn. In general, we can say that we know more about the material aspects of peasant life than about the economic ones. We know little about economic and financial decisions made by peasants and about their responses to economic change, such as fluctuations in the size of the harvest and in prices.[1] In particular, we have little knowledge of the connection between the economic and demographic aspects of peasant life. That connection must have been important, first, because the family constituted the main source of labour for a peasant farm and, second, because family members were the principal recipients of peasant farm products. We are well aware that the size and structure of any family is subject to change. Both the number of people to feed and the number of people who can work change during the family life cycle. It is interesting to discover to what extent those changes affected the economic activity of the peasant family and were in turn conditioned by the character of economic life.

This chapter is based on my paper prepared for the Polish–Hungarian seminar on historical demography held in Vesprem, Hungary in October 1978. I would like to thank all those who took part in the discussion, especially Dr Irena Gieysztorowa.
[1] W. Kula tries to analyse in this way both peasant and demesne economy in his *An economic theory of the feudal system* (1976): esp. 62–75.

For the Polish economy, these problems have been studied only for the twentieth century. A. Szemberg, for example, has indicated that in parallel with changes in the structure of family farm manpower, that is of a peasant family, we can observe the changes in the area of land used by that farm and the changes in the level of capital expenditure.[2] Szemberg's thesis is that the level of family economic activity was determined by the productive capabilities of its manpower. In his studies of village structure in overpopulated regions of southern Poland, W. Styś has shown how demographic factors caused a reduction in the size of holdings.[3] Girls from richer families got married at an earlier age than those from poorer ones; consequently they had more children, and so there were more potential heirs.

In his magnificent work, A. V. Chayanov tried to bring together economic and demographic analyses of the peasant family farm.[4] He maintained that demographic factors played a dominant role. The peasant family had to determine a certain level of exploitation of family labour on the farm. The peasant always tried to achieve a kind of equilibrium between a rising marginal drudgery of labour and a declining marginal utility of income. However, the number of family members and the structure of the family were changing with time (for example, children being born), and so, therefore, was the level of auto-exploitation. Chayanov used the concept of 'consumers/workers ratio' to show, on the basis of Russian material from the beginning of the twentieth century, how changes in this ratio were accompanied by changes in the volume of peasant economic activity, which he measured in work hours per day and work days per year. We can see that the larger the number of consumers (not, it should be noted, workers) and the greater the need of a family, the greater the volume of economic activity. And the greater the volume of activity, the greater the area of land cultivated. As a result, we have a strong correlation between the number of family members and the size of the holding.

Data from 23 villages of Little Poland in the eighteenth century

Our statistics for the Polish economy of the eighteenth century are not as good as those produced by Russian *zemstvos*; neither have we material similar to present-day statistics for rural areas. We therefore have to be

[2] Szemberg, *Przemiany struktury agrarnej gospodarstw chłopskich* (1966).
[3] Styś, *Współzależność rozwoju rodziny chłopskiej i jej gospodarstwa* (1959).
[4] Chayanov, *The theory of peasant economy* (1966).

content with the available evidence, namely a census of population from the end of the eighteenth century of two *starostvos*, which covered together 23 small villages in Little Poland. *Starostvos* Brzeźnica and Kłobuck were located not very far from the town of Częstochowa and had been given by the Polish monarchy to the convent of the Paulites.[5] We will attempt to interpret the results of our analysis, relying on other material and on our knowledge of the economic mechanisms of that time. Our interpretation will be to some extent conjectural, because of the inadequacy of the sources.

The census is part of a *lustracja*, an inventory of royal estates, of 1789. The document is in tabular form, combining the census with an inventory of holdings and of the obligations of peasants to the lord of the manor.

It is necessary to start with some methodological remarks. We use the term 'conjugal family' to mean married couples with or without children.[6] By the term 'household' we understand all the people living in the same house and, presumably, working on the same family farm. However, the households of landless peasants who lived together with the landed ones are treated separately, on the assumption that these households were separate. We analyse only those conjugal families whose heads are also heads of households. Only thus is it possible to establish a relationship between the size and structure of a conjugal family and its social position. Therefore, those members of households who are not members of such conjugal families are either relatives or domestics. The terms 'family labour' and 'non-family labour' are used to denote the manpower provided respectively by the members of the conjugal family and by the rest of the household. We assume that persons below the age of 15 are unproductive and that older persons are fully productive.[7] We also treat as fully unproductive the retired parent(s) of the head of a household or of his wife, if they lived together in the same household, and all the people described as cripples.

Some of these assumptions are, of course, debatable. On the peasant farm there are no people who perform no work at all. The working capability of a person rises gradually from childhood and diminishes

---

[5] Falniowska-Gradowska and Rychlikowa (eds.), *Lustracje województwa krakowskiego, 1789* (1962–3). As far as censuses of this type are concerned, we should bear in mind the warning of Dr Gieysztorowa about the possible underestimation of both the number of children under 15 and women, especially those in the lower strata of the population. Gieysztorowa, *Wstęp do demografii staropolskiej* (1976): 133.

[6] We use this term in a slightly broader sense than is usually done. See P. Laslett, 'La famille et le ménage' (1972a); also Flandrin, *Familles: parenté, maison, sexualité* (1976): 57–68.

[7] The same assumption is made by Chayanov (1966).

gradually as he or she grows old. However, the contribution of a child or
an old person to the revenue of a farm is probably less than his share in
the farm's consumption: they are more consumers than workers. One
of our aims is to discover whether larger farms could support more
unproductive persons, which is why the assumptions above seem to us a
justifiable approximation to reality.

We are interested in the relationship between the size and structure of
a family and its social and economic position, so a few words about social
stratification are in order. The problem is a complicated one, because we
have at least two independent criteria of social stratification: first, the
relationship between manor and peasant; second, the type of economic
activity pursued. According to the first criterion, we can divide the
population into serfs, who were obliged to perform labour services, and
free people. Included in the latter were some millers and innkeepers,
manorial officials, and landless day labourers. According to the second
criterion, people may be seen as farmers and as those who also pursued
some other kind of economic activity, such as millers, innkeepers,
craftsmen, blacksmiths, manorial officials, and so on.[8] Here we analyse
only serf families, who constituted 98% of all the families of our two
starostvos.

We can further divide peasants according to the size of the holding
each family cultivated. A traditional measure of land was the *rola*, on the
lines of the English virgate or bovate in the Middle Ages. We do not
know its exact equivalent in metric terms, but this is not so important, as
we are interested in the relative, not the absolute, wealth of peasant
families. The *rola* was not only a measure of land but also a basis for the
amount of service due to the lord of the manor; in particular, the
number of days per week the peasant was obliged to work on demesne
lands.

The census listed peasants with holdings of 1, $\frac{1}{2}$, $\frac{1}{3}$, $\frac{1}{4}$, $\frac{1}{6}$, $\frac{1}{8}$, and
$\frac{1}{12}$ of a *rola*; in addition, there were a number of landless peasants. We
shall divide these peasant households, perhaps somewhat arbitrarily,
into three categories. The first includes holders of 1 *rola* or $\frac{1}{2}$ *rola* of
land: they were obliged to provide the demesne with labour together
with work animals. We shall assume that these farmers were able to
produce not only the subsistence for their families but also some surplus
for the maintenance of draught animals. The second category comprises
the holders of $\frac{1}{3}$, $\frac{1}{4}$, or $\frac{1}{6}$ *rola*, and we assume that they were able to
provide their families with a mere subsistence. The third category in-

[8] An interesting reconstruction of the social structure of the Polish peasantry can be found
in Ćwiek, *Z dziejów wsi koronnej XVII w.* (1966).

Table 4.1. *Social structure of the peasant population of two starostvos:*
Brzeźnica and Kłobuck

	Persons		Families	
Category	No.	%	No.	%
Free population	87	1.85	18	1.81
Millers and innkeepers	77	1.64	15	1.51
Manorial officials	10	0.21	3	0.30
Serf population	4,608	98.15	976	98.19
Millers and craftsmen	41	0.87	8	0.80
Manorial officials	15	0.32	3	0.30
Rich peasants	763	16.25	133	13.38
Middle peasants	3,354	71.44	721	72.54
Poor peasants	435	9.27	111	11.17

cludes holders of ⅛ or ¹⁄₁₂ *rola*, together with the landless peasants, none of whom were self-sufficient. Those in the last two categories had only to give their labour to the landlord.

We shall label the three categories 'rich', 'middle', and 'poor' respectively. These are, of course, conventional terms. Were the bigger farms in fact richer, in the sense that they provided better living conditions? It has been argued that they were not because of the very heavy burden of labour and services they had to render.[9]

Table 4.1 shows the social structure of the selected villages, and the number of people and families. Table 4.2 indicates the relationship between the size of household and conjugal family and the social position of the household head. The differences in the sizes of conjugal families are smaller than those of the households because the number of relatives and domestics was greater in richer households. Table 4.3 shows the number per household of those who were neither members of a conjugal family nor workers. We see from this table that the richer families had a greater welfare burden to carry in that they had to support more unproductive persons than the poorer families. We realize, of course, that it is very difficult to draw a line between help to an unproductive person, such as a retired parent, a child, an orphan, a cripple, a person mentally retarded, and so on, and the exploitation of such a person. But the fact that there were more of such people in the richer households seems to indicate that it was relatively easier for these households to support them. To the extent that this is what one would expect, it does suggest that our crude definition of 'rich' does correspond to reality.

[9] Kula (1976).

Table 4.2. *Relationship between social position of household
and its average size and structure*

Category (1)	Size of household (2)	Size of conjugal family (3)	(3) as proportion of (2) (4) (%)	Non-family members per household (5)	(5) as proportion of (2) (6) (%)
Millers and craftsmen	5.13	4.25	82.93	0.88	17.07
Manorial officials	5.00	5.00	100.00	—	—
Rich peasants	5.74	4.35	75.88	1.38	24.12
Middle peasants	4.65	4.24	91.12	0.41	8.88
Poor peasants	3.92	3.57	91.04	0.35	8.96

Table 4.3. *Relationship between the average number of non-working, non-family
members and social position of household*

Category (1)	Non-working, non-family members per household (2)	(2) as proportion of the size of household (3) (%)
Millers and craftsmen	0.13	2.44
Manorial officials	—	—
Rich peasants	0.55	9.57
Middle peasants	0.22	4.68
Poor peasants	0.22	5.52

We can pursue the same issue by taking a count of the number of children per household according to social category, as in table 4.4. It will be seen that the number of children was greater in the richer families. Rutkowski made the same observation on the basis of more abundant material in inventories of private estates.[10] In his opinion the fact was to be explained by the greater demand for manpower on large farms, so that the children were older when they were allowed to leave

[10] Rutkowski, *Studia z dziejów wsi polskiej XVI–XVIII w.* (1956).

Table 4.4. *Relationship between average number of children and*
social position of household

Category (1)	No. of children per household (2)	Children of non-productive age per household (3)	Children of productive age per household (4)	(4) as proportion of total household manpower (5) (%)
Millers and craftsmen	2.38	1.88	0.50	8.33
Manorial officials	3.00	3.00	—	—
Rich peasants	2.44	1.88	0.56	17.25
Middle peasants	2.32	1.98	0.34	7.33
Poor peasants	1.75	1.44	0.31	7.82

the farms. Our material seems to support his thesis, for the number of children of productive age is greater in the richer households. Rutkowski thought that there was no significant difference in fertility or in infant mortality between households of different categories. However, it seems conceivable that there might have been some difference caused by a combination of better living conditions in richer households, variations in infant mortality, and poorer girls on average marrying later. Unfortunately, this problem has not been well researched by Polish historic demographers, so that we can only speculate. For peasants of southern Poland in the first half of the twentieth century Styś does document a small number of children, caused by the delayed marriage of poorer girls.[11] However, to return to table 4.4, the larger number of children at the productive age on bigger farms can be interpreted as caused by the greater demand of those farms for manpower. As pointed out above, these farms were obliged to supply not only labour, but also draught animals.

Non-family labour served first of all as a substitute for family labour. This is illustrated by table 4.5. When there were too many children on a farm, they were sent to serve in other households; when there were not enough of them, the family tried to hire their neighbours' children.[12]

[11] Styś (1959).
[12] Rutkowski (1956): 212; see also Michalski, Woliński, and Rostworowski (eds.), *Materiały do dziejów Sejmu Czteroletniego*, I (1955): 472; Łysiak (ed.), *Księga sadowa kresu klimkowskiego, 1600–1762* (1965): entry 1152.

Table 4.5. *Households with no children of productive age as a proportion of the total number of households having non-family labour*

Category	Households	
	Having plough-boys (%)	Having maids (%)
Millers and craftsmen	100.00	100.00
Manorial officials	—	—
Rich peasants	85.11	86.67
Middle peasants	94.4	71.67
Poor peasants	100.00	85.72

Table 4.6. *Family and non-family labour*

Category (1)	Family labour per household (2)	(2) as proportion of total household manpower (3) (%)	Non-family labour per household (4)	(4) as proportion of total household manpower (5) (%)
Millers and craftsmen	2.25	75.00	0.75	25.00
Manorial officials	2.00	100.00	—	—
Rich peasants	2.39	74.13	0.83	25.87
Middle peasants	2.17	91.74	0.20	8.26
Poor peasants	2.05	93.83	0.14	6.17

Peasants with both family and non-family labour used the former for their own holdings and the latter for the *corvée*.[13] Table 4.5 also shows that male labour played a greater role in the substitution of non-family for family labour.

On all categories of peasant farms the proportion of non-family labour was very small. The reason for this is that non-family labour was first and foremost a substitute for family labour. We can see this from table 4.6. The proportion of non-family labour was greater on richer farms, as was also the number of children of productive age. The explanation is the same: the greater demand for manpower.

[13] Michalski, Woliński, and Rostworowski (eds.), I (1955): 26; Leskiewiczowa and Michalski (eds.), *Supliki chłopskie XVIII w. z archiwum prymasa Michała Poniatowskiego* (1954): *passim*.

Table 4.7. *Male and female labour*

Category (1)	Male hands per household (2)	(2) as proportion of total household manpower (3) (%)	Female hands per household (4)	(4) as proportion of total household manpower (5) (%)
Millers and craftsmen	1.50	50.00	1.50	50.00
Manorial officials	1.00	50.00	1.00	50.00
Rich peasants	1.78	55.24	1.44	44.76
Middle peasants	1.24	52.26	1.13	47.74
Poor peasants	1.12	51.03	1.07	48.97

When we look at the part played by male and female labour on different categories of farms (table 4.7), we see that the smaller the farm, the greater the role of female labour. The reason is probably that corn production was of less importance on the smaller farms and such activities as raising poultry and growing vegetables, mainly carried out by women, played a greater part.

Family size and structure related to size of holding – social and economic mechanisms

We shall now attempt to interpret our findings with the help of other sources of qualitative rather than quantitative character, as, for example, records of local courts in villages where some sort of peasant autonomy had remained from earlier times: petitions of peasants to owners, records of royal courts on royal estates, and instructions from owners to their administrators. We have found that certain relationships exist between the size and structure of a family and the size of a holding, and we shall proceed to describe the social and economic mechanisms underlying these relationships.

First of all, there is the role of the lord of the manor to be considered. We must bear in mind that we are dealing with an economic system in which labour, not land, was the scarce commodity. The manor was interested in having as many serfs as possible because the produce of the demesne resulted from the number of peasants working the *corvée*. So the lord forbade serfs to leave the village and forbade girls to get married off the estate.[14] At the same time he encouraged inter-marriage among the estate population.[15] The lord of the manor was convinced that married people provided a stable element in village society, showing a much stronger attachment to a place than would unmarried persons. We can find many examples of such policies in instructions written for the officials of great landed properties. As was stressed by Kula, this practice reduced the freedom of peasant marriage, especially on the estates of the petty nobility.[16]

The lord tried to settle on the land everyone who was capable of working. As far as possible, orphans were cared for, and when they reached maturity they were given a farm and assistance in the running of it.[17] It was not to the manor's advantage to have several adult males in one household, because obligations were proportional to the area of a holding, not to the number of people on a farm. Therefore, the lord tried to settle the men on separate plots. But this was against the interests of the peasants, for it was to their advantage to have more working hands on the farm.[18]

The lord was particularly interested in having as many large peasant farms as possible because labour with draught animals was more important to him than manual labour. The peasants, on the other hand, wanted to divide their holdings after the death of the head of the family, so that manorial policy again ran counter to their interests. Moreover, not only the number of farms but the structure of farm labour was of importance to the lord.[19] If a farm was without some elements of its manpower, it ceased to be fully productive. Therefore, the lord required widowers and widows, and especially the latter, either to remarry or to leave the plot.[20] In this case the lord's interests coincided with those of the peasant. Farms, especially the larger ones, could not function properly even if lacking only in female labour.[21] Women were usually younger than their spouses at first marriage, with the result that the population

[14] Baranowski, Bartyś, and Sobczak (eds.), *Instrukcje gospodarcze dla dóbr magnackich i szlacheckich z XVII–XIX w.* (1958–63): II, 240, 252, 499, 630, 635; Michalski, Woliński, and Rostworowski (eds.), I (1955): 270.

[15] Pawlik (ed.), *Polskie instruktarze ekonomiczne z końca XVII i XVIII w.* (1915): 99; Baranowski, Bartyś, and Sobczak (eds.) (1958–63): II, 35.

[16] Kula, 'La seigneurie et la famille paysanne en Pologne au XVIIIe siècle' (1972).

[17] Baranowski, Bartyś, and Sobczak (eds.) (1958–63): II, 458.

[18] *Ibid.* I, 438; Michalski, Woliński, and Rostworowski (eds.), I (1955): 26.

[19] Baranowski, Bartyś, and Sobczak (eds.) (1958–63): I, 464, II, 46; Keckowa and Pałucki (eds.), *Księgi Referendarii Koronnej z drugiej połowy XVIII wieku* (1955–7): II, 287.

[20] *Ibid.* II, 664; Michalski, Woliński, and Rostworowski (eds.), I (1955): 43.

[21] Łysiak (ed.) (1965): entry 1130; Wierzbicka-Michalska, 'Małżeństwa wśród chłopów w drugiej połowie XVIII w.' (1959).

contained more widows than widowers.[22] Even so, more men remarried than women.[23] Sometimes a lord tried to reduce the number of unproductive persons in a peasant household, for example by forcing children of a widow to leave the farm.[24]

As was indicated earlier, when there were no children of productive age, their place was filled by farm servants. In this respect the interests of lord and peasant ran to some extent parallel, for both wanted to maintain the farm in full production. However, when the peasant devoted himself to his own farm work and set the hired hands to work the *corvée*, he ran into opposition from the lord, who found it easier to force a serf to do the required work than a servant, who might be a free man.[25]

According to Kula, the lord tried to respect the inheritance rights of peasants. The argument is that he did this to foster the peasants' confidence in the future and to make them feel that by working well they worked for their children. However, such a policy was contradictory to the lord's aim of maintaining as many big peasant farms as possible. He therefore tried to resolve the problem by promoting marriages between the sons and daughters of rich peasants.[26] At the same time he tried to discourage subdivision of land through inheritance by making money payments to younger children.[27]

Yet the demographic characteristics of the family were not determined solely by the lord. It was possible for the family to act, to some extent, autonomously. The peasant, like the lord, tried to influence the size and structure of his family in order to keep a balance between the size of his holding, family consumer needs, and available manpower. We have already considered some of the ways in which the peasant dealt with shortages in family manpower by remarriage, hiring of servants, and so on, topics about which we know most. It was noted by some writers of the time that hired hands were necessary on the bigger peasant holdings.[28] We also come across cases of adoption which, from the economic point of view, might be treated as another way of hiring servants.[29] Another method of managing labour was, most probably, to

---

[22] Among the 3,481 marriages studied by Wierzbicka-Michalska, the wife was older than the husband in under 10% of the cases.
[23] Gieysztorowa (1976): 250.
[24] Baranowski, Bartyś, and Sobczak (eds.) (1958–63): II, 459.
[25] *Ibid.* I, 456; Keckowa and Pałucki (eds.) (1955–7): II, 669. In spite of the existence of serfdom, there were some free peasants in Poland. Most of them lacked land and worked as hired hands.
[26] Kula (1972).
[27] Vetulani (ed.), *Księga sadowa Uszwi dla wsi Zawady, 1690–1788* (1957): entry 229.
[28] Michalski, Woliński, and Rostworowski (eds.), I (1955): 470.
[29] Łysiak (ed.) (1965): entry 1152.

vary the degree of work intensity. That a certain freedom of manoeuvre existed is evidenced by information about more intensive work done by peasants on their own plots, as opposed to their efforts when rendering labour services to the manor.[30] There are, of course, no statistics on work-time utilization for the period, so this remains a matter of speculation.

From what has been said so far, we may conclude that the lords, and to a certain extent the peasants, were trying to adjust family structures to the productive capacity of the plots. We might ask whether there is not an opposite tendency, that is the adjusting of the size of the farm to the needs and opportunities of the peasant family, as has been suggested by Chayanov, Styś, and Szemberg?[31] In eighteenth-century Poland such a tendency would have been in the interests of the peasant rather than of the lord. Thus the question implies a further question concerning the extent to which peasants had the freedom to make economic decisions. This freedom was not very great. Nevertheless, there were certain differences among different types of estates, affecting both the selling of land and inheritance. The best known are the differences between crown and private lands. For example, in Little Poland the peasants on royal estates were allowed to sell land to 'strangers' and to divide it among their children, a practice forbidden on noble and church lands.[32]

How might it be possible for a peasant to increase the area of land used? In the first place, he could try to buy it; second, he could rent abandoned land from the lord; and, third, he could take under cultivation land that had not previously been tilled. Evidence relating to the selling and buying of land by peasants which can be found in village court records[33] shows that this type of transaction occurred more frequently than was officially allowed by the manor.[34] The sources are more revealing about the motives to sell than to buy land. Among the former may be cited a decrease in consumer needs and in productive

[30] Baranowski, *Gospodarstwo chłopskie i folwarczne we Wschodniej Wielkopolsce w XVIII w.* (1958): 140, 142.

[31] Of course it was easier for such a mechanism to operate in Russia because of periodical divisions of communally owned land among peasant families made by *obshchina*; see Chayanov (1966); also Laszczenko, *Historia gospodarczá ZSRR* (1954): 522. See also the English translation, Lyashchenko, *History of the national economy of Russia to the 1917 Revolution* (1949).

[32] Bobińska (ed.), *Studia z dziejów wsi małopolskiej w drugiej połowie XVIII w.* (1957): 286; Dobrowolski, *Włościańskie rozporządzenia ostatniej woli na Podhalu w XVII i XVIII w.* (1933): 62.

[33] Especially in the records of village courts where such transactions were registered. See e.g. Vetulani (ed.) (1957): entries 1097, 1101, 1105, 1203; Vetulani (ed.), *Księgi sadowe klucza łackiego, 1526–1811* (1962–3): I, entry 670.

[34] Rutkowski (1956): 294.

capacity of a family, because of disease, death, and so on[35] or because the farmer had fallen into debt and had difficulty in rendering labour services.[36]

The peasant was keen to take abandoned land into cultivation without control from the lord of the manor and, of course, without rendering him any service.[37] However, we also come across instances of the lord taking over abandoned land, especially if it was worked by fugitive peasants.[38] As it was in the lord's interest to keep farms fully productive, he often relieved such peasants for a certain period from labour services, providing them with building materials etc.[39]

Owners were definitely opposed to the uncontrolled taking into cultivation of new lands. It was explicitly forbidden, for example, on the royal estates.[40] The frequency with which this phenomenon occurred depended on the possibility of enlarging the arable land, and this varied from locality to locality. The peasant could put under cultivation a strip of new land by rooting out thickets, by ploughing unplanted land, and by tilling pastures and meadows that were not used intensively.[41] Such actions were usually revealed in the course of periodical measurements of estates, carried out on the occasion of transfer to the heir or sale to another nobleman,[42] or when settling an argument between the village community and the lord.[43] As was noted by Kula, the taking of new lands into cultivation was a form of investment by the peasant aimed at increasing his productive capacity. Kula stated that these investments did not depend at all on the volume of overall production or on the market situation, as happens in a market economy. Rather they depended 'on the amount of labour, primarily family labour, [and] on the amount of service due to the landlord from this available manpower. These two elements together could be called the labour balance of the peasant plot.'[44]

In conclusion we can say that the peasant family in eighteenth-century Poland may be seen as a social unit within the feudal society. Family size and structure were mainly determined by productive

---

[35] Ćwiek (1966): 118; Vetulani (ed.) (1957): entries 151, 177; Łysiak (ed.) (1965): entry 1702.
[36] Rutkowski (1956): 294.
[37] *Ibid.* 174.
[38] See for example Vetulani (ed.) (1957): entry 216.
[39] Rutkowski (1956): 304; Vetulani (ed.) (1957): entry 213.
[40] Keckowa and Pałucki (eds.) (1955–7): II, 417.
[41] Rutkowski (1956): 320.
[42] Kula (1976): 70; Kula, *Szkice o manufakturach* (1956): 801–4.
[43] Rutkowski (1956): 347.
[44] Kula (1976): 69.

capacity and the amount of land under cultivation. The latter was mostly a variable outside the peasant's control. In his constant endeavour to satisfy the needs of his family, the peasant fought a continuing battle with the lord of the manor in order to enlarge his holding of land and to loosen the bonds of serfdom.

5

The familial contexts of early childhood in Baltic serf society

ANDREJS PLAKANS

The Baltic Provinces: some comparisons

By the end of the eighteenth century a series of five tax censuses carried out by the government of the Russian Empire had created for later generations of social historians a vast body of primary sources in the form of household lists. These 'revisions of souls' (Russ. *revizskie skazki*), as they were called, contained the names of taxpaying Russians, as well as those of a host of other peoples annexed by a succession of tsars and tsarinas in the course of the century.[1] One non-Russian territory consisted of the three so-called 'Baltic Provinces' (Russ. *Pribaltika*): Livland and Estland, which had been acquired from Sweden in 1720, at the conclusion of the Great Northern War; and Kurland, which was incorporated into the Empire during the territorial adjustments accompanying the Third Partition of Poland in 1795 (see fig. 5.1). The landed nobilities (*Ritterschaften*) of these Baltic lands were German-speaking, as was nearly all of the minuscule town population. The enserfed peasantries, on the other hand, consisted of Estonian-speakers in Estland and the northern half of Livland, and of Latvian-speakers in southern Livland and in Kurland. Both landowner and peasant in this area had seen changes of sovereigns several times before the eighteenth century, together with the waxing and waning of threats to landowners' powers. The Swedish Vasas in particular had tried to alter traditional lord–serf relations, but with little permanent effect. Even under reform-minded Romanovs such as Catherine, the Baltic provinces remained a land apart, with their regional and local laws and customs well

Parts of the research described in this chapter were supported by NEH grant RO-29144-78-643. The author also wishes to thank the Iowa State University Graduate College for covering the costs of preparing the map on p. 168.

[1] Kabuzan, *Narodnaselenie Rossii v XVII-pervoi polovine XIX vv.* (1963).

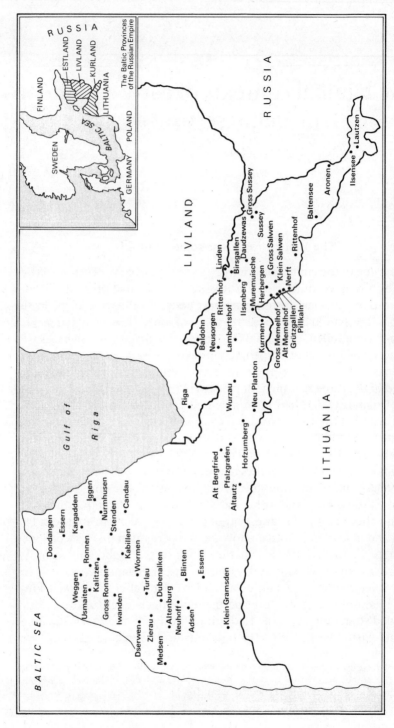

Fig. 5.1. Kurland province, 1797: location of serf estates mentioned in the text. *Note*: The three estates of Neuguth, Tigwen, and Essern-Neuguth could not be located (cf. table 5.3).

guarded against royal interference by Baltic German influence in St Petersburg.

Post-Second World War analyses of population surveys from the Baltic Provinces appeared first from the pens of Estonian historians who were interested, however, only in the Estonian-speaking districts of the region.[2] Somewhat later, the first (1797) tax revision of the Latvian province of Kurland began to yield comparative statistics on the size and structure of rural domestic groups, as well as on links between such groupings.[3] For these two peasant populations (Estonians and Latvians, that is; the Baltic Germans have not been investigated so far) the standard comparative measurements of mean group size, proportion of complex groups, proportion of three-or-more-generation groups, etc. have produced results generally higher than comparable figures for western European communities but not as high as those obtained for Russian localities.[4] This suggests, in Peter Laslett's words, that in the eighteenth century the Baltic belonged to a 'large intermediary area, stretching from Latvia and Estonia in the north, including Poland, the Czech lands, north-eastern Austria and transdanubian Hungary, [and] south as far at least as Florence', which did not exhibit in a straightforward manner the familial characteristics of either the west or the east.[5] It must be noted, of course, that neither Baltic nor, generally speaking, eastern European research has produced sufficient information for the boundaries of such an area to be drawn with precision. The studies mentioned above have been of localities chosen not because they were deemed representative of their areas, but because of the relatively high quality of primary sources; and a reliable assessment of local variation in these matters has yet to be produced. Thus a precise cartographic presentation of past familial attributes is here as much a thing of the future

---

[2] Vahtre, *Eestimaa talurahvas hingeloenduste andmeil 1782–1858* (1973); Palli, 'Historical demography of Estonia in the 17th–18th centuries and computers' (1971).

[3] Plakans, 'Peasant farmsteads and households in the Baltic littoral' (1975a), 'Seigneurial authority and peasant family life' (1975b), and 'Identifying kinfolk beyond the household' (1977).

[4] Evidence from rural Lithuania, south of the Baltic Provinces proper, is interpreted by recent Lithuanian scholars to suggest the presence of the 'individual family' as the dominant form from the thirteenth century onward, and the 'undivided family' as a persisting secondary form due to 'feudal exploitation at various periods' – see Vyšniauskaite, 'The development of the Lithuanian peasant family' (1964). Analysis of list-type population surveys in Lithuania appears to pre-date similar work in Latvia and Estonia. Though these three peoples emerged in the twentieth century as the three independent 'Baltic States', regional history prior to the First World War distinguishes between the 'Baltic Provinces', where the Latvians and Estonians lived on estates owned by a German-speaking nobility, and the regions south of this area, where the Lithuanian peasantry lived on estates owned by Polish or Polonized Lithuanian nobles.

[5] P. Laslett, *Family life and illicit love* (1977a): 16–17.

as it is in most other European national societies, save perhaps England, possibly France, and maybe also the Balkans, where the early researcher Philip E. Mosely sought to work out a geographic distribution of the *zadruga*.[6] Yet as a general statement, based on research results known at present, Laslett's observation is accurate.

What specific meanings should be attached, at this early phase of research, to the phrase 'intermediary area'? Since this problem is not the main subject of the present essay, I shall not explore it thoroughly. Three things, however, can be noted by way of preliminary answer and as an introduction to the topic at hand. There are, to begin with, the statistics now available for several Estonian and Latvian peasant communities.[7] These show more than half of all analysed rural residential units to be extended or multiple in structure, in terms of the typology proposed by Hammel and Laslett.[8] But the totals here do not reach in most instances the 84.3% of complex units (extended plus multiple) on the Russian estate of Mishino in 1814.[9] Similarly, three-or-more-generation residential units in the Baltic made up more than twice the proportion of their counterparts in western countries, but did not reach the 64.9% of the Russian estate. These numbers by themselves suggest the presence in the Baltic of domestic groups in which co-residence of married siblings, of parent and offspring families of marriage, and of representatives of non-adjacent generations was far more frequent than in the west, but not as frequent as in Russia proper. But there is more. Efforts to describe the household developmental cycle by reference to the age of the unit head show these Baltic groups to be resistant to precise cyclical analysis. Their first appearance in the population was not necessarily the result of the marriage of any of their inhabitants, including the head; their expansion and contraction were not necessarily linked only to the arrival and departure of members of the head's family of marriage; and their dissolution was not necessarily an event that followed automatically from the death of any member, including the head. The 'western' assumption of a new household with each new marriage, with expansion or contraction the result of the birth or departure of the married pair's offspring, cannot easily be made with groups such as these.

Similarly, one cannot easily employ in the Baltic an analytical model based on what is now likely to be described as the Russian peasant

[6] Mosely, 'The distribution of the zadruga within southeastern Europe' (1954).
[7] Palli, *Perede struktuurist ja selle uurimisest* (1974); Plakans (1975a and b).
[8] Hammel and Laslett, 'Comparing household structure' (1974).
[9] P. Laslett (1977a): 22–3. See also ch. 3 above.

experience, in which all surviving married sons remained with the father, whose authority over them lasted until his death. There was in the Baltic, among both the Estonian and Latvian peasants, an important subpopulation which was described by the enumerators in terms connoting 'servant' status, most frequently the term '*Knecht*'. A large computer file called 'Kurland', to which we shall refer again later, reveals that in 1797, married *Knechte* and their families made up some 26.5% of the total population of 40 estates selected from Kurland province. This means that the Baltic estates had within them a subpopulation which was very different from western 'servants', who were seldom married. Also, these married farmhands render the Baltic listings different from those of Russia proper, in which 'servant' designations were very rare. The Baltic *Knechte* were landless in the sense of not possessing the use rights enjoyed, though tentatively, by farmstead heads (*Wirthe*); both kinds of peasants were, however, hereditary serfs (*Erbuntertänige*). The farmstead heads could hope for some continuity of residence over generations, whereas the *Knechte* tended to be mobile within the estate, could assure nothing by way of a permanent place for their offspring, and very likely lost parental authority over them as soon as the offspring married and took up positions elsewhere. The membership of neither group was permanently fixed, however, and inflow and outflow can be documented in the relations between the two groups. Yet, from a comparative perspective and with due caution, the familial characteristics of the two groups can be thought of as pointing in different geographical directions: the *Wirthe* families with their patterns of co-residence of married siblings and of non-adjacent generations towards the Russian, and the *Knechte* families with their early dispersal and high incidence of neolocal marriages towards the western experience. It is therefore conceivable that when the full implications of the characteristics of intermediariness are finally understood they will have to be expressed in terms of the co-existence, in the same population, of several familial patterns, rather than in terms of a single pattern replicating imperfectly the dominant characteristics of the west or the east.

Children in the Baltic revisions

As we focus our attention on the Kurland farmstead we must keep in mind that beyond the interesting topics of size, composition, and structure there are numerous other aspects of group life we would like to know about. It would be useful, for instance, to be able to tell how exactly group size and structural features were experienced by individuals in their life cycles, and what role they played in the history of generations.[10] Such questions implying the passage of time are difficult to frame in relation to available empirical evidence, especially since it is now clear that only in rare instances in pre-modern European history will there be sufficient evidence – cross-sectional and longitudinal, synchronic and diachronic – to answer them satisfactorily. Nonetheless, the linking of structures and individual and group biographies is desirable, for in its absence we are left with, on the one hand, forms lacking content, and on the other the human content of historical change without specific structural contexts. In the present essay we shall focus on the familial contexts of the youngest element of the 1797 Kurland population – children aged 0–4 – for two reasons. First, as Peter Laslett has suggested, it is at this age 'when parents and their entirely dependent children are perpetually in company, a condition in which interaction between human personalities is at its most intense, and the human grouping at its solidest'.[11] Because it now appears that in the pre-industrial centuries throughout large areas of western Europe most children at this early stage of personality formation had a familial environment consisting of the simple-family household, there is every reason to look closely at areas where evidence suggests the presence of more complex early environments. Second, speaking particularly of the Baltic cultural setting of our sources, the youngest children enumerated in 1797 were important because they were to come of age at a turning point in the Baltic peasant experience. In 1797 these children were still in a condition of hereditary servility; 20 years later, in 1817, serfdom was abolished and freedom of the person instituted. Ironically, the first enumeration of Kurland had come at a moment after which the social structural involvements experienced during their lifetimes by the youngest age groups were not likely to be the same as those the grandparental and parental generations had gone through. The youngest persons in 1797 were serfs until about their twentieth year, and free though landless peasants thereafter; the hardier among them would even live into a period when the rural under classes began to challenge Baltic German hegemony over the region. The early life context of the cohort aged 0–4 in 1797 is thus as useful for a comparative look at the familial experience of European peasants at the end of the eighteenth century as for an understanding of the opening chapter of a new phase of Baltic history as rural reforms began to change the structure of communities and of collective motivations.

[10] Hareven, 'The search for generational memory' (1978b).
[11] P. Laslett (1977a): 13.

The title of this inquiry – 'the familial contexts of early childhood' – places 'childhood' in a secondary position, for our main concern will not be childhood itself but the kinds of familial structures the very young were enmeshed in. To learn about childhood we would need to know far more about the affective content of these involvements than can be inferred from a listing of inhabitants, and perhaps more than historical evidence will ever be able to yield about people who did not keep records about themselves. In this sense the present study is a prolegomenon to the study of childhood, but it is no less important for that, for, without a detailed scrutiny of structural involvements, whatever we say about the affective content of peasant family life would remain disembodied. To identify these structures properly is time-consuming, as we shall see, especially when the data are far from being unambiguous. Even so simple a task as determining which of a particular enumeration's listed children were orphans, and which had parents living elsewhere, can be arduous.[12] In the present study the first subject to be taken up will be the mean size of domestic groups; from there we shall go on to the problems of composition and structure and of the informativeness of the 'co-resident kin of head' analysis. Two concerns will be paramount: how these various kinds of description inform us about the immediate circumstances of children up to 4 years of age, and how the characterization of groups is supplemented by ties which individuals had with people outside their residential groupings. This last problem will lead into a discussion of the question of kinship and kinship groups, and whether the evidence adduced here justifies further exploration of those uncharted waters.

In due course the post-1797 social structure involvements of the youngest 1797 generation will be studied in as great detail as is permitted by the source (the soul revision) of that year. We will then know where the last decade of the eighteenth century stood in relation to subsequent developments. But it may be that we shall never be able to connect that decade with the earlier history of the region, for in Kurland we are dealing with a population the social structures of which can be studied thoroughly no earlier than the late eighteenth century. There are sources for earlier periods identifying the various social orders of the pre-1795 Duchy and their privileges and obligations, but none that allow for any reliable statements about less inclusive groupings. This makes it difficult to evaluate the assertion of Marxist historians that the rural social structures of late-eighteenth-century Baltic society had

[12] Plakans, 'Parentless children in the soul revisions' (1978a).

come about as a result of an impasse in the further exploitation of serf estates for profit.[13] In terms of this interpretation, the local domestic groups – the farmsteads – which the 1797 revisions allow us to look at in such detail would need to be understood as containing more residents than at some earlier date, since farmsteads are said to have expanded their labour force to meet the labour norms which had been increasing during the eighteenth century. They would also need to be viewed as more complex in composition, since an expanding population in an economy that was seeking to consolidate farmland and do away with peasant holdings would have provided few alternatives for married sons but to stay with a father, and married siblings to stay with their brothers who had become heads. We are not prepared at this time to admit as close a link between landowner policy and domestic group composition as this interpretation asks for; that is to dismiss the notion that frequent co-residence of married patrilineal males could have been due to other than economic reasons. It is perfectly conceivable that the structure of the domestic groups we find in the 1797 record was the consequence of the drawing together of cultural norms of Kurland peasants and the goals of seigneurial decisions. Yet this would not have needed to extinguish cultural norms (whatever these might have been), for though the political structure of a serf estate was authoritarian, it was by no means totalitarian, and could not have been, given the high ratio of serfs to administrative personnel. Moreover, estate owners and most of their administrators were Baltic Germans, whereas the peasant population was Latvian-speaking. In such circumstances it is not necessary to postulate a coherent culture of the under classes to be able to accept the idea that there were areas of everyday life and social intercourse which the landowner's will did not try to and perhaps could not regulate. We are thus left with less certainty than we would like to have about the extent to which the structure of our 1797 'base-line' population was influenced by economics.

The farmstead context of childhood

The earliest analyses carried out on the 1797 Kurland revision showed that the basic residential unit of the countryside – the farmstead – had in that year a mean size that was substantially greater than the mean household sizes available for comparison in the west. The single estate of Daudzewas yielded a mean farmstead size of 14.4 persons; the 16 estates of the south-eastern parish of Nerft, in which Daudzewas was included,

[13] Strods, *Lauksaimiecība Latvijā pārejas periodā no feodalisma uz kapitalismu* (1972).

Table 5.1. *The Kurland serf population, 1797*

Districts, 1797	No. of serfs	No. of farmsteads	Mean no. of serfs per farmstead
Mitau	102,460	6,567	15.6
Selburg	78,931	5,116	15.4
Tuckum	56,251	3,779	14.8
Goldingen	76,595	5,556	13.8
Pilten	44,879	2,729	16.0
			[mean of means 15.1]
Kurland province	359,116	23,747	15.1

Source: Keyserling (1805): appendix.

yielded a mean size of 13.8.[14] Subsequent averaging of farmstead sizes of a yet larger number of estates has confirmed the general range of these figures while suggesting that for Kurland as a whole a somewhat higher figure would be more appropriate. These measurements of mean farmstead size are likely to continue to vary within a range of a few points above a minimum of 13 or so, depending as they do on differing selections of what is to be measured. Thus, for example, in 1805 Peter Ernst von Keyserling published a general description of the province, including a population table which presented a series of aggregate statistics for the whole province based on the *Generalverzeichnis* (summary) of the 1797 revision.[15] The figures in table 5.1 have been taken from Keyserling's compilation. Keyserling's numerator of 359,116 serfs and denominator of 23,747 farmsteads produces a mean size of 15.1 persons. Were even half of the 41,808 free peasants (*'freie Leute'*) in Keyserling's table added to the numerator (since the revision books themselves tell us that a significant proportion of these lived on farmsteads among the serfs), the mean size would rise to 16.0.

To verify Keyserling's figures we compared the calculations above with the results obtained from manipulating the totals of the 40-estate file mentioned earlier (see p. 171). Keyserling's table does not tell us as precisely as we would wish the total number of peasants living in farmsteads, but in preparing the computer file it was possible to include or exclude individuals in the farmstead population by reference to the exact location of each person in each estate. The 49,210 persons in this Kurland file represented (in terms of Keyserling's figures) 12.7% of the

[14] Plakans (1975a and b). See also the appendix below, which shows the comparative figures for the 16 estates of Nerft parish.
[15] Keyserling, *Beschreibung der Provinz Kurland* (1805).

total rural population and 12.0% of the total provincial population. The mean of means for the 40 estates was 16.1 persons per farmstead, with a range of 22.5 at one extreme and 10.2 at the other (see table 5.3, below). It would appear, therefore, that the mean farmstead size of 15 ± 1 is the most useful figure to adopt for Kurland in 1797 when quick reference is needed. At the same time one has to underline that this figure describes the experiential reality of only the farmstead population. We cannot say much at this time about the mean size or typical composition of residential units in Kurland towns; and, though they were also rural co-residential groups, of the taverns (*Krügen*), foresters' dwellings (*Buschwächtereien*), sextons' homes (*Küstereien*), 'worker residences' (*Arbeiterwohnungen*), and the other different groupings not described in the revision books with the term '*Gesinde*' (farmsteads). These are likely to have been smaller than the farmsteads. What we are after at this time are quantitative statements about the co-residential experience of the rural majority, and for that purpose only the farmsteads will serve.

There can be no doubt that in the decades immediately before serf emancipation the farmstead setting was the backdrop of the everyday experience of the vast majority of the provincial population. Again using Keyserling's table, nearly all of the provincial population (94.6%) lived on landed estates, and at least 88.2% of that proportion (the heriditary serfs: *Erbbauern*) were bound to farmsteads. Thus about 8 out of every 10 people of Kurland had the farmstead as the principal location of their everyday movement, and a cluster of farmsteads within an estate as the locus of most of their personal ties of a compelling nature. This number would have included most of the 11.8% of the population which fell into the age range 0–4 (and of the 23.1% in the age range 0–9). Though movement in and out of the estate was restricted, it was not absent; but even if most people did not live out all their lives on the farmsteads on which they were born, they were more likely to relocate to other farmsteads of a size roughly comparable to that in which they had grown up than to enter residential units of a dramatically different nature.[16]

A mean size of 15 ± 1 for rural residential groups seems very large if we remember that research for the western parts of Europe has shown convincingly that there people generally lived in groups half this size or even smaller. We are still faced with the question of what precisely is being referred to when we speak of the farmstead and its constituent population. Were the farmsteads in fact family households, so that their mean size and the say 4.75 mean for English family households, can be

[16] Plakans, 'Population turnover in a serf estate' (1978b).

allowed to stand at the beginning of east–west comparisons? Or were the farmsteads, in Laslett's terminology, 'housefuls',[17] consisting of identifiable household subunits each of which had its own sphere of privacy? Should we rest with the assumption that in studying the farmsteads we are as close as we can ever get to a fundamental familial structure of Baltic rural life, in the sense that the *zadruga* was for the Balkans? Or should we take it that the Baltic farmstead was an artificial entity which, when created by the estate economy, twisted beyond recognition the domestic groups the Latvian-speaking peasantry would have preferred to live in? These questions (quite apart from the problems of comparison they raise) are of exceptional importance if we are ever to identify precisely the personal context in which the young moved during their most impressionable period of life.

Earlier analyses of the composition of the Baltic farmsteads, which will not be repeated here, showed that the population of a typical farmstead contained a head, who was as a rule a married male; a group of people with consanguineal or affinal kin links to the head; a group of male and female farmhands, married and unmarried, some of whom were on occasion also kin-linked to the head; and a lesser number of peripherals such as orphans, retired people, resident artisans, and the like. The 1797 revision is not as unambiguous as we would like in stating all existing links between heads and their subordinates. Some estate revisions use linking terminology based only on relations of authority (head–farmhand), others depend more heavily on kinship terms (head–son-in-law), while a smaller number note carefully the presence of a dual link (head's brother, who is also a farmhand). These varying enumeration practices render very difficult generalizations about the precise internal boundaries within the population of a large number of farmsteads and suggest that the analyst would be safer, when comparisons need to be made, in referring to the farmstead as a 'houseful' rather than as a 'household'. What we would expect to find in a farmstead would be several clusters of related people, together with a handful of individuals who had no identifiable kin links with the other residents of the group.

Thus the residents of a farmstead were involved in several kinds of relationship simultaneously. They were all subordinates of the head, though not necessarily his kin; they were frequently members of a conjugal family unit; and they could also have ties of family and kinship beyond the farmstead. The experiential significance of such ties would have varied with age, the ties of dependency being more important in

[17] Hammel and Laslett (1974); P. Laslett and Wall (eds.), *Household and family* (1972).

Table 5.2. *Status of children 0–4, Kurland file, 1797*

Parent(s) in co-residence	%
Children of heads or of relatives of heads	48.6
Children of married farmhands or of relatives of farmhands	43.1
Children of 'lodgers' (artisans, paupers, etc.)	4.9
Children of widow(s) and widower(s)	1.5
Foster children (*'Aufzöglinge'*)	0.9
Parent(s) not in co-residence	
Children of independent status (*'Jung'*, *'Magd'*, *'Hütter'*)	0.9
TOTAL	99.9
N = 5,823	

earlier years and ties of subordination in later phases. As we would expect, over 90% of the children 0–4 in our Kurland file were identified by the enumerator unequivocally as living with their fathers (table 5.2). The proportion of children in this age group who were designated with a term connoting independent status (such as *'Jung'*, *'Magd'*, *'Hütter'*) was small, less than 1%, though these terms when used for children in the 0–4 age group must have meant something different than when they were used for older youngsters. In any case, these children were not with their parents. It is also significant that only a minority of the children 0–4 were identified as offspring of the head of the farmstead, which is a strong argument for recognizing within the farmstead the existence of other familial units with their own spheres of authority. Judging by the wording of the enumeration, estate officials were never tempted to differentiate a farmstead listing in some simple fashion, say by reference to sex only. The husband–wife and the parent–child ties were for these officials, and presumably for the peasants themselves, ties of significance.

The farmstead, then, was more likely than not to have in it more than a single married couple, though only one husband ever bore the title of head (*'Wirth'*). This structural feature creates some difficulty in comparing the farmsteads (even if they are seen as housefuls) with western groups, where the assumption is that there will be one obvious, dominant family in reference to which group characteristics – structural type, generational depth, etc. – will be stated. But what if in the farmstead the head's group contained two conjugal family units (say the married head and his married brother), whereas the two or three farmhands' families, together comprising a larger number of people, were all of the simple variety? Were we to categorize the farmstead as complex (multiple), the reference point would have been a subgroup which did not include a majority of the farmstead's population even if it did include its most important members. Or, conversely, what if the head's group were in fact a simple-family unit (head, wife, children), but two married farm-hands were noted as brothers to each other? There is really no easy way out of these classificatory difficulties except to specify clearly which grouping within the farmstead is being used as the reference point in a particular kind of measure. Only in this way will we be able to place the Baltic domestic group into comparative perspective. One of the tabulations which our Kurland file of 40 serf estates allows us to produce on this basis is contained in table 5.3, where the 2,824 farmsteads are allocated among the structural types proposed by Hammel and Laslett[18] on the basis of the characteristics of the head's family only, i.e. in the manner employed in the construction of similar tables for western communities. Averaging the proportion of farmsteads in each category for all the estates, we are confirmed in the conclusion, as already stated elsewhere for a smaller number of estates, that the Baltic rural co-residential group stood very high in a ranking of complexity, with a total of 49% of the farmsteads being extended (one conjugal family unit plus some unmarried relatives) or multiple (two or more conjugal family units).

We present table 5.3 in full recognition of the fact that while it provides guidance on the question of relative complexity, it also raises questions about variation within a single region which cannot be dealt with here. We would like to use it now primarily to locate Kurland in a spectrum of societies characterized in this fashion. With nearly half of its farmsteads being either extended or multiple, the Kurland population should be located closer to the eastern pole of a west-to-east continuum than to the western, even though that proportion is not very far away from the figures of some southern French communities and is in fact less than the proportions found for the Italian communities of Pratolino (1721) and Chianti (1790). The 49% of complex units, however, does not come even close to the figure for the Great Russian estate of Mishino (84.3% complex) as reported by Peter Czap.[19] If individual estates are examined, however, we find some very high proportions: Gross Ronnen, with a population of 800 persons, had 85.7% of its farmsteads complex; and Baldohn, with a population of 2,000, had a proportion of 64.1% complexity. Some of the estates, on the other hand, match up with western figures. As is evident, the range of variations in our group of 40 ethnically homogeneous estates is as great as that which exists

[18] Hammel and Laslett (1974).
[19] P. Laslett (1977a); 22–3. See also Czap, ch. 3 above.

Table 5.3. *Mean size of farmstead and structure of heads' groups, Kurland file, 1797*

Name	N	Mean farmstead size (persons)	Simple (%)	Extended (%)	Multiple (%)	Other (%)
Stenden	87	17.1	31.0	18.4	50.6	—
Iggen	18	18.1	5.6	27.8	66.7	—
Nurmhusen	125	19.3	38.4	16.8	44.8	—
Kabillen	107	18.9	92.5	—	5.6	1.9
Baldohn	103	17.2	35.9	9.7	53.4	1.0
Ronnen	33	15.8	24.2	21.2	51.4	—
Medsen	36	14.1	50.0	36.1	13.9	—
Klein Gramsden	24	15.5	41.7	20.8	37.5	—
Neuguth	109	17.0	45.0	15.6	38.5	0.9
Pfalzgrafen	27	18.9	51.9	18.5	25.9	3.7
Alt Bergfried	35	20.4	42.9	20.0	37.1	—
Altautz	122	16.2	94.3	2.5	1.6	1.6
Neu Plathon	23	19.1	34.8	34.8	30.4	—
Wurzau	45	21.2	35.6	24.4	40.0	—
Dserwen	66	14.8	89.4	9.1	1.5	—
Dubenalken	75	13.8	50.7	14.7	34.7	—
Zierau	88	16.7	89.8	3.4	6.8	—
Blinten	16	16.1	37.5	25.0	37.5	—
Neuhoff	17	15.0	58.8	17.6	23.5	—
Adsen	15	17.2	26.7	40.0	33.3	—
Iwanden	53	15.7	50.9	18.9	30.2	—
Wormen	42	15.6	31.0	10.0	50.0	—
Turlau	29	14.3	48.3	27.6	24.1	—
Gross Ronnen	49	14.6	14.3	6.1	79.6	—
Tigwen	26	13.4	50.0	30.8	19.2	—
Weggen	9	17.2	66.7	11.1	22.2	—
Kargadden	6	22.5	100.0	—	—	—
Usmaiten	22	15.7	31.8	4.5	63.6	—
Essern-Frauenberg	430	13.7	74.4	11.9	13.5	0.2
Essern-Neuguth	56	16.2	42.9	19.6	35.7	1.8
Dondangen	293	16.1	63.5	17.4	18.8	0.3
Baltensee	50	12.6	52.0	12.0	36.0	—
Lautzen	147	13.2	33.3	13.6	41.5	11.6
Ilsensee	133	10.2	59.4	16.5	24.1	—
Aronen	46	10.9	42.2	15.2	32.6	—
Candau	71	16.1	52.1	8.5	39.4	—
Hofzumberg	79	21.8	55.7	26.6	17.7	—
Lambertshof	44	14.5	50.0	20.5	29.5	—
Neusorgen	47	15.5	59.6	6.4	34.0	—
Altenburg	20	16.7	55.0	15.0	30.0	—

No. of farmsteads = 2,824
Farmstead size: mean of means 16.1
Means of proportions of structural types = Simple   50.4
                                                       Extended 17.2
                                                       Multiple 31.8
                                                       Other   0.6

when measurements for individual communities from all over Europe are brought together into a single table.

It makes sense to use the structure of the heads' groups in a table meant primarily for a general characterization of an area and for a comparison of the area with others, even when we know that in a given farmstead the likelihood was great that non-heads, too, were surrounded by structured clusters of other people. The use of non-heads' groups (those of *Knechte*, for example) for this purpose would be unwarranted, and the creation of a new structural typology based on the relationships of groups within the farmstead would render comparisons with other European areas very difficult if not impossible. But in using the standard typology developed by Hammel and Laslett we should not forget that the statistical yield does not allow us to get as close to the immediate familial environments of children 0–4 as the Baltic data in fact permit. The generalization possible at this first step is that the young children of these 40 estates lived in a farmstead regime which exhibited strong tendencies toward complexity in the developmental cycle of the dominant (heads') groups. We cannot infer from this, however, the proportions of the young actually residing in groups of certain types; for this information reference has to be made to table 5.4, which states as proportions the number of children of different kinds living in groups of different structures. The reference point this time is not the farmstead as a whole, nor the structure of the dominant group, but the make-up of the group of people in immediate proximity to a young child and related to him.

Tables 5.3 and 5.4 suggest that when we speak of the familial context of children in the Baltic region and try to describe the likelihood of their growing up in and having contact with groups of certain types, the

Table 5.4. *Distribution of types of children 0–4 in groups of differing structure, Kurland file, 1797*

Type of group structure	Children related to head (N = 3,016) (%)	Children not related to head (N = 2,807) (%)	All children (N = 5,823) (%)
Solitary	—	1.6	1.6
Simple	51.8	93.5	71.8
Extended	15.1	3.5	8.9
Multiple	33.0	1.3	17.7
TOTAL	99.9	99.9	100.0

status of the adults surrounding the child and the inclusivity of the group about which a generalization is made become very important. In table 5.4 there are surveyed the forms of that group in which, in terms of Peter Laslett's description cited earlier, 'the interaction between human personalities is at its most intense'. Within this group were to be found the child's parents, grandparents, and siblings and other kin-related persons co-residing with him. The consequences of the social standing of the most important adult in the child's group (normally a male) are revealed clearly. The child had about a one in two chance of being in a complex group if that significant adult was the farmstead head or a relative of the head, but less than a one in ten chance of being part of such a configuration if that adult was a 'servant' type. Yet we know that 'servant' types and their children also lived in farmsteads, so that these children would not necessarily have remained completely unfamiliar with the phenomenon of multigenerationality or complex-family life as they were growing up and becoming aware of who else was in the farmstead and how these people were related to each other. And later, as these children came to participate fully in the life of the whole estate, their chances of coming into contact with complex-family life still remained strong, as we can infer from table 5.3.

It becomes clear that in the Baltic area no claim can be made for the universality of a particular kind of familial experience at any of the levels at which generalizations can be stated on the basis of the 1797 revision. Even the introduction into the analysis of the concept of the developmental cycle of the domestic group would offer only a partial solution to this problem. This procedure would lead to the conclusion that heads' (and heads' relatives') groups experienced prolonged phases of complexity, whereas the subunits of 'servants' did not. Yet both kinds of groups were in co-residence with each other, and could have communicated the advantages and disadvantages of either kind of familial context to all of the impressionable children in the farmstead. The consequences for the human personality of familial experience of this sort – if indeed there are consequences that flow from the structural involvements in the earliest phase of the life cycle – remain to be worked out.

Kalitzen: a case study

In order to make clearer the social reality that underlay the kinds of statistics presented in tables 5.2 to 5.4, we can look more closely at the relationships obtaining among the residents of a particular estate. It is the purpose of fig. 5.2, in which we have reconstructed the genealogical connections of the residents of the estate of Kalitzen, to allow the reader to have in his mind's eye a set of particular relationships as he scrutinizes the tabular presentation of more general information. Among the many hundreds of estate revisions reviewed for coding purposes, only three provided information on the relationships among people living in different domestic units: Kalitzen in the parish of Zabeln was one of these.

We should think of fig. 5.2 as the kind of chart an anthropological fieldworker might have produced after observing who in Kalitzen lived with whom, and what ties these co-residents had with each other and the relational terms used to describe them; and after noting the replies to the questions, addressed to specific individuals, about what relatives they had in other farmsteads and beyond the borders of the estate. The precision with which a trained observer would have carried out such a task would have exceeded that used by the 1797 enumerators, of course; a line of inquiry would have been pursued until the informant confessed ignorance, enabling the fieldworker to produce far more complete networks of connections than we have been able to do. The result aimed for, however, is roughly the same in both cases: a 'map' of the relationships of the inhabitants of the estate, with the help of which individuals can be located on grids more inclusive than the co-residential grid. Such a map, when based on only the 1797 revision, has some obvious shortcomings. We would like to have known, for instance, how the farmsteads were distributed spatially so as to be able better to interpret scattered but kin-linked sets of people. Also, it must always be remembered that in the Baltic setting the 'mapping' of social relationships in the pre-modern period has to be carried out with the aid of relational terminology expressed in a language different from that spoken by the people whose relations were being portrayed. (We are, in this essay, using English terminology and its special connotations to discuss German-language terms that purport to describe relationships among a people whose everyday language was Latvian.) While this feature of the investigation does not present much of a problem in understanding certain kinds of relational categories (e.g. farmstead head–farmhand), it does raise complex problems in the realm of kinship terminology. Unfortunately, we do not have access, in this source, to the kinship terms used by the community under study.

Nonetheless, there are advantages to having such a map, however crude. Because the revision document, a report by the landowner to the Imperial government, had affixed to it the landowner's signature and

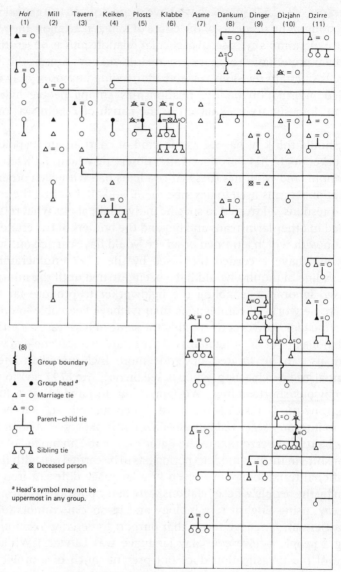

Fig. 5.2. Kalitzen residential groups, 1797.

seal, we can be fairly certain that the document (and our map based on it) contains the whole universe of individuals living in Kalitzen in April of 1797: a clear advantage for statements about proportions of people in different categories. We can tell at a glance from such a map precisely how an individual was involved in different social configurations and

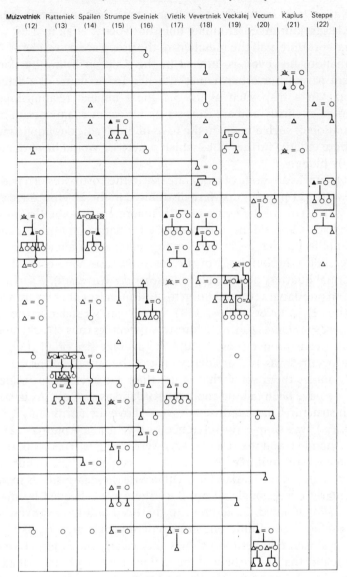

Fig. 5.2 (*cont.*).

whether he was or was not involved in more than one; a very difficult task if only a normal listing – a succession of self-enclosed blocks of names – is available, as is the case in the rest of the estates. A listing of inhabitants gives us, with certainty, residential membership only; conjugal, parent–child, and sibling ties are not evident if an individual is living apart from his family of birth or of marriage, and membership in some larger kin-linked grouping does not appear at all in a list of the normal sort unless all the members of the group are co-residents. Such information, however, is implied in the Kalitzen listing by non-co-resident parents' or other names attached to the name of a listed individual. In a map such as fig. 5.2 these implied relationships are presented explicitly and are thus set up for easier examination. In the preparation of such a map, on the basis of the dyadic ties implied in the list, there emerge further links which otherwise would have remained entirely hidden.

Kalitzen was an estate of moderate size in the north-western parish of Zabeln. Its 321 inhabitants were distributed in the 22 groups we see in fig. 5.2. The core of the estate was the manor house – the *Hof* (no. 1) – which had as its residents the owner Carl Johann von Mirbach and his wife Sophia Juliana; a German serving maid; and a female serf with a young child. The buildings of the *Hof* must also have contained the residential quarters of the bailiff (*Aufseher der Wirtschaft*), a serf with a wife and one daughter. In addition to these premises, there were a water mill (no. 2), 2 taverns (nos. 3, 4), a raftsman's residence (no. 5), a *Handwerker Wohnung* (no. 6), 2 foresters' dwellings (nos. 21, 22), and the 14 farmsteads proper (nos. 7–20). The average size of all the groups taken together was 14.3 residents; that of the farmsteads proper 18.8, which makes them somewhat larger than the average co-residential units we have been talking about for Kurland as a whole. As in size, so also in structure, these farmsteads were above the norm: only 1 of the 14 (7.1%) was simple (in reference to the head's group), 3 (21.4%) were extended, and the rest (71.4%) were multiple. This proportion of farmsteads with multiple heads' groups was higher than all but one of our 40 estates in the Kurland file. Otherwise these farmsteads were not particularly exceptional: all but 1 of them were headed by married males; all contained, in addition to the head and his relatives, farm-hands' subgroups of different sizes, retired people and the like.

The Kalitzen enumeration shows very clearly the different kinds of social reality that can lie behind the characterization of a farmstead with reference to the structure of only the head's group. In farmstead no. 13, for instance, all but one of the co-residents are in fact members of a very complex grouping which includes the head, and therefore the attribution of complexity would be appropriate. Yet in farmstead no. 18, which has a complex family of the head, most of the co-residents are in fact members of formations of other kinds: two childless married couples, a pair of siblings, and five 'solitaries'. This feature of the farmsteads

Table 5.5. *Proportions of children in groups of differing sizes, Kalitzen, 1797*

Type of group	No. of persons								
	1–3 (%)	4–6 (%)	7–9 (%)	10–12 (%)	13–15 (%)	16–18 (%)	19–21 (%)	22 (%)	Total (%)
Conjugal family units	35.3	61.7	2.9	—	—	—	—	—	99.9
Groups of co-residential kin	28.4	30.2	10.8	13.7	13.7	3.1	—	—	99.9
Farmsteads	—	—	10.8	7.8	7.8	22.5	50.1	2.9	99.9

suggests that when we state a measurement of the groups children were involved in, the statement is likely to be more informative if made in a multiple fashion, as in table 5.5, where the involvements of the 34 Kalitzen children aged 0–4 are summarized. All of these 34 children were in fact living in conjugal family units, which had in them between two and eight persons; yet about a fourth of these same children had co-residing with them, in addition to parents and siblings, other kinsfolk whose presence expanded the co-residential kin group substantially. And of course all these children were also living in farmsteads, regardless of whether or not they had kin beyond the conjugal family unit, which meant that the co-residential context, used in this wider sense, has to be described with a higher measurement. Difficulties of this nature appear inevitable when we are dealing with enumerations of peasant populations in which all members of a residential unit are not the kin of some senior male and those are not are as likely to be married as not married.

The Kalitzen enumerator knew enough, or was told enough, about the internal relationships of these groups to be able to sort out fathers, mothers, and children; siblings; and kin of the wife from kin of the husband. We can depict these relations ideographically, separate conjugal family units from each other, distinguish between those farmhands who were kin of head and those who were not, and in other ways draw distinctions between subgroups. But did these formally stated distinctions also mean that subgroups lived apart and ate apart? Did they have for themselves areas of privacy in a common dwelling unit, or did they live in separate dwelling units within a larger physical structure? In other words, can these farmsteads, when considered as housefuls, be taken as having had within them delineated households? Apart from the format of the 1797 census, we have no empirical data to answer these questions for that year, but we might venture a few guesses by reference to later enumerations before we return to a further exploration of the Kalitzen reconstruction.

The nature of co-residence: an unresolved issue

In 1885, some 88 years after our revision, the Statistical Committee of the province of Livland published the results of an inquiry about the co-residential patterns (*Wohnverhältnisse*) on farmsteads.[20] Livland was the middle Baltic province, lying between Kurland to the south and Estland to the north. Its rural population was divided into an Estonian-speaking peasantry in the northern districts and a Latvian-speaking one in the southern parts. Thus the data from the southern districts were likely to reflect the situation as it existed in Latvian-speaking Kurland in that decade. The inquiry listed a number of questions among which there were two that bear directly on our attempt to define the farmstead in 1797: namely did farmhands as a rule (*in der Regel*) take their meals together with or separately from the farmstead head; and were the living quarters of the two separate or joint? As the tabular presentation of the answers shows, in none of the Latvian districts in 1885 were farmstead practices such as to produce the internally segregated unit as the *only type*. That such internally segregated units were present is very likely; the columns reporting separate meals and separate living quarters must have included a number of farmsteads with both of these characteristics. But even then the internally segregated co-residential group was only one of four possible different types of arrangement, and probably not the dominant type at that. In most of the Latvian districts, joint living quarters and joint meals were still, by the 1880s, frequent practices, though we have no way of determining, at this point, why these should have been less frequent in some districts than in the others. In the Estonian districts, jointness in both living and eating arrangements was more pronounced than in the southern Latvian region. To the historians for whom internal segregation in farmstead life was a sign of the increasing modernity of the Baltic peasantry, the 1885 situation would suggest a much smaller amount of such segregation in earlier generations. By 1885 much had happened to make farmstead heads more conscious of their improved status: many were now owners of the land they farmed and of the farm buildings, which they could now redesign at will to emphasize the differences between themselves and

[20] Baltic Provinces, Livland Statistical Committee, *Materialien zur Kenntnis der livländischen Agrarverhältnisse* (1885): 233–6.

Table 5.6. *Farmer–farmhand co-residence, Livland, 1885*

Latvian districts	No. of farm-steads	Living quarters				Meals			
		Separate (%)	Joint (%)	Not reporting (%)	Total (%)	Separate (%)	Joint (%)	Not reporting (%)	Total (%)
Riga	3,243	40.8	55.8	3.3	99.9	32.9	63.4	3.6	99.9
Wolmar	2,945	64.8	27.5	7.7	100.0	60.2	33.2	6.5	99.9
Wenden	5,682	18.3	72.3	9.3	99.9	11.6	82.0	6.3	99.9
Walk	4,542	26.7	69.2	4.0	99.9	24.8	71.4	3.7	99.9
Mean		37.6	56.2	6.1	99.9	32.4	62.5	5.0	99.9
Estonian districts									
Dorpat	5,287	13.4	82.7	3.8	99.9	2.5	93.8	3.6	99.9
Werro	3,456	11.5	76.9	11.5	99.9	10.4	78.0	11.5	99.9
Pernau	2,361	12.9	78.8	8.2	99.9	4.0	90.1	5.8	99.9
Fellin	3,262	16.3	78.7	4.9	99.9	11.7	83.5	4.7	99.9
Mean		13.6	79.3	7.0	99.9	7.3	86.3	6.4	100.0

Source: Baltic Provinces, Livland Statistical Committee (1885).

their hired hands. In an earlier period, at the time of our 1797 revision, all peasants – heads and farmhands alike – were serfs, and redesigning of living space would have run into the unwillingness of the estate owners to allow lumber to be used for what to them would have appeared frivolous purposes. These changes may eventually be shown, on the basis of empirical evidence, to have been a trend. But at the moment, in the absence of longitudinal data, we must be satisfied with the observation that if in 1885 direct questions about internal arrangements of living space produced a variety of answers, the same kind of response would very likely have obtained in 1797.

But did the internal arrangements in 1797 concern people living under the same roof? The ground plans of surviving eighteenth-century farmsteads suggest this, since they show no other building except the main living quarters having been designed for continuous human habitation. We might normally allow the case to rest there, were it not for some data available in the 1881 Baltic provincial census, which was the first modern enumeration of the population of the Baltic provinces.[21] We shall have more to say about this census later, but at this point it will be informative to report on what it has to say about Kalitzen. In 1881, some eight decades after our 1797 census, Kalitzen still had 1

[21] Baltic Provinces, *Ergebnisse der baltischen Volkszählung von 29 December 1881* (1884): vol. III.

manor farm (*Hof*), 2 taverns, and 1 water mill. But there had been additions: there were now 3 units the census designates as '*Industrielle Establissements*', 1 smithy, 4 (instead of 2) foresters' dwellings, and 17 (instead of 14) farmsteads. The 30 inhabited premises ('*bewohnte Punkte*') had in total 55 inhabited dwellings ('*bewohnte Häuser*') and a total population('*Wohnbevölkerung*') of 472, of which number 300 persons lived on the 17 farmsteads ('*Wohnbevölkerung in den Gesinden*').

It is frustrating in the extreme not to have the number of inhabited dwellings for 1797 and thus not to be able to tell whether the 55 houses in 1881 in Kalitzen reflected a rise of material prosperity that was of very recent origin. The farmsteads, as we have observed, were now no longer all the property of the landowner, since land purchase by the peasantry had started in the 1860s; nor were the peasants of Kalitzen now serfs. Even in 1881 we are left with several possibilities in reporting mean sizes. The mean farmstead size had dropped from 18.8 in 1797 to 17.6 in 1881; the mean size of all inhabited premises had risen from 14.3 in 1797 to 15.7 in 1881. Yet in 1881 we also have a measure – 8.5 persons per inhabited house – for which we do not have an equivalent in 1797. Indeed, we cannot tell, even in 1881, whether the additional houses had been built on the farmsteads or on the manor farm or on the other inhabited spots of the estate. The nature of the 1881 census thus defeats our effort to describe precisely the internal arrangements of the 1797 farmstead; but at the same time, the census suggests enough to force us to pull back from the easy assumption that in 1797 all inhabitants listed for a farmstead were everywhere and at all times living under the same roof.

Kinsfolk in the farmstead and beyond

If we cannot assume, in a particular peasant society, that the rule of one family per household will hold true most of the time; and further, if we cannot fix firmly the internal boundaries of subunits of a co-residential group, then the need for multiple measurements becomes obvious. In the Baltic farmsteads, most children aged 0–4 had their parents and siblings in co-residence, and the size and composition of this group had to be measured, to be sure; but the evidence suggests also that this measure alone would not be sufficient, since an appreciable proportion of children had in co-residence kinsfolk other than parents and siblings. Granted that these additional people appeared far more in the case of children related to the head than in the case of children not so related, and granted also that very young children might not have been able to distinguish co-resident aunts and uncles from other co-resident non-parental adults; still, an adequate description of 'familial context' in the inclusive sense needs to take cognizance of the presence of such people, especially since further exploration of these rural groups most certainly would have to include the question of substitutability, e.g. who was likely to be placed in charge of young children when parents were temporarily unavailable. The analytical concept of 'co-resident kin of head' is one way of looking at the nature of such enhanced groups.

The 'co-resident kin of head' category has been used for the most part in analysis of co-residential groups in which it can be assumed that persons not related to the head will be unmarried and will not have co-resident relatives. The measurement counts the kinsfolk (other than spouses and offspring) of the head and the head's spouse and presents the number of certain types as proportions of all co-resident kin, and the total number of such kin as a proportion of the total population. In the Baltic context this procedure cannot be used without the risk of dropping from the calculation co-resident relatives of non-heads, and thus has to be revised accordingly. It is more appropriate for us to take as the points of reference not the heads of farmsteads, but the heads (male or female) of each of the several clusters of kin-related people in a farmstead. Thus, for example, the co-resident brother of a farmhand needs to be a part of the statistic, along with the co-resident brothers of a farmstead head.

Table 5.7 shows the results of applying this revised version of the 'co-resident kin' analysis to the Kalitzen population, as reconstructed in fig. 5.2. Fully a quarter of the estate population were co-resident kin of a head (in our sense); the reader, if he wishes, can see for himself how

Table 5.7. *Co-resident kin, Kalitzen, 1797*

Type	Proportion of all co-resident kin (%)
Parent	15.8
Sibling	25.6
Nephew	12.4
Niece	6.0
Son-in-law	7.3
Daughter-in-law	3.6
Grandchild	8.5
Other	20.7
TOTAL	99.9

Proportion of co-resident kin in population of 321 = 25.5%.

these ties were articulated in each of the residential groups of fig. 5.2. This figure of 25.5% is close in size to the proportion of co-resident kin in the Hungarian community of Alsonyek (1792: 24.1%) and the Japanese community of Nishinomiya (1713: 23.4%), but is considerably higher than the proportion in the community of Vändra (1682: 15.7%) in the northern Baltic province of Estonia. By comparison, western European communities have yielded a low proportion of 'co-resident kin of head': the English village of Ealing, about 3% (1599); the French village of Longuenesse, 6.6% (1779); and the German village of Grossenmeer, 7.9% (1795).[22]

The figure of 25.5% for Kalitzen is not strictly comparable to the others, for in Kalitzen we have used several reference points ('heads') in a co-residential unit, thereby increasing the numerator in the calculation. Moreover, the Kalitzen reconstruction allows us to track down kin connections among co-residents through non-residents, which would also tend to increase the numerator. Assuming, however, that the 25% proportion is somewhere near to the truth, the finding strengthens the possibility that the developmental cycle of rural Baltic families contained relatively slower dispersion of members than the cycles in comparable western societies. Correspondingly, the youngest age cohort had here a greater chance of having relatives other than parents in co-residence, as a result of the slower dispersal of the parents' families of birth.

Table 5.7 is calculated so that the kinship link between two individuals registers itself only once, even though we know that in a thoroughgoing analysis of kinship we would have to consider each link twice; that is from the viewpoint of each partner of the dyad. This is a more elaborate analysis than we can attempt here. To proceed further in this direction on the basis of table 5.7, moreover, would involve dealing with incomplete information, since we know from the Kalitzen reconstruction that for any given *ego* co-residential kin were not the only identifiable kin present in the estate. Because of the superior nature of the Kalitzen enumeration, we can ask whether for example the farmstead head and his wife had kinsfolk beyond the farmstead, how many of each kind there were, and the proportion they formed of the total population. Yet when we ignore the farmstead boundary as the limit on the kinds of people to be considered as kin, a host of analytical problems arise immediately. In a relatively highly endogamous peasant community, in which a genealogical grid encompasses a large number of persons, where is the line to be drawn between kin and non-kin,

[22] All comparative statistics from P. Laslett (1977a): 30–1.

Table 5.8. *Kin residence in and beyond the farmstead, Kalitzen, 1797*

Farmstead head's and/or spouse's	No. within farmstead	No. in other farmsteads and within estate
Parent	6	1
Sibling	15	13
Nephew	5	9
Niece	7	6
Son-in-law	5	1
Daughter-in-law	3	0
Grandchild	9	0
Other	7	6
TOTAL	57	36

Kin in same farmstead as head and/or spouse as proportion of total population of 321	17.7%
Kin of head and/or spouse anywhere in estate as proportion of total population of 321	28.9%
Kin in same farmstead as head and/or spouse as proportion of all kin anywhere	61.2%

between those who were undoubtedly kinsfolk (such as brothers, aunts, and uncles) and those (such as siblings of say brothers-in-law) for whom there were no special kinship terms but who did not stand so far from an *ego* on a genealogical grid as to make recruitment on that basis entirely impossible? The criterion of co-residence makes the measurement neater yet at the same time limits our understanding of 'familial context', especially when we have the Kalitzen reconstruction to look at.

In order to estimate approximately how much the number of kinsfolk expands when farmstead boundaries are ignored, we shall use as reference points only the heads of farmsteads and their spouses, eliminating from the category of 'relative' all those whose relationships to these two *egos* lay at a distance of more than one intervening marriage. A similar analysis could be carried out, on the basis of clearly specified conventions, by reference to any other married pair, or eventually by reference to all individuals. Table 5.8 shows that only 61.2% of all identifiable kin of the farmstead heads and their wives in Kalitzen resided in the same domestic group with them: about 4 out of 10 of such kinsfolk did not. There were nearly as many siblings outside the co-residential unit as within; nearly as many nieces, but not as many nephews. Parents of the heads (and heads' wives' parents) continued to reside with the married couple, as did all the grandchildren of heads.

The relative scarcity of sons-in-law and daughters-in-law outside the farmstead is due to the fact that the Kalitzen record does not always specify the parentage of a wife who is dependent on her husband. All in all, if kinship is looked at in the context of the whole community, the number of kin of heads (and of any other specified person) can be expected to rise. In the case of Kalitzen heads and their spouses, a multiple measurement would again appear to be warranted; without it, we would have little sense of whether or not the 'familial context' of these *egos* stopped at the household boundary.

An analysis similar to the one we have carried out for farmstead heads can be used to gain a better understanding of the 'familial context' of the very young. The questions can be posed not only in terms of group sizes and general structural characteristics (as we have already done), but also in terms of the specific types of kinsfolk and their frequency of appearance. Fig. 5.3 presents the results of this examination. There we have represented ideographically all the kin types to which children aged 0–4 in Kalitzen were found to be linked, with the numerator of each fraction attached to a type standing for the frequency of the appearance of that type within the farmstead and the denominator standing for the frequency within the remainder of the estate population. The appearance of a symbol for a specified type means that this type was found at least once somewhere in the population. A black coloration indicates that the type was found at least once among the persons the children were linked to within the farmsteads in which they resided. Thus, for example, the 34 children aged 0–4 of Kalitzen had a total of 22 fathers' brothers, 5 in co-residence with the children and 17 living apart from them. None of the siblings of the children's grandparents were in co-residence with the children; and the whole group of young children had a total of 22 types of kinsfolk in co-residence.

The statistics derived from this ideograph do not upset the conclusion, arrived at earlier, that most of the significant kin relations of young children had as their locus the farmstead in which the children were living. Nearly all surviving grandparents and parents, and some three-quarters of all siblings were in co-residence with the youngest cohort (see table in fig. 5.3). Yet the 24.6% of siblings who were living elsewhere constitute an important datum for evaluating the extent to which the 'co-resident kin' measure, when used in this way, needs to be supplemented by another datum reporting 'kin in the community' if we are to arrive at an accurate assessment of the 'familial contexts'. The size of sibling groups could not be accurately determined without knowledge of this non-resident group, nor could one calculate, for later phases

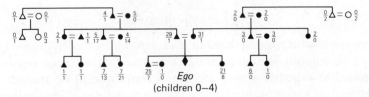

Number of children aged 0–4 = 34

Type	N_1	Proportion in farmstead with child (%)	Proportion in other farmsteads (%)
Parent	62	96.7	3.3
Sibling	61	75.4	24.6
Aunt	26	42.3	57.7
Uncle	27	33.3	66.7
Cousin	59	38.9	61.1
Grandparent	14	92.8	7.1
Other	10	0.0	100.0
TOTAL	259	62.5	37.5

Fig. 5.3. Relatives of children aged 0–4, Kalitzen, 1797.

of the life cycle, the size of the marriage pool from which these children could draw their spouses if marriage were endogamous. If the term 'family' is used in a very inclusive sense, the need for such multiple measures is shown even more forcefully. More than half of all uncles and aunts (putative parent substitutes in a high-mortality demographic regime) and of all cousins (putative sibling equivalents) were not in the same residential group as the children to whom they were related. Even though we are not now in a position to characterize the proportion of relatives not in co-residence as high or low (in the absence of comparative statistics for Europe), we can at least conclude that the strands of relatedness that led from a particular young *ego* to important adults had a significant proportion of terminal points beyond the farmstead. The existence of such strands might not have altered in any identifiable way the consciousness of these youngest children. But at the other end of these strands there stood adults whose role repertoire had been enlarged by the arrival of the children on the scene. Whether these roles were ever 'activated' by these adults themselves, by the parents of the children, or by the children themselves later in their life cycles must be important questions for future research.

Kinship groups

We have used the terms 'kinship' and 'kin' rather loosely in the fore-going paragraphs, without considering systematically even so basic a question as whether a network of ties reconstructed on the basis of kinship data and genealogical data together can be used for generalizations about kinship as such. In the Kalitzen enumeration, for example, an aunt of A was not normally designated as such, but rather as the sister of the father of A, or A's father's brother's wife. The 'map' allows us to 'read' an aunt–nephew relationship effortlessly, because in so interpreting the map we have made several assumptions which no anthropological fieldworker would normally make. This problem of the relationship between genealogy and kinship is so complex that we cannot discuss it fully here.[23] We can, however, make some observations on an 'as if' basis, and indeed must do so, since an examination of the familial contexts of the Kalitzen young would not be complete without some consideration of the question of whether an *ego* and those genealogically connected to him can be said to have constituted a kinship group. The Kalitzen reconstruction suggests the presence of the necessary personnel for such groups: large numbers of people linked to each other consanguineally and affinally. We have already shown that the presence of relatives outside the residential group can make a difference to how we assess quantitatively such matters as co-residential kinsfolk and other important groups surrounding the young. But so far we have dealt with these external relatives only to note their propinquity to an *ego* (and sets of *egos*), that is, their presence in the same estate; we have not looked at them as components of some larger grouping.

The literature on kinship and kinship groups in non-European settings is, of course, immense; but empirically grounded studies of the history of kinship in non-European and European areas alike are few. The social sciences, which might have been expected to produce empirical longitudinal studies after recognizing the unsound basis of earlier pseudo-histories, have not done so. Instead, according to one observer, 'considerations of long-term change often [have] appeared to be a distraction' and if the developmental perspective is in fact used, 'the accounts . . . are mainly of recent societies, which are then placed in some overall sequence using the archaeologically based model of progression from hunting to agriculture to industrial modes of production'.[24] For the researcher concentrating on particular European

[23] J. A. Barnes, 'Genealogies' (1967).
[24] Goody, *Production and reproduction* (1976).

localities in the past and trying to make sense of the kinship structures explicitly or implicitly presented in a single-year enumeration, the existing corpus of kinship literature is helpful in suggesting general approaches, but distinctly unhelpful concerning what an enumeration of a specific people at a specific point in pre-industrial time can be expected to contain.

The theoretical literature on kinship has entered historical scholarship mainly through the study of historical societies of western Europe, and within these of kinship groups and personal kinship networks among the relatively easily identifiable people of the upper social orders.[25] Speaking empirically, we are still left with the question of whether the hypotheses developed on this basis – that European cultures shifted from a patrilineal to a bilateral orientation towards the end of the Middle Ages, that marriage alliances eventually became as important or more important than corporate unilineal kinship, that personal kinship networks were far-flung and far less compelling for individuals than obligations arising from the nuclear family – fit the experiences of the anonymous masses of people, particularly in those eastern reaches of the continent where the socio-economic character of general society was markedly different from the west. The interpretation of our Kalitzen reconstruction is such a case in point. Even when it is accepted that in this serf estate, the very young were surrounded by members of their nuclear families – parents and siblings – we still know by looking at ages that a proportion of the adults in the parental generation, and a larger proportion, if not the majority, of a child's contemporaries (siblings, cousins) would continue to be around in later phases of the child's life cycle. They would be in the estate as the child became able to distinguish between different sets of adults, to recognize those sets of other children with whom marriage was or was not permitted, and to appreciate the material benefits that could accrue from behaving in certain prescribed ways towards elders who were designated as kin but were not living in the same household. The question in Kalitzen (as elsewhere in the Baltic) is whether, in the developing consciousness of a child, perceptions of obligations to specific persons eventually became perception of 'membership' with obligations and constraints sanctioned by the rules or 'constitution' of a group.

What then should we be looking for in the enumeration to test for the presence of such groups? The co-residential pattern involving married

---

[25] E.g. Kent, *Household and lineage in Renaissance Florence* (1977); Macfarlane, *The family life of Ralph Josselin* (1970); Heers, *Le clan familial au moyen age* (1974); Wheaton, 'Bordeaux before the Fronde' (1973).

couples in Kalitzen expressed itself most frequently in the father–son and brother–brother combinations, both of which tend to be character- istics of a kinship system that stresses the importance of the patrilineage and patrilocal marriage.[26] Of the 17 married offspring living with their fathers, 12 were sons and only 5 were daughters; and among the five groups of married co-resident siblings, only one is a brother–sister combination. Consequently we shall focus on the question of the patri- lineage, and we shall be further encouraged to do so by the frequent appearance in the oral tradition of the Latvian peasantry of the term '*dzimta*', which by itself is translated as 'lineage' but is most frequently used in connection with the term '*tēvs*' (father).[27] Oral traditions are notoriously anachronistic, of course, and there is no guarantee that the term, as used in folklore collected in the nineteenth century, had to have an empirical referent then, or even a century earlier. We shall first try to establish some general characteristics of the male population in regard to the question of lineage membership, and then go on to review one other feature that might suggest patrilineage activity.

For a kinship group to be effective locally it needs to have a local membership that has some continuity over time. All secondary litera- ture about Baltic serfdom (and serfdom elsewhere) makes much of the idea of a local, immobilized, closed population that was supposed to have been created when an increasingly larger proportion of the eastern European peasantry came to be attached to specific serf owners and their heirs, or to specific estates and their successive masters.[28] In the west, local population turnover was, by contrast, rapid, as we have been taught to expect by the pioneering research of Peter Laslett on Clayworth and Cogenhoe.[29] Yet if we turn to the Kalitzen reconstruc- tion and begin the inquiry about kinship groups by identifying the putative patrilineage connections of males, we find that of the 160.males the very high proportion of 32.3% would have had the bulk of their patrilineal relatives outside Kalitzen. We cannot identify the lineage connections of 2 elderly beggars. Of the others, there were 7 freemen (*Freigeborene*) with German surnames: the *Erbherr* himself, a shoe- maker with 4 young sons, a young farmhand, and an old carpenter from Riga. One young farmhand bore a Polish surname. And altogether 43 of the Latvian male serfs (*Erbuntertänige*) were listed as having come into the estate from the outside, most of them from the estate of Postenden

---

[26] Murdock, *Social structure* (1949): 16–18.
[27] Švābe, 'Latviešu dzimta un lielǧimene' (1965).
[28] Revesz, *Der osteuropäische Bauer* (1976).
[29] P. Laslett (1977a).

(of which Kalitzen was a subsidiary estate, i.e. *Beihof*) and the rest from other estates in the area. These serfs did not lose their servile status for having moved away from the estates (and farmsteads) of their births; but they must have weakened, through their move, the constraints their own patrilines were able to place on them. In any case, even this one statistic prevents us from thinking about Kalitzen as a closed kinship community.

Nearly all of the non-agricultural occupations in Kalitzen were filled by outsiders. The peasant elder of the estate (*Älteste*) was one such 'foreigner', as were the miller, the tavern-keeper, the shoemaker, the cooper, the mason, the carpenter, and all of their sons (for a total of 16 males). The rest of the 'outsiders' (36 altogether) had come to take up residence in the farmsteads, 4 as married farmhands (*Knechte*) and 5 as unmarried farmhands (*Jungen*). The rest were dependent children of the married in-migrants, some of them having been born after the arrival of their fathers. From these characteristics of the male population we would gather that even with respect to individual farmsteads we cannot think in terms of closed groups. There was a 'core' population to the estate, to be sure, composed of those peasants who were 'tied to this soil' by virtue of the fact that their fathers and grandfathers had been, and there were 110 males in Kalitzen who appear to have had this kind of rootedness. But living side by side with these, in statuses of greater and lesser importance, was a block of recent in-migrants who may indeed have been candidates for eventually becoming part of the 'local' population but at this time had their patrilineal ties outside the estate. Thus, we cannot seek to explain the composition of all farmsteads – considered as residential groups – entirely in terms of patrilineal principles, which have been so useful for understanding, for instance, the Balkan *zadruga*.

As for the core (or 'native') male population of 110, there was considerable potential within it for the creation of large, multi-unit co-residential groups of patrilineally connected males. What is of interest is the extent to which this potential was not realized. The best opportunity to build up a lineally based co-residential group would have belonged to those males who had come to occupy the farmstead headships, but how far this actually happened can be seen in table 5.9. Of 14 farmstead heads, 10 had a total of 15 brothers in the estate. Four of these brothers were unmarried: 2 lived with their brother (the head), but 2 lived apart from their brothers in subordinated positions to other heads. Of the 11 married brothers, 4 lived with their brothers who were heads, whereas 7 lived in other farmsteads, again in subordinated positions. Six out of the

200 *Andrejs Plakans*

Table 5.9. *Brother co-residence, Kalitzen, 1797*

Type of brother	In co-residence with brother head	In other farmsteads
Married	4	7
Unmarried	2	2

total of 15 brothers (40.0%) had stayed with their brothers (heads), but the rest had dispersed, thus diminishing considerably the degree of complexity that would have been obtained had farmstead heads been able to keep all these lineal male relatives with them. Moreover, nearly all the farmstead heads who had brothers elsewhere also had in their farmsteads married or unmarried farmhands.

This imperfectly realized potential of lineal co-residence suggests several things about the nature of the farmstead. First, even though the ideographic depiction of many of the heads' groups produces structures that are very similar to the Balkan *zadruga*,[30] these two types of co-residential groupings are not comparable if they are seen, as Hammel has suggested, in terms of processes. In the developmental cycle of the *zadruga* there came a point at which this patrilineally based co-residential group divided because of size and/or disagreements between adults. The result usually was two residential units, each following a separate course of further development. The departing unit did not normally lose status in the eyes of the community by doing so.[31] But with the Baltic farmstead heads' groups we cannot really speak of division in this sense, as an act freely entered into by all parties. This leads us to the second observation, which is that in the Baltic case we apparently encounter a local patrilineally oriented society which has had superimposed upon it an economic regime (the serf estate) with strong antilineal managerial proclivities. The serf estate was a system of land exploitation in which the owner apparently permitted one and only one of a group of male siblings to inherit a father's commanding status (the headship), thus raising him in the sibling group and *vis-à-vis* other lineal relatives to a position that was potentially far more powerful than he would have enjoyed otherwise, were his prerogatives based only on lineage membership. In Kalitzen, then, which had a limited number of farmsteads and headships, the opportunities of excluded brothers were few: they could stay with their brothers who were heads;

[30] Hammel, 'The zadruga as process' (1972): 353–5.
[31] Mosely, 'Adaptation for survival' (1943).

they could depart to take subordinate positions as farmhands in other farmsteads; or, to a limited extent, they could migrate out, as those males who had come into Kalitzen had done from their estates. The departure of brothers did not, however, mean division of land or resources: the disposition of these goods was under the control of the estate owners, who, in this period, did not countenance splintering of peasant holdings. The departing brothers did not necessarily remain in subordinate statuses for their whole lives. In other estates examined there is evidence of such brothers (siblings of heads) serving as farmhands for a time and then assuming headships when these fell open. But even this restitution of high status continued to point to the fact that the practice of kinship and the managerial economics of the estate were intertwined. The farmstead, to repeat, was not a co-residential group which can be understood by reference to patrilineal principles alone.

Whether the departure of brothers was preceded by, or caused by, animosity arising from very different statuses of members of the sibling group is not possible to answer on the basis of a population enumeration, but there is one piece of evidence that suggests that even after male siblings were separated kinship ties continued to play a role. The very important question of whom parents entrusted their unmarried children to when these left the family circle and took up positions elsewhere can be answered by looking at table 5.10, in which can be seen the residential context of those children who still had parents in the estate but were no longer living with them. There were altogether 39 such unmarried children of differing ages living away from their parents. Of these, 21 had no identifiable relatives other than parents in the parental generation in the estate; and 4 of them had senior relatives but were not living with them. Thus, of the 18 unmarried children who could have been placed with relatives, 14 had been; and of those 14, 8 had been

Table 5.10. *Unmarried children not living with parent(s), Kalitzen, 1797*

	Male	Female
Living with kin		
With brother	0	3
sister	2	0
father's brother	4	4
sister's husband	0	1
Not living with kin		
No parental kin available	5	16
Parental kin available	1	3

placed with a father's brother. The reappearance of the father's brother
as an employer of sorts and a mentor of some of his brothers' sons and
daughters would signify that the co-residential separation of adult male
siblings was not necessarily accompanied by the dissolution of lineage
ties.

As long as we continue to have listings of inhabitants as our only
evidence for kinship structure, the most significant questions cannot
be answered with any degree of finality. Even so, the evidence from the
Kalitzen reconstruction is suggestive enough for the question to be
posed (even if it cannot be answered here) of whether there might not
have been active in the Baltic estates a kinship grouping similar to the
vamilija in Serbia: 'a common descent group', according to the anthropologist Joel M. Halpern, '[which] was not a lineage in the strict sense of
the term since it was not a corporate group, nor a livestock nor landowning group . . . Geographic proximity combined with knowledge of
relationships in the male line . . . meant, and continues to mean, that
the *vamilija* has a sense of solidarity reflected in work exchanges, mutual
help, and lending, and a general sense of unity reinforced by common
attendance at crisis rites such as weddings and funerals.'[32] As our
empirical evidence for Kalitzen shows, a significant proportion of the
estate population would have had such 'lineage' involvements elsewhere; and numerous persons who must be taken as 'natives' of the
estate had no identifiable kinsfolk at all, perhaps because of the impact
of mortality on their families of birth and marriage. Yet for an equally
impressive number, as a glance at the reconstruction reveals, the personnel for such a group was present. Nor can it be entirely insignificant
(at least for Kalitzen) that the fathers of the 18 children who had come to
be placed under the authority of other males had frequently chosen
their own brothers as quasi-parents for their sons and daughters.

Before some final remarks on the later history of the farmstead
context, a few summary observations, if not conclusions, are in order
about the pre-emancipation decades. In this discussion of the familial
contexts of early childhood we have dealt far more with the nature of
the contexts than with childhood itself, since the latter calls for more
evidence than is found even in as rich a source as the Kurland soul
revision. In any ultimate sense we do not know at this point whether
primary socialization[33] occurring in complex residential units produced
in the end a generation of adults who behaved differently from adults
having grown up in simpler familial contexts. And this is so because

[32] Halpern and Halpern, *A Serbian village in historical perspective* (1972): 22.
[33] Cf. P. Laslett (1977a): 13.

among the societies that can be brought into a comparative framework only pre-industrial England has been examined with sufficient geographic coverage for the transition to be made from a discussion of localities to a discussion of 'society'. Even so small a corner of historic Europe as Kurland reveals very clearly how varied familial involvements among a specific cohort of the young could be. Thus it becomes very difficult to accept hypotheses in these matters that are based on single cases, or even a handful of cases, when it is not clearly known how the case represents the population universe being generally characterized, what proportion of the people of that universe participated in the familial system (or systems) posited as typical, and the duration of such participation. It can hardly be argued that at this point we have enough evidence about the complex family areas of Europe to be able to make statements in such a way. Because of this we are as far from being able to write an empirically grounded 'history of European childhood' as we are from having a 'history of European family life'. In order to write such histories, we shall need to know far more than we know now about the microstructures in which people were bound up, about the geographical distribution of the practices that created such structures, and about the timing of the transition from one set of practices to another. To be able to talk about these matters without endless caveats to the reader, we shall need many more of the kind of detailed data-linking study that has been launched by Alan Macfarlane for several pre-industrial English communities.[34]

With respect to pre-emancipation Kurland society, very young children there had as the immediate setting of their primary socialization – that is, the largest setting they could have been aware of – the polynucleated population of the farmstead, living under the authority of a male farmstead head who was not always the oldest male present nor always a kinsman to all his subordinates. The least-inclusive familial context for such children was the nuclear family within the farmstead with its members linked to the head as kin or as subordinates or as both. Not infrequently, the nuclear family within the farmstead was part of a more complex co-residential kinship unit in the same farmstead, as it was within the serf estate part of a more inclusive kinship grouping the activities of which remain shadowy at this point. It is not likely that very young children were aware of the roles they would eventually occupy in these larger structures; at the same time, of course, the existence of such children expanded the role repertoire of the adults who were kin-linked to them, so that, from a structural viewpoint, the young

[34] Macfarlane with Harrison and Jardine, *Reconstructing historical communities* (1977).

cannot be written off as unimportant even if they had no conception of
their own standing. Though the aggregate figures for 1797 are not as
precise as we would like, it is more than a fair guess that nearly all rural
children in Kurland spent the first years of their lives in such settings,
receiving their first impression of human social existence from a group
of people that included more than the members of their nuclear families.

After serfdom

To conclude, we would like to make reference once more to the provincial census of 1881 for what it might yield on the questions of how long
the conditions we have been describing for 1797 actually lasted. At this
moment the tax censuses that followed 1797 (in 1811, 1815, 1833, and
1857) are still in the archival state. In the intervening decades between
1797 and 1881 the administrative boundaries within the province were
redrawn, and the Kurland peasantry experienced changes in personal
legal status (from serfs to freemen, starting in 1817), mobility patterns
(growing rural-to-urban migration, starting in the 1850s), land ownership rights (from limited use rights before the 1860s to outright
ownership), and consciousness of nationality (the 'national awakening'
of the 1850s). These changes must have affected the motivations of the
generations coming of age in the decades after the 1830s (when emancipation was completed) in ways only partially susceptible to quantitative measurement. They must also have pointed the Latvian-speaking
population towards the relatively high ages at first marriage indicated in
both the 1881 provincial census and the 1897 Imperial census. But they
seem not to have changed the population dimensions of the farmstead
much, for, surprisingly, the 1881 census presents us with a mean of
means (of 9 of the 10 Kurlandic districts) of 14.8 persons per farmstead
(table 5.11), which is well within the 15 ±1 range we found for 1797.

There was, however, in that census the problem of farmstead size and
inhabited house size, which we encountered in talking about Kalitzen
alone. Table 5.11 is meant to be informative on that question as well,
though it is now clear, as it was not in 1797, that we are dealing with
two separate measurements. In 1881 we have in fact five numbers to
work with for each estate of the province: the total population of the
estate ('*Wohnebevölkerung*'), the total living in all inhabited premises
('*bewohnte Punkte*'), the total living in farmsteads ('*Wohnebevölkerung in
den Gesinden*'), the total number of farmsteads ('*Bauergesinde*'), and the
number of inhabited dwellings ('*Zahl der bewohnte Häuser*'). The last of
these would include not only the living quarters of the farmsteads, but

Table 5.11. *Mean sizes of farmstead and house, Kurland, 1881*

Districts, 1881	Mean farm-stead size (persons)	Mean size of inhabited house (persons)
Doblen	15.5	14.2
Bauske	15.9	12.4
Talsen	15.5	14.1
Windau	16.6	13.9
Hasenpoth	14.5	14.5
Grobin	9.4	13.4
Friedrichstadt	14.3	15.3
Tuckum	14.9	9.9
Goldingen	16.7	11.2
Mean of means	14.8	13.2

Source: Baltic Provinces (1884).

also those in the *Höfe* (manor farms) as well as the ancillary premises termed in the census *'Häuslerein'*, *'Ansiedlungen'*, *'Armenhäuser'*, etc. Thus in table 5.11 we see that in most cases the mean population per inhabited dwelling is smaller than the mean size of farmsteads. A precise statement of the quantitative dimensions of the co-residential group still remains elusive, but at least we now have a reason to think that the houseful containing upwards of 14 persons was a part of the residential experiences of the Kurlandic countryside well beyond the period of serf emancipation. But by 1881 it was no longer the experience of the bulk of the province's inhabitants. The total population residing in farm-steads in 1881 was 58.2% of the provincial population, a drop of about 30% from the maximum of about 88% we assessed for 1797. This represented, too, a drop in absolute numbers from about 385,000 farm-stead inhabitants in 1797 to about 311,000 in 1881. The 1881 census thus was very likely the last to reflect the traditional farmstead as the experience of the majority. The long-term trend was in the direction of small single-family farms, as poorer farmers acquired land and as the state-directed agrarian reforms of the third decade of the twentieth century redistributed parcels of agricultural property to the absolutely landless.

APPENDIX

Size of estates of Nerft parish, Kurland, 1797

Estate	No. of farmsteads	Farmstead size (persons)		
		Mean	Median	Range
Linden	111	15.5	17	6–27
Nerft	98	15.8	15	9–24
Gross Salwen	84	16.3	16	5–34
Herbergen	63	13.1	13	7–19
Ilsenberg	59	13.9	13	7–20
Kurmen	54	12.3	12	4–20
Daudzewas	53	14.4	14	7–23
Sussey	49	16.3	15	10–28
Pillkaln	29	12.1	12	7–18
Muremuische	29	12.6	13	6–17
Gross Memelhof	29	13.7	14	10–19
Gross Sussey	27	13.3	13	8–17
Klein Salwen (crown)	25	13.7	15	9–20
Grützgallen	25	11.0	11	9–14
Alt Memelhof	20	14.3	14	8–19
Rittenhof (crown)	12	12.2	11	9–19

6

Estonian households in the seventeenth and eighteenth centuries

H. PALLI

During recent years considerable progress has been made in the study of household structure in the U.S.S.R.,[1] especially in Estonia. Several studies have been published on the structure of Estonian households,[2] and more are to appear in the near future.

Estonian households are on the whole more complex than those in western Europe. Households with farmhands, whether male or female, are very common, and some even contain the families of such farm servants. On the south Estonian mainland during the seventeenth and eighteenth centuries, complicated houseful systems existed, with two or more farmers' households on one farm (*poolemaamehed* in Estonian, *Hälftner* in German, but here we call them 'co-farmers'). In these circumstances Peter Laslett's standard classificatory table on the typology of households[3] cannot be applied without some slight changes. However, a full picture of Estonian households in those days can be given if we allocate the categories and classes of this table to smaller groups: households without farmhands; households where the farmhands are unmarried or without their families; and households containing farmhands together with their families. For south Estonia four categories have to be distinguished: one household to a farm; one farmer's household together with one or more cotters' households to a farm; the households of co-farmers on a single farm; and the households of co-farmers together with cotter(s)' households on a single farm (see table 6.5 below).

[1] Minenko, 'Russkaia semia na Obskom Severe v XVIII–pervoi polovine XIX veke' (1971); Baklanova, *Krestianskii dvor i obshchina na russkom Severe* (1976): 1–46; Minenko, 'Gorodskaia semia Zapadnoi Sibiri na rubezhe XVII–XVIII vv' (1977).
[2] Palli, 'Perede struktuurist ja selle uurimisest' (1974); Kakhk and Uibu, 'K voprosu o sotsialnoi strukture semi i mobilosti krestianstva v Estonii vo vtoroi chetverti XIX v.' (1977); Linnus, *Maakäsitöölised Eestis 18. sajandil ja 19. sajandi algul* (1975): 102–10, 193–5.
[3] P. Laslett and Wall (eds.), *Household and family* (1972): 31.

Most sources from the fourteenth to the seventeenth century give only the name of the head of a farm and no information about the number of inhabitants, let alone their ages or other details. The land revisions in the first half of the seventeenth century mention only the male population, and it is not known whether the information they give is complete or not. The only more or less complete listing of inhabitants during this period is dated 1683.[4]

The land revisions (German *Hakenrevision*) were largely carried out from 1712 to 1778. The Swedish inquisition (1686–9) was similar to the land revision, but it did not cover all manors and in most cases only described certain categories of the peasant population. The land revisions of the eighteenth century gave the name of the head of the household and the numbers of household members divided into sex and age groups, that is children, persons of working age (15–60), and the old and infirm.

Registers, known in German as '*Personalbücher*', for Otepää (1763–99), Noarootai (1744–1860), and Suure-Jaani (1716–1851) provide relatively good information about the inhabitants of these parishes. The names of all inhabitants are given, their relationship to the household head, some information about their ability to read, and their distribution by families, households, villages, and manors. These listings, however, are not always complete, and therefore need to be supplemented with information obtained from family reconstitution forms.

Not until the soul revisions (Russian *reviziya dush*, German *Seelenrevision*) of 1782 and later do we get a complete picture of household structure in most Estonian parishes. In these listings the whole population (excluding nobles and some other small categories) was described farm by farm, household by household, family by family. Names, ages, and relationships to the household head were given for every person.

The Estonian social system was one in which the peasants were serfs who were obliged to work for the manor. The *corvée* system was highly developed, and the manorial economy was based on the labour dues of the enserfed population. Usually one of the farmer's sons or daughters or his brothers or sisters worked for the manor. But if, for this or other reasons, the farm had insufficient adult manpower, the head of the farm had to employ one or more farmhands or maids.[5] Some farm workers lived on the farm with their families. In most cases the farm workers living on the farm did not work for the farmer, but for the manor. Of course, there were some exceptions.

[4] Palli (1974).
[5] '*Sulane*', '*teenijatüdruk*' in Estonian; '*Knecht*', '*Magd*' in German.

In an Estonian parish there were several manors. Some of these manors might overlap a neighbouring parish. The peasant population lived in small villages or, especially in south-west Estonia, on single farms.

The soul revisions were compiled by people who had different conceptions of their task. As a result, the information they provided varied from one place to another. It is therefore necessary to compare the listings with family reconstitution forms. Such a comparison often helps to correct the ages given in the listings and clarifies the status of persons in the family and in the household, as becomes clear from the following examples from Karuse in the country of Lääne in north Estonia.

First, the ages of 12% of the persons listed in the soul revision for Karuse in 1782 had to be corrected by reference to the family reconstitution forms. Second, the same soul revision showed that the farm of Paewelia Michkli Michel in Karuse parish, Lihula manor, Peanse village, also housed his wife, their three daughters, his father, and his sister (see fig. 6.1). The family reconstitution form, however, showed a different household composition (see fig. 6.2). Two of the three girls shown in the soul revision as daughters of Paewelia Michkli Michel and his wife turned out to be offspring of a previous marriage of the wife, while the man shown as Paewelia's father in fig. 6.1 proved to be the father of his wife's first husband.

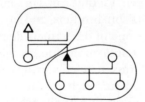

Fig. 6.1. The household of Paewelia Michkli Michel as shown by the soul revision, 1782.

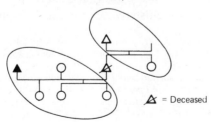

△ = Deceased

Fig. 6.2. The household of Paewelia Michkli Michel corrected after family reconstitution.

The offspring from two different marriages of one of the spouses are only very rarely distinguished in the soul revisions. There are other differences too. For example, in most manors in Karuse the sons and other relatives of the head of a farm who were working for the manor are described by their relationship to the head of the farm, but in Saastna ('Sastenhof' in German), they are described as farmhands or maids.

In the second half of the seventeenth century and in the eighteenth century a great number of so-called co-partners' or co-farmers' housefuls were to be found on the south Estonian mainland. Two or more co-farmers tenanted a single farm. Often one or more cottagers ('*vabadikud*', '*saunikud*', '*pobulid*' in Estonian; '*Lostreiber*', '*Einwohner*' in German) would be living on the farm's land. In most cases these cottagers were obliged to 'help' the farmer or farmers by working for them. In north Estonia, in most cases, the cottagers lived away from the farm property and not on it, as in south Estonia.

The origin of co-farmers is not clear. They were to be found in the first half of the sixteenth century, even in north Estonia.[6] At the end of the sixteenth century and the beginning of the seventeenth century there were co-farmers' farms on the south Estonian mainland.[7] In the first half of the seventeenth century co-farmers were also established on the island of Saaremaa (German Ösel).[8] In 1774 25.3% of all farms in the county of Pärnumaa and 36.1% in Tartumaa were co-farmers' farms.[9]

In most cases co-farmers had separate households, but they had jointly to pay the feudal rent for the farm. On some farms the co-farmers were relatives (father and son, brothers, and so on); in other cases, not. It is not known whether one of the farmers dominated in the partnership. This institution was not confined to Estonia. There is evidence of similar organization of farms in neighbouring countries.[10] It seems that during the sixteenth and first half of the seventeenth century co-farmers disappeared from north Estonia, while in south Estonia their numbers actually increased. It was not until the middle of the nineteenth century that this institution disappeared in the south.

We can therefore distinguish two areas with different houseful group-

[6] P. Johansen, 'Siedlung und Agrarwesen der Esten im Mittelalter' (1925): 19 and *Eesti majandusajalugu* (1937): 104; Ligi, *Eesti talurahva olukord ja klassivõitlus Liivi sõja algul (1558–1561)* (1961): 199–201.
[7] Tarvel, *Adratalupoegade olukorrast Lõuna-Eestis XVI sajandi lõpul ja XVII sajandi algul* (1964a): 21–3 and *Folvark, pan i poddannyi* (1964b): 140–7.
[8] Blumfeldt, 'Jooni taaniaegse Saaremaa agraarajaloost' (1931): 83.
[9] Tarvel, *Adramaa* (1972): 176.
[10] In Latvia, Bielenstein, *Art und Geschichte lettischen Siedlung* (1897): 281; Dunsdorfs, 'Der grosse schwedische Kataster in Livland 1681–1710' (1950): 144. In Finland, e.g. Jutikkala, *Suomen talonpojan historia* (1942): 246.

Table 6.1. *Size of households in Karuse*

Date	No. of persons per household											Mean house- hold size
	1	2	3	4	5	6	7	8	9	10	≥11	
1726	3	17	11	23	32	24	25	23	11	13	6	5.7
1739	2	6	10	14	19	41	31	28	13	22	14	6.9
1795	8	9	8	16	21	34	43	69	58	41	51	8.0

ings for the end of the seventeenth century and the whole of the eighteenth century. Housefuls with one household were typical of north Estonia, while housefuls made up of either one household or two or more households were found in south Estonia.

Let us take Karuse in 1782 as an example of the first type of parish and Vändra ('Fennern' in German) in 1683 to illustrate the second type. We have more information about the first parish. In four manors in Karuse the mean household size (MHS) in 1686 was at least 6, and probably more. There were approximately 3,000 inhabitants at this time. After the plague epidemic in 1710–11 the number of inhabitants fell to 950–1,000 in 1712. By 1782 the population of the parish again numbered about 3,000. At the same time the mean household size also rose, from 5.7 in 1726 to 6.9 in 1739 and to 8.0 in 1795 (see table 6.1).

During the eighteenth century a gradual growth in mean household size can be observed in Karuse, largely as a result of economic and social factors. The number of households in the parish rose from 200 in 1739 to 358 in 1795, a slower rate of growth than that experienced by the total population. As there was no opportunity for people to move to the towns, they had to live together on a farm or in a cottage. According to the soul revision of 1782, Karuse's 2,360 inhabitants lived in 304 peasant households.[11] Of these 2,360 inhabitants, 1,168 were male and 1,192 female.

The social structure of the village population in Karuse in 1782 is demonstrated by the following figures: farmers and their kin made up 82.75% of the population; servants (farmhands) and their kin, 11.86%; cotters, 4.66%; and lodgers, 0.72%.

The ages of all the inhabitants are known, except for 12 persons, 2 males and 10 females. Children in the 0–14 age group accounted for a large share of the total population – 39.7% – but there were few old

[11] Central State Archive of the Estonian S.S.R. (*ENSV RAKA*), fond 1864, list 2, file iv-9: 213–70, 426–71; st. u. V-64: 102–93.

people, the age group of 60 and over making up only 5.6% of the population. More than 54% were persons of working age (see table 6.2).

In Karuse, just over 34% of the whole population and 57.4% of those aged 15 and over were married. The 40–9 age group contained the highest proportion of married males and the 30–9 age group the highest proportion of married females. A considerable proportion of females aged 50 and over were widowed (see table 6.3).

Of the 304 households, 278 were headed by farmers and 26 by cotters. Most of the farms (51.8%) had one or more farmhands or maids. Cotters rarely had servants, who were found in only 11% of such households. The three main categories of household shown in table 6.4 varied considerably in the numbers of farm helpers they contained: farm workers were present in 77.1% of farmers' households falling into category 3; in 54% of farmers' households in category 4, and in 42.4% of such households in category 5.

The distribution of households by structure in Karuse was as follows: out of 304 households, 146, or 48%, were simple-family households containing only one family (married couple, married couple and children, or widowed person with children), with or without farmhands (see category 3 in table 6.4). Nearly two-fifths of all households in Karuse were multiple-family households (category 5 in table 6.4). In this group, class 5b was the largest, comprising 59 households out of a

Table 6.2. *Age structure in Karuse, 1782*

Age group	Males (no.)	Females (no.)	Total (no.)	Males (%)	Females (%)	Total (%)
0–4	166	185	351	14.21	15.52	14.87
5–9	150	149	299	12.84	12.50	12.67
10–14	152	135	287	13.01	11.33	12.16
15–19	124	103	227	10.62	8.64	9.62
20–4	94	114	208	8.05	9.56	8.83
25–9	80	84	164	6.85	7.05	6.95
30–4	79	107	186	6.76	8.98	7.88
35–9	86	80	166	7.36	6.71	7.03
40–4	45	53	98	3.85	4.45	4.15
45–9	42	40	82	3.60	3.36	3.47
50–4	46	34	80	3.94	2.85	3.39
55–9	37	30	67	3.17	2.52	2.84
60–4	25	29	54	2.14	2.43	2.29
65–9	25	29	54	2.14	2.43	2.29
≥70	15	10	25	1.28	0.84	1.06
Unknown	2	10	12	0.17	0.84	0.51
TOTAL	1,168	1,192	2,360	100.00	100.00	100.00

Table 6.3. *Marital status by age and sex in Karuse, 1782*

	15–19 (%)	20–4 (%)	25–9 (%)	30–4 (%)	35–9 (%)	40–4 (%)	45–9 (%)	50–4 (%)	55–9 (%)	60–4 (%)	65–9 (%)	≥70 (%)
					Male							
Single	99.2	77.4	39.5	24.7	10.6	4.4	4.9	4.3	2.7	—	—	—
Married	0.8	22.6	60.5	75.3	88.2	95.6	95.1	91.4	86.5	60.0	68.0	73.3
Widowed	—	—	—	—	1.2	—	—	4.3	10.8	40.0	32.0	26.7
					Female							
Single	98.1	71.7	29.4	12.2	5.0	11.1	5.1	5.9	3.5	3.4	3.4	—
Married	1.9	28.3	67.1	86.9	90.0	85.2	79.5	61.8	65.5	55.2	41.4	40.0
Widowed	—	—	3.5	0.9	5.0	3.7	15.4	32.3	31.0	41.4	55.2	60.0
					All							
Single	98.7	74.3	34.3	17.6	7.9	8.1	5.0	5.0	3.0	1.9	1.9	—
Married	1.3	25.7	63.9	81.9	89.1	89.9	87.5	78.75	77.3	57.4	53.7	60.0
Widowed	—	—	1.8	0.5	3.0	2.0	7.5	16.25	19.7	40.7	44.4	40.0

Table 6.4. *Household structure in Karuse, 1782*

Household category[a]	Without farmhand/ maid	With unmarried farm- hand(s)/ maid(s)	With farmhands and his/their family/ies	With farmhand(s) and his/their family/ies and one or more unmarried farmhand(s)/ maid(s)	All No.	%
3a	5	2	—	—	7 ⎫	
3b	63	52	12	3	130 ⎬ 146	48.0
3c	1	—	—	—	1	
3d	8	—	—	—	8 ⎭	
4a	5	16	6	2	29 ⎫ 40	13.2
4c	7	3	1	—	11 ⎭	
5a	16	13	3	1	33 ⎫	
5b	38	17	4	—	59 ⎬ 118	38.8
5c	5	4	—	—	9	
5d	11	6	—	—	17 ⎭	
All	159	113	26	6	304	100.0

[a] For description of household categories, see table 3.8 above.

total of 118. Extended-family households (category 4) were not so numerous: only 40 such households (13.2%) could be found in Karuse.

In most cases (85.8%) the household was headed by a married

couple. Two-thirds of the household heads fell into the 35–59 age group, and only 17.7% of heads were between 20 and 34 years of age, none being younger than 20. So in most cases the chances of getting a farm were greater when a person attained middle age.

The household structure of Karuse is taken here as representing the situation in north Estonia. As an example of the more complicated houseful system in south Estonia, we may take the parish of Vändra in 1683. We have no information about the ages of the inhabitants of Vändra at this time, so we cannot give such a full picture of the whole population of this parish as was possible for Karuse. In Vändra in 1683 there was a population of 976 persons, 48.6% of whom were males and 51.4% females. Married people accounted for 34.4% of the total population. The social structure was as follows: farmers with their relatives and children numbered 727 (75.2%); cotters, 91 (9.4%); and servants (farmhands, maids, and their families), 149 (15.4%).

This population lived on 89 farms, which contained 132 households; the mean household size was 7.4, with an average of 11 persons on a farm. One farm actually had 5 households on it, while another farm had 4 households. There were 56 farms which contained only 1 farmer's household; 19 farms with 1 farmer's household and with 1 or more cotters' households; 10 co-farmers' farms (2 or more farmers on a farm); and 4 co-farmers' farms with 1 or more cotters. Among the 132 households there were 75 farmers', 30 co-farmers', and 27 cotters' households. More than half the farmers' households had servants. In 10 households farmhands or maids were to be found with their families. Cotter households had servants in only 3 cases (11.1% of all cotters' households).

Simple-family households were dominant in Vändra. There were 86 such households (65.2%), but in many cases servants, sometimes with their families, were living in such households along with the family of the head of the household, or houseful, as it should perhaps be called. The number of multiple-family households was quite high too, numbering 31, or 23.5%, but extended-family households were rare, numbering only 9 (6.8%). The full characteristics of all households in Vändra are given in table 6.5.

In this chapter the households of two Estonian parishes have been examined, one typical of north Estonia and the other of south Estonia, at the end of the seventeenth and in the eighteenth century. It is clear that household composition in Estonia in those days was characterized by a relatively high proportion of multiple-family households and

Table 6.5 *Household structure in Vändra, 1683*

Household category[a]	Individual farmers without cotters			Individual farmers with cotters					Co-farmers without cotters			Co-farmers with cotters			All	
	Without servants	With unmarried servants	With servants and their families	Farmers			Cotters					Farmers		Cotters	No.	%
	(1)	(2)	(3)	(1)	(2)	(3)	(1)	(2)	(1)	(2)	(3)	(1)	(2)	(1)		
1b	2	—	—	—	—	—	—	—	—	—	—	—	—	3	5	3.8
2a	1	—	—	—	—	—	—	—	—	—	—	—	—	—	1	0.7
3a	1	1	2	—	—	—	6	2	—	—	—	—	—	—	12	
3b	14	7	—	7	7	1	10	1	8	6	3	3	4	3	74	65.2
4a	2	1	—	—	—	—	—	—	1	—	—	—	—	—	4	
4c	1	—	—	1	—	—	1	—	—	—	—	1	—	—	4	
4d	—	—	—	—	—	—	—	—	1	—	—	—	—	—	1	6.8
5a	—	2	—	—	—	—	—	—	1	—	—	—	—	—	3	
5b	7	9	3	1	1	—	1	—	—	—	—	—	—	—	22	
5c	—	1	—	—	—	—	—	—	—	—	1	—	—	—	2	
5d	—	2	—	—	—	—	—	—	—	—	—	—	1	—	3	
5e	—	—	—	—	1	—	—	—	—	—	—	—	—	—	1	23.5
Subtotal	28	23	5	9	9	1	18	3	11	6	4	4	5	6		
All	56			19			21		21			9		6	132	100.0

Braces in the "All" column group the categories as follows: 3a + 3b = 86 (65.2%); 4a + 4c + 4d = 9 (6.8%); 5a–5e = 31 (23.5%).

[a] For description of household categories, see table 17.1 below.

215

households with servants.[12] A further interesting feature is the system of co-farming in south Estonia.

Material for a comparative study of the evolution of household structure in eastern Europe is as yet insufficient. Nevertheless, there seem to have been great differences between different regions. Thus in Daudzeva (Kurzeme, Latvia) the proportion of multiple-family households was 64%, while in Mishino (Riazan province, Imperial Russia) it was 73%.[13] In Vologda province in 1678 simple-family households were 58.5% of all households and in 1717 39.2% of all households.[14] In the west Siberian district of Beriozovo in 1761, on the other hand, their proportion rose to 85% and to 76% in Surgut.[15]

[12] Compare P. Laslett, *Family life and illicit love* (1977a): 22–34.
[13] *Ibid.* 22–3, and see Czap, ch. 3 above.
[14] Baklanova (1976): 32–3.
[15] Minenko (1971): 123.

7

Family and *familia* in early-medieval Bavaria

CARL I. HAMMER, Jr

Introduction

In the late autumn of 820 the Frankish Empire stood at the beginning of a difficult short-term climatic cycle and hence, for an agrarian society, a possible crisis of subsistence. According to the semi-official Frankish Royal Annals, the entire year 820, which began for the Franks at Christmas (i.e. Christmas 819–Christmas 820), had been cool and wet, leading to crop failures.[1] This was accompanied by epidemic disease amongst both men and cattle. Flooding prevented the sowing of winter corn in many places, and these misfortunes were compounded by a ferocious winter in 821, during which many major rivers, including the Danube, froze over. The following year, 822, seems to have been without a major catastrophe of its own, although the situation could not have been good owing to the reduced harvest of winter corn in 821. In 823 again the annals of the great Bavarian cathedral monastery of St Emmeram in Regensburg report an exceptionally hard winter, followed by widespread drought and starvation,[2] to which the Frankish Royal Annals add crop-destroying hailstorms and epidemic disease throughout the Empire.

Research for this article was supported by simultaneous grants from the American Philosophical Society and the German Academic Exchange Service (DAAD) in both 1976 and 1978. For advice and support I would like to thank especially Professor J. Ambrose Raftis of Toronto; Professors Friedrich Prinz and Wilhelm Störmer and State Archaeologist Dr Hermann Dannheimer, all of Munich; and Professor Michael Mitterauer of Vienna. Professors Horst Fuhrmann and Hans Martin Schaller and the staff of the *Monumenta Germaniae historica* in Munich were gracious hosts to an unexpected guest in 1978. Professor Laetitia Boehm and Drs Rainer and Elizabeth Müller of Munich took me on a damp but memorable expedition to Lauterbach in June of the same year.

[1] Kurze (ed.), 'Annales regni Francorum' (1895): 152–64. See also Curschmann, *Hungersnöte im Mittelalter* (1900): 93–4.
[2] Bresslau (ed.), 'Annales s. Emmerammi maiores' (1934): 733–41 *passim*.

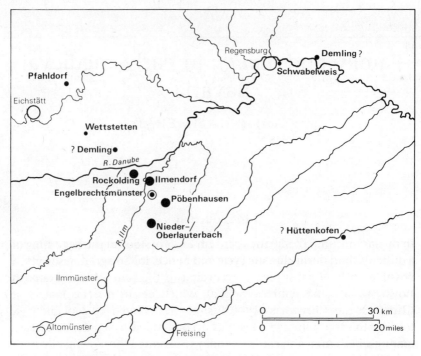

Fig. 7.1. Location of estates mentioned in the text. (*Sources:* Heinzelmann, 'Beobachtungen zur Bevölkerungsstruktur' (1977): 211; Klingsporn, 'Beobachtungen zur Frage der bayerisch-frankischen Beziehungen' (1965): 80.)

On the first Sunday in Advent, 2 December 820, before the full effects of these calamities could have been felt amongst the rural communities of the Empire, an event occurred which allows us to describe and to analyse a group of settlements in the south-eastern frontier province of Bavaria, far away from the relatively well-mapped west Frankish heartlands.[3] On that day Sigifrid, abbot of a small proprietary monastery dedicated to St Benedict and located on the Ilm River at Engelbrechtsmünster north-east of modern Munich, carried out a transaction at the altar of the monastic cathedral church of St Emmeram in Regensburg.[4] There he made over to St Emmeram his entire inheritance, an extensive lordship comprising nine places in Bavaria as well as the body of servants at the monastery itself (see fig. 7.1). In return for his generosity,

[3] Gutmann, *Die soziale Gliederung der Bayern zur Zeit des Volksrechtes* (1906) provides a good older study of Bavarian society in this period. See also Dollinger, *L'évolution des classes rurales en Bavière* (1949).

[4] Widemann (ed.), *Die Traditionen des Hochstifts Regensburg und des Klosters S. Emmeram* (1943): 17–22.

Sigifrid received back his possessions as a life benefice (*beneficium*), augmented by St Emmeram's estate at the vill or township of Lauterbach where Sigifrid himself had his largest estate. By this device, technically known as a *precaria remuneratoria*, Sigifrid was able to augment and to consolidate his possessions at Lauterbach and to enjoy his entire patrimonial lordship for the rest of his life. At his death it would then revert to the monastery of St Emmeram, where the newly combined seigneury of Lauterbach remained until the secularization nearly a millennium later in 1803.[5] The document, preserved in an eleventh-century copy in the Regensburg cartulary, ends with a list of the names of 41 witnesses to the transaction, all tugged by the ear in accordance with Bavarian legal practice as certification of their status.

Following the ceremony of donation at Regensburg, the properties and persons involved were probably surveyed separately, and independent inventories were drawn up.[6] Certainly the existing deed is a conflation of at least two separate documents: first, the donation of Sigifrid (41v–44r) and then the reinvestiture by the abbot–bishop, Baturich, representing St Emmeram. Perhaps the surveying process had been delayed by the inclement weather, for it was not until Friday 8 February 821 that the original deeds were finally combined into their present form by the deacon, Ellenhard, at Regensburg.

Such remunerative donations were not uncommon in Carolingian Bavaria, as the many extant cartularies show. The specific interest of this deed resides, therefore, not in the nature of the transaction itself, but in its particulars, for it is the first comprehensive census-like document to survive for Bavaria, possibly for Germany as a whole and even for Europe as well.[7] Historians have long noted, if not fully appreciated, its importance.[8] Excerpts from a part of it appear in a standard collection of early-medieval Bavarian documents, and much of its content has been summarized in a recent article.[9] Nevertheless, its full potential for illuminating both the general social history of the early Middle Ages and also the origins of the western European family has not been realized. To

---

[5] Volckamer, *Das Landgericht Pfaffenhofen und das Pfleggericht Wolnzach* (1963): 63–6.

[6] E.g. the lists of inhabitants in Hauptstaatsarchiv, Munich, Trad. Regensburg, no. 17: St Emmeram, Lit. 5 1/3, fols. 41v–42v (*nam* Beffonem . . . Berhta), 44r–45r (*nam* manentes . . . Deonaot). Cf. Heinzelmann (1977): 202 n. 2.

[7] The famous polyptyque of the Abbey of Saint-Germain-des-Prés, for example, is probably from the latter part of the decade.

[8] See Inama von Sternegg, *Deutsche Wirthschaftsgeschichte bis zum Schluss der Karolingerperiode*, I (1879): 514–15; Fastlinger, *Die Wirtschaftliche Bedeutung der bayerischen Klöster* (1902): 73; Dollinger (1949): 277n.

[9] Ay (ed.), *Dokumente zur Geschichte von Staat und Gesellschaft in Bayern*, I, 1, no. 104 (1974): 125–6, 169–70; and Heinzelmann (1977): 202–17.

appreciate this we must turn now to a detailed examination of the document itself and to the places, people, and institutions which its contents describe.

Settlements and structures

There are three main reasons why the surveys contained within this deed of gift are so valuable. First, as we noted above, Abbot Sigifrid's lordship, as his inheritance, represents a lay seigneury, the type about which we are least well informed in comparison with those of the king and the church.[10] Second, to borrow a high-medieval English distinction, this is a true 'survey' comprising both the tenant and the demesne (home farm) populations rather than a 'custumal' which includes only the former. Finally, the twin enumerations at Lauterbach allow us to study by comparative method a complex community based upon settlement rather than an exclusively administrative community composed of a single manor.[11]

Lauterbach, which occupies by far the largest portion of the document, lies about 50 kilometres north of Munich. Today it is divided into the twin settlements of Ober- and Niederlauterbach (Upper and Lower Lauterbach), which, like their medieval predecessor, take their name from the tiny Lauter-Bach, or Crystal Creek, which has its source by the upper settlement and then meanders north and west to the lower settlement some three kilometres away, dropping 20 to 25 metres in its course. From there it flows into the Ilm, a southern tributary of the Danube. The landscape is hilly and the elevations rising back from the stream as high as 50 to 60 metres above it. These contours form the natural boundaries of the modern settlements, particularly of Niederlauterbach, which today stretches for almost one and a half kilometres along the twin lines of the stream and the parallel road. The physical topography of the site, therefore, makes it likely that most, if not all, of the early-medieval settlement too was concentrated in the valley of the stream, as its name implies, rather than being highly dispersed with homesteads scattered individually and in small hamlets throughout the entire vill as has been plausibly suggested for many other places in

---

[10] See Störmer, *Früher Adel* (1973): 118–56.

[11] Other attempts to analyse settlements in this period have concentrated on townships, which were highly fragmented seigneurially and which produced a large number of small donations in ecclesiastical cartularies over varying periods of time: Caro, 'Zwei Elsässer Dörfer zur Zeit Karls des Grossen' (1902); Dannenbauer, *Grundlagen der mittelalterlichen Welt* (1958): 271–83; Schwind, *Das Dorf der Eisenzeit und des frühen Mittelalters* (1977): 444–93. All of these tell us more about tenurial than about social structures and processes.

Bavaria in this period.[12] We do not know whether the early-medieval settlement was divided like the modern one into upper and lower parts, possessing two distinct nuclei based upon the separate estates and probably clustered around the manor house and proprietary church mentioned for each. This is not improbable, since many other Bavarian settlements in this period were apparently 'bifocal'.[13] However, the only documentary clue to spatial arrangements is the statement that the third tenant holding on Sigifrid's estate adjoined the second, implying a topographical principle underlying the surveys.

Although the settlements now lie within the prosperous hop-growing region of the Hallertau or 'Holledau', this lucrative speciality is a relatively modern phenomenon. The general district itself, that of Pfaffenhofen an der Ilm, is characterized by much marginal soil, and moorish bottom-lands alternate with gravelly and sandy heights.[14] There are, however, small pockets of loess bed, and our area, the Holledau between the middle Ilm and the upper Aben rivers, has very good stretches of sandy loams. The site is still extensively wooded, as it was in the Middle Ages, and even in the late nineteenth century more than one-third of the two parishes was woodland.

The apparent early settlement history of the place is consistent with the topography. Lauterbach does not seem to be a site of great antiquity. It was probably innocent of Celtic and Roman occupation; at least, no archaeological evidence has yet come to light. The scarcity of early Germanic row-grave cemeteries and the nature of place-names in the immediate area both point to the secondary wave of internal Bavarian colonization rather than the initial period of establishment in the sixth and seventh centuries.[15] The only absolute chronological evidence is that provided by a small row-grave cemetery in Upper Lauterbach partly excavated in the mid-1930s. The six graves (including one child's) yielded a knife which allows a very rough dating to the late Merovingian period, probably the early eighth century in this context.[16] Clearly, ninth-century Lauterbach was something of a backwoods village, and

[12] Dannheimer, 'Aus der Siedlungsarchäologie des frühen Mittelalters in Bayern' (1974): 629–57.

[13] Gebhard, 'Zur Frage der frühen dörflichen Siedlungen in Bayern' (1962): 351–69, esp. 364, 367.

[14] For the following see Götz, *Geographisch-historisches Handbuch von Bayern*, I (1895): 364–75.

[15] A short account of early-medieval settlement is provided by Kurt Reindel in Spindler (ed.), *Handbuch der bayerischen Geschichte*, I (1968): 86–92. See esp. map 9a in Diepolder (ed.), *Bayerischer Geschichtsatlas* (1969), with commentary, 56–7.

[16] The report of the excavations, which were carried out in 1935–6 by V. Herberger, is deposited in the files of the Landesamt für Denkmalpflege (Upper Bavaria) in Munich. The dating of the knife was done by P. Reinecke.

it is unlikely that it had been settled for much more than a century before it was captured by a comprehensive documentary description.

Sigifrid's donation at Lauterbach (hereafter called Lauterbach I) included a proprietary church and a manorial complex attached to it, together with its residents and the tenants of the dependent holdings, as well as all the other normal appurtenances of the great estate: arable, woodland, meadow, pasture, waters, and watercourses. It then provides a detailed listing by name of the entire tenant population divided strictly according to holdings or hides, for which it uses the term '*domus*'. Altogether the 11 tenant hides contained 57 persons, 47 of whom were immediate members of the tenant families themselves and called '*manentes*' (sing. *manens*), while the other 10, distributed amongst only 3 of the hides, were servant workers or boarders called '*mancipia*' (sing. *mancipium*), allotted to the tenants and, to judge by their names, sometimes related to them.[17] The head of the eleventh hide is further designated as a freeman and a smith. No doubt he practised farming as well as his craft and occupied the hide on some exceptional basis about which we are not informed; his family, however, were regular dependants of Sigifrid.[18]

The survey continues with a list of 37 named *mancipi(a) intra domum*. The *domus* within which these *mancipia* were contained was clearly not the ordinary hide, since the wording of the deed sets this section distinctly apart from the preceding one. Rather, it is '*domus*' used in a second sense, as it was at the beginning of the document, to designate the manor house itself. But these 37 undomiciled workers on the home farm or demesne were not a homogeneous group, since the last 23 (at least 21 of whom were women, in contrast to the first 14, who were all men) were engaged in craft work, or *negotium*. A clue to their situation is provided by the famous contemporary survey of the very large Augsburg episcopal manor at Staffelsee in south-west Bavaria, where we find 24 female occupants of the *gynaeceum*, or women's cloth workshop, within the central manorial complex.[19] Hence, by analogy, the last 23

---

[17] The division by hide and household with the name of the 'head' of each household is as follows: (1) (a) Beffo, (b) Baldvinus, (2) Elilandus, (3) Rihbertus, (4) (a) Liubgisus, (b) Hrudhardus, (5) Wolfbertus, (6) Ceizfridus, (7) Beringisus, (8) Ebarhardus, (9) Berthridius, (10) Albuni, (11) Afbaldus. For the *mancipia* allotted to the hides see Lehmann, 'Bemerkungen zur Sklaverei im frühmittelalterlichen Bayern' (1965): 1378–87.

[18] For example, in 828 the smith, Engilmar, paid his rent (*censum*) to the Bishop of Freising for the *beneficium* which he held. See Bitterauf (ed.), *Die Traditionen des Hochstifts Freising* (1905–9): no. 577: I, 495. Clearly, the children at Lauterbach I followed the condition of the mother: *cuius uxorem et infantes donamus*. Strictly speaking, we ought to except the smith himself from the *traditio* (transfer), but for our social analysis we must consider him a part of the total population.

[19] Boretius (ed.), 'Brevium exampla' (1883): 250–2.

mancipia at Lauterbach I must be inmates of the *gynaeceum* there, and their numbers indicate that they must have been producing cloth on a relatively large scale, certainly for the entire lordship and the monastery at Engelbrechtsmünster and possibly even beyond. The 14 male *mancipia*, in contrast, must have been the permanent work force for the home farm. In sum, Sigifrid's estate at Lauterbach represents a classical bipartite manorial structure comprising both demesne and tenant land and ranking somewhere between the large complex at Staffelsee, on the one hand, with 740 *jurnales* of demesne arable and 42 dependent tenant hides, and the small church manor at Bergkirchen, on the other hand, which when it was surveyed in 842 had only two dependent holdings and the equivalent of another three in demesne land.[20]

St Emmeram's estate at Lauterbach (hereafter Lauterbach II) was similar but not identical to Sigifrid's property. The abbot–bishop began by excepting the hides and their appurtenances, not described, which were being held as benefices from St Emmeram by a certain Deotili and Altwart, probably retainers, whose names occur together as freemen in the witness list to the deed. Sigifrid, however, clearly received the overwhelming bulk of St Emmeram's possessions there. These included the manorial complex with its proprietary church, all the lands of various types, and whatever else pertained to the place including a total of 93 dependent inhabitants.[21]

Of these 93 persons, 78 were *manentes*, that is, members of the tenant families. Here at Lauterbach II there is no explicit listing by hide as there was at Sigifrid's estate, but clearly St Emmeram's possessions had experienced at least some form of division by hide, as the terms of the grants to Deotili and Altwart imply. Indeed, the final listing of *mancipia*, following that of the *manentes*, begins with 3 persons who are said, rather cryptically, to be 'without children, not possessing a hide'. The implication is that the preceding tenants listed together with their children did have hides, and the document can easily be interpreted in this sense. St Emmeram's *manentes* are divided into 23 subunits which were evidently familial or household groupings, and these are further combined by grammatical connectors, '*quoque*' and '*et*', into between 17 and 19 larger, intermediate units.[22] As we shall see presently, it is not

---

[20] Bitterauf (ed.) (1905–9): no. 652: I, 550–1. See also Prinz in Spindler (ed.) (1968): 288–92.

[21] I take the fact that their number is the same as that for Lauterbach I (94 less the free smith) to be a coincidence, since there would be no incentive to equalize shares in a *precaria* as opposed to a straightforward exchange.

[22] Cf. Heinzelmann (1977): 209, and n. 23 below.

unreasonable to suppose that these latter intermediate units represent the hides which in several instances were subdivided or shared between two or more households.[23]

Amongst the 15 *mancipia* at Lauterbach II only 2 were attached to tenant households, each to a different one. The other 13 are headed by the group of three, a *scutarius* (probably a dishmaker or potter (*scutellarius*) rather than a shieldmaker) and a husband and wife, who were explicitly said not to possess hides.[24] Presumably the latter were maintained directly within the manor house in contrast to the following 10 *mancipia*, who are designated as prebendaries or cottagers, that is persons who lacked sufficient land to support themselves and who received basic rations (*prebends*) at extended but regular intervals in return for their work on the demesne.

Our knowledge of these estates at Lauterbach can be enlarged by examining two later documents from St Emmeram. The first is a remarkable rental from 1031 covering all the monastery's properties.[25] For Lauterbach, if we except the 10 hides of demesne and the 1 hide of church glebe listed in the rental, on the basis that they were disposed of in the blanket introductory sections of our document from 820–1, we are left with 28 tenant hides for the now combined seigneury including 2 held by the reeve. If we subtract from this number the 11 enumerated hides of Sigifrid's estate, we are left with 17 hides, that is the smaller number which we estimated for St Emmeram's estate on the basis of internal, textual evidence alone, not too surprising a situation, because administrative land units such as the hide tend to be very stable. This would, in turn, imply that the hides earlier held by Deotili and Altwart had been lost to the monastery in the intervening years. This possibility is likewise not difficult to accept, because it is well known that much ecclesiastical property was alienated, particularly under Duke Arnulf in

---

[23] The proposed division (as in n. 17) is: (1) Isanman, (2) (a) Selbrat, (b) Kisal, (3) Werinberht, (4) Meginbald, (5) Amalunc, (6) Eparhart, (7) Kerbald, (8) Sindrih, (9) Berafrid, (10) (a) Brunic, (b) Ratolt, (11) (a) Abo, (b) Aotmunt, (12) Waltheri, (13) (a) Waltberht, (b) Wolfleis, (c) Herideus, (14) (a) Kerhart, (b) Sigebaldus, (15) Ratgoz, (16) Traostilo, (17) Burcsvind.

[24] Heinzelmann reckons them amongst the preceding *manentes* (1977: 209), but, aside from their lacking hides or holdings (the key criterion for a *manens*), they are separated from the *manentes* by a '*nam*' ('but' or 'on the other hand'), and the following group of *mancipia* is prefaced by the words '*et hec* (these) *mancipia*' implying the existence of '*illa* (those) *mancipia*'. Professor Bachrach (Minneapolis) originally suggested to me the possibility that '*scutarius*' was not a shieldmaker.

[25] Mai, 'Der St. Emmeramer Rotulus ... 1031' (1966): 96–7 for Lauterbach. Professor Mathias Thiel (Göttingen) kindly supplied me with corrections to Mai's printed version; he is preparing the St Emmeram material for publication. Another version of the rental appears in Dollinger (1949): 504–12, esp. 508–9.

the early tenth century in response to the pressures of the Hungarian invasions.[26]

Conceivably, we may have the conclusion of this episode in another remarkably informative deed from the late twelfth century (*c.* 1186–90).[27] There the monastery acquired back some freehold and a benefice in Lauterbach from the son of a former ministerial with the explicit aim that 'we might not be vexed in the future when no one aside from our church possesses anything within the aforesaid vill'. In this property we can perhaps imagine the benefices of Deotili and Altwart finally coming home to rest.

In any case, granting the inevitable uncertainties which arise from the lacunae of early-medieval evidence, it is difficult to believe either that the deed of 820–1 excludes extensive possessions from the two manors or that other significant estates or properties existed at Lauterbach in the early ninth century. Certainly the later evidence does not suggest this; indeed, it indicates just the opposite. Essentially, therefore, in the deed of 820–1 we have before us an entire vill or township, the population of which was divided fairly unevenly between two manors. Surely the numbers involved alone make it likely that we have almost the entire population. The 187 enumerated inhabitants and almost 30 tenant hides already bring Carolingian Lauterbach to a level alleged for the supposedly larger settlements of western Germany.[28] With Deotili's and Altwart's hides (assuming they were inhabited), we would easily reach a total population of about 200; this is certainly surprising in view of the marginal nature of the area noted above.

The rest of Sigifrid's properties described in the deed were considerably smaller. Other classical bipartite manors with proprietary churches are found at Pöbenhausen, about six kilometres to the north-east of Lauterbach, and at Rockolding, slightly more than twice as far to the north-north-west (see fig. 7.1). These two estates seem to have contained together about 68 *manentes* and 25 *mancipia*, the latter confined entirely to the central manorial complexes, which appear to have lacked an institution comparable to the *gynaeceum* at Lauterbach.[29] Their division into hides and households is more problematical, since the document here and elsewhere lacks the clear distinctions of Sigifrid's Lauter-

[26] See Reindel in Spindler (ed.) (1968): 209–10.
[27] Widemann (ed.) (1943): no. 988: 502–3.
[28] Schwind (1977), *passim*.
[29] Pöbenhausen: 25 *manentes*, 15 *mancipia*; Rockolding: 43 *manentes*, 10 *mancipia*. Note again the number (93) (see n. 21). I have rejected the editor's emendation at Rockolding ('*et Taomgiso*' to '*Etta, Orngiso*') as superfluous.

bach estate, but some plausible suggestions can be made.³⁰ At Ilmendorf,
the final estate within the cluster directly adjoining Engelbrechtsmünster, there was likewise a church, but the demesne complex was either
excluded, or there was none, so that only 18 tenant *manentes* are listed.
No proprietary churches occur further afield at Demling with its 4
manentes in a single house and its 6 *mancipia* within the manor; nor at
Hüttenkofen and at Pfahldorf with 8 and 6 demesne *mancipia* respectively. Individual tenant households are found at Wettstetten and at
Schwabelweis. Finally, 28 *mancipia* were attached directly to the monastery.

Aside from the free smith at Lauterbach I, the only person mentioned
on these estates who was not a direct dependant of Sigifrid was the
unnamed wife of the tenant Henricus at Pöbenhausen, where it is stated
rather graphically that 'she isn't mine'.³¹ Altogether Sigifrid's lordship
embraced 264 persons divided between 144 *manentes*, that is tenants
and their families, and 120 landless *mancipia*, a few of whom were
assigned to tenancies at Lauterbach but most of whom were occupied
within the central manorial complexes, whether in craft work or in
agricultural work on the demesne lands. Adding the 93 residents of
Lauterbach II, we arrive at a total deed population of 357 persons.

Although it is clearly the best, this is not the only source for studying
the interrelationships amongst family, village, and manor in early-
medieval Bavaria. From 773 we have a Freising deed concerning 32
members of tenant families of preferred status settled on eight free hides
at Buch am Erlbach, probably not far from Hüttenkofen.³² For 930 we
have an extensive deed of exchange from the Salzburg cartulary involving again 106 tenants of preferred status from the area around Salzburg
arranged largely by family and 105, mostly tenant, *mancipia* settled in
the Nordgau north of the Danube.³³ About a quarter of a century later
(*c*. 947–70) a Passau deed records more than 80 *mancipia* arranged by
family as part of an exchange involving six places in Lower Bavaria near

³⁰ For Pöbenhausen the tentative divisions (as in n. 17) are: (1) Liubrandus, (2) Aotmarus,
(3) (a) Winnibaldus, (b) Wolfmundus, (4) (a) Engilradus, (b) Henricus. For Rockolding:
(1) (a) Wolfbero, (b) Wolfmunt, (2) Reginhelmus, (3) Irminbertus, (4) (a) Rihhelmus,
(b) Rihmundus, (5) Wolfuni, (6) Waningus, (7) Liubun(i).
³¹ Like the free smith at Lauterbach I, she has been included in all statistics. Of course we
do not know whether she was free or had a master herself. This point is of some
importance, since the other master may have claimed the couple's children; none is
listed in our deed.
³² '*Serviantes et altiones*'; Bitterauf (ed.) (1905–9): no. 58: I, 85–6; c.f. no. 15: I, 42–3 (AD
760).
³³ '*Parscalchi*'; Hauthaler (ed.), *Salzburger Urkundenbuch* (1910–16): I, no. 85: 147–50. See
also n. 34 below.

Passau;[34] and from the early eleventh century (*c.* 1010–20) a final Regensburg deed preserves the names of 82 members of dependent families at the settlement of (Alten-)Schwand, 20 of whom had commuted their servile obligations to periodic renders of honey, whereas the rest had commuted theirs to money payments.[35] One non-Bavarian source is also highly useful for our purposes: the very detailed set of surveys made between 968 and 973 for the monastery of Fulda concerning its estates at nine places in Thuringia.[36] Other Bavarian and non-Bavarian sources can also be used on an *ad hoc* basis, but before we proceed to new materials and new topics it might be good to summarize and to compare what we have learned from our initial examination of the great deed of 820–1. In doing so, we shall concentrate here (as later) on Lauterbach, the population of which was, paradoxically, both more diverse and more homogeneous than we might have expected.

Leaving aside for the moment the fundamental division of the settlement into two manors, we may say that the population of ninth-century Lauterbach was diverse, first, in the sense that although we have before us an essentially agrarian society, the vill nevertheless possessed two skilled (but not necessarily full-time) craftsmen, the smith and the *scut(ell)arius*, one on each estate. Additionally, Sigifrid's estate included, in the *gynaeceum*, a large, highly specialized work force which must have produced for the entire lordship and even beyond. Second, while the population as a whole was divided into only two basic groups according to tenure and life style – the *manentes* with tenancies or hides, the *mancipia* without, regardless of actual residence – this latter group of *mancipia* was hardly monolithic. They might be established either on the holding of a tenant or within the manorial complex itself in varying capacities, or they might even enjoy a certain independence with a small dwelling and plot (but no holding) as prebendaries. Finally, the two estates within the vill seem to have been somewhat differently organized. Sigifrid's estate was more thoroughly manorialized from two points of view. First, the clear division of the tenants by *domus*, discussed above, indicates that the hidation of tenant land, its systematic organization into a coherent administrative structure linking holding and home farm, had been carried out more rigorously here than at Lauterbach II –

---

[34] Heuwieser (ed.), *Die Traditionen des Hochstifts Passau* (1930): no. 91: 78–9. 'Mancipium' here as in the previous document (n. 33 above) seems to have acquired a broader meaning to include tenants, presumably of the lowest status. Cf. Staab, *Untersuchungen zur Gesellschaft* (1975): 331–51.

[35] Widemann (ed.) (1943): no. 298: 236–8 (cf. nos. 295, 296: 235).

[36] Dronke (ed.), *Traditiones et antiquitates Fuldenses* (1884): 133–7 (cc. 48–55, 57). Identifications and dating in Werner-Hasselbach, *Die älteren Güterverzeichnisse* (1942): 46–9.

Table 7.1. *Distribution by seigneurial status*

Status	Lauterbach I		Lauterbach II		Total	
	No.	%	No.	%	No.	%
Manens	47	50	78	84	125	67
Mancipium	47	50	15	16	62	33
TOTAL	94	100	93	100	187	100

or anywhere else in Sigifrid's lordship, for that matter. Second, both the separate, sexually and occupationally segregated demesne establishment and the total labour force of landless *mancipia* were much larger on Sigifrid's estate than on St Emmeram's. This can easily be seen from table 7.1. If, for illustrative purposes, we analyse these relative figures by the chi-square (X^2) test of statistical significance, we arrive at a result so large, 24.1, that we can be confident that the differences are real.

This organizational fact about Sigifrid's estate at Lauterbach, together with its location, its size, and the presence there of groups of *mancipia* on the hides, the smith, and the *gynaeceum* all point towards its unique position within Sigifrid's lordship. In line with classical manorial organizational theory we may identify it as the main or head manor (*Haupthof*) from which administrative lines led to a number of dependent, secondary manors (*Nebenhöfe*) such as Pöbenhausen and Rockolding. For example, we would expect the *Haupthof* to be the most 'advanced' component of the lordship organizationally and to provide specialized goods and services to other parts. Thus at least a substantial part of Sigifrid's lordship should be seen not as an accumulation of discrete units, but as an interdependent system.[37]

Returning to our initial comparison, we may note finally that there was also an impressive uniformity and simplicity within these large, discrete seigneurial blocks. This internal coherence derived from the direct, personal bonds of servitude which linked all the inhabitants of the estates (with the two exceptions noted above) to their respective masters, the abbot and the saint. Thus, these estates were based on what German constitutional historians call *Leibherrschaft*, a form of slavery implying direct authority over persons, rather than *Grundherrschaft*, a form of serfdom where authority was exercised indirectly through tenure. This distinction explains, for example, why the tenant *manentes*

[37] This practice seems to have been a characteristic of fiscal estates. See Ganshof, 'Manorial organization in the Low Countries' (1949): 29–59, esp. 40–1.

were listed by name, exactly as were the *mancipia*: both enjoyed the same status as valuable personal property.

Indeed, the extent of this personal servitude appears to have been so great that it seems, at first sight, to have produced almost entirely endogamous seigneurial communities. This illustrates one way in which the structural and ecological questions which we have been considering are a prerequisite to the examination of demographic and social characteristics, since the latter do not develop in isolation but are adapted to specific environments.

Demographic characteristics

Lauterbach's population seems to have been thoroughly Germanic, if personal names can be taken as a reasonable guide to ethnicity. This point is not so unremarkable as it may seem at first sight, because a sub-Roman population of varying, often high, social status and coherence, bearing distinctive Latin names, occurs regularly in the former territory of the provinces of Raetia II and Noricum Ripense (most of modern Old Bavaria and Austria) throughout the ninth century. This was the case not only in the area around Salzburg, the heartland of the villa region of late-Roman Noricum,[38] where such Latin names occur in large numbers, but also stretching far out into the countryside north of the Alps.[39] In Sigifrid's lordship, for example, a Justina occurs at Wettstetten as the sister of Usso, possibly itself a corruption of the common late-Latin provincial man's name Ursus (the bear). In the earlier survey of the tenants at Buch am Erlbach in 773, the tenant Wolfdregi had a female slave named Adsonia.[40] Similarly, as late as the Salzburg exchange of 930, the names of Victor and his wife, Victoria, occur along the Salzach River. Moreover, this latter group seems to include Slavic names as well.[41] Thus ethnic homogeneity cannot be taken for granted in a province occupying old Roman territory and located on the eastern frontier of the Empire. Still, Lauterbach's backwoods location and its probable colonization only in the previous century make the situation there seem reasonable.

Names are also a regular guide to sex, since gender is not always explicit in our surveys through a *-us/-a* ending or a supplementary

---

[38] See Alföldy, *Noricum* (1974): fig. 18: 130 and text *passim* for Salzburg.
[39] Sturm, 'Romanische Personennamen in den Freisinger Traditionen' (1955): 61–80.
[40] *Ibid.* 73–4.
[41] E.g. 'Enzi'. The contrast with the *mancipia* in the Nordgau, who consistently bear recognizably Germanic, two-element names, is strong.

designation such as *'uxor'* (wife) or *'filius'* (son).[42] However, this is not a completely satisfactory criterion, since some Germanic names were bisexual; accordingly, extreme caution must be exercised. Even this test often fails us. In Sigifrid's lordship all of the inhabitants are named, but at Lauterbach II there are large numbers of unnamed and sexually unspecified 'children' as well as two unnamed, presumably adult, *mancipia* who could be of either sex. Still, some reasonable conclusions can be drawn when due care is taken.

The normally high sex ratios of early-medieval populations have recently attracted considerable attention.[43] At Lauterbach I, the population settled on the tenancies, including *mancipia*, had a virtually even sex ratio of 97, or 28 males to 29 females.[44] As we argued above, the first 14 demesne *mancipia* there were the male farm workers; the next 23, with two exceptions, the female inhabitants of the *gynaeceum*.[45] Thus the home farm had a low ratio of 16 males to 21 females, or 76, and the combined ratio for the whole estate was likewise a low 44 : 50, or 88. At Lauterbach II, amongst the sexually identifiable adults the tenant population was evenly divided (26:26), but the demesne *mancipia* (listed *in toto*) gave the edge to the men (9 : 4), yielding a total of 35 : 30, or 117, a high but not impossible figure, especially considering the age bias.[46] At Sigifrid's other agricultural estates the overall ratio was somewhat higher than at Lauterbach I, 74 : 68, or 109,[47] and the demesne population there, as at Lauterbach II, was heavily male (30 : 15, or 200). The combined ratio for all of these estates within Sigifrid's lordship was an even 118 : 118, or 100. However, the separate group of monastic servants at Engelbrechtsmünster was highly skewed towards the male, 23 : 5, or 460, yielding a final ratio of 141 : 123, or 115. For comparison we have only the purely tenant populations at Buch am Erlbach in the late eighth century (18:42, or 129) and at Schwand in the early

[42] It should be noted here that the plural form of *'filius'* often merges with *'filia'* to indicate children of both sexes rather than sons, e.g. *'cum filiis'* (with offspring).

[43] Herlihy, 'Medieval children' (1978): 116–17, 133–4; Ring, 'Peasant households' (1979): 5–8.

[44] Parents: 13 males, 13 females; children: 11 males, 10 females; *mancipia*: 4 males, 6 females. If we exclude the *mancipia*, as we shall do later, the *manentes'* ratio is 24 : 23, or 104.

[45] Hasnaot (*manc.* 21) and Fridiric (24) were almost certainly male, probably offspring of the females who preceded them in the list.

[46] It has been argued that ratios as high as 120–30 were common amongst adult medieval populations. See Russell, 'Population in Europe, 500–1500' (1972): 58.

[47] I here differ from Heinzelmann (1977): 212 nn. 47–8, in identifying three names in Pöbenhausen ending in '-mot' as female (hide 3b; *manc.* 15) and likewise a 'Rat-liub' at Rockolding (hide 1b). Even if all four were in fact male, it would not affect our argument significantly.

Table 7.2 *Distribution by sex*

(a)	Sigifrid's mancipia		Sigifrid's manentes		Total	
Sex	No.	%	No.	%	No.	%
Male	73	61	68	47	141	53
Female	47	39	76	53	123	47
TOTAL	120	100	144	100	264	100

(b)	Lauterbach I		Other Sigifrid estates		Total	
Sex	No.	%	No.	%	No.	%
Male	44	47	97	57	141	53
Female	50	53	73	43	123	47
TOTAL	94	100	170	100	264	100

(c)	Lauterbach I demesne		Other Sigifrid estates demesne		Total	
Sex	No.	%	No.	%	No.	%
Male	16	43	30	67	46	56
Female	21	57	15	33	36	44
TOTAL	37	100	45	100	82	100

(d)	Pöb./Rock. demesne		Pöb./Rock. tenancies		Total	
Sex	No.	%	No.	%	No.	%
Male	17	68	31	46	48	52
Female	8	32	37	54	45	48
TOTAL	25	100	68	100	93	100

eleventh century (40:42, or 95), neither of which is so exceptional as to draw attention or to call our ninth-century figures into question.

What does this information tell us about manorial society, aside from the improbability of systematic infanticide in early-medieval Bavaria? We may approach this question by returning to the fundamental distinction which we noted earlier in all the estates, namely that between the members of tenant families or *manentes*, and the landless *mancipia*, regardless of the latter's domicile. The difference in the sexual composition of these two groups within Sigifrid's lordship (table 7.2a) is a significant ($X^2 = 4.9$). Clearly, neither the predominantly male *mancipia* (sex ratio 155) nor the predominantly female *manentes* (89) can be considered as a complete, autonomous social group, segregated from the other.

This problem is most evident amongst the monastic *mancipia* at Engel-brechtsmünster. The extreme male bias there is easily explained by the prohibitions against female contacts imposed on the celibate male monastic community.[48] In spite of the inclusion of a husband, wife, and child, it is impossible to conceive of this group as a self-sustaining population; clearly, the bulk of its numbers had to be recruited and replaced from outside. At the other extreme, Lauterbach I's population exhibits a noticeable bias towards the female. If we compare the number of male and female inhabitants there with those on the rest of Sigifrid's properties (see table 7.2b) we can, for example, compute a chi-square statistic of 2.6, which, although it would not be conclusive statistically, is nevertheless so high that it would be extremely difficult to dismiss it as inconsequential. The demesne population with its strong female bias due to the presence of the *gynaeceum* was quite distinct from the other demesnes on Sigifrid's properties, which had twice as many male in-mates as female (table 7.2c: $X^2 = 4.6$). Indeed, at Lauterbach there was not the marked sexual contrast between the predominantly female tenancies and the male demesne which one finds, for example, at the other large bipartite manors at Pöbenhausen and Rockolding (table 7.2d: $X^2 = 3.7$). In sum, the differing sex ratios within the various subpopulations on Sigifrid's properties suggest three types of mobility or net circulation within the lordship: (1) the social and geographical movement between *manens* and *mancipium*; (2) the correlate but not identical movement between tenancy and demesne; (3) movement from one property or estate to another, particularly to those with specialized populations such as the *gynaeceum* or the body of monastic servants.

Since sex ratios predetermine marriage opportunities, we must now consider nuptiality. This is especially appropriate, because nuptiality can be associated with a fourth type of mobility: that from one lordship or seigneury to another.

Earlier we noted that with only two exceptions, the deed of 820–1 gives the overwhelming impression that endogamy was the rule, both on Sigifrid's properties and on St Emmeram's estate at Lauterbach. Our other materials do not contradict this impression. Now, while it is easy to suppose that marriage inside the lordship was both encouraged from above and was far simpler for the participants than was marriage out-side, the highly dispersed nature of early-medieval lordships, both lay and ecclesiastical, makes it unlikely that a suitable partner was always

[48] If we compare the sexual composition of Engelbrechtsmünster with the rest of Sigifrid's properties, we obtain a large and significant chi-square statistic of 10.3.

readily to hand.[49] Thus the static character of our documents may lead us to false conclusions. Indeed, there is evidence for an alternative hypothesis.

In the later tenth century, between 957 and 972, Bishops Abraham of Freising and Michael of Regensburg met at Lappach, halfway between their properties at Isen and (Gross) Helfendorf, to carry out an exchange.[50] Bishop Abraham exchanged 23 (the manuscript indicates 21) *mancipia* by birth from Isen including 7 single women with between 1 and 5 children each; Bishop Michael, in return, made over to Freising 20 similar servile dependents from Helfendorf including 5 single women with between 1 and 4 children each. The motivation for this transaction was the bishops' mutual convenience in dealing with those servile dependants who had intermarried with the other's seigneurial 'family'. Thus, the wives and children from one lordship were now being united seigneurially with their (unnamed) husbands and fathers from the other lordship. In this way, the administrative confusions caused by seigneurial intermarriage could be resolved periodically, restoring at any given time the sort of homogeneous lordship which we encounter in 820–1. We should probably apply this interpretation to the numerous deeds of exchange which, especially in the tenth century, involve single women and children, rather than view them as evidences of illegitimacy.[51]

The rate at which these servile populations married seems to have varied widely from estate to estate, if, in fact, we may speak consistently of 'marriage' within a strict seigneurial environment in the early Middle Ages, where, as we have seen, slavery was the rule. We can, with some confidence, posit a conjugal bond in those cases where a male is followed by a female designated as his '*uxor*' (wife). This was so in 11 cases amongst the tenants at Lauterbach I and in 9 cases at Lauterbach II; at Pöbenhausen and at Rockolding there were 6 and 4 couples respectively. Not all such bonds were confined to the *manentes*, however. We have already mentioned couples amongst the *mancipia* at Engelbrechtsmünster and at Lauterbach II. At the latter place there was another

[49] See Störmer (1973): 118–56 for the geographical disposition of such estates.
[50] Bitterauf (ed.) (1905–9): no. 1166: II, 89–90. Cf. the eleventh-century deeds nos. 1427 and 1470: II, 282–3, 320.
[51] E.g. Bitterauf (ed.) (1905–9): nos. 966, 1040, 1061: I, 737, 784, II, 11. See Staab (1975): 332–3. Cf. Boutruche, *Seigneurie et féodalité*, I (1968): 146–7. This, of course, raises the further possibility that the single parents who frequently occur *in situ* in the surveys and deeds may, likewise, be an optical illusion; that is, the family may have been socially complete but seigneurially divided. Clearly we cannot control for this, but the references in 820–1 to the two spouses, one male, one female, who did not belong to Sigifrid is an encouraging indication of completeness (cf. n. 31 above).

couple amongst the prebendaries as there also was amongst the demesne *mancipia* at Pöbenhausen. Regardless of the distribution, however, it is clear that these numbers yield very low rates of married persons to total document population, exceeding one-quarter (12/40 or 30%) only at Pöbenhausen.

Even a quick examination of the list for Lauterbach II, however, will show that not all female mates were explicitly designated as wives. In 8 cases a man and a woman are linked together grammatically (*cum, et*) and are followed by a varying number of children. These couples must also be considered even though the scribe may have been signalling some variation in status, as was probably the case half a century earlier at Buch am Erlbach. There, amongst the eight identified couples, the woman was called a '*coniux*', or spouse, in five instances, a clear counterpart to '*uxor*' at Lauterbach. But in three cases, two where offspring were present, the female mate was designated as a '*mulier*', or woman. Finally, by extension, we may suspect that other male–female pairs in 820/1, lacking children and unlikely to be child dependants themselves but joined by the scribe through a conjunction, shared some form of connubial association, whether voluntary or arranged.[52] These pairs are included in our statistics, as is a last group, single parents, who must be considered in any estimate of marriage opportunities, assuming that they represent real, not administrative, phenomena.[53]

The number of married and single parents as a proportion of population shows considerable variation, but a broad comparison is still possible (see tables 7.3 and 7.6). On the one hand, we have a group of properties at Buch am Erlbach, Lauterbach II and in the Salzburggau with rates around one-half. On the other hand, on Sigifrid's large estates and in the Nordgau we find considerably lower rates, between about one-quarter and one-third. Comparing only the two Lauterbach estates we find a pronounced difference between the combined number of married persons and single parents in each (table 7.3a: $X^2 = 13.2$). The other contemporary comparison a century later (in 930) between the

[52] The household economy of old Europe was built around the fundamental division of labour between the man/field and the woman/farmstead. See Brunner, *Neue Wege der Verfassungsund Sozialgeschichte* (1968): 103–27. Thus a tenancy, to function properly, would have to be staffed by at least one member of each sex as a team. Compare the two pairs on hide 4 at Lauterbach I with the eight pairs assigned to four hides in an 899 Freising deed (Bitterauf (ed.) (1905–9): no. 1031: I, 775–6). These pairings may have been quite transitory.

[53] See n. 51 above. The presence of single parents is also indicated by the definition of the conjugal family unit (see p. 239 below). Unfortunately, we can only deal with this group on the tenancies and not in the manor house itself, even though, as was pointed out above, mothers with children seem to occur there.

Table 7.3. *Distribution by marital status*

(a)

Status	Lauterbach I		Lauterbach II		Total	
	No.	%	No.	%	No.	%
Married[a]	26	28	50	54	76	41
Single	68	72	43	46	111	59
TOTAL	94	100	93	100	187	100

(b)

Status	Nordgau		Salzburggau		Total	
	No.	%	No.	%	No.	%
Married[a]	27	26	52	49	79	37
Single	78	74	54	51	132	63
TOTAL	105	100	106	100	211	100

(c)

Status	Lauterbach I & II		Salzburggau & Nordgau		Total	
	No.	%	No.	%	No.	%
Married[a]	76	41	79	37	155	39
Single	111	59	132	63	243	61
TOTAL	187	100	211	100	398	100

[a] Includes single parents.

Salzburggau and the Nordgau yields a comparable distinction, with the former exhibiting a much higher marriage/parent rate than the latter (table 7.3b: $X^2 = 12.2$). Comparing the two periods, 820–1 and 930, however, we find that the overall rates are not significantly different (table 7.3c: $X^2 = 0.43$).

The variations noted at given times were probably not unrelated. We argued earlier that seigneurial organization and authority at Lauterbach II seemed to be less systematic and extensive than at Sigifrid's estate, which was thoroughly manorialized. Similarly, the dependent tenants in the Salzburggau (and at Buch with an identical rate) enjoyed a preferred status and were presumably less dominated by seigneurial authority than were their *mancipia* counterparts in the Nordgau. Thus in both comparisons opportunities for marriage and seigneurial control seem to have been related inversely to one another. At Lauterbach II even the demesne *mancipia* had opportunities for marriage, although we cannot say at what stage these marriages were – perhaps a crucial question. In any case, the manor and matrimony seem to have been at odds with one another.

The inclusion of single parents in our marriage rates has already raised

the extremely difficult question of fertility, which is normally associated
with nuptiality. This problem can only be approached obliquely from
two directions: children in relation to total population (age ratio) and in
relation to parents only (conjugal family units), both of which paths are
strewn with obstacles.

An examination of this complex problem must begin at Lauterbach II,
where the children, without being named, are enumerated with some
care.[54] Amongst the tenant population there (counting the two *mancipia*
as adults), the ratio of adults to children was 49 : 31, or 1.58 adults to 1
child. Put another way, about 61% of the tenant population seem to
have been adults and about 39% children. At Buch am Erlbach in 773,
where the tenant children are likewise carefully enumerated, the ratio is
20 : 12, or 1.67; in the Salzburggau it is 62 : 40, or 1.55.[55] Thus in all three
surveys the tenant population is divided between slightly over 60%
adults and slightly under 40% children. This would be consistent with a
situation where the division between child and adult and departure
from the family normally occurred in the early to mid teens, say between about 14 and 15 years, as was the case in many traditional
European societies.[56]

The question of age ratios at Lauterbach I is further complicated by the
fact that the children of the tenant couples were not explicitly identified
as such except on the eleventh hide, where, due to the smith father's
free status, there was a special need to be precise lest the offspring escape
the lordship. Clearly, however, both this fact and the inclusion of
children at Lauterbach II demonstrate that they were considered to be
an integral part of the arrangement. Hence it is reasonable to suppose
that the 19 undesignated names directly following the 'uxorated'
tenant couples on six hides must be those of their children.[57] Neither
their numbers, averaging 3 when combined with the smith's 'infants'

---

[54] For purposes of computation I have reckoned the children (*'cum infantibus'*) of the
couple on hide 10a as 2, the median number for known children (average 2.3). We
should point out here that children are not necessarily the biological offspring of both or
even one of the parents because of the frequency of mortality-induced remarriage in
pre-industrial societies. These and other complexities of analysis are developed in
exemplary fashion by Mitterauer, 'Zur Familienstruktur' (1973): 168–222 and *Familiengrösse–Familientypen–Familienzyklus* (1975a): 226–55.

[55] In the contemporary Nordgau survey it is difficult to distinguish consistently between
the tenant and demesne *mancipia*, but the number of children is at least 43 and, hence,
not lower than 41% of the entire deed population.

[56] See Riche, 'Problèmes de démographie historique du haut moyen âge' (1966): 41,
although it is difficult to accept his argument for an early age of marriage corresponding
to the attainment of adulthood; and Weinberger, 'Peasant households in Provence'
(1973): 252.

[57] See Heinzelmann (1977): 206.

(median, 3.0; Lauterbach II average, 2.3 and median, 2.0), nor their sex composition (11 : 10, or 110) raises any suspicions. They cannot have been *mancipia* who were clearly identified as such, nor are they likely to have been mature co-resident relatives. If they were, we should expect the usually careful scribe to note this as he does with the sister and the brother resident with their tenant siblings at Wettstetten and at Schwabelweis respectively.

A final, more likely, possibility is that some might be foster or adopted children, including orphans. This was perhaps the case at Lauterbach II where an unnamed *'puella'* (girl) was attached to an otherwise childless tenant couple; at Buch am Erlbach too a girl and a boy (*'puerulus'*) were each attributed to a tenant couple who, in both cases, lacked other children. Of course such an arrangement does not exclude some form of service (i.e. under-age *mancipia*). In any case, this possibility would not affect our age ratio for the inhabitants of the tenancies at Lauterbach I, which is 36:21, or 171, roughly the same as our earlier calculations elsewhere. But if we apply the same set of assumptions to Sigifrid's two other largest estates at Pöbenhausen and at Rockolding, we find a very even ratio of 12 : 13 and 22 : 21 respectively, or 100 for the two estates combined: that is half adults and half children. This difference from Lauterbach I is suggestive if not conclusive (Table 7.4a: $X^2 = 2.2$), but any contrast is weakened by the fact that the ratio for the *manentes* alone at Lauterbach I was 26:21, or 124.

The foregoing argument is liable to two major objections as well. First, the notion of 'child' is ambiguous, since, as we have seen with the *'puella'*, it has a social component in addition to a chronological one.

Table 7.4. *Distribution by age group*

(a) Group	Pöb./Rock. tenancies No.	%	Lauterbach I tenancies No.	%	Total No.	%
Adult	34	50	36	63	70	56
Child	34	50	21	37	55	44
TOTAL	68	100	57	100	125	100

(b) Group	10th–11th C. estates No.	%	8th–9th C. estates No.	%	Total No.	%
Adult	208	56	217	69	425	62
Child	165	44	98	31	263	38
TOTAL	373	100	315	100	688	100

Thus a person beyond the chronological boundary of early adolescence
might still be considered a social child, i.e. a dependant, if he or she
remained in the parental household, say as a prospective heir or as a
spinster. I suspect that this is why the survey at Lauterbach II abandons
the neutral and chronologically specific term *'infans'* in four instances
for one *'filius'* (son) and three *'filia(e)'* (daughters), two of them sisters on
the same holding. This suspicion is strengthened by the fact that the son,
Adalolt, and the lone daughter, Lantsvind, are the only two children
named in the entire survey of the estate. It is not hard to imagine Adalolt
waiting for his parents to die or go into retirement so that he could take
over the holding and marry, a situation which may have occurred
recently on a nearby holding (see below); or Lantsvind managing the
household, in place of her mother, for her evidently widowed father. If
this analysis is correct, it would yield a revised age ratio of 53 : 27, or 196,
for the tenancies at Lauterbach II, with adults outnumbering children
almost two to one. As we shall see, the different social arrangements at
Lauterbach I make it unlikely that the same argument could be applied
to it or to Pöbenhausen and Rockolding, however.

A second major objection arises from the fact that the tenants were
not a complete population. A proper age ratio would have to take
account of the demesne population as well. Thus the maintenance of
the proposed age ratios would require a symmetrical distribution
amongst the manorial *mancipia*. This is not inherently impossible. Because of the implications for work capacity and maintenance requirements, contemporaries were not indifferent to age.[58] A Freising deed of
829 singles out the six *mancipia* within a manor house, three men and
three women, as all still being young, implying that such uniformity was
unusual.[59] Likewise, we have already pointed to the two male names
within the *gynaeceum* at Lauterbach I as evidence of small children there.
But, in the final analysis, the age composition of these bodies cannot be
specified precisely, or even grossly.

However, it is probably the case that the demesne populations would
weight the age ratios more decisively in favour of adults, and this is not
without possible consequences. For example, in a 'worst case' situation
where all were assumed to be adults, Pöbenhausen and Rockolding
would still be able to maintain proportions of children between one-

[58] *C.* 838–40 a list was made of the *mancipia* which a certain Luitbald held as a *beneficium*
from the Bishop of Freising. The first seven men and women were evidently fit for
service; the next four were 'unfit for work on account of infirmity or blindness or old
age'; and the last seven concerned 'small children'. Bitterauf (ed.) (1905–9): no. 632: I,
538.
[59] Bitterauf (ed.) (1905–9): no. 579: I, 496.

third (27 : 13) and two-fifths (32 : 21) respectively, but we would have to assume that at least 10 demesne *mancipia* at Lauterbach I, more than one-quarter of the total (37), were children to achieve the lower of these two figures. This fact, together with the relatively low incidence of nuptiality at Lauterbach I, emphasizes the difficulty of viewing Sigifrid's central estate as a closed reproductive system, a conclusion that previously had been suggested by the analysis of sex ratios.

Finally, the composition of the demesne population bears upon any estimate of population growth which we might wish to derive from our sources stretching over two and a half centuries. By assuming it to be entirely adult, we can identify a noticeable shift towards children occurring between the earlier, eighth- and ninth-century, group of estates at Buch, Lauterbach, Pöbenhausen, and Rockolding, and the later, tenth- and eleventh-century, group in the Salzburggau and Nordgau, in Lower Bavaria, and at Schwand (see table 7.4b: $X^2 = 12.4$). But the tentative nature of any such exercise in demographic expansion should be evident by now.[60]

The other indirect approach to fertility, the conjugal family unit, is not completely satisfactory either, since it only indicates the number of children co-resident with their parents at a given time, not the total number of children produced by the couple, much less those surviving to maturity as replacements. Moreover, there is normally a tendency for poor families to expel offspring earlier than rich ones and, hence, to be smaller on average. Thus socio-economic factors play an important role in this concept, but the conjugal family unit is still useful as another index to the social if not the biological family, and will serve as a good introduction to the household, its size and its structure, which we shall consider presently.

For our purposes, the conjugal family unit may be considered to be of two types.[61] *Complete* conjugal family units consist of a male and a female, either with or without children; *incomplete* conjugal family units consist of a single man or woman with children. Thus the latter category does not distinguish between the widow and the unmarried girl with illegitimate offspring.

The results of our calculations (table 7.5), which again consider the tenant populations only, seem to reveal certain regularities when

[60] Nevertheless, note the difference between the purely tenant populations at Buch in 773 (20 : 12, or 167) and at Schwand two and a half centuries later, when European society is generally assumed to have been in an expansive phase. There the children actually seem to have outnumbered the adults (38 : 44, or 86).

[61] The terminology and classification schemes used here and below are those discussed by P. Laslett, 'Introduction' (1972b): 28–42.

Table 7.5a. *Analysis of conjugal family units: early group*

Tenant CFUs	Buch am Erlb. (773)	Lauterbach I (820–1)	Lauterbach II (820–1)	Pöbenhausen (820–1)	Rockolding (820–1)
No. CFUs/persons	8/26	13/47	21/70	6/25	8/39
Average CFU	3.3	3.6	3.3	4.2	4.9
Standard deviation	0.9	1.8	1.5	2.6	3.0
Median CFU	3.5	3.0	3.0	3.0	3.5
Modal size by no. persons in CFU/ household	4.0/4.0	2.0/2.0	2.0/4.0	2.0/9.0	2 & 3.0/10.0
Childless couples No./% CFU	2/25%	6/46%	8/38%	2/33%	2/25%
Incomplete CFUs Head M + F/% CFU	—	—	1 + 1/10%	—	2 + 0/25% ?

Table 7.5a (*cont.*). *Analysis of conjugal family units: late group*

Tenant CFUs	Salzburggau (930)	Nordgau (930)	Lower Bavaria (947–70)	Schwand (1010–20)
No. CFUs/persons	28/90	17/70	17/68	15/69
Average CFU	3.2	4.1	4.0	4.6
Standard deviation	1.0	1.7	1.5	2.4
Median CFU	3.0	4.0	3.0	4.0
Modal size by no. persons in CFU/ household	3.0/3.0	2 & 5.0/5.0	3.0/3.0	4.0/4.0
Childless couples No./% CFU	4/14%	1/6%	1/6%	1/7%
Incomplete CFUs Head M + F/% CFU	2 + 3/18%	3 + 4/41%	1 + 2/18%	1 + 4/33%

Table 7.5b and c. *Distribution by size of CFU*

(b) Size	L I/P./R./N'gau No.	%	Buch/L II/S'gau No.	%	Total No.	%
2–3 persons	21	48	34	60	55	54
4+ persons	23	52	23	40	46	46
TOTAL	44	100	57	100	101	100

(c) Size	L I/P./R./N'gau No.	%	Buch/L II/S'gau No.	%	Total No.	%
2–4 persons	26	59	50	88	76	75
5+ persons	18	41	7	12	25	25
TOTAL	44	100	57	100	101	100

Table 7.6. *Proportion married of total population and size of CFU*

Place	Degree of seigneurialization	Married (%)	Average size of CFU
(1) Lauterbach II	Moderate	54	3.3
(2) Buch am Erlbach	Moderate	50	3.3
(3) Salzburggau	Moderate	49	3.2
(4) Lower Bavaria	Extensive ?	39	4.0+
(5) Pöbenhausen	Extensive	35	4.2
(5a) Freckleben[a]	Mixed	32	4.7
(6) Schwand	Moderate	30	4.6
(7) Lauterbach I	Extensive	28	3.6
(8) Rockolding	Extensive	≥26	4.9
(9) Nordgau	Extensive	<26	4.1

Correlation coefficient: $r = -0.79$.
[a] Not calculated in correlation coefficient (r).

viewed together with manorial organization and marriage. For example, when we consider the average size of the conjugal family unit against the marriage/single-parent rate (table 7.6), it is clear that there is a pronounced inverse relationship between the two.[62] Thus the higher the incidence of nuptiality, the lower the size of the average conjugal family unit seems to be. It is very easy to accept this notion on purely historical/theoretical grounds. It would be consistent, on the one hand, with a situation where the existence of many small, perhaps subdivided, holdings would make the establishment of an independent household possible for a relatively large number, but where the limited resources of each holding would support only a few inhabitants; and, on the other hand, with a situation where a few larger or more productive holdings were reserved for a small number of tenants, but enabled this privileged minority to support more children and other co-residents (cf. p. 246). On the whole, the first of these 'ideal types' seems to characterize the less-manorialized estates such as Lauterbach II, where poverty-induced emigration could account for the relatively high age ratios noted above; the second, the more thorough manorialized ones such as Lauterbach I with its large number of inhabitants, held off the tenancies as celibate, if not chaste, *mancipia*. Thus, while the classical bipartite manor may have

---

[62] Additional evidence is provided by the *mancipia* families given to the Alsatian monastery of Weissenburg in 774; almost half of the population was married or a parent (49/101), but the average conjugal family unit size was under 3.0 (73/25); 28 were solitaries. Bruckner (ed.), *Regesta Alsatiae aevi Merovingici et Karolini*, I (1949): no. 235: 144. Two instances of plural children counted as three.

hindered marriage and the establishment of an independent family, it may equally have enhanced the situations of those who were able to marry and set up a household.

However, we should not make too much of the difference in the size of the conjugal family units. As the standard deviations indicate, even apparently large average differences are not necessarily significant,[63] and the preoccupation with averages tends to obscure interesting anomalies such as the relatively high numbers of childless couples on several estates, including both at Lauterbach. Earlier, in our discussion of nuptiality, the possibility arose that these couples might represent administrative pairings, possibly transitory, created for seigneurial convenience. But a full discussion of this vital topic, the degree of intervention in and manipulation of domestic arrangements in early-medieval Bavaria, is better shifted to a broader concept than the conjugal family unit, that is to the household.

Household structure and hide

The household, taken as a co-resident domestic group including servants, the members of which share location, kinship, and activity in varying degrees, appears in the 820–1 survey as a discrete unit, usually, though not always, centred on a conjugal family unit or nuclear family.[64] Altogether, I count 13 households amongst the *manentes* at Lauterbach I, all of them containing a conjugal family unit, and 23 at Lauterbach II, 2 of which did not contain such a unit. Additionally, amongst the *mancipia* at Lauterbach II, we may take the four couples and the *scut(ell)arius* to constitute 5 households.[65] Thus, there were more than twice as many households in Lauterbach II as in I, even though the two estates had equal populations. This follows, of course, from our discussion of nuptiality. At Pöbenhausen and Rockolding, also within Sigifrid's lordship, there were an additional 15 households, only one of which, at Rockolding, could be construed as not containing a conjugal family unit.

[63] For example, if we compare the distributions of conjugal family units between our 'seigneurialized' group and the 'non-seigneurial' one for the number of conjugal family units up to the combined median (3.0) and average (3.6) and those above (table 7.5b), the chi-square statistic derived, 1.5, may be suggestive of a real difference but is neither conclusive nor striking. On the other hand, the seigneurialized group clearly had more very large conjugal family units (5.0+ inhabitants − table 7.5c: $X^2 = 10.9$).

[64] P. Laslett (1972b): 28–42.

[65] See Heinzelmann (1977): 213 n. 49. I am reluctant to classify the manorial barracks (or equivalent) as a household, although the case could be made for it. This would only strengthen the argument below, raising the average household sizes in Sigifrid's lordship, especially at Lauterbach.

Looking at Sigifrid's three principal estates, at Lauterbach II and at Buch, the only comparable source, the distribution of household types seems to provide striking confirmation from the early ninth century for a recurring feature of early-modern family history: the simple or nuclear family was the overwhelmingly dominant type (table 7.7a). In Lauterbach as a whole, no fewer than 31 of the 36 tenant households exhibit simple-family structures in one form or another, and they contain 122 of the 137 inmates. In particular, at Lauterbach I, and within Sigifrid's lordship at Pöbenhausen and Rockolding, there is scarcely a hint of complexity or extension. At the other extreme, there are apparently no solitaries, and there is only one possible no-family household at Rockolding. Similarly, on these three estates there are only a couple of possible instances of single-parent households, both likewise at Rockolding.[66] Thus we are left essentially with a population of couples having either offspring/child dependents or *mancipia* attached to them. At Sigifrid's other properties only the isolated extended-sibling households at Wettstetten and at Schwabelweis clearly break the pattern of 'simplicity'.

This degree of simplicity is hard to accept, especially when we look at Lauterbach II. There eight different types of households occur across the spectrum, even though (as we would expect) simple households are the most common type, both in frequency and in numbers of inmates. The two *mancipia* on hides are found, not in groups with childless couples as at Lauterbach I, but rather, in one instance, in a household with three children and, in the other, with a solitary man. In one household, brothers were co-resident (2a – no family) and in two instances a brother and a sister were each co-resident with a married sibling (4c – laterally extended). Likewise, we find one instance of parents resident with a married child (5a – multiple, secondary unit up), and even in the simple households, as we have seen, it was likely that adult children were present in three, yielding an intermediate type between simple and complex. Finally, there were two instances of a widow and a widower. The absence of three-generation households in these and other Bavarian documents is not surprising of itself.[67]

---

[66] The exceptions at Rockolding, type 2a (hide 2) and type 3c *bis* (hide 4a and b), are very uncertain. There are onomastic indications of sibling relationships: Reginhelmus–Reginhelm (2); Rihhelmus (4a)–Rihmundus (4b). Dependants at the latter hide (4) are inferred by analogy with hide 3. Thus, aside from the possibility of scribal errors, which always exist (see hide 2), it is clear that these interpretations should be approached with caution. Even if they are wrong, my argument would not be weakened.

[67] Such households are exceedingly rare in all the early-medieval records which I have examined. See Stengel (ed.), *Urkundenbuch des Klosters Fulda*, I (1958): no. 200: 297; Wartmann (ed.), *Urkundenbuch der Abtei Sanct Gallen*, I (1863): nos. 103, 155: 97, 147.

Table 7.7a. Distribution by household type

Household type and description	Lauterbach I Households (no.)	Lauterbach I Persons (no.)	Pöb./Rock. Households (no.)	Pöb./Rock. Persons (no.)	Lauterbach II Households (no.)	Lauterbach II Persons (no.)	Buch am Erlbach Households (no.)	Buch am Erlbach Persons (no.)
1. Solitary								
b. Single + servant	—	—	—	—	1	2 (1 servant)	—	—
2. No family								
a. Co-resident siblings	—	—	1	4 ?	1	2	—	—
2a. + servant	—	—	—	—	—	—	1	3 (1 servant)
3. Simple family								
a. Childless couple	2	4	4	8	5	10	2	6
3a. + servant(s)	4	18 (10 servants)	—	—	—	—	—	—
b. Couple + child(ren)	7	35	8	50	10	43	5	19 (2 servants)
3b. + servant(s)	—	—	—	—	1	6 (1 servant)	—	—
c. Widower + child(ren)	—	—	2	6 ?	1	2	—	—
d. Widow + child(ren)	—	—	—	—	1	4	—	—
4. Extended family								
c. Lateral extension	—	—	—	—	2	7	1	4
5. Multiple family								
a. Secondary unit up	—	—	—	—	1	4	—	—
TOTAL	13	57	15	68 ?	23	80	9	32

244

Table 7.7b. *Distribution by household type*

Household type	L I/Pöb./Rock.		L II/Buch		Total	
	No.	%	No.	%	No.	%
Simple	27	96	25	78	52	87
Other	1	4	7	22	8	13
TOTAL	28	100	32	100	60	100

With such low expected numbers of non-simple households, the chi-square statistic (table 7.7b: $X^2 = 4.2$) is not as informative here as we might wish, although it is consistent with the proposed contrast, and, if it were legitimate to compare, rather, the numbers of persons within households, it would be 16.3. Thus when comparing lordships the question of household structure rather than size seems to be the more crucial one. For example, the two major groups of Fulda dependants in Thuringia in the later tenth century, the more privileged *lidi* and the inferior *servi*, had virtually identical family sizes. The average size of conjugal family units for all *lidi* was 4.6; for all *servi* it was 4.5. At the comparable large estates of Freckleben and (Grosse-)Örner with a total of 120 households, the median household size was 5 for both *lidi* and *servi* who held tenancies from Fulda. However, if we look rather at structures, there is a consistent difference between these two groups. Although *servi* possessing tenancies often had *mancipia* assigned to them, as did the *manentes* at Lauterbach I (sometimes many *mancipia*), no *servi* had co-resident relatives, and none with a tenancy was a solitary, again as at Lauterbach I. On the other hand, at least one (possibly more) *lidus* with a tenancy was a solitary, and there were nine clear instances of *lidi* households, both with and without Fulda tenancies, having co-resident relatives. Although there are a number of complexities in these documents which we cannot consider here, it seems clear that preferred status and familial complexity went together. Obviously this fits in well with our discussion of Bavarian materials.

It would require great ingenuity to fit either Sigifrid's *manentes* or Fulda's *servi* into any normal cycle of household development, although this would not necessarily be the case for St Emmeram's (or Buch's) tenants. But perhaps this is only an apparent problem. If we cease to expect Sigifrid's households to develop in some autonomous way consistent with the natural rhythms of birth, puberty, marriage, and death and see them, rather, as a product of administrative manipulation, then their uniform structures make some sense. If, for example, the lord or his agent boarded or allotted his excess or useless *mancipia* to new tenant couples still without children or to older couples whose children had departed, both of whom could use additional manpower and had the resources to support it; if children of *manentes* were circulated off the holding at maturity, say about 15 years, and transferred as *mancipia* to the demesne work force or perhaps to relatives' or other households with excess capacity; finally, if the holding were not strictly hereditary and the injection of a new tenant couple (or couples), probably drawn from the *mancipia*, normally involved the ejection of their ageing predecessors, unfit to work or unable to remarry, who would retire either to the demesne or in a dependent status on a holding as *mancipia* – in short, if the optimal allocation of human and agricultural resources throughout the entire estates' complex were the primary consideration and the holdings and home farm were merely units or stages in a total circulatory system – then we might expect a situation very much like that on Sigifrid's properties.

This should not surprise us. It is in line with our earlier structural analysis and complements the demographic indications of mobility. Moreover, such seigneurial manipulation of family groupings, if carried out with some intelligence and delicacy, would not necessarily be to the disadvantage of its subjects and would probably involve co-operation more often than coercion. It would ensure that each holding was exploited to its limit, but that no individual holding would be burdened with too many mouths to feed; that all children would be provided for, especially daughters who had access to the servile version of the aristocratic nunnery in the *gynaeceum*; and that old persons would be cared for regardless of the presence or the willingness of heirs. In short, in a world of scarce resources, an environment dominated by a seigneurial life cycle (fig. 7.2), covering the entire lordship and in which *manens* and *mancipium* formed the significant stages, might look quite attractive to those at the bottom, in comparison with a fragmented peasant household environment and cycle. The advantages to the lord are just as

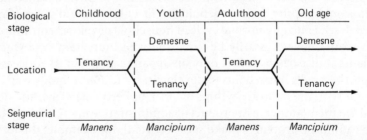

Fig. 7.2. A simple model of the seigneurial life cycle.

evident. Apart from flexibility, the circulation of large numbers through the central manor would ensure a uniform socialization of dependants, and the possibility of receiving a tenancy and the connected chance to establish a family would have served, for demesne *mancipia*, as an incentive to work. Nor does this interpretation do violence to contemporary conceptions of seigneurial life. Indeed, we can now see more readily why the pre-eminent meaning of *'familia'* in the early Middle Ages did not refer to 'family' in our modern sense but rather to the totality of the lord's dependants.[68] Sigifrid's lordship was literally one big family.

Conclusion

It is unlikely that the crude, sparse, and fragmented evidence of the early Middle Ages will ever yield conclusive answers for the subtle and complex problems which we have just raised, and for which we have suggested a possible comprehensive solution. Accordingly, our conclusions must be considered provisional. Still, the fact that three major lines of inquiry all converge at the same point is encouraging.[69] The traditional structural components of Sigifrid's lordship, the demographic characteristics of its inhabitants, and the social ecology of their familial arrangements all present an intelligible and consistent picture when viewed as parts of an integrated social system animated by what we have called a seigneurial life cycle. This is about as far as we can expect to go: we now have a dynamic social model of rural society in the early Middle Ages to supplement and, to an extent, replace the older static, hierarchical model developed for us by the constitutional and legal historians of the nineteenth century.

Similarly, our conclusions may have some implications for the study of the modern western European family, characterized by relatively mature partners and by simple structures together with (in earlier periods) a high incidence of unmarried persons.[70] Perhaps Lauterbach I provides us with a model for understanding the origins of these peculiarities

---

[68] See Bosl, 'Die "familia" als Grundstruktur der mittelalterlichen Gesellschaft' (1975); and Weizsäcker, 'Die Familia des Klosters St. Emmeram' (1951). A parallel, albeit much later, to our hypothesis is Peter Laslett's notion of the 'life-cycle servant' ('Characteristics of the Western family' (1977b): 104). Remarks consistent with ours can also be found in Duby, *Rural economy and country life* (1968): 38.

[69] A fourth line of inquiry, a detailed analysis of the onomastic material, also leads to a comparable conclusion. This highly technical discussion has been omitted for reasons of space, as has much of the critical apparatus of interest primarily to medievalists.

[70] P. Laslett (1972b), (1977b) and *The world we have lost* (1971): 84–112; Hajnal, 'European marriage patterns' (1965): 101–43, esp. 133.

which have been noted back into the later Middle Ages. After all, this family type is most evident in northern and western Europe, precisely the areas of the classical manorial regime. Thus, the western family may be a function of another aspect of our western heritage: slavery. The social arrangements and cultural patterns imposed by the aristocracy (including the church) on its plantation slaves for administrative efficiency may have been so deeply implanted and pervasive that they survived the decline after the eleventh century of the institutional environment which had nurtured them. The lords planned and tended, but it was amongst the enslaved masses of early-medieval Europe that the modern family emerged.

Still, these speculations run far ahead of our present concerns, and the value of the great deed of 820–1 and related documents is independent of their validity, for with their aid we can finally begin to get at the realities of life for the vast majority of early-medieval people. Bodo and his family can be seen from a new perspective, and we can obtain more nourishing fare in the 'kitchens of History'.[71] About the year 180 BC the Jewish scribe Joshua ben Sira wrote down his thoughts about the human condition. When he came to consider the history of his people, he set forth a historiographical programme to which many medievalists would still subscribe. Beginning with the famous exhortation 'Let us now sing the praises of famous men, the heroes of our nation's history', he goes on to recount the mighty deeds of rulers, the wisdom of counsellors and prophets, the achievements of artists, and the dignity of the mighty. 'All these', he continues, 'won fame in their own generation and were the pride of their times. Some there are who have left a name behind them to be commemorated in story. There are others who are unremembered; they are dead, and it is as though they had never existed, as though they had never been born or left children to succeed them.'[72] By all odds the nearly 200 inhabitants of Lauterbach (and their counterparts at Buch, Schwand, and elsewhere) ought to be amongst those 'who are unremembered', whose annihilation is so complete that 'it is though they had never existed'. Yet one cold day in February eleven and a half centuries ago a deacon named Ellenhard preserved a record of their little community, and two centuries later an anonymous scribe passed it on to us. Thus, unlike the mass of their fellows, they have – barely – 'left a name behind them to be commemorated in story', and it is that story which I have tried to tell.

---

[71] This is, of course, a friendly salute to Eileen Power's marvellous 'Bodo, a Frankish peasant in the time of Charlemagne' – see Power, *Medieval people* (1924).
[72] Ecclesiasticus 44: 1–9 (trans. NEB).

8

The property and kin relationships of retired farmers in northern and central Europe

DAVID GAUNT

Introduction

The structure of modern industrial societies shows an ageing population. In most countries in Europe there are more old age pensioners than ever before, and the proportion of people who have retired from the labour market because of age is steadily growing. Even in countries, like those of Scandinavia, where the proportion of aged persons is so high already that it cannot increase, there will be a great expansion in the number of the very old, that is those over 80 years of age, continuing into the next century.

This situation leads to difficulty in planning ahead for payment of old-age pensions based on social security funds deducted from the working population. In addition, traditional ways of coping with the problems of the very old by putting them into special institutions or hospitals have been extremely costly. There is, therefore, a considerable interest in alternative solutions to the problems of old age; a search for cheaper but perhaps even more humane ways of treating the elderly. Some social workers have tried to stimulate sons or daughters to take the old people back to their homes and build some sort of extended family. In countries like the United States, where institutional care for the elderly has not been given priority, more than one-third of all aged single people live with relatives, usually adult children. In Sweden, however, the number of old people's homes has rapidly expanded since

The writing of this essay has been aided and supported by many people and institutions. Foremost is the Max-Planck-Institut für Geschichte which gave me the opportunity to go through German-language works at Niedersächsisches Staats- und Universitätsbibliotek in Göttingen. Palle O. Christiansen of Copenhagen and Henry Rask of Helsinki helped me obtain Danish and Finnish literature.

   Professor Birgitta Odén of the Swedish group for the study of the aged has supported this work since its inception.

the Second World War. In the early 1970s only 7% of 70-year-olds in the large city of Gothenburg lived with relatives, and of those living alone and needing help only 9% received such help from their own children.[1] Other social workers concentrate on taking measures so that the elderly do not need to leave their own homes for basic care, and so on.

In Sweden, these kinds of interest have led to the formation of an interdisciplinary research group for the study of the problems of the aged in the future. An essential part of making a judgment on future development lies in properly evaluating long-term historical trends. This research group, therefore, includes not only sociologists, physicians, statisticians, social workers, and engineers, but also historians.[2] As a historian within this group, my task has been to present the cultural and social history of the aged.

Here, I want to treat the problem of retirement in the past in a very broad way. First, I wish to show that there are some interesting aspects of retirement which have previously been neglected and which demand attention. I want, moreover, to stimulate discussion, because the nature of the sources and the actions to be interpreted are quite complicated and may be seen in many ways. Further, the geographical variations are considerable. But in this chapter I particularly want to show how the problems of retirement in peasant households were integrated into all the other problems of family life which we know so much better: marriage and building of families, inheritance and other forms of succession to a farm or cottage, relationships between generations, and the way the number of mouths to be fed regulated the way the household was organized to meet these needs.

This chapter concentrates on a widespread system of peasant retirement whereby an aged farmer gives over his property in his lifetime to a relative, generally his own child, in return for food and lodging for the rest of his days. In early modern England such a retired person was sometimes called a 'sojourner', and the relationship between the retired person and his successor was recognized by the community as involving definite rights and responsibilities. I shall go back to the Middle Ages as far as sources allow us some insight. Since this relationship appears to cover places where Germanic law gained a foothold, I shall present data not only from Scandinavia, Germany, Austria, and England, but also

---

[1] U.S. Bureau of the Census, *Current population reports* (1977): 306; Svanborg, 'Seventy-year-old people in Gothenburg' (1977): 8, 12.

[2] Aldre i Samhället – Förr, Nu Och i Framtiden (The Aged Society – Past, Present, and Future) supported by the Delegationen för Lång Siktsmotiverad Forskning, headed by Birgitta Odén, Alvar Svanborg, and Lars Tornstam.

from non-Germanic countries where German law early became influential, like Bohemia, Moravia, and Finland.[3]

Medieval retirement

The Scandinavian medieval provincial law allows us to picture how old people were cared for from about the twelfth century.[4] Unfortunately, while there are a great number of laws and revisions of law codes, the actual conditions which they regulate are unknown. Court records are very rare outside the towns until the late sixteenth century. Several key factors emerge in the medieval legislation: the old or infirm persons themselves; the property and whatever wealth they have; and their kin. These factors could be combined in various ways, as some of the examples brought forward here will indicate.

The most common method for caring for the elderly was through sons and daughters and their households – though in principle even more distant relatives could participate. The old peasant, who at the time of the medieval provincial laws almost always owned his own land, was required to go to the *thing*, the local court, and announce a wish to retire. Those relatives interested in maintaining him or her and in assuming possession of his or her wealth also had to make themselves known to the court. The old person was then set to wander at intervals between these relatives. The length of time he stayed was in direct proportion to the amount of wealth each relative would inherit. If all were to inherit equally, he would begin with the eldest and finish with the youngest. In this way he kept rotating until he died. This system can be found in all the early Danish laws: Scanian law from about 1210, Valdemar's Zealand law from about the same time, Erik's Zealand law from the second quarter of the thirteenth century, and the law of Jutland dated 1241.[5]

In Danish law the person who retired in this way was called a '*fledfør-ing*', that is a person who goes (*fara*) from his own household, symbol-

[3] For the expression 'sojourner' see Spufford, 'Peasant inheritance customs' (1976): 174–5. In Sweden the terms are *sytning, undantag,* and *förderåd*; in Norway *kår, framførsle, föderåd, hold,* and *kost*; in Denmark the most common term is *aftaegt.* In Germany and Austria there are many names: *Altenteil, Ausbehalt, Auszug, Ausgedinge, Ausnahme, Austrag, Leibzucht, Leibgedinge, Winkel.* In Finland the word was *syytinki*; in Czech it was *wýměnek.* Lutz Berkner gives a description of how these relations functioned in Austria in 'The stem family' (1972a) and in northern Germany in 'Inheritance, land tenure and peasant family structure' (1976): 78–86, 92–5.

[4] A good survey of the medieval laws on this subject is found in Charpentier, *Om Sytning* (1895): 5–42. There are short articles by Helland-Hansen, 'Kår' (1955–76) and Hasselberg, 'Flatföring' (1955–76). See also Schultze, 'Die Rechtslage des alternden Bauers' (1931).

[5] Juul, *Fledføring* (1955–76); Charpentier (1895): 16–17.

ized by the floor (*fled*), into another's household. This term was also used in one of the early Swedish provincial laws, Västgöta law, which was written down around 1280. Most of the other provincial laws did not have any special term for the retired individual, though they did refer to the act of giving over inheritance during one's lifetime in return for room and board. Hälsinge law from the second quarter of the fourteenth century, which was used throughout the northern part of Sweden and in parts of Finland, used the term '*sytning*' for these relationships. '*Sytning*' comes from the verb '*syta*', which is dialect for 'to nurse' or 'to care' for someone.[6]

Generally, the people who maintained the elderly were the adult children. However, it was quite possible for children to refuse to maintain parents if they so wished. Only a few Swedish laws had clauses specifying an obligation on the part of descendants to care for parents – Uplands law, Västmanlanna law, and Södermanna law, all dating from the late thirteenth century. As soon as laws for the whole realm were composed in the mid-fourteenth century, however, this obligation was made clear.[7]

Relatives who did not participate in maintaining the elderly kin could not be cut off from their part of the inheritance. Their rights to succession were always recognized. In some ways, the early-medieval laws seemed to view the peasant not as the true owner of the land but merely as an administrator for a kin-based interest group. However, it is very easy to exaggerate the importance of the kin group at this time. Most laws had to deal with the situation in which an old and infirm person was refused care by relatives and was forced to seek maintenance elsewhere. There were several solutions.

The Swedish Ostgöta law on sojourning begins 'If children will not take over, so to the next heirs; if the proper heirs will not take over, then they shall ask their other kin.' But if all the relatives refused, the old person could turn over all his wealth to a non-kinsman and become a type of thrall (*gävträl*). This would involve the removal of the old person into a new dwelling and recognition of his dependence on the household head. The kin would be cut out of the inheritance. However, this sort of retirement involving a removal of wealth from the kin group was forbidden by Earl Birger (reign 1248–66) in the mid-thirteenth century.[8] The normal form of a caretaker relationship with non-kin involved a yearly payment to the care-giving household head. This would amount on average to 3 or 4 marks for each year, more if it was

[6] Charpentier (1895): 6–9.   [7] *Ibid.* 10–15.
[8] Hemmer, 'Vad förstår Östgötalagen med en gävträl?' (1932); Charpentier (1895): 32–6.

for an old man but less if it was for an old woman. This sum was to be withdrawn from the old person's property upon death and before distribution to the heirs. There was a definite risk, if the property was very small, or if the retired peasant lived a long life, that nothing would be left in the estate for the kin.[9]

In Iceland, where, despite the impression the sagas give, kin relations were weak because of settlement patterns, a rotation was set up within the neighbourhood. The old person transferred his wealth to non-kin and became what was known as '*arfsal*' and was then rotated among neighbours in what was called an '*umgang*' (lit. 'going around'). There was something similar in Friesland, where the free peasants retired through a system known as '*evelganc*' (*evel* means 'sick' or 'poorly', *ganc* 'to go') to non-kin.[10]

Retirement in twelfth- and thirteenth-century northern Europe thus had the following aspects. The foremost was a wandering or moving between various kin or neighbours in return for food or lodging. Where the old persons owned property, this was not transferred in a sort of anticipated inheritance to those who supported them at the moment the relationship began. Retirement was thus more an alimentation system than a property transfer. The old farmers were obliged to ask all heirs to participate in maintaining them; however, the heirs were not always obliged to participate. They might be fined for failing in this civil duty, but they were not disinherited.

The situation of the landless gives a glimpse of how little value was attached to the qualities of old age. Emancipated thralls were the largest landless group at the beginning of the Scandinavian Middle Ages. These people, at least according to the eleventh-century Norwegian Gulating law, could expect brutal treatment when they became old. If an emancipated couple fell on hard times in old age, they were termed '*gravgangsmän*' (lit. 'Grave-going-men'). 'For them shall they dig a grave in the church yard and set them there and let them die there. [The former] Owner shall take home the person who lives longest and then feed him.' From this legislation one can conclude that whatever good treatment an elderly Scandinavian received in the Middle Ages was probably based more on his landowning than on any high esteem for older folk.[11]

The relative absence of feudalism was a special feature of Scandinavia

[9] Charpentier (1895): 24–8.
[10] Lárusson, 'Hreppr' (1955–76a) and 'Umagi' (1955–76b); Schultze (1931): 292–309; Piepenbrock, *Die Entwicklung des Altenteils* (1926): 27–8 and literature cited there; Weiland, *Die geschichtliche Entwicklung des bäuerlichen Altenteils* (1939): 21–4.
[11] Gulating law §63. See discussion in Hovstad, *Mannen og samfunnet* (1943) and Robberstad, 'Litt meir um gravgangsmennene' (1948).

at the time of the codification of the provincial laws. The main concern
in these property transfers was with property-owning peasants. The
number of peasants dependent on the church and noblemen increased
greatly, however, in the following centuries. Unfortunately, it is not
possible to say much about intergenerational transfers of rights to land,
movable property, or 'authority' for these Scandinavian peasants.

Some insight can be gained by studying German law codes both at the
provincial and local court levels. Probably the earliest mention of
peasant retirement there is an article in the laws of the court of Stadt-
Lohn from the early fourteenth century. It states that retiring peasants
should be entitled to take 'the best bed, the best kettle, the best pot, the
best plough, the best horse, the best wagon and so on' from the former
dwelling. There was a further clause that the successor should assume
the debts of the retired who was to move to a *Leibzucht*. Obviously the
Leibzucht was a smaller plot of land with a dwelling; otherwise the need
to remove the farm equipment, draught animals, and furnishings would
be difficult to explain. This special plot was taken from the existing farm,
and upon the death of the elder peasant was to return directly to the
new peasant. There are similar articles in the Privileges of the Reichhof
Westhoven in the County of Mark about 1300.[12]

In England transfers of tenements during the lifetime of the peasant to
a younger relative can be found in estate records. George Homans has
published several examples in *English villagers of the thirteenth century*;
they usually involve a small plot of land and a separate room or dwelling
on the tenement.[13]

Among the wealthy Scandinavian landholders a new principle came
into use, and it was gradually adopted by the free peasantry. This was
the Augustinian soul gift of property made to the church by a person
who moved into a monastery to be cared for there until death. In
Denmark the soul gift was regulated in the following way: on the wish
of the elderly to move into a monastery, land was divided between
parents and children so that each was allocated an equal plot. If there
were one parent and four children, the parent received one-fifth of the
wealth. This part, called the '*hovedlod*' or '*head-lot*', could be given for
ever to the church, or ultimately to any third party who would support
the elderly person.[14]

[12] Runde, *Die Rechtslehre von der Leibzucht*, I (1805): 27–9.
[13] Homans, *English villagers* (1941): 144–59. Richard Smith of the Cambridge Group for
the History of Population and Social Structure is now analysing a number of similar
medieval transfer documents.
[14] See Schultze (1931): 271–3, 289–92 for the general development; Juul, *Faellig og
hovedlod* (1940): 84–7, 102–24; Kock, *Om hemföljd* (1924): 17–19, 37–9, 63–6, 75–9.

In Germany anticipated inheritance does not appear to have come about through the influence of a soul-gift institution. There the kinship group resisted the wishes of both the church and the crown to receive landed donations. Such land transfers could only occur with the consent of the heirs, and if they contested a donation the giver was to be considered 'as if he was dead'. The wealth was then divided among the heirs. This process is clear from Sachsenspiegel and other thirteenth-century legal codes. In addition, the kin group could force out a peasant who was no longer physically able to manage the land. This eviction was known as '*Abmeierung*'. One test of the peasant's ability was whether or not he could plough a *morgen* of land (two-thirds of an acre) in one day. If this could not be done the heirs would take over. This, in the opinion of Helmut Weber, was the origin of the anticipated inheritance in Germany.[15]

The emergence of inheritance *inter vivos*

By the end of the fifteenth century anticipated inheritance had become rather common in Denmark and Sweden. For instance, there were a considerable number of land transfers to ecclesiastical institutions where the principle of the soul gift was used. However, this does not mean the disappearance of the older view of a transfer first becoming ownership on death. In 1508 the district court of Häme in Finland recorded that Kirstin Olofsdotter from Kutila gave over her farm to her son Thomas for management; he was to receive land to the value of 3 marks yearly for the service he had provided up to then, and would in the future give her in the way of food and clothing to her dying day.[16]

The system of anticipated inheritance probably came earlier and was more widespread on the Continent and in England than in Scandinavia. The greater importance of feudalism meant that many more peasants were under manorial rule, and one can imagine the lord of the manor having an interest in replacing older tenants with more physically able sons and daughters. Indeed, one of the various German theories about the origin of the retirement system states specifically that it grew up in manors where the tenants had a recognized right to hereditary posses-sion. The Austrian writer Karl Schmidt is the main proponent of this view. However, really convincing proof has not been presented.[17]

[15] Weber, *Der deutsche bäuerliche Uebergabevertrag* (1941): 43–5, 48–50 and literature cited there.
[16] Hausen (ed.), *Dombok för sydvästra Tavastland 1506–1510* (1881): 163 and Charpentier (1895): 7, 24.
[17] Schmidt, *Gutsübergabe und Ausgedinge* (1920): 12–18.

If we ignore the origins of the system and look only at the structure, we can see peasant retirement in northern and central Europe during the Middle Ages developing in the following way. Gradually, the principle that the elderly should rotate among all willing heirs was abandoned. They could choose to remain with the heir they thought would best provide for them. The wandering specified in Icelandic, Friesian, Danish, and Swedish laws ceased. In addition the legal status of the property of the retired was ambiguous, at least for those who actually owned land. In the beginning, wealth changed owners only at the death of an ancestor. But other alternatives implying change of ownership during the life of the old possessor, like soul gifts and *Abmeierung*, became more influential. The changes in the way peasant retirement was treated in the Reformation period are unclear. In Scandinavia, at any rate, legislation and documents surviving from this time are very few. But basically the ambiguity in ownership which remained at the end of the Middle Ages disappeared. By the mid-seventeenth and the beginning of the eighteenth century the wealth of the old people was clearly transferred to the younger generation at retirement. Retirement was therefore connected with legislation on gifts of landed property or sale of such property. The care and maintenance due to the old couples or individuals were often specified in the documents of sale or gift.[18]

There was still, however, the matter of what the heirs who did not assume title to the property were to get. Throughout the seventeenth century in Sweden these co-heirs were entitled to a proportion of the wealth. But the heir with the title to the land was in a privileged position, since he could draw from the wealth an annual amount, set either by the transfer document or by custom, before redistribution took place. The judges in Kopparbergslan in 1695 reported that there common people went to kin or strangers for maintenance either in illness or age. 'But it is their greatest desire to stay with just one of the children who can best provide for them, and let the children therefore have a certain compensation from the property.' The other co-heirs, however, could nullify this compensation by delivering food or money to the caretaking heir.[19]

The Swedish law codification of 1734 completed the process of ownership change upon the registration of a retirement caretaking agreement. This was the first codification of Swedish law since the Middle Ages and was heavily influenced by the Roman law transmitted through Germany. This influence probably explains why such a widespread

---

[18] See documents cited in Charpentier (1895): 56–60.
[19] Charpentier (1895): 48, 52.

popular institution as the retirement contract is not even mentioned in the text of the law. This was surprising, since the commission which prepared the law had many proposals and presentations about the contracts. The law of 1734 did not abolish the retirement contract, but it is implied that it was not a separate legal institution. This meant that the laws regulating sales were to be used for such contractual situations.[20]

It should be mentioned that Swedish law was also used throughout Finland. In addition, there was a similar codification of Danish law made under Roman legal influence in 1682. However, the majority of Danish peasants did not own their land. The laws regulating sales had little relevance for tenant retirement and therefore will not be discussed here. The situation of the Danish peasants can be likened to that of the tenants in Germany with hereditary claims to a farm.

The change brought about by the law of 1734 dictated a new form for the retirement contracts registered at the local courts in Sweden and Finland. Before that date, old people still had a tenuous claim to ownership of their farms and so had some power to control their situation. Retirement contracts therefore could be quite simple: that son A takes over the property of B and C and that the latter are to receive room, board, and care from A for the rest of their lives. In the new situation, where property was really transferred, such simple contracts were unsatisfactory, and the elderly found that they had to specify certain resources, such as land, housing, animals, clothing, heating, and so on, which would be reserved from the property immediately exchanged. Sometimes these reservations began to be utilized directly, this being especially the case if a non-kinsman took over, but sometimes the specifications were only a guarantee to guard against the creation of a situation wherein daily troubles between the generations became so serious that the two couples had to live and eat separately. Thus the size of the amounts stipulated in the contract had less to do with constituting a minimum standard of living for the old people than with creating an effective sanction against allowing small problems to blow up into an insoluble conflict.

On manors, resources for retired farmers were specified in tenement contracts earlier than was the case with independent farm sales. But even in such cases there were many changes in the idea of property during the seventeenth century which paralleled developments for the independent farmers. Some examples from German territories will illustrate the point.

In Westphalia there was a tendency during the seventeenth century

[20] *Ibid.* 61–9.

for peasant retirement to cease being a matter of what might be called communal and family relationships. This development was part of the general worsening of the legal conditions of the peasantry in central and northern Europe. Various pieces of legislation like the Eigenthums-Recht und Ordnung of Ravensburg in 1669, the Eigenthums-Ordnung of Osnabrück in 1722, and the Royal Prussian Eigenthums-Ordnung for Minden and Ravensburg in 1741 bear witness to the new situation.[21]

The position of the lord of the manor as the party most affected by the retirement and takeover is emphasized to a much greater extent than in the previous *Hofrechte*. According to the law of 1669, the lord was to fix the size of the retirement share in land, animals, and furnishings in accordance with custom and fairness, though never to a value of more than one-sixth of the total value. Thus it became important to specify in detail what the pension was to comprise in relation to each tenement rather than to rely exclusively on the traditional custom of the manor. All the laws prohibited the elderly peasants and their children from making secret agreements involving larger pensions, or forcing the new peasants to make money payments. Such contracts were termed '*pacta contraria*'.

In Schleswig-Holstein, Sering found that retirement contracts among the free peasants were unknown before the sixteenth century and did not become common until the following century. When they did appear they had little to do with the Danish *fledføring*. On the contrary, they required the persons retiring to remain on the farmstead after retirement in a separate dwelling or room. There was a reservation of the use of certain resources and the delivery of food and clothing. The few cases where *fledføring* was used involved people who had no kin available to support them.[22]

The retirement contracts

Examples of Scandinavian retirement contracts from various times appear in the appendix below. They are very different internally: the few common articles are milk and grain, but otherwise they are rather individual. Even within the same parish there was no single standard, but the details of contracts varied considerably because of the size and specialization of the farm and the personal needs of the elderly retired.

About the time of the first detailed retirement contracts, one also

[21] Weiland (1939): 58–63.
[22] Sering, *Erbrecht und Agrarverfassung* (1908): 170–2.

begins to find the first complaints by governments, officials, churchmen, and academics about the way amity between parents and grown children was declining. Many pointed directly to the contracts as the cause, but from the evidence it is not easy to decide: it is a hen and egg problem. In Sweden and Finland complaints were very usual by the late eighteenth century. We can take an example from the agricultural reformer and traveller Anders Barchaeus. He reported in 1772 from one central Swedish parish that the priest considered the retirement conditions a great confusion. The young went about calling the retired 'the old devils' and demanding, 'What is their purpose in living?' The secretary of the provincial administration in Västmanland told Barchaeus that peasants retired at the age of 60 because in that way they could avoid the poll tax. It was of some importance to do so. The tax was not large, only 9 *daler*, but it had to be paid in cash, which was something of which most Swedish peasants had only too little.[23] Barchaeus reported that on one farm a widower annually received six barrels of grain plus a cow and a pig; on another farm the retired man and wife got eight barrels of grain. He goes on: 'I record this as a reminder of a cause of so much disorder and ungodliness in the relationship of children to their parents among peasants. Curses, fighting and murder of parents are not so rare among High Court cases.' The parish priest of Monktorp said that in the last 30 years he had buried no more than five or six active peasants from a parish of over 100 homesteads, for 'all the others were retired'. Barchaeus even related a popular story later retold by Riehl about a farmer and his old, infirm father. The young man had tired of caring for the old fellow and sat down to make a cattle trough to pour the old man's food into – he meant clearly to humiliate him. As he was carving, his small son came by and, hearing his father was making a trough for his grandfather, said, 'Oh! father, I will make one for you when you are old too!' This was clearly part of a fright campaign which the gentry and the upper classes were using against the peasant retirement system. Barchaeus went so far as to suggest a law providing that children 'could never more be head of household over their parents'.[24]

In Germany there were similar attacks on the system or its symptoms. At times, retirement of peasants was forbidden in Saxony, Hessia, and Baden. In some of the cities of Mark-Brandenburg, for instance Frankfurt an der Oder, a large club was hung from the gates with the following inscription:

[23] Kjellberg (ed.), 'A. G. Barchaei resa 1772' (1923): 54, 88–9.
[24] *Ibid.* 62, 63, 81, 88.

Wer den Kindern giebt das Brod
und leidet selber Noth,
Den soll man schlagen mit dieser Keule tod!

(He who has made himself dependent on his children for bread
and suffers from want
He shall be knocked dead by this club!)

One of the more realistic suggestions of what to do with peasant
retirement did not advocate abolition. An anonymous writer in the
Westfälisches Anzeiger in 1798 proposed the establishment of a Court for
Morality to settle conflicts between peasant parents and children.[25]

Throughout Europe there were a number of tales about old peasants
and clubs used to kill them. In Sweden these stories spread widely
during the late seventeenth century. A classic example tells of a farmer
who had turned over his property to his grown son and daughter-in-law
and was being treated badly. Eventually he hit upon an ingenious plan
and told the young couple that he hadn't given them all his wealth, but
that he had more hidden away in a chest which he would leave to them
when he died. From that moment his treatment became much better
and continued good up to death. After burial the son and his wife rushed
to open the chest, but the only thing they found was a long-handled
club on which a verse was written:

He who gives so that he must beg
Ought to be clubbed until he lies out flat.[26]

A Scottish version of this verse is:

Here is the fair mall
To give a knock on the skull
To the man who keeps no gear for himself
But gives all to his bairns.

There is an element of cultural conflict in reports about peasant
retirement in early-modern Europe. Literate people were in agreement
that the practice was demoralizing and improper. Did they really have a
base for these claims? There may have been some truth in the impression that relationships were not friendly between retired parents and
their children. Many other people close to the peasantry at that time
gave witness that young farmers often wished for the death of their
retired parents as an economic relief to the burdens of the farm. In the

---

[25] Runde (1805): viii n. a.
[26] Granberg, 'Släktklubban' (1934); Trotzig, 'Ätteklubban' (1938). For the Scottish version see Gomme, 'A Highland folk-tale' (1890): 197.

mid-eighteenth century, a priest in a parish in southern Sweden re-corded several occasions of cruelty towards pensioned manorial peasants by their children.[27] He described one case in 1783 of a man so badly neglected by his daughter and son-in-law that the matter came to the attention of the countess, who then went down into the village, entered the farm dwelling, and removed the old man to another of his children further away. This, wrote the priest, 'caused great excitement. For it is a shame which no one has overcome. This action has done great service for the old people, who in many places are suffering.' Retirement was the rule in this parish also. The priest, Severin Schlyter, mentioned that in the 19 years he had been in the congregation he had buried only eight peasants still farming. It was usual for them to retire after 20 years' farming and live on a pension. He stated that this led to real trouble: 'the young who take over the farm are fed up with the elderly, whereby much fighting, conflict and quarrelling comes up'.

A few decades before the incident of the countess, Schlyter wrote down the episode of an old widow who was on bad terms with her daughter-in-law. When the widow became very sick the daughter-in-law would not take care of her any longer. She persuaded her husband to throw the widow into the street. This was done and the widow died soon after. In the neighbouring parish there was a complaint over a daughter and son-in-law who totally refused to maintain an old cot-tager. Instead he had to fend for himself and lived in a horrible shack – 'the worst in the district' – and his death bed was 'an ant-hill crawling with vermin'.

The priest blamed the old for having created the situation which must inevitably lead to conflict. They had not planned for retirement, and had brought up children to be disrespectful. 'He wrongs himself who turns over the farm to his children, if they are badly brought up.' However, he does not go into the difficult economic situation faced by the children immediately on assuming possession of the tenement. For they had to support both their own small children and their aged parents.

The detailed recordings in these church books give a relatively solid background to judging the seriousness of administrative concern over peasant retirement since the eighteenth century. There certainly was a problem, though it could not be solved by the most common proposal, namely abolition. And the problems of the unfriendliness between generations seemed universal, from Lithuania to Finland and southern Germany.

[27] Gaunt, 'I slottets skugga' (1977).

The structure of generational conflict

I shall now try to establish the structural aspects of conflict over peasant retirement and leave aside psychological matters, such as improper upbringing. I shall concentrate on the age of retirement, the size of retirement portions, and the length of time for which maintenance was paid out, together with other economic topics.

In Finland the situation was hardly better than anywhere else. Jacob Tengström, the bishop of Turku, was co-author in 1802 of a work on the disadvantages of peasant retirement. He stated that peasants there usually retired at 50 or 60 but that it was not uncommon for them to do so at 40. They left possession to a son or son-in-law but demanded such a large maintenance fee that the new farmer could hardly pay it. The old people did very little or no farm work, while the young couple with their small children had a disproportionately large burden to carry. The consequences were both economic, in that standards of farm and forest management declined, and moral, in that harmony between the generations disappeared.[28]

Again, the elderly were held to have the greatest responsibility for creating this situation. When setting maintenance levels, they considered only their own comfort. The young peasant 'becomes fenced in and falls into poverty'. The quarrels based on inability to pay the maintenance 'sometimes led to fights, and the children, who are not satisfied with just wishing their parents dead, lay criminal hands on them'.

Anders Schönberg, official historian from Gästrikland in northern Sweden, recounted that in his home parish during the 1790s it was common for a peasant to retire at 60 and leave the farm to the children. But from that moment 'the old are as strange servants on their own land. And if any insensitivity should be mentioned, it is in the treatment of old parents, especially when they have reached the age when they cannot work; then it is no longer hidden that the young wish them a quick departure.'[29]

Can we get behind these narrative descriptions to determine the age at which peasants retired? Was it 60, as Barchaeus says; was it 50, as other writers state; or did it occur after 20 years, as Schlyter mentions?

In many of the countries where peasant retirement was considered a major problem, official and private sociological investigations were

[28] Tengström and Wallenius, 'Underdånig hemställan' (1819).
[29] Presented in Hülphers, *Samlingar til en Beskrifning öfwer Norrland och Gefleborgs län* (1793): 259; a similar situation in the far south of Sweden is described in Öller, *Beskrifning öfwer Jemshögs Sochn i Blekinge* (1800): 56–8.

made. Most of them used survey techniques, and the investigators sent out questionnaires to administrators in different provinces. This was the method employed by Wohlin for Sweden, the Verein für Sozialpolitik for Germany, Karl Schmidt for the Austrian crown lands, and some others.[30] A different type of investigation consisted of an analysis in depth of a district or several villages over a long time. Here church records, probate inventories, court minutes, and land transactions were the sources. This technique was used by Horáček for Bohemia and Moravia and for a suite of works on parts of Finland by Högnäs, Kiviahlo, and Koskikallio.[31] Some of the findings of this latter type of investigation follow.

The Finnish works deal with court districts in three parts of the country – Ostrobothnia, where the population was Swedish-speaking at the time, and Häme and Proper Finland, where Finnish was spoken. These investigations were made between two world wars, but in several cases the historical evidence presented goes back to the beginning of the nineteenth century. At what age did farmers retire? In Ostrobothnia during the first half of the nineteenth century men retired at 57–8 years and women at 54–5. However, the tendency throughout the period up to the First World War was for retirement age to rise. Just before the war retirement age was 65 for men and 62 for women. In Proper Finland in the middle of the nineteenth century the retirement age was 53 for married men and just under 50 for married women. By the beginning of this century the ages had risen to 60 for husbands and 58 for wives. Because of the way the material is presented it is not possible to follow the rise in retirement age over time in Häme. But during the entire nineteenth century the average age on retirement was 58 for men and 54½ for women. The reason for the discrepancy between the two language groups – about five years lower for Finns at retirement age – has to do with the lower age of marriage of Finns during this period.[32]

It is common to believe that farmers in the past kept working until they died or retired only when death was very near. Such people probably existed, but the various in-depth investigations of retirement show that many pensioned themselves off a good time before infirmity

[30] Wohlin, *Faran af Bondeklassens undergräfvande* (1910): 31–55; Schmidt (1920); Verein für Sozialpolitik, *Bäuerliche Zustände in Deutschland* (1883) and an evaluation by Mias-kowski, *Das Erbrecht und die Grundeigenthumsvertheilung*, II (1884), esp. 163–92.

[31] Horáček, *Das Ausgedinge* (1904); Kiviahlo, *Maatalouskiinteistöjen omistajanvaihdokset ja hinnanmuodostus Halikon* (1927); Koskikallio, *Maatalouskiinteistöjen eläkerasituksesta Pirk-kalan ja Ruoveden* (1927); Högnäs, *Sytning och arvslosen i den folkliga sedvänjan* (1938). In eastern areas of Finland, where swidden agriculture was universal, there were seldom any retirement contracts. See Jutikkala, *Bonden i Finland genom tiderna* (1963): 354–6.

[32] Högnäs (1938): 186–9; Koskikallio (1927): 226–30; Kiviahlo (1927): 94–5.

264 *David Gaunt*

set in. In Proper Finland during 1851–5 fewer than a fourth of those retiring were over 60. And retired people lived a good while after they had turned over the farm. In Ostrobothnia, for instance, a young farmer who had contracted to support both his aged parents could count on continuing to care for at least one of them for the next 16 years. Ordinarily one of the parents would have died after 7 or 8 years. The longest period an Ostrobothnian retirement contract was in effect was 52 years. Because people retired earlier among Finnish-speaking populations, the average lifetime of retirement maintenance was longer. In Häme during the second half of the nineteenth century it was 24 years for at least one parent. Usually one of the parents had died after 14 years of care.[33]

A similar pattern emerges from Horáček's study of parts of what is now Czechoslovakia. Here early retirement may have been encouraged by the lords of the manor, since under the *robot*, or special type of serf obligations in use in Bavaria, peasants were liable for very heavy day-labour services. Few lords would tolerate the economic loss involved in having the day labour performed by very old people. As in Finland, marriage age was lower here than amongst western European populations, and this also favoured early turnover. Even the rise of the standing army, which was recruited from the unmarried peasantry, was an impetus to early retirement. If a son could take over the farm and marry he avoided conscription.[34] This is, however, a factor which was not influential in Finland, where soldiers remained in the parish on special farms.

In 1899 the Bohemian Landeskulturrat sent out a questionnaire to functionaries in the districts with questions about the extent of retirement practices, whether pensions were paid in cash, the value of the annual maintenance, the length of time farmers were retired, and the length of time farmers actually cultivated their property. Among other things, they found that peasants worked their lands for between 25 and 35 years, but that they retired early enough to spend 15 to 25 years as pensioners.[35]

Horáček found this presentation methodologically unconvincing and set about a study in depth of four parishes with different economic conditions, in order to shed more light on the retirement problems. In one of the parishes data were unobtainable, and in another, which was a suburb of Prague, there were very few farms burdened with retirement

[33] Högnäs (1938): 192–5; Koskikallio (1927): 227–30.
[34] Horáček (1904): 7–21.
[35] Summarized in Horáček (1904): 29–35.

contracts. Such contracts were, however, much more frequent in the two parishes with prosperous farming – Senomat and Kožušan. In the first parish a full third of all real estate with a net annual produce exceeding 25 florins had a retirement maintenance liability, while in the Moravian parish of Kožušan the proportion was about one-fifth. In Senomat farmers retired on average at 56½ and in Kožušan at 51½ years of age. In the latter place, 8 out of 19 retired persons were under 50 when they retired. The length of retirement was about 8 and 12 years respectively, although it should be noted that these figures do not record the total length of retirement but only the number of years already experienced up to 1899.[36]

In both Finland and Czechoslovakia, early marriage was common. One may wonder whether the retirement age was appreciably higher in areas where marriage came later. In Mönsterås on the south-east coast of Sweden the average age for retirement of men in 1860–90 was 59, and by 1930 it had risen to 60 years. The average total length of retirement was 26 years.[37]

The age at which a farmer turned over his farm during his lifetime was connected with the desire of the younger generation to take control and marry. The earlier the age of marriage, the earlier the retirement. It does not seem that physical infirmity was the decisive factor; otherwise the average length of retirement support would not amount to the 15 to 25 years reported from various places.

But there is a conflict here. If maintenance of the elderly was to be given over a score or more years without the full work input of the parents in the field, then the economic conditions of the new farm couple could have been very depressed. The working capacity of the aged naturally became less and less as the years went on. A decisive element in a structural description of the retirement system must therefore be consideration of the size of the pension given to the elderly.

Calorie calculations on the few total inventories of the food intake in the contracts indicate that many retired people specified deliveries larger than they could consume. A nutritional expert has analysed a

---

[36] Horáček (1904): 38–49.
[37] Cederlund, 'Undantagsinstitutionen i Mönsterås' (1964): 45. Western European areas with relatively early retirement were the south German Schwarzwald and Odenwald – see Miaskowski (1884): 206–7. In Upper Bavaria retirement frequently came between 45 and 50 – see Fick, *Die baüerliche Erbfolge* (1895): 63, 70–1, 74, 87–90. These were places where a cash economy had early made its influence felt. Schmidt (1920): 75–81 mentions that there were few places inhabited by non-Slavs where retirement came before 55–60, but even so the length of retirement was seldom less than 15–20 years. Less precise Norwegian data also show a high age at retirement. See Hovdhaugen, 'Frå det gamle bondesamfunnet i Gudbrandsdalen' (1962): 53.

relatively meagre Danish contract of 1792. It involved only 1 barrel of
rye flour, 20 kilos of pork, ½ bushel of peas, and ¼ barrel of barley
yearly plus a pot of milk for one person daily. Along with beer, it gave a
daily intake of 2,275 calories.[38] This is quite satisfactory today for an
elderly person who is not especially active. However, almost all contracts involved very much more food, as may be seen from those set out
in the appendix to this chapter.

When one Swedish aristocrat at the turn of the last century went
through the archives of one of his estates he was surprised to see the size
of the contracts registered. He took up an example from 1826 in which a
son was to deliver to his father annually 7 barrels of grain, fodder for the
cows, 1 swine, 2 sheep with fodder, and much more. When all this was
given a monetary value, the pension to the father amounted to much
more than double the yearly rent paid to the lord of the manor. The
writer was also convinced that his ancestors had not taken the size of the
retirement contracts into consideration when settling the rent for the
new peasants, 'so it was inevitable that the consequence would be the
ruin of the farmer'.[39]

On Danish estates, however, at least during the eighteenth century,
lords of the manor did take the size of the pension into account. The new
tenant could sometimes be freed from entrance fees or have previous
debts removed. On most estates in Jutland grain was an important
element in the retirement contracts. But the contracts were only to
come into effect in the event that the old and the new tenants could not
agree to eat and live together. The amount of grain was so large that the
old farmers could both eat from it and have some over for sale. Generally
the retired also received a garden, even though it was not always
mentioned in the contract. Usually two persons would receive 2 barrels
of rye and 2 barrels of barley annually. Elderly solitaries might receive a
little over 1 barrel of each sort of grain.[40]

In Finland during the nineteenth century the amount of grain in the
contracts was somewhat larger. The difference between Finland and
Jutland is systematic; in Finland the farmers themselves could to a great
extent determine the size of the retirement payments, whereas in the
Danish cases the lord of the manor intervened to limit the retirement
support. In Ostrobothnia a married elderly pair would receive on aver-

[38] Lemche, 'Kan aftaegtskontrakter tjene til belysning af ernaeringsproblemer?' (1940):
    791–2.
[39] Trolle-Bonde, *Trolleholm förr och nu*, III (1906): 412.
[40] Skrubbeltrang, 'Faestegården som försørger' (1961): 255–63, 272–4. During the eight-
    eenth century 35–40% of the peasants on Danish estates remained active until death,
    30–5% retired on pension, and 25–30% were evicted.

age 3½ barrels of rye and 3 barrels of barley annually. The same amount was delivered in the Carelian part of Kuopio län. Smaller amounts were provided in other Finnish areas, as, for instance, 5 barrels of rye and 1 barrel of barley in Eastern Uusimaa, 5–5½ barrels of rye and 1–1½ barrels of barley in Proper Finland, 3 barrels of rye and 2 barrels of barley in Häme. In addition, throughout the entire nineteenth century there was a steadily increasing supply of potatoes, a product very rarely found as part of retirement deliveries at the start of the century.[41]

The size of food deliveries increased throughout the nineteenth century and up to the First World War. A retirement support for two persons in Ostrobothnia in 1810–24 averaged 3⅓ barrels of rye, 3⅙ barrels of barley, and 2½ barrels of potatoes. By 1900–14 the amounts had increased to 4⅓ barrels of rye, 3¾ barrels of barley, and 6¼ barrels of potatoes.[42]

The hope must have been that the old people and their children would never quarrel with each other so that the contracts would not need to be put into effect. Unfortunately, however, it was not at all uncommon for this necessity to arise, either because of conflict or because the property was not transferred to a kinsman but to a stranger.

Another aspect of retirement economics was the burden of debt on the farm. Originally the turning over of the farm or tenement to a son or son-in-law with the reservation of certain rights and resources had the advantage that little money was involved. A very low value was put on the farm, and the proportions allotted to co-heirs not succeeding to the land were either proportionately low or even lower. Ideas of the farm as a family asset kept the claims of the co-heirs in check.

However, Roman law concepts of civil inheritance which began to permeate the peasantry in the nineteenth century stood in opposition to the relatively inferior treatment of co-heirs. The new ideas involved giving each co-heir an exact proportion of the actual value of the farm, and this value was to be set on the market or sale value of the real estate, not as before on the value of the farm's production. This principle had little influence in central Europe as long as the peasants were under manorial control; but with the freeing of the peasantry at various points throughout the century, it became the most important complication in land transfers during the lifetime of the peasant.[43] Demographic change

[41] Högnäs (1938): 94–105; Ilvonen, *Maataloudellisista oloista Kuopion läänin Karjalan osassa paitsi Kaavin pitäjää* (1888): 12–13; Forsell, *Udenmaa lännin itäinen puoli* (1887): 12; Koskikallio (1927): 64–80; Kiviahlo (1927): 105.
[42] Högnäs (1938): 102–3; similar tendencies are described in Kiviahlo (1927): 105 and Koskikallio (1927): 74–90.
[43] Weber (1941): 55–63.

during the century, resulting in more and more children surviving to inherit, added to this problem.

Horáček found that in the prosperous farming communities of Bohemia and Moravia in 1899 the real estate encumbered with deliverances to elderly retired farmers had a very much greater debt burden than farms without retirement conditions. Those without retired people had a debt burden of less than one-third of the capitalized net produce of the farm, while those with retired people had a debt burden (even when the retirement burden was drawn away) of four-fifths of the capitalized net produce.[44]

Högnäs's study has shown that in the nineteenth century the values put on Ostrobothnian farms at their transfer from parents to children were only about 5% under their market value. In 1810–24, at the beginning of his investigative period, the farms being handed over had on average less than one co-heir to be bought out (i.e. 0.9 co-heirs per farm). This average rose steadily to 2.7 co-heirs not succeeding to the landed property by 1900–14. With a single co-heir, it was relatively easy to persuade the sibling to relinquish claims on a part of the farm, since a co-heir was very likely to marry a main heir somewhere else. But by 1850 the average number of co-heirs had risen to over 2, and then problems were created.[45] This meant that the burden of debt on the young farmer was successively increasing, and that it was more and more often necessary for him to borrow money, even from credit institutions, to pay off brothers and sisters. The same tendency was present in Germany. In Brandenburg in 1883 officials complained: 'The fathers are no longer able to control the wishes of the co-inheriting children, who use the inheritance laws to their own advantage and demand a higher proportion of the wealth. This increases the debt of the farm and, along with wills, causes the sale and splitting up of the farms.'[46]

Retirement in the family cycle

If we look at the family-life-cycle aspect of a peasant economy with a retirement system we can get a further idea of the problems involved in the retirement contract. Here we shall look especially at the ratio be-

[44] Horáček (1904): 44, 49.
[45] Högnäs (1938): 65–8: 77% of male and 91% of female co-heirs received a cash payment. Payment to a sister not succeeding to the farm averaged 10–12% of its declared total value.
[46] Miaskowski (1884): 196.

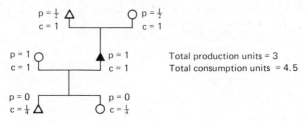

Fig. 8.1. First stage of a possible retirement cycle.

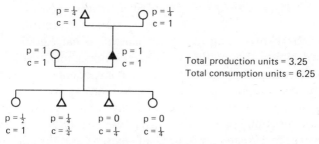

Fig. 8.2. Second stage of a possible retirement cycle.

tween the productive forces – in this case reduced to labourers – and the number of mouths to feed.

We can assign a hypothetical value to each household member's productive capacity and the quantity of food each consumes. These will be called here production and consumption units and will not really be defined in clear terms. What is essential is that each member's units vary somewhat with age. In this manner we can see how different stages in the family cycle would be affected by the retirement contract coming into effect.

Fig. 8.1 shows a newly formed household comprising the retired couple and the young farmer, his wife, and young children. The retirement contract is not in effect, and all live and eat together. The retired pair still do some work on the farm, but eat for a full adult.

After ten years the picture of the same household might be as shown in fig. 8.2. The older children take care of the younger, and in addition may also help in production. However, the productive capacity of the elderly has decreased.

But what happens if there is a conflict between the retired and the active generations and the elderly decide to live separately and take out all the food rations specified in the contract? For simplicity we can assume that they take out twice what they can consume. The situation

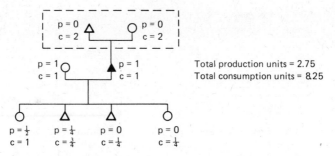

Fig. 8.3. Third stage of a possible retirement cycle.

would be that shown in fig. 8.3. At the same time that the elderly double their food ration, they withdraw from the household. They refuse to participate either physically or with their experience in running the farm. The consumption burden of the farmer, his wife, and children remains unchanged. However, to meet the new situation, either the farmer and his family must work much harder to produce the amount of food needed, or a greater amount of any existing surplus must be taken away from the supply which would normally have been sent to market. A conflict leading to a split between generations could force a farmer in a marginal economic situation to the brink of ruin. Furthermore, this situation could be changed in only one way, namely by the removal of the retirement pension through the death of the parents.

The disappearance of retirement contracts

It will come as no surprise that from the end of the nineteenth century the retirement contract form of land transfer quickly fell out of use throughout Europe. When a survey was made in Sweden just before the First World War it was found that only in the far north and in isolated forested areas of the south were retirement contracts still the rule. In many other places they occurred occasionally, but in important areas they had disappeared entirely.

This did not mean that families were again living so harmoniously that there was no need of contracts. It was rather that the transfer of landed property between generations, if it happened at all, was regulated by money sales. The old people put the money into the bank and pensioned themselves on the interest from the capital, as they would have done in any business relationship.

The areas in Sweden where the contracts first disappeared were those affected by progress in commercial agriculture and by the boom in forest products after the middle of the nineteenth century; that is to say in the southern plains and the western woods. Obviously, money played a role in the disintegration of the retirement contract system. We have already touched on the importance of the new ideas on heirship and the use of market values for real estate instead of productive values in setting inheritances.[47]

In Denmark, where agriculture was geared to the export of bacon and dairy products, mainly to Great Britain, farmers generally had abandoned the retirement contract practices, which were earlier very common, by the end of the nineteenth century. In the eighteenth century, over a third of all changes of tenancy on estates involved the retirement of a peasant on special conditions. In 1891 a law was passed to give economic support to the elderly, but proud farmers preferred not to accept this money. In such cases, where an aged mother or father remained on the children's farm, she or he was maintained not by food deliveries but by a mortgage on the farm which they held. They received the interest on this, and the entire debt was written off on the death of the parent. Still others moved from the isolated farms into the villages and lived off the same sort of interest, buying food and services there.[48]

In Austrian territories, Karl Schmidt found that just before the First World War retirement contracts were not being used in the transfer of farms in those areas most affected by the money economy. In areas with small holdings and much industry one seldom finds farms where parents lived with their children in a contractual relationship. However, where agriculture prospered and holdings were large, such a system still flourished. This would agree with the findings of Horáček for Bohemia and Moravia (see p. 265).[49]

It is a little more difficult to generalize about the developmental pattern in German territories. On prosperous farms in West Prussia in 1883 it was reported that the elderly did not remain on the farm but retired to the city. They were paid an annual interest by the son or son-in-law. Those who were less prosperous stayed on and received room and board together with some interest on the sale. But retirement contracts were not in use, even though these aged people might build their own cottages on the farm land. Here ethnic differences were also perceptible; while the German farmer retired into the city, the Polish

---

[47] For this and the preceding paragraphs see Wohlin (1910): 34–8 on the spread of change through different regions; 48–51 on credit and banking.

[48] Christensen, 'De gamles forsørgelse' (1928): 77–8 for cash pensions; 84–5 for mortgages; 87–8 for reaction to the pension law; 93–5 for movement into towns. See also Siggaard, 'Aftaegtskontrakter og deras Aendringer gennem Tidene' (1944).

[49] Schmidt (1920): 43–50; Horáček (1904): 37–40.

farmer remained at home. Retirement to the city was a relatively new phenomenon:

> Earlier, up to 30 years ago, the peasant proprietor stayed as farmer until 70 or 80, saw to the provisioning of his children from the wealth he had assembled and turned over the farm to the youngest with a retirement pension. Today [1883] when the prices of farms have shot up, most proprietors are well off, but still forgetting their heirs turn over the farm at 40 to 50, seldom later, to the eldest son, who has the unenviable duty of providing for the younger children and supporting the retired farmer for another 20 to 30 years.

Commentators were certain that the retirement payments were higher than the old farmers' needs. In Posen there was a similar ethnic division. 'The smaller the farm, the more Polish the possessor, the earlier he retires.'[50]

In places where movement to towns or large villages was impossible, other substitutes for retirement contracts came into use. On the wealthy Scanian plain in Sweden, one large landowner forbade his tenants to make retirement agreements. Instead, at the will of the landowner, tenants were awarded yearly old-age support, for instance 24% or 15% of the yearly rent they had paid.[51] For those who were less fortunate there was a great expansion in the number and size of Poor Houses, which just before the First World War began to change their names from Poor Houses to Homes for the Aged.

If the new farmer got into economic difficulties because of the problems involved in taking over from parents and meeting the claims of his siblings, he still had one trump card to play. He could avoid the whole predicament by selling the farm anew to someone else and simultaneously specifying a retirement maintenance to be given to his own household. In this manner one farm could be burdened by several 'retired' households. This procedure of passing on debts to another, of course, put the new farmer into an even more difficult situation. In Nykarleby district in Ostrobothnia a full 123 of 572 farms had more than one retired household of elderly to support.[52] The peasant retirement system began to be used as a universal method to avoid rural bankruptcy. An anonymous writer in *Finlands Allmänna Tidning* of 1850 gave a detailed description of this trick. When peasants were in such straitened circumstances that they could neither pay off old debts nor

---

[50] Verein für Sozialpolitik (1883), 23: 236, 243 (the long quotation), 327; 24: 28, 29 (the short quotation).

[51] Trolle-Bonde (1906): 415–16.

[52] Högnäs (1938): 210–11. Similar conditions in East Prussia are mentioned in Verein für Sozialpolitik (1883), 23: 297; and in Silesia and Moravia by Schmidt (1920): 55, 58–9, though in Schmidt's opinion the figures in these provinces were too high (see 61–2).

get any more credit, they had a way of preserving at least a minimum standard of living. The debtor would sell his property, which had been previously mortgaged up to the full market value, for a very low price but on the condition that the buyer took over the debts and gave a retirement portion. Sometimes the seller even mortgaged this retirement portion. The buyer was, of course, enticed by the low price in relation to the market value of the property. But this price could even have been totally imaginary and no real money have changed hands. Often the buyer and seller were in collusion, and the retirement settlement, which must be respected in the courts, was made large enough for both the buyer and seller to live off. Since the buyer assumed the old debts, he was in just as bad a situation as his predecessor, and ultimately the farm was repossessed or went for public auction (excluding the retirement portion). Those who bid, however, took account of the large retirement settlement and made very low offers. The former buyer moved in with the original seller, and they lived off the retirement sum and continued at a minimum standard. The mortgage holders, of course, suffered a great economic loss. This sort of transaction, the writer stated, was constantly becoming more common throughout southern Finland.[53]

The examples presented here give a good impression of how the transition to an economy where cash played a major role changed the function of the traditional retirement contract. In some places the elderly were retiring earlier than before and moving into towns to live off interest as *rentiers*. In other places farmers could use retirement contracts as a dodge to get out of embarrassing financial situations. The young farmer who took over found that he was increasingly getting into debt because of demands by his parents for support and by his siblings for a more equitable portion of the sale value of the real estate.

The rural retirement contract system, at least for farmers who owned their own land, developed during the centuries before industrialization as an integral part of peasant-economy ideology such as that described for Russia by Chayanov. In this system individual comfort was continually sacrificed for the good of the family farm. Parents and adult children remained together as long and as often as possible; siblings not inheriting the main portion of the farmer's property were expected to accept very small amounts of wealth when they left home and on inheritance; the value of the farm at the moment of transfer was never calculated on the actual market of the real estate but rather on the

---

[53] 'Om sytning och dess betydelse' (1850); Högnäs (1938): 218–19; Charpentier (1895): 79.

productive capacity; on many occasions the conditions specified in the retirement contract were not put into effect, existing simply as a guarantee that the farm should not be sold by the children to strangers and that harmony should exist among generations. However, by the middle of the nineteenth century, even in a place like Finland, which was not then noted for being economically advanced, this sort of ideology was breaking down.

When reformers late in the nineteenth century made proposals to better farm conditions, they often tried to reintroduce the old 'peasant economy' morality. A good representative of this movement is the German professor of political science August von Miaskowski, a member of the Verein für Sozialpolitik. In the 1880s he made several proposals, for instance that farms should once again be evaluated on productive value and not on real-estate value on the free market; that siblings not taking over the farm should get only small inheritances and portions; that farmers should not be allowed to retire before they had reached 60; and so on.[54]

The form of the retirement contract developed in the 'peasant economy' had remained the same once a money economy had permeated the rural world. But the meaning and the consequences of the retirement contract system were quite changed. One of the gloomiest and most drastic descriptions of how devastating the contract system was for the peasantry comes from the writings of a schoolteacher and local politician in northern Finland, Anders Svedberg. In 1868 he wrote a brochure entitled 'On the destructive consequences of the emburdenment of farms with retirement' against the background of the massive famine then raging.[55] He noted that there had been famines before, for instance in the 1770s and the 1840s, to name only the worst. But each time, the farm communities had managed to control the crisis; farmers had not lost their possessions even though they starved. The crisis of the 1860s, however, led the peasantry to economic ruin and destitution. Many had lost their farms and would never be able to regain them.

Svedberg attributed this new destitution to the debts rooted in the retirement contracts. He noted that there were many farms with more than one retired household. First were the grandparents, who had the usual large retirement settlement. Thereafter there were the parents, who had just as large a retirement portion when they had become too deeply indebted. They had passed on the farm to a son, who had also not been able to pay the debts or make the farm profitable. Even the son, still

[54] Miaskowski, 'Altenteil, Altenteilsverträge' (1909): 421–2.
[55] Svedberg, *Om de förderfliga, följderna af jordbrukets betungande med sytningar* (1868).

in his 30s, had retired and passed over the property to a stranger. By this time the actual farm was in a poor condition, many resources having been taxed to the limit in a vain attempt to remove the debt while paying the retirement portions. When the crops failed in several successive years all the households were affected, but with a time lag. The first to be brought to ruin was the actual farmer, who was already in debt and had only a marginal standard of living already. He could not make the retirement payments and was evicted. But this meant that the retired households could not be paid in the long run. So one after the other, first the farmer and then the retired families, were forced onto the roads, begging. Svedberg admittedly neglects population growth in his analysis of why the 1867–8 famine took such a large toll. But it is quite conceivable that the retirement system, when used in the way described to pass on debts to successors and preserve one's own position, intensified the effects of a poor harvest by making preparedness for a bad year more difficult.

Occasionally old-age insurance had been proposed as an alternative to the retirement contract. In Germany people like Albert Schäffle and Eugen Jäger in the 1880s suggested that farmers pay yearly instalments towards an old-age pension fund which would give a decent standard of living by the time the farmer had reached 60.[56] Thus there would have been no need for a retirement contract attached to transfers between parents and children. The new farmer would not need to borrow money to finance the old age of his parents. But these proposals could not be put into effect, since few farmers had the type of stable extra income each year that such a scheme demanded.

In Austria, too, there was very active agitation for a general old-age insurance for farmers as a substitute for the retirement contract. As early as 1873 a meeting of agriculturalists recommended the creation of an insurance system. Demands steadily increased in the 1890s, and a large public opinion campaign formed itself around the wandering teacher Stephan Richter.[57]

However, even if these insurance schemes had been launched, it was highly unlikely that the farmers could ever have received more than symbolic annual sums. They might have improved the situation somewhat by making retirement contracts smaller or enabling the retired to pay the children for their upkeep. But most farmers had already seen the solution to their problem in the very practice which most reformers

---

[56] Miaskowski (1909): 414–22.
[57] Habermann, 'Das bäuerliche Ausgedinge und sein Ersatz' (1908): 627–30; Richter, *Das bäuerliche Ausgedinge* (1891).

wanted to stop, namely the selling of farms at market value followed by retirement on the bank interest. From the end of the nineteenth century retirement contracts have been abandoned in most parts of central and northern Europe.

Conclusion

As far as possible I have tried to simplify the very complicated relations among generations in farm families in the past. Only through simplification can the structural features of the historic changes be seen. This chapter has covered conditions in many countries over many centuries, and it has attempted a synthesis of social, economic, and legal historical literature. There will, therefore, obviously be points in the argument which can be challenged, expanded, or further developed. But such a discussion must centre on the structure of relations between parents and children, the ideologies of property and evaluation of wealth, and the function of the written retirement contract, rather than individual details.

Throughout this presentation the conditions of old farmers have been related to the prevalent type of economy, to the organization of inheritance *inter vivos*, and to the way family property was esteemed. In the Middle Ages, old farmers were either subject to living in the households of strangers or kin, or they were put into new households through the intervention of the manorial lord. They often rotated among various households. When no lord owned the land, ownership stayed in the parents' hands and was not transferred to the adult children until death. But this ownership really differed from the modern conceptions of the word, since disposal and running of the farms were subject to the consent of many others.

During early-modern times a new view of property came into play both among independent farmers and manorial peasants. From this time the lord of the manor was seen as the party most affected if the tenants retired and encumbered the tenement with a pension on its transfer. Among farmers owning their land, retirement transfers were seen as involving a real change of ownership to the younger generation. Therefore, the interests of both the manorial lord and the independent retired peasant combined in the emergence of documents for change of title which specified, in considerable detail, the items to be reserved for the old farmer's use. In the two situations the decisive persons were different: in one, the lord of the manor determined the size of the ration and the moment of retirement; in the other, the decisions lay with the old farmer himself. Thus the pensions of independent farmers could be much larger than those for manorial serfs. However, with the freeing of the peasantry in the nineteenth century the number of farmers owning their own land expanded greatly.

The gradual permeation of rural society by cash, which occurred at various times in different places, placed great strain on the retirement system developed after the Reformation. As noted above, this system was based on peasant-family ideology with no room for thought of individual well-being among the members of the farm household. The main objective of the retirement system may even have been to hinder the entrance of individual economic thinking into family life. The transfer *inter vivos* could be used to circumvent laws on equal inheritance passed by enlightened governments. There were certainly attempts to keep the stated price of the farm low, and portions going to the few co-heirs were minimized.

But new ideas came with the blossoming of the market economy. Chief among them were that farms had not just a value based on production, but also a speculative free-market value. And the latter was higher in most places than the capitalized value of production. At the same time co-heirs were no longer satisfied with the minimal portions they had accepted before. There were many more of them, since more were surviving to adulthood, and the likelihood of their getting married to a main heir somewhere else was thus constantly decreasing. The Roman law ideas of equal inheritance applied first to males, then to females at stages throughout the nineteenth century. And these co-heirs had a direct advantage in getting their portions evaluated on the market value of the real estate.

The old people were also attracted by money. Many looked forward to 20 or more years of retirement. If the pension was large enough, a part could even be sold, or the whole thing could be paid in money. But in any case they preferred to take a mortgage on the old farm and move into rapidly expanding towns and buy services and foodstuffs from the interest paid them.

Both the equal or larger payments to co-heirs and the mortgaging of farms for pensioning could hardly have come into existence if the farms were not involved in a money economy. For the farmer taking over, this was not so much a matter of going to market and selling produce, although this happened all the time. It was rather a question of money borrowed all at once from somewhere to meet the claims of his closest relatives. It meant getting into debt to meet family obligations. This was a condition which was unproductive and enervating and led to the abandonment of the entire contractual rural retirement system.

APPENDIX
Types of retirement contract

I. South-east coast of Sweden, 1904

When I today, with the consent of my wife, sell our property ¹/₁₂ of Garö number 1 to our son Oskar, so we have reserved for us the following retirement privileges to be given yearly for the rest of our lives, namely free care and attention as needed plus:

(1) Free use of the two small rooms on the ground floor plus parts of the kitchen and cellar and woodshed.
(2) three piles of fir-wood, two piles of pine-wood, all dry and of good quality delivered to the woodshed.
(3) three barrels of rye, four barrels of potatoes.
(4) one and a half pitchers of sweet milk daily during the summer reckoned from 1 May to 1 November and a pint of sweet milk daily during the other six months.
(5) fodder for one sheep both summer and winter.
(6) a fourth of the produce of the garden, yearly.

The advantages specified in the above shall be yearly delivered to us, and should be of good quality. The year shall be reckoned from the 1st of October.

Source: Cederlund (1964): 47.

II. North-west coast of Finland, 1816

Hereby we give to our son Jonas our property ⁵/₂₄ of Ållandt farm in Nykarleby parish. In return he will give the following pension (*sytning*) namely: two barrels of rye and two barrels of barley, one firkin of *strömming* (salted small herring), a *lispund* of butter, two shirts, one pair of stockings, a pair of winter boots, a pair of Bothnian shoes, a striped linen handkerchief, a padded vest and two *kappelands* for planting potatoes yearly, plus one-half pitcher sweet and one-half pitcher sour milk daily throughout the year. A good sheep slaughtered each autumn and a pitcher of *brännvin* on all the Christmas holidays. Every third year a new padded sweater and long trousers, a new church-going scarf and a linen long shirt. Every sixth year a new padded coat.

Ride to church and to the mill and other necessary travel when needed.

In payment for the farm Jonas will give to his sister Brita Lena one thousand *dalers* plus one cow and two sheep. This is to be given to her either at her marriage or our deaths – there will be no other inheritance. To his sister Maria after either of us dies: yearly as long as she lives one barrel of grain, a cow, and a sheep to use plus two and a half loads of hay. A batch of rye straw, a summer load of barley straw plus one and a half barrels of chaff for their annual feeding. But in case she marries, the hay and other items disappear. If she remains on the farm she will get for her services 8 *dalers* yearly plus room and heating.

To our son-in-law, Anders, Jonas shall give upon his moving into the cottage two cows and two small and two large sheep.

Jonas will be sole owner of all remaining chattels of animals, farm equipment, etc. except one-third of the *brännvin* distillery.

Should Jonas turn over the farm to a stranger, the other heirs have the right to take back the whole property according to the above-mentioned terms.

Source: Högnäs (1938): 229–30.

III. Northern Zealand, Denmark, 1785

Our son-in-law Peder will pay to us for the farm Gentofte once and for all 100 *rigsdaler*. We reserve the use of the old large house and Peder will build a new one for himself.

In addition he will pay us yearly a pension of 20 *rigsdaler*, 3 barrels of good rye flour, 3 barrels of malt brewed into good quality beer, 1 barrel of unmilled rye, 1 barrel of barley, 1 barrel of oats. Four geese with their goslings well fatted, 4 sheep with their lambs fed winter and summer, 2 fresh swine yearly and 1 barrel of good butter. Two pots of milk daily when the cows are milking and 8 loads of peat-turf. Care and maintenance with woollens, linens, and cleanliness.

Source: Lemche (1940): 791.

9

Pre-industrial household structure in Hungary

RUDOLF ANDORKA and TAMÁS FARAGÓ

Introduction

Hungarian social anthropologists[1] have tended to assume that in pre-industrial times Hungarian peasants lived in large households containing at the same time families of parents and several married children. But when the size and structure of households were investigated by historians by means of listings of inhabitants of villages and of large estates in past centuries, the average size was found to be small.[2] Using the published summarized results of the first census in 1784–7, J. Tamásy, a demographer, found that the average size of households in Hungary, Transylvania and Croatia together was 5.28 persons.[3]

Laslett found that in England and in parts of north-western Europe, contrary to the assumption of many sociologists and historians, the average size of households was small and the proportion of households with a complex structure – that is, extended- and multiple-family households – was also low.[4] On the other hand, research into the nature of Serbian households revealed that in Serbian society complicated households of the *zadruga* type were very common,[5] while Peter Czap's

---

[1] See e.g. Morvay, *Asszonyok a nagycsaládban* (1956) and 'The joint family in Hungary' (1965).

[2] Veress, 'A jobbágycsalád szervezete a sárospataki uradalom falvaiban a 17. század közepén' (1958); Taba, 'Baranya megye család és lélekszáma 1696-ban' (1962); Kosáry, 'A paraszti familia kérdéséhez a 18. század elején' (1963); Zimányi, *A rohonc-szalonaki uradalom és jobbágysága a XVI–XVII. században* (1968).

[3] Tamásy, 'Az 1784–1787. évi első magyarországi népszámlálás család- és háztartásstatisztikai vonatkozásai' (1963).

[4] P. Laslett, 'Introduction' (1972b).

[5] Halpern, 'Town and countryside in Serbia' (1972); Hammel, 'The zadruga as process' (1972); Laslett and Clarke, 'Houseful and household in an eighteenth-century Balkan city' (1972); Hammel and Laslett, 'Comparing household structure' (1974).

chapter in the present volume presents results on nineteenth-century Russia showing very large and complex households among serf peasants (see chapter 3).

Thus the type of household structure and the size of households prevalent in pre-industrial Hungary are open questions, and it would be interesting to ascertain whether Hungarian household structure resembled the western rather than the eastern European pattern. The question is complicated by the fact that in the eighteenth and nineteenth centuries the populations of Hungary, Transylvania, and Croatia were very heterogeneous in social status (serfs, cotters, artisans, etc.), ethnicity, and religion.

Sources

The published results of the first census of Hungary, 1784–7, make it possible to investigate the mean size of households and the average number of men aged 18 or over per household.[6] The original census lists are, unfortunately, available only in exceptional cases. When these original census sheets can be found, they provide a good source for investigating not only the size, but also the structure of households and their variations.[7] In addition, *status animarum*-type listings of the population of certain communities were prepared from the mid-eighteenth century to the first years of the nineteenth century by priests and pastors, sometimes on their own initiative and sometimes at the request of higher authorities. Many listings of this type are available, for example the complete listings of the diocese of the Bishop of Veszprém,[8] as well as those of individual parishes.[9] Some earlier listings were prepared for administrative purposes. The listing of Szigetvár, for instance, was prepared in order to provide data on the number of people who fled to the town to seek protection from the invading Turkish armies, while the lists of the settlements of Baranya were prepared to assess the number of people residing in the area after the expulsion of the Turks.

---

[6] Tamásy (1963); Faragó, 'Household structure and rural society in pre-industrial Hungary' (1976); Dányi, 'Háztartás és család nagysága és strukturája az iparosodás előtt Magyarországon' (1977).

[7] Thirring, 'Jászberény népessége és társadalmi viszonyai II. József korában' (1935a), 'Kecskemét népessége és társadalmi viszonyai II. József korában' (1935b), and 'Egy alföldi falu népessége viszonyai II. József korában, Magyarcsanád' (1935c); Danyi, 'Városi háztartások és családok a 18. század végén' (1965).

[8] Dávid, *A családok nagysága és összetétele a veszprémi püspökség területén 1747–1748* (1973); Faragó, 'Household structure of Nagykovácsi in the eighteenth century' (1975).

[9] Mándoki, 'A kölkedi népszámlálás 1816' (1971); Bárth, 'Fajsz népessége a 18. század közepén' (1975); Andorka, 'Peasant family structure' (1976a).

Fig. 9.1. Location in Hungary of the communities studied.

These listings are extant and have been analysed.[10] Investigations by social anthropologists also provide insight into household structure in past centuries.[11]

Thus sources of data on household structure are relatively plentiful. Unfortunately, however, the studies carried out in earlier years did not use uniform methods, and it is therefore difficult to compare the results of the different studies and to see clearly the types and varieties of household structure in Hungary. The typology elaborated by Peter Laslett[12] makes it possible to use a standardized method by which results of different Hungarian studies can be compared with each other and with the household structures of other countries.

Micro-studies

The communities investigated by the Laslett method are shown in fig. 9.1, and are as follows:

[10] Taba (1962); Szakály, 'Sziget mezőváros, Somogy megye, lakosságának "connumeratiója" 1551-ben' (1970).
[11] Fél, 'A nagycsalád és jogszokási' (1944) and 'A magyar népi társadalom életének kutatása' (1948); Fél and Hofer, *Arányok és mértékek az átányi gazdálkodásban és háztartásban* (1967) and *Proper peasants* (1969).
[12] P. Laslett (1972b): 31.

Nagykovácsi is a village near Buda and Pest, two urban centres in central Hungary which were developing rapidly in the eighteenth century. In the seventeenth century the village was inhabited by Roman Catholic German peasants, who immigrated after the liberation from Turkish occupation in 1686. Situated in a valley, Nagykovácsi is surrounded by forests.

Perbál, a village in the neighbourhood of Nagykovácsi, was a new settlement dating from around 1720–30 and inhabited partly by Germans who came from the neighbouring villages, including Nagykovácsi, and partly by Hungarian and Slovak peasants. Perbál is situated on a plain, and the surrounding land is more fertile than that around Nagykovácsi.

Pilisszántó, also near Buda and Pest, was inhabited mostly by Slovak peasants who immigrated around 1700 after the Turkish domination. Situated in a mountainous area, it had little arable land and was very poor.[13]

The fourth village, Fajsz, in southern Hungary on the river Danube, was inhabited by Roman Catholic Hungarian peasants who claimed to be noblemen. The ecclesiastical landlord did not have much influence over them. Arable land was very scarce, because the village was situated in an area often inundated by the Danube; animal husbandry and fruit growing were therefore important.[14]

Sárpilis and Alsónyék are two neighbouring villages in the Sárköz region of southern Transdanubia, also on the river Danube and not far from Fajsz but on the other side of the river. They were inhabited by Hungarian Calvinists. Here arable land was very scarce because the area was marshy and often inundated. In such a situation animal husbandry, hunting, and fishing provided a livelihood.[15]

Kölked is also in southern Transdanubia, on the river Danube but somewhat to the south of the Sárköz region. It was inhabited by Hungarian Calvinists, and the ecological conditions were very similar to those of the Sárköz country.[16]

In addition, we can utilize data on the distribution of households by size in four other communities: Magyarcsanád, a village in the southeastern part of the Great Plain area, inhabited by a population of mixed

[13] The listings of these three villages were prepared in the framework of the *status animarum* enumerations ordered by the Bishop of Veszprém.
[14] The *status animarum* enumeration was ordered by the Bishop of Kalocsa. The listing was first published by Bárth (1975).
[15] The listings were prepared by the local pastors.
[16] The listing was prepared by the local pastor and was first published by Mándoki in 1971.

Hungarian–Serbian–Rumanian ethnicity;[17] two agricultural market towns in the north-central parts of the Great Plain, the first, Jászberény, being inhabited by Roman Catholic Hungarians and the second, Kecskemét, by Calvinist Hungarians, the population of both being more or less free from the bonds of serfdom;[18] and, finally Győr, a town in western Hungary, inhabited mostly by Roman Catholics of mixed German and Hungarian ethnicity, occupied only for a very short period by the Turkish Empire and therefore continuously under the influence of western Europe. Of the Hungarian communities investigated by us it was in every respect the most like a western European town.[19]

In most studies using the Laslett method it is a problem to know for certain whether those who were listed together did in fact constitute a household, that is whether they were really living in one dwelling or house, or formed one unit for the purposes of housekeeping. For ancient peasant communities an additional criterion of the household might be suggested, namely common production. As Fél and Hofer point out,[20] common housing, consumption, and production were not necessarily linked, many different combinations being possible, such as common dwelling, separate consumption, common production.[21] In the first Hungarian census, as well as in the subsequent enumerations of the non-noble population from 1804 to 1847, the basic principle applied was that those who cook together constitute one *familia*, even when they dwell separately, that is in separate houses on the same plot. In those decades it was customary for married children of serf peasants to live in separate houses built near to the main house of the parents, often on the same plot. It may therefore be considered that the first census and the non-noble enumerations give a true picture of household structure. In the case of enumerations carried out by other institutions, for example *status animarum*-type listings, we mostly do not know the enumerator's instructions, that is the principle on which people were grouped in the listing. Thus we are bound to accept that those who were listed as living together, mostly indicated by serial numbers, by letters, by horizontal lines, or in some cases by stating the number of persons in the given unit, formed a household.[22]

The classification of servants and of those cotters who did not have

[17] Thirring (1935c).
[18] Thirring (1935a) and (1935b).
[19] Dányi (1965).
[20] Fél and Hofer (1967).
[21] Cf. Plakans, ch. 5 above, pp. 188–90.
[22] See P. Laslett (1972b): 86–8.

houses[23] causes additional problems. They were treated differently in various listings. In some cases houseless cotters and servants were simply enumerated at the end of the list;[24] in others the household to which they belonged was indicated;[25] and in still others they were listed within the household to which they belonged.[26] It is difficult to decide whether they formed separate households or were members of the household of the serf peasant to whom they were attached.[27] Probably there were many intermediate situations. It seems that they shared the plot, residing in a second house or in the stable on the plot, or lived, at least in summer, in the serf's second house built on land somewhat distant from the village. It seems likely that they shared in some of the consumption and participated in the production of the serf farm. On the other hand, at least some of them may have worked also for other serf peasants. In earlier publications these houseless cotters and servants were treated differently,[28] but in this paper we have adopted the principle that servants and houseless cotters who have no family are treated as members of the households to which they belong, except when it is stated explicitly that they live independently, and that servants and houseless cotters with a family (a spouse and/or children) are treated as separate households.[29] In table 9.5 below, however, these families of servants and houseless cotters, which were treated in other tables as separate households, are shown in separate columns in order to give an idea of their household structure and of the influence their treatment as households may have had on our results.

Mean household size and the distribution of households by number of members (table 9.1) was highest in the three southern Transdanubian

[23] 'Cotter' is essentially a legal category, meaning a non-noble member of the village community, having no serf farm but participating in some other rights – for example, pasture – and duties of the village community. From a sociological point of view the category was heterogeneous: (a) some cotters owned some land, but in the form of non-serf land, for example, cleared woodland; (b) others had very little or no land, but owned a house; (c) some cotters had no house of their own, but lived in the house of a serf peasant, working for the serf and possibly also for others; (d) the legal category 'cotter' also included artisans; cf. below, p. 294.
[24] E.g. Sárpilis, 1792.
[25] E.g. Sárpilis, 1804.
[26] E.g. Fajsz, 1762.
[27] Compare Plakans (1975a) and Palli, 'Perede struktuurist ja selle uurimisest' (1974).
[28] In earlier publications the servants and houseless cotters were consistently included in the household of the serf in whose house they lived, even if they had a family of their own. Consultations with ethnologists convinced us that these servant and cotter families might have had separate households, for example preparing and eating food as separate family units, even if they lived in the house of the serf family.
[29] In the three villages of Nagykovácsi, Perbál, and Pilisszántó, where the listings enabled us to distinguish cotters from servants, we have been able to class all cotters as forming separate households.

Table 9.1. *Distribution of households by size*

No. of persons in household	Perbál 1747 (%)	Pilis-szántó 1747 (%)	Nagykovácsi		Fajsz 1762 (%)	Magyar-csanád 1787 (%)	Jász-berény 1787 (%)	Kecskemét 1787 (%)	Györ 1787 (%)	Sárpilis		Alsónyék 1792 (%)	Kölked 1816 (%)
			1747 (%)	1769 (%)						1792 (%)	1804 (%)		
1	2	3	6	3	1	3	2	2	6	3	1	2	—
2	11	19	12	10	8	18	10	11	15	4	3	4	5
3	16	21	17	9	9	12	15	15	20	11	9	9	12
4	20	11	11	19	13	14	20	17	20	10	22	18	17
5	18	11	14	15	17	15	17	17	15	27	17	20	22
6	18	11	17	12	18	11	16	14	10	17	11	15	15
7	5	10	9	12	11	13	9	10	6	16	13	14	6
8	6	10	6	10	10	5	6	} 12	4	5	11	11	9
9	2	3	6	4	6	3	3		2	3	10	4	4
10	2	—	1	3	3	2	1		1	—	1	1	2
11	—	1	—	1	1	1	1	} 2	} 1	1	1	1	5
12	—	—	1	—	—	—	} 1			1	—	—	1
≥13	—	—	—	—	3	3				2	1	1	2
TOTAL[a]	100	100	100	100	100	100	100	100	100	100	100	100	100
N	105	98	140	190	173	239	2,117	453	2,982	82	91	122	122
Mean size of household	4.67	4.61	4.82	5.28	5.91	5.13	4.92	5.08	4.30	5.53	5.77	5.80	5.75

[a] In this and subsequent tables the rounding up or down of individual percentage entries has resulted in some cases where the columns do not total exactly 100%.

287

288 Rudolf Andorka and Tamás Faragó

Table 9.2. *Distribution of households by generational depth*

No. of generations in household	Perbál 1747 (%)	Pilis-szántó 1747 (%)	Nagykovácsi 1747 (%)	1769 (%)	Fajsz 1762 (%)	Sárpilis 1792 (%)	1804 (%)	Alsónyék 1792 (%)	Kölked 1816 (%)
1	10	21	19	15	7	6	3	5	4
2	81	69	71	73	65	80	66	58	59
3	8	10	10	12	27	14	31	36	36
4	—	—	—	—	1	—	—	1	2
Not known	1	—	—	—	—	—	—	—	—
TOTAL	100	100	100	100	100	100	100	100	100
N	105	98	140	190	173	82	91	122	112

villages, Sárpilis, Alsónyék, and Kölked, and in Fajsz, which is situated on the opposite bank of the Danube in the Great Plain but very near to Sárpilis and Alsónyék and in similar ecological conditions. In the account that follows, therefore, these four settlements will be referred to as the southern Transdanubian villages. In the three villages around Buda, Perbál, Pilisszántó, and Nagykovácsi, the mean size was lower and large households much less common, as they were in the two towns Jászberény and Kecskemét and the village of Magyarcsanád in the Great Plain. The lowest mean household size was found in Győr, a town in western Transdanubia. It is remarkable that in both the villages for which two listings survive the mean household size increased considerably between the date of the first listing and the date of the second, although very different ecological and economic conditions obtained and they were inhabited by people of different ethnicity and religion.

Similarly, the proportion of three- and four-generational households varied in different geographical areas (see table 9.2). The four southern Transdanubian villages had many more three-generational households than the three villages around Buda. In Sárpilis the proportion of three-generational households grew considerably between 1792 and 1804, resulting in an increased average household size.

The composition of households was also analysed by calculating the average number of heads and spouses, their never-married children and other kin (including married children), and servants.[30] The number of other kin was clearly much greater in southern Transdanubia, while the

---

[30] For tables made out on similar principles for rural Denmark, rural India, and rural China see above, Hajnal, tables 2.1–3, 5; for rural West Flanders see below, Wall, table 12.5; and for south-east Bruges see below, Wall, table 14.7.

Table 9.3. *Mean number of household members by their relationship to the head of the household*

Village	Head of household and spouse	Offspring of head in conjugal family unit	Other kin of head, including ever-married offspring	Servant	Lodger and unknown	Mean size of total household	Mean size of head's conjugal family unit
Perbál, 1747	1.93	2.38	0.23	0.10	0.04	4.68	4.31
Pilisszántó, 1747	1.90	1.71	0.66	0.33	0.01	4.61	3.61
Nagykovácsi, 1747	1.89	2.19	0.35	0.38	0.01	4.82	4.08
1769	1.92	2.36	0.42	0.58	—	5.28	4.28
Fajsz, 1762	1.84	2.31	1.67	0.08	0.01	5.91	4.15
Sárpilis, 1792	1.83	2.61	1.07	0.08	—	5.53	4.44
1804	1.85	2.33	1.50	0.09	—	5.77	4.18
Alsónyék, 1792	1.67	1.86	2.03	0.21	0.03	5.80	3.53
Kölked, 1816	1.55	1.70	2.48	—	0.02	5.75	3.25

Table 9.4. *Mean number of servants, houseless cotters, and lodgers per household*

Village		per household	
	Servant	Cotter	Lodger
Perbál, 1747	0.10	0.39	0.02
Pilisszántó, 1747	0.33	0.19	—
Nagykovácsi, 1747	0.38	0.49	0.01
1769	0.58	0.46	—
Fajsz, 1762	0.08	0.17	0.01
Sárpilis, 1792	0.08	0.17	—
1804	0.09	0.33	—
Alsónyék, 1792	0.21	0.04	0.01
Kölked, 1816	—	—	0.02

number of servants was much greater around Buda, with the exception of Perbál. Also the number of other kin increased in Sárpilis between 1792 and 1804, while in Nagykovácsi the greatest increase came in the rise of servants from 1747 to 1769, causing a growth in average household size. Families differed, therefore, mostly in the number of other kin (including married children) and of servants they contained (table 9.3).

However, when the number of cotters belonging to the households were considered (table 9.4), another difference was discovered. In the poor Slovak village of Pilisszántó very few houseless cotters living in other households were found, while their number was high in the two villages around Buda, where the population was largely or entirely of German origin. In Fajsz and Sárpilis the majority of cotters were married couples, often with children. Therefore the mean number of cotters per household was fairly high, but not as high as in the two German villages near Buda. It is not clear why no servants and cotters were found in Kölked.

When we compare these characteristics of Hungarian communities with those of western Europe, more particularly of England and France on the one hand,[31] and with communities in Serbia[32] and in Russia[33] on the other, we find that household size was somewhat higher in southern Transdanubia than in western Europe, but approximated western European levels in the villages near Buda and in the towns of the Great Plain. In the town of Győr, household size was particularly low. But households in all the Hungarian communities which we have investigated were on average smaller than in Russia and in the true *zadrugas*.

In the villages around Buda three- and four-generational households seem to have occurred with about the same frequency as in western Europe, but the frequency was much higher in southern Transdanubia, although not as high as in Russia.

The number of servants per household was similar to western Europe in Nagykovácsi, but much lower in southern Transdanubia. Another important difference was that in Nagykovácsi servants were not married, while in southern Transdanubia they were often married and had children. In the latter region they cannot always be distinguished from cotters, as their designation in the lists is often ambiguous. Clearly in southern Transdanubia the number of adult servants and cotters (omitting their children) was much lower than in western Europe. This could be interpreted as due to a different organization of work. Even before the Industrial Revolution the mobility of manpower was much greater in western Europe than in Hungary, since it was not inhibited by law as it was in Hungary until 1785. In the west wage labour supplied the needs of farms and workshops to a high degree. But in Hungary, because of the more rigid feudal conditions, the lower population density, and the underdeveloped infrastructure, the manpower demand of familial

[31] P. Laslett and Wall (eds.), *Household and family* (1972).
[32] Halpern (1972); Hammel (1972).
[33] See Czap, ch. 3 above.

economic units was for the most part met by members of the family. It may be inferred that the German immigrants and their descendants imported western European patterns of work organization and lived under better economic conditions than the peasants of southern Transdanubia.

Although this information on the size and composition of households in Hungary provides an interesting insight into their distinguishing features, their differences, and their tendencies to change, the analysis of households by means of the typology elaborated by Peter Laslett[34] elucidates these features even better (tables 9.5 and 9.6).

For Hungary it seems useful to introduce a further distinction, namely to divide multiple-family households (type 5) into three groups, as shown in table 9.7: (1) those containing one parental conjugal family unit and only one conjugal family unit of one of their ever-married offspring (stem family type); (2) those containing in addition to the parental conjugal family more than one conjugal family unit of their ever-married offspring (patriarchal family type); (3) those containing several conjugal family units of brothers or sisters, but no parental conjugal family unit (frérèche type, this being identical with types 5c and 5d of the Laslett typology).

In the three villages around Buda the distribution of households by types was very similar to western Europe, the overwhelming majority being of the simple-family household type. On the other hand, in the four southern Transdanubian villages the proportion of extended- and even more of multiple-family households was much higher than in western Europe, but about the same as in Estonia,[35] lower than in Latvia,[36] lower still than in Russia,[37] and probably also lower than in the Serbian *zadrugas*.[38] Another difference between southern Transdanubian and western European households was the marked absence of solitaries in the four Transdanubian villages.[39]

The frequency of households of the patriarchal and frérèche type among multiple-family households was also very different in the villages of southern Transdanubia from those around Buda. In the former region we find an important number of these, although households of the stem type predominated, while around Buda they were very rare.

[34] (1972b): 28–34.
[35] Palli (1974).
[36] Plakans (1975a).
[37] See Czap, ch. 3 above.
[38] Hammel (1972); Halpern (1972).
[39] This may have been caused by our treatment of unmarried persons without children attached to some of the serf households. We included them in the household, except for those cases where it was explicitly stated that they had a separate household.

Table 9.5. *Household structure: number of households by type*

Household type	Perbál 1747	Pilisszántó 1747	Nagykovácsi 1747	Nagykovácsi 1769	Fajsz 1762 Independent households	Fajsz 1762 Servant families	Sárpilis 1792 Independent households	Sárpilis 1792 Servant families	Sárpilis 1804 Independent households	Sárpilis 1804 Servant families	Alsónyék 1792 Independent households	Alsónyék 1792 Servant families	Kölked 1816 Independent households	Kölked 1816 Servant families	Kölked 1816 Lodger family
1. Solitaries															
1a. Widow(er)	1	3	6	5	1	—	—	—	—	—	2	—	—	—	—
1b. Single	—	1	2	—	—	—	2	—	1	—	1	—	—	—	—
2. No-family household	1	—	—	—	1	—	—	—	—	—	—	—	—	—	—
3. Simple-family household															
3a. Married couple alone	10	17	16	24	7	2	3	—	1	1	2	1	4	—	—
3b. Married couple with child(ren)	77	49	89	115	74	5	52	1	39	5	49	1	42	—	—
3c. Widower with child(ren)	—	—	1	1	1	—	—	—	1	—	1	—	2	—	—
3d. Widow with child(ren)	3	3	5	7	7	1	—	3	1	2	—	—	4	—	1
4. Extended-family household															
4a. Extended upwards	5	6	6	6	11	—	2	—	4	—	13	—	13	—	—
4b. Extended downwards	1	—	1	—	4	—	—	—	—	—	—	—	1	—	—
4c. Extended laterally	—	1	2	5	3	—	2	—	3	—	5	—	1	—	—
4d. Combinations 4a–c	—	1	1	—	—	—	—	—	—	—	—	—	—	—	—
5. Multiple-family household															
5a. Secondary unit(s) up	2	1	4	18	1	—	11	—	2	—	2	—	2	—	—
5b. Secondary unit(s) down	1	11	2	6	39	—	—	—	25	—	30	—	34	—	—
5c and d. Units on one level	1	3	2	2	13	—	4	—	5	—	11	—	4	—	—
5e. Other multiple families	1	2	1	1	3	—	2	—	1	—	4	—	4	—	—
6. Not classifiable	2	—	2	—	—	—	—	—	—	—	—	—	—	—	—
Total no. of households	105	98	140	190	165	8	78	4	83	8	120	2	111	—	1

Table 9.6. Household structure: proportion of households by type

Household type	Perbál 1747 (%)	Pilis- szántó 1747 (%)	Nagyko- vácsi 1747 (%)	1769 (%)	Fajsz 1762 (%)	Sárpilis 1792 (%)	1804 (%)	Alsón- yék 1792 (%)	Kölked 1816 (%)
1. Solitaries	1	3	6	3	1	2	1	2	—
2. No-family household	1	1	—	—	1	—	—	—	—
3. Simple-family household	85	71	79	77	56	72	54	44	47
4. Extended-family household	6	8	7	6	10	5	9	15	13
5. Multiple-family household	5	17	7	14	32	21	36	39	36
6. Not classifiable	2	—	1	—	—	—	—	—	4
TOTAL	100	100	100	100	100	100	100	100	100
N	105	98	140	190	173	82	91	122	112
Proportion of complex households categories 4–6)	13	25	15	20	42	26	45	54	53

Table 9.7. Number of multiple-family households by the kinship relation of the conjugal family units contained in them

Village	1 parental conjugal family unit 1 conjugal family unit of ever-married offspring	1 parental conjugal family unit More than 1 conjugal family unit of ever-married offspring	Several conjugal family units of brother and/or sister and their spouses only	Total
Perbál, 1747	3	1	1	5
Pilisszántó, 1747	12	1	4	17
Nagykovácsi, 1747	7	—	2	9
1769	24	—	2	26
Fajsz, 1762	34	8	14	56
Sárpilis, 1792	11	2	4	17
1804	24	3	5	32[a]
Alsónyék, 1792	32	4	11	47
Kölked, 1816	20	16	4	40

[a] One of the 33 multiple-family households in Sárpilis in 1804 shown in table 9.5 is not included here, as the relation of its nuclear families is unclear.

Again, the tendency for household structure to become more complicated can be seen clearly in the case of the two villages for which we
have two listings. The change is fairly dramatic in Transdanubian Sárpilis, where the two listings are separated by 12 years, but it is also
pronounced in Nagykovácsi, near Buda, where 18 years elapsed between the two listings. It seems as if household structure in the village
inhabited by German immigrants became gradually more akin to that
prevailing in the autochthonous Hungarian villages.

A note should be added about the servant and cotter families in Fajsz,
Sárpilis, and Alsónyék. All of them were of the simple-family household type. If we were not to treat them as separate households, but as
members of the households who owned the house in which they lived,
the proportion of simple-family households would be even lower and
the difference from western Europe would be greater.

In sum, household structure in Hungary in the eighteenth century
and in the first two decades of the nineteenth century seems to have
been intermediate between western Europe on the one hand and Serbia
and Russia on the other hand, but important differences existed within
the country: some parts resembled western Europe; others, eastern
Europe. However, differences in household structure did not exist only
between regions, but also between social classes. In the three villages
around Buda it was possible to discover the social status of the majority
of households, so that social differences in household structure could be
analysed.

Some clarification of the definitions of the social categories used is
necessary:

Serf peasants were peasants who held possession of their land on the
basis of the feudal landlord–serf relationship. They were amongst the
wealthiest peasants.

Cotter peasants were those who either held possession of their land
on some other legal basis (for example, because they cleared the woodland) or had a smaller amount of land than the prescribed minimum of
serf land.

Cotters having a house were those who had no land, but worked on
the farms of others; they did have a house of their own with a small
farmyard and perhaps a small garden.

Cotters having no house were those who had no land and no house
and usually worked for those in whose house they lived, but conceivably also for others.

Artisans were the small rural artisans.

Table 9.8. *Distribution of households by type and social status, Nagykovácsi, 1769*

	Social status of household head						
Type of household	Serf peasant (no.)	Cotter peasant (no.)	Cotter with house (no.)	Cotter having no house (no.)	Artisan (no.)	Other (no.)	Total (no.)
1. Solitaries	—	—	—	5	—	—	5
2. No-family household	—	—	—	—	—	—	—
3. Simple-family household	30	37	15	26	25	14	147
4. Extended-family household	4	4	—	—	2	1	11
5. Multiple-family household	15	9	—	—	1	1	26
6. Not classifiable	—	—	—	—	—	1	1
TOTAL	49	50	15	31	28	17	190

Table 9.9 *Mean number of members of households by relationship to the head of household and by social status of head, Nagykovácsi, 1769*

	Mean number of persons per household					
Social status of household head	Head of household and spouse	Offspring of head of household	Other kin of head of household	Servant	Mean size of household	Mean size of nuclear family of head of household
Serf peasant	1.96	2.88	0.83	1.86	7.53	4.84
Cotter peasant	1.96	2.90	0.58	0.12	5.56	4.86
Cotter with house	1.93	2.27	—	—	4.20	4.20
Cotter having no house	1.71	1.10	—	0.03	2.84	2.81
Artisan	2.00	2.57	0.25	0.25	5.07	4.57
Other	1.94	1.29	0.24	0.29	3.76	3.23
TOTAL	1.92	2.36	0.42	0.58	5.28	4.28

Serf peasants tended to have the largest households, and complex households were more frequent in this class. Cotters with no house of their own had the lowest average household size, and complex households were the exception among them. Cotter peasants, that is cotters having some land, seemed to be similar to the serf peasants, and cotters having a house were similar to the houseless cotters. Artisans seem to have had moderately large, but only rarely complex, households. Households consisting of one solitary person did not occur in the peasant class, but were frequent among houseless cotters.

When households are analysed according to the mean number of heads and spouses, children, other kin, and servants, it appears that the most important factor in the differentiation of household size was the number of other kin and of servants per household. Approximately 80% of all servants and 90% of all other kin (including married children) in Nagykovácsi in 1769 lived in the households of serf peasants and cotter peasants. The reason for this social difference is obviously that wealthier peasants needed extra labour and could afford to accommodate in their households not only married children and other kin, but also servants. Both relatives and servants supplied the manpower needed on the farms.

The analyses above show the distribution of households by different characteristics in cross-section at given points in time. Clearly it would be most interesting to follow individuals and households over a period in order to discover the changes in household structure occurring in the life cycle of individuals. For this purpose we would need a number of successive listings separated by short intervals. In the absence of such a series, we tried to determine to which types of household individuals belonged at different ages according to their position in the household. The analysis was based on the listing of Kölked, which stated the ages of the persons concerned.

Table 9.10. *Age distribution of the inhabitants of Kölked by type of household and family status, 1816*

Type of household and family status	Age group							Age un-known	Total
	0–9	10–19	20–9	30–9	40–9	50–9	≥60		
Males									
Simple-family household									
Never-married off-spring	30	32	3	—	—	—	—	—	65
Husband or father in the conjugal family unit	—	—	5	12	21	8	2	1	49
Extended-family household									
Never-married off-spring	9	9	1	—	—	—	—	—	19

Type of household and family status	Age group							Age un-known	Total
	0–9	10–19	20–9	30–9	40–9	50–9	≥60		
Husband or father in conjugal family unit	—	1	1	6	4	1	—	—	13
Outside the conjugal family unit	—	—	—	—	—	—	5	—	5
Multiple-family household									
Never-married offspring	25	18	4	—	—	—	—	2	49
Husband or father in the parental conjugal family unit[a]	—	—	—	—	6	13	8	—	27
Husband or father in the ever-married offspring's conjugal family unit[a]	—	1	28	16	4	—	—	—	49
Husband or father in the brother's or sister's conjugal family unit[a]	—	2	4	6	4	1	—	—	17
Outside the conjugal family units	—	—	—	—	—	1	1	—	2
Unclassifiable household[b]									
Never-married offspring	2	2	2	—	—	—	—	—	6
Husband or father in the conjugal family units	—	—	4	1	2	1	1	—	9
Outside the conjugal family units	—	—	—	1	—	—	1	—	2
Of unknown status	—	—	—	—	—	—	—	1	1
TOTAL	66	65	52	42	41	25	18	4	313
Females									
Simple-family household									
Never-married offspring	31	23	5	—	—	—	—	—	59
Wife or mother in the conjugal family unit	—	1	7	18	18	4	—	1	49
Extended-family household									
Never-married offspring	6	6	—	—	—	—	—	—	12
Wife or mother in the conjugal family unit	—	—	6	3	4	—	—	—	13

Type of household and family status	Age group 0–9	10–19	20–9	30–9	40–9	50–9	≥60	Age un-known	Total
Outside the conjugal family unit	—	—	—	—	—	3	5	—	8
Multiple-family household									
Never-married offspring	40	24	4	—	—	—	—	1	69
Wife or mother in the parental conjugal family unit[a]	—	—	—	1	14	13	6	—	34
Wife or mother in the ever-married offspring's conjugal family unit	—	7	27	11	2	—	—	1	48
Wife or mother in the brother's or sister's conjugal family unit	—	—	6	7	3	1	—	—	17
Outside the conjugal family units	—	—	—	—	—	—	2	1	3
Unclassifiable household[b]									
Never-married offspring	4	—	2	1	—	—	—	—	7
Wife or mother in the conjugal family units	—	1	1	1	3	1	—	—	7
Outside the conjugal family units	—	—	—	—	—	1	1	—	2
Of unknown status	—	1	—	—	—	1	—	—	2
TOTAL	81	63	58	42	44	24	14	4	330

[a] Those husbands or wives, fathers or mothers who are members of conjugal family units but who are also parents of ever-married offspring who have formed their own conjugal family units in the same household have been entered as being in the parental conjugal family unit. These ever-married offspring (and/or their spouses) have been entered as being in the ever-married offspring's conjugal family unit. In cases where the conjugal family units within the household consist solely of those of siblings, brothers-in-law, or sisters-in-law and the parental conjugal family unit is absent, the husbands, wives, fathers, or mothers within these conjugal family units are recorded as members of the brother's or sister's conjugal family unit.

[b] In the case of unclassifiable households it was impossible to find out the family relationship between the conjugal family units.

From the data in table 9.10 it is evident that approximately half of the children aged 0–19 lived in simple-family households and half in extended- or multiple-family households. After their marriage most young adults lived in extended- or multiple-family households with their parents for a certain number of years. With increasing age, however, the proportion of those living in their own simple-family households, or in their own extended-family households with one of the parents, rose to a maximum in the age group 40–9. In this age group, too, and increasingly at higher ages, there appears a new household form, namely living together with married children in multiple-family households, or, after the death of the spouse, in extended-family households and, in due course, together with grandchildren. After the age of 60, the number of widows or widowers, particularly the former, who lived with their married children in extended-family households increased. Thus a family or household cycle can be discerned: young married couples first lived in the households of their married parents for some time, but later most of them established their own independent households, at first simple-family households or extended-family households with one of the parents; later, however, after the marriage of their own children, the household reverted again to a multiple-family household.

Obviously, this cycle did not apply universally. Some families lived their whole lives in multiple-family households, while others always lived in simple ones. As stated earlier, the dominant type of household varied according to socio-economic class. Nevertheless, it would seem that there was, as individuals grew older, a certain cyclical pattern of moving from a multiple- into a simple- and back again into a multiple-family household.

It has already been hinted that the distribution of households by type was not stable over time. In the case of Sárpilis, the two listings were separated by only 12 years, and as a family reconstitution of the village was also carried out, it was possible to follow households from the first listing to the second and to discover how their structure changed and what demographic events took place parallel with these changes. Of the households in Sárpilis in 1792, 56 could be unambiguously identified with households there in 1804. However, 11 of them split during these 12 years, so that in 1804 the number of households whose forerunners in 1792 could be identified amounted to 70 (see table 9.11).

The growth of complex households is clearly shown: more than half of the simple-family households in 1792 had become extended- or

Rudolf Andorka and Tamás Faragó

Table 9.11. *Changes in household type, Sárpilis, 1792–1804*

Household type, 1804	3a. Married couple alone	3b. Married couple with children	4a. Extended upwards	4a. Extended laterally	5b. Multiple; secondary unit down
Households^a which were not split					
3a. Married couples alone	—	—	—	—	1
3b. Married couples with child(ren)	1	15	1	—	1
4a. Extended upwards	—	2	—	—	1
4c. Extended laterally	—	—	—	1	—
5a. Multiple; secondary unit up	—	1	—	—	—
5b. Multiple; secondary unit(s) down	—	14	—	—	3
5c and d. Multiple; units on one level	—	2	—	—	1
5e. Other multiple	—	1	—	—	—

Households which were split, listed individually

1792	3b	3b	4c	5b	5b	5b	5c	5d	5d	5d	5e
	╱╲	╱╲	╱╲	╱╲	╱╲	╱╲	╱╲	╱╲	╱╲	╱╲	╱╲
1804	3b 4c	3b 5a	3b 3b	3b 3b	5b 3b	5b 3b	3b 5b	3b 3b	5b 3b	3b 3b	5b 3b

^a Only households that could be unambiguously identified have been included in this table.

multiple-family households by 1804. The reason was in all cases the marriage of a child, mostly of a son (in two cases of two sons), who brought his wife to live in the household of his parents. In two cases a daughter married and brought her husband into the parental household, but in these instances there was no son in the family.

On the other hand, the change from a multiple- to a simple-family household was rare. In eight cases a multiple-family household was split, but only in two did the split result in the formation of two simple-family households. In the other six instances one of the new units was a multiple-family household. The demographic happenings were various: sometimes one of the parents, or both, died and the married children split off their households. In one instance the widowed father married again and the son from the first marriage formed an independent household. The multiple-family households of the frérèche type separated when a child of one of the brothers married. Thus it would seem that in Sárpilis there was a clear tendency for simple-family households to become complex ones.

Macro-studies

Micro-studies make it possible to investigate types of household struc-ture and changes in these structures over time, as well as the demo-graphic, social, and economic factors that underlie such changes. They cannot, however, give us a representative picture of a whole country. This is particularly true of Hungary, where the regions differed widely in their ecological, economic, social, ethnic, and religious aspects. In order to generalize from the results of the micro-studies, we need to under-take parallel macro-studies, using cruder methods. This can be done by using the census of 1784–7 and the non-noble enumerations carried out between 1804 and 1847. From these sources it is possible to calculate mean household size and the number of adult household heads, as well as the number of adult sons and sons-in-law per household, for the counties (administrative units) or other regional units and communi-ties. The same sources also yield information on social structure (for example, the distribution of peasants or cotters).

These data were calculated and analysed by counties for the historical territory of Hungary, Transylvania, Croatia, and the military border areas at the southern frontier,[40] in relation to the non-noble part of the population, by excluding the noble households from the census of 1784–7. The free towns were also excluded. A similar study of house-hold structure was carried out by using village data for the present territory of Hungary.[41]

At the end of the eighteenth century, the social structure of village males aged 18 and over was as follows: 33% serf peasants; 46% cotters (partly peasants with very small farms, partly agricultural workers as well as people living from cottage industry); 3% artisans; 18% persons having no independent household but living as son or son-in-law in the household of the father or father-in-law.

The size of the household, as well as the number of adult men and adult sons and sons-in-law per household, was particularly high in three areas: first, in the mountainous northern parts of Hungary; second, in the relatively sparsely populated southern part of the Great Plain area; and third, in Croatia and Slavonia, as well as in the neighbouring parts of southern Transdanubia. On the other hand, western Transdanubia and the north-eastern part of the Great Plain were characterized by smaller households and fewer adult men per household. It can be stated with

[40] Faragó (1976), and 'Háztartásszerkezet és falusi társadalom-fejlödés Magyarországon 1787–1828' (1977).
[41] Dányi (1977).

Table 9.12. *Changes in non-noble household structure, Hungary,[a] 1787–1828*

Year	Mean size of household	Mean no. of adult[b] males per household	Mean no. of adult[b] sons and sons-in-law per household	Adult[b] sons and sons-in-law living in the households of fathers and fathers-in-law as a proportion of the total adult[b] male population
1787	4.95	1.17	(—)[c]	(—)[c]
1804	5.11	1.36	0.25	18%
1819	5.16	1.36	0.25	19%
1828	5.54	1.47	0.35	23%

[a] Excluding the free towns, Croatia, Transylvania, and the military border area.
[b] Aged 18 years or over.
[c] Figures not available.

confidence that the predominance of large and complex households was not characteristic of the country as a whole in the years 1784–7. But there seems to have existed a clear correlation between the proportion of serf peasants on the one hand and the size of households and the proportion of complex households on the other.

The size and structure of households, as well as their regional differences, gradually changed between 1787 and 1828. Mean household size and the number of adult men and adult sons and sons-in-law per household increased overall (see table 9.12 and fig. 9.2). At the same time the area characterized by a higher proportion of complex households increased, while the area where simple households prevailed gradually decreased.

Hypotheses on the interrelation of demographic, social, and economic conditions and household structure

The main findings of our micro- and macro-studies may be summarized as follows:

1. In pre-industrial Hungary the majority of households were probably of the simple-family type, but there were many more extended- and multiple-family households than in western Europe.
2. Extended- and multiple-family households were much more common among serf peasants than among landless cotters.

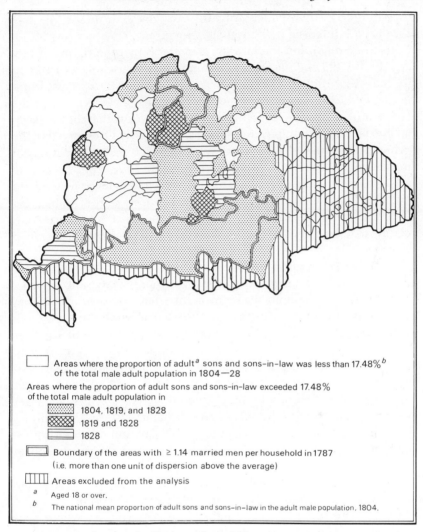

Fig. 9.2. Areas characterized by complicated households, Hungary, 1787–1828.

3. There were important regional differences in household structure.
4. The size of the households and the proportion of extended- and multiple-family households gradually increased from the last decades of the eighteenth century to about 1830.

On the basis of these findings certain hypotheses can be put forward concerning the economic, social, and demographic factors that may have influenced household structure and which, in their turn, may have been influenced by household structure.

First, one might put forward the hypothesis that the comparatively large household and the relatively complicated household structure in pre-industrial Hungary as compared with western Europe was not a permanent feature, as is often supposed, but that it evolved during the eighteenth and nineteenth centuries. It would follow that the break-up of large families in complex households, which may be observed in the second half of the nineteenth century, did not change a pattern of household structure which had been dominant for centuries among peasants, but merely altered a structure which had developed only in the preceding three or four generations. This does not, of course, exclude the possibility that some elements of the functions and customs relating to large and complex households had in fact existed for several centuries.

As for the variations in household structure found among different social classes, the fact that the highest proportions of large and complex households existed among the serf peasants, that is those having a farm, and mostly among the wealthier of these, tallies with the findings of anthropologists[42] and with local results.[43] If the households of Szigetvár in 1551 are grouped according to wealth, a positive correlation of household size and wealth is found.[44] In Győr households were larger in the centre of the town where the more affluent burghers lived than in the outer districts.[45] Comparison of different parts of Hungary indicates that large and complex households were characteristic of the counties which had a numerically strong serf-peasant class, but that such households occurred less frequently in counties where the proportion of landless cotters was higher.

Considering next the regional distribution of different household structures, two kinds of area with large and complex households may be observed. The first lay in mountainous or hilly country where poor economic and ecological conditions prevailed, and where the population density was relatively high. This type of area is found in southern Transdanubia and in the north of the country. Second were the sparsely populated 'frontier'-type areas in the southern part of the Great Plain.[46] These border regions had two characteristics in common, namely that

---

[42] Fél (1948); Morvay (1965); Szabó, *Munkaszervezet és termelékenység a magyar parasztságnál a 19–20. században* (1968); Fél and Hofer (1969).
[43] Veress (1958) and 'Háztartás, telek és termelés viszonya hegyaljai és bodrogközi jobbágyfalvakban a XVI. század derekán' (1966); Faragó (1975).
[44] Szakály (1970).   [45] Dányi (1965).
[46] Hollander, 'The great Hungarian plain' (1960–1).

there were few towns and that the economy was based on peasant subsistence farming. On the other hand, large and complex households were less in evidence in the counties of Hungary, especially those of western Transdanubia and the central region around Buda and Pest, where market production by the peasants and urbanization prevailed. In these areas there was a higher proportion of cotters (landless workers) in the village population.

On the basis of these regional features we may hypothesize that complex household structure might have had two functions. First, by embracing more male manpower and thus allowing a greater division of labour, it enabled peasant households to maintain a larger land area and a larger number of domestic animals than a simple-family unit could manage. Second, it avoided the danger of fragmentation of land, and thus the pauperization and proletarianization of serf peasants. The second function might have been more important in the densely populated southern Transdanubian and northern areas where land was scarce, while the first might have predominated in the sparsely populated Great Plain areas where land was relatively abundant.

In order to compare the demographic background of household structure in Hungary with that of western Europe, mortality, nuptiality, and fertility should be analysed. Levy and Burch have shown that under mortality and nuptiality conditions prevailing in western Europe, the proportion of extended- and multiple-family households could not be very large.[47] From the family reconstitutions[48] and from the crude death rates noted in the official vital statistics of the 1870s, we may deduce that life expectancy was somewhat, but not much, lower in Hungary in the eighteenth and nineteenth centuries than in western Europe. On the other hand, the average age at marriage was much lower. Most women married at about the age of 20, several years earlier than in the western European marriage pattern.[49]

The family reconstitutions of Sárpilis and Alsónyék suggest that about 50% of ever-married men and women were alive when their children married and the first grandchildren were born. The chance of a married couple both being alive when their first grandchildren were born was about 30%. Effectively, this is approximately the proportion of those multiple-family households in Alsónyék and Sárpilis in which married children lived with their married parents.

[47] Levy, 'Aspects of the analysis of family structure' (1965); Burch, 'Some demographic determinants of average household size' (1972).
[48] Andorka, 'La prévention des naissances en Hongrie' (1971) and 'Un exemple de faible fécondité légitime dans une région de la Hongrie' (1972).
[49] Hajnal, 'European marriage patterns' (1965).

As to the connection of complex households with fertility, the family reconstitutions of Sárpilis and Alsónyék[50] have shown that, contrary to the opinion expressed in demographic literature,[51] the high proportion of extended and multiple households was correlated to a relatively low level of marital fertility, which can only be explained by the widespread early practice of birth control in marriage. Several Hungarian authors dealing with birth control have pointed to the role of the parents, mostly of the mother-in-law, in forcing birth control on the young married couple.

Finally, we would put forward the hypothesis that household structure, marriage patterns, and marital fertility were interrelated and together constituted a strategy by peasant families to deal with the ecological, economic, and social conditions prevailing in Hungary at that time. With the exceptions of western Hungary, where, under the influence of western Europe, market production gradually developed, and of the southern Great Plain area, where land was still relatively abundant in the nineteenth century, Hungarian economy and society in the second half of the eighteenth and the first half of the nineteenth century were characterized by a growing scarcity of land and by an almost complete lack of industrialization and urbanization, as well as by the absence of an emerging capitalist and bourgeois state and society.

As large-scale emigration began only in the last decade of the nineteenth century, the peasants were forced to make the best of existing conditions. In southern Transdanubia, where Alsónyék, Sárpilis, and Kölked are situated, the strategy was to allow young people to marry and live in the parental household and to provide employment and livelihood for them on the parental farm, but to control excessive increase in population and in the members of individual families by strictly enforcing birth control within marriage. Thus the peasants hoped to avoid fragmentation of land, pauperization, and proletarianization.

This strategy would have been critical in a patrilineal and partible system of inheritance,[52] where all sons obtained an equal share of the

[50] Andorka, 'Fertility, nuptiality and household structure of peasant communities of Hungary in the XVIIIth–XIXth centuries' (1976b).
[51] K. Davis, 'Institutional patterns favouring high fertility in underdeveloped areas' (1955).
[52] The system of inheritance was not investigated in the villages studied. There is some evidence, however, from other parts of Hungary that a partible system of inheritance was rather widespread among Hungarian serf peasants, though landlords tried to limit it by stipulating that subdivision must not exceed one-quarter of an original serf plot (Fél and Hofer 1969). In a southern Transdanubian micro-region, near to the Sárköz and Ormánság, Andrásfalvy observed a partible system of inheritance among Hungarian

wealth inherited from the parents. According to Goldschmidt and Kunkel,[53] this system of inheritance was associated with patrilocal joint households, that is, in the terms of the Laslett typology, with multiple-family households containing several married brothers and/or sisters. This system of inheritance, however, would have led, if unchecked, to a rapid fragmentation of the serf plots and to pauperization of the families. But this was counteracted by the landlords setting a limit below which serf plots could not be subdivided, and by the families themselves controlling the number of heirs through birth control in marriage. In this way the peasants avoided an excessive growth in peasant households, and at the same time increased the average size of the households and the number of extended- and multiple-family households.

The rate of population growth resulting from this strategy was similar to that resulting from the pattern of late marriage, high celibacy, no birth control in marriage, stem families and/or simple-family households that was employed by some western European peasant communities in similar circumstances.

These two strategies are obviously only 'ideal types', rarely occurring in pure forms in real communities, either in Hungary or in western Europe. Further micro-studies of other Hungarian communities, possibly combined with family reconstitutions, as carried out for Sárpilis and Alsónyék, would be necessary to discover how widespread this 'ideal type' was in Hungary and how common were other strategies or adaptations to different ecological, economic, and social conditions.

peasants and an undivided system of inheritance among German peasants, where the eldest son inherited the whole farm and the younger brothers were compensated by money (*Ellentétes értékrendek összeütközése és a polgárosodás*, 1973).

[53] Goldschmidt and Kunkel, 'The structure of the peasant family' (1971).

10

The reconstruction of the family life course: theoretical problems and empirical results

REINHARD SIEDER and MICHAEL MITTERAUER

The family life course in history: sources and methodological problems

The importance of the developmental approach to the history of family life and to the changing structure of the individual family during its life cycle would now appear to be undisputed.[1] It has not been easy, however, to adapt empirical study to meet the requirements of this approach, mainly because of the different sources available to researchers in different countries.[2]

Our aim in this paper is to outline the possibilities and problems involved in the developmental approach when using serial household lists, a source common in Austria and elsewhere. The family life course, as we see it, embraces the entire household. Changes in household form we define as the family life course. The household lists are a type of annual census taken over long periods of time and not, as is more usual, perhaps once a century.[3] This particular source therefore enables us to investigate households and their development over several generations.

There are detailed lists for a long series of years for the districts now known as Lower and Upper Austria. We have used lists for Andrichsfurt in Upper Austria,[4] Gmünd in the Lower Austrian Waldviertel,[5] Rappol-

---

[1] For the theoretical concept of the family life cycle and its use in sociology, anthropology, and history see Cuisenier (ed.), *The family life cycle in European societies* (1977).
[2] For a survey of sources and methods of historical research into the family life course see Mitterauer and Sieder, 'The developmental process of domestic groups' (1979).
[3] For Austria see Mitterauer, 'Familiengrösse – Familientypen – Familienzyklus' (1975a).
[4] Seelenbeschreibungen der Pfarre Andrichsfurt, 1813f, Parish Archive, Andrichsfurt (Andrichsfurt is about 10 miles east of the Bavarian border); Schmidtbauer, *Modell einer lokalen Krise* (1978a); Sieder, 'Strukturprobleme der ländlichen Familie im 19. Jahrhundert' (1978); Mitterauer and Sieder (1979).
[5] Beschreibung der Seelen in der Stadtpfarre Gmünd, 1801f, Diocesan Archive, St Pölten (Gmünd, about 75 miles north-west of Vienna, is only a few miles from Heidenreichstein, where the peasant family structure has been analysed by Berkner); Berkner, 'The stem family' (1972a) and 'Family, social structure and rural industry' (1973).

tenkirchen in the Vienna Woods,[6] and Maria Langegg in the Dunkelsteiner Wald,[7, 8] limiting the study to rural areas in the nineteenth century.[9]

The possibilities of analysing serial household lists are many. Like single listings, serials throw light on the population according to age, marital status, and household position, whether spouse, child, servant, etc. Moreover, serial lists enable us to follow the composition of a local population over a considerable period of time. Although they do not always give precise ages, they have the advantage over the classic historical–demographic sources of birth, death, and marriage registers in that they enable us to see the connections between household structures and their development on the one hand and demographic changes on the other. It is possible to correlate changes in the age of marriage with structural changes in the domestic economy, changes in the timing of retirement, and so on, and thus to proceed beyond the mere description of demographic events.

Especially important for the reconstruction of the family life cycle, or family life course, as we prefer to call it, is the question of duration. From the serial lists one can recognize the exact duration of a particular household structure and of certain phases in the individual life course. Serial lists can also help one to estimate the average duration of marriage and of widowhood. Service was an important aspect of any agrarian society, and we may learn how long servants stayed on the same farmstead, and how much of an individual's life was spent in service.

The timing of family events ('family time') such as marriage, birth, generational change, and so on thus shows a group-specific pattern of a dynamic familial nature, incorporating individual life courses ('individual time').[10] If 'family time' and 'individual time' are not synchronized, one may assume conflict and disregard of personal interest

[6] Seelenbeschreibung der Pfarre Rappoltenkirchen, 1842f, Diocesan Archive, St Pölten (Rappoltenkirchen is in the Wienerwald, about 12 miles due west of Vienna).

[7] Seelenbeschreibung der Pfarre Maria Langegg, 1788f, Diocesan Archive, St Pölten (Maria Langegg is in the Dunkelsteiner Wald, a hilly woodland south of the Danube approximately 45 miles north-west of Vienna).

[8] The authors are indebted to Franz Meisl, Eleonore Krabicka, Gertrude Ostrawsky, and Peter Schmidtbauer for the transcription and arrangement of some of the sources used here.

[9] As we will show later, the close connection of the family life course with material resources of the rural household gave rise to a specific sequence of phases in the developmental process. For urban families different models of the family life course would probably be apposite. Detailed research into this for Austria is a matter for future studies.

[10] Hareven, 'Family time and historical time' (1977).

behind the collective façade of the family, or vice versa. To discover this, one has to unravel social, economic, kin, neighbourhood, and village relationships, manifesting themselves in the choice of a marriage partner, the engaging of servants, the coming and going of persons, and the other social events which may be reconstructed from the lists. The methods we shall employ will vary, of course, according to the size of the sample and the particular event under investigation. In one case, the analysis may be confined to a single family; in another, we may encompass several families caught in a network of interrelationships; in a third, we may concentrate on an individual life whose course runs through several families and households.

In the following paragraphs the most important changes of role, position, and status within and among the rural households of our area of research will be presented and analysed. In this exercise we have mixed our methods of presentation. Events which happen in nearly all families, such as changes in the headship of the household, are presented in their numerical frequencies within the areas in question. More complex and special connections can only be comprehended by presenting examples. We consider that the causal nexus between the regional labour and marriage markets, and between the developmental process of domestic production and the individual life course can be better clarified by means of this special 'family biographical' method than by relying on necessarily simpler quantifiable data for the community as a whole.

Phases in the family life course in past time

Succession in the household

In literature the change in the headship of the household is mostly held to accompany a generational change, the transfer of the farmstead from the father to one of his children. Furthermore, prevalent legal customs are supposed to have led to forms of succession typical of different regions. In the light of serial lists of households, both assumptions would seem to be too facile. Certain family customs of handing over property do hold sway in the countryside, not only among peasants, but also among cottagers ('*Haüsler*'), but analysis so far shows a far broader spectrum of sequences than the generally postulated sequence of father to son.

The number of those families where peasant property passed, according to custom, from the father to either the eldest or the youngest son is

Table 10.1. *Changes of headship in peasant households*

Headship		Andrichsfurt (51 farmsteads, 1813–62) N = 70 (changes) (%)		Rappoltenkirchen (49 farmsteads, 1842–76) N = 81 (changes) (%)	
Father	→ eldest son	34.3		3.7	
	→ middle son	1.4	35.7	4.9	18.5
	→ youngest son	—		9.9	
	→ son-in-law	10.0		3.7	
	→ stepson	1.4	14.3	—	3.7
	→ foster son	2.9		—	
Mother	→ eldest son	10.0		4.9	
	→ middle son	—	12.9	6.2	14.8
	→ youngest son	2.9		3.7	
	→ son-in-law	1.4		1.2	
	→ stepson	—	4.3	—	1.2
	→ foster son	2.9		—	
Head	→ his widow		14.2		25.9
Widow	→ 2nd husband		4.3		2.5
Former head's daughter	→ 1st husband		1.4		—
Head	→ kinsman	8.6	8.6	1.2	2.4
Widow	→ kinsman	—		1.2	
Head	→ unrelated person	2.9	2.9	24.7	27.2
Widow	→ unrelated person	—		2.5	
Head	→ inmate	1.4	1.4	1.2	1.2
Widow	→ inmate	—		—	
Head	→ servant	—	—	1.2	2.4
Widow	→ servant	—		1.2	
TOTAL			100.00		99.8

surprisingly low in those areas studied to date. In Upper Austrian Andrichsfurt, a prosperous agricultural village where the farmers produced grain on quite large plots and primogeniture was prevalent, 34.3% of all transfers of the parental farm were from father to eldest son (see table 10.1). In Lower Austrian Rappoltenkirchen, with small vineyards and ultimogeniture, the parental property was taken by the youngest son in only 9.9% of all cases. Where at the time of the transfer there was only a single son, we counted him in areas of primogeniture as the oldest and in areas of ultimogeniture as the youngest. Our results are therefore, if anything, biased in favour of the norm implied by the inheritance customs.

In 10% of all cases in Andrichsfurt the farmstead was transferred from the peasant to a son-in-law; in about 3%, to a foster son; more rarely, to a stepson. But a great number of peasants died before a son was old enough to marry and take over the farm. In about 14% of all cases the management of the household went in the first place to the peasant's widow. In 17.2% of all these cases the widow handed over to a grown-up son, mostly after a short period: in 43%, she married again. Although the developmental processes of those rural families in the nineteenth century so far analysed suggest that the widow managed the farm single-handed, mainly because at the time she assumed control there was no heir of a fit age, the situation was one where potential conflict was likely. Certainly, those widows who married again might have encountered a conflict of interest with the presumptive heir, who had to reckon at best with not being able to lay hands on his inheritance for a considerable time, and at worst, should the woman have children from her second (or third) marriage, with likely usurpation by an heir chosen from among these. Faced with this prospect, the heir presumptive from the first marriage very often left the farm at the remarriage of the mother.[11]

The customary concept of a father–son conflict on the occasion of the transfer of the farm is therefore only partly true; conflicts between father and daughter and between mother and son have also to be taken into consideration. According to inheritance customs, the widow was supposed to hand down to the eldest son, but this occurred in only 10% of all cases. Other transfers were made to a younger son. This might occur because the elder brother had left the farm or because he was unwilling to wait for his inheritance.[12] Succession by more distant relatives was also quite frequent (8.6%), and in about 3% of cases a change involving unrelated families occurred.

In comparing succession practices of prosperous arable farmers of Andrichsfurt with those of poorer viniculturists in the parish of Rappoltenkirchen, we are struck by the considerably smaller number of father–son sequences in the latter, and the nearly 10 times more numerous changes involving non-related families (see table 10.1). In Rappoltenkirchen, ownership on the death of the husband passed more frequently than in Andrichsfurt to the widow, and thus the property was often

[11] Sieder (1978): 181–2, tables 8, 17, 18.
[12] Cole and Wolf (*The hidden frontier* (1974)) hint at this connection: 'Of the thirty-three current holdings in St Felix [a South Tyrolean village], where male heirs were available, seventeen of these had forgone their inheritance . . . The eldest son often leaves his father's home and the village . . . Thus, it is often one of the youngest sons who inherits the estate – one who was still young enough to be uncommitted in a life career at the time the eldest made the final break.'

handed down by the widowed mother to one of the children. Interestingly, the mother evinced no distinct preference for one son over another, although this was said to be an area of ultimogeniture. In this she differed from the father, who gave preference to the youngest son in the matter of transfer.

Kin relationship generally and inheritance customs in particular seemed to play a smaller role in the transfer of family property in Rappoltenkirchen than in Andrichsfurt. More frequent changes involving non-related families in Rappoltenkirchen point to an important difference in the economic structure of the two districts. Whereas in Andrichsfurt the plots were large, there were vineyard owners in Rappoltenkirchen whose small plots could be bought with little capital. As the viniculturists were dependent on a strong market for their produce, property transactions were often effected in hard cash, whereas among the wealthier arable farmers of Andrichsfurt possession of land was mainly obtained by inheritance.

Property transfers among cottagers and artisans have rarely been studied, because the changes pose special methodological problems. Such families were far less bound to a particular place than were peasant families, and, as they frequently moved house, it is often very difficult to follow their fortunes over generations. The movement of non-peasant families depended on the economic structure of a certain region and on the regional possibilities of living without owning a farmstead.

In the vinicultural parish of Rappoltenkirchen, cottagers ('*Haüsler*') were mostly day labourers in the vineyards; they often owned a small plot of land, which could not, however, provide for all their wants. Artisans, such as shoemakers, tailors, joiners, cartwrights, blacksmiths, bakers, who all owned their own houses, were another section of the non-peasant population, as were the employees of the manor (steward, gardener, gamekeeper, hunter, innkeeper, etc.). The family life course of those employed on the manor and in village administration was determined by special factors which are discussed in greater detail below (see p. 325). The tenants of cottages we shall also disregard for the moment (see p. 326). Sixty-nine per cent of all changes in the cottage-owning group, as distinct from cottage tenants and married or administrative employees, occurred between totally unrelated families (see table 10.2). Only in 5.4% of all cases did the father, and in 7.4% the mother, hand down to a son. There is a marked difference compared to the peasant inheritance customs of this area, for amongst the cottagers there is no instance where the inheritance was handed down to the youngest son.

Table 10.2. *Changes of headship in cottagers' households*

Headship		Andrichsfurt[a] (1813–67) N = 22 (changes) (%)		Rappoltenkirchen[b] (1842–82) N = 149 (changes) (%)	
Father	→ eldest son	27.3		3.4	
	→ middle son	4.5	31.8	—	3.4
	→ youngest son	—		—	
	→ son-in-law	—		1.3	
	→ stepson	—	—	0.7	2.0
	→ foster son	—		—	
Mother	→ eldest son	4.5		4.7	
	→ middle son	—	4.5	0.7	5.4
	→ youngest son	—		—	
	→ son-in-law	4.5		1.3	
	→ stepson	—	4.5	0.7	2.0
	→ foster son	—		—	
Head	→ his widow		4.5		14.8
Widow	→ 2nd husband		—		—
Former head's daughter	→ 1st husband		—		—
Head	→ kinsman	18.2		1.3	
Widow	→ kinsman	4.5	22.7	—	1.3
Head	→ unrelated person	18.2		63.1	
Widow	→ unrelated person	13.6	31.8	6.0	69.1
Head	→ inmate	—		1.3	
Widow	→ inmate	—	—	0.7	2.0
Head	→ servant	—		—	
Widow	→ servant	—	—	—	—
TOTAL			99.8		100

[a] Changes of headship in 23 cottages are included. Thirty-three tenanted cottages, in which the same tenants usually stayed for only a few years, have been excluded. Often several tenant families lived together. In such circumstances it would be meaningless to talk of a 'headship' of the house.
[b] Seventy-two cottages have been included. Fifteen cottages inhabited only by inmates have been excluded.

The cottagers of Andrichsfurt, on the other hand, transferred property from father to son in the same way as did the peasants of that area. The non-peasant population consisted mainly of tradesmen and artisans. In 31.8% of all cases the headship of the household passed from father to son, the eldest son being preferred in accordance with the inheritance customs of the district. In 22.7% of cases the cottage went to a kinsman, and in 31.8% to someone not related to the family. The fact that the inheritance went to kin in two-thirds of the transfers of headship between cottagers was probably due to the structure of the rural economy and of property-holding. It is also possible that attitudes prevalent among the social class of the peasants percolated down to the sub-peasant groups.

To grasp the meaning of the succession in household headship as an element of the family life course, we must look beyond the immediate protagonists – father and son – to the preparations for the succession and their influence on the changing structure of the household. This is only possible if we can reconstruct the development of the household over long periods both before and after the change in headship, the most critical event in its development. Serial household lists enable us to do this and provide us with the following examples, which we believe are typical.

The first example comes from the village of Grillenstein in the parish of Gmünd in the Waldviertel of Lower Austria (see fig. 10.1). It concerns a family of peasant weavers. The farm was transferred to the son while the parents were still only in their early fifties; they went into retirement (*Ausnahm*) together with the sisters of the young household head. But all stayed together on the farm. It was usual in the Waldviertel to hand over the property while both parents were still living. It was also not unknown, as in our example, for the heir to marry shortly before take-over, so that an intermediate phase might occur during which the old couple lived together with their married offspring, the heir apparent. These are the only circumstances in which the 'classic' stem family, in the sense of Fréderick Le Play's definition, occurred. However, this form of household structure lasted only a very short time, after which the young farmer took over the headship and the old couple went into retirement.[13]

This three-generational family, with the young farmer as head, presents us with a totally different social entity from that of the family with a married child completely under parental authority. But this un-

<hr>

[13] See Berkner (1972a): 406 for the manor of Heidenreichstein, which is very near to the Grillenstein of our example. 'In those households headed by men over 58 a small proportion lived with a married child. But as none of these married sons or daughters had children who were more than two years old, the status of "married son" probably lasted only a few years before the parents retired.' An ethnologist reports for the Waldviertel in the nineteenth century that the young wife often remained with her parents after marriage for a certain time, the interval varying between a few days and several weeks. When she then moved to her husband's house, the old and the young couple at first worked together for some time and also ate at the same table. However, this did not last long, and the old ones moved to the *Stübl* (a room set apart for the retired). See Rauscher, 'Volkskunde des Waldviertels' (1926): 51.

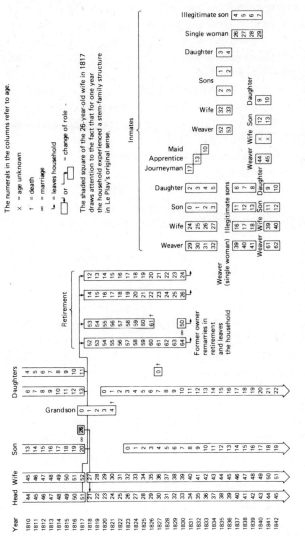

Fig. 10.1. Family life course of a peasant-weaver household, Grillenstein, parish of Gmünd, 1810–42.

doubted difference has hitherto been ignored in the literature for the sake of a formal concept of the stem family.[14]

In Upper Austrian Andrichsfurt we find no intermediate periods when married children lived under the headship of a father before he handed over control. Indeed, the father would hand over the headship at a comparatively early age. Many retired peasants were therefore of an age when they were perfectly able to work; it was the economic capacity of the farm which made longer periods of retirement possible. The timing of the transfer of the farm was probably determined not so much by the declining working capacity of the old couple as by the demands of the heir. Again, the predominance of primogeniture strengthened the tendency to early succession. Retirement was therefore a common experience and constituted a lengthy phase of the family life course. In a comparison between regions of the Habsburg monarchy, the area round Andrichsfurt shows the highest proportion of retirement contracts during the nineteenth century.[15] Here too, because of the early demise of one of the parents, it frequently happened that there was no available heir and that the widowed parent managed the farm single-handed or married again.

It was very rare in Austria for a widower or widow to manage a farm for a long period of time. The widowed household head either remarried or found an heir. Usually in a rural household the central roles of two adults, one male, one female, had to be filled permanently because of a domestic economy where the family as a whole engaged in the production process. But under certain conditions of labour organization this compulsion to fill the roles within the household might be less pronounced.[16] This was the case in Andrichsfurt. The economic capacity of the farms, clearly developed inheritance customs, weak manorial influence, and demographic change led to longer periods when the farm was managed by unmarried or widowed household heads.

The working of these factors in combination may be illustrated by the following example (see fig. 10.2). At Mayer zu Pötting, the largest farm

[14] Berkner (1972a: 407) speaks of a 'complete stem family' when the old couple had withdrawn and handed down to a son 'while another child is still living at home'. However, even when the young farmer's siblings had left and the father had died, so that only the mother was living with her son's family, Berkner still speaks of a stem family ('but the stem family organization remains nevertheless'). Berkner thus stretches the concept of the stem family from the patriarchal three-generational family with the old father as overlord to family forms of a totally different character.
[15] Schmidt, *Gutsübergabe und Ausgedinge* (1920).
[16] Mitterauer, 'Zur Familienstruktur' (1973): 186, 'Vorindustrielle Familienformen' (1975b): 172, and 'Auswirkungen von Urbanisierung und Frühindustrialisierung' (1976): 62f.

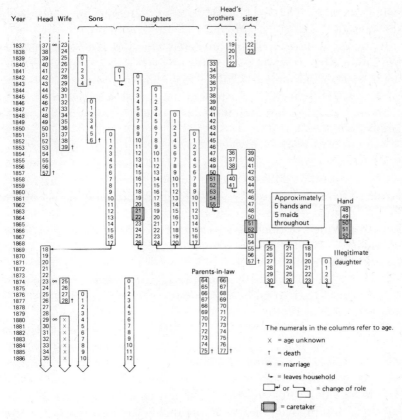

Fig. 10.2. Family life course on the farm Mayer zu Pötting in the parish of Andrichsfurt (see also fig. 10.8 below).

The numerals in the columns refer to age.

× = age unknown
† = death
∞ = marriage
⌐ = leaves household
⌐ or ⌐ = change of role
▢ = caretaker

in Andrichsfurt, the wife died at the early age of 39. After her death the widowed farmer managed the farm single-handed for four years. Besides his older daughters, two brothers and a sister stood at his side. The last-mentioned might have filled the role of the housewife. After the early death of the farmer, no suitable heir was available, because the eldest son was only 7 years old. Therefore an interim solution had to be found. One after the other the uncle of the heir apparent, a sister, and then an aunt, together with a farmhand, took over the running of the farm as caretakers (*Wirtschafter*). At 18 years of age the heir took over the farm himself. For five years the young master remained single, three of his sisters staying at home. Only after he had married did they leave the parental house. In their stead the farmer's parents-in-law entered the household. Two children were born from the first marriage; then the wife died. After two years of widowhood the farmer married for the second time.

In this family life course one can detect a near-dynastic conception of the family. After the early death of the parents, successive attempts were made to keep the property in the male line in accordance with the inheritance system, thus illustrating the causal connection between economic capacity and testamentary strategy in this rich farming family.

The peasants of the parish of Maria Langegg in the Dunkelsteiner Wald were far poorer than those in Andrichsfurt. For other reasons too, we must presume a different family life course. In particular, there was a greater difference in age between father and inheriting son because of the prevalence of ultimogeniture, and retirement occurred less frequently. Farmers or their wives who had become widowers or widows often tried to avoid the heavy economic burden of retirement by remarrying. Unlike their richer brethren of Andrichsfurt, these farmers, if widowed or single, could not afford the help of relatives and servants to run the farm. Unmarried heads of households are missing altogether, and widowers as household heads are met with only rarely.

Nevertheless, a variety of ways existed in which a farm might be handed over, which may be demonstrated by the following example (see fig. 10.3). The farmer of Wolfenreith 13 of the parish of Maria Langegg went into retirement after the death of his wife and handed over to his eldest son. Five years later, however, the farm was sold, and another family moved into Wolfenreith 13. The new head died after only three years, and his widow married again shortly afterwards. Within ten years three different types of headship change occurred in this house: father to son, purchase, and marriage into the property by a third farmer.

Let us now follow the adventures of the 14-year-old brother of the second head of Wolfenreith 13. After his father's death he went into service at Schenkenbrunn 22, not by chance, it would seem, for he was related to the farmer there. He stayed on as a farmhand for two years. Meanwhile the question of succession had become important to the old couple at Schenkenbrunn 4. They had no children and were therefore looking for another solution. Our farmhand, now 16 years old, was related through the wife of his master to the farmer of Schenkenbrunn 4, who took him on as farm servant, possibly with the intention of appointing him his successor. The maid there was of the same age as the farmhand; she probably occupied a position of trust, for she had been on the farmstead for some years, which was unusual. When man and maid

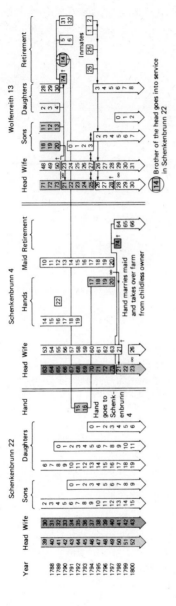

Fig. 10.3. Family life courses of three closely connected farms in the parish of Maria Langegg.

321

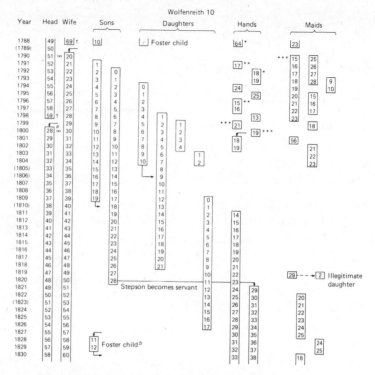

^a The second husband is a foster brother of the wife, being a son of Wolfenreith 2, although absent in the section of that family's life course represented in this figure.
^b A grandchild of the wife and a step-grandchild of the farmer.

Fig. 10.4. Family life courses of two closely connected farms in the parish of Maria Langegg.

were 20 years of age they married, and the old farmer handed over the farm. Sadly, however, the young wife died in the same year, and the widowed farmer soon married for a second time.

The example above suggests, first, that younger sons entering service preferred to join the households of relations.[17] Second, the importance of kinsman ties in the selection of the heir is shown in those cases where there was no immediate heir. It is evident that succession to the farm was not determined by household structure alone, and that changes in family structure must be seen in the light of the wider network of kin relations, workers' recruitment, and so on.

The next example also demonstrates how relationships between different houses might shape the single family life course on the basis of kinship, marriage, and service. After his wife died, the farmer of Wolfen-

[17] See detailed examination, pp. 328–31.

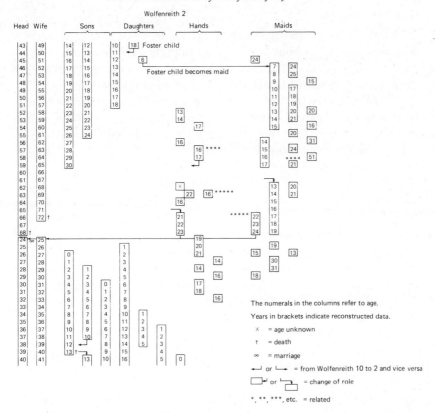

Fig. 10.4 (*cont.*).

reith 10 (see fig. 10.4) married 19-year-old Theresia Stiegler, a foster daughter of the farmer of Wolfenreith 2. When he died after ten years, his widow, Theresia, married her foster brother, Michael Speiser, two years her junior, the own son of her foster father, the farmer at Wolfenreith 2, where, within three years, the question of the succession presented itself, for all the children had left home. The eldest daughter of the farmer at Wolfenreith 10 then came to No. 2 as a maid. She was related to her master, because her mother was his foster daughter, and his son, Michael, the present farmer at Wolfenreith 10, was her stepfather. Four years later her elder brother, Johann, also a child of the head's foster daughter, arrived at the farm as a servant, and at the same time his future bride was taken on as a maidservant. The settlement of the succession had become urgent, for in the same year the wife died, and the farmer shortly afterwards. Farmhand and maid married and took over the farm.

Some years later the succession of Wolfenreith 10 became an acute problem. A stepson of the farmer's was still living at home, but he was probably not the intended heir, for in the later listings he was named only as a farmhand. After the last of their own children had left home, an 11-year-old son of the farmer of Wolfenreith 2 was taken on as a foster child. He was the farmer's wife's own grandchild. Probably he was intended to take over the farm in due course, but when the eldest son at Wolfenreith 2 died, his younger brother returned to the paternal farm to fill the place of the dead heir. At Wolfenreith 10 they therefore had to look for another solution to the succession.

Two elements in the histories of these interrelated families are typical of Austrian rural conditions at this time. Foster children and servants were frequently related to the couple heading the household, and their acceptance into the family was often part of the strategy of marriage and succession. We become aware of these family connections only by examining a number of households over a period of time. The serial listings enable us to gain an insight into domestic policies aimed at the organization of labour and the retention of the property within the family.

Each of the two family life courses presented in fig. 10.4 gives some interesting indications of the forms which succession to the headship of an individual household could take. The fact that the farmer at Wolfenreith 10, in the early lists of the series, was 20 years younger than his wife would suggest that this was the wife's second marriage. After her death the farmer married a girl 30 years his junior,[18] so that she, in her turn, became a widow and married a second time. Over a period of about 60 years the headship of this farm never devolved from parent to child. The vacant positions of the household head and of the wife were always filled by the remarriage of the widowed person. Such a form of succession occurred very frequently, especially in Lower Austria, and may be traced even in the thirteenth century.[19] Frequent remarriage of widows on the basis of marital joint property was one of the reasons why rural multigenerational families were not very common in Lower Austria.[20] To speak of the stem family with reference to the peasants of Lower Austria would not therefore in our opinion be justified.[21]

Similar conditions obtained in the Lower Austrian vineyard village of Rappoltenkirchen. Here ultimogeniture was the custom, although

---

[18] For the possible consequences of great age differences between spouses see Sieder (1978): 177–83.
[19] Feigl, 'Bäuerliches Erbrecht und Erbgewohnheiten in Niederösterreich' (1967).
[20] Mitterauer (1973): 213 and (1976): 143–6.
[21] Berkner, 'Rural family organization in Europe' (1972b): 145.

much modified in practice, as we have seen. Some special features of the household arose because the area was given over to viniculture, which was characterized by a less pronounced division of labour between the sexes than was the production of grain and the raising of stock. In particular, widowed persons more frequently headed households and occupied such positions for longer periods.[22]

Property in the area was divided among 49 quite small farmsteads and 87 cottages of the non-peasant population. Because inheritance customs were in practice not very strong, there were relatively frequent changes of ownership, and the social barrier between peasants and cottagers was not as marked as, for instance, in Upper Austrian Andrichsfurt. Children of peasants who did not inherit the parental farm quite frequently married children of cottagers. On the other hand, peasant sons and daughters who did not inherit might marry and set up cottager households. In some cases the status of cottager was only a passing phase for peasant children.

At the age of 55, the farmer at Kogel 9 in the parish of Rappoltenkirchen (see fig. 10.5) handed over to his eldest son, who married in the same year. His wife bore him seven children. The brother and sister of the new head continued to live with their father in his retirement. At 25 years of age the younger son married the only child of the neighbouring farmer, but as her parents were not yet prepared to hand over the farm, the young couple had to seek an interim solution. They first moved to a cottage owned by the husband's family, where they stayed for some years and where the first children were born. Then, when the father-in-law was ready to hand over the farm and go into retirement with his wife, the son-in-law moved as owner into the vacated farm. In this or similar ways prospective heirs sometimes found the material resources to start their own households. Frequently they lived as tenants or as inmates until they were able to buy a cottage or to take over a farm. However, when an individual's desire to marry and start his own household could not be realized within his own social class, he was compelled to join a lower class, if only for a time. The individual life course therefore frequently ran across several social groups in rural society.

The families of manorial and village officials form a special group. In the parish of Rappoltenkirchen these would include the households of the steward, the castellan, the gardener, the gamekeeper and others. Serial listings show that these families stayed only a short time in one place and would seem to have been moved frequently by the lord of the

[22] Mitterauer (1976): 76 and table 3b.

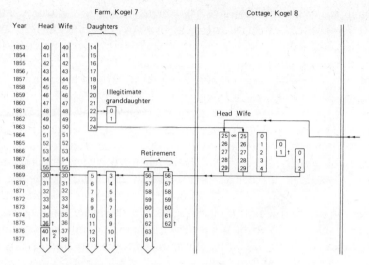

^a Younger son of first head of Kogel 9 marries only daughter of Kogel 7. They live for a while in cottage Kogel 8, before moving to Kogel 7, where he takes over his parents-in-law's farm.

Fig. 10.5. Family life courses of two farms and one cottage, closely connected, in the parish of Rappoltenkirchen.

manor. Similarly, the lessees of the manorial mills, inns, and such like changed often. Less importance was probably attached to inheritance strategies amongst these families than among peasant families, and consequently their attitude towards children and the relationship among spouses would have been less subject to the restraints of a domestic economy.

In the regions that have been under consideration, inmates were to be found on farmsteads and in cottages, generally as tenants. The usual pattern was for people to move every couple of years, and there was no permanent attachment to a particular house. It is our opinion that there is little difference between the role of inmate of a farm and inmates of shared cottages, whom we shall term tenants. Fig. 10.6 sets out the situation in the parish of Andrichsfurt. A change of occupants took place at least every four or five years, although some returned after several years to a particular cottage. It is noticeable that few children were listed, probably because they left their parents at an early age to go into service with a farmer.

In this respect different conditions prevailed in those regions where outwork, as for example amongst weavers in the environs of Gmünd, or daily labour, for instance in the vineyards, offered a comparatively secure income to these propertyless groups. This is illustrated by the

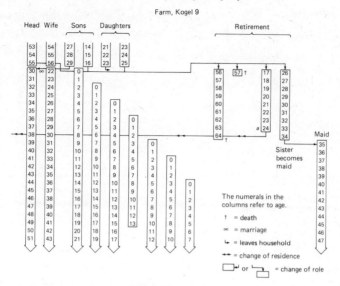

Fig. 10.5 *(cont.).*

example of a cottage in the vineyard area of Rappoltenkirchen (see fig. 10.7) where several tenant families lodged during a 40-year period. Five of them consisted of widows with their children, and it is particularly interesting that the sons remained at home for a long period. Their daily labour in the vineyards probably secured the means of subsistence for these incomplete families.

The status of tenant or inmate would have been lifelong and immutable for some of the population and only temporary for others. There are instances of married children of peasants living as inmates for only a few years and then taking over either the parental farm or a cottage. They found their partners mainly within their own class but often also among cottagers, although it is notable that peasants rarely married the daughters of inmates.

Servants: their exits and their entrances

The serial listings allow us to observe the coming and going of servants, which leads us to the conclusion that, for Austria at any rate, the traditional picture of the faithful, long-time servant is a false one. The general impression is one of constant movement among the servant population. Servants often changed their farm annually, with only a

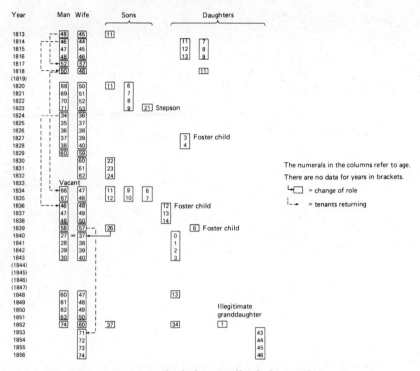

Fig. 10.6. Cottage, Andrichsfurt 8, all inhabitants being tenants.

few staying for several years.[23] On the larger farms, however, there was some continuity. Hands taken on for one year were sometimes retained for a second year. It was probably customary to try and establish an age and social hierarchy within the servant group. An almost unchanging age structure may be observed, especially among farmhands. For instance, on the farm Mayer zu Pötting (fig. 10.8) there was nearly always an older farmhand of over 40 and a very young one of between 12 and 18 as well as two or three farmhands between the ages of 20 and 30.

On the basis of the serial listings one can discover whether servants bore the same name as the farmer or his wife and were therefore probably related to them. Sometimes the kin relationship was noted in the listing; in other cases it may be deduced from the development of the household. Frequently foster children and stepchildren were listed only after a certain age as servants (see Wolfenreith 2 and 10, fig. 10.4). It seems legitimate to conclude from this that it was not their kin rela-

[23] Mitterauer and Sieder (1979): 271.

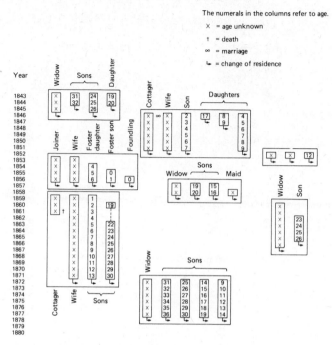

Fig. 10.7. Cottage, Penzing 8, in the parish of Rappoltenkirchen, all inhabitants being tenants.

tionship with the couple at the head of the household that was of primary importance for their social position, but their function in the domestic economy.

Fig. 10.4 also gives some indication of the way servants were obtained. On both farms shown here the high proportion of servants who were related to each other is evident. Immediately after a girl left Wolfenreith 10, where she had served as a maid for nine years, two of her brothers were engaged as farmhands. This suggests that farmers were inclined to take servants from certain families, or rather that siblings and other relatives procured jobs by recommending each other to the farmers.

It would seem that parents tried to place their children with kins-people at the beginning of their period of service, as is shown in fig. 10.9. On the farm of Georg Streif of Andrichsfurt a number of servants related to him served over a period of 30 years. Many were very young, so that it would probably have been their first position. Some, we know, were the children of Georg Streif's brother who headed a neighbouring farm.

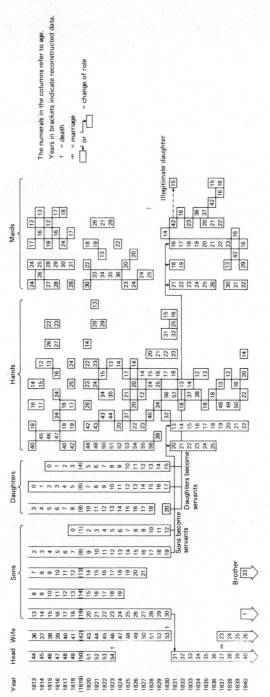

Fig. 10.8. Family life course of the farm Mayer zu Pötting (see fig. 10.2) in the parish of Andrichsfurt.

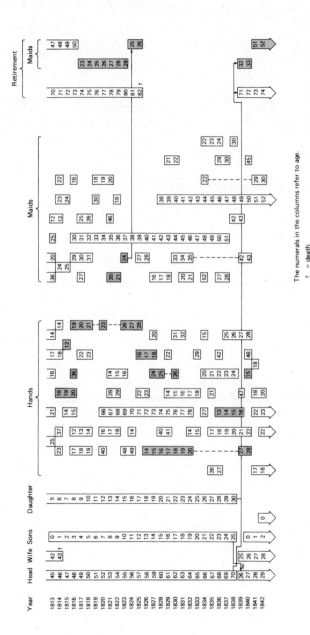

Fig. 10.9. Family life course of the farm Bruch 1 in the parish of Andrichsfurt.

331

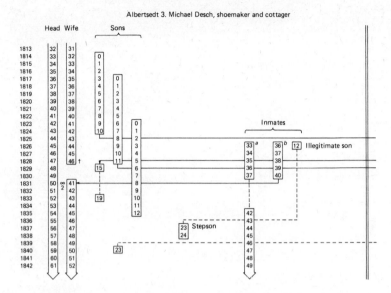

a Brother of the inmate in the adjoining column.   b Midwife with illegitimate child; later marries widowed head.
Returns later as brother-in-law of the head.   Her son returns for two years as stepson of head.

Fig. 10.10. Family life courses of two related shoemaker families in the parish of Andrichsfurt.

Cottagers were also frequently interrelated, as is shown by two shoemaker families in the parish of Andrichsfurt (fig. 10.10). The two household heads were probably brothers. At 10 and 11 years of age the sons of the one moved into the family of the other, where they were listed as foster children, but, considering their ages and the general situation, they were undoubtedly sent into service with their uncle. Servants who had kinship ties with the household often stayed longer and returned more often to the same house than those servants who were not related (see fig. 10.9).

The serial listings also show that the demand for servants depended on the ages of the children in the household. At Wolfenreith 10 (fig. 10.4) the farmhand was replaced by the son when he was 11 years old, and the maid left when the two elder daughters were 10 and 7 years of age. Conversely, when children were old enough to leave home, they were often replaced by servants. Again, examples may be found in fig. 10.4. But sometimes relatives were kept as servants when, from an economic point of view, they were not needed at all, which suggests that the keeping of servants did not always correspond to labour requirements but was sometimes a means of supporting indigent kinsfolk.

Finally, we give an example of a life cycle of a servant which shows

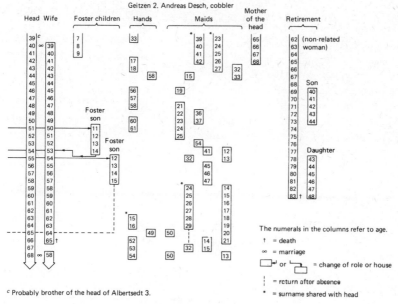

c Probably brother of the head of Albertsedt 3.

Fig. 10.10 (*cont.*).

clearly that 'home and family' could have a totally different meaning for certain rural servants than for children of peasants and cottagers (see fig. 10.11).

Barbara Tischler was an illegitimate child born in 1819 into an inmate family consisting of her mother and her mother's 71-year-old father. Soon after her birth, grandfather, mother, and child moved to another hamlet within the parish. When the girl was 6 years of age, she was separated from her mother and was taken into an uncle's family as a foster child. Together with the whole family Barbara Tischler moved house several times. At 14 years of age she went into service as a maid with a shoemaker. She stayed eight years and then moved to another village. One year later she changed her job again, and in two years' time she bore an illegitimate child. She and her offspring stayed in the same place for a further four years, and then moved to the house of a blacksmith. After a year of service there, Barbara Tischler finally returned to the house of the shoemaker where she had started life as a servant 16 years earlier. After two years she and her child probably left the parish for good, for there is no further trace of them.

Such was Barbara Tischler's life cycle, typical of that of many offspring of inmates in that there occurred an early separation from her mother

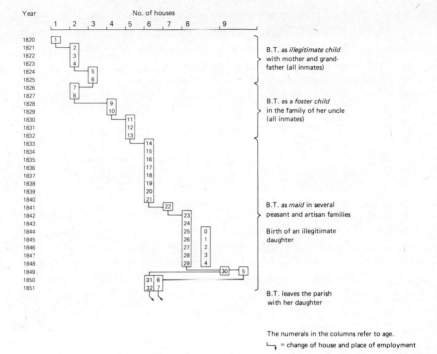

Fig. 10.11. Individual life course of a female servant (Barbara Tischler) from the parish of Andrichsfurt, 1820–51.

(at the age of 7) and in the frequency of moves from house to house. That an illegitimately conceived child should in turn bear an illegitimate child is also a common phenomenon. In this way a section of the servant population reproduced itself.

Siblings, grandchildren, and foster children

The serial household lists show that the whole period of female fertility was utilized from the date of marriage onwards. In most of the family life courses we have analysed so far, the last birth occurred in the fifth decade of the woman's life, with the youngest child frequently born when the eldest was already grown up. In the peasant family of Wolfen-reith 10 (see fig. 10.4), the eldest child was 19 at the birth of the youngest. The life course of this family also indicates how it might happen that there were still small children after the wife's fertile phase had ended. The illegitimate child of a maid or a grandchild taken in as a foster child enlarged the circle of growing children. Because men frequently remarried, the fertile periods of two or more mothers were linked together, producing a still larger number of children and a still greater disparity of age between the children.

This may be illustrated by the family life course of the peasant household of Rappoltenkirchen 13 (Fig. 10.12), where the eldest daughter of the first marriage was already 26 years old at the birth of the youngest of the second marriage, giving an overlap in the generations of children and grandchildren. The farmer's children of the second marriage grew up alongside two illegitimate children of the eldest daughter, while the second daughter also bore an illegitimate child. The farmer's youngest daughter was born three years after her eldest nephew.

The acceptance of illegitimate grandchildren was, as our sources make clear, a widespread phenomenon in Lower Austria. It led to the emergence of a special type of three-generational family.[24] Seen in the light of the family life course, it meant a prolongation of the phase in which children were being reared. Frequently these illegitimate grandchildren were listed expressly as foster children of the grandparents. The rearing phase often stretched beyond the death of one or both parents. In many cases minors were still at home when the farm or cottage was taken over by the heir. Parents moving into retirement not infrequently had under-age and even adult children with them (see fig. 10.1).

In such a household there could have been no constant focus of affection for the children. Within their own group too, relationships were always changing, as did the size of the group itself. Fig. 10.12 shows that older siblings might leave the farm, though not necessarily permanently. Of the sons of the first marriage one returned home four times and another, three times, and a daughter was absent for two short periods before she left finally. The sources show that the usual purpose in leaving home was to enter service in another household, but it is not always possible to discover the motive behind the return. When a child came home shortly before the death of a parent, it was probably because of the parent's illness. Unmarried daughters often came home after a period of service to have a child[25] and to seek family care and protection in and after their confinement, while an additional motive here might well have been the hope of leaving the child with the grandparents.

Frequently daughters bore illegitimate children after the parents had already handed over to the heir and were living in retirement (see

---

[24] Sieder (1978): 188f, tables 1, 6, 9, 11, 12, 13, 14, 20; Mitterauer (1976): 121.
[25] Sieder (1978): table 14.

Reinhard Sieder and Michael Mitterauer

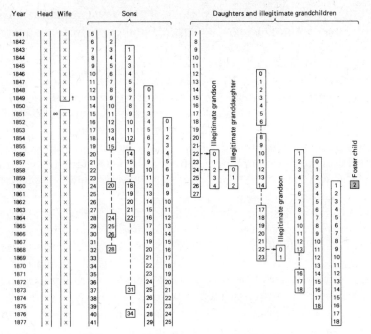

Fig. 10.12. Family life course of the farm Rappoltenkirchen 13 in the parish of Rappoltenkirchen.

fig. 10.13). Indeed, in some areas retirement seems to have been regarded as an institution providing shelter for unmarried daughters and their children. If the daughters left home again after some time, their offspring often remained with the grandparents as foster children. Many of those entered only as foster children in the lists would therefore have been illegitimate children of members of the family. Some unmarried mothers, termed in the source '*Inwohner*', or 'inmate', continued in the house after the death of the parents. In this way the household offered protection to unmarried mothers and illegitimate children. But amongst the poor, the cottagers and tenants, where the resources of the farm household were lacking, unmarried mothers suffered social and economic insecurity. They frequently became separated from their children or moved with them as inmates from place to place and from house to house.

One point above all is deserving of emphasis. The serial listings show that a child might leave home more than once. There was no clear distinction between a 'rearing phase' and an 'empty-nest phase' in the family life course in this period, any more than there was a clearly defined phase of childhood separate from a phase of extra-familial occupational training and employment.

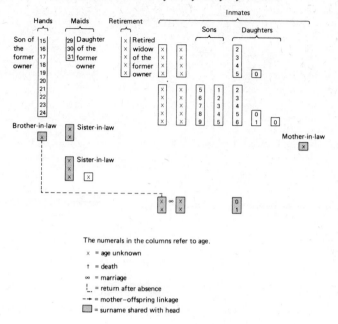

The numerals in the columns refer to age.

x = age unknown

† = death

∞ = marriage

⌐ = return after absence

--→ = mother–offspring linkage

▥ = surname shared with head

Fig. 10.12 (*cont.*).

Theories and concepts of the family life course in historic times

Our analysis of the serial lists of households allows us to advance certain general hypotheses concerned with the nature of the family life course in historic times.

Lutz K. Berkner outlined a concise model based on source material from Lower Austria.[26] He believed he was able to distinguish 'three parallel developmental cycles' – of the individual, of the family, and of the household. Although he saw the developmental cycle of the household as being 'dependent upon the phases of the family cycle', it was, nevertheless, clearly distinguishable from it. The household cycle he characterized by the 'presence or absence of non-family members' such as servants and lodgers. The household cycle was determined by economic necessities, 'a stable labour force on the farm', and 'the availability of living space'. The family cycle, on the other hand, was determined by demographic events, such as birth, marriage, and death.

Berkner thus makes a distinction within the household group be-

[26] Berkner (1972a): 418.

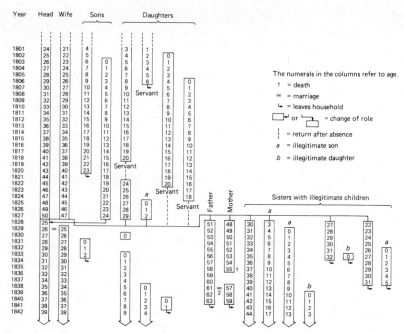

Fig. 10.13. Family life course of the farm Ehrendorf 4 in the parish of Gmünd.

tween the immediate family of the household head and non-related persons. This immediately gives rise to the difficult problems of the definition and delineation of historical family forms, problems with which we have dealt extensively elsewhere.[27] We repeat here what we held on those occasions, that it is not justified to use the criterion of kinship to delineate, define, or typify the family.[28] A delineation of the family on the basis of kin and marriage relationships draws arbitrary division lines across a group of persons who lived and acted together intensively as one complete unit.

Indeed, it is precisely from such units of intensive interaction that one has to proceed to a definition of the historic family. A strictly kin-based concept of the family by itself does not accord with social reality, as the examples given above demonstrate. Kinship ties cannot be equated with certain constant social relationships. To be related to someone means very different things in different circumstances. To avoid arriving

[27] Mitterauer (1973): 173, (1975a): 231, (1975b): 130, (1976): 58; Mitterauer and Sieder, *Vom Patriarchat zur Partnerschaft* (1977): 31.
[28] The discussion about the stem family and the nuclear family has contributed considerably to the fact that types based on the criterion of kinship dominate international research into historical family forms. See P. Laslett, 'Introduction' (1972b): 31.

at a totally artificial concept of the 'family', one has to define it primarily according to its functions; for example, its tasks of production and socialization. By carrying out these tasks, related and non-related persons were integrated into the social group of the rural household community. We must not put the cart before the horse. The concept of a kinship group held together by specially intensive interaction and distinct from the totality of the rural household should be put forward as a result of empirical research, not as an *a priori* definition.

In this chapter we have analysed the development of the household group as a whole and have made no *a priori* distinction between family and household. The examples we have given show clearly that it is not possible in most circumstances to make this distinction. We must ask whether, for instance, the sons and daughters of the Mayer zu Pötting farm (fig. 10.8) no longer belonged to the family cycle when they stayed on as servants after the succession to the headship by their brother. Was the daughter of the retired peasant in Kogel 9 (fig. 10.5) to be counted as 'family' only as long as her father was alive, and not when she was listed as a maid after his death? How does one class a widow who was living in retirement after the death of her husband while someone to whom she was not related owned the farm? Did she become a member of the 'family' again when one of her daughters married the farmer? Should one count siblings, children, and grandchildren listed as servants and inmates as 'non-family' members regardless of their kinship ties? Every attempt to separate a 'family cycle' or a 'conjugal family unit' from the household community leads to an artificial dismemberment of a social unit of interaction.

Berkner's distinction of the 'family cycle' as demographically determined and the 'household cycle' as economically determined seems problematic too. The break, so important in the peasant family life course, which occurs on the handing over of the farm to the heir, and on his marriage, is mainly dependent on economic circumstances and is in no way comparable to such demographic events as birth or death.[29] It is therefore questionable whether we would be justified in looking at demographic occurrences in isolation from the socio-economic background when tracing the development of the domestic group.

As the modern sociological concept of the family has no validity for the historian, he must wonder whether this is not also true of the family cycle, which sociologists divide into phases according to co-residence or not of parents and children. In this they are following the currently fashionable theory about the role of the family in primary socialization.

[29] Sieder (1978): 185f.

The cycle is generally divided as follows: young married couple without children; parents with children at pre-school age, with pre-adolescent children, with adolescent children; parents alone after the children have left home until the death of one partner ('post-parental companionship', 'empty nest') and the final stage in which the widowed parent lives alone.[30] The modern pattern is of births mainly falling within the first years of marriage and succeeding each other at short intervals. The children pass through the 'rearing phase' as a close-knit group and generally leave the family at much the same age. Education and training necessitate the 'withdrawal' of the children from the family. This happens at an earlier age in the lower classes and at a later age in the higher classes,[31] but it rarely varies within the same milieu. Finally, withdrawal from the family very often coincides with the foundation of a household of one's own.

On the other hand, the rural family of the nineteenth century presents a totally different picture, with neither a rearing nor an empty-nest phase. As we have seen, there were nearly always some children without prospects in the household. Children who were neither destined to inherit nor used as labourers on the farm often left the parental home to receive their training by serving in the house of a relative or of a stranger. However, many returned home from time to time. The length of the period of service did not depend on a definite training programme but could end at very different points of time, depending on the possibility of marriage and the founding of a household. Sons and daughters who were to take over the parental property did not, with few exceptions, leave the family at all. Where at least one child remained at home with its parents until succeeding to the headship, the phase of post-parental companionship was missing altogether.

Again, the death of one parent did not mean that the other one remained a solitary, as in the modern family cycle. While today the majority of widowed elderly people live alone and have to fend for themselves, in the nineteenth century there were hardly any solitary people in country districts. On the contrary, most elderly people lived in large households. Even in widowhood they lived in the family of the heir, frequently together with their other non-inheriting offspring, servants, and other kinsfolk.[32] The generations mingled and were linked by the dependence of family members on the house for living space and

[30] König, 'Soziologie der Familie' (1969): 115f.
[31] *Ibid.* 117.
[32] On the situation of old people in the family life course of past centuries see Sieder, 'Probleme des Alterns im Strukturwandel der Familie' (1977).

on the household economy for subsistence. Patrimonial inheritance ensured an enduring family life course which was not terminated by the death of the surviving parent. The 'perenniality of the peasant family' is the term coined by the agrarian sociologist. But here also the concept of the family cycle is questionable, for it presupposes a certain regularity in the sequence of phases and a clear delineation of the cycle by marriage and death of the surviving partner. Therefore we think it preferable to refer to family situations of past centuries not as 'family life cycles' but as 'family life courses'.

Breaks in the family life course were brought about not so much by the bearing and rearing of children as by the 'critical event' of inheritance of the household headship. In the preparatory stage, and again after the event, this occasioned the coming and going of people, and changes in status and roles. All these family events were dependent on the overriding purpose of the household economy, namely to secure subsistence for the family with the aid of related and non-related work people.

The requirements of domestic production demanded a reproduction policy, as well as a policy of ensuring that a proper balance was kept between producers and non-producers. This expressed itself in the first place in the search for a marriage partner. It was not so much a personal matter as the need for an 'alliance between two families' of great importance to all members of both families.[33] The chances of marriage depended mainly on the ownership – or the likelihood of eventual ownership – of the agricultural or commercial means of production (house, land, tools, etc.). The fitness of the marriage partner for the task of the domestic economy was an inherent condition of the marriage. Accordingly, social and professional endogamy was common. In addition to the geographical limits of the marriage market, the potential number of suitable candidates was often too restricted to make it possible for the individual to make emotional and personal demands on the marriage partner. Often, therefore, it was necessary to accept considerably older partners, provided they could meet the important ma-

---

[33] Hareven (1977): 64; Rauscher (1926): 45: 'Therefore the parents tried to arrange that the match should, at any rate according to their notion, be a good one, that is that the future son- or daughter-in-law should be well situated, be an industrious worker, and be of good reputation. In contracting the marriage it was therefore not so much love as economic considerations which were of importance. Nevertheless, these business marriages were in most cases good and lasting ones. Love marriages were, however, not entirely unknown and were often entered into against the parents' wishes. These marriages were consequently frequently not so happy as the more prosaic ones. The daughter-in-law was often accused of not having contributed anything to the union, and quarrels resulted.'

terial and occupational requirements.³⁴ Because of these differences in age,³⁵ the younger partner might become widowed relatively quickly and then marry a second time, so that children of the first marriage became stepchildren. These were rarely designated heir, for normally children of the last marriage were favoured.³⁶ Remarriages must often have led to tension and emotional stress. The threatening figure of the fairy-tale stepmother has a socio-historical background.

On balance, it would seem that conflict within the family principally arose when the rationality of either the domestic economy or collective norms could not be reconciled with individual interests. The problems of inheritance, especially, must have led to tension between parents and children and also between siblings, for the succession of the heir might force his siblings to leave home, with a consequent loss in their social status. The most important causes of family conflict must have lain in the distribution of material resources and of power and prestige, a conflict which was most likely to erupt at the handing over of the farm. The economic interests of all were affected when the ageing farmer, and sometimes also the widowed mother, clung to power. Retirement also was not without its problems. In the nineteenth century rising life expectancy frequently brought about long periods of retirement which threw a heavy economic burden on the farm. Signs of these burdens are the many retirement contracts relating to the areas that we have studied.

The reconstruction of family life courses from the serial lists highlights the frequent changes in the composition of the household brought about mainly by the movement of servants, of inmates, and of children – by their departure from, and frequent return to, the parental home. High mortality often led to the reconstruction of the household. Frequently members of the family simply disappeared, leaving us to assume the migration of that person from the district.

This must be the principal difference between the historic and the present-day family life courses. One might perhaps go further and suggest that the experiences of death and separation must have had a different quality in the nineteenth century. What did people feel on the death of parents, a marriage partner, or a child? How did parents react to parting with a child at an early age? It would seem that, because there was little stability, there were also little privacy and intimacy among

³⁴ For differences in ages of partners see Sieder (1978): 177f.
³⁵ An older wife, on average 5.15 years older than her husband, was present in 23.4% of all peasant couples. *Ibid.* 180.
³⁶ *Ibid.* 192.

members of the nineteenth-century rural family, certainly less than what would be true of many present-day middle-class families. The need to ensure that the household fulfilled its prime task of production would have the effect of constraining individual emotions. Ethnologists report that, even at the turn of the century, in the Lower Austrian Waldviertel, relations between parents and children lacked every sign of tenderness. They conversed in a sober and matter-of-fact manner; they had an aversion to showing affection, because this would have been interpreted as a sign of weakness and indulgence. Children experienced kisses and caresses only when very small babies. The young never addressed their parents with the intimate '*du*' but with the more formal '*Sie*'. There was certainly little intimacy or affection in the 'socialization' of children.

On the other hand, such problems as children emotionally tied to their parents and vice versa, 'the over-protective family', did not exist to the same extent in the past. For these problems arise from the relative isolation, the intimate relationships, and the proneness to psychic disturbance of present-day families. Research into the historical family should allow one to test the validity of model explanations based on particular temporal and cultural conditions put forward by psychologists and sociologists.[37]

The analysis of serial listings shows that certain family life courses were characteristic of certain social groups. Such differences arose because the nature of ownership of the means of production and of other material resources also differed. If the owner of a farm or cottage was normally tied to house and status, the non-heirs frequently moved into a lower social class to experience mobility and social instability. Contrary to the conventional view, however, marriage was not dependent on the ownership of a farm or cottage, though without such a base a couple might have to join the class of multiply dependent inmates. While among peasants the continuity of the family life course was preserved, though perhaps at the cost of crises affecting all persons in the household and transforming its structure, there were frequent changes of house amongst cottagers, some making a further social descent into the group of inmates. This points to the more stable existence of peasant

[37] Kriedte, Medick, and Schlumbohm, *Industrialisierung vor der Industrialisierung* (1977): 100. The specific conditions of the domestic economy are not dependent on the subjective preferences of the members of the family. 'The rationale is the structural and functional coherence of the "whole house", founded as a socio-economic entity, which organizes and unites members of the family into a common way of life through production, generative reproduction, and consumption.'

families as compared with the wage-dependent and more crisis-prone non-peasant families.

Our analysis requires that connections among all persons, both within and without the household community, should be taken into consideration. Links among households were forged either alone or in combination by marriage, kinship, and the recruiting of work people, by sheer proximity, and by ties of patronage and dependency. Taking the family life course beyond an individual household marks the beginning of a fresh assessment of the socio-economic function of kinship ties.

Andrejs Plakans has pointed to the necessity of joining kinship networks to socio-economic models of stratification.[38] However, we consider that kinship ties and social roles cannot be placed on the same level.[39] The reconstructed family life courses present us with a number of examples where kinship could lead either to a higher or to a lower social position: one brother of a farmer might become a farmhand; another might marry and become an inmate. But even though kin relationship might occasionally have improved an individual's position, it was primarily his economic position which determined his social status. On the other hand, it cannot be denied that kinship ties could assist in mitigating antagonism among social groups, moderating conflict between farmers and servants, or facilitating a solution of their differences. By dealing with the family, not in isolation, but in its social and economic context, the analysis of family life courses may well assist in shedding light on the stratification of social classes in pre-industrial societies.

Family life courses provide clear evidence of the influence on the family of regional patterns of property and mobility, economic and cultural trends, and habits of behaviour. Together with other historical sources, such as retirement contracts, betrothal and marriage agreements, or descriptions of villages and regions, serial lists can give us a region-specific picture of family structure, differentiated according to social group, in historical time. But the reconstruction of family life courses also shows that household structure is more than the composition of the household at a particular date. Such types of household

---

[38] Plakans, 'Identifying kinfolk beyond the household' (1977): 3f. See also ch. 5 above.
[39] Plakans writes (1977:17): 'Many household members possessed more than one kind of link to the head and therefore it follows that each person also must have had more than one role in the community at large. Thus, if the community is examined for the kinds of social ranks or strata it contains (however these be defined), care must be taken that the hierarchy in which these strata seem to fall must not be conceived in so simple a fashion as to foreclose from the outset the investigation of the manner in which allegiance to kin interacted with the cleavages due to permanent or temporary occupation of socio-economic ranks.'

structure as the 'simple', the 'extended', and the 'multiple' are all phases of the family life course. Over several generations each family might experience several of these phases. If we start from a concept of dynamic structure, these various phases will be seen as elements of the same family structure, whose sequences are determined, as our examples show, mainly by the circumstances of the domestic economy in which family property, inheritance strategies, and so on each makes its own contribution.[40]

[40] Medick, 'Zur strukturellen Funktion von Haushalt und Familie' (1976a): 254f, esp. 258.

11

The changing household: Austrian household structure from the seventeenth to the early twentieth century

P. SCHMIDTBAUER

Introduction

Since Berkner drew attention in 1972 to Austria's then as yet un-touched sources for the structure and history of the family, much work has been done by Austrian historians, and today one can fairly say that the main difficulties in studying family structures in Austria since 1600 are caused not by lack of sources but by the problem of coping with the great quantity of material available. It is, however, possible to give a broad outline of how work on this material has progressed and of the problems which have arisen.

One of the most interesting features of the Austrian sources is the series of annual *Seelenbeschreibungen* or *libri status animarum*, literally translated as 'soul descriptions'. These are census lists with additional remarks on the religious and sometimes on the moral behaviour of the people. They may cover quite long periods, so that it is possible to follow domestic groups throughout their developmental cycle. Analysis of these lists have led us to definitions of 'family', 'household', and 'house-ful' differing slightly from those propounded by Peter Laslett.[1] Basically, we place the greatest importance on the social roles within the family and household, and prefer not to stress biological or purely matrimonial connections unduly. However, the authority of the head of the house-hold and/or the spouse would seem to be a very important factor in binding different members of family and household together.

Looked at from this last point of view, there can be no clear distinction among family, household, and houseful, but only a gradual diminishing of authority outwards. At the centre of authority and partaking in practically all family functions are the head of the household and the

---

[1] P. Laslett and Wall (eds.), *Household and family* (1972): 1–88.

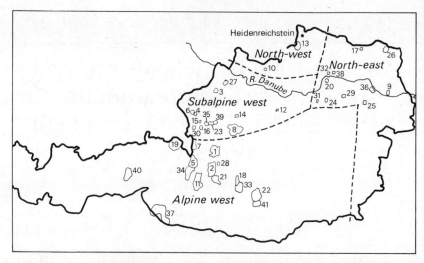

Fig. 11.1. Austria: distribution of places for which listings have been used. The places numbered above are listed under corresponding numbers in the appendix at the end of this chapter.

spouse; next come children; then servants; and on the outskirts one finds the *Inwohner*, lodgers or 'inmates' in Gregory King's sense. Kin may be placed in any position, depending on their social role. With decreasing familial functions and familial authority, the outer groups become more and more independent and finally emancipate themselves from their old centre. Thus the inmates move from being obvious members of the household in the older rural listings to a state of structured housefuls, where they form something like a household of their own but still depend upon the main household and partake in some of its functions, and finally to the unstructured housefuls of the large industrial towns, where the relationships among the households sharing a flat are impersonal and businesslike. It is very difficult, however, to delimit these phases, because to do so depends on whether or not the inmates share productive functions with their central household, and this is not easily discovered from the sources.

The position of servants undergoes a similar development, but slightly later and with the difference that their working position is clear and it is their place of living that changes. Their process of emancipation is therefore easier to follow. It is noteworthy that over the years children too have lost many familial functions, so that the pattern of their emancipation from the family today differs from that of the past.

The soul descriptions that are dealt with in the following pages come from four different areas of Austria (see fig. 11.1). First is the north-east, where the pattern of settlement is in villages; farms are rather small, and there is a fair amount of viniculture, especially in Poysdorf. The second area lies in the uplands of the north-west, a rather poor farming area with some domestic industry, settled like the rest of Austria in hamlets or single houses with small market towns as local centres. The third area is the subalpine west, containing some of the richest farming areas in all Austria (Raab), nowadays with a mixed economy but in historic times mainly producing grain. Fourth is the alpine west, a stock-raising area with often very isolated farmsteads and parishes spread over great distances. Manorial rights tended to be greater in the east than in the west but varied widely.[2] In several regions it was possible to distinguish between central townships and rural environs. Furthermore, there are enumerations for big towns and industrialized areas: Salzburg, the residence of the prince-archbishop; Ebensee, a centre of salt-processing; Perchtoldsdorf, an industrial town south of Vienna; and parts of Vienna itself (see fig. 11.2), ranging from the upper-class Herrengassen quarter (8.3% of all households headed by the higher nobility) to the very working-class Gaudenzdorf (in 1857 85% of households headed by industrial workers of different descriptions).

Inmates

Numbers and characteristics of inmates vary considerably, not least because they are treated differently in different sources. Such inmates may include relatives who have not been described as such, but more often they are connected with the household as servants or cotters, in that they may either be aged or married servants; or they may belong to a class of people living for a time with a peasant family on a farmstead and then again for a time on their own in a cottage. Inspection of consecutive listings over a period of years shows that there is one class of inmate whose average length of sojourn on a farmstead is similar to that of a servant, that is hardly ever more than two years. Unlike servants, however, at least in some areas of Austria, such inmates tend to return frequently, and it seems that there they simply rotate among several farmsteads. In the north-east this happens less often. A second class of

---

[2] Thus the tendency to pass over a direct heir who was a minor in favour of an adult collateral or even a stranger was certainly influenced by the insistence of the lord of the manor on a capable management of the farm. Similarly, manorial influence can be detected in retirement patterns.

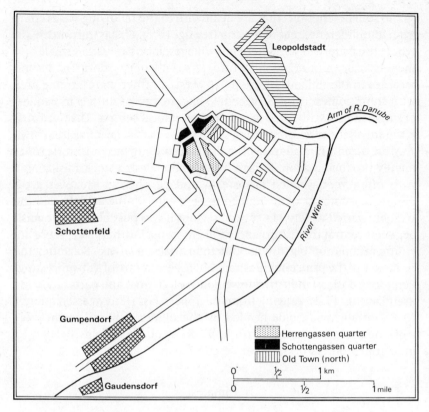

Fig. 11.2. Selected areas of Vienna, 1857.

inmate, more often to be found among small peasants, rural artisans, and cotters than among the richer farmers, stays for a very long time (ten years or more). It might be thought that this second class has always been more emancipated from the central household and that its members are nearer to being lodgers than those in the first category. Thus it would seem that in the country the inmates are far more integrated into the household than in the central townships.

Groupings which occur among the inmates do not at first seem to arise from differences of roles, though one can observe that nuclear families within groups of inmates are the first to emancipate, settling in newly built cottages. While in rural areas in the seventeenth century there was an average of 0.58 inmate children for every adult inmate, and on average 43.6% of all inmates were married, the proportion fell in the eighteenth century to 0.25 (23.9% married), but rose again in the nineteenth century to 0.32, mainly because of a change of attitude towards illegitimate children who were more frequently retained within the family (see table 11.1). The whole development can be observed especially clearly in Abtenau, Thalgau, and Dorfbeuern, all in Salzburg province.

During the first phase of industrialization, the proportion of biological families among what would now be called lodgers rose again in several cases, as can be shown, for instance, in Gmünd and Weinzierl, the last-named being a village near the developing industrial town of Krems. But this was a transitory phase, resulting from the predominance of home industry and lack of dwellings, and in the fully industrialized places most of the lodgers were persons without dependants. In 1857 the industrial areas of Austria had a ratio of children to adult lodgers of 0.14; 11.3% of the lodgers were married.

Numbers and proportions of inmates vary greatly with the regions, but there is a close connection between rural architecture and the number of inmates: extended farmsteads with outhouses normally contained a greater proportion of inmates than buildings forming a single complex, which were common in the north-east of Austria. Series of soul descriptions suggest that a favourite place for inmates was the room set apart for the retired. The village centres and market towns usually contained more inmates than the surrounding countryside, because cotters and rural artisans more frequently had inmates. The same applied to the poorer peasants as compared with the richer ones, but whereas it can be argued that cotters' and artisans' inmates more nearly approached the status of lodgers, this might not necessarily be so in the case of the poorer farmers, because they might have taken inmates in lieu of servants, as they certainly did with relatives.

It is interesting to look at the distribution of inmates in Raab in 1834. The mean number of inmates per household was 0.74 for the environs and 1.79 for the market town, but the mean for peasants with 40 or more units of land (a unit is probably an Austrian acre) was only 0.23, and it rose to 1.21 for peasants with 9 units or less. Country cotters had 0.90 inmates; country artisans with a small farm, 0.25, almost the same as the richest group; but in the case of country artisans without a farm, the number rose to 0.96. The farmers in town, all of whom were quite prosperous, had on average 2.33 inmates, whereas the town's cotters had the largest number, with 3.05. The mean for the town's artisans was far lower at 1.45.

We can therefore assume that the average of 0.25 inmates per household represents about the level this area required as a result of popula-

Table 11.1. *Inmates from the seventeenth to the twentieth century by ratio of children to adults, marital status, and household distribution, Austria*

Place and date	No. of children per adult inmate	Proportion of married inmates (%)	Proportion of households with inmates (%)
1. Rural areas			
Abtenau, 1632	0.56	43.1	36.2
1790	0.24	21.6	41.6
Thalgau, 1647	0.54	60.9	—
1750	0.28	18.3	—
Dorfbeuern, 1648	0.58	26.9	14.0
1772	0.08	14.0	18.5
Altenmarkt, 1755 (country)	0.58	24.0	14.1
Metnitz, 1757 (country)	0.30	7.8	26.8
Zweinitz, 1757	0.25	19.4	29.2
Zell am Ziller, 1779	0.46	34.5	63.1
Villgraten, 1781	0.18	31.0	21.1
Obergrafendorf, 1788	0.51	50.3	48.0
Zweinitz, 1811	0.46	7.5	31.3
Andrichsfurt, 1813	0.20	—	—
Raab, 1834 (country)	0.22	42.0	25.0
Andrichsfurt, 1863	0.33	—	—
Poysdorf, 1890	0.32	27.6	9.2
Andrichsfurt, 1909	0.24	48.6	25.5
17th century ⎞	0.58[a]	43.6[a]	16.7[a]
18th century ⎬ All listings	0.25	23.9	32.8
19th century ⎠	0.32	25.7	21.8
2. Industrializing areas			
Weinzierl, 1751	0.50	76.0	20.4
1867	0.67	66.7	7.7
Gmünd, 1801	0.41	49.1	20.2
1842	0.81	57.8	33.8
Perchtoldsdorf, 1754	0.29	37.1	10.5
1857	0.19	15.0	12.6
Stein, 1762	0.85	48.5	10.9
1857	0.12	3.0	10.5
3. Vienna, 1857			
Herrengassen quarter	0.14	9.1	30.6
Schottengassen quarter	0.11	12.2	35.0
Old Town	0.10	9.2	43.8
Leopoldstadt	0.14	11.3	55.9
Gumpendorf	0.21	15.5	39.0
Schottenfeld	0.14	15.2	37.9
Gaudenzdorf	0.30	21.5[b]	45.2

[a] In some places the listings were defective.
[b] Plus 1.0% common-law couples.

tion development, custom, and the need for specialists' labour. This was the level experienced on the larger farms and by the more prosperous artisans in the country. Smaller farms and the households of poorer rural artisans as a consequence had more inmates, because their rent or their work was needed. That the inmates in the country did probably work for their hosts to a certain degree is shown by the fact that the cotters, who were in need of money but not of labour, had fewer inmates than the small peasants. Of course inmates working with their central household were far more integrated with it than those simply paying rent. In the town, however, where there was much greater opportunity to earn a living, the general level of inmates was considerably higher. It seems as if inmates in town were more willing to pay in money, thus accounting for the high level of inmates attached to the town's cotters; whereas the number of inmates attached to the town's farmers is simply explained by the size of their houses.

As the majority of married inmates disappeared in the later seventeenth century, those they left behind were predominantly female and ageing; this predominance became more and more pronounced up to the first half of the nineteenth century. In particular, average age rose steeply. In rural listings of the seventeenth century about half the inmates were aged 40 or more, and about 15% were 60 and over. In the eighteenth century more than two-thirds were 40 and over, and more than a quarter, 60 or more, while in the rural listings of the nineteenth century nearly three-quarters of all inmates were 40 and over and about 40% were 60 years old or more. The sex ratio did not change as much, but where direct comparison is possible it can be seen to have fallen from about two men to three women to one man to two women from the seventeenth to the eighteenth century. Obviously women, being less emancipated, were prone to remain in a role that, for those areas and times, must be regarded largely as still within the familial authority of the head of the household.

When we turn from rural inmates to lodgers in the towns, we see that age and sex ratios also changed quickly; not only did the average age decrease sharply, but the number of male lodgers rose, so that males formed the majority of lodgers in Vienna in 1857, though not as yet in other industrialized towns. The proportion of inmates aged 40 years or over in the industrializing areas stood at 56% around the year 1800, a figure not very different from the contemporary rural mean, but while it rose sharply in the countryside, it dropped to 30% for the industrializing areas by the middle of the nineteenth century. The sex ratio, too, changed from 68 males to 100 females in about 1800 to 88 : 100 50 years later, while Vienna had a male surplus at 152:100 with roughly the same age distribution. It is, however, not only industrialization that produced this distribution, but the greater economic opportunities of a big town, because Salzburg in 1794 also showed a male surplus at 114:100. Of course details vary widely according to the degree and the kind of industrialization experienced by a particular area.

It is true both for industrialized towns and for rural areas that the number of inmates rose as the social status of the households to which they were attached sank. In the absence of clear economic data for individual Viennese households, one can check frequency of lodgers against frequency of servants. By so doing, a strong inverse relationship is shown. In areas where 80% or more of all households had servants, only 31.6% had lodgers; areas containing 60–79% of households with servants had 44.6% with lodgers; areas containing 40–59% of households with servants had 53.1% with lodgers; and in areas where under 40% of households had servants, 61.3% had lodgers.

In industrializing or industrialized places, most inmates maintained a very independent status in relation to their central households and must therefore be regarded as lodgers, though their pattern of distribution hints that structures of dependency, especially of origin and profession, might still exist. A remarkable number of lodgers shared a profession and/or place of origin with a member of the central household, so that the possibility of kinship or another kind of connection remains in some cases. This applies especially to Jews. Although Jewish households had fewer lodgers than average, most of the housefuls formed by the attachment of these lodgers to the household seem to have been structured (see p. 348).

Servants

While there will always be room to speculate as to what extent inmates shared activities and authority with their central family, there is no such doubt regarding servants. Servants were certainly under the authority of the head of the household; they shared consumption and production with their central family; and furthermore they very rarely formed subsystems within the household (and then mainly with their illegitimate children). Only in very few cases did persons in a servant-like position live in their master's house while having a household of their own, thus forming a structured houseful. This happened only with the servants of the richest aristocrats and some wealthy merchants. Otherwise servants lived in their master's household, and their role as well as their number depended primarily on the household's place in the organization of production. As time went on, families became less concerned with production, and so servants became more expendable.

Servants also became expendable at particular stages in the development of households, at least in rural areas. It can be shown that households with more grown-up children, other things being equal, had fewer servants than those with younger children. The village of Villgraten provides a clear example. Peasants of equal economic standing, that is all owning between 10 and 14 cattle and/or horses, who had no children above the age of 10 years had, on average, 2.71 servants (28 cases); with one child they had 2.45 servants (11 cases); with two children, 1.64 servants (14 cases); with three children, 1.06 servants (18 cases); with four children, 0.72 servants (18 cases); and with five children, 0.07 servants (14 cases). None of the five peasants with more than five children or grandchildren over 10 years of age employed a servant.

As for social status, it is a truism that the richer people had more servants, though the correlation is not quite linear, because above a certain limit the differences among production personnel such as apprentices, domestic personnel such as cooks and so on, and prestigious personnel such as ushers, musicians, and pipers became more important. The number of servants was therefore highest, not among the princes, but among well-to-do artisans. If one considers only households with servants, upper-class Herrengassen quarter (Vienna, 1857) came third with an average of 2.59 servants per household, after upper-middle-class Schottengassen quarter with 2.91 servants per household and Schottenfeld, where many rich artisans and industrialists lived, with 2.99 servants per household (see table 11.2). It may be worth mentioning that keeping up with the Joneses is not an entirely new phenomenon, because it seems that peasants of a certain standing were expected to have a certain number of servants, regardless of whether or not this was an economic necessity.[3]

In north-eastern and north-western Austria, where farmsteads were smaller and peasants poorer, the number of servants was considerably lower than in the west, only 0.48 servants per household being found in the former areas compared with more than 1 in the latter. Settlement structure may have been of importance in the north-east and north-

[3] Andrichsfurt in Upper Austria provides an interesting example. A farm which had been extremely prosperous all through the nineteenth century, employing eight to ten servants, ran into difficulties at the beginning of the twentieth century. The large number of servants, however, was retained for as long as it could be managed. When this became impossible the number of servants dropped to zero within a few years.

Table 11.2. *Servants from the seventeenth to the twentieth century by household, Austria*

Place and date	Servants per household (no.)	Servants per servant-keeping household (no.)
1. Rural areas		
North-east		
Maria Langegg, 1788	0.45	1.19
1828	0.51	1.23
1875	0.38	1.45
Obergrafendorf, 1788	0.53	1.77
Poysdorf, 1890	0.51	1.80
West, sub-alpine		
Thalgau, 1647	0.94	1.97
1750	1.24	2.60
Dorfbeuern, 1648	0.57	1.67
1772	0.66	1.93
Andrichsfurt, 1813	2.15	3.75
1863	1.96	3.56
1909	1.43	2.70
1947	c. 0.70	1.67
Raab, 1834 (country)	1.87	3.42
(town)	0.83	2.18
West, alpine		
Abtenau, 1632	0.93	2.19
1790	1.15	2.04
Altenmarkt, 1755 (country)	1.88	3.42
(market)	0.60	2.43
Metnitz, 1757 (country)	3.58	4.66
(market)	1.00	2.03
1796 (country)	3.21	4.22
(market)	0.98	2.52
Zell am Ziller, 1779	1.21	2.78
Villgraten, 1781	0.68	1.92
2. Industrializing areas		
Gleink, 1799	0.98	—
1856	1.00	—
Gmünd, 1801	0.27	1.12
1842	0.35	1.13
Perchtoldsdorf, 1754	0.63	2.05
1857	0.50	1.92
Stein, 1762	1.09	2.41
1857	0.56	2.38
Ebensee, 1809	0.22	c. 1.45
3. Vienna, 1857		
Herrengassen quarter	1.76	2.59
Schottengassen quarter	1.61	2.91

Table 11.2 (*cont.*).

Place and date	Servants per household (no.)	Servants per servant-keeping household (no.)
Old Town	1.50	2.42
Leopoldstadt	1.24	2.33
Schottenfeld	0.47	2.99
Gaudenzdorf	0.50	2.25

west and a fair number of agricultural workers may have lived in their villages as cotters. In the west one finds great differences. Subalpine grain farmers had most servants, 1.35 per household overall, with an even higher mean in the rich Innviertel (Raab, Andrichsfurt), whereas the average was slightly lower in the alpine areas outside Carinthia (1.17). Carinthia presented an outstanding feature in its huge households with their enormous numbers of servants. In 1757 rural Metnitz had an average of 3.58 servants per farmstead, and its farms were by no means the largest.

If one considers only those households with servants, then the averages are naturally much higher, but the pattern is the same. The difference among the individual regions, however, are not as big as before, which indicates that there were more servantless farms in the northeast (see table 11.2).

Changes over time are strongly connected with economic developments and short-term fluctuations: there are indications that numbers of rural servants increased slightly during the seventeenth and eighteenth centuries and the first half of the nineteenth century. In the second half of the nineteenth century, when more and more rural areas came within travelling distance of big centres, the numbers of servants fell sharply. Agricultural labourers did not, it seems, move directly into industrial work, but only indirectly, first replacing urban domestic personnel and moving into industry only later in life and sometimes not until the second generation. The total collapse of agricultural labourers as a class did not occur in Austria until the 1950s.

Turning to non-agrarian production, a distinction has to be made between domestic and non-domestic servants. The first group declined somewhat during the nineteenth century, or rather it became more exclusively female, with the disintegration of the great households into structured housefuls. On the other hand, the weakening and final disappearance of the guild system opened the way to concentrating people involved in production into groups. In Austria industrialization did not take place at first on a large scale, but was developed by middle-class artisans, who used to treat their workers as living-in journeymen. An interesting example is the distribution of apprentices and journeymen among masters in Leopoldstadt in 1857: of the 189 masters who had any employees living in, 63.5% had between 1 and 3, but these account for only 34.8% of all 652 employees, while 6 masters (3.2%) shared 90 employees (13%) among them. This gives a mean of 3.45 employees per master, but with a variance of 8.4. The variance would be still higher if one were to take into consideration the 3 carters employing drivers, because they had respectively 7, 9, and 46 (*sic*) drivers living on the premises, which would give a mean of 3.78 and a variance of 17.85.

This concentration of work people within the household was a prelude to their emancipation, as increasing numbers transformed earlier personal relationships between servant and master into more business-like ones, thus removing servants more and more to the outskirts of the household. Later the same became true for domestic servants, and the second half of the nineteenth century saw the rise of the charwoman, who lived out and came in daily to work.

Servants may be considered as an age group as well as a social class. Up to 55% were in their 20s, while on average no more than 16% were 40 years of age or more. There was quite a clear age pattern. More female

Table 11.3. *Servants of known age as a proportion of all servants of known age from the seventeenth to the twentieth century, by age group and sex, Austria*

Age group	Male (%)	Female (%)
0–9	0.6	0.4
10–19	25.9	24.0
20–9	37.3	43.1
30–9	19.6	18.2
40–9	8.9	7.8
≥50	7.7	6.4
TOTAL	100.0	100.0[a]
Servants of unknown age as a proportion of all servants	2.4	2.2

[a] Because of rounding, the actual totals in this and further tables are not always 100%.
Source: Schmidtbauer, 'Daten zur historischen Demographie und Familienstruktur' (1977) and fig. 11.3.

Table 11.4. *Servants of known age as a proportion of all servants of known age from the seventeenth to the twentieth century, by age group and residence, Austria*

Age group	In towns (%)	In countryside (%)
0–9	0.2	0.8
10–19	29.4	27.1
20–9	41.7	37.4
30–9	17.4	17.3
40–9	6.7	9.1
≥50	4.5	8.2
TOTAL	100.0	100.0
Servants of unknown age as proportion of all servants	1.4	3.0

Table 11.5. *Proportion of servants of known age as a proportion of all servants of known age, by age group and century, Austria*

Age group	17th century (%)	18th century (%)	19th century (%)	20th century (%)
0–9	0.8	0.9	0.1	—
10–19	33.7	25.3	28.1	38.8
20–9	46.3	42.4	37.3	27.8
30–9	13.1	16.0	19.7	17.7
40–9	4.1	8.7	8.3	5.5
≥50	2.0	6.6	6.5	10.2
TOTAL	100.0	100.0	100.0	100.0
Servants of unknown age as a proportion of all servants	9.4	2.0	0.7	—

Source: Schmidtbauer (1977) and fig. 11.5.

servants than male were to be found in the 20–9 age group (43% against 37%; see table 11.3 and fig. 11.3). There were also more town servants than country servants in this age group (42% against 37%; see table 11.4), though the overall proportions decreased with each century from the seventeenth to the twentieth. Servants aged 20–9: seventeenth century, 40.2% rural, 51.9% town; eighteenth century, 39.9% rural, 45.2% town; nineteenth century, 34.2% rural, 37.9% town; twentieth

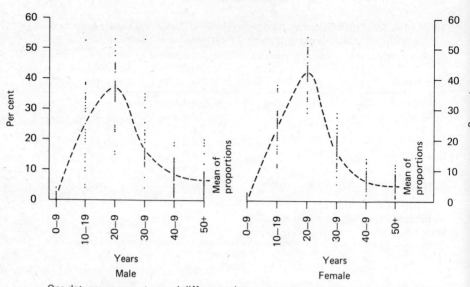

One dot may represent several different values.

Fig. 11.3. Age distribution of servants (means) by community, for 49 communities in Austria, seventeenth to twentieth century. (*Source:* Schmidtbauer (1977).)

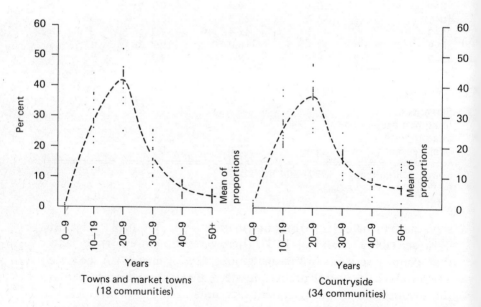

Fig. 11.4. Age distribution of urban and rural servants by community, Austria, seventeenth to twentieth century. (*Source:* Schmidtbauer (1977).)

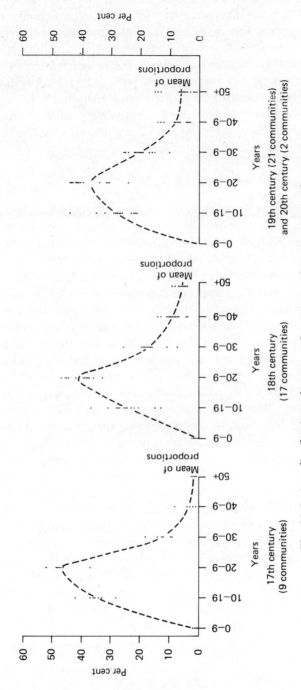

Fig. 11.5. Age distribution of servants by community, Austria, in the seventeenth, in the eighteenth, and in the nineteenth and twentieth centuries. (*Source:* Schmidtbauer (1977).)

century, 27.8%. It has been noted that servants had households of their
own in only a very few cases, but it is also true that only very few
servants brought their relatives into the central household. This usually
happened only with illegitimate children and more frequently in rural
areas than in towns. On average there were only 1.3 dependants of
servants per 100 servants living in the same household: 1.7 in rural
areas and 0.5 in towns.[4] Only in the Herrengassen quarter of Vienna did
the number of dependants increase to 4.2 per 100 servants. The percentage of widowed servants was negligible.

Kin

Inmates as well as servants include a number of relatives of the household whose status cannot be established with certainty, and who therefore pose an important theoretical question which makes it difficult to
approach problems of family structure on a predominantly kin basis.
The question is whether they are to be regarded as kin, and whether the
households in which they lived are therefore to be treated as extended
or multiple households, simply because we now know that a kinship
relationship existed; or are they not to be regarded as kin, with everything that follows from such a classification, because the contemporary
source did not consider this kin relationship of primary importance?
Furthermore, difficulties arise over comparability, because it may be
possible to identify nearly all kin in one source and hardly any at all in
another. The problem is not a trifling one, for the Andrichsfurt serial
listings suggest that about 10% of all servants might have been relatives.
There were fewer inmates in Andrichsfurt who were related to members of the household, but more elsewhere. When one compares Zell am
Ziller in 1759 and 1779, one finds that the proportion of kin falls from
11.2% of the population in the first listing, which notes relationships
with care, to 6.7% in the second. In the latter case, more households
were affected, as often only one relative was to be found in a household.

   If the social role is regarded as most important – and this is probably
best represented in the contemporary record – one will be reluctant to
pay too much attention to differences in the number of extended
families, and yet one cannot ignore kin entirely, because when one
examines kin servants closely, one finds that their situation was somewhat different from that of non-related servants.

[4] There are, however, two freak results. In Duerrnberg in 1647 there were 331 dependants of 100 servants, and in Gastein market in 1690 there were 69. Both were mining
   areas, and these features are probably the result of the special organization of production. I have omitted them when calculating the mean.

As the series of listings indicate, non-related servants rarely stayed longer than two years on a farm: in Andrichsfurt, for instance, 88.6% had left after two years, the mean length of stay being 1.56 years, and they only occasionally came back; 94.6% did not. Kin servants, on the contrary, frequently returned and usually stayed longer. In some areas they sometimes remained a very long time. This does not necessarily imply that they occupied a special status among the fringe members of the household, because their behaviour may have resulted as much from a desire to remain in a place where they had close associations as from necessity, but their pattern is sufficiently different to warrant consideration of the households where kin have been detected.[5]

As the number of detectable kin depends mainly on the quality of the sources, the variances which occur are enormous; with a mean of 12.1% of all households containing kin, the variance is 64.8, but this rises to over 120 for certain subgroups. This makes interpretation hazardous, but even so, and relying primarily on sources that probably give all related people as kin, one can say that the north-east had far fewer kin living in the household than the alpine west and that therefore the proportion of extended households was far higher in the Alps than in the north-eastern lowlands. The Tyrolean Alps in particular seem to be an area with an outstanding proportion of households with kin. The listing of Zell am Ziller for 1759 shows that 48.2% of all households contained relatives of some sort[6] (see table 11.6). But the Zell listing was out of the ordinary in that one of the enumerator's principal tasks would seem to have been the notation of all kin. In Villgraten, too, 34.7% of households included kin, and there were even more unusual features in this town which will be discussed later. Another region with a large number of kin was Innviertel, but here we meet the problem mentioned above. From the series of listings one can calculate that about 30% of all households of Andrichsfurt contained kin in 1863, but apart from parents and a few other relatives of a special sort none were explicitly given as kin in the source; even kin servants were not listed as such, and one would not recognize them as kin, if one only had a single description. It is not surprising, therefore, that the number of detected siblings rises from 0.9% of the population in the first year of the series to 6.8% after 60 years of uninterrupted observation.

[5] I have included among such households those in which only co-resident siblings or relatives of other kinds were present (P. Laslett and Wall (eds.) (1972): 31, table 1.1, categories 2a, b). In Austria, at least, such kinship groupings represented a very transitory phase, not deserving special attention. Households of this kind were very few, under 0.5%.
[6] Only three households (2.2%) contained parents but no other kin.

P. Schmidtbauer

Unlike these areas with a high kin rate, Poysdorf in 1890 had only 6.1% of its households with collateral kin (10.5% when parents are included), although this listing gives relationships in great detail.

Table 11.6. *Household composition in the eighteenth and nineteenth centuries, Austria*

Place and date	House-holds (no.)	Multiple households as a proportion of all households (%)	Extended households as a proportion of all households (%)
Villgraten, 1781			
Agrarian population			
0–4 cattle	103	1.9	14.6
5–6 cattle	71	14.1	22.5
7–9 cattle	116	21.6	20.7
10–14 cattle	105	25.7	22.9
15+ cattle	40	47.5	27.9
Non-agrarian population			
0–4 cattle	68	7.4	27.9
5+ cattle	19	26.3	21.1
TOTAL	522	17.8	21.6
Raab, 1834			
Country			
Cotters	29	3.4	
1–19 land units	61	9.8	
10–39 land units	69	13.0	22.9
40+ land units	31	12.9	
Artisans with farm	24	8.3	
Artisans without farm	25	4.0	
TOTAL	239	9.6	22.9
Town			
Cotters	20	5.0	—
Peasants	9	11.1	—
Artisans with farm	33	6.1	—
Artisans without farm	54	5.5	—
TOTAL	116	6.0	17.3
Metnitz, 1757, market town	68	1.4	10.1
country	245	1.2	20.4
TOTAL	313	1.3	18.2
1796, market town	59	3.4	30.5
country	192	2.6	28.6
TOTAL	251	2.8	29.1

Table 11.6 (*cont.*)

Place and date	House-holds (no.)	Multiple households as a proportion of all households (%)	Extended households as a proportion of all households (%)
Zell am Ziller, 1759	137	2.2	48.2
Poysdorf, 1890	620	0.3	10.5
Vienna, 1857			
Herrengassen quarter	623	0.5	8.3
Schottengassen quarter	717	1.0	4.6
Old Town	940	0.6	6.7
Leopoldstadt	1,750	0.5	5.7
Gumpendorf	2,255	0.4	4.3
TOTAL	6,285	0.6	5.5

Market townships and their environs are directly comparable. The result is surprising, because it seems that centres of population had a higher proportion of kin compared with surrounding villages when the general level was low, and a lower proportion when the level was high. In the five cases where the centres had a higher proportion of kin, the mean was 8.6% (centres, 10.4%; environs, 6.8%). In the four cases where the centres' share was lower, the mean was 16.6% (centres, 14.1%; environs, 19.0%).

The evidence of change over time is unconvincing, because of the high variance among the individual listings, but one gets the impression that households with kin increased in numbers from the first observation in the mid-seventeenth century until the early part of the nineteenth century, when there was a sudden change. Industrialized areas had a very low number of kin, though in the early stages of industrialization there was a brief upsurge in living-in kin. The distribution in Vienna suggests that living-in kin, and therefore extended-family households, occurred more frequently among the well-to-do than among the poor: 8.3% of the households in the Herrengassen quarter had this type of structure, while working-class areas had only 5.1%. As many as 10.2% of the aristocratic households had kin living in.

One kinship role, that of parent, is always given. This leads us to the difficult problem of the Austrian stem family. There can be no doubt that a considerable proportion of households in historic Austria contained at least one of the central couple's parents and that this obtained particularly for rural households and for many non-rural ones as well. This situation does not necessarily constitute a stem family, because the parent was in most cases not at the centre of the household. His participation in the production process was inconsiderable or non-existent, and, most important, he had no authority and therefore no control over the life and economy of the farm. But a stem-family situation demands that the authority rests, if not exclusively, at least partly, with the older generation, while the younger man is at best joint owner but never has sole authority over the household's economy. In all Austria, save in a single area, the younger man with very few exceptions owned the farm, had control over its whole economy, and exercised authority over all its people. The old people had reserved for themselves nothing more than their means of livelihood, in case the young did not provide these voluntarily.[7]

As the hand-over might take several weeks, one occasionally finds an old and a young farmer on one farm, but this occurred but rarely. The one exception, however, is Villgraten, where true stem families, complete with married sons working under the direction of their father, grown-up grandchildren, and other relatives did form a considerable proportion of households.

That Villgraten was indeed extraordinary is clearly shown by the number of multiple-family households (see table 11.6). Of all Villgraten households, 17.8% were multiple, and this proportion becomes even more striking if one breaks down the households according to wealth. Only 1.9% of those possessing 0–4 cattle and/or horses were multiple (103 cases); 14.1% with 5 or 6 cattle (71 cases); 21.0% with 7–9 cattle (116 cases); and 25.7% with 10–14 cattle (105 cases); while a staggering 47.5% of the 40 richer households were multiple. Of course not all the multiple households were stem families, but of the 98 subordinate couples only 1 was probably an uncle, 7 were brothers of the owner, and 6 were parents, corresponding to the usual Austrian form of retirement, while 84 (85.7%) were married children: 79 sons and 5 daughters. So one can reckon that about 15% of all Villgraten households were centred upon a stem family, and that, at least for the wealthier peasants,

7 Written retirement agreements are very often purely a matter of form, made according to custom or the model provided from the manor. Sometimes one finds provisions granted that were clearly impossible for the farm to supply. In one place, for instance, retirement contracts regularly provided for beehives, even if none had ever been owned by the farm in question.

the stem family must be regarded as a usual or even as the most characteristic form of family.

In all the other Austrian enumerations, however, multiple households were far rarer, and there were practically no stem families. Raab in 1834, taking country and town together, had the second highest number of multiple households, making up 8.5% of all households, but this was mainly because the peasants were wealthy and could afford to retire while the old couple were both still living. Of the 31 subordinate couples, 27 (87.1%) were parents and 3 were other relatives, and there was only 1 married son (3.2%), so that only 1 of Raab's 355 households contained a stem family (0.3%). In Raab as in Villgraten, richer farmers had more multiple households than the poorer ones, but the difference was not really marked, rising from 3.4% to 12.9%. Among artisans who also did some farming, 7% had multiple households (4% in the countryside and 5.5% in the town) compared with 26.3% for the similar group in Villgraten, while artisans without land in Raab had about 5% multiple households (4% in the countryside and 5.5% in the town) compared with 7.4% in Villgraten. Even Raab's cotters had some multiple households. In all the other places analysed in table 11.6, fewer than 4% of households were multiple, and this figure drops to 1% in Poysdorf and Vienna.

Except in the rich Innviertel, most peasants retired only when one of the old couple had died or was about to die. Manorial pressure sometimes forced them out earlier, but, given their own choice, this was their usual behaviour, not least because double retirement was a heavy burden on the farm's economy. Nevertheless, quite a high proportion of households contained retired parents. In pre-industrial times, except in the great cities, 12% of all Austrian households contained at least one retired parent. There were, however, quite big differences; very few cotters and only some artisans had parents with them, compared with about a fifth of all farmers.[8] As a result, fewer parents lived with their children in the central townships than in the environs.

There were also quite important regional differences. In the northeast, where ultimogeniture was frequent, only 9% of all households contained parents; in the Alps the figure was 11.2%, whereas in the subalpine west (with Raab) and the north-west (with Heidenreichstein)

---

[8] Raab is one of the places with the highest proportion of retired parents in Austria. In 1834 the distribution was as follows: 29.4% of peasant households contained parents, compared with 18.4% of artisan households and only 8.2% of cotters' households. Of households in the town, 18.1% contained parents, compared with 24.3% in the environs. It is to be noted that the very richest peasants were less likely to have parents at home. They were probably rich enough to buy a little house in town for them.

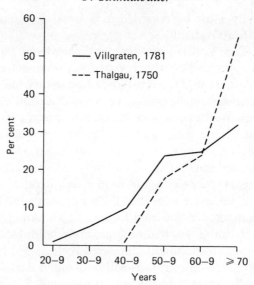

Fig. 11.6. Age distribution of retired people, Villgraten, 1781 and Thalgau, 1750. (*Source*: Schmidtbauer (1977).)

there were a large number of retirements, with about 18% of the households containing parents. There was a major difference between the two regions, as in the poor north-west such parents were usually widowed, whereas in the subalpine west a considerable number of peasants retired while the couple were both still living. The development over time is difficult to trace, and one would need more material to make definite pronouncements. But while in the subalpine region the number of households with parents did not change very much, in the Alps their number dropped from the seventeenth to the nineteenth century. As the province of Salzburg is overrepresented in the sample, this may have been a consequence of the economic stagnation Salzburg experienced in the eighteenth and nineteenth centuries. In the north-east there was a marked increase from the eighteenth to the nineteenth century. Big cities like Salzburg and industrial towns had a very low proportion of households with parents (about 2%).

Children and heads of households

Let us finally turn to the central roles of any European family: children and the couple or single individual at the centre of the household. It is important to stress that 'children' are not limited to biological children, but include all persons who are in a child-like position, thus embracing not only offspring, but also stepchildren and foster children and even adult persons living in a household with their parents as head. Detection of stepchildren depends to a certain degree on whether they are indicated as such in the source, but their numbers tend to decrease from the very beginning of the period of observation, because the pressure to remarry lessened with the decrease of manorial rights and with the change of production patterns, thus enabling peasants to replace the deceased wife with hired servants. As a result, areas with more servants show a markedly lower rate of remarriage than areas with fewer servants, where the economic pressure for remarriage was higher. In the second half of the nineteenth century the impact of rising life expectancy was also being felt. On the other hand, numbers of foster children, who were mostly illegitimate grandchildren or other relatives, increased considerably until the middle of the nineteenth century.[9] The mean age of children increased too, a fact that is, strictly speaking, not altogether due to longer life expectancy (although this might account for the last part of the rise, when deaths in childhood decreased) but also to the tendency to keep children at home longer rather than sending them away as servants to some neighbouring farm. Thus the proportion of children of 20 years of age and over rises from 11.2% in the seventeenth century to 16.3% in the eighteenth and to 19.6% in the nineteenth century. For children of 30 years and over the increase is even more marked: 1.8% to 4.0% to 4.6%.

Differences among regions were not great, except perhaps in the Alps, where children were kept at home somewhat longer. The same is true for townships as compared with their environs. Interestingly, the mean age of children in cities and industrial towns did not differ from that in the country. Still, in Vienna the better-off could afford to keep their children far longer. Schottengassen and Herrengassen quarters had a mean age of over 13 years, 13.29 and 13.04, compared with working-class Gumpendorf with only 10.87.

The proportion of households with children was remarkably uniform. Regional differences ranged from 83.3% in the north-west, 79.9% in the north-east, and 79.3% in the subalpine west to 76.1% in the Alps. In all regions the townships showed a lower proportion than in the country (78.6% to 80.7%). For the rural areas the mean was constantly falling: 81.9% in the seventeenth century, 79.0% in the eighteenth, and 78.4% in the nineteenth, but there was stability in the townships in the

[9] Their working power might have helped to set servants free to fill a possibly missing role.

seventeenth and eighteenth centuries (75.2% and 75.7% respectively) and even an increase to 79.6% in the nineteenth century.

The position in the big cities, however, was quite different. Whereas industrializing places showed a slight increase in households with children, the proportion in the big cities was always far below average: Salzburg did not exceed 66.7% in any of its three censuses: 1569, 62.3%; 1647, 66.7%; 1794, 49% (*sic*). Vienna in 1857 had a mean of 61.7%, with the lowest proportion (51.8%) in the Schottengassen quarter and the highest (81.5%) in Gumpendorf (see table 11.7). This low proportion of households with children is perhaps the most significant feature which modern society has in common with pre-industrial urban society. Closely connected with the proportion of households containing children is the proportion of nuclear-family households: at around 65% they followed the same pattern of change.

Table 11.7. *Proportion of households with children from the sixteenth to the twentieth century, and mean age of children, Austria*

Place and date	Households with children (%)	Mean age of children (years)
North-east		
Obergrafendorf, 1788	76.7	9.86
1855	80.7[b]	—
Maria Langegg, 1788	82.2	10.3
1875	87.0	12.2
Rappoltenkirchen, 1872	84.7[b]	—
Poysdorf, 1890	76.9	12.97
Mean[a]	79.9	
North-west		
Gmünd (Land), 1801	88.8	
(Stadt), 1801	85.2	11.01
(Land), 1842	78.7	10.49
(Stadt), 1842	80.4	
Mean[a]	83.3	
West, subalpine		
Dorfbeuern, 1648	82.0	10.22
1772	70.9	10.33
1876	67.3	11.30
Thalgau, 1647	80.9	9.61
1750	80.9	11.64
Berndorf, 1647	81.4	12.39
Andrichsfurt, 1813	c. 79	10.04
1863	c. 81	17.33[c]

Table 11.7 (*cont.*)

Place and date	Households with children (%)	Mean age of children (years)
1909	*c.* 82	11.47
1947	*c.* 68	14.44
Raab, 1834 (country)	77.9 ⎫	11.24
(town)	75.7 ⎭	
Mean[a]	79.3	
West, alpine		
Abtenau, 1632	89.2	10.50
1790	79.4	10.56
Tamsweg, 1635 (country)	70.1[b]	—
(town)	77.3[b]	—
Altenmarkt, 1755 (country)	87.5 ⎫	10.18
(market)	69.9 ⎭	
Taxenbach, 1622	81.5[b]	—
1794	72.2[b]	—
Metnitz, 1757 (country)	81.2	12.12
(market)	72.5	11.25
1796 (country)	72.4	13.02
(market)	76.3	15.05
Zell am Ziller, 1759	87.6	13.07
Villgraten, 1781	76.2	13.33
Mean[a]	76.1	
Cities		
Salzburg, 1569	62.3[b]	—
1647	66.7	9.78
1794	49.0	13.85
Vienna, 1857		
Herrengassen quarter	54.8	13.04
Schottengassen quarter	51.8	13.29
Old Town (north)	56.7	12.42
Leopoldstadt	68.7	11.93
Gumpendorf	81.5	10.87
Schottenfeld	70.3	12.07
Gaudenzdorf	70.4	10.14
Mean[a]	64.9	

[a] The mean of all listings in the area, not only those places named above.
[b] Partial or no information on ages.
[c] Exceptionally high average, due to untypical circumstances; see Schmidtbauer, 'Modell einer lokalen Krise' (1978a).

The central figures of the household were, in the great majority of cases, married couples. There were, however, changes in distribution. While in the early listings the number of central couples was extremely high, it fell off considerably in later centuries. The proportion of married couples at the centre in the seventeenth century was 89%, falling in the eighteenth century to 84.2%, in the nineteenth century to 82.4%, and in the twentieth century to 73.5%. Although until comparatively recently the rural economy in Austria depended on two persons at the centre, each with a distinctive role to play, peasants showed a growing tendency to replace a deceased spouse not by remarriage but by employing servants and kin, who would temporarily fill the vacant role. Where this was not possible, because the farms were too poor to keep additional personnel or where manorial rights were stronger, so that the landlord could insist on either remarriage or retirement, remarriage would occur more frequently. If one compares subalpine Salzburg province, where manorial rights were stronger and there were fewer servants, with alpine Salzburg, one finds that the proportion of married couples at the centre of the household in the seventeenth century was 94.5% for the subalpine area and 86.6% for the alpine region.

It is therefore not surprising that the proportions were higher in the north-east and north-west, where farms were poorest, lower in the subalpine west, and lowest in the alpine west. In this last region, only about 75% of the households in Metnitz, with its great number of servants, and Zell am Ziller and Villgraten, with their high proportion of kin, were headed by married couples at the end of the eighteenth century. Most of the rural households not headed by couples were centred on single or widowed men, whose proportion as household heads was constantly growing, as was that of widowed women. Townships followed a different pattern, as they always had a lower proportion of married couples, somewhat under 80%. This figure did not change very much until the mid-nineteenth century, when it dropped sharply. Here women were normally more likely to form the non-married centres than men were, though there were also places where men predominated as unmarried heads of household.

The two early enumerations of Salzburg (1569 and 1647) do not show any great differences from the distribution pattern in lesser centres, but the census of 1794, taken at the end of a long decline in the city's importance, shows a unique situation in that less than half of all households were headed by a married couple: 48.9%, against 15.9% of single or widowed males and 35.3% of single or widowed females. Vienna too shows a very low proportion (66.3%) in 1857, which accords with modern developments. Poorer areas had a higher rate than richer ones: Herrengassen quarter, 57.6%; Gumpendorf, 73.1%. For the first time there was a marked rise in the number of non-married couples. For example, in Gaudenzdorf their proportion rose from 0.8% in 1857 to 9.4% in 1880.

Conclusion

Starting with a model of the family that stresses the importance of social rather than biological roles, not only in its composition, but also in its functions of production and consumption, in the authority of its head, and in the general interdependence of its members, one can reach a fairly clear concept of the development of the familial household in historic Austria. Our first sources show the household, with a few exceptions, as a fairly complicated structure, consisting of the two central figures, husband and wife, together with children, servants, and groups of inmates who might sometimes have distinct substructures but who shared in the life of the household to a sufficient extent to enable one to think of it as a single unit. It is, of course, impossible to discover how far this represents an advanced state, developed over centuries; our sources do not enable us to make any pronouncements on medieval conditions.

Change of economic opportunities as well as of the general ideology of the family allowed the inmates to be the first to emancipate themselves from the authority of the head of their household to form new, smaller and nuclear households, sometimes after an intermediate state of a structured houseful. This emancipation of the inmates signals the end of one of the household's former functions, namely to give protection to outsiders who could not, for various reasons, form a household of their own.

The drift away of the inmates was closely connected with a change in the familial organization of production. As this changed further with urbanization, industrialization, and constantly improving communications, especially in the country, production servants emancipated themselves as a second group, as finally did the domestic servants, first in the towns and after about 1850 in the country, where the process was considerably slower. This again shows that the family had lost its function as the unit of production of goods for non-domestic consumption. The exodus of members of the household as well as ideological change and technical development obviously also affected the status of children and householders, so that children remained at home longer and the possibility of being a householder became less bound to the married state.

In all this development industrialization played an important role, but not a causal one, because the first instances of the emancipation of inmates and servants can be observed far earlier; in some households the growing demand for paid labour was apparent even before industrialization proper. Inmates and servants were gradually enabled to set up households of their own, mainly in urban centres, thus forming a broad group of people living in small families without being dependent and without many dependants. It was from this group that industry, when it was later established, could draw recruits.

Different factors served to produce different aspects of this general development. Most important were the economic possibility of hiring servants and the varying strength of the landlord's rights. Retirement age, succession, and remarriage rates were fundamentally dependent upon these factors. A second feature influencing the composition of the household was the pattern of settlement and traditional forms of house-building; the number of inmates who could be accepted depended largely on the available space in the house. In areas with village settlements the mean number of servants was markedly lower than in areas with small hamlets or single farms, where it would be difficult for the servant to live out. A third important point that differentiates household structure is the more or less central position of a given geographical place. The larger the area for which a place is the centre, the more the non-agrarian population is concentrated in that place, with all the economic and social impact that results. Furthermore, the more central a place, the more opportunity for casual work and hired labour and therefore for people to emancipate themselves economically. This can be seen both in the township of 300 souls and in the capital city of many thousands. These were the centres where the small family abounded and whence the concept of the nuclear family spread all over the country.

APPENDIX
Listings used

Place and date	Population	Households	Mean household size
1. Abtenau, 1632	4,112	536	7.67
1790	3,916	508	7.71
(both PA Abtenau)			
2. Altenmarkt im Pongau, 1755, market	367	67	5.48
country	1,978	264	7.49
Other listings: 1733, 1762			
(all PA Altenmarkt)			
3. Andrichsfurt, 1813	806	108	7.46
1863	702	98	7.16
1909	622	98	6.35
Other listings: 1814–62, 1864–97, 1901, 1910–17, 1923, 1942–56			
(all PA Andrichsfurt)			
4. Berndorf bei Salzburg, 1647	747	163	4.58
(PA Berndorf)			
5. Dienten am Hochkoenig, 1726	619	87	7.11
Other listings: 1711, 1756			
(all PA Dienten)			
6. Dorfbeuern, 1648	991	168	5.90
1772	747	157	4.76
Other listings: 1671, 1862, 1876			
(all PA Michaelbeuern)			
7. Duerrnberg, 1647	510	79	6.46
Other listing: 1685			
(both LA Salzburg)			
8. Ebensee, 1809	3,092	596	5.19
1829	3,950	767	5.15
1868	5,634	1,120	5.03
Other listings: 1779–1808, 1821, 1826–8, 1830–67, 1870, 1879, 1883, 1892			
(all PA Ebensee)			
9. Eckartsau, 1766	1,329	218	6.10
(Haus-, Hof- und Staatsarchiv, Herrscharch. Eckartsau, Vienna)			

Notes:
Not all data could be made available for all places.
Numbers correspond with numbers in fig. 11.1
DA: Dioezesanarchiv (Diocesan Archive).
LA: Landesarchiv (Provincial Archive).
PA Pfarrarchiv (Parish Archive).

Appendix (*cont.*)

Place and date	Population	Households	Mean household size
10. Freistadt, 1919	2,956	834	3.54
(LA Linz, Stadtarch. Freistadt)			
11. Gastein, 1497	2,294	599	3.83
(copy, LA Salzburg)			
1690, market	594	105	5.66
(PA Markt Hofgastein)			
12. Gleink, 1799	1,054	168	6.27
1856	922	155	5.95
Other listings: 1800–55			
(all LA Linz, Stadtarchiv Steyr)			
13. Gmünd, 1801	2,342	364	6.43
1842	3,300	453	7.28
Other countings: biannually 1802–38			
(all DA St Pölten, PA Gmünd)			
14. Gmunden, 1762	1,824	378	4.83
(LA Linz, Stadtarchiv Gmunden)			
15. Koppl, 1647	647	76	8.51
1805	307	82	3.74
(both PA Koppl)			
16. Koestendorf, 1648	2,556	319	8.01
1665	2,306	291	7.92
(both PA Koestendorf)			
17. Laa/Thaya, 1867	2,161	415	5.21
(PA Laa/Thaya)			
18. Lessach, 1811	—	87	—
(LA Salzburg, Pfleg Tamsweg)			
19. Lofer, 1593	—	141	—
(LA Salzburg, Konsistorialakten)			
20. Maria Langegg, 1788	530	93	5.70
1828	616	97	6.35
1875	625	100	6.25
Other listings: 1789–1827, 1829–74			
(some years missing)			
(all DA St Pölten, PA Maria Langegg)			
21. Mauterndorf, 1774	—	174	—
(PA Mauterndorf)			
22. Metnitz, 1757, market	371	69	5.38
country	2,222	250	8.89
1796, market	334	59	5.66
country	1,634	192	8.51
(two listings; both DA Klagenfurt)			
23. Mondsee, c. 1740	—	154	—
(LA Linz, Stiftsarchiv Mondsee)			

Place and date	Population	Households	Mean household size
24. Obergrafendorf, 1788	1,980	268	7.39
1855	2,152	281	7.66
Other listings: 1789–1854 (some years missing)			
(all DA St Pölten, PA Obergrafendorf)			
25. Perchtoldsdorf, 1754	1,685	293	5.75
1857	2,930	579	5.06
(both Marktarchiv Perchtoldsdorf)			
26. Poysdorf, 1890	3,113	620	5.02
(PA Poysdorf)			
27. Raab, 1834, town	869	126	6.90
country	1,882	239	7.87
Other listings: biannually 1816–32, 1860			
(all PA Raab)			
28. Radstadt, 1752	952	127	7.50
(PA Radstadt)			
29. Rappoltenkirchen, 1862	—	128	—
Other listings: biannually 1842–82			
(all DA St Pölten, PA Rappoltenkirchen)			
30. Salzburg, 1569	—	975	—
1647	7,245	1,478	4.90
1794	5,851	1,383	4.23
(all LA Salzburg, Geheimes Archiv)			
31. St Leonhard am Forst, 1756	—	53	—
Other listings: 1737–55			
(all DA St Pölten, PA St Leonhard a. F.)			
32. Stein, 1762	978	192	5.09
1857	2,274	507	4.49
(both Stadtarchiv Krems)			
33. Tamsweg, 1635	1,207	199	6.07
(PA Tamsweg)			
34. Taxenbach, 1622	—	184	—
1794	—	180	—
(both PA Taxenbach)			
35. Thalgau, 1647	2,949	404	7.30
1750	2,570	397	6.47
(both PA Thalgau)			
36. Vienna, 1857			
Herrengassen quarter[1]	3,517	623	5.65
Schottengassen quarter[1]	3,857	717	5.38

[1] Herrengassen quarter and Schottengassen quarter are divided differently in later operations, so that Herrengassen quarter contains 976 and Schottengassen quarter 303 households (61 households dropped). See fig. 11.2.

Appendix (*cont.*)

Place and date	Popula-tion	House-holds	Mean house-hold size
36. Vienna, 1857 (*cont.*)			
Old Town (north)	5,579	940	5.94
Leopoldstadt	10,994	1,750	6.28
Gumpendorf	13,323	2,255	5.91
Schottenfeld	3,194	586	5.45
Gaudenzdorf	1,238	230	5.38
Vienna, 1880: Gaudenzdorf	1,466	323	4.54
(all Archiv der Stadt Wien, Konskriptionen)			
37. Villgraten, 1781	3,420	525	6.51
(LA Innsbruck)			
38. Weinzierl, 1751	544	99	5.41
1867	653	133	4.91
(both Stadtarchiv Krems)			
39. Wildenegg, 1740	—	771	—
(LA Linz, Stiftsarchiv Mondsee)			
40. Zell am Ziller, 1759 (partial)	1,182	137	8.63
1779	2,581	278	9.28
(both PA Zell am Ziller)			
41. Zweinitz, 1757	637	89	7.16
1811	676	99	6.83
Other listings: 1770, 1786, 1798			
(all PA Zweinitz)			

12

Does owning real property influence the form of the household? An example from rural West Flanders

RICHARD WALL

Marriage and inheritance

In a paper written in 1972 Lutz Berkner listed the factors that might prevent inheritance customs from influencing the form of the household.[1] Some factors made inheritance lore inoperative, for example if the family had no property or only 'movables', in which case there would be no link between their possession and a particular residence; or if land was held on a temporary lease. On the other hand, there were certain factors such as the development cycle of the household and the property arrangements surrounding marriage which might simply conceal the effect of inheritance. When to all this has to be added differences among inheritance law, custom, and practice, it becomes a very difficult matter to predict what forms of household might underlie a particular inheritance system. Indeed, in a more recent paper, written jointly with Franklin Mendels, Berkner has specifically identified an area where an egalitarian inheritance system had little effect on the partibility of land, and in turn on demographic and household patterns, because the nature of the local economy required large farms.[2] This area comprised the polders of West Flanders.

So far, however, the arguments have been advanced in the absence of hard data on the structure of the household, and it seems worth while to try and establish whether there is a particular form of household that one might associate with rural West Flanders. For this purpose we will divide the households not only by the occupation of the head but according to whether they were owner-occupiers or tenants. For

---

[1] Berkner, 'Rural family organisation in Europe' (1972b): 151. Cf. Sabean, 'Aspects of kinship behaviour and property in rural western Europe' (1976): 103–6.
[2] Berkner and Mendels, 'Inheritance system, family structure and demographic patterns' (1978): 218.

380 *Richard Wall*

though inheritance practices may affect them both (the tenants may be the minor heirs of the previous generation),[3] it will do so unequally. Before we proceed with the examination of the household, though, we need to set out what is to be expected in the particular circumstances of West Flanders. About this Berkner and Mendels, although warning about the flexibility allowed by partible inheritance practice, have been clear, up to a point. Two factors that they say positively preclude the subdivision of property are a heavy soil requiring a large plough, and dairy farming. Both apply to this area of West Flanders.[4] We would therefore expect, though Berkner and Mendels do not tell us, that one of the farmer's sons would stay on in adulthood to help work the land and that he would eventually succeed his father, as he would have done in an area of impartible inheritance. There is a possibility, even, that the farmers were operating a form of the stem family.[5] Tenant farmers, one suspects, would be in quite a different situation. Without real property of their own, they would be unable to prevent their sons leaving when opportunities arose for them to become tenant farmers in their own right. The only constraint on the sons' actions would be a shortage of land created by the need to work land in large units.[6]

There is, however, another factor affecting owners rather than tenants that we need to consider: the nature of the marriage system. Thanks to the work of Yver and its popularization by Le Roy Ladurie,[7] we now know a good deal about the geographical spread of 'lineage' and 'community' arrangements and the differences between them. Flanders is interesting for the emphasis placed on the lineage principle in contrast with what is now the French-speaking part of Belgium, where the community system was in operation.

Flemish customary law favoured the individual at the expense of the household community. In lineage marriage, two features may be

[3] *Ibid.* 213.
[4] *Ibid.* 214, 218. For dairying in West Flanders see van der Maelen, *Dictionnaire géographique de la Flandre occidentale* (1836).
[5] The definition of the stem-family household is in terms of the relationship between the existing household and its successor on the same plot, a process that can only be explored by matching households at named addresses between successive lists. For an example of this technique applied to one of the rare repetitive lists for Flanders see the contribution to this volume by Luc Danhieux, ch. 13 below.
[6] Unfortunately, it is difficult to obtain precise information about farm size. Land registers which would give this information seem not to have survived for the nine villages chosen for detailed study below. See van de Haegen, 'Bronnen voor de Reconstructie van de agarische Struktuur' (1979).
[7] Yver, *Egalité entre héritiers* (1966); Le Roy Ladurie, 'Family and inheritance customs in sixteenth century France' (1976): 65–70. Yver, 'Les deux groupes de coutumes du Nord' (1953–4) documents considerably more variation in Flemish custom than is implied by Le Roy Ladurie's summary.

singled out for special attention. First, the marriage partners maintained separate rights to whatever property they brought into the marriage. On the death of one of them, any property passed to that individual's heirs (collaterals in the absence of children) and not to the surviving spouse, as in Wallonia. Secondly, offspring of a second marriage shared equally in the inheritance with the offspring of a first marriage. These practices were reversed in community marriage.

The principles of lineage marriage, if adopted in practice, would in the long term reinforce any trend towards the subdivision of landholdings.[8] When assessing the relationship between the marriage system and the shape of the household, however, we have to take account of the different circumstances of individual members of the household, circumstances that could alter depending on the point in their life cycle and the family's life cycle when the property became available. Under the lineage system the interests of head, spouse, and offspring were dissimilar. The recently widowed farmer, who may have 'lost' some property on the death of his wife, had a strong incentive to remarry. So had the widow, although unlike the widower she would not be able to bring her new spouse to the farm which she had occupied during her first marriage, as in most cases she would have no further claim on it. We can therefore expect a high remarriage rate on the part of property owners.[9] In the meantime their offspring would have to wait for the remaining pieces of their inheritance. Unless they were themselves successful in the remarriage market, this would seem likely to have resulted in a prolongation of the period of dependency in the parental household. Again a contrast with the offspring of tenant farmers seems likely. They had no inheritance to await and could choose their moment to leave home, whether for marriage or a period of service in someone else's household.

Of course, if farm tenants enjoyed as much security as farm owners, then one would not anticipate any major difference between the households of owners and tenants, other factors being equal. A leading authority on the agricultural history of Belgium, however, Hubert van Houtte, makes clear that in West Flanders the rule was short leases which could be extended beyond nine years only by the negotiation of a new contract or by special agreement.[10] Admittedly, some of the farmer-owners in the nine villages were also tenants. In the extreme case of

---

[8] Yver's suggestion is that the correlation between partible inheritance and the egalitarianism of the lineage system is universal, but this is refuted by Sabean (1976): 106.

[9] Remarriage might also occur under the community system, but then it would be designed to keep the property intact rather than to reconstitute a viable holding.

[10] Van Houtte, *Histoire économique de la Belgique à la fin de l'Ancien Régime* (1920): 427.

Table 12.1. *Proportion of owners of real property residing in parish of birth*
(married couples only)

	Residing in parish of birth			
	Husbands		Wives	
Occupational group of husband	Owning real property[a] (%)	No real property (%)	Owning real property[a] (%)	No real property (%)
Artisans	26	8	44	18
Farmers	32	21	29	20
Labourers	24	17	16	16

Property owners: Artisans N=22   Farmers N=31   Labourers N=69
Non-property-owners: Artisans N=45   Farmers N=45   Labourers N=226
[a]Ownership of real property is ascribed in the census to one individual within the household, almost invariably the head. Wives are never described as property owners in their own right.

ownership being confined to the farmhouse, the farm owner's security could be little better than that of a tenant farmer, since the farmhouse was of little value without the surrounding farmland. No direct measure of this security is available. However, if one takes the proportion of married couples (from the case study below) still living in their parish of birth as a crude indicator of security, then it would appear that the ownership of land did have a certain stabilizing influence (table 12.1). A certain but not a great influence, since the majority even of property owners were born outside the parish of current residence. Nevertheless, artisans and labourers as well as farmers were less likely to have been mobile if they were the owners of real property.

The case study: nine villages in West Flanders in 1814

So far we have been content to refer to rural Flanders in general terms as though it can be treated as a unity, but even within a group of villages within a few miles of each other, there can be surprising differences in land ownership patterns. In fact one can see very easily from an analysis of structure of land ownership at village level that a number of assertions made by Berkner and Mendels[11] are in need of extensive qualifications. Farmers may not generally have owned their farms, but the distribution of owner-occupiers from village to village was very uneven.

[11] Berkner and Mendels (1978): 218.

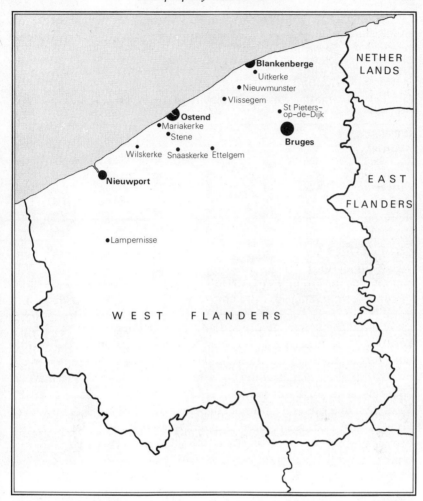

Fig. 12.1. West Flanders, showing the location of the nine villages and Lampernisse (see chapter 13 below).

Commercial agriculture may have required large farms, but in some places land fragmentation seems to have occurred nonetheless.

Nine villages have been selected for analysis, all within 25 kilometres of Bruges (see fig. 12.1).[12] In terms of occupational structure (with one

12 The lists have been chosen from many others relating to West Flanders because of the detail offered on relationships within the household. Lists that referred to 'children' rather than to sons and daughters have been rejected because of the possible confusion between the use of the term 'child' to indicate age and 'child' as a relationship to the head. Even so, some problems remain (cf. n. 18 below), and cross-checking the lists with the parish registers would no doubt bring to light some further errors in the recording of

Table 12.2. *Male-headed households by occupational group of head*

Parish of residence	Households with male head (no.)	Proportion of all male household heads: Artisans (%)	Commerce (%)	Farmers (%)	Labourers (%)	Other (%)	Total (%)
St Pieters-op-de-Dijk	97	12	15	18	46	9	100
Uitkerke	79	8	2	20	64	6	100
Nieuwmunster	38	16	0	18	60	6	100
Vlissegem	100	14	3	24	52	7	100
Mariakerke	63	10	5	17	62	6	100
Stene	60	10	5	28	47	10	100
Wilskerke	26	15	4	42	23	16	100
Ettelgem	69	14	0	25	56	5	100
Snaaskerke	69	10	4	23	58	5	100
All parishes	601	12	5	23	54	6	100

exception to be noted later), the differences between the villages, bearing in mind the possibility of random variation due to their small size, were not in themselves particularly remarkable (table 12.2). All the villages contained some artisans, and commerce was represented in all but two, but most men heading households were described as farmers or labourers, with the latter predominating except in the smallest parish, Wilskerke. In terms of the number of people owning property, however, it is very clear that we are faced with two types of village (table 12.3). In four villages about 1 in every 10 household heads owned real property, while in the remainder never less than 3 and more often 4 in 10 household heads were property owners. In the four villages where there were fewer owner-occupiers, St Pieters-op-de-Dijk, Uitkerke, Nieuwmunster, and Vlissegem, not a single labourer owned land (table 12.4). Nor were there many owners amongst the artisans and female-headed households. The other five villages had much larger proportions, often a majority, of labourers, artisans, and women heading households who were property owners.

This second group of villages lay somewhat to the west of the others, close to Ostend, while the others were closer to Blankenberge. There is the opportunity, therefore, to explore in two quite different contexts the relationship between the ownership of real property and the form of the

relationship and age. The version of the lists that has been used is the transcription published by the Vlaamse Vereniging voor Familiekunde, Afdeling Brugge, *Volkstelling 1814*, vols. I, III, V (1976–7).

Table 12.3. *Proportion of heads of household owning real property by parish of residence*

Parish of residence	Household heads (no.)	Owning real property (%)
St Pieters-op-de-Dijk	109	10
Uitkerke	86	13
Nieuwmunster	44	9
Vlissegem	106	5
Mariakerke	70	48
Stene	63	30
Wilskerke	29	52
Ettelgem	81	48
Snaaskerke	79	43
All parishes	667	28

household. In Mariakerke, Stene, Ettelgem, and Snaaskerke, either through the fragmentation of inheritances or through labourers having bought their way into the community, the land had passed into many hands, whereas elsewhere the ownership of real property had remained the privilege of the few. From the present sources, it is impossible to discover how land had fallen into many hands in the one case and not the other. If one group of landowners had divided their property among their sons, who had then sunk to the level of agricultural labourers, it would of course mean that the economic circumstances precluding partible inheritance were less relevant or less regarded in these five villages than in the other four. At present we can do little more than hint at what these circumstances might have been.

The fact that the nine villages selected for analysis all lay on the Belgian polder, an area reclaimed from the sea in early-medieval times and not subject to major flooding after the seventeenth century, would seem to place a natural limit on any diversity. Reference to van der Maelen's geographical dictionary, published a couple of decades after the census of 1814, does, indeed, confirm only limited diversity among the villages.[13] In 1836 the area was by and large devoted to cereals,

[13] Van der Maelen (1836). The suggestion of a difference in farm economy comes from the fact that in the parishes of Uitkerke and Nieuwmunster he substitutes the acreage devoted to grain cultivation for the head of livestock. St Pieters, Uitkerke, and Nieuwmunster are also the only villages where there were day labourers (*dagloners*) as well as general labourers (*werkmen*) in 1814. The correlation is not perfect. There were no day labourers recorded in the remaining parish of the group, Vlissegem, and there is no entry for this parish in van der Maelen. The latter also provides no figures at all on the agriculture of St Pieters.

Table 12.4. *Proportion of heads of household owning real property by occupational group, sex, and parish of residence of household head*

	Male household heads								Female household heads All	
	Occupational group									
	Artisans		Farmers		Labourers[a]		Others[b]			
Parish of residence	Total (no.)	Owners (%)	Total (no.)	Owners (%)	Total (no.)	Owners (%)	Total (no.)	Owners (%)	Total (no.)	Owners[c] (%)
St Pieters-op-de-Dijk	12	17	18	6	46	0	21	33	12	8
Uitkerke	6	17	16	44	51	0	6	33	7	14
Nieuwmunster	6	0	7	43	23	0	2	50	6	0
Vlissegem	14	14	24	8	52	0	10	10	6	0
Mariakerke	6	50	11	54	39	46	7	14	7	86
Stene	6	33	17	18	28	36	9	11	3	100
Wilskerke	4	75	11	36	6	50	5	40	3	100
Ettelgem	10	40	17	24	39	69	3	0	12	33
Snaaskerke	7	86	16	25	40	42	6	67	10	30
All parishes	71	32	137	25	324	23	69	28	66	32

[a] Includes 'workmen' and 'dagloners'; cf. n. 13.
[b] Includes tradesmen, minor officials (sexton, constable), and those not actually employed (described in the census as rentier or independent).
[c] For the sake of consistency, proportions have been calculated for all categories, although because of the small number of cases involved in certain cells only the most general inferences about ownership patterns are justified (see text).

although there were some livestock to be tended. This was a feature of all rather than just some of the villages. On the other hand, there is just a hint in van der Maelen's statistics of arable farming being rather more important in those villages where land was in few hands, and of live-stock farming being more important in villages where labourers as well as farmers were owners of real property. It is just possible, therefore, that it was more feasible to divide properties in dairying areas than in arable areas that had to be worked with a heavy plough and that this allowed the ideal of partible inheritance to become a reality.

Nor is this the only way in which the association of the inheritance pattern with a particular type of farming might influence the formation of households and the combinations of people found within them. As an example of the sort of interrelationship that could apply, we can point to the work on English populations by Keith Snell, particularly on the composition of the agricultural work-force in the eighteenth century.[14] There was less of a demand for living-in servants, and particularly for female servants, in grain-growing areas than in dairy-farming areas, and this affected not only these particular farming households but also those of the labourers and other farmers whose offspring provided most of the servants. One might also expect to replicate van der Woude's findings on the relative absence of extended-family households in live-stock as opposed to arable-farming areas of the Netherlands in the middle of the eighteenth century.[15] Before we can test these various hypotheses by looking in detail at the households of property and non-property owners, at the households of property owners who were farmers and of property owners who were labourers, and at the two types of village, it is useful to complete an overview of household structure in all nine villages.

Members of the household

Table 12.5 is laid out to show the composition of the household and houseful[16] according to the sex and occupational group[17] of the head.

[14] Snell, 'The standard of living, social relations, the family and labour mobility' (1980).
[15] Van der Woude, 'Variations in the size and structure of the household' (1972): 306–7.
[16] The household includes the head and, where present, his spouse, offspring, relatives, and servants. Inmates lie outside the household but within the houseful. It is possible that some of the 'inmates' may have constituted separate households which were not identified as such by the listmaker, as seems to have been the case with Bruges (ch. 14 below). The circumstances of Bruges, however, are very different, particularly in regard to the number of inmates. Therefore, while we have thought it advisable to adopt the term 'houseful' to describe the blocks of names in Bruges, the term 'household and attached inmates' has been accepted for the nine villages.
[17] Further division of the occupational groups would have been desirable, particularly the

Table 12.5. *Mean membership of households by occupational group and sex of household head (per 100 households in each occupational group)*

Relationship to head	Male heads					Female heads
	Artisans	Farmers	Labourers	Other	Subtotal	
Head	100	100	100	100	100	100
Spouse	90	95	92	81	91	0
Offspring	289	324	261	190	271	226
Relatives[a]	35	26	12	28	20	17
Servants	55	260	20	59	84	68
Attached inmates	20	12	27	40	24	36
TOTAL	589	817	512	498	590	447
Households	71	137	324	69	601	66

[a] Includes servants related to the head, and married offspring.

Farming households were by far the largest. This was principally because of the large number of resident servants, averaging more than 2.5 per household. Farmers also were more likely to be married and had more offspring resident than other groups. On the other hand, the number of relatives in farmers' households was certainly not excessive, even though all servants who could be linked to the head through a common surname[18] have been counted as relatives and not as servants. In fact it is the artisans, who might seem an almost alien element in the Flanders countryside,[19] who had the most relatives. As for the wider perspective, households looked quite different from those in the neighbouring city of Bruges, which has been analysed below in chapter 14. For example, male-headed households in the villages contained more

separation of commerce from 'Other' as in table 12.2, and some division of the female-headed households into those who were farmers and those who were labourers. The small size of the population made such steps impractical and also precluded the separation of day labourers from other labourers, a minority (24 of 120) even in the parishes where they occurred; cf. n. 13 above. One advantage to the present classification scheme is that it is almost identical to that used in a recent independent study of West Flanders. See Costenoble, 'De Bevolking van Adinkerke in de 19de Eeuw' (1978).

[18] Identifying relationships through a common surname is more practical than is the case with English lists, because in Flanders women retained their maiden names after marriage. There is no problem, for example, in tracing the in-marrying son-in-law. Admittedly the relationship between a widow and the rest of the household would be uncertain if the only information available was her maiden name, but the better lists fortunately include the late husband's name.

[19] Artisans were involved in a wide range of trades associated with a rural community. Shoemakers and carpenters were to be found in eight of the nine villages, millers in seven, and cartwrights in six; and it might seem odd to regard them as an alien element. However, they were less likely than farmers and labourers to have been born in the parish of current residence (see table 12.1 above), and unlike the household heads in other occupational groups they were less likely than their spouses to be locally born.

Table 12.6. *Sex ratios by relationship to household head and head's occupational group and sex*

Sex of head	Occupational group of head	Offspring ≥ 20 No.	Offspring ≥ 20 Sex ratio	Relatives No.	Relatives Sex ratio	Servants No.	Servants Sex ratio	Attached inmates No.	Attached inmates Sex ratio
Male	Artisans	27	107.7	25	212.5	39	290.0	14	75.0
	Farmers	80	128.6	35	169.2	356	220.8	17	88.9
	Labourers	88	83.3	39	105.3	68	44.7	87	102.3
	Other	13	85.7	19	111.1	41	41.4	28	64.7
	Subtotal	208	101.9	118	143.8	504	155.8	146	89.6
Female	All	60	140.0	11	120.0	45	221.4	24	118.2

than three times as many servants and a quarter more offspring but had many fewer relatives, and there were fewer inmates.[20]

The household can also be examined in terms of the sex ratio (number of males per 100 females). The principal contrast is between farmers and artisans on the one hand and other male household heads and labourers on the other, with the former group having the higher proportion of males whether the focus is on offspring over the age of 20, relatives, or servants.[21] However, the composition of farming households did not exactly parallel that of the artisans. Farmers retained rather more male offspring but had, in relative terms, fewer male kin and male servants.

In addition, two points in particular repay special attention. First, the majority of all relatives were male, in contrast to what has emerged for English communities (even rural ones) at the close of the seventeenth century (see ch. 16 below). Second, although all occupational groups in some sense shared the same characteristics, for instance in that they all included some households with relatives and some with servants, it is now clear that they were not calling on the same people. When labourers and those in public service and commercial employment[22] had servants, they were predominantly female; when they had relatives, it was more likely that they would be female than was the case for farmers; and when their offspring stayed in the parental home beyond the age of 20, it was their daughters rather than their sons who did so.

[20] Figures for Bruges comparable to those in table 12.5, derived from tables 14.7 and 14.8, are 216 (offspring), 33 (relatives), 27 (servants), and 82 (inmates). For female-headed households the urban–rural contrast is even sharper.

[21] On the other hand, labourers were the occupational group with the highest proportion of male inmates.

[22] See n. *b* to table 12.4.

The sex ratio of the inmate group also varied with the occupation and sex of the household head. There were more female inmates than male inmates attached to male-headed households except where the household head was a labourer. Inmates attached to female-headed households were predominantly male. Reference back to table 12.5 reveals that there were rather more inmates attached to households headed by labourers and by women than to other households. Labourers and women heading households may well have accepted these inmates as a means of supplementing their meagre resources, but otherwise it is not easy to know what interpretation to put upon these figures. Inmates constituted a varied group. They were not named as such in the census, and the term is used here as a residual for all those persons whose relationship to the head was unspecified. It can be suggested, however, that it is unlikely that inmates performed a similar function in regard to the household as relatives or servants or that the inmates were misclassified servants or relatives. The basis for this assertion is the fact that the variation in the sex ratio of inmates by head's occupation differs so markedly from the variation for the sex ratio in the case of relatives and servants.

The life cycle of the individual and household

Further evidence on the meaning to be attached to the roles of relative, servant, and inmate comes from consideration of figs. 12.2 and 12.3. In these figures, each relationship to the household head is expressed as a proportion of all relationships recorded for a particular age group, males and females being taken separately. The 'life cycle' attributes of certain roles are immediately apparent, not only those of offspring or head, which are naturally conditioned by age, but also those of servant and, in the case of females, of inmates as well. There is, however, little visible life-cycle trend in regard to relatives, who were represented by rather small numbers in most age groups. There would, indeed, have been even fewer relatives but for the fact that all servants found to be related to the household head have, for the purposes of figs. 12.2 and 12.3, been classed as relatives. As they represent about a quarter of the total identified co-resident relatives, it can be said that the service function contributed an important element to the kin structure of these Flemish households. However, the converse is not true. Servants were not as a rule directly recruited kin. Indeed, under 6% of male and female servants in these villages were related to the household in which they served.

Figs. 12.2 and 12.3 show that the frequency of service, together with a general late age at coming to head a household, stand out as the most distinctive characteristics of the life cycle of the individual. The two features are, of course, closely connected in that it was partly because so many men remained in service in their 30s that almost half of the men in this age group still occupied a subordinate position within the household. In addition, there are clear differences between the male and the female life cycle. During early adulthood, service was more important for men than for women. Conversely 'family' roles (daughter and spouse of head) were more important for women than the equivalent male roles of son and head were for men. In later life, however, this ceased to be the case. Whereas the vast majority of men over the age of 40 were household heads and married (compare fig. 12.2 and table 12.5), an increasing proportion of women headed their own households.[23] This increase would have been all the larger but for the absorption into the 'inmates' of a not negligible number of women presumably unable to support households of their own.

In regard to this last point there is certainly a parallel to be found with the population of neighbouring Bruges (see chapter 14 below), despite the wide difference in absolute terms in the proportion of female-headed households and female inmates. Equally instructive, however, is the contrast with the life-cycle patterns of English rural communities. There is a tendency to speak of north-west Europe as embracing a common marriage and household system. Broadly speaking, this is true. Thus West Flanders and pre-industrial England share in the predominance of nuclear-family households, a late age at marriage for both sexes, and life-cycle service. Nevertheless, within this overall framework there was room for considerable variation. In Flanders, the period of living-in service occupied a longer period of the life cycle than was the case in England, and people came to the headship of the household at a later date. It was fairly general in England that 8 out of 10 men in their 30s would be heading households (only 6 out of 10 in Flanders), and there were even some English parishes at the end of the eighteenth century where more than half of the men aged 25–9 headed households.[24] The significance of all this lies in the fact that new house-

---

[23] Of all household heads aged 60 and over, 15% were women. Comparable proportions for other age groups were: 50–9, 14%; 40–9, 9%; 30–9, 5%; < 30, 0%.

[24] Corfe Castle (Dorset) listed in 1790 and Ardleigh (Essex) listed in 1796. Of the nine English pre-1801 local censuses which contain information on age, only in the earliest, listed in 1599 (Ealing, Middx.), are the headship rates of young adults as low as the Flemish ones. Calculations of headship rates are included in the tabular analyses of these lists in the library of the SSRC Cambridge Group, but only the Ealing ones have

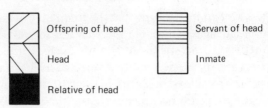

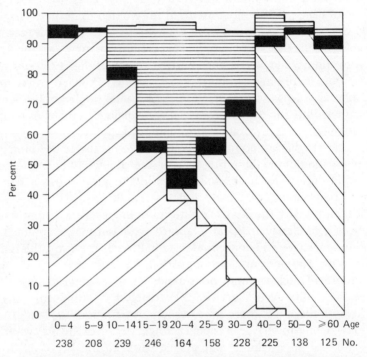

Fig. 12.2. Male population by age group and relationship to household head. The number under each age group is the total number of persons in the age group. Note that in figs. 12.2 and 12.3 the age groups are in five-year blocks until age 30.

holds could be formed at a very much faster pace in England. There are possible implications too for the degree of responsibility exercised by young adults and the nature of the impact of youth on society as a whole. To some extent this would depend on the actual power enjoyed

been published. See P. Laslett and Wall (eds.), *Household and family* (1972): 79, and cf. above, pp. 36–41. For the proportion of servants in various age groups see P. Laslett, *Family life and illicit love* (1977a): 44.

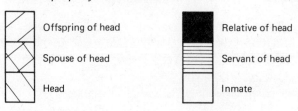

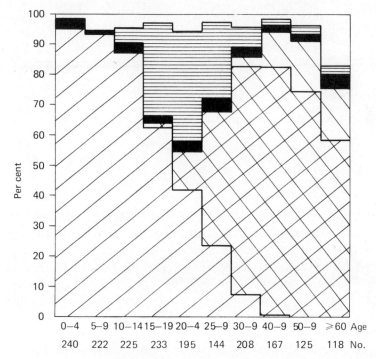

Fig. 12.3. Female population by age group and relationship to household head. The number under each age group is the total number of persons in the age group.

by household heads, a subject on which it is difficult to get hard information. Yet it is not unreasonable to regard West Flanders as a society in which, for many, dependency continued into middle life.

Figs. 12.2 and 12.3 detail the individual life cycle, but it seems a reasonable assumption that households too will have a cycle, that is to say that when the head is young the household will have a different shape from when he is old. Table 12.7 tackles this question for the two major groups in the population, farmers and labourers. Apart, however,

Table 12.7. *Mean membership of households by occupational group, sex, and age group of household head (per 100 households in each age group)*

Farmers

Age group of head	No. of household heads	Offspring <20	Offspring ≥20	Relatives	Male servants	Female servants
<30	6	183	0	50	267	133
30–9	29	217	14	24	134	86
40–9	52	317	27	31	221	81
50–9	25	332	108	20	160	64
≥60	25	172	140	16	140	80
All	137	266	58	26	179	81

Labourers

Age group of head	No. of household heads	Offspring <20	Offspring ≥20	Relatives	Male servants	Female servants
<30	25	136	0	12	0	16
30–9	61	247	6	18	6	20
40–9	108	294	14	6	4	17
50–9	73	251	49	12	12	7
≥60	57	137	58	16	7	14
All	324	234	27	12	6	14

from the variation in the number of offspring and a predictable rise with the age of the head in the mean number of offspring aged over 20, there is no cycle to be seen. The absence of a cycle has been noted before in connection with nineteenth-century populations and could be the result of having to rely on the age of the head as a reference point for the life-cycle stage of the household rather than on, say, the date of marriage.[25] Otherwise, the points to note in connection with table 12.7 are that it was the 50-year-old farmer who had most resident children and that even when he had passed 60, his household contained on average three resident children. Farmers, not surprisingly, had more resident children, particularly older children, than labourers. Nevertheless, labourers aged 60 and over also had on average two children at home, although they might seem to have little to inherit and to be of an age when they might easily have found places as farmers' servants.

The last major feature of the social structure that we need to examine

[25] See e.g. Anderson, *Family structure in nineteenth century Lancashire* (1971): 202 n. 46, and Chudacoff, 'Newlyweds and family extension' (1978). Anderson's alternative classification based on 'life cycle stage' divides households according to whether the spouse of the head was above or below 45 and is not likely to translate well to a rural area where remarriage was common (see n. 26 below).

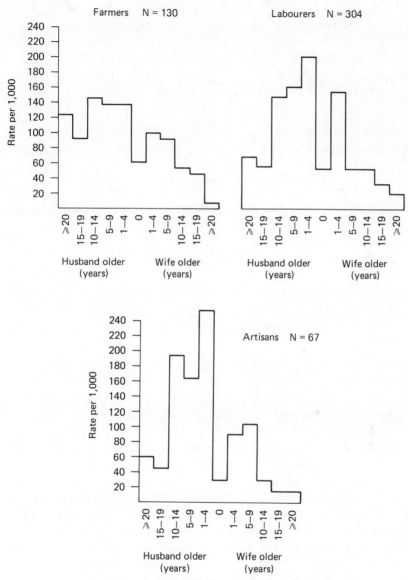

Fig. 12.4. Age gap between spouses as a rate per 1,000 married men in each occupational group.

is that of the age gap between spouses. The range was particularly wide. In about a quarter of the existing marriages, the wife was older than her husband, but these were more than balanced by marriages where the husband was the elder by more than 10 years (fig. 12.4). Each major

Richard Wall

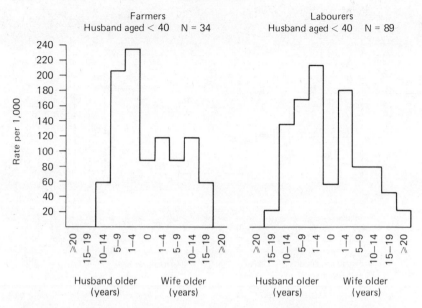

Fig. 12.5. Age gap between spouses as a rate per 1,000 married men aged under 40 in each occupational group.

group in the population (farmers, labourers, and artisans) had its own distinct pattern. The age gap was widest in the case of farmers (12% were more than 20 years older than their current spouse) and narrowest in the case of labourers. An artisan was the least likely to be younger than his wife.

Fig. 12.4 represents a cross-section of the life cycle. Some of the married partners were in their second or even third marriages; others, in their first. Only the tedious procedure of linking the census and parish register could clear this up, but it is possible to gain a greater insight into the different marriage strategies by dividing married couples into two groups according to whether the husband was under 40 or over 50. About as many farmers as labourers initially chose an older spouse, but there the similarities end (fig. 12.5). Most of the younger farmers either had a spouse little removed from their own age or had married a much older woman. Indeed, it is notable that there were as many such farmers with a wife 10 to 14 years older as with a wife 1 to 4 years older. The marriage pattern would seem to be symptomatic of the need for the farm to be subject to the controlling influence of a mature woman and of a shortage of farms in relation to the number of potential farmers. Labourers, on the other hand, were much more prepared to choose a

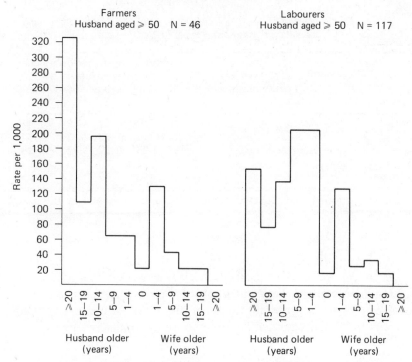

Fig. 12.6. Age gap between spouses as a rate per 1,000 married men aged 50 or over in each occupational group.

considerably younger wife. In 13% of the cases there was an age difference of more than 10 years even though the husband was under 40. Even if the wife were the elder, it was more often by a modest amount than was the case with the farmers. The younger labourers, it could be argued, were freer than the farmers in their choice of a spouse.

Later in life the situation altered somewhat (see fig. 12.6).[26] Labourers as well as farmers remarried, but farmers more often had the opportunity of choosing a much younger spouse. A third (twice as many as the labourers) were married to women more than 20 years younger, and close to two-thirds had a spouse who was 10 or more years younger. The marriage pattern of Flemish farmers certainly suggests no unwillingness

[26] From a cross-sectional analysis it is impossible definitively to differentiate a recent shift in marriage patterns from change over the individual's life cycle (i.e. the farmers aged 50 and over in 1814 may never have had a marriage pattern approximating to that of the farmers under 40 in 1814). However, the difference between the two cohorts, the size of the age gap, and the identification of many stepchildren in the population make it unlikely that temporal change has produced the age pattern that can be observed in the 1814 data.

Table 12.8. *Proportion of household heads who were owner-occupiers by age, occupational group, and sex of household head*

| Sex of head | Occupational group of head | Proportion of owner-occupiers in age group | | | | |
		<30 (%)	30–9 (%)	40–9 (%)	50–9 (%)	≥60 (%)
Male	Artisans	(20)	12	52	24	47
	Farmers	(0)	14	25	36	32
	Labourers	8	25	27	18	28
	Other	(25)	12	40	31	31
Female	All	—	(50)	37	24	35

Note: Proportions based on fewer than 10 cases are indicated by the use of brackets.

on the part of the ageing farmer to burden the property with the claims of relicts and minor heirs. Indeed, this is how we felt lineage marriage arrangements might work out in practice for owner-occupiers. However, we have not yet established that there was a difference between owners and tenants in regard to their household and marriage patterns.

Property-owning and the household

The first necessity is to discover whether there is any association between owning property and the age of the household head. This is a vitally important step, because the number and age of resident offspring correlates with the age of the head (see table 12.7), and there could be a danger of identifying with owner occupation aspects of the household that might more properly be tied to the age structure characteristics of property ownership. From table 12.8, however, it is clear that while the frequency of owning property was certainly not constant across all age groups, the variation was random rather than systematic. There is every chance, therefore, that any differences between the households of property owners and the propertyless will reflect the effect of property owning on the rules governing the formation of households.

At this stage it may be useful to refer back to the hypothesis about the relationship between the need for large farms, inheritance practices, and the household with which we began this paper. The expectation was that, despite the preference for partibility, the economics of large-scale farming would predispose some of the heirs to stay on in the parental homes beyond the age of 20. A consideration of table 12.9

Table 12.9. *Mean membership of households by head's ownership of real property (per 100 households in each occupational group)*

Sex of head	Occupational group of head	Sons < 20 Owner-occupier	Sons < 20 Non-owner	Sons ≥ 20 Owner-occupier	Sons ≥ 20 Non-owner	Daughters < 20 Owner-occupier	Daughters < 20 Non-owner	Daughters ≥ 20 Owner-occupier	Daughters ≥ 20 Non-owner
Male	Artisans	130	121	43	8	109	135	30	12
	Labourers	120	109	12	12	120	124	15	15
	Farmers	118	141	32	33	123	134	26	25
	Other	58	96	0	12	58	96	0	14
Female	All	100	47	71	44	86	64	57	29
All		112	110	26	20	108	119	23	18

Sex of head	Occupational group of head	Male relatives Owner-occupier	Male relatives Non-owner	Female relatives Owner-occupier	Female relatives Non-owner	Male servants Owner-occupier	Male servants Non-owner	Female servants Owner-occupier	Female servants Non-owner
Male	Artisans	13	29	4	14	22	50	4	19
	Labourers	4	7	8	5	5	7	15	14
	Farmers	6	19	6	11	206	170	70	84
	Other	32	8	21	10	42	8	74	30
Female	All	0	13	5	9	43	49	24	20
All		8	12	8	8	56	49	32	32

suggests that this hypothesis is of limited validity for an understanding of the West Flanders population. It was artisans who had more sons aged 20 or over resident when they were property owners than when they were not, and the same holds for those women who headed households. In both cases the ownership of property also seems to have promoted the continued presence of older daughters (though it might not be immediately apparent what an artisan's daughter would inherit).[27] The evidence on farmers is much more difficult to accommodate.[28] Farmers owning their own farms are the key group, having a tangible asset to pass on to their heirs, yet there is no sign of their having any more resident sons over 20 than non-owning farmers. Instead, the fact that they owned their farms seems to be associated with a greater number of resident male servants, who would have been non-relatives; and they actually had fewer resident children younger than 20 and relatives of both sexes than tenant farmers.

The influence of the head's owning property on the composition of the household emerges, therefore, as neither very dramatic nor predictable, with considerable variation between one occupational group and another.[29] In other words, property-owning did influence the composition of the household but only through interacting with the head's occupation and not in the way predicted. Even so, the labourers seem untouched. The households of labourers who were property owners look just like those of labourers who were not property owners. The clear implication is that factors other than the ownership or not of real property determined the membership of labourers' households.

From table 12.10 we can see that the age difference between spouses also seems to be associated in some way with the ownership or not of real property. For both farmers and labourers it increases the number of occasions on which the wife was the elder partner. At the same time, for

[27] One possibility is that a daughter thereby improved her chances in the marriage market, perhaps with an artisan who would carry on her father's trade. Certainly artisans were more often outsiders than were men in other occupational groups (cf. n. 19 above), but there is a missing link in the chain of evidence, namely information on the occupation of the fathers of artisans' wives, which can only be supplied by extensive work with the parish registers.

[28] All figures are for the mean number of sons and daughters per household, but exactly the same effect appears if a count is made of the number of households without any sons or daughters over the age of 20. A further check also revealed that daughters were staying on in the parental home whether or not there was a son (heir) of equivalent age in residence.

[29] An example additional to those given above is that while the propertied artisans had fewer relatives and servants than propertyless artisans (though more offspring over the age of 20), the opposite applied in the case of the heads with commercial or minor public appointments, who constitute the 'Other' male-headed household category of table 12.9.

Table 12.10. *Age gap between spouses by occupational group of head and ownership of real property*

	Owner-occupiers Artisans (%)	Farmers (%)	Labourers (%)
Age difference			
Husband ⩾10 years older	32	48	22
Husband 1–9 years older	37	10	30
Same age	4	3	7
Wife older	27	39	41
TOTAL	100	100	100
N =	22	31	69
	Non-owners Artisans (%)	Farmers (%)	Labourers (%)
Age difference			
Husband ⩾10 years older	29	33	28
Husband 1–9 years older	45	33	38
Same age	2	8	4
Wife older	24	26	30
TOTAL	100	100	100
N=	45	98	226

farmers alone, it increases the proportion of wives more than 10 years younger than their spouse. The ownership of property, it can be said, is again interacting with occupation to create the differences between the occupational groups. Thus there is considerably less difference in the marriage strategies of farmers and labourers when they were property-less than when they were owner-occupiers.[30]

On this occasion, then, there is some support for the initial hypothesis. The ownership of property and a high remarriage rate do appear to be associated, as seemed likely if the lineage took precedence over the household community in any transfer of property. Illustrating marriage patterns this way is, of course, but a first step. Two very different mechanisms could be at work. The first runs from property-owning to marriage. In this case the argument would be that a man as a property owner was more likely to need or to be able to attract a wife of an age group far removed from his own than could a non-property-owner. An alternative mechanism would reverse the relationship between property and marriage. In the second example the couple would begin marriage propertyless but through having contracted a prudent mar-

[30] Compare the range of variation across occupation in the two panels of table 12.10 for 'Husband ⩾10 years older' and 'Wife older'.

Table 12.11. *Mean membership of farmers' households by head's ownership of real property and parish of residence (per 100 households in each category)*

Relationship to head	Group A[a]		Group B[b]	
	Owners	Non-owners	Owners	Non-owners
Sons <20	38	113	167	169
Sons ≥20	38	44	28	22
Daughters <20	85	136	148	131
Daughters ≥20	23	33	28	18
Male relatives	15	19	0	20
Female relatives	15	4	0	18
Male servants	369	175	105	165
Female servants	108	85	48	84
N (households) =	13	52	21	51

[a] Parishes of St Pieters, Uitkerke, Nieuwmunster, and Vlissegem.
[b] Parishes of Mariakerke, Stene, Wilskerke, Ettelgem, and Snaarskerke.

riage, represented by the man choosing a woman older than himself, they would soon move up in society. At present we lack the evidence to decide between these two mechanisms.[31] In particular there is the absence of a running check on the incidence of property-owning over the individual's life cycle. Conceivably the 'prudent marriage' hypothesis might represent the situation of the labourer and possibly of the younger farmer (less likely than older farmers to be property owners; see table 12.8), while the 'marriage prospect' hypothesis represents the situation of the older farmers.

We should not forget, however, that the nine villages do not constitute a homogeneous set. On the contrary, it was possible to divide them into two distinct groups according to whether fewer than 13% of the household heads or over 30% were property owners (cf. table 12.3 above). It is necessary, therefore, to repeat the tabulations of household membership and age gap between spouses for each subpopulation. For this purpose, in the following tables the parishes of St Pieters, Uitkerke, Nieuwmunster, and Vlissegem, where there were very few resident property owners and no labourers owning land, have been labelled 'Group A', and the remaining parishes 'Group B'.

In looking at the figures in tables 12.11–13 it is important to proceed warily because of the small number of cases which underlie some of the calculations. Too much attention should not be paid to small differences,

[31] In addition there is the possibility (considered above) that the property might have been inherited through the wife.

Table 12.12. *Mean membership of labourers' households by head's ownership of real property and parish of residence (per 100 households in each category)*

Relationship to head	Group A[a] Non-owners	Group B[a] Owners	Group B[a] Non-owners
Sons <20	116	120	94
Sons ≥20	15	12	6
Daughters <20	120	120	131
Daughters ≥20	17	15	10
Male relatives	7	4	6
Female relatives	5	8	4
Male servants	8	5	4
Female servants	19	15	5
N (households) =	172	75	77

[a] See notes to table 12.11.

Table 12.13. *Age gap between spouses by ownership of real property and parish of residence*

	Farmers Group A[a] Owner-occupiers (%)	Group A[a] Non-owners (%)	Group B[a] Owner-occupiers (%)	Group B[a] Non-owners (%)
Age difference				
Husband ≥10 years older	25	24	63	43
Husband 1–9 years older	17	27	6	38
Same age	0	14	5	2
Wife older	58	35	26	17
TOTAL	100	100	100	100
N=	12	51	19	47

	Labourers Group A Non-owners (%)	Group B Owner-occupiers (%)	Group B Non-owners (%)
Age difference			
Husband ≥10 years older	26	22	32
Husband 1–9 years older	35	30	43
Same age	5	7	3
Wife older	34	41	22
TOTAL	100	100	100
N=	154	69	72

[a] See notes to table 12.11.

since a couple of individuals more or fewer in a certain category can have an appreciable impact when the number of households at issue falls below 20. For example, it was almost certainly because of random variation that the largest absolute difference between owning and non-owning farmers in Group A parishes, apart from the number of male servants, was in the number of sons under the age of 20. Nevertheless, we do find that Group A farmers had more sons over 20 resident than Group B farmers, which would be in line with a more frequent subdivision of property in Group B than in Group A parishes. There is, however, a complication. Although farmers and labourers with property in Group B parishes had slightly more sons over 20 co-resident than did farmers and labourers without property, this was not true of the farmers in Group A parishes, who should have been the most concerned to keep their holdings intact. In addition the non-property-owners in Group A parishes had more sons resident than did the property owners from Group B. The conclusion to draw from this is that it is not the ownership of property that is the key determinant of residence patterns but the grouping of parishes and hence, by implication, the nature of the local economy. It is difficult even to claim that owner occupation is interacting with the local economy in the same sort of way that it did with occupation to produce the result on the age gap between spouses that is discussed above in connection with table 12.10. Although there are cases where the differences between the owners' households in the two groups of parishes are greater than between the non-owners, notably in the case of male farm servants (see table 12.11), there are other key variables – the number of resident sons over 20, for example – where the non-property-owning households in the two groups of villages are rather more dissimilar than the property-owning ones.

Moreover, even within each group of parishes, the strongest associations with the ownership of property are not those involving celibate adult offspring of farmers, but with servants (positively in Group A, negatively in Group B) and negatively with relatives of farmers in Group B. The fact that Group A farmers had many more resident male servants than did Group B farmers, taken in conjunction with Keith Snell's findings on the differences between the agrarian and pastoral areas of England, suggests that we were correct in identifying Group A as predominantly a grain-growing area. On the basis of table 12.11, one could also say that the chief difference between the households in the two areas is in this question of servants.

We must, however, add a few words about relatives. We can now dismiss for West Flanders the association between arable farming (type

A parishes) and extended-family households that has been identified in connection with the Netherlands in the eighteenth century.[32] In fact, in all nine villages there was only one farmer who shared his household with a married son.[33]

The final set of figures on which we have to comment concerns the age gap between spouses. There is a more definite association between property-owning and marriage strategies than between property-owning and the composition of the household. As table 12.13 shows, the ownership of property is consistently associated with a higher proportion of wives being older than their husbands. It applies whether the husband was a labourer or a farmer, or lived in a type A parish or a type B parish. There is also some interaction between the type of parish and property-owning, seen in the fact that the differences between the two groups of owner-occupiers are greater than those between the two groups of non-property-owners. All the same, one has to add a similar qualification to that made above in connection with the presence in the household of sons of the head over the age of 20. The differences between the owners and non-owners of real property are smaller than those between the groups of parishes. There are more Group A non-owning farmers than Group B owners younger than their wives.

Conclusion

We began this chapter by setting out how the lack of viability of small farms should have caused the offspring of the owner-occupiers of West Flanders to have stayed on in the parental home after the age of 20. The offspring of tenant farmers, it was predicted, would not be bound to their parents to the same extent. Yet in fact celibate adult offspring are as much in evidence in the households of tenant farmers as in those of owner-occupiers. But if the existing theory about the relationship between the composition of the household and the owning of property by its head is inadequate, is there any other explanation that one might put in its place? Certainly much of what we have had to say has been in the direction of qualifying the relevance of property-owning for the composition of the household. The occupation of the head and the type of parish in which the household resided seem much more potent influences.

[32] Van der Woude (1972).
[33] The artisans and 'Other' male-headed households had five married sons from about the same number of households. Four of the five resident married daughters were the daughters of labourers.

Nevertheless, there is some evidence, especially for farmers, of a different set of relationships between property-owning and household forms; in fact two sets, corresponding to the frequency with which household heads held land. In parishes where there were few resident property owners, the result of a farmer being an owner-occupier was felt not in terms of the numbers of adult celibate offspring or resident relatives, but in the presence of an increased number of unrelated servants. In the second group of parishes, where property-holding was relatively well distributed, the associations were quite different. Farmers who were property owners had fewer servants and fewer resident relatives than tenant farmers. They were also likely to be at least 10 years older than their spouses (see table 12.13). The evidence is fragmentary, but it is possible that these behavioural traits were connected: that it was through remarriage that the farm maintained its productive capacity and that that was why fewer servants or relatives were present. Where repetitive censuses survive so that it is possible to trace the evolution of particular households over time, this suggestion could be tested more fully than is possible here. There is a need also to discover which of the two sets of relationships we have identified apply generally outside the immediate area of study; indeed, whether other relationships existed between property-owning and the household, as the present small data base has already produced evidence of considerable variety. The study of Flemish owner-occupiers, however, would lead us to expect that a relationship between an individual's owning property and his choice of a marriage partner would be closer than that between his owning property and the residence patterns of his offspring.

The relationships among inheritance practice, economic necessities, and lineage marriage are intricate, and it is not easy to single out which has the more significant impact on household and marriage patterns. Berkner and Mendels were inclined to dismiss inheritance as irrelevant because of the needs of the farm economy. We have questioned in this chapter whether the need to avoid the subdivision of farms made that much difference to the migration patterns of offspring, suggested that the partibility of inheritances was practised more often than those two authors allowed, and traced strong links between a wide and variable age gap between spouses and the lineage marriage system. Now these are not necessarily culturally induced as opposed to economically induced behaviour patterns. First, it is possible that the offspring of tenant and owner-occupier farmers were responding to common circumstances in the labour market rather than sharing in a cultural pattern despite the economic and social differences between the parents.

Second, the immediate participants may well have stood to gain something from their behaviour, from partible inheritance where it was practical, from a remarriage that would restore the viability of a landholding, and so on. Yet it would be surprising if this was not so. The mere fact of gain goes not mean that the cultural element is unimportant.[34] Berkner and Mendels have perhaps been too hasty in writing off the significance of the cultural factors enshrined in the legal code of inheritance.

Our final thoughts we will devote to the consequences of the patterns we have been describing. There is no doubt that partible inheritance and lineage marriage are egalitarian in intention. Le Roy Ladurie, this time interpreting rather than paraphrasing Yver, was inclined to draw a direct association between lineage marriage and the advent of modernity, rural unrest, individualism, and egoism.[35] This seems just a little too simple. In West Flanders, households were decidedly unequal in size, composition, and resources. Many individuals spent much of their early adulthood in a state of dependency. We do not, of course, know how these individuals felt, but a more convincing interpretation would see unrest as stemming from the unequal distribution of resources within the community, an inequality which jarred with the spirit of equality that pervaded the communal norms.

[34] The argument is used by J. Davis in the context of kin links among households. Davis, *People of the Mediterranean* (1977): 206f.
[35] Le Roy Ladurie (1976): 69–70.

13

The evolving household: the case of Lampernisse, West Flanders

LUC DANHIEUX

Lampernisse: economy and household structure

Lampernisse is a small village in the canton of Pervijze (see fig. 12.1, p. 383). Before the French occupation in 1796 it was one of the villages of the region known as Veurne-Ambacht. Its population under the Ancien Régime was quite stable at around 210 persons, but after the French occupation which ended in 1815 the number of inhabitants rose steadily from about 350 to a maximum of 462 in 1846. According to van der Maelen, writing in 1836, the same range of crops (wheat, rye, oats, barley, oil-producing plants, vegetables, and fruit) was to be found in Lampernisse as elsewhere in West Flanders.[1]

Studies by Dalle have illuminated certain structural elements of the West Flanders society of which Lampernisse forms a small part.[2] Dalle found, for example, that the majority of servants outside the town of Veurne were male (sex ratio 144). Male children over 12 outnumbered female children, although not to such a marked extent (sex ratio 107). But we know nothing of the role of kinship in the household beyond the nuclear family, nor has it been possible to throw any light on the process by which offspring succeeded their parents as heads of households. One list on its own may show the place of the old and of the young in the household, but it cannot tell us how individuals moved from one position to another, nor what other opportunities they might have taken up had they wished or the occasion demanded.

My thanks are due to Richard Wall for reading an earlier version of this chapter and to M. Eric Huys, who, as my research assistant, helped in the preliminary analysis of the data.
[1] Van der Maelen, *Dictionnaire géographique de la Flandre Occidentale* (1836). A concentration on dairying is suggested by a greater number of animals per head of the population and a higher ratio of cows to horses than in the other Flemish parishes studied by Wall in ch. 12 above.
[2] Dalle, 'De Bevolking van de Stad en van de Kasselrij Veurne in 1796' (1964): 143.

In Lampernisse we are able to follow the household through at least part of its life cycle, using census documents that survive for the years 1814, 1824, 1826, and 1829.[3] Since the quality of the lists is somewhat uncertain, the accuracy of the information given has been checked wherever practical. In particular, ages were compared with those in the baptismal register of Lampernisse, or that of the home parish in the case of in-migrants. One of the surprising results of this analysis was that, although parish of birth was given accurately, recorded age was only approximately correct.[4] Since age will be one of the major variables to be considered, the recorded age has been corrected wherever appropriate. Where the exact age could not be traced, age at first census was assumed correct, and appropriate adjustments made to the later returns.

To see the evolution of Lampernisse in context, we will set out the major attributes of its households as they appear in the first of the successive censuses. The choice of the 1814 census is an appropriate one, since it allows a comparison with the figures supplied by Wall for nine other villages in West Flanders. The first obvious difference concerns occupation. In Lampernisse there were more farmers than labourers, whereas labourers predominated in all other villages with the exception of the minute village of Wilskerke. On the other hand, like the other settlements, Lampernisse had its quota of artisans and tradespeople (14% of all male household heads). More significant are the differences in the structure of households of farmers and labourers in the two areas. The households of Lampernisse farmers were more likely than those of farmers in the nine villages to contain relatives, but were less likely to contain offspring or servants.[5] The sex ratio of the servant population was also much lower (119 males to 100 females).

As for the labourers of Lampernisse, the fact that there were no servants at all in their households suggests that the people we have classed as labourers were generally poorer than the comparable class in the nine villages. There is some direct evidence on poverty in Lampernisse from a document dated 1812 which refers to 77 paupers in the

[3] Rijksarchief, Bruges, Volkstelling 1815, no. 101 and Gemeentearchief Lampernisse, no. 244 (1824), no. 245 (1826), no. 246 (1829). Two earlier lists (for 1796 and 1799) have been deemed a little too far removed from the others to be used in this particular study.
[4] There are a number of reasons for these inaccuracies, among which one may note age-rounding, less precision after persons reached adulthood and after marriage, and even complete ignorance of age. There may also have been special reasons for particular individuals to conceal their ages from either the local or the central authorities: for example, fear of the conscription laws.
[5] In Lampernisse 62% of farmers' households contained offspring; 33%, relatives; and 62%, servants (N = 24). Comparable figures for the nine villages were 84%, 18%, and 80%. For the sex ratio of servants see table 12.6 above.

parish,[6] and a further pointer in this direction is that there was also only 1 household headed by a labourer (out of a total of 20) with a child over the age of 20. Indeed, even this case involved a daughter living with her widowed father. In contrast, in the other villages there were 27 offspring aged 20 or over resident in every 100 labourers' households (cf. table 12.7 above).

Some of these differences, particularly the near equality in the number of male and female servants, probably arose from the fact that dairy farming was more important in Lampernisse than in the other villages. There is at least a possibility, though, that other differences between Lampernisse and the rest are best accounted for by variations in property arrangements made at the time of a marriage. Wall argued above (chapter 12) that Flemish farmers relied on marriage and remarriage to build up their holdings. In Lampernisse the offspring group did not disband on the death of the surviving parent.[7] Presumably the parental holding was still intact in these cases. And there is evidence to show that those Lampernisse farmers who did marry were less likely than farmers elsewhere to pick a spouse widely removed from their own age.[8]

The chief concern of this paper, however, is to follow individual households over that part of their life cycle that is encapsulated within the period covered by the four censuses of Lampernisse. We will try and establish whether their kin structure changed over time. In addition we will measure how many households passed through extended-, simple- or no-family phases even when they were not of long duration. Working from one census, it is possible only to say how many households there were of each type at a particular point in time.[9] Here, with four censuses available, we can add to this total the households that were simple, or extended earlier or later in their evolution. The second measure naturally yields the higher frequencies. The interest is in the difference between the two sets of figures. Some scholars have argued in particular that a low proportion of extended households in one census is easily misinterpreted, because households spend such a short period of time in this particular phase,[10] but this has never yet been directly tested.

To examine households solely from the point of view of their kin

---

[6] Rijksarchief, Bruges, Gemeentearchief Lampernisse.

[7] One in five of the farmers' households consisted of unmarried siblings, a form of household that occurred rarely in the other villages, 95% of the farmers there being married (cf. table 12.5 above).

[8] Of Lampernisse farmers, 32% were separated from their spouses by more than 10 years, compared with 47% of farmers in the nine villages.

[9] The household types are based on the Hammel–Laslett categories; see P. Laslett and Wall (eds.), *Household and family* (1972): 85.

[10] Berkner, 'The use and misuse of census data' (1975).

structure would, however, be of limited value. Accordingly, the analysis of the four censuses has been extended in order to look at the households as economic units. This we can do in a crude way simply by recording the number of adults per household. It can be shown, for example, that households would be more likely to be without an adult male than an adult female. We can then proceed to relate these patterns to the various types of household, to discover whether no-family or extended-family households contained more adults than simple-family households and, if so, how many more. Finally, we can test whether servants unrelated to the head are only brought into the household in the absence of family members of equivalent age and sex. Advantage can be taken of the fact that four censuses rather than one have survived to examine how the individual household modified its labour requirements as well as its kin structure over time.

Households: types and successors

Table 13.1 shows that about one-third of the household heads aged 50 and over in 1814 had no traceable successor in the community by 1829, that is to say the head of the household was no longer resident in the village, nor had the succession passed to a clearly identifiable successor, such as a son, son-in-law, or spouse. The figures show that continuity of families over time was far from universal. Taking the 22 household heads of 50 and over in 1814 probably gives a good measure of the extent to which households of the younger generation replaced those of the older; close to 1 in 3 disappeared in the 15-year period.[11] Not surprisingly, where the heads were below 50 years of age, continuity of the household over the 15 years was much stronger, only about 1 in 10 neither surviving nor having a successor.

However, it is important to consider also the head's occupation as a factor in encouraging the continued existence of a household in the village. Only 13 out of 20 labourers' households were present for all four censuses against 20 out of 24 farmers' households. The extinction rate of labourers' households was therefore close to double that of farmers'. For the latter, persistence was the norm if not the universal experience, whereas just over a third of labouring households could not be found in the parish 15 years later. Age differences between farmers and labourers

[11] Of course we must expect some families without heirs (as many as 20%), but with succession going to stepchildren and spouses, persistence rates must be considered on the low side. Wrigley, 'Fertility strategy for the individual and the group' (1978): 140–1, table 3 calculates the possibility of one or more direct heirs for given rates of mortality and fertility.

Table 13.1. *Lampernisse: age of male household heads in 1814
by persistence of households*

Age of head in 1814	Total households[a]	Households persisting in 1829	
		No.	%
Under 30	2	2	100
30–9	14	13	93
40–9	18	16	89
50–9	11	7	64
60–9	6	4	66
≥70	5	3	60
All	56	45	80

[a] Female-headed households (N = 10) are excluded.

cannot affect the issues, since the median age of farmers was 44.5 and of labourers, 43.5.

For those households that remained throughout the 15 years, it is possible to measure the extent to which their structure was constant. As defined by the continuous presence or absence of kin other than the members of the head's nuclear family, one can say that over one-third of all households remained constant in basic structure throughout the period.

Extended households were ephemeral, showing, as has been demonstrated for other communities, that the presence of a relative in addition to the nuclear family represented but a short phase in the life cycle of the household. On the other hand, kin ties within the household could be more enduring when the head was not married. Two of the 5 no-family households retained this structure over the 15-year period. Table 13.2 also contains a certain amount of information on the persistence of various forms of nuclear-family household. None of the households consisting of a lone parent and child retained this form, showing that this truncated type of household, too, was often of short duration. As might be expected, the group consisting of married couple and child proved the most lasting: 54% of all these households maintained this form. This type of household probably provided the most continuous familial experience for the majority of inhabitants.

Another approach to the problem of continuity is to record the number of households which at some stage in their history passed through particular phases. For example, 9 out of 10 households were of the simple-family type at some time between 1814 and 1829. This can

Table 13.2. *Lampernisse: constancy in household type*

	Household type[a] in 1814 (no.)	Constant in type	
		(no.)	(%)
1. Solitary	1	0	0
2. No family	5	2	40
3a. Married couple alone	2 ⎫	0 ⎫	0 ⎫
b. Married couple with child(ren)	26 ⎬ 35[b]	14 ⎬ 14[b]	54 ⎬ 40[b]
c. Widowers with child(ren)	2 ⎪	0 ⎪	0 ⎪
d. Widows with child(ren)	5 ⎭	0 ⎭	0 ⎭
4. Extended	9	0	0
5. Multiple	1	0	0
All	51	16	31

[a] Based on P. Laslett and Wall (eds.) (1972): 85. Households not present in all four censuses are excluded.
[b] Types 3a to 3d collectively are termed simple-family households.

be compared with the third which were extended by the addition of a relative during the same period. Even fewer passed through a solitary or no-family stage, while the experience of living in a multiple-family household (two or more co-resident conjugal family groups) was rare, being experienced over a 25-year period by only 4% of all persisting households.

The interesting point is that if we had been able to study these households only in 1814, we would have reported that 69% were simple and 18% extended (see table 13.2). The chance, therefore, that a household would at some stage be confined to parents and unmarried children (i.e. simple) was extremely high, while the chance of extension at some time was almost double that for one census. The difference between the two sets of figures would probably be greater still if there were more than four censuses providing observation points.

When households changed in type there was often a transfer of headship.[12] This process is crucial to our understanding of Flemish society, since it raises questions regarding the transfer of responsibility from generation to generation. The role of direct lineal transmission of property and responsibility from father to son is central to much of what

[12] This is not absolutely inevitable, given the categories we have used to distinguish households. For example, a son might succeed his mother as head of the household, and as long as she continued to reside with him and he remained unmarried and no other relatives joined them, the household would remain in structure a widow–child unit as it was before.

Table 13.3. *Lampernisse: succession to household headship by age of head in 1814*[a]

| Age of head in 1814 | Relationship of new head to his/her predecessor | | | | | No change of head | |
	Son	Stepson	Son-in-law	Wife	Total successors	No.	%
Under 30	0	0	0	0	0	2	100
30–9	0	0	0	3[b]	3	10	77
40–9	0	2	0	2[c]	4	12	75
50–9	1	0	1[d]	0	2	5	36
60–9	0	0	2	0	2	2	50
≥70	2	0	0	1	3	0	0
TOTAL NO.	3	2	3	6	14	31	69
%	21	14	21	43	99	—	—

[a] Excludes households not present in all four censuses, and the 6 households headed by women which persisted from 1814 to 1829.
[b] Including one case where the wife's second husband is head in a later census.
[c] In one of these cases the son becomes head in a later census and his mother establishes a new household.
[d] In a later census the son has left and his mother has assumed the headship.

has been written about the family. It is thus natural to think that it will be the son who succeeds the father as household head in Lampernisse. Yet, as table 13.3 shows, in 43% of the cases it was the wife who assumed the headship, and in a further 14% the headship went to the son of the wife by a previous marriage. Only in a fifth of the cases did the headship pass directly to the son of the former head,[13] and in as many it was the son-in-law who emerged as the new head. Admittedly, 15 years is not long enough to give us the total picture we would like. Nevertheless, the importance of women in the transference of headship is very clear. Nor would it be correct to think of the wife as always exercising temporary authority during the minority of the heir. In one case where a second transfer of headship occurred during the 15-year period, it was the second husband rather than a son of the first marriage who finally became head of the household. In another instance, where the son had acquired the headship from his father, he later relinquished it to his mother.

It is impossible to say at this stage whether the transference of headship also involved transference of property. It seems a reasonable

[13] Cf. Sieder and Mitterauer above on succession in Austrian households, tables 10.1 and 10.2. Any comparison of the two studies needs to take account of the fact that it was possible to record the succession of non-related households in Austria but not in Lampernisse. Nevertheless, there does appear to be a real difference in the proportion of successions by widows (higher in Lampernisse than in any of the Austrian populations).

hypothesis, however, that the rules governing inheritance were of some consequence in conferring the headship on the wife and occasionally on her own children or her second husband. Yet the rules may have been effective simply because they accorded with the demographic circumstances. The son-in-law, for example, succeeded when there was no co-residing son in 1814 who might have taken over. Similarly, the transfers to stepsons occurred first when there was no co-resident child in 1814 and second when there was only a daughter in the household. In the first case there could be no conflict between step-siblings, and in the second it was unlikely.

The situation in regard to widows who succeeded their husbands is a little more ambiguous. A number took over when their offspring were still young, but there were others who were accorded the title 'head' when there was a co-resident son in his 30s. In the latter cases the widow was possibly not more than a titular head. The instances in which a mature son was deliberately and permanently passed over in favour of the wife's second husband, a stepson, or son-in-law were probably very few indeed, although perhaps not entirely unknown even in a village as small as Lampernisse. Yet, as a widow or even a stepfather did assume temporary headship, the potential for conflict between stepparents and step-siblings was always there.

The household as an economic unit

We can introduce our second measure – the household as a viable economic unit – at this stage. It has become common to think of households in terms of their kinship structure, in other words to focus on the various relationships between the individual members and the head. However, if we think of the household as a whole, one good measure of its strength is the number of adults, both male and female, of prime working age. Relationship here is not of crucial importance, providing all concerned can be assumed to work in one capacity or another, paid or unpaid, to support the household. It is our contention that by including all family members and servants in the following calculations, we have met this condition.[14] If we further define a productive member as either a male or female aged between 20 and 59, we find that close to half of all households contained only one productive male, whilst rather more than half contained only one productive

---

[14] Inmates are excluded, although they may have made an important contribution to the household income in the form of rent. It is accepted also that a few adult children will have been physically or mentally incapable of supporting the household.

female. Only very rarely was a household found without any productive female. The maximum number of households of this sort in any one year was 2 out of a total of 51 households in observation. On the other hand, the number of households lacking a productive male was never less than 4 and reached 13 out of 51 in 1829. In contrast, there were a number of households consisting of three or more productive males, as many as 20% in some years. Households containing three or more productive females were much rarer, only once exceeding 10% in any of the censuses.

We can also measure, by following the same household from census to census, how often a household might have to survive a period without either a productive male or productive female. It emerges that a third of households might at some stage be without a male aged 20–59, but that not even 1 household in 10 would experience a period without a female in this age group.

Many households, however, contained two or more productive persons. These individuals might include more distant relatives and servants in addition to the household head, his wife, and offspring. The circumstances under which these 'extras' were brought into the household are far from clear, apart from a general awareness that more relatives and servants are to be found in higher-status than in lower-status households.[15] The final section of our survey will therefore be devoted to a consideration of service in relation to the amount of labour already provided by members of the family (head, spouse, offspring, and kin). Only farming households, of course, are at issue here.[16]

The first point to focus on is the extent to which the recruitment of servants helps to explain the presence of kin beyond the nuclear family. Taking all four censuses together, about 21% of farming households contained a relative in addition to a conjugal family unit, and a further 19% were of the no-family type, consisting of unmarried siblings. However, if we consider only those kinsmen who are not described as servants, then the proportion of extended households falls from 21% to 10%. The number of no-family households and the few instances of multiple-family households are not, however, affected, implying that these forms of households existed independently of the need of living-in labour, explicitly carrying the status of servant.

It is also the case, though, that co-resident unmarried siblings were more likely to need the labour of strangers to support the economic

---

[15] Cf. P. Laslett, 'Mean household size in England' (1972c): 154.
[16] The number of artisans is negligible, and servants are rarely found in labourers' households.

Table 13.4. *Lampernisse: farmers' households with servants by number of male and female family members of equivalent age[a]*

No. of male family members[a]	No.	With male servants		No. of female family members[a]	No.	With female servants	
		No.	%			No.	%
0	15	15	100	0	18	18	100
1	54	30	56	1	54	27	50
2	8	3	38	2	18	5	28
≥3	8	0	0	≥3	3	0	0
All	85	48	56	All	93	50	54

[a] Excludes all households not present at all four censuses, and persons aged 0–14 and 60 or over. For the purpose of the calculation of equivalent age, family members and servants were divided into two age groups: 15–19 and 20–59. Households are counted on every occasion when a family member fell into either of these age groups. Six servants under 15 were not included, nor is any account taken of the possibility that farmers' offspring between 10 and 14 may have been carrying out some of the tasks that otherwise might have been performed by somewhat older servants, such as the herding of livestock. Family members include the head, spouse, offspring, and relatives of the household head when present and of equivalent age and sex. Relatives of the head who were servants, however, are counted as servants and not family members.

activities of the household. Only 1 of the co-resident sibling groups was without servants, whereas 19 of the 49 nuclear-family and 5 of the 8 extended-family households were servantless. There is a need, therefore, to explain why no-family households relied more on servants than did family households. Two explanations seem possible, either separately or in combination. First, it might be thought that no-family households would be smaller and would mostly contain fewer adults than simple-family households and would thus have more need of extra-familial labour. The second possibility is that their members might be wealthier, either through inheritance or because they were without the burden of a growing family. This in turn would allow them more space and more resources to accommodate living-in servants.

There is evidence that might suggest that the first explanation is the correct one. Table 13.4, for example, shows that a servant was most likely to be taken into the household when there was no family member of equivalent age and sex already present. The point is clearly brought out in the contrast between the households with no male or female equivalent family member, all of which took in at least one servant of the appropriate sex, and households where there were three family-member equivalents, when servants were never taken in. Obviously

Table 13.5. *Lampernisse: distribution of productive family members of farmers'*
households by sex and household type

Household type[a]	No. of male productive family members[b]					No. of female productive family members[b]				
	0	1	2	≥3	Total	0	1	2	≥3	Total
1. Solitary	0	5	0	0	5	4	1	0	0	5
2. No family	1	4	5	5	15	0	10	4	1	15
3. Simple family	11	34	2	2	49	0	41	7	1	49
4. Extended family	1	6	1	0	8	0	5	3	0	8
5. Multiple family	0	3	0	0	3	0	2	1	0	3
All	13	52	8	7	80	4	59	15	2	80

[a] This table excludes households not present in all four censuses, and all servants, whether or not related to the household head. It should be noted that the latter exclusion reduces the number of extended households.
[b] Males and females aged 20–59.

some households needed more labour than others, for close to 40% of households with two male members in the appropriate age groups still felt the need of a male servant.

However, although families did balance familial against imported labour, this does not explain why no-family households more often contained servants than did households of other types. Table 13.5 shows the distribution of adult family members by household type. It emerges that the no-family households already contained more adults of both sexes before they started importing additional servants. One-third of no-family households contained three or more adult males, but only 4% of simple-family households did so. One is forced, therefore, to assume that these households were indeed wealthier than the others and that this wealth supported a different family structure which also required more servants. The reverse of this argument, that it was the peculiarity of their household structure that gave them their wealth, seems far-fetched. A greater number of adult family members may have carried with it the potential for greater wealth, but as the majority of the heads of these households were relatively young (three out of four were aged 35 or under in 1814) there would not appear to have been much time to build up appreciable reserves.

Two further observations must be made concerning the use of servants in relation to the life cycle of the household. First, it should be noted that only a minority of farming households contained servants at each of the four censuses. Out of a total of 20 households, 6 were without a servant at one census and 3 at three censuses, while 2 never had a servant. Flexibility in labour requirements is further suggested by the fact that only 2 out of the 15 households who were employing servants on at least three occasions restricted themselves to servants of one sex. A further 4 households employed servants of both sexes in all years, but the remainder were divided equally between those that employed females always and males sometimes and those that employed males always and females sometimes. The nature of the local economy with its emphasis on livestock, the necessity to complete a variety of household tasks, and the requirements of individual households all apparently worked together to give both men and women opportunities for service in the parish.

Conclusion

We must now pull together the main threads of the arguments. A study based on just one village carries with it both disadvantages and advantages. One of the disadvantages is not knowing whether Lampernisse village is typical of its area. To this must be added that there are only a small number of households in observation, with the result that the creation of subcategories such as occupational or age groups all too often leads to comparisons between groups of some half-dozen households. Yet, there are positive advantages to a small-scale study. It enables us to see precisely which factors were important in a particular situation, revealing the way in which individual households in Lampernisse changed shape over time. It has led us to four general conclusions. First, strict lineal descent of household headship from father to son was not the usual mode of transmission. The second conclusion is that over a 15-year period almost all households would experience a simple-family phase but only a third an extended-family phase. Third, the number of extended households is inflated by the need of these households for servants. This does not occur in the case of the no-family households. Finally, the presence of servants is only partially accounted for by the absence of family members of equivalent age. Indeed, the inequality in resources between households is on occasion intensified by the inclusion of servants in those households which had an above-average number of productive family members. However, it is evidence of the individuality of behaviour that abounds in Lampernisse, some of it prompted by demographic circumstances, such as the death of a wife or the absence of a mature son to carry on the farm.

14

The composition of households in a population of 6 men to 10 women: south-east Bruges in 1814

RICHARD WALL

Introduction

Cities by their very size pose considerable problems for those who wish to understand their social structure. The present study involves a detailed examination of the household and familial patterns of the inhabitants of the south-east sector of Bruges at the end of the Napoleonic period. Bruges was chosen because it is known to have exhibited an extreme imbalance between the sexes, a situation that the Napoleonic Wars had only served to intensify. Yet although women heavily outnumbered men, such a situation was not at all uncommon in European cities. In some cases this was the product of the flooding in of domestic servants to serve in the households of wealthier masters. In others it was associated with a particularly important textile industry – in the case of Bruges, lacemaking. Yet although this occupation had co-existed with the surplus of women in Bruges over a long period, it would be precipitate to assume that lacemaking was the sole or even the principal cause of the city's population structure. As will be pointed out later, the case for direct movement into Bruges of women seeking employment as lacemakers is very difficult to establish.

Bruges's tradition of lacemaking can be said to be world-famous, but surprisingly little is known of the family circumstances of those who were engaged in this production. Lacemaking qualifies as one of those activities which have in recent years come to be termed 'proto-industrial'. A number of diverse employment situations can be com-

Revisions to this chapter were completed while I was attached to the Institut für Wirtschafts und Sozialgeschichte, and I have benefited from discussions with Professor M. Mitterauer, J. Ehmer, P. Schmidtbauer, and R. Sieder. My thanks are also due to Professor E. Hélin of the University of Liège and L. Danhieux, Archivist of the Rijksarchief, Bruges.

prised under this head,[1] but usually they carry the sense of employment in the home rather than in a factory and of employment that was additional, if not subsidiary, to the (sometimes different) occupation of the head of the household, yet with the involvement of members of the household from an early age. In a rural area the household head, if not himself fully involved in proto-industrial activity, might be a peasant. In Bruges, where lacemaking was a female activity, any males would be artisans or day labourers. At the same time, however, a considerable number of households were entirely dependent on proto-industrial employment and had to compete with others in which such activity was supplementary to what male members of the household might earn. The majority of lace workers fell into the latter category.[2]

The theory of the proto-industrial family does not take one very far in considering what effect all this activity had on the form of the household. Those who have written about proto-industrialization, while agreeing on its relevance for an understanding of the household, have often been less than explicit about its impact on household membership. Such ideas that have been thrown out, principally in connection with proto-industrialization in a rural setting, are that labour, being family based, would encourage complex households as families sought to maximize their labour power. Parents would seek to keep their children at home instead of sending them out into service and would try to draw into the household any additional cheap labour, of relatives or of non-relatives, that was available. However, as the basic working unit was the family, the existing working units could not indefinitely maintain all their labour. Mature offspring, in particular, would seize opportunities to found households (and new work units) of their own, a process which the older generation was powerless to prevent.

With only limited modifications, those expectations about household forms might be carried across to Bruges. As lacemaking was specifically a female occupation, parents would be more anxious to keep their daughters at home than their sons, other factors being equal. On the other hand, marriage would be early, at least for women, because of this potential for supplementary earnings. In practice, although it is possible to show an excess of females amongst relatives and non-relatives as well

[1] The following account relies heavily on my reading of Medick, 'The proto-industrial family economy' (1976b) and Mendels, 'Agriculture and peasant industry' (1975): 179–203.
[2] Preliminary analysis of the census of 1814 suggests that 43% of all lacemakers were neither household heads nor inmates, i.e. they were daughters or relatives. No servants or wives were specified as lacemakers.

as amongst offspring, there is no sign of women marrying particularly early.[3]

It is a mistake, however, to consider household patterns from a single perspective, in this case the one of a particular proto-industrial activity. It is the converse of the more usual practice of examining the structure of the household solely in terms of the occupation of the (usually male) household head. A lacemaker had to be trained, but very little capital was required in order to commence employment.[4] There were no expensive tools to acquire, as there were with many other hand crafts, and no stock, as with commercial activity. At first sight lacemaking would seem to offer women an alternative to remaining in the parental home, an alternative even to marriage, provided lodgings could be found. However, these opportunities are easily exaggerated. Lacemaking is unlikely to have been particularly profitable, or it would not have remained an exclusively female activity. Detailed statements of earnings are difficult to locate. Figures given by Duceptiaux suggest that women in Bruges in about 1850 could earn not much more than a third of that earned by a labourer in Bruges.[5]

If household patterns are to be understood, therefore, it is necessary to come back to a consideration of male as well as female occupations and the distribution of the population by age and sex among the various occupational groups. Through seeing which elements of the household – relatives, offspring, servants, or attached inmates – change with the occupation of the head, it is possible to gauge how occupation influenced the household and houseful. First, however, it is essential to make clear what is meant by the terms 'family', 'household', and 'houseful' in the context of the census of 1814, which is the medium for our view of Bruges.

Families, households, and housefuls and their neighbours

Censuses provide firm boundaries for families, households, and housefuls. Even if the census is ordered by house rather than by household, it is a fairly straightforward matter to identify smaller units within it on the basis of relationship or service. It has long been recognized, however, that the boundaries of these units may be more fixed at one time than another. There may be other loyalties, to kin across the street or to

[3] See below, table 14.3.
[4] Duclos, *Bruges: histoire et souvenirs* (1910): 299, 405–6; Diderot, *L'encyclopédie ou dictionnaire raisonné des sciences, des arts et des métiers* (1763); Briavoinne, *De l'industrie en Belgique*, II (1839): 369.
[5] Duceptiaux, 'Budgets économiques des classes ouvrières' (1855): 318.

fellow workers, which compete with those of the resident family and the household. In a large town where the majority of household heads were in artisan or commercial employment, home and workplace are often assumed to be synonymous. At the same time, the pressure of poverty forced households to subdivide the existing housing stock. Considerable care therefore must be exercised to make sure that a label for a form of co-residential domestic group, whether the preference is for 'household' or 'houseful', is not interpreted rigidly.

No census, of course, is going to be entirely accurate, and detailed cross-checking of references to families in other sources such as parish registers would no doubt bring to light a number of errors, such as the omission of some infants and the misclassification of some other persons, particularly stepchildren. This sort of operation is tedious enough in the context of a small village, and is scarcely practical in the case of Bruges, where it is doubtful if the improvement in reliability would justify the amount of work involved. More serious for the argument of the present chapter is the possibility that there might be confusion involving the principal categories – head, spouse, offspring, relatives, servants, and inmates – into which the population has been divided. There is very little of a problem in the case of spouse, offspring (referred to in the list as 'son' or 'daughter' and not by the more ambiguous term 'child', which might include grandchildren), and servants.[6] The major difficulty comes with the category 'related persons'. The precise relationship to the head is not always indicated in the list, and in such cases it has been necessary to rely on the possession of a surname shared with the head to distinguish 'relatives' from inmates.[7]

Inmates are not referred to as such in the 1814 census but are simply a collective term for all those for whom it has been impossible to identify a relationship with the head. In the Cambridge scheme of household analysis, the choice of the term 'inmate' would place them outside the household but within the houseful.[8] It is impossible in the present circumstances to be certain about this, but thinking purely in terms of

---

[6] In order to simplify the analysis, all identified stepchildren have been counted in the total of offspring. Married offspring have been included in the count of relatives. There were a few cases of servants identified as relatives, and these have been classed here as relatives. In the count of housefuls with relatives and servants (table 14.6 below) they were, on the other hand, included in both categories.

[7] The fact that in Belgium women retained their maiden names after marriage helps with the identification of the kin relationship.

[8] P. Laslett and Wall (eds.), *Household and family* (1972): 34–9. The subclassification into familial and non-familial inmates in table 14.7 is adopted in this chapter for the first time. It distinguishes those inmates with some other related person present (spouse, offspring, or relative) from those apparently on their own.

the problems of enumeration in a town such as Bruges, listing by houseful, rather than household, seems more probable. Inmates, even subhouseholds, are therefore to be expected. The argument is certainly not negated by the fact that the composition of the inmate group varied with the composition of the household, as will be shown later. The concept of the houseful is intended to be suspensive in character; it does not preclude associations between inmates and the household.

It becomes clearer whether such 'inmates' constitute separate households when there is detailed information on the layout of the house. The presence of some families amongst the inmate population of Bruges (see table 14.7 below) is by itself no indication that they were living separately from the household (e.g. cooking separately and with distinct living quarters). Conversely, the fact that many inmates shared an occupation with either the head or a member of the household is no proof that the inmates were associated with the activities of the household or even had access to a common workroom. Something on the lines of the latter seems inherently probable[9] but must await further evidence, even if it has to be the impressionistic accounts of travellers passing through Bruges and dropping a comment or two on working conditions as they admired the remains of the city's earlier glory.

Two factors, however, might suggest a rather different conclusion about the position of inmates *vis-à-vis* the household. First, there is the occasional multiple grouping of families into one unit in streets such as the Kraanrei. This could indicate a substantial building, possibly with annexes, divided among a number of households whose connections with each other were not particularly strong. On the other hand, such cases are exceptional in south-east Bruges according to the census of 1814, and this is confirmed by an examination of the many surviving houses and the late-nineteenth-century record of pictures and photographs.[10] Meriting more consideration is the evidence in the census of distinct rights of residence within the houseful. The enumerators of 1814 took pains to note not only the names and ages of the inhabitants, but also whether they were the owners, tenants, or under-tenants

[9] Pictures and photographs of Bruges laceworkers (*c.* 1895 and 1910) in Duclos (1910): 187 show them working in the street, either in groups or singly but within conversational distance of neighbours. However, these groups were subject to the exigencies of the weather and possibly also of the camera.

[10] The drawing of the Rolweg (*c.* 1895) even shows a number of single-storey buildings (Duclos (1910): 187). In 1814 the Rolweg ran from St Anna's Church to the periphery of the built-up area; see fig. 14.1 below.

of the buildings they occupied. For the first-named person in every name block, who are unequivocally heads of households, this information on ownership is a useful piece of additional knowledge, and there will be occasion to refer to it below. In addition, however, the census identified tenants and under-tenants (though never owners) within the blocks of names.

This identification would appear at first sight to provide an inner dividing line separating one household from another. When the first person listed in the block of names is called a tenant and none of the familial inmate groups or individuals are interrelated, then there may indeed be a case for thinking of them as constituting separate households. Even if they did not live entirely separately (for example through sharing a workroom), they had by implication taken up residence there as distinct units. But the situation becomes progressively less clear when the head of the first group is a tenant and the others are under-tenants, or when related individuals are involved. Careful perusal of the census showed that tenancies and under-tenancies were specified for related as well as unrelated persons. In the case where two sisters shared a house and an occupation and yet each was styled tenant, it seems improbable that they were 'living' separately. More plausible is the suggestion that they had jointly inherited the rights to the tenancy and with it perhaps the rights to the business. Without further evidence, therefore, it would seem unwise to insist on the existence of smaller residential groups than the name blocks which are clearly indicated in the census. For this reason, we shall refer to housefuls, not households, throughout the remainder of the chapter, as far as Bruges is concerned.

There is also, however, the question of relationships beyond the houseful. These are much more difficult to establish, particularly in towns, than are even the connections within the houseful. To pursue this question in detail would be impractical here, but to take a first step towards the sort of community study which is needed is a subsidiary aim of this chapter. Of the need for such a study there can be no doubt.

The anatomy of a city has usually been considered either in terms of its administrative divisions or in terms of grid squares. From such work it is possible to map the social topography of the pre-industrial city from the location of the wealthier areas in the centre to the poorer areas on the periphery. Unfortunately, concentration on areal units along these lines misses much of the diversity. For the inhabitants of the time, adjoining streets, a single street, or even a section of a street is likely to have been the important universe, constituting the locale for many of the daily activities.[11] One of the more important points of contact is likely to have been common work experience. In this study of Bruges the intention is to look at the occupational structure within individual streets.

Immediately, there arises the problem of the precise measure of occupational segregation which should be used. It would be all too easy to repeat the mistake of the aggregate approach and get a general impression of segregation by singling out streets where one or other occupation was dominant, in that more than a given proportion of houseful heads, or alternatively of individuals, had that occupation. Instead, the decision was taken to note all the streets where two or more heads possessed occupations of the same type. It is quite deliberately the weakest measure of occupational segregation that could be devised. If occupational 'areas' show up on the basis of this method, then there can be no doubt that occupational groups were residentially segregated.

Yet the difficult issue is not whether there was, or was not, occupational unity at the level of the street but what importance should attach to such unity or, alternatively, to its absence. To be able to answer this, it would be necessary to know much more than we do at present about the characteristics of contact between individuals in the street and in the home. Much of this may never be recoverable, but by a determined use of other sources, noting the frequencies of marriages between individuals from neighbouring housefuls and the nature of disputes between neighbours, some idea of an individual's network of contacts can be gauged.[12] To establish this network even in the context of a village takes time. For the present, such considerations must be put aside, and it will be necessary to rely on inferences drawn from the proximity of housefuls with common characteristics. For example, it can be noted on the basis of the patterns of occupational segregation (see figs. 14.1–8 below) that this segregation was to some extent a matter of choice. Poverty necessarily excluded some housefuls from the hub of the city, but there was choice in the sense that occupational groups were not excluded by poverty from residing in all areas, yet were to be found, like with like, in particular streets. This grouping, it can be argued, would not have taken place unless it was of material benefit to the respective parties. Admittedly, the pattern might have had its origin in a common workplace (although the evidence is rather for the individual home and

[11] Cf. n. 9 above and the remarks on the street being 'the garden of the poor' in the large towns of Belgium. Duceptiaux (1855): 329, citing Ministry of the Interior, *Enquête sur la condition des classes ouvrières*, III: 230.

[12] For an example of what can be done in a rural context see R. M. Smith, 'Kin and neighbours' (1979b).

workplace being synonymous) or in mutual dependence on a common resource – water supply, for instance, or a major thoroughfare. Even in such cases, though, mutual dependence would soon become the base fostering personal contacts of a more general nature.

The inhabitants of south-east Bruges: age, sex, and marital status

The precise area involved in the present survey is a web of streets lying east and south of the central market place (Markt) containing about a quarter of the population of the entire town (see fig. 14.1 below).[13] For the residents of these streets the census yields information on age, sex, marital status, relationship to houseful head, occupation, and migration.[14] From all this it is possible to establish at what age people typically came to head a houseful, at what age they might marry, at what age they might find themselves living as a servant or relative in another person's houseful. First, however, it is necessary to examine with care the age, sex, marital, and occupational characteristics of the population.

The distribution of the population by age and sex is considered in table 14.1. The most marked feature is the surplus of females: after the age of 15 there were no more than 64 males to every 100 females. In their 20s women outnumbered men almost two to one. The male age pyramid is also quite different from that of the female. Of the males, 35% were under the age of 15; only 25% of the females. The imbalance between the numbers of males and females in the older age groups, notably

[13] Visits to the Rijksarchief und Stadsarchief in Bruges failed to reveal any detailed map of Bruges contemporary with the 1814 census. The use of a modern map brought to light one or two problems. Four streets which one might have expected to find in the census were missing (these may have been omitted by the enumerator), and three other streets, probably on the fringe of the built-up area in 1814, had clearly been lengthened at some later date. Fortunately, most of the other 78 streets referred to in the census were located without problem on the modern map even though some of them had experienced a change of name. The information on households in 1814 is taken from the first, and so far only, volume of the transcription, and part translation, by the Vlaamse Vereniging voor Familiekunde afdeling Brugge of the 1814 census of Bruges. The original (in French) is in the Rijksarchief in Bruges. The population of the whole town was 31,300 in 1796 and 30,826 in 1804. See van Houlte, *An economic history* (1977): 230; Duclos (1910): 105.

[14] The information in the 1814 census on migration has been analysed, but the result was extraordinary. There were more male than female in-migrants (8% against 5%) and even more migrant male than female servants (32% against 18%) in a context where females heavily outnumber males. The figures have, therefore, been set on one side. One possibility is that much short-distance migration was not noted by the enumerators, although sporadic references to neighbouring villages in the census show that this cannot be the full explanation.

Table 14.1. *South-east Bruges, 1814: distribution of the population by age and sex*

Age group	Males[a]		Females		
	No.	%	No.	%	Sex ratio
0–9	775	23.3	792	17.5	97.8
10–14	381	11.5	355	7.9	107.3
15–19	296	8.9	398	8.8	74.4
20–4	207	6.2	386	8.5	53.6
25–9	227	6.8	415	9.2	54.7
30–9	396	11.9	639	14.1	62.0
40–9	436	13.1	585	13.0	74.5
50–9	306	9.2	459	10.2	66.7
≥60	296	8.9	487	10.8	60.8
TOTAL	3,320	99.8	4,516	100.0	73.5
≥15	2,164	65.2	3,369	74.7	64.2

[a] Excludes 3 males of unknown age.

during the 20s, might in theory be produced, either alone or in combination, by the net in-migration of females or the net out-migration or non-registration of males anxious to avoid enrolment in Napoleon's armies. These are not matters which are easy to decide with only a single document to go upon, but the balance of probability is for major outflow of males due to the war and only a modest inflow of females. This argument is proffered on the basis of the size of the male age groups 20–4 and 25–9 in relation to earlier age groups and to the comparable female age groups but is not, and cannot be, decisive. The more intractable problem of the size of the male age groups has to be approached by a process of exclusion. For example, the misrepresentation of the ages of males would have produced a male surplus in other age groups, and there is little sign of this. Similarly, it is unlikely that many males had been registered as females, since the major adjustment of the totals necessary to raise the number of males aged 20–4 to a level compatible with that of males aged 10–14 (allowing for mortality) would simply reproduce the same problem in the case of females. This still leaves unresolved whether the males were missing due to omission from the census or because of involvement, direct or indirect, in the military campaigns. However, one would want hard evidence of the presence of these men in Bruges in 1814 to reject the latter hypothesis with confidence.

At this juncture it may be useful to consider whether south-east Bruges was exceptional in having a sex ratio in 1814 of 73.6 males to

Table 14.2. *South-east Bruges and nine neighbouring villages:*
proportions married by age group and sex

Age group	Proportion of married males[a] by age group in South-east Bruges (%)	9 villages in West Flanders (%)	Proportion of married females[a] by age group in South-east Bruges (%)	9 villages in West Flanders (%)
15–19	2.4	0.0	1.5	1.8
20–4	20.8	4.9	13.7	15.4
25–9	49.8	25.9	33.2	48.6
30–9	71.2	55.7	51.3	77.4
40–9	80.3	81.3	54.7	82.6
50–9	80.4	84.8	51.0	75.2
≥60	62.2	74.4	30.2	61.0
≥15	56.6	44.3	36.2	47.8

[a] N = 2,164 males, 3,369 females (Bruges); 1,284 males, 1,190 females (9 villages).

every 100 females. In 1784,[15] before the wars, the sex ratio of the entire town had been 84.7, but it had already fallen to 76.9 by 1801, a change that one might well impute to the direct or indirect effects of the war. It is of course well known that most European towns of this period contained more women than men, but it is the size of the female surplus that is the issue here. Reference to Mols's three volumes on European towns shows, however, that south-east Bruges, while clearly exceptional, was not unique.[16]

The second major characteristic of the population to be investigated is the age and incidence of marriage. The main features of the western European marriage pattern were delayed marriage by women, a high proportion of women never marrying, and the establishment of a separate residence on marriage by the new couple. Within this general framework, however, there was room for considerable variation, the significance of which has not always been appreciated. Consider, to begin with, the proportions of men and women who were married (table 14.2). A sharp contrast can be drawn between the population of Bruges and that of the villages in the vicinity. In the case of south-east

[15] Calculated from figures cited by Mols, *Introduction à la démographie historique des villes d'Europe* (1954–6), II: 188, 192–3.
[16] For example, some Swiss towns in the thirteenth and eighteenth centuries and some English towns in 1801 had sex ratios similar to that of Bruges in 1814. Mols (1954–6), II: 187–90.

Bruges, 57% of the men over the age of 15 were married but only 36% of the women. Yet in nine of the villages within a few kilometres of the town, the proportion of women married actually exceeded that of the men.[17] Second, in the town the proportion of married men in the population increased much more rapidly with age. Half of those aged between 25 and 29 were married; in the nine villages, only a quarter. On the other hand, the figures suggest that more men in the rural area than in the urban area would eventually succeed in marrying. Already for men over the age of 40 there was a higher proportion married in the villages, and the difference becomes significant in the case of men over 60. The final element in the urban–rural contrast is that men married earlier in the town than in the country, and women earlier in the country than the town. In terms of their marriage patterns Bruges and its hinterland were clearly poles apart.

Underlying such differences were the sex ratios of the two populations: 64 men to 100 women over the age of 15 in south Bruges; 107 men to 100 women over 15 in the rural area. This is not to say that one can simply 'read off' marriage patterns from differences in sex ratios. Although the balance between the sexes naturally produces constraints on how many of each sex may marry, similar proportions married can be found in populations with different sex ratios.[18]

Nevertheless, given the sex ratio of 64, it is scarcely surprising to find that in south-east Bruges marriage was the common, if not the universal, expectation for men, while for women the position was quite different. The proportions of women married were exceptionally low, barely rising above 50% even for women in their 30s, which, for a later-marrying population, was the prime age of bearing children. It is not the low proportion of women married in itself that was special, however, but that this co-existed in Bruges with an exceptionally high proportion of men married. This becomes clear by turning again to the data on other European towns reproduced by Mols.[19]

It is also apparent from a study of Mols's three volumes that towns subject to so many different influences, social, demographic, and economic, could exhibit similar proportions of married persons. It is a timely

---

[17] These are the nine villages analysed in detail in chapter 12 above. See also table 14.2.
[18] For example, the proportion of women aged 40–9 who were married was 55.0% in central Vienna in 1754 and 54.7% in south-east Bruges in 1814, while the sex ratio of the population aged 40–9 was significantly higher in Vienna at 86.2 compared with Bruges's 74.5. Data on Vienna are from Mols (1954–6), II: 191.
[19] For example, both in Bruges and in central Vienna in 1754 55% of females aged 40–9 were married, but whereas in Bruges 80% of the males in the same age group were married, only 65% of such males were married in Vienna.

reminder that there are limits to what it would be legitimate to infer from the existence of a particular marriage pattern. The significance of a marriage pattern in the demographic sense, that is the impact on population growth, is calculable. The influence of a particular pattern on the lives of the inhabitants is naturally more problematic, depending on factors on which the present sources cannot throw any light, such as the degree of segregation in sex roles. On the other hand, the extent to which people bound by the marriage bond predominate in a given society is, without doubt, one of the major characteristics of that society. Individuals may be conceived of as having loyalties to a variety of people in the community; a network beginning with the people seen most often, a spouse or offspring, and spreading out to relatives and neighbours. Many of the women of western European cities had to operate without the first of these ties. Apart from the relevance of this for the emotional, social, and economic life of these women, the effect on the social and economic life of the European town must have been considerable.

The proportion married in the population is contingent upon the numbers never marrying, the frequency of widowhood, and the opportunities for remarriage, as well as upon age at first marriage. It is impossible to consider all of these,[20] but there is some information available on the proportion of the Bruges population that never married. This imposes a much greater test of the quality of a census than does the calculation of the proportion married. Although most lists make it clear how many inhabitants were married, the widowed and single are seldom carefully distinguished, especially if they were not heads of housefuls, and if they were men rather than women. All too often the only information on widowhood is that which can be inferred when offspring lived with just one parent. Inevitably this links the definition of widowhood to a whole range of other factors, such as the number of surviving offspring, the frequency of offspring remaining with a widowed parent, the timing of widowhood in the individual's life cycle, and so on. Comparisons with the proportions never married as reported in other studies have therefore to be treated with care.

In south-east Bruges and two of the nine neighbouring villages it is possible to be sure that the lists are sufficiently rigorous and consistent in their identification of widowed women to allow an accurate account of

---

[20] Some idea of the importance of remarriage can be obtained from the variation in the age gap between the spouses according to the husband's age. See below, figs. 14.12 and 14.13.

Table 14.3. *South-east Bruges and two neighbouring villages, 1814: number and proportion of never-married females by age group*

Age group	South-east Bruges			Mariakerke and Nieuwmunster		
	Total in age group	Never married No.	%	Total in age group	Never married No.	%
15–19	398	392	98.5	38	36	94.7
20–4	386	333	86.3	25	20	80.0
25–9	415	265	63.8	24	9	37.5
30–9	639	258	40.4	39	7	17.9
40–9	585	185	31.6	26	0	0.0
50–9	459	130	28.3	18	0	0.0
≥60	487	133	27.3	18	2	11.1
All	3,369	1,696	50.3	188	74	39.4

the number of women never married.[21] This exercise, limited as it is, again brings out the different marriage patterns of town and country (see table 14.3). The vast majority of women in the countryside did eventually marry, and for some age groups there were no never-married women.[22] In south-east Bruges, in contrast, the proportion of never-married women fell only slowly with age, indicative of women entering marriage not only after 30 but also after 40. Even so, more than a quarter of women in their 50s had never married.[23]

Some of the women of south-east Bruges were attracted into irregular unions. More than 10% of single women in their 30s had co-resident offspring. In view of the recent development of interest in this subject, particularly in the relationship between bastardy and the norms regarding marriage,[24] it is worth examining the incidence of these irregular unions in some detail. Whatever may be the case elsewhere, there is

---

[21] For men it is only possible to produce the figures showing the maximal number never married (and the minimal number widowed) on the assumption that all widowers would have co-resident offspring in the same household. Since such figures, aside from any doubts about their utility, would not be compatible with those for never-married women, it has been decided not to reproduce them here.

[22] These proportions are within range of those drawn from the reconstitutions of parish registers within the Paris basin. See Dupâquier, *La population rurale du bassin parisien* (1979): table III, pp. 299–300. On the other hand, Austrian villages of the eighteenth and nineteenth centuries generally had higher proportions unmarried at age 50. See Schmidtbauer, 'Daten zur historischen Demographie und Familienstruktur' (1977) in the library of the SSRC Cambridge Group.

[23] Even higher proportions never married have been recorded for some Austrian towns. In Salzburg in 1794, for example, as many as 48% of the women aged 45–9 were never married. See Schmidtbauer (1977). In Austria proportions never married were very variable from place to place, with the result that even the claim that towns contained a higher proportion of unmarried women than did country areas is difficult to establish.

[24] P. Laslett, Oosterveen, and Smith (eds.), *Bastardy and its comparative history* (1980): 54.

Table 14.4. *South-east Bruges, 1814: number and proportion of never-married women with resident offspring by age*

Age group	Never-married women with resident offspring (no.)	Never-married women with resident offspring as proportion of		
		All never-married women by age group (%)	All ever-married women by age group (%)	All women by age group (%)
15–19	1	0.2	14.3	0.2
20–4	12	3.6	18.5	3.1
25–9	21	7.9	12.3	5.1
30–9	26	10.1	6.4	4.1
40–9	15	8.1	3.6	2.6
50–9	1	0.8	0.3	0.2
≥60	1	0.8	0.3	0.2
All	77	4.5	4.4	2.3

certainly some justification for the argument that implication in bastardy was in Bruges particularly the fate of the younger woman. For example, irregular unions were most marked among women aged 20–4, when they formed almost a fifth of all unions within the age group. However, the perspective changes if one measures instead the number of single women with offspring as a proportion of all women or as a proportion of all women still single. In the first case the maximum proportion of irregular unions is recorded by the age group 25–9. In the second, the maximum is postponed still further into the 30s (table 14.4). Beyond the age of 50 few single women were found with offspring.

Any general statement that might be made about the significance of these patterns has to be hedged about with qualifications, because it is not known how many of these women subsequently married (some obviously did so) and because the incidence of these unions can only be established when offspring and their mothers co-resided. The figures in table 14.4 are in that sense minimal. However, even when a generous allowance is made for irregular unions concealed by later marriage, irregular unions formed a higher proportion of the unions contracted by women under 30 than they did of unions contracted by women under 40.[25] The implication is that these irregular unions were not a repre-

[25] The estimate maximizes the number of irregular unions by making the assumption that all such unions recorded for a preceding age group(s) had been converted into regular marriages by the time of the following age category. Nor is any allowance made for

sentative cross-section of potential 'normal' marriages that had for some
reason 'gone wrong'.

Heads of housefuls and their occupations

A problem which any investigator of the social structure encounters is
how to make sense of the occupational diversity of the towns. In
south-east Bruges, houseful heads alone were engaged in no fewer than
73 distinct occupations which might broadly be termed 'artisan'. Some
of these occupations were represented in many housefuls, such as those
of the 148 weavers, but most had only a handful of adherents. Much of
the following analysis will therefore be in terms of broad-based groups
such as artisans and those in commercial employments, except where
the number of housefuls with a particular occupation such as weaving
or lacemaking permits otherwise. This both facilitates comparison with
other studies[26] and allows certain key elements in the Bruges population
to be distinguished. Considerable care has been taken to ensure that
housefuls headed by women are classified separately from those headed
by men, even when they fall within the same occupational category.
The reasons for this lie in the very different characteristics of female-
headed housefuls, not only in terms of the head's age but also in the
number and type of extra persons (relatives, servants, and inmates)
with whom they co-resided.

A classification of the occupations of houseful heads using this system
yields 14 categories, 8 for male heads and 6 for female heads (see table
14.5). Artisans, with 36% of all male heads, form by far the largest group
even without the weavers (13% of male heads). Otherwise the quarter
had the wide range of occupational types that one would expect of a city
the size of Bruges. Thus 16% of the male heads were in commerce,
engaged in buying, selling, and transporting various commodities,
sometimes in association with the three markets ('large', fish, and grain)
which lay within the area. Then there were 6% of male heads with
public appointments (directors of taxes, receivers of taxes, city officials
high and low, clerks, and policemen), and 4% were in personal service.
This last category embraces all those with a service to offer, including

---

mortality. On this basis irregular unions as a proportion of the total are 20.0%, 19.9%,
and 14.7% for the age groups 20–4, 25–9, and 30–9 respectively. Thereafter the
proportion rises, principally because the 'no mortality' assumption becomes increasingly unrealistic.

[26] See Hélin, 'Les codes socio-professionnels comme instruments d'analyse' (1970). There
is a fuller description in Hélin's contribution to Marcilio and Charbonneau (eds.),
Démographie Historique (1979).

Table 14.5. *South-east Bruges, 1814: distribution of housefuls in streets by occupational group and sex of houseful head*

Sex of head	Occupational group of head[a]	Housefuls by occupation of head Proportion of all housefuls with male or female head[b] (%)	Streets containing such housefuls[c] Proportion of all streets (N = 78) (%)
M	Agriculture	3.3	26
	Personal service	4.4	37
	Public service	6.2	36
	Non-active	7.3	47
	Weavers	12.6	46
	Day labourers	14.0	60
	Commerce	16.2	60
	Artisans	35.9	82
	All male heads	100.0	100
F	Miscellaneous[d]	4.6	17
	Commerce	13.0	33
	Seamstresses	13.0	31
	Non-active	13.3	32
	Day labourers	18.8	44
	Lacemakers	37.1	55
	All female heads	100.0	83

[a] The groups are arranged in order of ascending size. In later tables the arrangement is alphabetical. For an explanation of the groups, see text. The total number of male-headed housefuls was 1,172; of female-headed housefuls, 345.
[b] Proportions have been rounded to the first decimal place.
[c] Streets in which at least one houseful of each type was located. This complements figs. 14.1–8 below, which depict the streets in which at least two housefuls of each type were located.
[d] Occupations which did not fall into any of the other categories and which occurred too infrequently to tabulate separately.

lawyers as well as barbers, musicians, and servants in the strict sense (most of whom of course did not constitute independent housefuls but lived with the households to whose needs they ministered).

Of male houseful heads, 7% were without a distinct occupation, that is they had either retired permanently, or temporarily, from a named occupation or were described as independent (in Flemish *bijondere*) or as *rentenier*. The precise meaning of these terms, particularly the last, is not clear, yet the category of 'independent' represents quite a considerable section of the population of south-east Bruges; indeed, of other cities in western Europe. Many of these men may have been considerable property owners, living off rents or the interest on money at loan. On this point there is as yet no evidence, but it may not be altogether accurate to categorize them as 'non-active' in table 14.5. Another category difficult to interpret is that of the day labourers (14% of the male heads). The term in Flemish is *dagloner* (in French, *journalier*) and may not necessarily carry the connotation of 'labourer' – someone who is basically unskilled. Finally, 3% of the male heads were engaged in agriculture, either as gardeners or actually designated as farmers.

Between a fifth and a quarter of all housefuls were headed by women. Their occupational profile is quite different from that of male heads, principally because so many occupations were not open to them. Women are almost completely missing from the general run of artisan employment with the exception of the exclusively 'female' occupations of lacemaking and needlework. These two involved more than half of all women heading housefuls. Other women were employed by the day (the Flemish term is *dagloonster*), the nature of the work not being specified. Still others (13%) were engaged in commercial activities, and there were also 13% without a specific occupation. There is a contrast here with the male heads, only 7% of whom were non-active, but it should be borne in mind that female heads were older on average than their male counterparts. The difference is much less significant once an age control is introduced. Of the male heads aged 60 and over, 18% were non-active, compared with 21% of the female heads, and it is highly probable that even with this 'age group' the women were older on average than the men.

At this point it is possible to introduce the question of the spatial distribution of the occupational groups within that part of south-east Bruges selected for analysis. As was mentioned above, the procedure adopted was to consider an occupational group to be represented in a street, provided that at least two houseful heads from that group appeared there. This quite deliberately tips the balance against finding occupational segregation, because there is always the possibility of the chance presence of a couple of such housefuls, particularly in the longer street. It is the more remarkable, therefore, that very distinctive residential patterns of occupational groups are displayed on the series of maps appearing in figs. 14.1 to 14.8. Male and female heads are again considered separately.

The distribution of day labourers is represented in fig. 14.1. In conformity with the traditional picture of the early modern town, they were

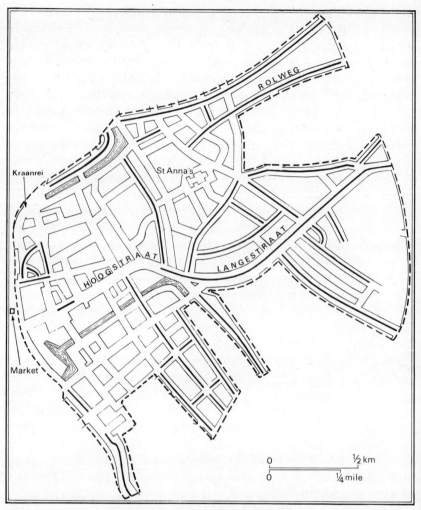

Fig. 14.1. South-east Bruges, 1814: streets containing ≥ 2 housefuls headed by
male day labourers (lined in black). The broken line indicates the study area.

principally to be found towards the probable margin of the built-up area
in 1814. They were completely absent from the streets of the central
area and around St Anna's Church (apart from a few to the north of the
central market). Yet they were not the most 'secluded' of the occupational groups. This distinction falls to the weavers (see fig. 14.2).[27]

[27] There are slightly fewer weaver housefuls than labouring ones (148 against 164), but
the difference is not enough to account for their concentration into a smaller area
(compare figs. 14.1 and 14.2). For the number of housefuls in other occupational
categories see table 14.6.

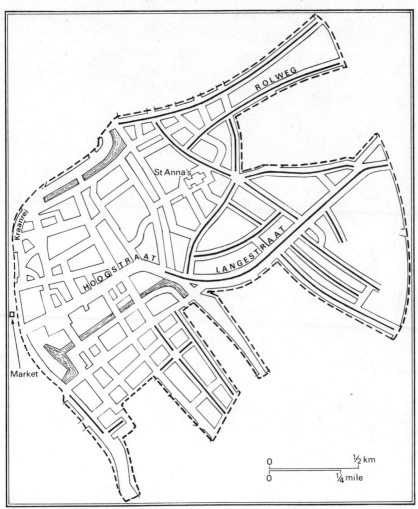

Fig. 14.2. South-east Bruges, 1814: streets containing ≥ 2 housefuls headed by weavers (lined in black).

Broadly speaking, the distributions of weaver and day-labourer house-fuls are similar in that they were both largely confined to the periphery of the town, but they are not in fact identical. Despite the wider distribu-tion of labouring than of weaver housefuls, and their slightly superior numbers, there were still streets where weavers but not labourers were represented.

For a contrast to these last two groups it is appropriate to select two other occupational groups, commercial and public-service employ-

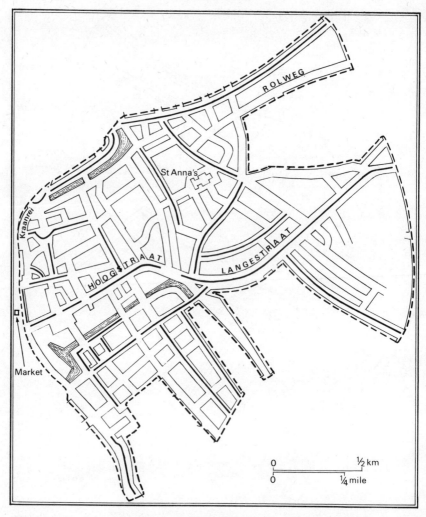

Fig. 14.3. South-east Bruges, 1814: streets containing ⩾ 2 housefuls headed by
males in commercial employment (lined in black).

ments. These contained within them, although they neither monopolized nor were monopolized by, the cream of Bruges society. Figs. 14.3
and 14.4 show them spread much more evenly than was the case with
either weavers or labourers. One would not have had to move far in the
south-east of Bruges to find a street with a male head with public-
service or commercial employment. On the other hand, public-service
occupations in particular were notable absentees from those sections of

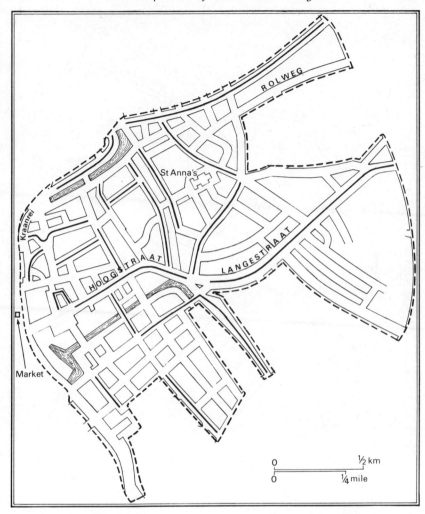

Fig. 14.4. South-east Bruges, 1814: streets containing ≥2 housefuls headed by males in public-service employments (lined in black).

south-east Bruges which showed the most marked concentration of weavers and labourers. There are suggestions too of a concentration of commercial occupations in the centre of the town (as one would expect) and, unexpectedly, of public-service employments to the north of the main thoroughfare Hoogstraat–Langestraat.

The remaining occupational groups of any size are best examined separately. Artisans (see fig. 14.5) seem virtually ubiquitous. Specifi-

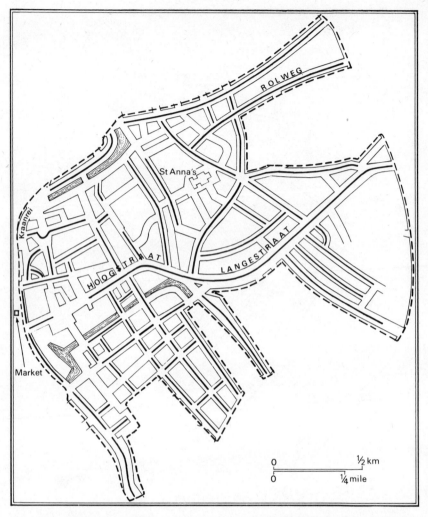

Fig. 14.5. South-east Bruges, 1814: streets containing ≥2 housefuls headed by
male artisans (lined in black).

cally, they feature in 82% of the streets in south-east Bruges, but the
artisan class as defined here may have included within it a number of
distinct groups. It might be quite misleading, for example, to place in the
same category cabinetmakers, knife-grinders, and locksmiths, but when
numbers are small it has to be accepted that some such grouping is
inevitable. Later, it will be possible to point to differences in the composition of artisan housefuls according to their location within the city.

Fig. 14.6. South-east Bruges, 1814: streets containing ≥2 housefuls headed by non-active males (lined in black).

These differences, it can be said, reflect in good measure some of the social differences among housefuls that have been classed here as simply 'artisan'.

Last of the male groups to be considered are the non-active (fig. 14.6). This is something of an age category as well as an occupational one, because as many as 44% of the heads were over the age of 60. This figure compares with 14% for the artisans, 12% for those in commerce, and

24% for the day labourers. In a present-day western European town the segregation of the elderly would be quite normal. Indeed, in Great Britain it is possible to find whole towns largely given over to the elderly.[28] In Bruges in 1814 retirement might be expected to depend, first, on exactly which occupations gave their holders sufficient opportunities for gain to enable them to live on their savings; and second, on the differential survival rates of these groups compared with other groups in the population, such as weavers and day labourers. The assumption would be that the latter would hold their occupations, at least in name, until death. Comparison of fig. 14.6 with figs. 14.1 and 14.2 shows that the non-active male heads were notably absent from the areas where labourers and weavers predominated. This means that if any labourers or weavers had moved into the non-active category they must have moved not only socially (assuming for the moment that the hypothesis on the standing of this group is correct) but also geographically. Another significant fact about the residential distribution of the non-active males is that they were also missing from the streets in the heart of the town where heads with commercial employment were located. In other words, the non-active heads congregated in the intermediate area between the heart of the town and the periphery. There was a distinct pattern to their distribution, just as there was to that of the heads with occupations.

Finally, in this connection two of the female occupational groups may be examined (see figs. 14.7 and 14.8). The housefuls of lacemakers, despite their dominant place in the list of female-headed housefuls, were not usually to be found in the central area, and the same is true, but to a much greater extent, of the housefuls whose women heads were day labourers. Since there were some housefuls near the town centre headed by females, who were employed chiefly in commerce or as seamstresses, it suggests that the same sort of social differences appear in female occupations as in male ones. A more general point, looking at the whole series of maps, is that the amount of segregation, while broadly compatible with the standard generalization of poor on the edge and rich in the centre, was very much more complex in practice than that generalization would lead one to believe.

Occupation and class

A doubt arises here as to the extent to which it is legitimate to infer high

[28] Law and Warnes, 'The changing geography of the elderly' (1976): 460 instance Grange over Sands, Lancs., with almost half of its total population over the age of 60.

Fig. 14.7. South-east Bruges, 1814: streets containing ⩾2 housefuls headed by lacemakers (lined in black).

to low status from the occupational groups which have been constructed. As should already be evident, the groups have been defined on the basis of economic sectors and not because the occupations were of similar social standing. Certain groups, such as day labourers, may correspond fairly well with a single social class, while others, for instance public employees and artisans, obviously straddle several. An independent assessment of social class, however, while clearly desirable, is not easily obtained. The problem is that while it is possible to

Fig. 14.8. South-east Bruges, 1814: streets containing ≥2 housefuls headed by
female day labourers (lined in black).

agree on the standing of certain occupations, others are more difficult to
place. In this sort of exercise it is all too often the case that present-day
values are consciously or unconsciously allowed to influence the definitions of classes. It is relatively easy to place some occupations above
others within a status hierarchy – attorneys above barbers, for example
– but the researcher's knowledge is often insufficient to place all occupations in their right order for the period in question.

There are in fact a number of ways in which some notion of the social distance between individual occupations might be obtained. The first, on the lines of the successful study carried out by Vivienne Brodsky on the population of seventeenth-century London,[29] would be to measure the frequency with which the offspring of the heads with these occupations intermarried. The second would use a measure of geographical distance between occupations by grouping together those which were practised regularly in adjoining residences. Since the Bruges census of 1814 does not make it clear where in the street, or indeed on which side of the street, a particular houseful was to be found, it would be necessary to rely entirely on the serial number of the houseful to determine proximity. Neither method is entirely satisfactory. The negotiation of a successful marriage for a son or daughter may simply demonstrate the wealth of a particular houseful, rather than its current social class. Further, holders of occupations of quite different status might live side by side where they depended for their livelihood on a common resource such as a major thoroughfare.

Instead, the connection between occupational groups as constructed here and social class can be pursued by considering two independent measures of social position: the frequency of taking in servants and the frequency of home ownership. These points are considered in table 14.6, along with information on the presence of offspring and relatives. Very clearly there were differences in social position between one occupational group and another and between male and female heads. Weavers and day labourers, for example, who were concentrated in those areas of the town typically thought of as poor, turned out to be almost uniformly poor. Not one of the housefuls headed by a weaver or a day labourer contained a resident servant, and they fell well behind all other male-headed housefuls in the matter of home ownership.

In certain other respects the measures of social standing are more ambiguous in that the message obtained from owner occupation does not tally with that from the presence of servants. Of male heads, the four groups most likely to have had co-resident servants were, in order, the non-active, those in public-service employment, those in personal service, and those in agriculture. On the other hand, in the case of home ownership, although the non-active again headed the field, they were followed this time by those in commerce and in personal service and by the artisans. The poor showing of those in public service in terms of home ownership is perhaps to be explained by the geographical mobility

---

[29] Brodsky-Elliott, 'Mobility and marriage' (1978): 83–115.

Table 14.6. *South-east Bruges, 1814: proportion of housefuls in owner-occupation containing offspring, relatives, and servants, by occupation and sex of houseful head*

Sex of head	Occupational group of head	No. of house-fuls	In owner-occupation (%)	With off-spring (%)	With relatives (%)	With servants (%)
M	Agriculture	39	15.4	87.8	30.8	35.9
	Artisans	421	25.4	74.6	20.4	14.2
	Commerce	190	37.9	69.0	22.6	20.5
	Day labourers	164	2.4	72.0	11.6	0.0
	Personal service	51	33.3	56.9	19.6	37.2
	Public service	73	23.3	57.5	23.3	41.1
	Weavers	148	2.7	73.0	16.2	0.0
	Non-active	86	62.8	53.5	19.8	66.3
	All male heads	1,172	24.0	70.1	19.5	20.2
F	Commerce	45	51.1	51.1	37.8	22.2
	Day labourers	65	4.6	60.0	33.8	1.5
	Lacemakers	128	8.6	50.0	35.9	0.8
	Seamstresses	45	11.1	40.0	28.9	0.0
	Miscellaneous	16	62.5	56.2	18.8	43.8
	Non-active	46	65.2	41.3	28.3	67.4
	All female heads	345	23.8	49.8	33.0	14.5

Header note: "Proportion of housefuls in each occupational group"

of this particular group,[30] but for some of the other differences there is no immediate explanation. This, however, should not occasion surprise. Status need not be one-dimensional, and it may be legitimate to use the frequency of servants and of home ownership as independent markers of social position.

There is more of a problem in the fact that the majority of the groups can be divided into those with servants and those without, with similar divisions in respect of home ownership. This yields a four-fold classification (owners with and without servants; non-owners with and without servants) for these occupational groups. But it is not in itself sufficient proof of the existence of fundamental divisions *within* occupational groups, particularly if either home ownership or the frequency of

[30] Of the male houseful heads in public-service employment, 27% were in-migrants, while the average for male heads was 14%. There is reason to question, however, the reliability with which migration was recorded (see n. 14 above), and it would be as well to bear in mind that public-service employment contained a number of low- as well as high-status occupations.

having resident servants could be shown to vary directly with the age of the head. It might then be agreed that these housefuls had progressed from a stage without servants to a stage with servants, or from being tenants to being owner-occupiers.[31] This is something that will be considered later (see tables 14.13 and 14.14), but it can be said here that there are a number of reasons why it would probably be misplaced to consider any of these groups as constituting homogeneous entities. There is also the fact that the differences among some of the occupational groups are relatively modest, for example between personal service and commerce in the matter of home ownership. It is therefore advisable to think of the groups as occupational rather than as social. That is, they represent a sector of the economy rather better than they represent status within society. The social-class element in the occupation remains of such importance, however, that further references to it will be made from time to time.

With this in mind, table 14.6 can be further examined, particularly for the impact which the presence of servants or house ownership might have on other elements in the houseful, such as relatives and offspring. Two broad conclusions follow. First, the sex of the head had a more powerful impact than either owner occupation or servants on the presence of relatives and offspring. Second, although there was considerable variation between one occupational group and another in regard to the frequency of relatives and offspring being present, it is impossible to relate this variation to the position of the occupational group in the hierarchy of owner occupation or servant keeping. There is a partial exception in that, with male heads, the presence of servants does seem to have varied inversely with the presence of offspring, if we except the small agricultural group. It is also the case that the housefuls of weavers and day labourers were the least likely to have contained relatives, the least likely to have been owner-occupied, and the least likely to have contained servants. Otherwise, however, it would seem that these differences among occupational groups must have arisen from some other factor in their construction, such as their age composition[32] or the nature of the work itself, rather than deriving from the extent to which they were owner-occupiers or took in servants.

The final point to note in connection with table 14.6 is that the

[31] One weakness in such an argument is that it is impossible to prove a progression through life-cycle stages from one list in isolation because of the confusion between 'life-cycle' change for the individual household with temporal change affecting the whole of society.

[32] The houseful can be analysed in terms of the age of the head or, more comprehensively, in terms of the number of persons present of various ages. The focus here is on the latter.

proportion of female heads who were owner-occupiers is almost exactly the same as for male heads. There is no sign, then, of women becoming heads because they had acquired a house of their own. At the same time, some further implications also emerge of the narrowness of the range of occupations available to women – witness, for example, the fact that female occupational groups with low proportions of owner-occupiers, such as lacemakers and day labourers, had rates of home ownership that were somewhat above those of lower-status male groups. For women, there was a greater disjunction between home ownership and occupation performed than was the case for men.

To sum up: the factor clearly identified as critical for the frequency with which the houseful contained offspring, relatives, or servants was the sex of the head, although there is a hint that the occupation of the head, divorced from its social-class overtones, could also be important in some circumstances. All other general statements about the determinants of the houseful would be unwise. This may seem unduly negative, but in fact it is valuable to be able to remove from the field (at least for south-east Bruges) some of the wider hypotheses concerning the frequencies of servants and relatives in households and the extent to which the composition of the entire houseful was determined by its wealth or status. Put very crudely, one hypothesis would say that the ownership of a house, as a proxy for wealth and representing a substantial investment of resources, would be a powerful factor attracting the co-residence of both relatives and offspring. Another set of factors working in the same direction would lead from wealth to early marriage or remarriage to more offspring and eventually to more relatives. The presence of relatives is to be expected, since remarriage provides the chance of an extra set of parents-in-law besides additional siblings-in-law, although relatives in direct descent are less likely, since the hypothesis rests on the initial assumption that the head married early because of acquired wealth, and it would be a little inconsistent to hold that this would not apply equally to his offspring. Yet it is quite conceivable that the difficulties of acquiring one's own house, through the necessity of saving or the waiting for an inheritance, could reverse the relationships between the variables. Home ownership in this case would be associated with later marriage and a reduced chance of offspring.

Similar lines of reasoning are possible in the case of servants. Resident servants might be a substitute for offspring or relatives, and vice versa, or an illustration of the economic or social opportunities in a particular houseful. These opportunities would both bring in relatives from outside and keep offspring at home who would otherwise be away. It is very

clear, however, from what was said above, that none of these hypotheses can deal satisfactorily with the existing evidence. On the other
hand, such factors might have had a greater impact on the number and
ages of offspring and relatives present than on the frequency with which
housefuls contained persons of these types. In order to assess the relevance of the factors, it is necessary, therefore, to look further at the age
and sex composition of these housefuls and to take account of the age of
the head. This must have had a very obvious impact on the frequency
with which housefuls contained resident offspring, and might influence
the frequency of having relatives as well.

The composition of the houseful

Examination of table 14.7 reveals that females who were heads of
housefuls had fewer offspring present and fewer servants[33] than did
males, but to some extent compensated for that by having more relatives and inmates. At the same time, there were also considerable
differences between one occupational group and another. The degree of
variation between occupational groups was particularly large in the case
of servants and inmates.[34] Even for relatives in housefuls where the
head was male, the range extended from the 0.38 relatives per houseful
of the artisans and agriculturalists to the 0.20 of the labourers. The
occupation as well as the sex of the head, therefore, helped to shape the
composition of the houseful.

Looking at occupational groups in detail, among the male heads those
in agriculture and the artisans had the most offspring and relatives; the
non-active and those employed in public service had the most servants,
and day labourers and weavers had the most inmates. Amongst female
heads, offspring were most numerous in the homes of women with
commercial employments, relatives in the housefuls of the day labourers, servants in the housefuls of the non-active, and inmates in the
homes of lacemakers.[35] The details of houseful composition throw

---

[33] The difference (0.20 to 0.27) servants per household) is perhaps less than might be
expected if female-headed households were at a particular economic disadvantage
compared with male-headed households.
[34] This applied independently of whether the head of the houseful was male or female.
Least variation occurred in the case of houseful size and, for male heads, in the presence
of a spouse. Variation in the number of offspring and relatives was in both male- and
female-headed housefuls less than one-sixth of the variation in the number of servants. In
each case variation is measured by taking the range as a proportion of the mid-point of the
distribution.
[35] The occupations that it was impossible to classify separately (referred to as 'Miscellaneous' in table 14.7) have been disregarded in view of the small number of cases.

Table 14.7. *South-east Bruges, 1814: mean membership of housefuls by occupational group and sex of houseful head*

| Sex of head | Occupational group of head | Housefuls (no.) | Persons (no.) | Mean number of persons in houseful by relationship to houseful head | | | | | | Mean houseful size[b] |
				Head + spouse	Offspring of head	Relatives of head	Servants of head	Inmates[a] Familial	Non-familial	
M	Agriculture	39	236	1.92	3.08	0.38	0.38	0.13	0.15	6.05
	Artisans	421	2,393	1.89	2.37	0.38	0.18	0.50	0.36	5.68
	Commerce	190	1,007	1.92	2.07	0.35	0.36	0.40	0.20	5.30
	Day labourers	164	843	1.90	1.92	0.20	0.00	0.82	0.30	5.14
	Personal service	51	242	1.70	1.76	0.27	0.41	0.31	0.27	4.74
	Public service	73	380	1.68	1.89	0.32	0.59	0.53	0.19	5.20
	Weavers	148	826	1.93	2.33	0.32	0.00	0.73	0.27	5.58
	Non-active	86	461	1.72	1.55	0.30	1.14	0.44	0.21	5.36
	All male heads	1,172	6,388	1.87	2.16	0.33	0.27	0.53	0.28	5.45
F	Commerce	45	172	1.00	1.27	0.47	0.22	0.44	0.42	3.82
	Day labourers	65	296	1.00	1.25	0.89	0.02	0.92	0.48	4.55
	Lacemakers	128	592	1.00	0.88	0.82	0.01	1.26	0.66	4.62
	Seamstresses	45	130	1.00	0.60	0.40	0.00	0.49	0.40	2.89
	Miscellaneous	16	72	1.00	1.25	0.94	0.69	0.06	0.56	4.50
	Non-active	46	189	1.00	1.04	0.74	0.98	0.04	0.30	4.11
	All female heads	345	1,451	1.00	1.00	0.73	0.20	0.77	0.51	4.21

[a] For the definition of familial inmates, see p. 424 n. 8.
[b] As a result of rounding, there are slight discrepancies between the figure for houseful size (last column) and the sum of the figures in the other columns.

valuable light on the nature of particular occupational groups. It might have been difficult, for example, to have predicted that large groups of inmates would be found in housefuls headed by day labourers, since it would be reasonable to assume that day labourers would occupy smaller houses and be unable to accommodate so many inmates even at the expense of some overcrowding. In Bruges, however, labourers appear to have occupied large houses. Even more unexpected is the difference between seamstresses and lacemakers, occupational groups that *a priori* one would have taken to be closely allied. In fact, housefuls headed by seamstresses contained on average no more than 2.89 persons, while those of lacemakers contained 4.62. The difference arises not from one element alone but from several. Lacemakers had, in descending order of importance, greater numbers of inmates, relatives, and offspring.

It is easy to point to these differences among occupational groups; more difficult to explain them. Some of the possibilities have already been raised. One might, for example, postulate the existence of two kinds of occupation – strong and weak. Where the former applied, the houseful would attract relatives and servants, offspring would be retained, and there might, with early marriage, be more surviving offspring. These would occupy all the surplus space. Inmates, as paying guests, would not be necessary. A houseful head with a 'weak' occupation would lose offspring to wealthier families in the form of servants, and there would be no incentive for the co-residence of relatives. Any available space would be occupied by people paying for the privilege of being there.

Some signs of such a difference can certainly be found. Male day labourers, for example, had the fewest relatives, were very low in terms of offspring, and had large numbers of inmates.[36] It is not, however, a general principle. 'Strong' occupations are particularly difficult to identify. Artisans, for example, score high in terms of the number of offspring, relatives, and non-familial inmates.

It is also useful to be able to reject some sweeping generalizations about household structure: that relatives were substitutes for servants or for offspring; that there was a clear relationship, either positive or negative, between the degree of owner occupation and the number of resident servants and offspring (see table 14.6). The strongest relationships identified for male-headed housefuls were between the num-

---

[36] It will be noticed that the relationships are quite different in the case of female day labourers. This would suggest that it was clearly not the status of the occupation (assuming that the terms '*dagloner*' or '*dagloonster*' are equivalents) that determined the composition of the houseful. It is possible that some further associations are obscured by the heterogeneous nature of some of the occupational groups; cf. above, pp. 445–9.

454 Richard Wall

bers of offspring and relatives (positive); between the fact that the houseful head was married and the number of servants (negative); and between the number of offspring and the number of servants (also negative).

These remarks are based on the variation in the rank order of each occupational group (male and female heads taken separately) in terms of the mean number per houseful of the head's spouse, offspring, relatives, servants, and attached familial and non-familial inmates. The correlations for female-headed housefuls are even weaker, the closest being a positive one between the presence of offspring and the presence of servants. Since the presence of a spouse and the number of offspring were themselves correlated, one or other of the correlations suggested in the preceding paragraph, spouse–servants and offspring–servants, might be spurious. Yet the association between the presence of the head's spouse and the number of offspring in residence was not in practice as strong as some of the others, for which the explanation might be the degree of remarriage, to which reference has already been made.

So far the sole concern has been with categories such as 'relatives' and 'servants', which are very general, encompassing persons of both sexes and a variety of ages. To get a better idea of the function of relatives and servants in particular housefuls it is necessary to examine in greater detail the age and sex compositions of housefuls together with attached inmates. Table 14.8 shows that in many subgroups in the population females were in surplus. They predominated among offspring over the age of 20, relatives, servants, and inmates. But the size of the surplus varied. Most highly feminized, perhaps not surprisingly, was service: 26.9 males to every 100 females in male-headed housefuls and 15.2 for every 100 in female-headed housefuls. There were twice as many female relatives as male ones and almost twice as many female inmates. For offspring the situation was a little more even. Sixty-eight sons over the age of 20 to every 100 daughters over the age of 20 resided with their fathers, which is above the mean sex ratio for this age group.[37]

Some females, then, formed what could be termed a submerged population. They were overrepresented in those sections of the population whose houseful roles look least prestigious and from where the prospects of advancement seem remote. Alternatively, they were to be found beyond the household in the world of inmates. Another aspect of this was the tendency for women to move into a houseful whose head

[37] Compare the sex ratios for the age groups 20–39 in table 14.1. There were very few offspring in these housefuls older than 40, in fact just 8 sons and 17 daughters, representing 5% of the sons and 7% of the daughters aged 20 or over.

Table 14.8. *South-east Bruges, 1814: sex ratios by relationship to houseful head and head's occupational group and sex*

Sex of head	Occupational group of head	Offspring (aged ≥20) of head No.	Sex ratio	Relatives of head No.	Sex ratio	Servants of head No.	Sex ratio	Inmates No.	Sex ratio
M	Agriculture	17	41.7	15	66.7	15	66.7	11	37.5
	Artisans	136	58.1	159	63.2	78	47.2	363	56.5
	Commerce	62	77.1	67	39.6	68	17.2	114	31.8
	Day labourers	45	73.0	32	60.0	—	—	184	47.2
	Personal service	16	128.6	14	40.0	21	0.0	30	66.7
	Public service	25	66.7	23	35.3	43	38.7	53	55.9
	Weavers	56	64.7	47	51.6	—	—	148	55.8
	Non-active	39	85.7	26	33.3	98	21.0	56	80.6
	All male heads	396	67.8	383	53.2	323	26.9	959	57.5
F	Commerce	26	52.9	21	16.7	10	0.0	39	56.0
	Day labourers	33	57.1	58	52.6	1	—	91	68.5
	Lacemakers	44	91.3	105	41.9	1	—	246	33.0
	Seamstresses	8	100.0	18	12.5	—	—	40	42.9
	Miscellaneous	10	66.7	15	66.7	11	83.3	10	66.7
	Non-active	16	100.0	34	32.0	45	7.1	16	45.4
	All female heads	137	73.4	251	39.4	68	15.2	442	43.0

was also female. It is a noticeable feature that more of the relatives, the servants, and even the inmates were female when the houseful head was female than when there was a male head. This can be seen as one of the consequences of the unbalanced sex ratio and of the high proportion of women never marrying. There was a huddling together of women in residential groups that were predominantly and sometimes exclusively female.

It is interesting, though, that there was one case where this did not apply, namely in connection with the older offspring of the houseful head. A different set of factors seems to have governed the continued co-residence of offspring with their parent(s), one in which a widow was likely to keep more sons at home than would have been the case for a two-parent family. Quite why this should be so is not clear, although the attempt to balance the sexes seems deliberate. This is also suggested by the fact that for male-headed housefuls there was a negative relationship between the sex ratio of offspring and the sex ratio of relatives. For example, housefuls headed by artisans and men employed in agriculture had the lowest proportions of sons in relation to daughters but the highest proportions of female to male relatives. The attempt to balance the sexes certainly is not a ubiquitous characteristic of western European social structure, for the only intensive study of urban family forms, that by Michael Anderson, revealed a clear trend of a higher proportion of daughters residing with widows than with widowers and two-parent families.[38]

Although the influence of the head's sex on the composition of the houseful was crucial, there was also space for the occupation of the head to operate on its form. This is best illustrated by a couple of examples. In female-headed housefuls it was most likely that it would be daughters rather than sons who would remain in the parental home after the age of 20 when their mothers worked in commerce. In addition, 9 out of 10 relatives were female in such cases, a much higher proportion than was customary even among female-headed housefuls. The explanation, no doubt, lies with the well-known dependence of the commercial sphere on female labour, a dependence which was reflected in the composition of the houseful.

Somewhat similar effects hold when a male houseful head was in commerce. He was particularly likely to be married (see table 14.7), and his relative and servant groups were heavily feminized. The relationships are not quite the same, however, since the sex ratio of the offspring group was above the average for male-headed housefuls, whereas the reverse was true in the case of female heads in commercial employment. This is a further illustration, therefore, of the importance of the sex of the head, over and above that of the occupation, in determining houseful composition. To take another example, the sex ratio of inmates in male-headed housefuls worked out at almost 6 men to every 10 women. For those in female-led housefuls it was about 4 to every 10, while when the head was a lacemaker it was little more than 3 to every 10.

There is another important factor, however, which ought to be taken into consideration, and that is the age composition of the houseful. This brings out a number of further differences among occupational groups. For instance, although on average 58% of males identified as relatives of the houseful head were above the age of 20, there was a considerable spread about the mean.[39]

These figures, and others relating to offspring, servants, and inmates, are set out in table 14.9. It should be borne in mind, however, that the

---

[38] Anderson, *Family structure in nineteenth century Lancashire* (1971): 126, but see also Wall, 'Age at leaving home' (1978): 197.

[39] For example, in the housefuls headed by the labourers and men in commercial employment, 75% and 90% respectively of the male relatives were over the age of 20. There are

Sex of head	Occupational group of head	Male offspring (no.)	Proportion of male offspring aged ≥20 (%)	Male relatives (no.)	Proportion of male relatives aged ≥20 (%)	Male servants (no.)	Proportion of male servants aged ≥30 (%)	Male inmates (no.)	Proportion of male inmates aged ≥20 (%)
M	Agriculture	59	8	6	50	6	33	3	67
	Artisans	460	11	62	58	25	24	131	66
	Commerce	202	13	19	90	10	40	48	54
	Day labourers	149	13	12	75	—	—	59	64
	Personal service	50	18	4	50	—	—	12	67
	Public service	66	15	6	83	10	70	19	58
	Weavers	175	13	16	31	—	—	53	55
	Non-active	73	25	8	88	17	47	25	52
	All male heads	1,234	13	133	63	68	40	350	61
F	All female heads	151	38	71	48	9	67	133	64
	TOTAL	1,385	16	204	58	77	43	483	62

Sex of head	Occupational group of head	Female offspring (no.)	Proportion of female offspring aged ≥20 (%)	Female relatives (no.)	Proportion of female relatives aged ≥20 (%)	Female servants (no.)	Proportion of female servants aged ≥30 (%)	Female inmates (no.)	Proportion of female inmates aged ≥20 (%)
M	Agriculture	61	20	9	67	9	0	8	50
	Artisans	537	16	97	84	53	30	232	75
	Commerce	191	18	48	75	58	36	66	71
	Day labourers	166	16	20	85	—	—	125	74
	Personal service	40	18	10	90	21	38	18	83
	Public service	72	21	17	94	31	61	34	59
	Weavers	170	20	31	77	—	—	95	70
	Non-active	60	35	18	61	81	51	31	71
	All male heads	1,297	18	250	80	253	42	609	72
F	All female heads	194	41	180	69	59	64	309	78
	TOTAL	1,491	21	430	76	312	46	918	74

457

numbers in some of the categories are small; too much should not be
presumed on the basis of these figures. Some of the correlations, however, are perfectly acceptable. For example, there can be no cause for
surprise that there should be a correlation between the presence of older
offspring and the fact that the houseful head was non-active or female,
since these heads were themselves older on the average. It is valuable
also to be able to identify certain correlations, such as those involving
inmates, as being very weak. There is no obvious connection, then,
between the occupation of the houseful head and the age structure of
the inmate population, as there was between the occupation of the head
and the sex ratio of the inmate population. In contrast, older servants
would appear to have been more prevalent in the housefuls of the
non-active, in those with public service employments, and where the
houseful head was female. That is older servants were associated with
the housefuls whose heads were concentrated into older age groups.
Housefuls from these occupational groups preferred a rather different,
and perhaps more costly, kind of servant.

The life cycle of the individual

The individual in a present-day western population follows a well-
defined life cycle. Critical events such as starting work, leaving home,
and getting married tend to occur within a few years of each other. The
vast majority of children leave home permanently only on marriage.[40]
One factor which is known to differentiate the present situation from
western European societies before 1900 is that the latter were characterized by a tradition of life-cycle service, a period of service in the
household of another which provided something of a hiatus between
leaving home and establishing one's own household. Yet there has been
little intensive study of the rest of the life cycle. To try and rectify this,
reference can again be made to the Bruges study. Of course, being based
on a single census, it cannot reveal how people moved on from role to

two possibilities: that they took in an above-average proportion of older relatives or, as
seems more likely, a below-average proportion of younger relatives. The latter is
suggested by the fact that there is little difference between one occupational group and
another in the mean number of male relatives aged 20 and over per houseful. The
pattern was broadly the same for females, with the dividing line drawn at age 15 rather
than age 20.

[40] The best study remains that of Christabel Young on Melbourne, Australia based on
information collected during 1971: 75% of sons and 85% of daughters left home to
marry. Young, 'Factors associated with the timing and duration of the leaving home
stage of the family life cycle' (1975): fig. 3, and 'Ages, reasons and sex differences for
children leaving home' (1974): fig. 2 and table 4.

role, but it can show how the frequency of relationships such as 'offspring of head' or 'servant' varied according to age.

In the case of the male life cycle there was a fairly orderly progression from being the son of a houseful head to houseful head, with the principal movement into headship occurring during the late 20s and the 30s (fig. 14.9). Service was relatively unimportant. There was very little 'cycle' effect in the case of relatives but rather more of a 'cycle' for inmates. To be an inmate was most likely during early adulthood (20–9) and again after 60. The prevalence of inmates, servants, and relatives during early adulthood rendered it the period in the life of the individual when residence outside a prime unit (houseful head or member of the head's nuclear family) was most to be expected. The same pattern can be discerned in the female life cycle, here intensified because of the higher proportions of relatives, servants, and inmates in the female population.

In other respects, though, the female life cycle was a little different (fig. 14.10). In the first place, the proportion who were daughters of the head declined earlier than did the proportion of sons. Daughters of the head constituted two-thirds of the female population aged 15–19; sons of the head, three-quarters of the male population aged 15–19. The second difference concerns relatives. Whereas there were comparatively few elderly male relatives, the proportion of females identified as relatives of the head remained fairly constant at around 10% after the age of 20 before increasing to 14% after 60 years. It was in old age, therefore, that women were most likely to join the household as a relative. Here, the household might be seen as exercising a supporting role in the care of the elderly.[41]

Yet a different explanation has to be sought for the consistency in the proportion of female relatives between the ages of 20 and 60. One suggestion could be that it resulted from the lack of opportunities in the marriage market following on from the unfavourable sex ratio. Perhaps for the same reason service was less of a life-cycle role for females than it was for males, women remaining in, or returning to, service, after 40. Even among women aged 50–9 the proportions in service were still a third of what they had been at their height. Finally, it is interesting that the proportion of females classed as inmates is above the proportion of males so classed even in the case of the under-10s, for whom the risks of becoming inmates should be equal. For this there is as yet no explanation.

---

[41] On the other hand, the proportion of inmates also rose sharply after age 60, suggesting that a considerable proportion of elderly women may have moved out of the household altogether.

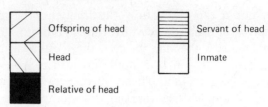

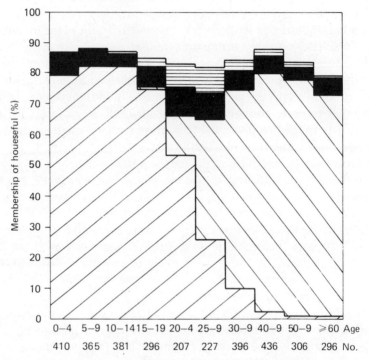

Fig. 14.9. South-east Bruges, 1814: male population by age group and relationship to houseful head. The number under each age group is the total
number of persons in that group. Note that in figs. 14.9 and 14.10 the age
groups are in five-year blocks until age 30.

Age gap between spouses

In contrast to the attention devoted to other aspects of marital behaviour, the age separating husband from wife has attracted little notice
apart from Peter Laslett's use of it as one of the defining characteristics of
western European families past and present. According to Laslett, the
age gap between spouses has generally been insignificant in the west,

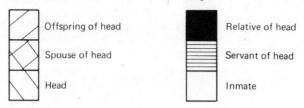

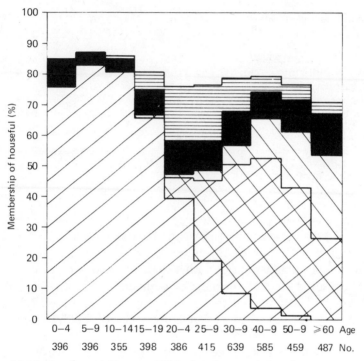

Fig. 14.10. South-east Bruges, 1814: female population by age group and relationship to houseful head. The number under each age group is the total number of persons in that group.

with a relatively high proportion of wives older than their husbands. The difference between the 'western' and 'eastern' experience was between a mean age gap in favour of husbands of about 3 years in the west and 10 in the east. A fifth of wives were older than husbands in the west, almost none in the east.[42] The inference was that marriages were

[42] P. Laslett (1977a): 13, 27. The western pattern is represented by the English village of Ealing and the nothern French village of Longuenesse, listed in 1599 and in 1778 respectively, and the eastern by Belgrade (1733–4) in Serbia and Nishinomiya (1713) in Japan.

Table 14.10. *Proportion of wives older than husbands and age gap between spouses:* '*western*' *and* '*eastern*' *patterns and south-east Bruges, 1814*

Area	No. of couples	Mean age gap between spouses (years)	Proportion of wives older than husbands (%)
'Western'[a]			
England: Ealing, 1599	62	3.50	21.0
France: Longuenesse, 1778	48	2.35	27.0
'Eastern'[a]			
Serbia: Belgrade, 1733–4	192	10.82	0.5
Japan: Nishinomiya, 1713	105	10.36	1.9
South-east Bruges, 1814[b]	839	1.16	41.0
Artisans	377	0.51	44.3
Commerce	173	3.71	29.5
Day labourers	147	0.92	42.2
Weavers	142	0.00	45.1

[a] P. Laslett, *Family life and illicit love* (1977a): 26 (table 1.4).
[b] Selected occupational groups only, as specified.

likely to be companionate in the west. Laslett had available only four community studies on which to base these statements, and more recent work has introduced a certain amount of variation into the picture. For example, more than a quarter, rather than a fifth, of wives were older than their husbands in a wide range of towns and villages in eighteenth- and nineteenth-century Austria. At the same time there was a substantial minority (15–20%) of husbands over 10 years older than their wives.[43]

For the south-east of Bruges the age gap between spouses can be examined in relation to the occupational groups to which reference was made above, although the following analysis will be restricted to those groups – artisans, commercial employees, day labourers, and weavers – which include at least 100 married couples. Table 14.10 sets out the relevant details, and it will be seen that Bruges in 1814 represented an extreme form of the 'western pattern'. Indeed, in regard to the proportion of wives older than husbands, three of the four occupational groups that have been selected (artisans, day labourers, and weavers) were almost as far above Laslett's western examples (Ealing and Longuenesse) as the latter were above his own eastern examples.

[43] Schmidtbauer (1977).

Summary as they are, measures such as mean age gap and proportion of wives older than husbands do illustrate some important differences between one occupational group and another. Men in commerce, for example, were much less likely than others to have an older wife.[44] The mean age gap declined from more than 3½ years in their case to just under 1 year for labourers, ½ year for artisans, and 0 for the weavers. These differences become more intelligible if the distribution of age gaps rather than the mean is examined (see fig. 14.11). Nearly 60% of the weavers were within 5 years of their spouse's age, as were 56% of the artisans, 53% of the day labourers, and 46% of the men in commercial employment. Only in the case of the latter were a substantial number of the husbands (23%) more than 10 years older than their wives.[45]

Fig. 14.11 represents a cross-section of the life cycle of the married couple. Some couples were still young; others had been married 20 or 30 years. Some were first marriages; others involved second or third marriages for one partner, or even both. By dividing each occupational group according to whether the husband was under 40 or 50 or over, it is possible to establish whether the age gap between spouses varied with the husband's age. Specific objectives were to judge how many men, married under 40, had chosen a wife approximately the same age as themselves and how many in later life had, on remarrying, picked a much younger spouse.[46] The first point to be made about the men under 40 (fig 14.12) is that the majority were younger than their spouses. This was true regardless of occupation, again if the exception is made of those in commerce. The degree to which the wife was older than her husband was sometimes substantial; a quarter more than 5 years older, a tenth more than 10 years older. Second, it has to be emphasized that the differences among occupational groups were slight, apart from that between commerce and the rest which has already been mentioned.

Something of an occupational hierarchy emerges, however, if one considers instead the number of marriages where the husband, although himself under 40, had chosen a wife who was more than 5 years younger. About 18% of the marriages by men in commerce were of this sort, and they are followed by the artisans with 15%, the day labourers with 12%, and the weavers with under 8%. For weavers, such

[44] Schmidtbauer confirms this for commercial versus industrial or artisan employment in the Schottengassenviertel of Vienna in 1857.
[45] The next highest were the day labourers, with 13% more than 10 years older.
[46] The assumption underlying the cross-sectional approach used here is that the marital behaviour of the group of men aged 50 or over roughly represents the future experience of the survivors of the younger cohorts. In practice, from cross-sectional data (i.e. from a single point in time) it is impossible to exclude the alternative possibility of a temporal shift in marital behaviour.

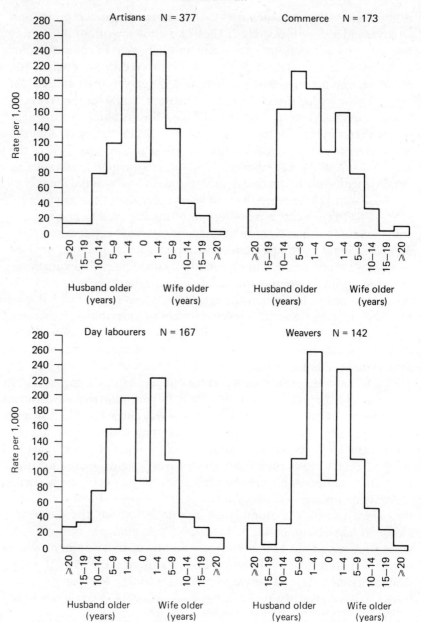

Fig. 14.11. South-east Bruges, 1814: age gap between spouses as a rate per 1,000 married men, in different occupational groups.

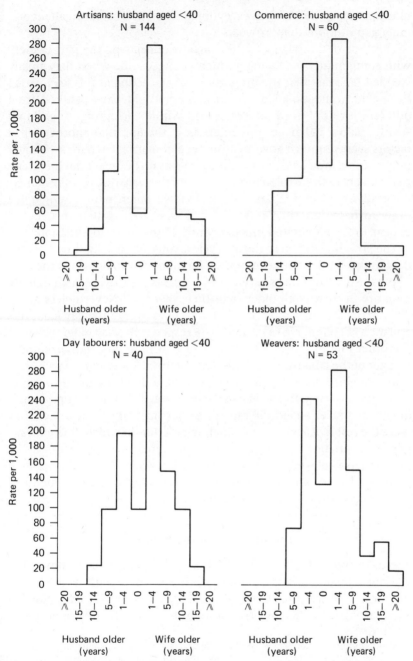

Fig. 14.12. South-east Bruges, 1814: age gap between spouses as a rate per 1,000 married men aged under 40, in different occupational groups.

marriages were clearly very exceptional. There were none at all involving a gap of more than 10 years.

This type of marriage was the outcome of delay on the part of men,
who compensated by taking a much younger bride when they finally
wedded. The fact that the proportion of men acting in this way varied
from one occupational group to another could have resulted from
different levels of need (or even wish) within each group to build up
savings before marriage. It is interesting, though, that another set of
factors seems to have governed the type of marriage where a younger
man chose a much older wife, for there was no occupational hierarchy
here. Even if the explanation lies with the vagaries of inheritance,
illustrative of no more than the luck of a few women in the demographic
draw to have inherited property, it is still puzzling that this should
appear to have operated independently of the man's occupation.

The position later on in the life cycle is considered in fig. 14.13, which
depicts the age gap between spouses for men aged 50 or over at the time
of the census. The effects of remarriage are plainly to be seen, in that the
majority of men were older than their spouses.[47] Nevertheless about
40% of the weavers and artisans and rather fewer of the day labourers
and men in commerce (25% and 20% respectively) had older wives. At
the other end of the distribution, a third of those in commerce and a
quarter of the labourers, but only 15% of the artisans and weavers, had
a spouse more than 10 years younger. The differences among occupational groups when the head had passed the age of 50 were considerably
greater than those identified for an earlier stage of the life cycle. They
were the result of a whole combination of factors in which the initial age
gap, and variation in life expectancy, and remarriage opportunities by
occupation all played a part. If to have a wife much younger than oneself
might be deemed an asset, then it was in later life that a man's pursuit of
certain occupations had its reward.

The life cycle of the houseful

Just as the individual has a life cycle, so, it has come to be assumed, has
the household. Inspired by the modern household with its celebrated
empty-nest phase (the period when all the children have left home but
the marriage remains intact), historians have searched for appropriate

---

[47] Another interpretation that would fit the figures is that older men marrying for the first
time would more often choose women younger than themselves than men who had
married earlier in life. The presence of so many stepchildren in the population (not
examined in this chapter) indicates, however, a considerable amount of remarriage.

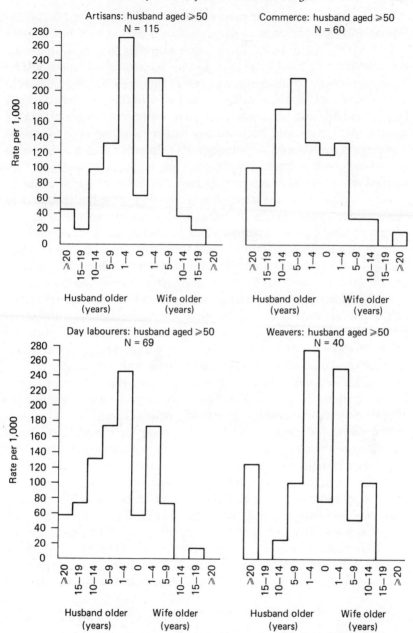

Fig. 14.13. South-east Bruges, 1814: age gap between spouses as a rate per 1,000 married men aged ≥ 50, in different occupational groups.

cycles for households from past societies. Such cycles would, for instance, link the presence of servants to the period in a household's history when there would be no adult offspring to contribute to the household's well-being. The cycle in the classic form first identified by Rowntree is both familial and economic in that there are phases early in the married life of the head and again in his (or her) old age when outgoings are particularly high in relation to resources.[48] For poorer families these crisis points could wipe out any earlier gains and even for others involve a cessation or a slowing down of the process of accumulating household goods. Further complications are introduced if assets are subdivided when the adult offspring move away from the parental home.

To try and measure the strength and direction of the household, or in this chapter's terminology houseful, cycle in south-east Bruges, two 'economic' indicators, servants and the frequency of owner occupation, have been added to two familial ones (offspring and relatives) in tables 14.11–15. The stage in the cycle has been determined by reference to the age group of the houseful head, and on the assumption that this is a fair reference point, the effect of the houseful cycle could hardly be called strong. Indeed, even the drop in the frequency with which housefuls contained offspring once the head had passed 60 could be deemed relatively modest. The only other feature holding regardless of occupation would appear to be the increase in the frequency of relatives, again for housefuls where the heads were over 60.[49] In the case of servants, there is no sign that they were most frequent when adult offspring were unavailable; in fact rather the reverse.

The particular form of the houseful cycle may well have varied according to the occupation of the houseful head, and tables 14.11–15 have been laid out with this possibility in mind. There are differences, for example, in the timing of taking in of relatives. Labourers were most likely to take in relatives early in the life cycle of the houseful (when the head was under 40) and again when he had passed 60. With weavers, on the other hand, there was no sign of the earlier peak. The head's occupation also made a clear difference to the timing of the headship. Headship was achieved early by men working in commerce, in personal service, and as weavers, and by women who were seamstresses (table 14.15).[50]

---

[48] The study relates to York at the beginning of the twentieth century; see Rowntree, *Poverty* (1902).

[49] Even so, there were some exceptions: among male heads, those in commerce; and among female heads, the lacemakers.

[50] Based on a comparison of the proportion of heads (males and females taken separately) in the various occupational groups under the age of 30 (under the age of 40 in the case of females) with those aged 40–59.

Table 14.11. *South-east Bruges, 1814: proportion of housefuls with offspring by age, sex, and occupational group of houseful head*

Sex of head	Occupational group of head[a]	No. of of heads	Proportion of housefuls with offspring where the head is aged				
			Under 30 (%)	30–9 (%)	40–9 (%)	50–9 (%)	≥60 (%)
M	Artisans	421	67.6	82.5	82.2	67.9	56.9
	Commerce	190	56.5	75.6	77.0	62.5	60.0
	Day labourers	164	75.0	72.0	79.1	73.2	61.5
	Personal service	51	(25.0)	58.8	70.0	54.6	(80.0)
	Public service	73	(40.0)	64.7	83.3	60.0	34.8
	Weavers	148	64.0	76.7	86.0	75.0	45.4
	Non-active	86	(50.0)	(83.3)	61.1	50.0	47.4
F	Commerce	45	(0.0)	(100.0)	(77.8)	67.1	29.4
	Day labourers	65	—	(85.7)	76.9	63.2	42.3
	Lacemakers	128	(87.5)	75.0	53.7	31.0	46.9
	Seamstresses	45	(33.3)	30.0	50.0	(14.3)	(75.0)
	Non-active	46	—	(80.0)	(66.7)	(50.0)	25.9

[a] Male heads in agriculture and female heads with miscellaneous occupations are excluded, as there are insufficient cases to justify a breakdown by age. Figures in brackets indicate proportions based on fewer than 10 cases.

Table 14.12. *South-east Bruges, 1814: proportion of housefuls with relatives by age, sex, and occupational group of houseful head*

Sex of head	Occupational group of head[a]	No. of heads	Proportion of housefuls with relatives where the head is aged				
			Under 30 (%)	30–9 (%)	40–9 (%)	50–9 (%)	≥60 (%)
M	Artisans	421	16.2	20.2	20.3	16.7	29.3
	Commerce	190	21.7	19.5	21.3	30.0	20.0
	Day labourers	164	25.0	12.0	4.6	4.9	20.5
	Personal service	51	(25.0)	17.7	50.0	0.0	(0.0)
	Public service	73	(0.0)	23.5	33.3	10.0	26.1
	Weavers	148	16.0	13.3	12.0	15.0	31.8
	Non-active	86	(0.0)	(0.0)	27.8	20.0	21.0
F	Commerce	45	(0.0)	(33.3)	(33.3)	28.6	52.9
	Day labourers	65	—	(0.0)	30.8	10.5	61.5
	Lacemakers	128	(25.0)	33.3	33.3	51.7	30.6
	Seamstresses	45	(50.0)	20.0	33.3	(28.6)	(0.0)
	Non-active	46	—	(0.0)	(16.7)	(37.5)	33.3

[a] See table 14.11, note *a*.

Table 14.13. *South-east Bruges, 1814: proportion of housefuls with servants by age, sex, and occupational group of houseful head (selected occupational groups only)*

Sex of head	Occupational group of head	No. of heads	Proportion of housefuls with servants where head is aged				
			Under 30 (%)	30–9 (%)	40–9 (%)	50–9 (%)	≥60 (%)
M	Artisans	421	10.8	20.2	11.7	7.8	13.8
	Commerce	190	0.0	31.7	34.4	37.5	28.0
	Personal service	51	(25.0)	23.5	60.0	54.6	(20.0)
	Public service	73	(20.0)	52.9	50.0	40.0	30.4
	Non-active	86	(50.0)	(100.0)	77.8	70.0	55.3
F	Commerce	45	(0.0)	(33.3)	(11.1)	28.6	23.5
	Non-active	46	—	(80.0)	(33.3)	(100.0)	63.0

Note: Figures in brackets indicate proportions based on fewer than 10 cases.

Table 14.14. *South-east Bruges, 1814: proportion of housefuls occupying own property by age, sex, and occupational group of houseful head (selected occupational groups only)*

Sex of head	Occupational group of head	No. of heads	Proportion of housefuls occupying own property where the head is aged				
			Under 30 (%)	30–9 (%)	40–9 (%)	50–9 (%)	≥60 (%)
M	Artisans	421	10.8	20.2	21.9	28.6	48.3
	Commerce	190	17.4	31.7	39.3	40.0	60.0
	Personal service	51	(12.5)	29.4	70.0	36.4	(0.0)
	Public service	73	(20.0)	29.4	22.2	20.0	21.7
	Non-active	86	(25.0)	(50.0)	66.7	75.0	60.5
F	Commerce	45	(0.0)	(66.6)	(22.2)	50.0	70.6
	Non-active	46	—	(20.0)	(50.0)	(100.0)	66.6

Note: Figures in brackets indicate proportions based on fewer than 10 cases.

One of the difficulties is undoubtedly the small number of cases in particular categories. Yet while this might account for some of the irregularity, it is doubtful whether it is an adequate explanation for all. There is the case of the 23 male houseful heads under the age of 30 engaged in commercial activity, not one of whom had a servant resident. About a third of the heads of all other ages working in commerce

Table 14.15. *South-east Bruges, 1814: houseful heads by occupational group and sex*

Sex of head	Occupational group of head	>25 (%)	25–9 (%)	30–9 (%)	40–9 (%)	50–9 (%)	≥60 (%)	All ages (%)
		Houseful heads by occupation as a proportion of all houseful heads in each age group (males and females separately)						
M	Agriculture	0.0	2.2	3.1	3.2	5.4	2.3	3.3
	Artisans	35.5	29.2	44.2	37.8	35.1	27.0	36.0
	Commerce	19.4	19.1	15.9	18.0	16.7	11.6	16.2
	Day labourers	12.9	13.5	9.7	12.7	17.2	18.1	14.0
	Personal service	9.7	5.6	6.6	2.9	4.6	2.3	4.4
	Public service	3.2	4.5	6.6	5.3	4.2	10.7	6.2
	Weavers	19.4	21.3	11.6	14.7	8.4	10.2	12.6
	Non-active	0.0	4.5	2.3	5.3	8.4	17.8	7.3
	TOTAL	100.1	99.9	100.0	99.9	100.0	100.0	100.0
	N	31	89	258	339	239	215	1,171[a]
F	Commerce	50.0	7.1	7.9	11.7	16.7	13.1	13.0
	Day labourers	0.0	0.0	18.4	16.9	22.6	20.0	18.8
	Lacemakers	0.0	57.1	31.6	39.0	34.5	37.7	37.1
	Seamstresses	50.0	35.7	26.3	23.4	8.3	3.1	13.0
	Miscellaneous	0.0	0.0	2.6	1.3	8.3	5.4	4.6
	Non-active	0.0	0.0	13.2	7.8	9.5	20.8	13.3
	TOTAL	100.0	99.9	100.0	100.1	99.9	100.1	99.8
	N	2[b]	14[b]	38	77	84	130	345

[a] One houseful head, age unknown, has been excluded.
[b] Proportions for females under the age of 30 are not to be depended upon because of the small number of cases on which they are based but have been included for the sake of completeness.

had resident servants. Was this how a head began in commerce, unaided by a resident servant? Or were those who had achieved headship early in life not representative of the rest of the commercial group? Until or unless such individuals can be followed over their own life cycles it is impossible to be sure. For the same reason it is necessary to be careful in interpreting the fact that the proportion of heads engaged in commerce (and artisans too) who were owner-occupiers rose with the age of the head (table 14.14). It is certainly possible that this represented economic advancement over the life cycle, through inheritance or graft. A similar effect, however, would be produced if the comparatively wealthy outlived the other heads in their occupational group or retained the headship, and at least nominally their occupation, while others moved in later life into other occupational categories[51] or descended into the ranks of the inmates. For a number of possible reasons, therefore, these occupational groups are again seen not to have constituted homogeneous entities: those who remained in them after 60 were not a representative selection of those who had been in the category earlier in life.

Conclusion

A study of this kind inevitably leaves a number of problems unresolved. The use of the age of the head of houseful as a sole reference point for the houseful life cycle is in many ways unsatisfactory, though it is an essential first step towards life-cycle analysis and does throw further light on the influence of the head's occupation on the shape of the houseful. Then there is the problem of deciding to what extent occupational groups were homogeneous entities and interpreting the links between inmates and their hosts. Nevertheless, the basic structure of south-east Bruges society is clear. Previous attempts to look at city social structures have relied on the convenient administrative divisions of the ward and quarter, or used grid squares. From this has emerged the image of the pre-modern city where the poor congregated on the periphery and the rich in the centre. Such a generalization misses much of the diversity of a city like Bruges. The Bruges study was conducted at street level with a technique deliberately aimed at minimizing occupational segregation. Yet occupational segregation is clearly visible. Weavers, day labourers, lacemakers, and men in public service were each concentrated into their own special areas. There was even something of an area for the retired.

On each individual occupation depended also the age at which one could expect to marry – indeed, the sort of person one would marry (younger or older spouse) – and the number and type of persons with whom one would co-reside thereafter. With the usual reservations about the difficulty of distinguishing 'life-cycle' from temporal change affecting the fortunes of the occupational group as a whole, the profile of all the occupational groups can be established. Weaving may serve as a convenient example. Weavers achieved headship early. Approximately a fifth of the male heads under 25 years of age were weavers,

[51] Table 14.15 shows that between the 50–9 and the 60+ age groups, the proportion of both artisans and houseful heads employed in commerce fell, while that of the non-active moved up from 8% to 18%. The proportion of day labourers remained approximately the same although the proportion of labourers in both groups was above average. For the increase in the population of male inmates after age 60 see fig. 14.9.

although only 13% of male household heads of all ages were weavers. Their choice of a spouse would customarily be one close to their own age (60% within 5 years). Weavers, together with day labourers, were the least likely to have relatives and servants in their housefuls. On the other hand, they had a very high number of inmates. In old age weavers were less likely than many other groups, notably artisans and men engaged in commerce, to have offspring still resident. In this way, differences in familial patterns went to reinforce the occupational segregation that already obtained. Admittedly the artisans were virtually ubiquitous, but even their familial patterns varied according to residence. For example, 85% of the artisans in the principal street, Langestraat, were married, the mean number of relatives present was 0.62, and the mean number of offspring present, 3.19. In the streets around the centre of the town only 74% of the artisans were married, and the mean number of resident offspring and relatives stood at 1.94 and 0.26 respectively. These figures can be compared with those for artisans as a whole in table 14.7.

Overshadowing the differences among occupations was the sex ratio: 6 men to 10 women above the age of 15. A quarter of the women were permanently celibate, and there was a substantial difference in the proportions of men and women who would eventually marry. The sex ratio was visible, too, in terms of houseful composition, the surplus women being absorbed in the ranks of the relatives, servants, and inmates. Women, it was noted, gravitated towards the housefuls whose heads were also women.

Finally there are some wider implications of the findings. Protoindustry has usually been viewed as an activity involving the whole family: the head, his spouse, and children of working age. The same sort of mistake was made by the mid-nineteenth-century investigators of working-class budgets who in pursuit of the average budget left out the many incomplete families, i.e. the widowers and widows with children and persons living only with relatives or non-relatives.[52] In 1814 female relatives and inmates represented a third of the total membership of the female-headed housefuls in south-east Bruges (cf. tables 14.7 and 14.9), and we need to know more about them. Might some lacemakers and other working women have pooled their incomes in order to minimize the burdens of supporting themselves and their dependants without the benefits of a male wage? The data on family budgets (admittedly for a later period) suggest that this was unlikely to have much impact on the

---

[52] See, for example, the criteria for the selection of representative budgets laid down by the Commission Centrale de Statistique, reproduced in Duceptiaux (1855): 264.

main expense, that of subsistence. On the other hand, women's earnings in these family budgets are somewhat stylized in that within each community a standard amount is quoted for a day's work. However, if the level of skill varied (and presumptively therefore earnings), as one would certainly expect it to do anyway in relation to age, then some sections of the female population might have had an economic motive for the patterns of co-residence which can be seen in the census.

15

The importance of women in an urban environment: the example of the Rheims household at the beginning of the Industrial Revolution

ANTOINETTE FAUVE-CHAMOUX

Introduction

Little is yet known about the history of the urban family. The study that I have carried out over the last few years into the social and demographic history of the town of Rheims in Champagne will eventually illuminate the fundamental characteristics of a non-rural society before the Industrial Revolution. I propose here to analyse the census of 1802, which has survived in its entirety, for this town of 30,200 inhabitants. This document provides the closing point for the family reconstitution of all Rheims parishes beginning in 1660.[1] The opening of the nineteenth century makes a fitting end to the study. By then, the tumultuous revolutionary period was over, and the town had recovered the demographic prosperity it had enjoyed in 1780. Yet no one suspected at the time that the century which was about to begin was to result in unprecedented population increase and the modification of all demographic and economic structures.

The economic situation at the beginning of the nineteenth century

Rheims in 1802 remained fundamentally as it had been under the Ancien Régime: it was dominated by an intensive artisan-based textile

---

[1] The procedure was to reconstitute the families whose surnames began with the letter B, using the parish and civil registers for the period 1660–1802 for each of 14 parishes of Rheims, together with the Hôtel-Dieu (the hospital). It was an advantage that the annual tax list made it possible to ascertain whether households were still present in the town, to follow their movements within the urban area (poor people often changed their residence), and to analyse over the years changes in their employment and standard of living. Computer analysis of the demographic information is in progress. This is based on 3,000 completed families, complete in the sense that there is information on the age of the wife and a date of end of marriage. For a more detailed description of this work see e.g. Fauve-Chamoux, 'La reconstitution des familles' (1972); 'L'enfance abandonnée à Rheims' (1973), and 'Town and child in eighteenth century Rheims' (1974).

industry involving the preparation and weaving of wool. In 1790 the town had contained 1,300 master drapers as well as serge, butter-muslin, and cheesecloth weavers working more than 3,000 looms among them. Those not actually concerned with weaving combed, spun, and set the warp for the looms. Men and women had their separate tasks. Unfortunately, circumstances were not propitious at the end of the eighteenth century. This Rheims 'industry' was burdened by too many regulations governing the production of the famous cloth and woollen goods, which had been exported widely ever since the thirteenth century. There was severe competition from northern French and English products. Small workshops multiplied in the country to the detriment of artisans in the towns. In effect, Rheims was suffering an economic crisis: of the 32,000 inhabitants listed in 1790, 9,159 were said to be in absolute poverty and without work. By 1802, the situation hardly seems to have changed, and two-thirds of the population were crammed into the high town under the shadow of the magnificent Saint-Remi Abbey, in dark streets and courts and sordid lodgings, while the wealthy families occupied vast mansions in the centre of the town, built on the ruins of the Roman town, near the cathedral which kings visited for their coronations.[2] Like all large towns Rheims was the more fascinating for the contrasts it offered. Our purpose here will be to delimit the demographic and social structures of the population, dominated politically and economically, as is always the case, by a powerful minority: in Rheims the superior bourgeois merchants. However, before considering the characteristics of the population of Rheims, a few notes on the source are in order.

The census of 1802

The 1802 census, often called 'the census of the year X', covered the whole of France. It is fortunate that for Rheims the original nominative list has been preserved in its entirety, in a rebound volume of considerable size and weight. The lay-out in columns is very clear, and the writing, easily readable, is in the same hand right to the end. The enumerator noted with care the surname, Christian name, age, place of

---

[2] The cost of the coronation of the kings of France had to be met by Rheims, but in consequence the town was excused payment of the poll tax. The rolls of these exceptional taxes dealing with the consecration have been preserved in the archives and make it comparatively simple to follow changes in population size and social development in Rheims from the Middle Ages. This special factor could have been an additional attraction to immigrants, who, like all inhabitants of Rheims, prayed for the long life of kings!

birth, marital status, occupation, and relationship to the head of the household for each individual. The various co-resident persons not related to the household head were always listed, whether they were male servants or fellow workers (*compagnons*), female servants or spinners. During the enumeration process documents were kept up to date: persons dying between the beginning and the end of the enumeration were deleted, any births were added, and changes of address were noted to prevent double registration. As ages were hardly ever omitted, and there was very little ambiguity about the specification of sex or of relationship, it can be concluded that the census was of high quality and worthy of a complete analysis. However, it was beyond our resources to undertake such an exhaustive operation. Instead an appropriate sampling method had to be found.

The sample

It was decided to consider all households headed by individuals whose surnames began with the letter B.[3] However, as I wanted to look at the composition of the household, it was also necessary to include individuals concerning whom I had no information other than that they were living in the home of a household head whose surname began with the letter B. The proportion of the population that was abstracted for 1802 (12.8%) was thus just a little larger than that of the population studied in the parish and civil registers (between 11% and 12%). In either case the sample is sufficiently representative. Since the familial background of the large majority of individuals was known, it was possible to throw light on some of the vaguely defined relationships, to provide information on relationship where this item was missing altogether, and to give exact ages and a certain amount of detail on occupations. The link back to the family reconstitution was indispensable in the case of women who had been married several times and had had children by a number of husbands, since these step-siblings had a variety of surnames. Altogether this sample produced a total of 1,003 households containing 3,883 individuals. Let us see what sort of population was involved.

Population in 1802: female surplus

The first obvious classification is the distribution according to sex and marital status, as shown in table 15.1. A quick glance at this table gives

[3] Cf. n. 1 above.

Table 15.1. *Marital status by sex, Rheims, 1802*

Marital status	Males		Females		All	
	No.	%	No.	%	No.	%
Single	936	53	1,194	56	2,130	55
Married	733	42	741	35	1,474	38
Widowed	67	4	178	8	245	6
Separated/divorced	15	1	19	1	34	1
All	1,751	100	2,132	100	3,883	100

Sex ratio = 82.13.

rise to the following comments. First, there were more women than men. Second, although the proportion of all non-married persons, whether single, widowed, separated, or divorced, to the total population was not unusual, standing at 62%, it was a different matter when children were omitted and only the adults were considered. Looking exclusively at the population of 15 and over, we find that no fewer than 49% were spouseless: for those of 20 or more, the proportion remained high, at 42%.

The difference between the numbers of men and women is particularly significant, in line with the very specific urban pattern that has been found elsewhere in France in large towns such as Metz and Rouen. It would appear that such a pattern is an urban constant caused by the immigration of servants and female workers. In an attempt to explain this excess of women, certain authors, such as R. Mols, have argued that the explanation lay with a greater number of male exits (emigration and excess mortality).[4] I think, for my part, that a more likely explanation is that the town was an important centre for female employment (before becoming a marriage market) and that young girls were more inclined than young men to migrate to the town. Whether workers or servants, many of them also married in town.

Immigration

Looking at the proportion of the population born outside the town according to age (table 15.2), it is immediately noticeable how many persons had moved into Rheims. Overall, 36% of the females had been born outside the city and 34% of the males. Female immigration took place later in life than male immigration. To put it another way, sons left

---

[4] Mols, *Introduction à la démographie historique des villes d'Europe* (1954–6): II, 220–1.

Table 15.2. *Proportion of the population not born in Rheims by age and sex, 1802*

Age	Males (%)	Females (%)
0–4	6	5
5–6	16	6
10–14	17	15
15–19	31	25
20–4	29	43
25–9	26	41
30–4	43	48
35–9	57	42
40–4	49	52
45–9	53	46
50–4	50	54
55–9	47	43
60–4	46	50
65–9	47	52
70–4	52	47
75–9	21	23
All ages	34	36
15–79	42	44

their parents earlier. As the Rheims-born had a tendency to leave, whether attracted in particular by Paris or for other reasons, it was the regular flow of immigration which guaranteed the replacement of the existing generation. It is not our intention here to enter into a discussion of the demographic characteristics of this population or its history. Rather our commentary focuses on a cross-sectional analysis of the census, at a point where the population, after a long stagnation, 'took off'. It was not on the base of old stock that it did so.

In such circumstances, it is appropriate to ask what sort of familial structure supported this population. We turn, therefore, to consideration of the household.

Households in Rheims: the importance of women

Mean household size by sex and marital status of household head

Table 15.3 shows clearly that household size varied markedly with the sex and marital status of the head of the household. The Rheims household headed by a married man had on average 3.88 resident members, which usually presupposes 2 other persons in the household apart

Table 15.3. *Mean household size by sex and marital status of the household head, Rheims, 1802*

	Married	Widowed	Separated	Single	All
Male-headed households	3.88	2.95	4.00	1.48	3.62
Female-headed households	—	2.46	2.06	1.26	1.96
Sexes combined	3.88	2.58	2.32	1.35	3.23

from the married couple. Female-headed households were always considerably smaller than male-headed ones: on average, 1.96 members compared with 3.62. As female-headed households were so much smaller, it is reasonable to suppose that there would also be a significant difference in terms of composition. We will therefore turn to the familial structure of these households, again paying particular attention to the differences between female- and male-headed households.

The frequency of household types by sex of head

Use of the Cambridge Group's typology yields table 15.4 to which we have added the frequency of household type by the sex of the head. The overall pattern shows first that 67% of all households were of the simple type, which was a relatively low proportion but not altogether surprising for a town. Second, we can point to the significant proportion of households (19%) consisting of solitaries. Third, it is necessary to stress the importance of couples without children. These amounted to more than 17% of the total number of households, a proportion which seems considerable. It is my impression that this proportion resulted primarily from the presence of elderly couples, remarried or not, whose children had left home. Unfortunately, this point cannot be cleared up satisfactorily in the context of the present contribution. However, certain comparisons with family reconstitution forms have made it clear that the absence of children should not be taken as an indication that the couples were infecund but rather that the children were no longer resident with their parents. The absences were caused by the placing of young children with a wet-nurse in the country, the apprenticeship of adolescents, and marriage or work outside Rheims for the adult offspring, without, of course, forgetting mortality. Fourth, the 8% of extended families was not negligible when set alongside proportions for other parts of the north of France. In towns, individuals could become

Table 15.4. *Household types by sex of household head, Rheims, 1802*

Household type	Male-headed households (%)	Female-headed households (%)	Sexes combined (%)
1. Solitaries	8	55	19
2. Households without familial structure	3	13	5
3. Simple-family households	79	27	67
4. Extended-family households	10	4	8
5. Multiple-family households	0.5	0.5	0.5
All	100	100	100

Note: In this and further tables, proportions >0.5 have been rounded to the nearest whole number. This accounts for any slight discrepancy between totals or subtotals and the sum of the figures in columns or rows.

very isolated or, fearing such isolation and anxious to avoid it, join the households of near relatives.

This classification can be repeated taking account of the sex of the head of the household. Solitaries were numerous primarily because of the number of unmarried women in the population, which resulted in a high proportion of female-headed solitary households (67% of all such households). Households without familial structure, although they were not very common, were also more likely to have a woman as a head (60% did so), but simple-family households (for definitional reasons) and extended-family households were more often headed by males. The overall figure of 67% for simple-family households is not very meaningful in itself, since it contains such very different types of household: 58% of all households could be called 'independent and unbroken conjugal family units' or 'couples', to use the modern terminology (with or without children).

Household composition

Another way of looking at this is to establish the different roles exercised by individuals within a household, that is whether they were household heads, relatives of the head, servants, or others. Table 15.5 shows for each age group of 15 and over what proportion of each sex held the positions of household head, son or daughter of the head, father or mother of the head, wife of the head, etc.

Table 15.5a. *Proportion of males in each age group (15–74) with specified relationship to household head, Rheims, 1802*

Age	Son[a] (%)	Father (%)	Other relatives[b] (%)	Resident employees (%)	Household heads			Others (%)	All (%)
					Non-solitary (%)	Solitary (%)	Sub-total (%)		
15–19	62	0	5	27	2	2	4	4	100
20–4	40	0	5	21	26	7	33	1	100
25–9	40	0	4	8	45	0	45	3	100
30–4	13	0	1	8	76	2	78	0	100
35–9	4	0	0	5	87	3	90	0	100
40–4	1	0	0	3	90	4	95	1	100
45–9	2	0	3	3	92	1	93	0	100
50–4	0	0	3	3	89	6	95	0	100
55–9	0	0	0	3	91	3	93	4	100
60–4	0	2	2	4	86	6	92	0	100
65–9	0	6	2	4	74	14	88	0	100
70–4	0	8	0	0	72	20	92	0	100
All age groups	20	0.5	2	10	62	4	66	1	100

[a] Includes stepson.
[b] Includes father of wife.

Table 15.5b. *Proportion of females in each age group (15–79) with specified relationship to household head, Rheims, 1802*

Age	Daughter[a] (%)	Wife (%)	Mother[b] (%)	Other relatives[b] (%)	Resident employees (%)	Household heads				Others (%)	All (%)
						Family head[c] (%)	Non-solitary (%)	Solitary (%)	Sub-total (%)		
15–19	76	1	0	7	11	0	0	2	2	3	100
20–4	32	22	0	8	29	0	2	7	8	1	100
25–9	18	48	0	5	20	0	1	8	9	0	100
30–4	6	64	0	2	16	3	2	5	10	1	100
35–9	2	63	0	6	12	5	2	8	16	0.5	100
40–4	1	65	0	2	9	10	2	8	22	2	100
45–9	2	69	0	3	9	8	0.5	7	16	2	100
50–4	0.5	60	2	6	6	8	3	12	23	2	100
55–9	0	48	4	3	9	9	1	20	30	6	100
60–4	0	45	7	4	10	8	3	16	27	7	100
65–9	0	40	12	6	6	10	10	14	34	2	100
70–4	0	18	16	12	4	14	8	20	43	6	100
75–9	0	20	33	20	0	0	0	14	14	14	100
All age groups	16	45	2	5	14	5	2	9	16	2	100

[a] Includes stepdaughter.
[b] Includes mother of wife.
[c] Women with co-resident children but no spouse resident (includes widows and unmarried, divorced, and separated women).

483

Household heads

Of the total population over the age of 15, 38% were heading their own households. The smaller the mean household size within a given population, the more likely it was that an individual would become a head. In Rheims in 1802, one of every two individuals between the ages of 30 and 75 was in this position. For older people, the probability of being a household head declined to one in three. Sex and age influenced the probability of an individual heading a household. It seems useful to carry the analysis further and consider how often these household heads were living as solitaries. The results show that only 6% of male householders were living alone. All the rest had responsibilities for others: spouse, children, relatives, or others. Should one perhaps regard these 94% non-solitaries as representing what are commonly termed 'family heads'? It would be wise to choose our terms carefully, because the family could take on a number of very different forms; of the total, only 41% of households had the classic shape: husband, wife, and at least one child.

It is noticeable that most of those male household heads living alone were either young (20–4) or over 50, constituting 20% of the oldest age group. For women too, old age increased the risk of solitude, although this was always more likely for women than for men. Of female householders, 55% lived alone (and 65% of these solitary women were unmarried). Young men might also live alone, but such isolation was particularly associated with women. Between the ages of 20 and 40, the large majority of female household heads were completely alone, but the chances of living as a solitary lessened over time, and at about age 40 the possibility that a woman would be living alone fell to its lowest point: the proportion of widows with attached children had been steadily increasing from age 20, swamping the remaining unmarried women. Later, when their children left home, women were once again isolated, a fact documented by a rise in the proportion of solitaries from the age of 55. The very old, however, appear to have given up solitude and sought shelter in another household.

To make the nature of the various types of husbandless living a little clearer, we may distinguish two groups among those female householders whose spouses were absent, for whatever reason. First were those who were bringing up at least one of their own children, who might be called 'family heads', and second, those who were living with other related or non-related persons, whom we might term 'non-solitary household heads'. The first category involved 30% of all female-headed households; the second, just under 15%. With whom, then, we can now ask, were these non-solitary female householders co-residing, and who was dependent on them?

Of these women, 65% were living with their offspring only; 12% co-resided with one or more siblings only; 7% headed no-family households containing other relatives. Five per cent were living with a daughter and that daughter's illegitimate child; a further 5% headed households which were extended by the presence of a nephew or a niece; and 5% lived with non-related individuals. What stands out here above all is the importance of family ties in bringing people together in a female-headed household, although one must always remember how many women lived alone. It is remarkable that it was particularly the older women (aged between 65 and 75) who took into their households individuals who were not their children.

Offspring

It seems reasonable to suppose that up to the age of 15 children would remain in the home of one or both of their parents, but what happened afterwards? Tables 15.5a and b show that 76% of the females aged 15–19 were described as 'daughters', while only 62% of the comparable male age group were 'sons'. At this period of their lives they were not yet married, and it is possible that they were apprenticed but still living at home. It can be no surprise that daughters were generally older than sons when they left the parental home but that eventually a higher proportion of them would leave. Although differences in marriage age explain part of this behaviour, it is clear that many of these young women did not immediately marry on leaving the parental home, nor was the proportion of women of all ages married to household heads a large one. It is my opinion that we have to look at immigration for another important explanation. In the older age groups the arrival of immigrants may lessen the proportion, though not of course the numbers, of daughters still living at home.

Spouse

Of the adult female population, 45% fell within the category 'spouse of head'. Spouses were a majority of the female population only in the 30–55 age group, and even then that majority was a small one. For these women it could be a second or later marriage. We have therefore to look elsewhere in the household for the 23% of females over the age of 15 who were neither spouse nor offspring of the head, nor heads themselves.

Parents of the head

Very few old people held the household position of head's parent, and this was particularly true of men, who, as long as they were able, continued to head their own households, even if it meant living on their own. Only when they had reached the age of 65 did they at last begin to accept lodging with a son or a daughter. Women were in a little different situation. The grandmother, as she was to the children of the household, already known to exist through folklore, is represented more frequently in the statistics, and on this fact we must dwell. Although only 1.7% occupied the position of mother of the household head, their importance had steadily increased from the age of 50 to reach 12% of all women aged between 65 and 69, 17% of those aged between 70 and 74, and 33% of those over the age of 75. Such a welcome for grannie was far from being universal, since many elderly women continued to run their own households, a number of these often living totally alone. Admittedly, the latter were more usually elderly spinsters rather than women who had been married. It is possible to see in this a tradition of family solidarity in actual operation. On the other hand, extended families formed by the presence of such old parents constituted no more than 2.7% of all households. It can also be noted that the presence of a grandparent was three times more likely in a male-headed household than in a female-headed household. The most frequently encountered grandmother, if one may put it like that, was thus the mother of a male household head.

Other co-resident relatives

Within the household, individuals can be found related in a variety of different ways to the household head. Let us take first of all the collaterals.

Brothers and sisters

It would appear in Rheims that siblings co-resided relatively frequently. Such combinations constituted almost half (45%) of all households without familial structure, or 2.2% of all households. This form of domestic group was more frequent in the case of female-headed households (5.5% of all such households) and in such instances particularly involved unmarried sisters. In the case of male-headed households, it was the presence of a brother or sister of the household head which produced 30% of the extended households, or 2.1% of all households. It should be emphasized again that such individuals were either unmarried or widowed. Frérèches involving married co-resident brothers or sisters did not exist in our area.

Nephews and nieces

The presence of nephews and nieces was responsible for 37% of extended families, and was particularly likely when the couple had no children of their own, although there were cases of shelter being offered to an orphaned nephew or niece when children were already present in the household. Nephews and nieces were found in 3% of households, more often in a male-led than a female-led household, and their presence often implies adoption by the otherwise childless couple.

Descendants

The co-residence of parents and a married son or married daughter was very rare. The stem family did not exist in northern France, in contrast with the situation in the south. Those who co-resided with their parents typically consisted of a widowed or unmarried daughter with her children. The presence of grandchildren without their parents was also unusual and when it occurred could well have been the result of orphanage, or of the death of the mother with the father absent and not remarried.

Other types of relationship to the household head did occur occasionally: widowed or unmarried uncles and aunts, and individuals sharing a surname with members of the family but whose exact relationship cannot be identified. The numbers involved here were too small to analyse as separate categories. Indeed, to provide a sufficient number of observations, it was necessary to group together in table 15.5 not only these relations, but also siblings, nephews, and nieces, under a general heading 'Other relatives'. Children, spouses, and parents of the household head were not included. The question we can now put is whether the age structure of this 3.8% of the population throws any light upon their position.

Up to the age of 30 these individuals were relatively numerous (6% of the appropriate age group), and the same is true for those over the age of 65, while they constituted 10% of the very old. However, it is the excess of women within this category which attracts our attention. Of the entire female population, 5% fell within it; twice as many women as men could be so categorized. Keeping in mind that this form of co-residence was particularly the fate of women, the overall distribution would indicate that it was in the age of maturity, between the ages of 30 and 69, that the individual was least likely to be in this sort of position in the household. What, then, can be said about other forms of co-residence?

Resident employees

Although the various types of servant were identified clearly and precisely in the census, it was decided to group together under a general term, 'Resident employees', all servants, apprentices, and fellow workers whose accommodation was provided by their masters. Indeed, they all lodged in the same house, sat round the same table, and ate with the family of their employer. Of the total resident employees, 70% were servants in the strict sense, the remaining 30% being employees, newly fledged artisans, shop assistants, or workers receiving board and lodging. It is my opinion that the unmarried spinner, living in her master's household, was comparable in social status to a female servant. She would certainly have helped the mistress of the house in the preparation of supper and attended to the fire when she wasn't sent to carry buckets of water from the public fountain. The female servant, for her part, being a true maid of all work, would also have had to spend some hours spinning and sewing for the members of the family. In the same way the female shop assistant could not have avoided helping in the domestic activities of the household. The proof of all this is that when an employee was resident in the household, no servant was resident. The familial nature of the terms of employment provides the justification for the present categorization system.

Table 15.6 shows that only 10% of households had resident employees (and in fact only 7.2% had servants in the strict sense). Although it might happen that a family would employ several servants (though this would have been rare), a higher proportion was expected, given that we are dealing with an urban population. Yet in the town of Preston in Lancashire the proportion of households with servants was no higher in the middle of the nineteenth century,[5] and comparable proportions of 8.2% in Rouen in 1770 and 11.6% in Tours have been found.[6] It would appear that much higher figures have frequently been recorded for the pre-industrial period, sometimes in excess of 30%, but such proportions are for rural areas where tasks performed by servants in the households of their masters were even more necessary than they were in towns in that their work was comparable with that undertaken by agricultural labourers.[7]

[5] Anderson, *Family structure in nineteenth century Lancashire* (1971): 46. The figure of 10% includes both servants and apprentices.
[6] Referred to by P. Laslett, 'Characteristics of the western family' (1977b): 103.
[7] *Ibid.* 102–5.

Table 15.6. *Proportion of households with resident employees by household type, Rheims, 1802*

Household type	Male-headed households (%)	Female-headed households (%)	Sexes combined (%)
1. Solitaries	18	6	10
2. Households without familial structure	4	0	2
3. Simple-family households	12	6	11
4. Extended-family households	10	9	10
5. Multiple-family households[a]	20	0	17
All	12	5	10

[a] As there were very few multiple-family households, the proportions calculated are of limited value.

We have yet to consider in what households such employees were most likely to be found. Of multiple-family households, 17% were thus served – an indication, probably, of their relative wealth. The comparable proportion for simple-family households was 11%. Households least likely to contain resident employees (2%) were those without familial structure, which without any doubt were also the poorest. In addition, households with a male head were more likely to have a servant or a worker resident than were female-headed households (12% compared with 5%). The households of the latter, reduced in size, stood a great chance of being poor, with the women having to undertake all the work themselves. Married couples were more likely to house employees when they had resident children (12% for households with children and 10% for households without children), but the widowers held the record as far as employment of servants went. When widowers were responsible for children, 26% of them had a resident servant, and when they were on their own, 44% had the assistance of a paid employee. For widows, the phenomenon was less marked, although the same pattern can be identified. Fourteen per cent of widows living on their own and 17% of the deserted wives had a resident servant. It is necessary to bear in mind that the most deprived section of the population could not avail themselves of this form of assistance, and that it was particularly men living alone who kept resident servants, and married couples who lodged apprentices, fellow workers, and other employees.

We must now shift our attention from the households employing resident employees to the employees and servants themselves. The first point to note is that female employees greatly outnumbered male employees, not only because the disequilibrium in the sexes was in their favour, but because they could, so much more easily than men, be called on to perform domestic tasks. Of the male population, 10% were resident employees, compared with 14% of the female population. One possibility is that rural women sought the role of servant within the town, on the grounds that it was less hard than the alternative of farm work, which, through its very nature, tended to demand male labour.

As far as Rheims men were concerned, it was particularly the young who were employed as servants. Between the ages of 15 and 25 a good quarter of them fell within this category (27% and 21% respectively for the age groups 15–19 and 20–4), but thereafter the proportions decreased until the age of 40, when the proportion became stable, although very low, at around 3%, to rise again for the very old (to 4%). In the case of women, the age distribution was quite different. Before the age of 20, only 11% of girls were placed as servants, as has already been remarked. Later, between the ages of 20 and 25, and before marriage, 30% of girls were so placed; this period they used to gather the resources for their dowries. The proportion fell steadily away thereafter to reach 6% at age 50, but then rose again to a new peak between ages 60 and 64. All servants were unmarried.

Several points have to be kept in mind in a search for an explanation of the decline in the proportion of male servants from the age of 25 onwards, that is before the mean age at marriage for men, and the contrast between the patterns of service for men and women. In the first place, the age structure of the population tells us that the male population had lost a far from negligible section of its population from the age range 25–34: there is a perturbation to the age pyramid that could correspond to the losses of the revolutionary wars. Furthermore, if one looks at the proportion of this age group born outside Rheims (see table 15.2), a similar perturbation appears at the same place in their age pyramid, although it is unclear whether this was caused by younger men returning to their natal villages after the expiration of their period of service (the majority of servants in the strict sense were not born in Rheims), or whether it was due to war losses similar to those experienced by those born in Rheims. Turning to the female servants, it was particularly after the age of 20 that the village girls came into the town. Thereafter the proportion of women born outside Rheims remains very high until extreme old age (see table 15.2). Those women who did not find suitable marriage partners remained as servants, even when they became rather old, rather than return to the rural area. This indicates a fundamental difference in behaviour from that suggested as the pre-industrial English model of living-in service – essentially a rural model, it is true, but one according to which servants over the age of 45 were unknown.[8]

Others

The group at issue here comprised persons whose presence in the household was due neither to relationship nor to a specific function. Most of them must have been tenants or individuals who were offered accommodation in return for certain services, but who did not receive a specific salary for the work undertaken which would then have led to the use of an unequivocal term in the document such as 'servant' or 'apprentice'. Like the individuals only distantly related to the household head, many more women than men were included (2.2% of the female population, compared with only 1% in the case of men). In addition, the age distribution was very different for the two sexes. The men in this category were relatively young. On the other hand, it was the women over the age of 55 who were strongly represented within the category, while as many as 14% of the very old women could be so placed.

Thus, while old age offered opportunities, particularly to men, to be household heads, women adopted other life styles and tried to avoid the isolation that awaited them, a particular danger if they were unmarried. It is possible that they knew how to make themselves useful within the household despite their age, in a period when day-to-day existence demanded so much in the way of effort.

Conclusion

Our overview of the variety of positions occupied by individuals within the household suggests that there may be a familial model specific to the urban situation, a model directly tied to the age structure of the population and to the surplus of women caused by massive immigration from rural areas. We would see this system as one in which the woman, whatever her age, had an important role to play, first of all as household head, then as mother or relative, and finally as a non-related member of the household, whether or not she was a servant in the strict sense of the term in that she received payment for work performed. The key to the system lay with the unmarried or widowed woman, as opposed to the woman as spouse, a role which was in the end heavily circumscribed. All these women occupied an important place in the process of urban

[8] *Ibid.* 104.

development, whether one is thinking in terms of their familial, social, or indeed even their economic role. The fact that the household was small resulted on the one hand from the presence of so many solitaries (households of solitaries, and those with no familial structure, constituted together 24% of the total) and on the other hand from the relative infrequency of married couples with co-resident children (41%) and the frequent absence of children from the households of married couples and widowers. The corollary was that elements of the family did regroup (as for example in the case of nephews and nieces) and that a household did not hesitate to welcome a close or even a distant family member when the need arose.

Thus, despite the break-up of families and the underlying poverty to which the greater part of the population was subject – a population, moreover, which had largely lost its roots – a certain willingness to take tentative steps towards familial regroupment can be discerned. In the society we have been portraying, which pre-dates the Industrial Revolution, the role of the 'conjugal family' was already much reduced. Nor is there any reason to think that this was a recent development, which cannot be without consequence for the transmission of behaviour patterns and the raising of each new generation.

16

The household: demographic and economic change in England, 1650–1970

RICHARD WALL

The basic structure of English households in the pre-industrial era is now well known. Households were small. The majority contained fewer than five persons, and membership was customarily confined to parents and their unmarried children. If the family was sufficiently wealthy, or involved in farming or trade, then the household might well contain servants, but there were remarkably few complex households containing grandparents, parents, and grandchildren.[1] Untimely death in the older generation and average age at marriage in the mid- to late 20s for both sexes naturally curtailed the number of three-generational households that it was possible to form. But the number that were formed never came anywhere near the potential number.[2] It was not because children married late while their parents died early that few households spanned three generations, but because the vast majority of children who had not already left the parental home to become servants in the households of others would establish separate households on marrying.

The implication of the link between marriage and the formation of a household is that English households must have varied in structure over time. Nationally, the crude marriage rate fell steadily to reach a low point in the late seventeenth century, from which it rose to a high plateau between 1771 and 1796 before falling again.[3] On each occasion the turning point followed a reversal in the trend of real wages some 30 years earlier, a sustained fall in real wages ushering in a fall in the

I would like to thank my colleagues Dr R. S. Schofield, Dr R. M. Smith, and Dr E. A. Wrigley for their comments on an earlier draft of this chapter.

[1] P. Laslett and Wall (eds.), *Household and family* (1972): 146–54.
[2] Wachter with Hammel and Laslett, *Statistical studies of historical social structure* (1978): 80.
[3] R. M. Smith, 'Fertility, economy and household formation in England' (1981b): 601, fig. 3. Marriages per 1,000 persons aged 15–34 derived from Wrigley and Schofield, *The population history of England* (1981), which contains the base data and an explanation of the procedures underpinning the calculations.

Table 16.1. *Headship rates and proportions ever married: males aged 20–9*

| | | Males aged 20–9 | | | Proportions | |
| | | No. ever married | No. heading households | All | Ever married (%) | Heading households (%) |
Parish	Date					
Ealing	1599	4	7	31	12.9	22.6
Grasmere	1683	2	2	21	9.5	9.5
Chilvers Coton	1684	17	19	43	39.5	44.2
Lichfield	1695	29	37	116	25.0	31.9
Ringmore	1698	3	2	13	23.1	15.4
Stoke	1701	38	39	116	32.8	33.6
Wembworthy	1779	4	5	18	22.2	27.8
Corfe Castle	1790	24	24	80	30.0	30.0
Ardleigh	1796	35	30	94	37.2	31.9
Elmdon	1861	20	20	37	54.1	54.1

marriage rate, a sustained rise in real wages prompting a comparable rise in the marriage rate. In terms of household composition this relationship would be reflected most obviously in the headship rate, that is the proportion of persons by age who headed their own households. The expectation would be that more men in their 20s and 30s would marry and form their own households in the late sixteenth and late eighteenth centuries than during the seventeenth century, this behaviour being occasioned, as with the marriage rate, by an earlier rise in real income.

The information that is available on headship rates in pre-industrial England is unfortunately limited.[4] It is derived from those nine listings[5] which give the ages of the inhabitants and is presented for men in their 20s in table 16.1. Contrary to expectation, there is no sign of higher headship rates in the late eighteenth century, or indeed in the one solitary example from the late sixteenth. However, it could be argued that this is caused not by any lack of correlation between headship rates and proportions married, since at the level of the community such an association is visible (see the final two columns of table 16.1), but

[4] One nineteenth-century community, Elmdon in Essex, has been included for comparative purposes and had a very high headship rate.

[5] Listings are population counts including surviving enumeration schedules of the first four national censuses of England (1801–31) in which the population is divided into households. A brief description of the information provided by each list can be found in the journal *Local Population Studies* beginning with issue 24 (Spring 1980). For a discussion of some of the issues underlying the identification of the blocks of names as households, see ch. 1 above.

because the extremely wide variation in headship rates between communities completely masks any shift in headship rates between the
seventeenth and eighteenth centuries. For example, the two large
towns of Stoke and Lichfield yielded high rates, with more than 3 of
every 10 men aged between 20 and 29 heading households. In the
nascent industrial centre of Chilvers Coton, the headship rate was even
higher. At the other extreme were Grasmere, nestling among the West-
morland fells, where only 9.5% of men aged 20–9 were household
heads, and Ringmore, a coastal parish in Devon, where 15% of men in
their 20s headed households.

These inter-community differences in headship rates, however, pose
a further set of problems. Movement over time in headship rates may be
explained by trends in the real wage, but it is less clear that such trends
account for the range of headship rates among communities. Other and
probably more relevant factors governing the process of household
formation are the period of training considered necessary before an
individual became free to pursue a particular occupation; the labour
requirements of other households, which might involve at certain times
a greater or lesser preference for labour within the household (i.e.
unmarried servants)[6] over out-labour (labourers, mainly married persons); even, as might be the case in Grasmere, ease of access to land.
Mortality too could vary markedly in level from place to place, altering
the speed at which land or employment opportunities could be taken up
by younger adults.[7]

The importance that should be given to each of these factors must
await the detailed examination of the local economies of these communities, and even so there will be a limit to what can be based on no
more than nine self-selected settlements. In practice, therefore, for
charting both temporal and spatial variation in the English household
before 1821 it will continue to be necessary to rely on the much larger
body of listings which do not give ages.[8] This material has now been

---

[6] Kussmaul, *Servants in husbandry in early-modern England* (1981): 97, 101.

[7] For example, unpublished estimates by the SSRC Cambridge Group, derived from 12
reconstitutions and relating to the period 1750–99, indicate that if the average chances
of a man surviving from age 25 to age 50 is expressed as 100, in Gainsborough, Lincs. his
survival chances were only 85.2, while in Gedling, Notts. they rated 112.7. The strength
of regional variations in mortality in the nineteenth century is assessed by Benson,
'Mortality variation in the north of England' (1980).

[8] 1821 was the first of the national English censuses to include a question on age, and a
number of enumeration schedules have survived giving the ages of the inhabitants. The
first national census for which a full set of enumeration schedules has survived is 1841,
but only in 1851 did it become standard to give the relationship to the head of the
household and the exact age of every individual.

thoroughly resurveyed,[9] and with the information now beginning to emerge from Michael Anderson's mammoth random sample of the 1851 enumerators' schedules, together with some near-contemporary sample surveys of households, it is possible to modify and add much greater detail to the overview of the household presented by Peter Laslett in 1969.[10] However, one major problem remains. There are simply too few listings to enable a random selection of communities to be drawn up for the pre-industrial period. General statements about the household based, as is inevitably the case, on the few lists of acceptable quality (cf. notes to table 16.2) need careful consideration. This is a difficulty to which further reference will be made below.

The main outlines of English households since the seventeenth century are set out in table 16.2. Two factors account for the fact that English households are now much smaller in size: the reduction in the number of children and the virtual elimination from the household of resident labour, represented by servants. On the other hand, the number of kin in the household seems to have declined only after 1947. Indeed, kin (relatives of the household head other than spouse or offspring) were at their maximum in 1947 rather than in some remote period in the past. It may be significant that the decade following 1947 saw a number of pioneering studies of the role of the kin group in working-class communities, studies that can be seen, in retrospect, to have unduly influenced expectations about the size and nature of the kin group in 'traditional' English households.

It is not possible to produce a fine measure of change in household composition when the evidence is contained in a series of snapshot

---

[9] The principles on which this fresh selection of listings was made were as follows: that divisions between households should be clearly identified, that the relationships of all or nearly all persons to the head of the household should be specified, and that the terms used should be unambiguous (for example some listmakers used 'child' as an age category rather than as a relationship indicating the offspring of the household head, and listings of this type were excluded). The differences between this selection and the one made in P. Laslett, 'Size and structure of the household in England over three centuries' (1969) is that Laslett made use of a variable number of listings depending on the subject under investigation (for example, 100 listings yielded information on mean household size but only 46 on kin), whereas the present selection uses fewer listings but has the same 'population' in all calculations. According to the new selection there were more households headed by married couples and more kin, but rather fewer offspring, servants, and attached lodgers than was previously suggested, but the revisions to the figures are generally slight; cf. table 16.2 below and P. Laslett and Wall (eds.) (1972): 83, table 1.13. Corrections of a similar order apply to the results in Wall, 'Regional and temporal variations in English household structure' (1977), in which Laslett's original selection of listings was rearranged according to time period (enumerated before or after 1750); cf. nn. 12, 26, 49 below.

[10] P. Laslett (1969). A revised and extended version formed ch. 4 of P. Laslett and Wall (eds.) (1972).

Table 16.2. *Mean number of persons per 100 households: England, seventeenth to twentieth centuries*

Relationship to household head	1650–1749	1750–1821	1851 Rural	1851 Urban[a]	1947	1970
Head + spouse	163	175	171	164	180	170
Offspring	177	209	210	191	134	109
Relatives	16	22	33	27	42	11
Servants	61	51	33	14	2	0[b]
SUBTOTAL	418[c]	457	447	396	358	290
Attached lodgers	26	24	24	50	9	3[b]
TOTAL	444	481	471	446	367	293
N (households)	866	1,900	2,467	1,961	5,997	796

[a] Excludes London.
[b] Servants and lodgers are not separately distinguished in the 1970 survey, and the division suggested here is entirely arbitrary.
[c] Proportions have been rounded to the nearest whole number. This accounts for any slight discrepancy between totals or subtotals and the sum of the figures in columns or rows
Sources:
1650–1749   Cambridge Group listings: Puddletown, Dorset (1724); Southampton, Holy Rhood and St Lawrence (1696); Southampton, St John (1695); Goodnestone, Kent (1676); London, St Mary Woolchurch (1695); Harefield, Middx. (1699); Clayworth, Notts. (1676).
1750–1821   Cambridge Group listings: Binfield, Berks. (1801); West Wycombe, Bucks. (1760); Littleover, Derby. (1811); Mickleover, Derby. (1811); Morley, Derby. (1787); Corfe Castle, Dorset (1790); Ardleigh, Essex (1796); Forthampton, Gloucs. (1752); Barkway and Reed, Herts. (1801); Heyford and Caldecote, Oxon. (1771); Bampton, Barton, Hackthorpe, Kings Meaburn, Lowther, Morland, Newby, and Great Strickland, Westmor. (1787).
1851   Calculated from data supplied by Michael Anderson in a personal communication, derived from a one-sixteenth subsample of enumerators' schedules.
1947   Gray, 'The British household' (1947).
1970   R. Barnes and Durant, 'Pilot work on the General Household Survey' (1970).

pictures of the household, but there are some very clear trends visible in table 16.2. The first phase (seventeenth to eighteenth centuries)[11] involved the decline in the number of servants in the household, but this was more than offset by a rise in the number of kin and, more particular-

[11] The time periods adopted for the analysis were 1650–1749 and 1750–1821, but most of the listings within the former period date from the late seventeenth century and within the latter period from the late eighteenth century; cf. notes to table 16.2.

Table 16.3. *Household members by relationship to household head:*
England, seventeenth to twentieth centuries

Relationship to household head	Proportion of total membership of household plus attached lodgers					
	1650–1749 (%)	1750–1821 (%)	1851		1947 (%)	1970 (%)
			Rural (%)	Urban (%)		
Head	22.5	20.8	21.2	22.4	27.3	34.1
Spouse	14.3	15.6	15.2	14.3	21.9	24.0
Offspring	39.9	43.4	44.4	42.8	36.5	37.2
Relatives	3.6	4.6	7.1	6.1	11.5	3.8
Servants	13.8	10.7	7.1	3.1	0.5 ⎫ ·	1.1
Attached lodgers	5.8	4.9	5.0	11.2	2.3 ⎭	
TOTAL	99.9	100.0	100.0	99.9	100.0	100.2
N (population)	3,850	9,133	11,630	8,734	21,985	2,337

Sources: As for table 16.2.

ly, in the number of offspring, with the result that households were, on average, some 8% larger in the latter period.[12] During the second phase (up to 1851) there was a much sharper fall in the number of servants and a further rise in the number of kin, but it was only in the third phase that there occurred a fundamental transformation with marked falls in the numbers of offspring, servants, and attached lodgers. Owing to the failure of successive generations of census officials to conduct inquiries into the structure of the household, and the 100-year closure period that operates before the enumerators' schedules can be examined, this third phase is unsatisfactorily long. It is unclear when exactly the household changed and difficult therefore to frame hypotheses as to why it changed. It may also provide a false perspective from which to view the fourth phase, the changes that occurred to the household after 1947.[13] On the figures as they stand, the decline in kin and the further falls in the number of offspring and attached lodgers during the quarter century

[12] Cf. Wall (1977): 94, which indicated a more modest rise in mean household size of 2.3% based on a different set of listings (and in particular more London parishes in the earlier period), a subdivision of the material used by Laslett for his 1969 study (cf. n. 9 above).
[13] The economic uncertainties of the 1970s and the decline in real incomes and the contraction of the housing market in the early 1980s suggest the possibility of a fifth phase: a reversal of the fall in household size and more households containing kin. However, the latest available figures covering 1979, on household size and gross type (two-, one-, or no-family households with some subdivisions showing some of the households with dependent children or retired people or headed by married couples), provide no evidence of a halt to the process of fragmentation. See the journal *Social Trends*, 11 (1981): 28.

after the Second World War seem the most dramatic in the English experience, as they have occurred in such a short period. Hidden perhaps in the nineteenth century or the early twentieth, however, there might be other periods of equally dramatic change, although it has to be said that the evidence of the headship rate is that the rules governing the formation of households varied little between 1861 and 1951.[14]

At the same time it is important to remember, when referring to aspects of the household that have changed over time, that some surprising parallels can be drawn between the households of 1970 and those of the seventeenth century. This becomes clear if the focus is placed on the proportion of persons of various types present in the household, as in table 16.3. Admittedly, the fact that households were so much smaller in 1970, with many persons living entirely on their own, means that more than half of the total membership of the household fell into two categories of household head and spouse of head.[15] On the other hand, the share of certain other persons in the household of the total membership was unchanged. This is true both for children and for kin despite the fact that the number of children and kin present was at an all-time low in 1970 (cf. table 16.2).

A more detailed examination of the structure of the household, however, is sufficient to bring out a further set of differences between the households of the seventeenth century and those of the present day. For example, an analysis of the range of kin accepted into the household (table 16.4) reveals that in both 1947 and 1970 a larger proportion of relatives could be defined as 'close kin' (parents and spouses of offspring) than had been the case in previous centuries.[16] In fact, looking at the kin group in detail, it is clear that this has been the most decisive shift in its composition. The earlier expansion of the kin group, even that between the late eighteenth century and the mid-nineteenth involving an increase in the number of grandchildren, nephews, nieces,

[14] My interpretation of the findings of Hole and Pountney, *Trends in population, housing and occupancy rates 1861–1961* (1971); see Wall, 'Regional and temporal variation in the structure of the British household since 1851' (1982a).

[15] Households containing just one person made up 23% of all households in 1979 compared with 5.7% in pre-industrial England; cf. *Social Trends*, 11 (1981) and P. Laslett and Wall (eds.) (1972): 142. Some data on the proportions of persons living alone in past and present populations are included in Wall, 'Woman alone in English society' (1981).

[16] Information on kin (resident relatives) in 1851 is derived from an analysis of the enumerators' schedules for the same settlements for which listings had been drawn up between 1750 and 1821 and avoids the problem of a comparison between a random sample of schedules, the source of the data for 1851 in tables 16.2 and 16.3, and a much smaller and non-random selection of listings. See also n. 40 below for an illustration of the differences in the composition of the households in the random sample and in the schedules selected to provide a 'match' with 1750–1821.

Table 16.4. Resident relatives by relationship to household head: England, seventeenth to twentieth centuries

Relationship to household head	Mean relatives per 100 households					Proportion of all relatives				
	1650–1749	1750–1821	1851	1947ᵃ	1970ᵃ	1650–1749 (%)	1750–1821 (%)	1851 (%)	1947ᵃ (%)	1970ᵃ (%)
Parentsᵇ	2	3	4	10	3	16	17	12	24	30
Siblingsᵇ	2	3	7	—	2	22	18	21	—	23
Sons- or daughters-in-law	1	1	2	8	2	8	7	8	19	14
Nephews or nieces	1	2	5	—	—	9	11	16	—	—
Grandchildren	3	7	12	—	2	27	38	39	—	19
Other relatives	2	1	1	24	2	17	8	4	57	15
TOTAL	11	18ᶜ	32ᶜ	42	11	99	99	100	100	101
N (households)	2,765	2,231	2,804	5,997	796 (Kin)	293	409	943	2,531	88

ᵃ Dashes in these columns indicate that persons with this relationship have not been separately distinguished and are subsumed into the category 'Other relatives'.

ᵇ Includes in-laws.

ᶜ Values have been rounded to the nearest whole number. This accounts for any slight discrepancy between totals or subtotals and the sum of the figures in columns or rows.

Sources: As for table 16.2 with the following exceptions:

1650–1749: additional listings of Stoke Edith, Herefs. (1647); Monckton, Kent (1705); London, All Hallows Staining and St Mary le Bow (1695).

1750–1821: additional listings of Braintree, Essex (1821); Leverton, Lincs. (1762); Hartsop and Sockbridge, Westmor. (1787); but excluding Ardleigh, Essex (1796); Barkway and Reed, Herts. (1801); and Heyford and Caldecote, Oxon. (1771).

1851: enumerators' schedules for same settlements as 1750–1821.

and siblings present in the household, produced no marked change in the proportion of kin of various types, other than a modest fall in the proportion of kin who were the parents or parents-in-law of the household head.[17] Put another way, the situation is one in which prior to 1851 the kin group expanded without materially altering the balance among the various types of relative present, whereas by 1947, despite the fact that the kin group grew even larger than it was in 1851, the range of kin in the household had already narrowed to what it was to be in 1970.

There has, therefore, been a considerable amount of change over the past three centuries in the structure of English households, and various suggestions can be put forward to explain the key elements of the process. For example, one explanation of the decline in farm service between the late eighteenth and mid-nineteenth centuries would be to see it as a consequence of the rise in population and fall in real wages which made labour relatively abundant and cheap at the same time as it made feeding that labour in one's home relatively expensive. It was, it could be argued, a natural response on the part of the farmers to switch from using living-in farm servants to day labourers who had to fend for themselves and could be employed on a more casual basis.[18] Similarly, reference is made to living standards in the twentieth century (only this time to rising standards) as a cause of the fragmentation of households.[19] It has to be recognized, though, that such explanations do not provide a complete solution.

The first issue is the question of timing. The decline in farm service cannot be charted precisely, because the surviving listings are too scattered both geographically and over time. Nevertheless, farm service lingered on, particularly in pastoral areas, as is evident from the census returns of 1851.[20] It is clear, therefore, that population growth in the eighteenth century by itself cannot provide an entirely satisfactory explanation for the decline in farm service. The management of live-

[17] Table 16.4 also records an expansion between the seventeenth and eighteenth centuries in the number and proportion of all relatives who were the grandchildren of the household head. The difficulty is to decide whether this change is genuine, because the category of 'other relatives' (kin whose relationship to the household head was not specified) was sufficiently large in the period 1650–1749 (and much lower thereafter) to account for much of the registered increase in grandchildren. It is an unfortunate feature that the specification of relationships is not more exact even in the most detailed English listings of the seventeenth century (cf. n. 9).

[18] Cf. R. M. Smith (1981b): 604, who also stresses the relevance of the agrarian economy (grain as opposed to pasture), though his argument is formulated a little differently from that of the present chapter.

[19] For example Michael, Fuchs, and Scott, 'Changes in the propensity to live alone' (1980), interpreting trends in the United States between 1950 and 1976.

[20] Kussmaul (1981): 20, fig. 2.3.

stock required, or at least benefited from, a resident labour force (i.e. the farm servant) in a way arable farming did not.[21] However, one of the indirect consequences of population growth was that it induced farmers to meet the increased demand for basic (grain-based) food and a reduced demand for high-quality dairy products by abandoning pasture for arable wherever the geographical situation did not preclude such a change. In other words the economic pressures produced by population growth that led farmers to shed resident labour were largely confined to the arable sector, though population growth also tended to increase the relative importance of that sector in agriculture as a whole.

The question of timing also arises, but in a different sense, in connection with the association between changes in household structure in the twentieth century and rising living standards. No one doubts that living standards have risen. The problem is that such a rise has occurred in other periods without promoting change in the household. It is necessary, therefore, to conceive of living standards as subject to a certain (but as yet undefined) threshold which has to be crossed before the structure of the household is to be transformed. The principal difficulty in the concept of 'threshold' is that there is evidence to suggest that the household is 'fragmenting' in much the same way over much of Europe, and indeed in the United States,[22] despite the fact that living standards could scarcely be described as uniform. It is necessary, therefore, to elaborate the hypothesis further to take account of the possibility that the point of change might differ from one country to another. Such differences might arise if a cultural pattern specific to a particular population discouraged members of families from breaking away to establish their own households, even though they had acquired sufficient resources for this purpose. A more plausible explanation, in my opinion, given the present ease with which ideas and tastes are communicated, is that once a particular pattern has established itself in a culturally dominant population, such as the United States, the pattern will spread rapidly to other populations in quite different economic

[21] Kussmaul (1981): 23 argues that farm servants were common in pastoral areas not only because dairy farms required continuous labour but because labour was often scarce in such areas as a result of the combination of dispersed settlements and alternative employment opportunities in rural crafts. A further possibility, however, is that the real cost to the farmer of providing board and lodging for his employees was lower in mixed farming than in wholly agrarian regions, and it is a pity that information on this point and on the level of real wages in pastoral as opposed to agrarian regions is still unavailable.

[22] Some of this evidence is discussed in ch. 1, and see also Wall (1982a) and references, but it has to be admitted that determining the exact point of change from decadal or even quinquennial censuses and the occasional survey must be subject to a considerable margin of error.

circumstances. A less economically developed population will adopt, or at least tries to adopt, a household formation pattern that has emerged in the economic context of a more affluent neighbour. Obviously such a process would impose considerable strain on the familial system in the poorer population.

Issues of timing apart, further problems of interpretation arise because changes in attitudes about the type of household that is considered desirable are often associated with modifications in the composition of households. It is often claimed today, for example, that family ties are looser; that people value their independence more than they did; that individuals may still want to see their relatives, but not too often, and that they certainly do not want to live with them if it can be avoided. What is not so clear, however, is whether these attitudes existed, perhaps in a latent form, prior to the onset of the fragmentation process, or whether such attitudes are really new, as is sometimes claimed.[23]

A comparable situation occurs in connection with the decline in farm service after the late eighteenth century. Farmers, it is said, came to value their privacy and were therefore glad to distance themselves, both socially and geographically, from their employees.[24] This, too, could have been a previously held attitude, merely awaiting the right economic climate to be put into effect, or, alternatively, it could be an attempt to rationalize a behaviour pattern that economic forces had made advantageous.

It is difficult to see how the conceptual difficulty is to be satisfactorily resolved, because of the problem of placing any attitudinal evidence in a sufficiently specific context. Nonetheless, changes in opinions about families and households are likely to be in evidence at a time when the shape of a household is undergoing modification, for whatever reason, and may well assist that process. On another front, however, further progress is possible in that there is much more information on the structure of English households that could be assembled, particularly for the nineteenth century.[25] A survey of the strength of regional variation

---

[23] A point raised in connection with the elderly in Britain by Hole and Pountney (1971): 26, and with one-person households in Austria by Findl and Helczmanovszki, *The population of Austria* (1977): 120.

[24] See the responses to Question 38 of the Poor Law Report of 1834 summarized by Kussmaul (1981): 128–9.

[25] The enumeration schedules of the mid-nineteenth-century censuses have been extensively analysed, but, as much of the work has been uncoordinated, it is often impossible to make direct comparisons between one study and another. It is the intention of the SSRC Cambridge Group to select a set of schedules representative of communities of diverse type and subject them to a standard analysis using the model tables to which Peter Laslett refers in ch. 17.

in the frequency with which households contained relatives of the head
(kin) has already been included in chapter 1 above, and in the present
chapter I intend to look in more detail at the degree of change in
household forms between the seventeenth and nineteenth centuries.
Apart from the fall in the number of servants, there is also the rise in the
number of offspring and kin to be explained (see table 16.2). In addition,
two results of a previous analysis of changes in the English household
need consideration: namely the fall from the seventeenth to the eighteenth century in the proportion of households headed by women, and a
rise in the proportion of households headed by non-married men
(whether by bachelors or by widowers could not be determined).[26]

How many of these developments can be ascribed to demographic
factors? First, variations in the age at contracting a first marriage, it has
already been argued, exerted a powerful influence on the whole process
of household formation (see above, p. 493). Second, there is the impact
on the age structure of a population of changes in fertility, themselves
the result primarily of the increase in nuptiality during the eighteenth
century.[27] In 1696, approximately the mid-point of the earlier period of
listings, fertility was low, and it has been calculated that some 9% of the
population was over the age of 60 and 31% under age 15. In 1786, the
approximate mid-point of the second period of listings, after several
years of rising fertility, the proportion over age 60 was little changed at
just under 8% , but the under-15-year-olds now made up some 35% of
the population; and the age structure was to become even more youth-
ful and remain so for much of the nineteenth century.[28] Since the type
of household in which one lives and one's relationship to the head of
that household are very much conditioned by age, it is to be expected,
on the basis of these figures alone, that households of the late eighteenth century would differ in composition from those of the late seventeenth, and, most obviously, that there would be a rise in the number of

[26] Wall (1977): 94 shows that the proportion of households headed by women fell from
18.3% to 13.9%, while the proportion of households headed by non-married men rose
from 11.5% to 13.4%. Other figures are subject to the slight discrepancies mentioned
above (nn. 9, 12). For example, it was stated in 1977 that for the period 1650–1749
children constituted 37.6% of the total population; servants, 18.4%; and kin, 3.2%,
whereas table 16.3 above suggests 39.9%, 13.8%, and 3.6% respectively.

[27] Nuptiality rose because age at marriage fell and the proportion ever marrying increased,
as did illegitimate fertility. The relative importance of these three factors in raising
fertility in the eighteenth century is calculated in Wrigley and Schofield (1981): 267,
table 7.29. Two other factors can be largely discounted. Changes in mortality have a
much less significant impact than changes in fertility on the age structure of a population (*ibid.* 443 n. 84), and the level of marital fertility changed very little between the
late sixteenth and later eighteenth centuries (*ibid.* 254).

[28] *Ibid.* 217 and appendix 3.1.

children in the household. This, of course, is exactly what is recorded by the listings evidence. Beyond this, however, the alteration in age structure helps one to understand some of the other changes that have occurred to the structure of households. For example, it was reported above that the proportion of households headed by women fell by 4.4% between the late seventeenth and late eighteenth centuries (n. 26). This was primarily caused by a decline in the proportion of households headed by widows (from 14.6% to 10.8% of all households), and it would be easy to jump to the conclusion that this followed from a reduced risk of prolonged widowhood because of a decline in mortality amongst younger adults.[29] However, the information that is now available from changes in the age structure of a population makes it clear that even without a fall in mortality the proportion of widows heading households would have fallen (other factors remaining constant) because of the declining share of those over the age of 45 in the total adult population.[30]

Of course, in reality other factors may well have played a role. For example, the Poor Law authorities might have modified their attitude towards paying maintenance to widows in their own households, or the economic situation might have changed in a way that made households headed by widows less viable or gave widows a role to play in other households, perhaps as child-minders.[31]

So far it has proved possible to identify three different links between changes in the demographic situation prompted by the level of the real wage and the structure of the household. Thus it was argued that earlier marriage promoted earlier household formation, while higher fertility led to an expansion of the child population and to a reduction in the proportion of households headed by widows, though the latter reflected also the fall in mortality, a trend less clearly linked to the level of the real

[29] The reconstitution evidence on this point is somewhat equivocal, suggesting between the late seventeenth century and the late eighteenth only a modest improvement in male survivorship chances in early adulthood, although there was a more marked improvement for women. However, estimates of adult mortality from reconstitution studies are bedevilled both by the small number of individuals in observation and by the fact that the period of observation is arbitrarily curtailed by the termination of reconstitutions in 1812 or 1837, and it is thought that the existing tabulations underestimate survivorship, particularly for the period 1750–99.
[30] Unpublished estimates of the age structure of England produced for Wrigley and Schofield (1981) suggest that of the population over the age of 25, those over age 45 were 47.6% in 1696, 43.8% in 1786, and 40.2% in 1851.
[31] See Anderson, *Family structure in nineteenth century Lancashire* (1971): 141, and cf. Thomson, 'Provision for the elderly in England' (1980): 350f for a demonstration of the extent to which changes in the operation of the Poor Laws during the nineteenth century affected family patterns.

wage.[32] To these can be added a fourth, but indirect, link: the decline in farm service that was discussed above. It has to be said, though, that these links are suggested rather than proved, since the only evidence put forward is that the upward movement in population and the changes in household composition occurred at approximately the same time. A much more precise statement of the relationship is required, for which it will be necessary to develop models of household structure to show how variations in nuptiality, fertility, and mortality within the range of the English experience might have produced various proportions of children, widowers, and widows in households, when children went into service in large numbers only from the age of 15 and two out of three widows lived with at least one other person (not counting lodgers).[33] Previous modelling of pre-industrial households has focused almost exclusively on variations in kin composition in relation to a variety of inheritance strategies.[34]

On theoretical grounds, too, one might well want to argue that the real wage exerted only a limited influence on the composition of the household. Admittedly, real income, as experienced in the parental household or indeed in service, in conjunction with any norms about ideal households,[35] might have given rise to certain expectations about the type of household in which an individual would want to live in later life. Further, real incomes, provided the younger generation were able to retain the profit of their labour, yielded the economic wherewithal to establish such households. However, whether the households would be formed in precisely the way intended depended on circumstances that could be outside the control of the individual, such as the number of openings in the village economy or other structural economic constraints. There is a classic example just after the end of the Second World War, when there was insufficient housing to satisfy demand.[36] This provides a more convincing explanation of why so many kin were present in the household in 1947 than the argument that the population

[32] Wrigley and Schofield (1981): 414–15.
[33] Wall, 'The age at leaving home' (1978): 190–1, tables 2, 3; and for the household position of widowed persons, Wall (1981), table 4. In any modelling exercise it would be necessary to allow for the considerable variations in the age at leaving home according to the sex of the child and occupation and marital status of the parent.
[34] For example, see Wachter with Hammel and Laslett (1978).
[35] This issue is discussed above in ch. 1, p. 28.
[36] Hole and Pountney (1971): 26, who argue, however, that the shortage of housing was less severe in 1951 than after the First World War; and see Wall (1982a). It might also be argued that experiences of the war years, when family members might be separated as a result of war service or evacuation, fostered a feeling for 'family togetherness' that persisted into the immediate post-war period when demobilization of the armed forces had not yet been completed. For this interesting suggestion I am grateful to Jean Robin.

had formed expectations during the war years or earlier as to the sorts of household it would be preferable to form. At such times, tensions between generations could become particularly acute if what had seemed realistic expectations in terms of the real wage were unexpectedly thwarted. Periods when this seems most likely occurred at the end of the First World War (a housing crisis again)[37] and in the last years of the eighteenth century, when a considerable number of houses seem to have been subdivided to accommodate the unprecedented growth in population, although households themselves were no smaller – were, indeed, somewhat larger (see above) than they had been previously.[38] In general, however, it is probably correct to think of such tensions as affecting individuals more often than they affected whole communities, and local communities more often than society as a whole. Of the 10 communities that appear in table 16.1, in 2 only, Ringmore, enumerated in 1698, and Ardleigh, enumerated in 1796, were there in the age group 20–9 more married men than there were heads of households.

Another possibility is that the rise in the number of relatives between the eighteenth and nineteenth centuries was caused because the division of existing houses failed to create sufficient additional accommodation for independent household units. Certainly there is no reason why one should have predicted an increase in the number of resident kin from the trends in population and overall real wages. It would be otherwise if it could be shown that the increase was limited to grandchildren or nephews or nieces who would, in most cases, be of those age groups that during the course of the eighteenth century expanded their share of the total population; but, as is clear from table 16.4, there was an increase in almost all types of relative. Only part of the increase in the size of the kin group could, therefore, be ascribed to changes in the age structure of the population, leaving the rest to be explained by an increase in communal living as household formation failed to keep pace with the expansion of the population. However, one should bear in mind also a point made in the introduction (p. 35 above), that some of the increase in kin may be more apparent than real, occasioned by a change in the basis of censuses from 'ideal' to 'real', that is from a description of where people usually resided to a description of where they were located on census night. This change was particularly likely to affect the recording of kin who might well be present in a household for a short period of time, for example after a bereavement or at a time of childbirth.

[37] Hole and Pountney (1971): 25.
[38] Wall, 'Mean household size in England' (1972): table 5.8.

At this point it is useful to introduce a final table, on the subject of kin. It was admitted above that, until the census of 1851, the evidence on the structure of the household has to come from listings of individual communities, and this imposes limitations on the analysis of the English household. The listings can be divided, as above, into broad time periods to provide an impression of change or stability, but since no community is listed in detail in both the seventeenth and the eighteenth century, there is always the danger that any variation (or lack of it) between periods has arisen because the comparison involved two quite distinct groups that would have differed in terms of household composition even if it had been possible to examine them at a single point in time. The fewer the listings that are selected for analysis, in order to increase the precision with which the household can be portrayed, the greater the danger that the set of communities will be atypical in some way. As far as change between the seventeenth and eighteenth centuries is concerned, there is no immediate solution,[39] but it is possible to side-step the problem for the period between the eighteenth and nineteenth centuries by selecting for analysis in 1851 the same communities for which listings survive from the eighteenth century. Such a selection has been used in the analysis of the composition of the kin group in table 16.4, and it indeed confirmed the increase in kin that was observed when comparisons involved different sets of communities.[40] One is, of course, still left with the problem of whether the few communities one can follow through time are representative of the general experience.

In table 16.5 the analysis is taken a stage further by measuring the variation in the proportion of multiple and extended households[41] between the eighteenth and mid-nineteenth centuries for the same group of communities and for the same occupational groups. The result is something of a surprise in that almost all social groups seem to have experienced an increase in the proportion of households that were complex in structure: from gentry and yeomen at the top of the social

[39] One might perhaps say a problem without any solution, unless many further listings can be located. Even if it were to emerge that the settlements enumerated before 1750 and after 1750 were similar in character at the time of the 1851 census, it would be dangerous to infer that this had been true at earlier times.

[40] The values, though, are a little different: from 18 (1750–1821) to 32 per 100 households in 1851 when the communities were the same, compared with 22 (1750–1821) to 31 (1851) when different communities were used for 1750–1821 and a random sample of schedules in 1851; cf. table 16.2 above, but averaging the figures for urban and rural areas in 1851.

[41] These are most but not all of the households that contained kin. Excluded are relatives in households without a conjugal family (for example co-resident siblings) and some in simple-family households (for example where a widowed parent co-resided with a son or daughter but was not herself the household head).

Table 16.5. *Complex households by occupational group of household head*

Occupational group of household head	1750–1821		1851	
	Total households	Complex[a] (%)	Total households	Complex[a] (%)
Gentry and clergy	40	10.0	108	15.8
Yeomen and farmers	185	18.4	298	24.8
Intermediate agriculture[b]	137	17.5	43	9.3
Tradesmen and craftsmen	395	12.1	478	16.3
Labourers	415	10.4	854	16.6
Paupers	18	11.2	56	17.9
Widows without specified occupation	116	10.3	63	26.9
Not classified and not given	64	14.0	64	12.5
All	1,370	12.9	1,964	17.8

[a] Extended and multiple (types 4 and 5) in the Laslett–Hammel classificatory system; see ch. 1 n. 33 for a brief description, and for a fuller account, P. Laslett and Wall (eds.) (1972): 28–31.
[b] Gardeners and husbandmen except for the parish of Ardleigh, where husbandmen have been classed as labourers, no labourers as such being listed in 1796.
Sources:
1750–1821   Cambridge Group listings: Littleover, Derby. (1811); Mickleover, Derby. (1811); Corfe Castle, Dorset (1790); Ardleigh, Essex (1796); Forthampton, Gloucs. (1752); Barkway and Reed, Herts. (1801); Bampton, Barton, Hackthorpe, Kings Meaburn, Lowther, Morland, Newby, and Great Strickland, Westmor. (1787).
1851   Enumerators' schedules for same settlements as 1750–1821.

pyramid to labourers and paupers at the bottom.[42] The similarity in trend does not, of course, mean that the causes of that trend are necessarily the same. The increase in kin residing in the household

[42] There are problems in defining occupational groups which are sufficiently flexible to cope with the degree of social change experienced during the late eighteenth and early nineteenth centuries. First, certain terms such as 'husbandman' disappear without being replaced by any other term of equivalent status. Whether this represents a real change (the disappearance of a particular class of person) or is simply a change of nomenclature is unclear, for differences within the group of labourers (the natural successors to husbandmen) can sometimes be discerned; cf. Wall, 'Real property, marriage and children' (1982b) on households and marriage patterns of two groups of labourers (occupiers of property above or below a certain value) in Colyton, Devon in the nineteenth century. The second major problem is that there is no guarantee that the same terms are used consistently in listings of similar date. The identification of gentry in particular is something about which opinions could differ, and the Rector of Ardleigh in drawing up the listing of 1796 seems to have used the term 'husbandman' in a different sense from that of other listmakers. In the latter case an appropriate correction has been made (cf. note to table 16.5), but detailed work on other parishes might bring to light other discrepancies.

could even be seen as the product of three quite different processes: changes to the age structure of the population; various attempts by the population to offset the effects of demographic expansion, for example when parents placed out one of their children with their own parents or took in a daughter's illegitimate child;[43] and a modification of familial and migration patterns as old employments decayed and new ones opened in areas where individuals could not immediately establish their own homes.[44] Much more detail on household patterns within particular occupational groups is required before the exact pattern of change can be established, but this combination of processes provides a credible interpretation of trends in the numbers of kin. Moreover, it would appear more convincing than the assertion of a general link between the increase in kin and urbanization or industrialization, whether attributed to the emergence of a new calculative element in attitudes towards helping others such as Michael Anderson associated with family relationships in mid-nineteenth-century Preston or, more simply, through the expansion of sectors of society where co-residence with a relative had always been above the average.[45]

However, the general relevance for household forms of the social and economic changes of the late eighteenth and early nineteenth centuries does merit further consideration. Indeed, it would be odd if the developments that characterized this period were without impact on the pace of household formation and the types of household that were created. In the middle of the nineteenth century the composition of households in urban areas was not the same as those in rural areas, as table 16.2 makes clear. Urban households were, generally, smaller. They were less likely to be headed by a married couple, and they contained fewer children and fewer relatives and servants. This last is something of a surprise, given that domestic service in the nineteenth century is often considered to have been the mechanism by which people were channelled into towns.[46] However, apart from the question of servants and the

[43] A study of nineteenth-century enumerators' schedules shows that a number of three-generational-family households arose through the presence of an illegitimate child. Given the rise in illegitimacy during the late eighteenth century and the possibility of a further rise between the 1830s and the 1850s (Laslett, Oosterveen, and Smith (eds.), *Bastardy and its comparative history* (1980): 18), it seems likely that this type of household will also have become more frequent over the same period.
[44] Judging from Preston in mid-nineteenth century, migrants usually went into lodgings rather than to kin, possibly because in many instances they had no kin with whom they could live. See Anderson (1971): 52. My argument is, however, that migrant kin would be 'extra' to any other households with kin that might be formed.
[45] Anderson (1971): 170f.
[46] Cf. McBride, *The domestic revolution* (1976): 34; Ebery and Preston, *Domestic service in late Victorian and Edwardian England* (1976): 77.

presence in towns of many more lodgers, the difference between urban and rural households is not large, and urbanization could not be said to have altered the general shape of the household. It has recently been claimed that there is no evidence in England to associate a particular mode of production with a particular nuptiality and fertility pattern.[47] Should one now go further and disclaim any association of a particular household type with either urbanization or industrialization?

From one perspective, the case is a strong one. Much of the temporal change in the composition of English households can be plausibly associated, either directly or indirectly, with demographic factors, responding in turn to variations in the level of the real wage, with a suitable allowance made for disjunctures in the local economy. Such an argument, however, ignores the considerable variation in household structure that is known to have existed among communities. For example, in the period 1750–1821 10% of settlements had a mean household size of 4.27 or less, while in another 10% it was more than 5.41. A similar situation arises in the case of kin: in a quarter of settlements, under 5% of all households spanned three generations, while in another quarter at least 10% were three-generational households. Other examples could be cited involving servants or children.[48] Admittedly the statistical modelling of household processes has still to be completed in order to reveal how much of such differences could be attributed to chance variation in small populations enumerated on one occasion (see n. 34 above), but it is possible, and perhaps more likely, that variation on this scale reflects the fact that particular communities operated within very distinct demographic and economic contexts.[49] Of

[47] R. M. Smith (1981b): 614.
[48] These examples are from Wall (1977): 97, table 4.4.
[49] Whether one takes this degree of variation as large or small is a matter of the perspective from which one views it. There is unfortunately no tabulation by district of all the households containing kin in contemporary England, but a very crude comparison can be made using the data on the proportion of households containing two or more families, since in the vast majority of cases it is known that such families were related in direct descent (Wall 1982a). This comparison indicates rather greater variability in the proportion of households that were three-generational in England in 1750–1821 than in the proportion of households containing two or more families in England and Wales in 1971 (15% of settlements within 10% of the median, range 0%–16% for England in 1750–1821; 23% within 10% of the median, range 0%–2.9% for England in 1971). Against Austrian experience in the past, the variation in household composition in late-eighteenth to early-nineteenth-century England looks more modest: in England in 1750–1821 kin formed between 0% and 10% of the population within households, and proportions in a third of settlements were within 10% of the median, whereas in Austria the range was 0.8%–17.9%, and proportions in only 15% of settlements were within 10% of the median. The figures for England and Wales in 1971 relate to the proportions of households containing two or more families in a random sample of county and municipal boroughs and urban and rural districts selected from *Census of England and*

the demographic factors, mortality was subject to most local variation (as a function of density and location), then nuptiality (reflecting differences in economic opportunities), while the variation in marital fertility among communities was relatively less well marked.[50] It does not necessarily follow, however, that it will be the variation in mortality that will have most impact on the household, since a modest variation in nuptiality will alter the pace at which new households are formed. Of the economic factors, access to land and the nature of the labour market were critical, but neither their influence nor the forms of household they helped to produce were constant over time. The fact that the relationship between economic change and household structural change has not been more visible is because the attempt to understand the transformation in economic relationships has so far been rather schematic, relying on generalized concepts, such as industrialization and proto-industrialization, that have somewhat obscured the intricacies of the changes that occurred within individual communities. The construction of a more refined set of concepts for the analysis of economic opportunities and developments at the local level will, it is anticipated, permit a fuller assessment of the role of economic combined with demographic factors in promoting the modification of the structure of the English household between the seventeenth and nineteenth centuries.

Wales 1971: household composition tables (1975): III, table 32. The sample N corresponds to the number of settlements for which information on three-generational households was available during the period 1750–1821; cf. Wall (1977): 94, table 4.3, and n. 9 above. Data on Austria are from Schmidtbauer, 'Daten zur historischen Demographie und Familienstruktur' (1977).

[50] The weighting of these three factors was suggested by Roger Schofield. See also n. 7 above, and for proportions of men married in the age group 20–9, table 16.1.

17

Family and household as work group and kin group: areas of traditional Europe compared

PETER LASLETT

In this final chapter we find ourselves returning to the issues raised in the introduction by Richard Wall and taken up by several of our contributors, especially by John Hajnal in chapter 2. If we are to compare family and household as work group and kin group among areas of traditional Europe, we shall have to lay down exactly what it is which is being compared. This means reopening the problem of the definition of the household, and the extent to which it is justifiable to suppose that it is best regarded, as we shall regard it, as a residential group. The resemblances, and the slight differences, between the view we shall take and that of earlier chapters should become evident as we proceed.

From residence we shall go on to the question of whether there were distinguishable areas of traditional Europe which can be contrasted with each other. An hypothesis will be put forward on this matter: that it is possible, and for our purposes useful, to distinguish four sets of tendencies in traditional Europe as to the composition of the family household in relation to work and to kinship, tendencies which can be tentatively labelled 'west and north-west', 'middle', 'Mediterranean', and 'east'. After this we shall proceed to our subject proper and marshal such evidence as we have space to consider on working relationships within families and households alongside reproductive and kin relationships. We shall end by facing the question of historical development.

Residence as a defining characteristic of the domestic group

Nearly everyone who lives or has lived on the continent of Europe has dwelt in a household, more familiarly a home. The assumption here will be that it is permissible to disregard the homeless and those in institutions. We shall also accept the claim that a man or a woman belongs or is attached to a household although he or she spends only the night or one

513

or two weekend days a week there. It will be further supposed that a person can belong to one household only, even if, as we shall find to be the case with a surprising number of people in some pre-industrial European countries, that person slept in one household, the one to which we shall allot him, and worked in another household. Although it is in general true that an individual can live in only one home at any one time, he or she can certainly work in several places, alone or in collaboration with others. To work permanently in the household to which one belongs, or in collaboration with others there, is only one of many possibilities, a special case, in fact.

Nevertheless, this special case is the one to which we shall devote particular attention in this chapter, and it is already evident that our topic can quickly become complex and difficult to discuss in brief compass. There are five matters on which it is necessary to comment for our present purposes. First, it must be made plain that a distinction will be drawn here between family, household, and what has been called 'houseful'. This last comprises all the individuals who reside in a house or in a defined set of premises. Residents in a houseful may make up a single household, and usually do, but they may make up more than one household, or as individuals or as 'families' they may be inmates, not belonging within any particular household but attached to one. A domestic group which is a work group can, then, be either a household or a houseful, and may or may not be composed of the family members of either of these unities.

Second, it must be recognized that in allotting every individual to a particular household or houseful it is not being supposed that he or she is a member of only one family, for family memberships have several senses and are usually plural. Third, we must be aware that it is possible for groups of persons who have the attributes usually thought of as describing the members of a household to be divided residentially, and that this happened particularly in south-east Europe in traditional times, and still happens there. So intricate is the task of defining the household by searching out common characteristics and functions that one of the authorities on the subject and on eastern Europe, E. A. Hammel, has been led to question whether we are in a position to apprehend the reality we have to do with. He denotes the task of trying to do so with a blank.[1]

In the fourth place, and as a consequence of such considerations, some anthropologists are prepared to define the household without

---

[1] Hammel, 'On the XX of investigating household functions' (1981), and compare Wall's introductory chapter to this volume.

referring to common residence at all.[2] Their interest seems to be in the nexus of rules and functions which interlink groups of persons as producers, reproducers, consumers, and so on. Residence has no necessary connection with such a nexus, although in practice the persons concerned find it convenient and desirable to live together. This would make it no longer possible to regard the household as always and necessarily intermediate, a unity coming between the individual on the one hand and the community on the other hand, the community which is also usually thought of in residential terms. But as we shall see, such an analysis sometimes comes closer to the facts of economic collaboration than an analysis which insists on each co-resident group being entirely discrete.

In the fifth place, moreover, there can be no doubt that societies and cultures have differed, and do differ, in their apprehension of the domestic group itself and have done so in ways which affect our discussion. Variation among parts of our continent may well have existed not only in what the domestic group performed in the past, but also in how that group and its functions were perceived. We shall suggest that there may have been a widespread tendency, a tendency still observable in the extant traditional societies of Africa, for the ideological stereotype of the household to maintain itself in spite of economic changes which have begun to undermine its autonomy and self-sufficiency, its apartness.[3] Familial and household ideology is an important part of our topic.

In taking a stand on residence, then, as a defining characteristic of the domestic group, we cannot be said to find ourselves on entirely secure ground for proceeding to the analysis of work relations. There are, however, anthropologists who also maintain the view that residence is everywhere and always primary, even if it has to be qualified for certain purposes. It seems to me that Michel Verdon is justified in the claim that residence is a 'distinct and autonomous social phenomenon' and not 'as is often claimed, simply an epiphenomenon of marriage, kinship or economics'.[4] In any case the historian has little or no choice in the matter. This is because those who have taken notice of domestic groups in the past, as well as in the present, seem always to have had residence uppermost in their minds. They have defined it inconsistently, as might be expected, especially on the question of how far absence while retaining rights in the household should count as residence, and they have

[2] See e.g. Carter, 'Household histories' (1981).
[3] Vaughan, 'Which family?' (1981).
[4] Verdon, 'Sleeping together' (1979).

shown bewildering confusion in their classifications, as is brilliantly demonstrated by Hervé Le Bras for contemporary European census offices.[5] But presence on the spot in the house or whatever counted as home, working there, reproducing there, or simply usually being there, has been the almost universal criterion of those who have written out household descriptions. Very seldom have they taken note of connections among households or among persons within separate households. A conspicuous exception has been that of Le Play and his followers, whose inter-domestic group observations have been made use of by Richard Wall.

Household typologies and a four-region hypothesis

In their commentaries on family forms in historic Europe most of the contributors to this volume have made distinctions on the basis of kinship composition. In this they have continued a practice going back to Le Play himself, Sir Henry Maine, and even Montesquieu, a tradition of analysis represented in *Household and family in past time* and codified in a table printed there.[6] Our contributors with one or two exceptions have used that scheme of analysis where occasion has arisen, and a slightly revised version of it appears in the first four tables below. They present kinship composition as it was at the places concerned during the latest phase of traditional European social structure, already fast fading in England in 1861.

It will be seen that the four sets of population come from widely separated areas. Elmdon is in middle-eastern England, Grossenmeer in the Oldenburg area of Germany, and Bologna in the north-central and Fagagna in the far north-east of Italy. Krasnoe Sobakino is one of the serf settlements in Great Russia which constituted the estate analysed by Peter Czap in chapter 3 above. The tables have been printed here so as to illustrate rather than to represent regions of Europe which seem to have had distinguishable forms of family and household, distinguishable in respect of their shape and structure for productive and reproductive purposes.

[5] Le Bras, *Child and family* (1979).
[6] P. Laslett and Wall (eds.), *Household and family* (1972): 31, table 1.1. See also the discussion by Wall in ch. 1 above. This typology, which includes an ideographic system for representing domestic groups, was considerably developed in Hammel and Laslett, 'Comparing household structure' (1974). It is now often referred to as the Hammel/Laslett or Laslett scheme, though in fact (see P. Laslett and Wall (eds.) (1972): 33 n. 48) it was adapted with only one important change from that devised by Louis Henry.

A more extreme contrast in familial organization could not be imagined than that between Elmdon in 1861 on the one hand, with nearly three-quarters of its households simple in composition and fewer than one-fiftieth multiple, and Krasnoe Sobakino in 1849 on the other hand, with four-fifths of its households multiple and not many more than one-eighth simple. The Italian and German villages can be seen as intermediate between the two in these terms. But it will be noticed that Grossenmeer resembles Elmdon much more than the other two, and that the Italian villages are more like Krasnoe Sobakino.

It may also be remarked that in Fagagna, the only example of repeated kinship analysis, the kin composition of households changed noticeably over time. That the proportion of complex households (extended plus multiple) should rise in the village by one-fifth between 1870 and 1890, the actual figures in the original annual data showing the rise to be steady throughout, may still surprise us after all that has been recently published against earlier suppositions that kin complexity decreases over time, especially as industrialization sets in. Equally interesting, and in accord with much of the discussion in earlier chapters, is the considerable difference between share-cropping and other households, especially those of labourers, in the Bologna area in the 1850s. But, as if to underline the complexity of our problems and their multidimensional quality, there were only one or two share-cropping households in Fagagna at any time although the level of kin complexity was so high. This is something of some importance to the present chapter, and we shall return to it in due course.

A fourfold tendency in household composition in traditional Europe

In putting forward his thesis of the uniqueness of the European marriage pattern, a pattern exemplified geographically in the British Isles, in the Low Countries, in Scandinavia, and in northern France, John Hajnal implied in 1965 that our continent was divided into two great regions, that which showed forth this pattern and that which did not.[7] The line of demarcation was suggested as running from Leningrad to Trieste, but with considerable geographical complication in France and in some other areas. Hajnal's position has by now been universally accepted and in chapter 2 above he extends it, as in my own study of 1977, to include the kinship composition of the domestic group in Europe and outside it.[8] The present object is to take the theory a little further, to propose a

---

[7] Hajnal, 'European marriage patterns' (1965).
[8] P. Laslett, *Family life and illicit love* (1977a): ch. 1.

Table 17.1. *Kinship composition of households at Elmdon, Essex, 1861*[a]

Population: 520

Table B3 (see appendix below). *Household structure: households by kin composition*

Household type	Class		No. of households	Proportion of all households (%)
1. Solitaries (singletons in households)	1a. Given as widowed		3	2.6
	1b. Given as non-married or of unknown marital status		4	3.5
		SUBTOTAL	7	6.1
2. No-family households (co-residents amongst whom no conjugal family unit can be discerned)	2a. Co-resident siblings		2	1.7
	2b. Other co-resident relatives		6	5.2
	2c. Co-residents with no familial relationship given			—
		SUBTOTAL	8	7.0
3. Simple-family households (conjugal family units only)	3a. Married couples without offspring		14	12.2
	3b. Married couples with offspring		57	49.6
	3c. Widowers with offspring		2	1.7
	3d. Widows with offspring		11	9.6
		SUBTOTAL	84	73.0
4. Extended-family units (conjugal family units having kin-linked individuals)	4a. Extension upwards (of which 3 have fathers and 3, mothers)		6	5.2
	4b. Extension downwards (of which 3 have grandchildren only)		3	2.6

518

4c. Extension sideways (of which 3 have brothers only and 0, sisters only)	4	3.5
4d. Combinations of 4a–4c, or any other form of extension	1	0.9
SUBTOTAL	14	12.2
5. Multiple-family households (two or more kin-linked conjugal family units)		
5a. Households with secondary units disposed upwards from head (of which 0 also extended)	—	—
5b. Households with secondary units disposed downwards from head (of which 0 also extended)	2	1.7
5c. Households with secondary units disposed sideways from head, member of parental generation being present (of which 0 also extended in other directions)	—	—
5d. Frérèches: households with secondary units disposed sideways from head; no member of parental generation (of which 0 also extended)	—	—
5e. Combination of 5a–5d, or any other multiple-household arrangement (of which 0 also extended)	—	—
SUBTOTAL	2	1.7
6. Indeterminate (Households where kin linkages are insufficient for classification in any category above)	—	—
SUBTOTAL	—	—
TOTAL	115	100.0

a Workings by Jean Robin.

519

Table 17.2. *Kinship composition of households at Krasnoe Sobakino, Mishino estate, Great Russia, 1849*[a]

Population: 516
Table B3 (see appendix). *Household structure: households by kin composition*

Household type	Class	No. of households	Proportion of all households (%)
1. Solitaries (singletons in households)	1a. Given as widowed	—	—
	1b. Given as non-married or of unknown marital status	—	—
	SUBTOTAL	—	—
2. No-family households (co-residents amongst whom no conjugal family unit can be discerned)	2a. Co-resident siblings	—	—
	2b. Other co-resident relatives	—	—
	2c. Co-residents with no familial relationship given	—	—
	SUBTOTAL	—	—
3. Simple-family households (conjugal family units only)	3a. Married couples without offspring	—	—
	3b. Married couples with offspring	5	11.1
	3c. Widowers with offspring	1	2.2
	3d. Widows with offspring	—	—
	SUBTOTAL	6	13.3
4. Extended-family units (conjugal family units having kin-linked individuals)	4a. Extension upwards (of which 0 have fathers and 2, mothers)	2	4.4
	4b. Extension downwards (of which 0 have grandchildren only)	—	—
	4c. Extension sideways (of which 0 have brothers only and 0, sisters only)	—	—
	4d. Combinations of 4a–4c, or any other form of extension	1	2.2
	SUBTOTAL	3	6.7

520

		No.	%
5. Multiple-family households (two or more kin-linked conjugal family units)	5a. Households with secondary units disposed upwards from head (of which 0 also extended)	—	—
	5b. Households with secondary units disposed downwards from head (of which 11 also extended)	20	44.4
	5c. Households with secondary units disposed sideways from head, member of parental generation being present (of which 0 also extended in other directions)	1	2.2
	5d. *Frérèches*: households with secondary units disposed sideways from head; no member of parental generation (of which 0 also extended)	4	8.9
	5e. Combination of 5a–5d, or any other multiple-household arrangement (of which 5 also extended)	11	24.4
	SUBTOTAL	36	80.0
6. Indeterminate	(Households where kin linkages are insufficient for classification in any category above) SUBTOTAL	—	—
	TOTAL	45	100.0

521

[a] Workings by Jean Robin from data supplied by Peter Czap.

Table 17.3. *Kinship composition of households at Grossenmeer, Germany, 1785[a]*

Population: 885
Table B3 (see appendix). *Household structure: households by kin composition*

Household type	Class	No. of households	Proportion of all households (%)
1. Solitaries (singletons in households)	1a. Given as widowed	1	0.7
	1b. Given as non-married or of unknown marital status	1	0.7
	SUBTOTAL	2	1.4
2. No-family households (co-residents amongst whom no conjugal family unit can be discerned)	2a. Co-resident siblings	1	0.7
	2b. Other co-resident relatives	—	—
	2c. Co-residents with no familial relationship given	—	—
	SUBTOTAL	1	0.7
3. Simple-family households (conjugal family units only)	3a. Married couples without offspring	9	6.3
	3b. Married couples with offspring	76	53.5
	3c. Widowers with offspring	2	1.4
	3d. Widows with offspring	10	7.0
	SUBTOTAL	97	68.3
4. Extended-family units (conjugal family units having kin-linked individuals)	4a. Extension upwards (of which 3 have fathers and 20, mothers)	23	16.2
	4b. Extension downwards (of which 0 have grandchildren only)	—	—
	4c. Extension sideways (of which 1 has brother only, 4, sisters only)	5	3.5
	4d. Combination of 4a–4c, or any other form of extension	—	—
	SUBTOTAL	28	19.7

522

5. Multiple-family households (two or more kin-linked conjugal family units)	5a. Households with secondary units disposed upwards from head (of which 1 also extended)	6	4.2
	5b. Households with secondary units disposed downwards from head (of which 1 also extended)	8	5.6
	5c. Households with secondary units disposed sideways from head, member of parental generation being present (of which 0 also extended in other directions)	—	—
	5d. *Frérèches*: households with secondary units disposed sideways from head; no member of parental generation (of which 0 also extended)	—	—
	5e. Combination of 5a–5d, or any other multiple-household arrangement (of which 0 also extended)	—	—
	SUBTOTAL	14	9.9
6. Indeterminate	(Households where kin linkages are insufficient for classification in any category above)	—	—
	SUBTOTAL	—	—
	TOTAL	142	100

a Workings by Jean Robin.
Note: Inmates are excluded from this table as not being members of households but attached to them. There were inmate groups attached to 24 households and containing 77 persons. See text.

Table 17.4. Kinship composition of households in Italy in the nineteenth century: villages around Bologna, 1853; village of Fagagna, 1870–90 Table B3 (see appendix). Household structure: households by kin composition

	Bologna area, 1853 (28 villages; 21,715 inhabitants)				Village of Fagagna, 1870–90 (vicinity of Trieste)			
	All (%)	Share-croppers (mezzadri) N= 9,256 (%)	Labourers (braccianti) N= 5,501 (%)	Others (altri) N= 6,958 (%)	1870 households N= 353 (%)	1876 households N= 341 (%)	1883 households N= 329 (%)	1890 households N= 316 (%)
1. Solitaries	} 2.6	} 0	} 3.2	} 4.0	5.9	4.1	5.2	7.6
2. No-family households					2.6	2.6	1.2	1.2
3. Simple-family households	61.0	41.6	73.9	64.4	48.4	44.6	41.9	38.9
4. Extended-family households	12.7	11.9	11.5	14.2	15.0	13.5	15.8	13.6
5. Multiple-family households	22.1	46.2	10.7	13.9	28.1	35.2	35.9	38.7
6. Unclassified	1.6	0.3	0.7	3.5	—	—	—	—

Sources: Bologna area: Angeli and Belletini, 'Strutture familiari nella campagna Bolognese' (1979): 160.
Fagagna: Morassi, 'Strutture familiari in un comune dell'Italia settentrianale' (1979): 205.

524

subdivision within each of Hajnal's European regimes, and to include criteria of work-group membership and status in the analysis.

Both Hajnal and Laslett recognized that the region where the 'western', or 'European', marriage and familial pattern has been an established historical reality was by no means uniform. Geographical variability in respect of demography has recently been illustrated by E. A. Wrigley, who writes: 'Both [France and England] possessed nuptiality characteristics clearly within Hajnal's "European" canon, but they differed so substantially as to demonstrate that there were significantly variant forms within it.'[9] Richard Wall insists in chapter 12 that Flanders did not share the narrow age gap between spouses propounded by Laslett as one of the marks of the western system. In his introduction he dwells on the possibility that the within-region variability might exceed the between-region variability in respect of a number of characteristics. Alan Macfarlane reiterates the existence of such differences, and emphasizes a divide within France itself, separating north from south.[10] It is because the 'western' or European region has been found not to be uniform, and for other reasons affecting areas beyond the western, that the fourfold classification set out in table 17.5 below has been worked out. The objects of making the fourfold division are to give some structure to a difficult and confusing subject of inquiry, and to call forth the further information which we so badly need. The architecture of the table itself is intended to bring out the interrelationship between kin-group and work-group characteristics in traditional European localities. Some of its provisions are uneasily classified in any one of its panels (for example, variable d 8 on household members of working age) which speaks of the close intermingling of kin group and work group in the traditional European household.

Domestic group tendencies and European geography

In table 17.5 domestic group organization for production as well as reproduction in traditional Europe is classified initially under 'Northern and western' and 'Southern and eastern' and then subclassified under the titles 'West', 'West/central or middle', 'Mediterranean', and 'East'. The relevance to the family systems of historic Europe of some of its variables, especially those in the two middle panels, is discussed in 'Characteristics of the Western family considered over time'.[11] The

---

[9] Wrigley, 'Marriage, fertility and population growth' (1981): 182.
[10] Macfarlane, 'Demographic structures and cultural regions in Europe' (1981).
[11] P. Laslett, 'Characteristics of the Western family' (1977b).

Table 17.5. *Sets of tendencies in domestic group organization in traditional Europe*

Overall criterion	Sets 1 and 2 Northern and western		Sets 3 and 4 Southern and eastern	
	1	2	3	4
	West	West/central or middle	Mediterranean	East
Occasion and method of domestic group formation				
a 1 Formed at marriage of household head	Always	Usually	Seldom	Never
a 2 Formed by fission or fusion of existent household(s)	Never	Sometimes	Frequently	Always
a 3 Marriage important to household formation	Always	Usually	(Seldom)[a]	Never
a 4 Takeover of existent household by new head	Occasional	Frequent	Frequent	Usual
Procreational and demographic criteria				
b 1 Age at marriage, female	High	High	Low	Low
b 2 Age at marriage, male	High	High	High	Low
b 3 Proportions marrying	Low	Low	High	High
b 4 Age gap between spouses at first marriage	Narrow	Narrow	Wide	Narrow
b 5 Proportion of wives older than husbands	High	Very high	Low	High
b 6 Proportion of widows remarrying	High	Very high	Very low	Very low
Criteria of kin composition of groups				
c 1 Proportion of resident kin	Very low	Low	High	High
c 2 Proportion of multigenerational households	Low	Low	High	Very high
c 3 Proportion of households headed by never-married women	High	High	(Low)[a]	High
c 4 Proportion of solitaries	Very high	High	Low	Absent

c 5 Proportion of no-family households	High	High	Low	Absent
c 6 Proportion of simple-family households	High	High	Low	Low
c 7 Proportion of extended-family households	Quite high	High	Low	Low
c 8 Proportion of multiple-family households	Very low	Low	High	Very high
c 9 Proportion of complex-family households (c7 + c8)	Very low	Low	High	Very high
c 10 Proportion of *frérèches*	Absent	Low	High	Very high
c 11 Proportion of stem-family households	Very low	High	Low	Low
c 12 Proportion of joint-family households	Absent	Low	Very high	Very high
Criteria of organization of work and welfare				
d 1 Addition to household of kin as workers	Rare	Common	Very common	Universal
d 2 Added working kin called servants	Rare	Common	?	Irrelevant
d 3 Addition to household of life-cycle servants	Very common	Very common	Not uncommon	Irrelevant
d 4 Married servants	Uncommon	Common	?	Irrelevant
d 5 Attachment to household of inmates as workers	Very rare	Common	?	Occasional
d 6 Mean number of adults per household	Low	High	Very high	Maximal
d 7 Mean number of households of ≤3 persons	Very high	High	Very low	Very low
d 8 Mean number of persons of working age (15–65) per household	Low	Medium	Very high	Very high
d 9 Household head described as labourer, journeyman, out-servant, cottager	Often	Sometimes	Never	Never
d 10 Household head described as pauper	Often	Sometimes	?	?
d 11 Attachment of secondary household to houseful	Absent	Common	Absent	Absent

[a] Exceptions to the suggested classification are known to exist.

Note: For meaning of entries in this table and the character of supposed regions, see text.

column titles are spatial expressions, but it will be understood that geographical boundaries separating distinct and fairly consistent areas can scarcely be meant, if only because our present knowledge is so scanty. Tendencies rather than demarcated practices are at issue, and these tendencies have a highly variable relationship with geographical distribution. This is perhaps what we ought to expect, bearing in mind the complex history of European populations, the extensive migrations and intensive cultural influences which have been at work. Such considerations make the comparative uniformity of some of the areas, especially of England, even more remarkable.

Moreover, the sets of characteristics which go to form the columns of our table are uneven in their composition. The first column, headed 'West', differs radically in its entries from the last column, headed 'East', and that for 'Mediterranean' differs significantly from both these two. But the second column, 'West/central or middle', is not so clearly marked in pattern, and the region where its tendencies have been found is even more miscellaneous. Some might wish to class its domestic group tendencies as constituting a variant of 'west', but in my view it is more useful to look upon it as forming an intermediate or perhaps a residual category, though closer to 'west' than to 'Mediterranean' or to 'east'. 'Middle', nevertheless, has an individual characteristic found in some of the populations which it covers. This is the presence of subunits or sub-households attached to domestic groups for the purposes both of work and of welfare, a feature absent elsewhere.

The village of Grossenmeer is located in that ill-defined European arena where households tended to have the characteristics we have called 'middle', and can be used to show how sub-households make their appearance. In addition to the 142 households anatomized in table 17.3 there were listed in the village 14 individual lodgers and 24 inmate groups, each attached to one or other of the 142 domestic groups composing village society.[12] When the inmate groups are analysed by the use of the appropriate tables it turns out that they were smaller than their host households, which themselves were of higher than average size and had some tendency towards kin complication. Further examination shows that only domestic groups of a particular description – descriptions quite exceptionally specified in the original document – had attached inmate groups, that is to say cotters, whether owners or

[12] In our typology, inmate groups are not regarded as households, and so do not appear on household composition tables. They are analysed, along with their relationship to their host households, in other tables belonging to the series, for example tables A7, B4, and G2 (see the appendix to this chapter).

renters, rather than farmers. To be confident of the position of these sub-households and the social structure of the village one would have to be an expert on the society of the region, and perhaps on Grossenmeer itself. But they certainly seem to have been ancillary work groups, co-operating with the work group in the household to which they were attached.

It is not certain, however, that these extra work groups were neces-sarily recruited by the host household themselves. They may have been attached by the village authorities for welfare reasons. We have no evidence at all that this was the case in Grossenmeer, and must not exclude the possibility that these sub-households represented a recog-nized method of extending a work force on the part of a household head who had more on his hands than his available working associates could carry out. He added to his houseful, in fact, for reasons of work. We do, however, know that some of the individual lodgers in the village were called 'pauper' in the list, and it is much more likely that they were placed in appropriate domestic groups for reasons of welfare. It is proce-dures such as these which help to explain why the fourth panel of table 17.5 is headed 'Criteria of organization of work and welfare'.

There is little information as to how widespread such practices were in the German lands, or even in Scandinavia, where it is known that pauper families and pauper individuals were attached to solvent house-holds for maintenance. The presence of spouses of servants in house-holds is an allied characteristic, also, we suspect, typical of domestic group tendencies we have labelled 'middle', but found too in the Baltic provinces of Russia, certainly in seventeenth-century Estonia.[13] Conspi-cuous as the presence of sub-households is, therefore, as a marker of the tendencies we have called 'middle', discussion of its prevalence and cognate arrangements soon brings us back to geographical and de-finitional uncertainties. Nevertheless we retain the view that eastern tendencies, classically shown forth in Great Russian serf villages, are justifiably associated with the domestic group structure of European Russia as a whole and of some of its surrounding areas; that Mediterra-nean characteristics probably marked the whole of Spain, and parts of Portugal too, and perhaps areas of the Balkan peninsula as well as the Italian peninsula, where the Mediterranean type is symbolized, as we have already hinted, by the share-cropping families of Tuscany and of Emilia Romagna. Countries, we must insist, cannot be expected to be uniform in these respects, nor national boundaries to be frontiers, in

[13] Palli, 'Perede struktuurist ja selle uurimisest' (1974), and see ch. 6 above.

spite of the homogeneity which has been called a distinguishing feature of England. Since the remaining countries of the British Isles, particularly Ireland, do not show forth the same homogeneity, the western pole, if that expression be permitted, does not lie in the westernmost part of the European land mass (cf. introduction). France has been found to be sharply divided between 'west' and 'west/central'; Germany to be very mixed; Hungary even more so. This last country seems to stand at the confluence of three of the four sets of tendencies and to partake of them all. Portugal is a puzzle.

Table 17.5 has accordingly to be regarded as inventory or checklist to be used somewhat as follows. A researcher, with a census or census-type document in front of him which makes it possible to answer all or most of the questions raised by entries in the table, should usually be able to decide where to place the population or settlement in question as to its tendency in respect of the household as work group and kin group. He should be able to do so even if he has no further information. But he should not be surprised if he finds the correspondence to be loose, or even that few of the implications of the table are borne out by his data. So intermingled in various localities were European familial systems and subsytems that it is quite possible to find a community which must be classed as belonging with 'west' situated where 'middle' or 'Mediterranean' tendencies could be expected to predominate. A possible judgment could, therefore, be that such a settlement had household characteristics associated with 'west', although it was situated in Poland, say, or in Italy.[14] It can also happen that settlements can show forth patterns of the nominated variables which cannot be classed in any column of the table, where the correlation among procreational, demographic, and kin composition criteria is apparently weak or even absent. This may turn out to be the case with Portugal.

But there seems to be some pattern of a north-west/south-east character even in these inconsistencies themselves. A settlement strongly marked by sets of characteristics typical of 'Mediterranean' or of 'east' has never made an appearance in England or the Low Countries. In these regions changes over time seem never to have gone so far as to introduce structures so different from their prevalent patterns. Nor have the economic, demographic, and other ecological variations set out by Richard Wall in his introduction and in chapter 16 above. The shape of households in fact has evidently been less stable on the southern and eastern than on the northern and western side of the continent. Nuclear

[14] See e.g. Lesnica in 1720 or Rome in 1621. P. Laslett (1977a): 20.

families can appear in any part of Europe or indeed of the world; multiple families do not. The question of whether it is economic development which was responsible for this interesting phenomenon will have to be left open, but we shall touch on it in our conclusion.

These are all issues of considerable importance, and it is essential that the meaning and theoretical intentions of our classificatory system should not be misunderstood. But we must not allow painstaking discussion of these details to obscure the general message of the table.

Neo-localism and its structural significance

The greatest emphasis is intended to be placed on the first section of table 17.5, laying down an overall criterion of household formation. The claim is that the outstanding point of differentiation among the postulated regional tendencies consisted for all the purposes we are considering in the extent of what the anthropologists called 'neo-localism'. This is a disposition in familial behaviour which can usually be inferred from census-type evidence, but which has to be confirmed wherever possible from evidence of other kinds. It requires each newly married couple to set up on their own, to live by themselves and not with the families of either set of parents – to take charge of their own domestic enterprise, as John Hajnal puts it in chapter 2 above. In the north and west this disposition was stronger than in the south and east; in a country like England it was very strong indeed. Weaker in the middle region, much weaker in the Mediterranean countries, this overall tendency was almost entirely absent from the extreme eastern pattern, where marriage practically never led to the formation of a new household. Households came into being by partition or by fusion, procedures certainly possible in the middle and the south of Europe, but almost unknown in the west. Neo-localism is a decidedly structural principle, and many of the other differences listed in the lower panels of the table are entailed by it. This is especially the case with those variables to do with kin composition, but it also applies to those to do with procreation, with work, and with welfare.

This is as far as we can go here in discussing the lineaments of these four hypothetical regions themselves, obviously a complex and difficult topic in which we hope much further work will be done.[15] There are

---

[15] Especially in countries where the familial system is so far illknown or entirely unknown, like Spain, Greece, and the countries of the south coast of the Mediterranean in North Africa. The Cambridge Group hopes to found the *Journal of Historical Sociology* to encourage research and publication on such topics. These are especially promising in countries like Italy where the records are good. A great deal of attention will no doubt

analytic features of the suggested classification system which are of equal interest.

We should be aware of the fact that the differences in the first part of the table imply differences in the family cycle itself. This is because a family cycle has to have a beginning point, and a beginning point is obviously likely to be affected by rules of household formation. In England, for example, household formation was predicted on marriage, but not quite universally. For in spite of the insistence on neo-localism, couples in the early years of marriage do seem occasionally to have lived with parents until their new home was ready for them. Moreover, it seems to have been possible for a young person who acquired the means simply to quit the parental household and set up by himself or herself without a spouse, so independent was the domestic tradition.[16] In England, then, a repeated family cycle proceeding within a domestic group which remained in being over time cannot have been frequent, and this must apply elsewhere in northern and western Europe, if in varying degrees, and in central Europe too. In Austria, however, it seems possible to assume that most peasant households outlasted the completion of one family cycle, or of several (see chapter 10 above), and structural durability seems to be essential to the stem-family notion, or stereotype, as expounded by recent scholarship.[17] Where Mediterranean or eastern tendencies prevailed and households were regularly taken over as going concerns rather than formed anew by their heads, such perdurance in the domestic group must have been the general rule, and Peter Czap has illustrated this vividly for Mishino in a recently published essay.[18]

Here we have a principal difference among European regions in the household as work group and kin group, for wherever neo-localism prevailed work groups tended to be dissolved when a household head died, but not in regions where household formation rules were different. Such an illustration of the implications of the statements in our table draws attention to the force of the statements contained in its cells. They are all relative rather than absolute, and judgments have to be made in strict regard to what has now become known about the variables in question. When it is implied in line b 1, for example, that the

have to be paid to frontier localities. The most interesting of all seems to be that including the Alpine region and stretching eastwards into Hungary (see chapter 9 above).

[16] On both these points, compare Anderson, *Family structure in nineteenth century Lancashire* (1971).
[17] See P. Laslett, 'The stem-family hypothesis' (1978a) and references.
[18] Czap, 'The perennial multiple family household' (1982), and see also above, pp. 138–41.

age at first marriage of women is high in the north and west (under both
'west' and 'west/central') and low elsewhere (under both 'Mediterranean' and 'east'), it has to be understood that mean marriage age on the
one side was usually above 22, and could be 27 or even 30. It was
practically never low enough for a majority of all the women present in
the population to be described as ever-married by the age of 20. The
tendencies we have named 'Mediterranean' and 'east', on the other
hand, were for mean female marriage age to be about 20 or below,
almost never as high as 25 or above, and often such that a majority of all
women could be described as ever-married by the end of their
nineteenth year. Here, then, the scale is fairly wide, but in other
variables it could be much narrower.

Frérèches, for example (variable c 10) could make up some 9% of all
households classed under 'east', as can be seen in table 17.2. This must
be regarded as a maximal figure, even when Italy is taken into account.[19]
Frérèches are almost never found in the north and west, so that the
general distribution of the values for this variable seems to have fallen
between 0 and 10%, with most of them lying between 0 and 3%.

In the same way, the expressions 'Absent', 'Always', and 'Universal'
are to be judged relatively. It is not impossible that persons living alone
will be found in Russia, even a *frérèche* in England, or a secondary
household like those at Grossenmeer attached to the domestic group
elsewhere than under the 'West/central' heading. It is notoriously bad
practice to argue by implicit numeration. It is true that for many, though
by no means all, of the cells in the table, we do have some numerical
information, and even an idea of how large a difference must be in order
to be significant.[20] But we must not be supposed to imply values on
a ratio scale. Rather, ordinal placings are intended, and in the fourth
and least-worked-out section of table 17.5, the language of order is
explicit.

Organization of work and welfare

It will be seen that the language used here is vaguer than in the other
sections, and the sense of a spectrum, between a polar west and a polar
east, is much less in evidence. Some of the cells have had to be left with
queries in them. This arises because we have much less information on

[19] Poni, 'Family and *podere* in Emilia Romagna' (1978).
[20] See Wachter with Hammel and Laslett, *Statistical studies of historical social structure* (1978),
where it is shown that the differences in kin composition variables have to be surprisingly large in order to be taken to indicate differences in household formation rules.

working relationships than on procreative and kinship relations, and also because working connections are less easily inferred from listings of inhabitants. Indeed, productive and economic connections are by their nature likely to involve or to imply interconnections transcending domestic boundaries or disregarding them. They require information on what the sociologists call society-level variables to a far greater extent than reproduction, and so are less susceptible to the somewhat simplistic analysis implied by our table.

As we proceed to our consideration of the familial work force as a subject in itself, the provisions schematically set out will have to be borne in mind. We have committed ourselves, for example, in table 17.5 to the statement (line d 1) that in northern and western Europe it was less common for kinsfolk to be present in a household as working members than it was in southern and eastern Europe. When it comes to unrelated persons taking part in the productive activities of a household, the table suggests that in the north and west standard practice was to add such persons as life-cycle servants to the working strength (line d 3). Such entries need no further explication, but that to do with welfare (d 10) perhaps requires a little further discussion. The reason for its importance to the familial work group should be clearer when we reach the question of how far the efforts of household members yielded sufficient income to support the whole unit (see below). A household in receipt of transfer incomes, we shall claim, was to that extent lacking in status as a work group.

In ways such as these, therefore, the whole of our consideration of the working household may be regarded as a commentary on the propositions set out in the table. But the variables it contains are for the most part a small selection of those present in the whole body of tables listed in the appendix. A complete comparison between two populations from the social-structural point of view would require, we believe, the filling out of all these tables, or of such of them as the listing or listings make possible. It would also demand, of course, as much information on matters not covered by tabular analysis as could possibly be obtained, both to inform and correct that analysis and to put it into historical proportion as well as to add information from society-level variables which listings of inhabitants cannot usually be made to yield. In the matter of welfare, for example, knowledge of the relief system established in the society at large, and of how it was administered in the place concerned, down to the personal history of the individuals receiving such payments, would take the inquirer much further than the bare title 'pauper' attached to the names of certain individuals in the listing.

Let it be insisted therefore that the object of table 17.5 and of all those listed in the appendix is to yield the greatest possible amount of principled, comparative information when only listings of the inhabitants of a community or members of any historic population are available. Listings vary enormously in the information they contain, and researchers should be aware that without ages, for example – and these are very frequently lacking – several of the lines of cells in table 17.5 will have to remain blank, including some of the important ones (b 1, 2, 4). The table may nevertheless also provide a framework of analysis when information of other types is present, even in the absence of a listing or listings. Such exercises, as we shall see, are profitable notwithstanding the disadvantage of cross-sectional materials, and in spite of the fact that an isolated static picture at a point in time can tell us nothing about change. Opportunities to look at social structure at different points in time do tell us a great deal about change, however, and here detailed tabular analysis has its greatest usefulness for historians. We shall have to return to the larger question of the historical status of such terms as 'west', 'middle', 'Mediterranean', and 'east' when we come to our final paragraphs. There a tentative remark or two will be ventured on such questions as these. How far do these tendencies go back in time in the various European regions? Is one of them prior to the others, logically or historically? Can we envisage a process whereby a population could transfer itself from one of our columns to another?

Summary of the issues bearing on European households as work groups and kin groups

We turn now to the working activities of traditional European households and to the extent to which they did indeed maintain as separate individual work groups the economy of our continent in traditional times. Since our interest is in the status of households as work groups, we concentrate our attention on what can be said to qualify sets of persons for that title. So miscellaneous and shapeless have we found the subject to be that it seems best to set out a list of household attributes bearing on this question.

List 1. *Attributes having the status of principles to which households as work groups should conform: the ideal type, or stereotype*

1. All households to be households must provide from amongst their members the requisite labour to maintain housekeeping independently of all other domestic groups. Collaboration among house-

hold members in the work of housekeeping does not itself create a
work group, nevertheless.

2. A work group must be wholly contained within the membership of
the household, though not necessarily, or usually, coterminous
with that membership. For example, very young children could not
be part of the work group. The work undertaken by the group must
go on by collaboration among household members, and must be
done within the house itself or within the boundaries of the plot
cultivated by its residents.

3. The whole subsistence of all members of the household must come
from the income created by the household work group.

4. To maintain the status of work group, households must be independent, autonomous, and self-sufficient as to income and at liberty to
make co-operative arrangements with other households, but must
be in no way subordinate.

5. To be work groups, households must produce one commodity or set
of commodities only, either agricultural products or manufactured
products of a particular kind, and all members of the work group
must be wholly and permanently engaged in these tasks and in no
others.

List 2. *Features which may be inconsistent with the principles of List 1 yet
are acceptable to varying degrees as compatible with the ideal type*

6. Extension of collaborative work relationships to include those with
persons not resident within the household (not sleeping within it)
but working within it full time; married journeymen, for example,
or inmates (lodgers, lodging groups).

7. Subsistence-gaining activities not classifiable as production and/or
not wholly or even partially carried on at the household site or on
the attached plot. Examples are transport; distribution and services
of all kinds, such as retailing, carriage of goods by land and water;
milling; barbering; innkeeping; peddling.

8. Voluntary assistance in the work of the household freely offered by
neighbours, relatives, or friends, particularly at times of heavy
workload (seed time, harvest) or of familial crises (death, illness,
marriage, etc.). When such assistance is reciprocal (the usual case)
it can be regarded as cancelling out in the short or long run. But it
seems to be acceptable within the ideal, even if this does not occur
and a degree of work dependency comes about.

9. Plural productive or other income-producing activities going forward within the household, one activity usually being the principal

source of subsistence and the others secondary, often called bye-employments. Such activities may be intermittent or continuous. Examples are farmers who are also miners, innkeepers who are also farmers.

10. Subordination of a household to another household or agency in such a way as to impair or destroy its independence or autonomy, including its enjoyment of its whole product. Such subordination and exploitation may restrict its liberty to constitute its work force in accordance with its own interest and require it to supply labour for no economic return. Examples are agrarian serf households, especially those performing labour services; share-cropping households; proto-industrial households.

11. Receipt of income arising from rents, investments, etc. not requiring work inside or outside the household; income additional to that gained by the work group within it. Examples are households of landowners or of capitalist clothiers.

12. Receipt of income derived from work outside the household, provided that this income makes up only a minor part of subsistence. Examples are payments from sons and daughters working elsewhere; petty or casual earnings of household members from miscellaneous sources.

List 3. *Activities not ordinarily capable of being undertaken by collaborative work among members of households even in traditional society, whose existence nevertheless is not regarded as anomalous with respect to the ideal type*

13. Communal economic undertakings, such as heavy ploughing with village teams or harvesting.

14. Construction of buildings larger than modest dwelling houses; most mining activities; manning of sea-going and ocean-going vessels; most production of metals, salt, armaments, etc.

15. All military and ecclesiastical operations; larger-scale political activity in so far as these involve 'work'.

List 4. *Attributes and activities of households which modify, impair, or negate their character as work groups and are inconsistent with the ideal type*
A household cannot be a work group if:

16. Although occupying its own premises, it lacks other characteristics of a household, such as a common fund maintaining all its members.

17. It does not contain at least two persons of working age.

18. Its head works outside and derives most or all of the subsistence of the household from such work.
19. The work of other members than the head undertaken outside the household provides more than a minor part of its subsistence, especially when such earnings are retained to any extent by household members and not contributed to the common fund.
20. Its means of subsistence, although it consists in a common fund, is gained from the miscellaneous activities of household members not acting as a group and not co-ordinated with each other. This is especially so if the activities proceed in whole or in part outside the household and if members fail to contribute all or most of their earnings to the family fund.
21. Its means of subsistence comes wholly or to a noticeable extent from transfer incomes.

We must hasten to put some flesh on the bones represented by the tables and lists we have been presenting by looking at some real working lives in the European past, giving instances and naming names. But something must be said in explication, even in defence, of the propositions just set out.

These propositions are, it is fully recognized, founded to a large extent on opinion and judgment rather than on inference. In spite of attempts at complete definition, important concepts have been left indefinite, as for example that of 'work' in item 15. Although the combined list is certainly long enough, there are no doubt possibilities in the work organization of households which are not covered, just as there are statements which might be rejected. Some might say that too much emphasis has been placed on the existence of an ideal type or a stereotype of the family household as a work group. Or they might maintain that such features as all work being contained within the household and only one line of production having to be pursued are not required by the stereotype, or that less importance should be attached to independence, autonomy, and self-sufficiency. They might find it less than adequate to qualify the stereotype in the way I have chosen to do, by setting out elements not strictly compatible with the ideal type in a list of their own.

Chimera of a natural economy and the entirely self-sufficient household

The reply here must be that there seems to be no very satisfactory way of presenting these considerations, and that the method chosen seems to be the least likely to lead to confusion. Perhaps the most contentious decision implied in the lists is the lack of any reference to the supposition, formerly very widespread amongst scholars of the organization of work, that the original state of Europe, and of the rest of mankind, has to be called a 'natural' economy, in which each family group itself produced everything it needed to satisfy its wants – items of manufacture as well as of nourishment. In such a condition there would have been no need for exchange or markets, or even for money, and nothing approaching what we think of as capital or capitalism.

It seems to me that all we have learned about Europe in historical times in every region makes the concept of a natural economy unrealistic. If it ever existed, then it must have been at a period far earlier than that of written record, and so does not belong to history in the strict sense. This is not to deny that households, especially agrarian households, did produce a great deal for themselves in traditional times or that the increase in the proportion of goods offered on the market and the growth of capitalism undermined familial work-group organization. It is simply to assert that a wholly natural economy, with complete familial self-sufficiency, is a concept so remote from our subject that it cannot be of use in helping us to discriminate. Now for some real-life examples.

Households as work groups in sixteenth-century Coventry

It is easy to show how misleading the ideal type of household work group would be if applied to the great English woollen manufacturing city of Coventry during the course of its headlong decline in the 1520s. Nearly two-thirds, over 60%, of the domestic groups in Coventry at that time were headed not by master craftsmen, but by journeymen, labourers, poor widows, and what were called out-servants.[21]

Virtually none of these households can have been units of production – composed, that is to say, in the way in which the operations of work within the household dictated. Married journeymen and labourers and out-servants did their daily work not in their own homes but in the establishments of their masters, which were usually, but not necessarily, also the residences of those masters and their families. Journeymen and labourers were poor, some very poor, and their jobs were precarious: complete self-sufficiency can scarcely have been characteristic of their households, and they were certainly not independent or

---

[21] Phythian-Adams, *Desolation of a city* (1979): esp. ch. 6.

autonomous. As for poor widows, they were in much the same position as labourers, except that such earnings as they secured, or income from any source, were even less adequate to subsistence. Their description as poor distinguishes them sharply from those substantial widows who were carrying on the occupations of their dead husbands as farmers or, in the case of trades, as 'honorary masters'.[22] Such more fortunate women could have headed household work groups, but they did not necessarily do so. In Coventry poor widows existed, no doubt, to a large extent as they did in the English countryside, on the proceeds of providing modest services to their neighbourhoods: nursing; needlework; shopkeeping; taking in lodgers; running extremely elementary schools – child-minding rather than instructing; or more demeaning tasks like housecleaning, or 'charring', as the English call it. Some women could be labourers or midwives or even artificers, like blacksmiths (see the widows so described in a list of the inhabitants of Denham, Bucks. in 1749). Only the last of these, who were very rare, can possibly be described as heading work groups.

The family households of poor widows, moreover, were liable to be so poverty-stricken that they lacked self-sufficiency entirely, especially if they had no resident earning children. In order to stay in existence their domestic groups were frequently dependent on transfer payments, some of which came from children working elsewhere or even from other relatives, but most from relief and charity. Begging, the clearest indication of economic dependency, was probably important to many others.

The smaller masters in Coventry may often also have been in a precarious position, especially at that time of depression, if nothing like as badly off. They were probably existing on miscellaneous activities, not all of them pursued within the dwelling, and the worst-placed dependent on the relief funds of their craft companies or of the city. A few of these married master craftsmen may have been reduced to living as inmates or lodgers rather than as householders, which could have been the position of even more of the poor widows and journeymen. Even if they had their own premises, they would have been denied the title 'householder' – a status term in that city and elsewhere – and be classified as cottagers.[23]

It is only the solvent and substantial Coventry masters, then, who seem to have conformed at all closely to the expectations raised by our ideal type. Though a minority – probably a small minority – of all

[22] P. Laslett, 'Le rôle des femmes dans l'histoire de la famille occidentale' (1978b): 459.
[23] Phythian-Adams (1979): esp. 80.

households, these large and prosperous units contained a dispropor-
tionate share of the working population, but almost entirely because of
the presence of servants and apprentices. Certain qualifications have to
be made even with these domestic groups, certainly with the largest of
them. The richer a citizen was, the more commercial rather than manufacturing his line of business, the less likely he was to live at his workplace or at one of his workplaces. There were London merchants with
country residences from medieval times,[24] and lock-up shops in the
early seventeenth century.[25] These big men were those in a position to
direct and exploit the households of small men by the use of capital, and
so to take away their independence and autonomy. It is noticeable how
miscellaneous the activities of these large masters were as well. The
establishments they owned and ran, or had run for them, were not
necessarily all engaged in one line of trade, and could have been engaged in several: 'business in the office' was already characteristic of
some of these capital-accumulating, capital-disposing establishments.
Indeed, it was not unusual for city notables to belong officially to
companies whose trade or 'mystery' they did not carry on at all. It is
uncertain how far the features of Coventry were due to its being in
decay. It is known, however, that French and Belgian cities at a later
date, but still in pre-industrial times, had similar characteristics, as can
be seen from chapters 14 and 15 above.

In 1802 Rheims had nearly a quarter of its households headed by
women, many of whom must have been like the 'poor widows' of
Coventry three centuries before, though some of them were solitaries or
spouseless women with children. Labourers and people corresponding
to married journeymen were common in Rheims as well, whilst in
Bruges in 1814, 50% of the housefuls were headed by women or men
described in such a way (as labourers, in service occupations, or as
non-active) that excludes the possibility of their heading work groups.
More remarkable perhaps is that Rheims seems to have resembled
Coventry in many of these respects as early as 1422.[26] The standard
work of Roger Mols on the urban areas of historic Europe seems to
confirm these impressions for the whole Continent.[27] An eighth of all
the households in Coventry in 1522 contained one person only,[28] and so

[24] Thrupp, *The merchant class of medieval London* (1948); Lang, 'Social origins and social
aspirations of Jacobean London merchants' (1974).
[25] Dale, *The inhabitants of London in 1638* (1931).
[26] See Desportes, 'La population de Reims au XVe siècle' (1966) and compare with
Phythian-Adams (1979): 247n.
[27] Mols, *Introduction à la démographie historique des villes d'Europe* (1954–6).
[28] Phythian-Adams (1979): 310.

by definition cannot have been work groups, and this was a feature fairly frequently found in European cities in traditional times.

For example, the famous Catasto of 1427 informs us that over 10% of the households of the city of Florence were of size one; at Salzburg in 1569 the figure was 6.3%, while at Rouen in the eighteenth century that for a particular parish apparently reached almost 40% in the case of *'journaliers et ouvriers'*. But the rural areas had solitaries too, and if we extend the count to include households of two persons, not all of which by any means can have had both of working age, or even to households of size three, a considerable minority of which cannot have been work groups either, we find the following. The English standard sample of predominantly rural settlements in 1571–1821 had 5.7% of its households of size one, 14.2% of size two, and 16.5% of size three, that is 36% of all domestic groups, containing 17.5% of all persons, were unlikely to have qualified for the status of work group. The figures for the Tuscan countryside, the hinterland of Florence, were about 10%, 14%, and 14.5% (about 16% of persons in all three); in southern France in the seventeenth and eighteenth century they were seemingly somewhat the same, but there is an indication of much higher proportions of households of size three and a sharper division between rural and urban areas.[29]

This brief numerical excursion falls far short of giving a concise impression, but it does demonstrate how misleading it would be to suppose that anything like the whole population, urban or rural, can have been living in domestic groups properly described as constituting or containing work groups. What is more, it suggests that this feature was common to the sets of tendencies we have named 'Mediterranean', 'middle', and 'west'; only the east may have differed in these respects. All the facts bearing on this point cited in previous chapters of this volume bear out these statements. In spite of its possible unrepresentativeness, therefore, it seems legitimate to make use of the evidence of Coventry in the 1520s to make a series of generalizations about the family household as work group and kin group, and to supplement that evidence with materials from various periods and places in the European pre-industrial past in illustration and support.

A series of generalizations

(1) *Social differentiation in relation to the household as work group.* The first and most important generalization concerns social differentiation. This

[29] P. Laslett and Wall (eds.) (1972): 142, table 4.6; Herlihy and Klapisch-Zuber, *Les Toscans et leurs familles* (1978): 473; Flandrin, *Familles: parenté, maison, sexualité* (1976): 242–3; Mitterauer, *Grundtypen alteuropäischer Sozialformen* (1979): 79.

must be supposed to have existed to some extent and in some form over the whole of Europe once the notion of a universal natural economy has been left behind. The overriding issue, therefore, is the degree of this social differentiation and its character, both of which are of crucial significance for our subject.

For it should now be clear that where rich and poor were to be found in the same community or area, and the bigger men and bigger households employed, directed, or exploited the smaller men and smaller households; where land was distributed among some large, some intermediate, and many small holdings, with some households holding no land at all; and where in consequence of such differentiation there were household heads who had to go out to work to gain or supplement the family living; where in fact a labour market existed in persons other than servants; in all such places and under all such conditions it cannot have been the case that every domestic unit was a work group. I am not well enough informed about productive activity and its history over the Continent as a whole even to guess where and at what times a labour market has been established and under what conditions. But it is acknowledged that market relations were of considerable weight in an eastern European country at the acme of its feudal epoch, in Poland in the eighteenth century.[30]

(2) *Domestic economy and wage economy.* The second generalization flows from the situation of journeymen and labourers in Coventry, working all day in the establishments of their masters, but living elsewhere in their own modest households. The principle asserts that such persons belonged to two domestic societies, one of which was an organized work group, and the other, that which each himself headed, decidedly was not. They could be said to have worked under a domestic economy in respect of their masters, but in respect of their own families, in some cases at least familial inmate groups, they were clearly existing under a wage economy, just as much as is the factory or office worker of our own day. Indeed, as concerns the separation of spouses, the resemblance is striking. We are told that journeymen in Coventry left their wives at 5 or 6 in the morning, and, if they were cappers, anyway, did not finish until 7 p.m.[31] All the daytime which they could spend at home was Saturday afternoons and Sundays. This must have been true of the labourers in Coventry as well, and according to the provisions of the English Statute of Artificers of 1563 it should have been true of English labourers at all times, in the town and in the country.

[30] Kula, *An economic theory of the feudal system* (1976).
[31] Phythian-Adams (1979): 76.

The existence of a wage economy in this sense in pre-industrial times, with its implications for the division of workplace and living place, is insisted upon by Rudolf Braun in the studies he has made of working households in Switzerland and has been well described for France in the eighteenth and early nineteenth centuries.[32] These scholars stress the great importance of the family fund for the working life of the wage earners they discuss, and this is significant for our subject too. Like the wage receivers of late-twentieth-century Europe, pre-industrial labourers had no guarantee of a job: how frequently they were un- employed is beginning to become known for English rural labourers in the eighteenth century.[33] When the wage-earning household head was out of work, he was at home, certainly, but this did not make his household a work group in respect of him, and his family had to rely on other sources of income. For the fortunate this would consist of the regular wages of other household members, grown sons and daughters, or perhaps even of wives who had outside jobs or even undertakings of their own, as shown by divorce cases in Revolutionary France.[34] It has to be said that these jobs were in most cases wretchedly paid or marginal.[35]

There were also the proceeds of modest services and of miscellaneous work outside the home, as we have seen. But a great part of the casual earnings undoubtedly came from the efforts of wives and children engaged in multifarious petty productive tasks within the household. The family fund thus engendered was administered to a surprising extent by the women, who may have received all or a fair proportion of their husbands' wages when they were at work. Such arrangements throw into sharp relief how entirely different these households were from a work group organized for collaboration in a particular productive activity undertaken in the household, even though the element of pooling earnings in a household fund was wholly or partially preserved.

Not all labourers were landless, however. Indeed, we have found that one labourer's household in fifty had servants.[36] Most labourers had garden plots, a pig or quite often a cow, even in the early capitalist, pre-factory England of the seventeenth and eighteenth centuries. They

---

[32] Braun, 'Early industrialization and demographic change in the Canton of Zürich' (1978); L. Tilly and Scott, *Women, work, and family* (1978).

[33] Snell, 'The standard of living, social relations, the family and labour mobility' (1980); Lindert and Williamson, 'English workers' living standards during the industrial revolu- tion' (1980).

[34] Clark, *The working life of women* (1919); Phillips, *Family breakdown in late eighteenth century France* (1981); Levine, *Family formation in an age of nascent capitalism* (1977).

[35] Hufton, 'Women, work and marriage' (1982).

[36] P. Laslett and Wall (eds.) (1972): 154, table 4.16.

themselves produced some of their means of subsistence at home, therefore. Even owners or renters of reasonably sized holdings might work elsewhere for wages. Such outside employment might be only intermittent, but it affected the autonomy and self-sufficiency of the household as a work group, and the extent to which its character was influenced or determined by its organization for production. 'Bye-employments' was the phrase used in our list for such activities, and this expression also covers petty production within the household, work on projects ancillary to, or quite different from, its main productive task.

Several questions are at issue here, all important to our theme, but we have quite inadequate information to be able to answer them. How much manufacture was done in this way by farming families engaged in it on the side? How far did Europe differ in this respect from other pre-industrial economies, as for example from Tokugawa Japan, whose 'farm family bye-employments' have been so well described by Thomas C. Smith?[37] Above all, how far did regions of Europe differ from each other? Did the serf settlements of the east in fact produce a greater proportion of manufactured goods from the bye-employments of serf households than was the case in the west?

We cannot say for certain at present whether more bye-employments went forward in solvent domestic groups, adding to their incomings, than in labouring households near the margin of subsistence doing all they could to stay above it. There were certainly great numbers of labouring households in the west. Gregory King seems to have assumed that over a quarter of English households were headed by 'labouring people and out-servants' in 1688 and that some 56% of all households subsisted on family funds of which wages would usually form a part.[38] Historians such as Hoskins have claimed that a majority of all English household heads earned wages even in the sixteenth century (compare Hilton for the preceding two centuries).[39]

---

[37] 'Farm family bye-employments in pre-industrial Japan' (1969).
[38] P. Laslett (ed.), *The earliest classics* (1973).
[39] See Hilton, 'Some social and economic evidence in late medieval English tax returns' (1974); and Professor Osamu Saito of Hitotsubashi University in Tokyo, whose interest is in bye-employments and labour force participation, in a personal communication makes the following comments on poverty, bye-employments, and dual occupations pursued in households. 'Poverty, whether the household is a work group or not, is likely to force it to yield part of its workforce to other economic activity, over which it has no control. This suggests that dual occupation can take various forms, according to the combination of the degree of impoverishment and the degree of independence.' He instances agricultural labourers whose wives and children engaged in lacemaking besides working occasionally in the fields, and subsistence farmers whose whole households engaged in weaving in the slack season under a putting-out system. As for the

In pre-industrial England, then, and in many other traditional European societies, the appearance of a work unit existing within households of wage earners, and especially of labourers, may arise from multifarious unco-ordinated and sporadic activities such as gardening, spinning, knitting, straw-plaiting, broom-making, and a whole range of other handicrafts which went forward within them, and which yielded the contributions to the family fund of wives, children, very occasionally relatives, and sometimes aged parents. A crucially important function of this fund was to keep the household going when the wage earner himself was unemployed. But we must be careful not to suppose that the work which went into its accumulation made of the household an organized work group in the sense we have laid down.

Although there is plentiful evidence of all this going on in English history back to medieval times, it is not until the very end of the eighteenth century that we have access to household budgets. Apart from documents made out for political reasons when a price rise had to be justified, as by the bakers of London in 1616, the earliest English examples are in the book of David Davies, rector of Barkham in Berkshire, and they belong to those on the margin of subsistence.[40] He gives us details of the finances of the hopelessly impoverished labourers' households of his own district – some of them had to use urine instead of soap – and also a series of comparable figures from other parts of England and Scotland. Similar labourers' budgets are printed in a much-better-known source.[41] Many of the women in these households brought in money, although they often had young children; it came to about a tenth of the earnings of the husband.[42] The children added little sums too, beginning at six years of age. Trifles of the same kind, mostly derived from knitting undertaken by every household member, including perhaps the wage earner himself when out of work, old people, and children, are detailed in a listing from the village of Corfe Castle in 1790.[43] One little lad earned a shilling or two turning a wheel, a job which he obviously had to do away from home.

(3) *The organization of production and the proletarian household.* A domestic group whose rationale consisted in a family fund like this, lacking the features of a co-ordinated work group, corresponds badly to the ideal, or

more prosperous, 'an extreme case is a household which combines an independent undertaking, like farming, with another one, like retailing. In this case two occupational activities are co-ordinated in the work of one group, with labour divided accordingly.'

[40] P. Laslett, *The world we have lost* (1971): 1; Davies, *The case of the labourers in husbandry* (1975).

[41] Eden, *State of the poor* (1797): vols. I and II.

[42] Lindert and Williamson (1980).

[43] Saito, 'Who worked when' (1979).

stereotype. It is not easy to see what its principles of structure and of continuity can have been, at least from the economic point of view. The family economy of the poor was not, in itself, a work economy.

These considerations bring us to our third generalization, which goes as follows. Households not organized as work groups did not have their constitution *determined* by the economics and imperatives of work, although they were of course profoundly influenced by economic conditions and class relations. It follows that the numbers, sexes, ages, and so on of the individuals present in a labourer's household had little to do with the work undertaken by the labourer himself any more than in the household of a gentleman. Unlike the gentlemanly household, moreover, that of the labourer was usually free of any influence from property or the rules of inheritance. Its structure could in fact have been quite arbitrary – a group of miscellaneous persons – unless there were other imperatives upon household formation and structure. The most important of these imperatives would be the absolute demands of food preparation and housework generally. Equally crucial in many ways would be the necessity of some, perhaps most, but not all, labourers' households undergoing a phase in which a man and his wife were together producing and rearing children. Accordingly we find that the households of labourers have to be placed under the heading 'west' in most relevant particulars, though subject to modification by the cultural norms prevalent in the area where they were found.

Their households seem universally to have been formed at marriage and tended to be simple in form and with few resident relatives. In every reproductive demographic particular, in fact, they were inclined to conform to the English model. When it comes to working characteristics, of course, they had a reciprocal relationship with work-group households, since it was labourers who went and joined the work groups in those households for daily labour, and their children who made up a high proportion, though not all, of the servants which both lived and worked in them. What applies to labourers' households seems to have applied to all those in what might be called a proletarian situation, like that of the married journeyman and poor widows of Coventry. The symmetrical reciprocity between the proletarian households defined in this way and the households of the possessors and employers is an eminent example of class determinism in domestic group composition – this in spite of the fact that the relationship did not dictate the membership and the activities of the families of the labouring and the impoverished in the way that imperatives of work organization clearly could.

This can be demonstrated in the following way. All over Europe the domestic groups of the subjugated and the exploited, some but by no means all of them justifiably described as proletarian, if and when they were engaged on co-ordinated work showed forth 'western' tendencies to a markedly smaller extent than labourers' households did, except of course in the western region itself. There are three conspicuous instances of this, the share-cropping households of historic Italy, the serf households of Imperial Russia, and the proto-industrial households found in so many areas. '*Mezzadri*', as the Italian share-croppers were called, appear to have been everywhere and at all times very much more disposed or perhaps compelled to live in large-scale, complex, and usually multiple households than any other occupational category.[44] As we have already seen from table 17.4, this could be so where other households in the same community had fewer, and labourers markedly fewer, households of this description. But important as their status as work group was, it does not seem that it was the sole reason for the huge size of *mezzadri* households, some of the largest and most complicated in structure in Europe west of the Baltic and of Russia. It seems to have been a convention shared among landowner and share-cropper, the village community and local society, even Italian society at large, as well as the imperatives of work, which ensured that these share-cropping arrangements should give rise to such huge fraternal joint families of the Mediterranean type.

That it was not necessarily the absence of a labour market is demonstrated by the very existence of labouring households in the villages where share-croppers were situated. It is confirmed by the fact that *mezzadri* could themselves have numbers of servants.[45] In the region of Bologna in 1853, even labourers' households, presumably lacking work-group organization as they did elsewhere, were of the multiple form (table 17.4) more than twice as often as is found in the English standard sample for household composition in the whole population.[46] 'Other professions' in the Bologna area had an even higher proportion than labourers. There seems to be little doubt, therefore, that a norm of household formation was affecting behaviour in the Bolognese villages in 1853 and in Fagagna between 1870 and 1890. Such a norm of behaviour was clearly in evidence amongst the 'factory' workers of Iaroslavl, north of Moscow, recently analysed by Mitterauer and Kagan

[44] Poni (1978).
[45] 35.6% of *mezzadri con servi e garzoni conviventi*; 18.5% of *altri*; 1.0% of *braccianti*. See Angeli and Belletini (1979): table 2.
[46] 10.7% as against 4.1%. See P. Laslett (1977a): 22.

and referred to in Wall's introduction. In this 'industrializing' province in the later eighteenth century, the households of serf artificers showed forth in a fascinatingly modified form the joint family form described by Peter Czap in chapter 3 for the agrarian serfs of Mishino.[47] A great deal depends here, of course, as always in this area of inquiry, on the exact meaning of terms such as 'labourer', both in the data and in the mind of the inquirer; 'proletarian' is an expression which is also far from precise, and slippery in use. But the conclusion seems to be that where households are not work groups, and so are not under an imperative to organize themselves in any particular way, although they tend to be decidedly 'western' in structure, they also take upon themselves something of the form and structure normative to the society which surrounds them. But it has to be added, as Mitterauer himself declares, that when domestic units are in fact organized as work groups they likewise show some tendency to do the same. The intermingling of cultural influence, economic determinism, and work-group imperatives here can only fascinate the observer, even if it makes his analytic task very difficult.

The same kind of inference can be made from the facts which are becoming known about the proto-industrial households of central and western Europe. The details of their composition as to the presence of children and of relatives and assistants (servantlike, but very seldom servants), as to age at marriage, as to parental authority, and as to many other circumstances are being extensively debated at the present time in relation to their clear status as work groups.[48] In spite of such discussions and the general interest of this subject, it cannot be said that any one of the positions taken up about the degree and manner in which proto-industrial households were determined by their work situation is yet entirely secure. This might be expected to be so where household tendencies could be classified as 'west' and where differences are so much less pronounced than they seem to have been in Italy.

(4) *Transfer incomes and the self-sufficiency of working households.* Our fourth general statement about domestic groups as work groups and kin groups in traditional Europe lays it down that when and where it is known, or can be inferred (as in the case of Coventry in the 1520s) that numbers of households existed which were in receipt of transfer incomes, the work-group principle has to be modified. In extreme ex-

[47] Mitterauer and Kagan, 'Russian family structures from a central European point of view' (1980).
[48] See Medick, 'The proto-industrial family economy' (1976b); Levine (1977); Kriedte, Medick, and Schlumbohm, *Industrialisierung vor der Industrialisierung* (1977).

550 _Peter Laslett_

amples, such as that of the ruined master craftsmen of that city, men so affected by the collapse of the market that they could provide work for no one living with them, work becomes altogether irrelevant to the household.

This further statement, like so much of our topic, would require a reconstruction of the entire English economy over time to appreciate in full. We do not know enough to venture upon the task as historians, but it so happens that a contemporary, Gregory King (1648–1712), made an attempt at just such a reconstruction for England for one particular year, 1688. Now King was in no doubt as to the extent and importance of transfer incomes in his own society at that time. He believed that a considerable majority (850,000 out of 1,350,000) of all the households which then constituted England were 'decreasing the wealth of the kingdom'. A minority, the remaining 500,000 households, so much larger than the others that they actually contained more persons living in them, were 'increasing the wealth of the kingdom'. It seems legitimate to infer that those decreasing the kingdom's wealth must have been receiving some at least of their means of subsistence from those increasing it. In King's view, therefore, transfer incomes must have existed on a large scale in his traditional European society.[49]

It is not easy to decide how seriously to take this principle of King's, and his reliability as an observer has often been questioned.[50] But we are here concerned with a matter of general principle and with the macro-structural features of English society rather than with detail. It is sufficient for us to know that there is evidence of impaired self-sufficiency throughout the whole society. The work organization of large numbers of households must have been affected by this, and there must have been a proportion, discoverable only for any part of a country by close investigation, where work was indeed of marginal importance to the structure of the household, or even irrelevant to it. We find evidence for this statement in our English records. For example, all six of the households at Glynd in Sussex, anatomized by Eden in 1797, showed a 'deficiency of earnings' even after their poor law 'pay' was taken into account.[51] These deficiencies were made up by 'frequent and great help from the charitable and considerable farmers'.

(5) _Identity of work group and kin group as an ideal type._ It is to the terminology used by our pre-industrial predecessors that we shall have

[49] King, _Natural and political observations, 1696_: 48–9, in P. Laslett (ed.) (1973).
[50] E.g. by Holmes, 'Gregory King and the social structure of pre-industrial England' (1976).
[51] Eden (1797): II, 734.

to appeal under this heading, to their attitudes as much as to their practices, in discussing the ideological overtones of the familial work group.

Although many domestic groups could not have been work groups for the reasons we have run over already, and some could not have been so for the physical reasons to which we shall now turn our attention, the people of the time showed a pronounced preference for looking at all production groups in domestic, familial terms. We begin our consideration of this principle with the word 'factory', which is used in reference to the non-agrarian production workers of the province of Iaroslavl in the 1760s.[52]

These Russian craftsmen did not live in household or familial work groups, because they engaged in their productive toil in the 'factory', the factory that is to say in its earlier, traditional sense of warehouse, or warehouse with offices and also with some productive activity, the type of factory which the colonial powers planted in Africa and Asia, America and Australia. But there were other more obvious instances of sites of production, of performance of services, or of work of every kind which could not involve co-resident domestic groups for physical reasons. These were spread all over pre-industrial Europe and are summarily indicated in our List 3 above.

We have at present no way of telling how widespread were all such practices and situations taken together, and, once again, there must have been differences among regions of traditional Europe. Some of the activities were undoubtedly universal, particularly those to do with building, mining, and transport. It is not satisfactory, in my view, to look upon such non-familial, teamlike work groups, or wandering working individuals, simply as exceptions to the general rule that all production was done by households. It would be better, I think, to look upon the union of workplace and living place as an ideal type of the Max Weber kind and to recognize that the purchase of that ideal type over the minds of the men of the past might have varied from region to region. Even in those examples we have cited where the workplace cannot have been literally where a family was living, it seems that contemporaries in England at least may have felt that the group concerned could, under most circumstances, be made into a fictive family for the purpose of mapping their social world. In England, in fact, familistic ideology may have been particularly strong. A day labourer, for example, with his own household, and only temporarily employed by a yeoman, would be

---

[52] Mitterauer and Kagan (1980).

referred to as a part of the yeoman's family whilst he formed part of the work group, especially if, as often happened, he took his meals with the rest of the yeoman's household. When Gregory King drew up his anatomy of a national society, he thought of it as consisting exclusively of families; no other form of association is allowed for. He and most of his contemporaries conceived of the state itself, the central bureaucracy, in family terms. This, however, was a widespread characteristic of pre-industrial polities.

Social historians, I should like to suggest, have tended to follow this usage of the past persons they have studied without being wholly aware of the consequences of doing so. In this way we may have accepted rather too readily the notion of a co-resident domestic group in traditional times as being both kin group and work group and have ourselves applied that notion, as did the intellectual of the pre-industrial past, to associations of other kinds. Here our rather intricate subject complicates itself even further.

(6) *Work groups as non-familial kin groups.* For it has to be further added that a kin group can be a work group, or make up a part of a work group, without being a family in the co-resident, housekeeping, or procreative sense, and that this can arise in our day as well as in historical times. Crews of boats, or even of ships of the sea-going kind, for example, seem to have consisted of related persons to some extent, and still may do so. Sometimes they have been the immediate families of the master of the vessel, but they have included less closely kin-connected persons, as well as neighbours and entirely unconnected work associates. Even the early factories, factories in our modern sense, were not unlikely to have amongst their work-force bodies of persons showing interlocking kin relationships. This is especially so if, as in the best-known case, that body of workers had been recruited through immigration.[53] All of which confirms what perhaps ought to be expected on general grounds, that kinship connection and collaborative work tend to go together at all times and places, whether or not the workplace is a family household.

But, as we have already pointed out, it does not follow from this that the familial image was the same for every European region. That image, it might be suggested, varied between the sets of tendencies assembled by column in table 17.5 as a variable partly independent of the others in the column, but also in relation to them, as their 'rationalization'. When we reach this point and allow for the varying attitudes of our ancestors, we recognize how elusive any finally satisfactory comparison among

[53] Hareven (ed.), *Family and kin in urban communities* (1977).

households, families, and familial work groups really is. The discussion of work and work groups here shades into the discussion of European regional social-structural differentiation as a whole; such differentiation in traditional times inevitably had its basis in agriculture.

(7) *The farm work force.* The overwhelming mass of our European ancestors always lived their lives in agrarian households. It can quite simply be said of the rural household that the model fits to a greater extent than it does in the case of the activities with which we have been concerned. In so far as every farming household made its living by working the land, then that household was a work group. The composition of that work group was affected by the size of the undertaking, by the crops grown, or the animals reared, though always within the limits imposed by the necessity for most domestic groups to procreate and raise their children and for virtually every household to be maintained by housework. All this seems to have been true all over the Continent, presumably for all of the time up to industrialization.

But it certainly does not follow from this that all of the work required to cultivate the plot or farm of the household head fell upon the members of his household. It is only in the very special conditions usually associated with Chayanov, the great Russian theorist of peasant family organization, that these further positions ever held.[54] And it would only be possible to argue, as Chayanov does and as many subsequent scholars have tended to do, that family size and demographic conditions determine the size of the agrarian enterprise under the quite individual circumstances which he assumes were indeed present. The inverse proposition, still more often assumed but never so far as I know defended in principle by Chayanov, though referred to by him – the proposition that size of holding and conditions of agriculture determined the size and composition of the agrarian domestic group workforce – falls under the same criticism.[55] It could only have held in highly special, indeed entirely unlikely, situations.

Once more, regions of Europe must have differed in these respects from time to time and place to place, but no attempt to estimate these differences has so far been made, at least to my knowledge, in a fashion which might make it possible to record them in table 17.5. Even in the late-nineteenth-century Russia which Chayanov himself had under his view, it seems unlikely that the familial work force was ever the whole body of labour engaged in exploiting a family's land over any length of time, even in the course of one year. Let us take the example best known

[54] Chayanov, *The theory of peasant economy* (1966).
[55] *Ibid.* 64.

to an English scholar, the agrarian structure and history of his own country, and set down the consequences of trying to apply Chayanov's very influential theory, or its inverse, to the agrarian history of the English household.

(8) *Choices open to English landholders.* The English landholder, that is to say the English gentleman, farmer, yeoman, husbandman, copyholder, or even in earlier times the English peasant serf, especially the *kulak*, had a long series of choices open to him when it came to the working of his land. The higher he was in the scale of property and social consequence the greater the range of choice would be, but even a modest copyholder with a lease for three lives, say in the early seventeenth century, had some options under English economic conditions. It would by no means necessarily be the case that those persons who resided in his cottage were the whole work-force of his farm. We can try to survey these multiple choices in a series of descriptions.

An English landholder could choose to carry out all the operations on his farm with the aid of his own immediate family, if its members were adequate to carry out the necessary tasks, both outdoor and indoor. Alternatively, he might hire servants and add to his labour force. Or he could hire labourers by the year, month, or even day, and dispense with servants; or have both labourers and servants in various combinations. Or, if he did not wish, or was not able, to direct the farm operations himself, he could put them 'out to task'. In this case another householder would contract with him to do the ploughing or part of it; to do the harvest, or part of that; or to do all that had to be done for a part of the farm in question. All this could go on at the same time as the landholder continued to work some of the land himself, probably that round his residence, with the aid of his family with or without servants and labourers.

We must not forget that the household head might be a widow, presumably less disposed to direct a work group, or less able to do so, and so more likely to hire labourers or put operations out to task. A landholder was at liberty, if she or he wished to do so, to let out part of the plot for rent, or even its whole area, and live on the proceeds. This might be done for some years, perhaps when the children were young, and the land be resumed 'into his own hand' when they were grown up. A landholder might also choose to take up bye-employments, like brewing on a comparatively large scale. Substantial English peasants are known to have behaved in this way in the High Middle Ages. If a man were of the entrepreneurial type, perhaps on his way up in the world from a modest beginning, and not necessarily a village landholder, he could be the 'tasker', the man who undertook to work land held by others, providing his own servants, hiring his own labourers, and so on for these purposes.[56]

Men of this type, of course, might choose to buy or to rent land if they were able to get hold of it, and the policy of landowners which we have set down would often make this possible. Such a renter could also give up a part of his rented land if and when it became too burdensome or unprofitable. He could sell parts of his farm as well, or all of it, if that suited him; when he wished to retire, for example. He could also get into debt and be sold up; this is a persistent theme both of the English novel and of English agrarian history.

For these reasons a feature of what is usually thought of as peasant farming was decidedly absent in England, and this because of the principle of neo-localism. The assumption that a man on taking over a farm would keep it the same size until he relinquished it to his successor, preferably his son, did not hold in England. A farmer's land varied very considerably in size over his working lifetime, especially if he was markedly successful or a profound failure. Much of the land a prosperous farmer bought he used to set up his sons as farmers during his own lifetime, and some of that which he sold was to pay portions to his daughters. Some of it he used to retire upon. The holding of a farmer who failed would undergo even greater vicissitudes as to area and shape. The family plot in England was to a surprising extent disposable by the man who had control of it. Since the notion of designated heir was much vaguer with us than it seems to have been elsewhere in Europe, the concept of a family plot or even a family house was weaker too. Inheritance was not the only, indeed not the usual, title a landowner had to all or to parts of the area which he occupied.

In such a situation as this we can see that there would be no necessary relationship whatever between the size of a farm and the nature of agricultural operations upon it, on the one hand, and the size and composition of the farming work group, on the other hand, even though that group did itself engage in work. We find nevertheless that bigger farms and bigger estates in England did tend to have larger households. The households were larger as a result of their having more servants, but this seems to have been as much a matter of status as of the demand of agricultural work. It cannot be shown, for example, that the numbers, ages, and sexes of English servants bore a consistent rela-

---

[56] See Hilton (1974), extended and with much further discussion in Razi, 'Family, land and the village community' (1981), and esp. in R. M. Smith, 'The peasant family labour farm and English medievalists' (1982).

tionship with the numbers, ages, and sexes of the children of the landholder. The principle with which we began, that the number of members of the household had to be kept in constant relation with the enterprise, just did not apply in the English countryside.[57]

The Chayanov model, then, will not fit the English case, and it would seem to me to be difficult to use as a way of discriminating area from area in Europe. At the present time, anyway, we do not know enough about the social structure of our continent to begin to make the necessary comparison.

Traditional households as work groups and kin groups: original character and historical development

Having made it evident how partial, how uncertain, and how subject to ideological double-talk are the assumptions with which we began – that all households in traditional society must have been work groups and that all work must have been done in such households – we have to consider change in time and space. It will not be expected that we shall get very far in such a context as this, and I shall confine myself to a few very general observations.

Little can yet be confidently offered as to the original character of the familial map of Europe in its entirety, from its western seaboard to its Asian frontier. Nevertheless, the fragments of information which we have do make it possible to speculate, a temptation not easy to resist. In chapter 7 Carl Hammer presents the earliest hard evidence so far discovered, coming from Bavaria in the ninth century, where the form of the household could be classed in the column 'West' of table 17.5 as to kinship composition. It is known from the famous Catasto of 1427 that the simple-family household predominated in Tuscany, even though a fifth of all domestic groups were multiple in the countryside, and still more of those of the wealthiest city dwellers. Some authorities on the institutional history of Russia have maintained that before the establishment of serfdom in the early modern period the Russian household also had western traits. The suggestion might conceivably be made, then, that the rise of serfdom in the eastern regions, along with the changes which came with share-cropping in the Mediterranean, specifically in the Italian arena, were finally responsible for the differences among the four sets of tendencies which have been described in the data. They had recognizable historical origins.

[57] Kussmaul, *Servants in husbandry* (1981).

There is persuasive evidence, moreover, to which reference has been made several times, that in England western familial forms were present in the fourteenth and thirteenth centuries to a much greater degree than in Tuscany in the fifteenth century. Under such circumstances it might further be argued, though even more tenuously, that if a decision had to be made about the original position, original historically and logically, then northern and western tendencies should be nominated as a more likely choice than southern and eastern. Northern and western Europe would thus be the region which preserved original familial lineaments to the greater extent.

A conjecture like this has the advantage that it requires the examination of assumptions which seem to have gone almost entirely unchallenged until recently. The lineaments of the domestic group in the west, both as to production and reproduction, have always been thought of as the outcome rather than as the point of departure of historical development. Development here has consisted in the decline of feudal attitudes and in the spread of wage labour, of concentrated land ownership, of capitalistic productive organization, of proletarianization, and finally of factory industrialization. It must be clear that such processes could not account for the earliest English evidence. We should have to suppose that social-structural changes of this kind by 1200 transformed the familial situation, not only of the cottager on the margin of subsistence, but also of the due-paying landholder and even of the landowner himself.

If the western familial model turned out to be prior, further claims might be advanced. Settlements outside the northern and western region, yet displaying markedly western characteristics, like Kassa and Sziget in central Europe in 1549 and 1551,[58] could be explained by one more heroic assumption, that these were places where institutions like enserfment had never appeared, or that there had been reversion. Reversion of this kind, if the hypothesis were pushed to the extreme, would be at issue whenever western familial forms began to be adopted by people with different institutions.

It is only necessary to go as far as this to recognize the inefficacy of a simplistic, unilinear model of this kind. It belongs to an attitude to these questions which we were at pains to dispose of in *Household and family in past time*. For one dogma about an original Europe uniformly displaying a particular form of familial life and work it substitutes another. As a general proposition it simply will not do. The notion of reversion,

[58] Laslett (1977a): 22.

however, draws attention to an intriguing feature of the evidence. Settlements or populations with non-western familial characteristics could not only move quite far towards the western pole; they could subsequently move backwards and resume southern and eastern characteristics. In the western region itself, however, change of neither type was possible except to the strictly limited extent described by Richard Wall for England since the seventeenth century and for Britain in very recent years.

A conspicuous example of reversion of this kind has been documented in Hungary by Rudolf Andorka, and Lutz Berkner has pointed to an exactly similar example in Saxony.[59] Fagagna is to be seen moving rapidly in a 'non-western' direction in table 17.4. The great interest of such circumstances as these is that they fasten our attention on the character of the principles which inform such behaviour, and on the position of these principles in the cultures concerned in the social structures themselves.

A cultural element in the shaping of the domestic group organization both as to production and reproduction seems inescapable. There seems to be no reason whatever in the present state of our knowledge to prefer an original cultural unity over our continent in these respects over an original pluralism. We cannot yet say whether any of the four sets of tendencies charted in table 17.5 is older than the earliest date of the documents from which its existence has been inferred. This means that we simply do not know which of them came first, or which had institutional priority. With our fragmentary data and our imperfect understanding of their meaning, and our very clumsy instruments of measurement and analysis, we can have little confidence that the range of possibilities has been covered. There seems to be no point in speculating about an archaic Mediterranean tradition, along with a German and perhaps a Slavic, independent in their origins but contending with and influencing each other over the centuries in a way which would produce the four sets of tendencies which have been distinguished.[60] We cannot even be confident that when we observe a change from one column to another in table 17.5 the reasons for it were necessarily of a 'developmental' character, nor can we be sure of how cultural diffusion or imitation might come about.

What we do know about the relationship of historical change to

---

[59] Andorka, 'Peasant family structure' (1976a) and Berkner, 'Inheritance, land tenure and peasant family structure' (1976). See also Laslett (1978a): 106n, with a further reference to a similar case for Estonia.

[60] Compare Macfarlane (1981).

family forms in historic Europe is that the western set of tendencies makes two appearances in the story. It has as much claim as any of the others to be 'original' in the sense just laid down, but it also appears as the end, the goal, of 'developmental' history. There is a sense, then, in which the end was present at the very beginning. This must have been so in ninth-century Bavaria if the production of cloth, almost universally associated with the familial work group in traditional times, was organized there in a non-familial, factory-like fashion. Here we have a telling illustration of a point made repeatedly in this essay, that work organization and domestic organization properly so called were contingently rather than necessarily related. This was so in spite of the content of patriarchal ideology, and in spite of the fact that it was usually convenient at all times and in all places to take advantage of familial relationships and of domestic premises for productive purposes.

There are two connected generalizations which seem at present likely to survive discussion. One is that the inability of the domestic group to control its own labour tended to lead to a western-type procreative and kinship organization in the group itself, although it was also the case that entirely independent domestic groups, wholly in control of their resources, could show forth such an organization, as they certainly did in northern and western Europe. The second generalization is that western familial tendencies may themselves have disposed towards factory industrialization. This seems to have been so however we place proto-industrialization in the historical account. Directly industrial culture of a factory kind established itself in the world, however, western institutions, the western domestic group amongst the rest, became the subject of imitation, of mimesis, on the part of societies anxious to industrialize themselves. It would seem that the spread of industrial culture has become, at least to some, a matter of cultural diffusion.

The so-called convergence theory, whereby all 'advanced' countries inevitably take on the same western-type institutional forms, is not our subject here. For us the point of importance is that the Japanese, the Russians, or even the Italians and the Poles, in so far as they have adopted industrialism as a way of life, may not be in the same position in respect of the industrial culture as the west Europeans themselves. The evidence we have surveyed would seem to imply that neo-local tendencies were never part and parcel of the historical social structure of these societies as they have been for the west Europeans. It is not impossible, therefore, that there will come a time when one or other of them may revert in the way we have described. It is already apparent that various types of social structure can exist alongside established industrialization, even if it may also be true that only one particular social structure could give rise to industrialization in the first place. This brings us back once again to the question of where in cultural or national life such behaviour-regulating, behaviour-defining principles do in fact belong.

Until we can understand this problem — and the effort of comprehension could be called one of the most demanding of all the challenges faced by historical sociology — we shall not be able to get much further with the final questions raised by family and household as work group and kin group in traditional Europe. The multiplication of comparative cases, the pushing back of the frontiers of our knowledge in time, and a general familiarization with analytic problems of this type will no doubt help us a great deal. But the final questions faced by social scientists, as all of them are very well aware, are not easily susceptible of final solutions.

APPENDIX
Model tables for analysing families, households, and housefuls

Prepared by Peter Laslett, Richard Wall, and Jean Robin of the SSRC Cambridge Group for the History of Population and Social Structure

Section A. Population and domestic group divisions

A1 Population by sex and marital status
A2 Population by age and sex
A3 Marital status of population by age and sex
A4 Conjugal family units, households, housefuls by size
A5 Count of individuals in conjugal family units, households, and housefuls
A6 Distribution of households by age and sex of members
A7 Membership of household and houseful
A8 Dual roles
A9 Visitors and persons of unspecified relationship to the household head

Section B. Composition of domestic groups

B1 Marital status of heads of households
B2 Size of households by age of heads
B3 Household structure: households by kin composition

B4   Household structure: household types by presence or absence of servants and inmates

B5   Household structure: households by conjugal family units

B6   Generational span of households

B7   Numbers of persons in or attached to households of various types by relationship to household head

B8   Distribution of individuals by household type and by age

B9   Household types by age of head

B10   Households with resident servants by age and sex of household head and by household type

B11   Households with attached inmates by age and sex of household head and by household type

B12   Individuals by sex and in age groups by relationship to household head

B13   Age gap between spouses

B14   Household structure: augmentation

B15   Age-specific headship rates by marital status: male heads of households

B16   Age-specific headship rates by marital status: female heads of households

Section C. Children

C1   Children in households and familial inmate groups

C2   Resident offspring: count of offspring by marital status of parent(s)

C3   Resident offspring: size of offspring group by marital status of parent(s)

C4   Resident offspring by sex and marital status of parent(s)

C5   Resident offspring: numbers and proportions

C6   Households with resident offspring of head by age and sex of head

C7   Age of father by ages of resident offspring

C8   Age of mother by ages of resident offspring

C9   Bastards, bastard-begetters, and bastard-bearers

C10   Familial position of bastards

C11   Orphans and one-parent families (excluding bastards)

Section D. Elderly and widowed persons

D1   Familial position of widowed persons

D2   Familial position of elderly persons

D3   Widowed persons and their co-residents by sex

Section H. Occupational status

H1   Household heads and heads of familial inmate groups by occupational group
H2   Household heads and heads of familial inmate groups by category of social status (traditional England)
H3   Household hierarchy (traditional England)
H4   Household heads and others in or attached to the household, by occupation and sex
H5   Working population by relationship to household head (or to head of attached familial inmate group)
H6   Working population by sex and marital status
H7   Households by working and dependent persons, excluding resident servants of the household
H8   Households with working males by number of working females, excluding resident servants of the household
H9   Working wives by social status of husband (traditional England)
H10 Working population by sex and age
H11 Distribution of working population by sex and age in households
H12 Ages of those in specified occupations
H13 Working wives by age
H14 Working wives by number and age of resident offspring
H15 Working male offspring by social status of parent (traditional England)
H16 Working female offspring by social status of parent (traditional England)

Section I. Migration

I1   Distance between place of birth and place of residence by marital status and sex
I2   Birthplaces of household members by relationship to household head; and of attached inmates

References

Åkerman, S., Johansen, H. C., and Gaunt, D. (eds.), 1978. *Chance and change: social and economic studies in historical demography in the Baltic area.* Odense.

Aleksandrov, V. A., 1976. *Selskaia obschina v Rossii (xvii – nachalo xix v.).* Moscow.

Aleksandrov, V. A. (ed.), 1967. *Russkie: istoriko–etnograficheskii atlas: karty.* Moscow.

Alföldy, G., 1974. *Noricum.* London.

Anderson, M., 1971. *Family structure in nineteenth century Lancashire.* Cambridge.

Andorka, R., 1971. 'La prévention des naissances en Hongrie dans la région d'Ormànsàg depuis la fin du XVIIIᵉ siècle'. *Population,* 26, 1: 63–78.

  1972. 'Un exemple de faible fécondité légitime dans une région de la Hongrie. L'Ormànsàg à la fin du XVIIIᵉ siècle et au début du XIXᵉ: contrôle des naissances ou faux-semblants?' *Annales de Démographie Historique*: 25–53.

  1976a. 'The peasant family structure in the eighteenth and nineteenth centuries (data from Alsónyék and Kölked in international comparison)'. *Acta Ethnographica Academiae Scientarum Hungaricae,* 25, 3–4: 321–48.

  1976b. 'Fertility, nuptiality and household structure of peasant communities of Hungary in the XVIIIth–XIXth centuries'. Paper presented at the colloquium on agrarian structure and regional development in the XIXth century, Gödöllö.

  n.d. 'Micro-demographic researches in Hungary (family reconstitution and types of household structure)'. Mimeographed.

Andrásfalvy, B., 1973. 'Ellentétes értékrendek összeütközése és a polgárosodás' [The collision of contradictory value systems and the development of embourgeoisement]. *Tiszatáj,* 27, 8: 105–10.

Angeli, A., and Belletini, A., 1979. 'Strutture familiari nella campagna Bolognese a meta' dell'Ottocento.' *Genus,* 35, 3–4: 155–72.

Arrivabene, G., 1843. *Sur la condition des laboureurs et des ouvriers belges.* Brussels.

Austria, Diocesan Archive, St Pölten. Beschreibung der Seelen in der Stadtpfarre Gmünd, 1801f.

  Diocesan Archive, St Pölten. Seelenbeschreibung der Pfarre Maria Langegg.

  Diocesan Archive, St Pölten. Seelenbeschreibung der Pfarre Rappoltenkirchen, 1842f.

Parish Archive, Andrichsfurt. Seelenbeschreibungen der Pfarre Andrichsfurt, 1813f.

Ay, K.-L. (ed.), 1974. *Dokumente zur Geschichte von Staat und Gesellschaft in Bayern*, I, 1. Munich.

Baklanova, E. N., 1976. *Krestianskii dvor i obshchina na russkom Severe: konets XVII – nachalo XVIII v.* Moscow.

Baltic Provinces, 1884. *Ergebnisse der baltischen Volkszählung von 29 December 1881*, vol. III. Riga.

Livland Statistical Committee, 1885. *Materialien zur Kenntnis der livländischen Agrarverhältnisse*. Riga.

Baranowski, B., 1958. *Gospodarstwo chłopskie i folwarczne we wschodniej Wielkopolsce w XVIII w.* [The peasant and the demesne: farming in Eastern Great Poland in the eighteenth century]. Warsaw.

Baranowski, B., Bartyś, J., and Sobczak, T. (eds.), 1958–63. *Instrukcje gospodarcze dla dóbr magnackich i szlacheckich z XVII– XIX w.* [Economic instructions for the estates of the nobility during the seventeenth and eighteenth centuries]. I, Wrocław; II, Wrocław–Warsaw–Cracow.

Barclay, G. W., 1954. *Colonial development and population in Taiwan*. Princeton.

Barclay, G. W., Coale, A. J., Stoto, M. A., and Trussel, T. J., 1976. 'A reassessment of the demography of traditional China'. *Population Index*, 42, 4: 606–35.

Barnes, J. A., 1967. 'Genealogies'. In: A. L. Epstein (ed.), *The craft of social anthropology*. London.

Barnes, R., and Durant, M., 1970. 'Pilot work on the General Household Survey'. Held by Cambridge University Library, OP 1100 20 013(1).

Bárth, J., 1975. 'Fajsz népessége a 18. század közepén' [The population of Fajsz in the middle of the eighteenth century]. In: *Bács-Kiskun megye multjából*, I: 81–131. Kecskemét.

Bartmuss, H.-J., 1964. 'Die Genesis der Feudalgesellschaft in Deutschland: Bemerkungen zu einigen neuen Hypothesen von E. Müller-Mertens'. *Zeitschrift für Geschichtswissenschaft*, 13: 1001–10.

Bartyś, J., 1958. *See* Baranowski *et al.* (eds.), 1958–63.

Bavaria, Hauptstaatsarchiv, Munich. Trad. Regensburg: St Emmeram, Lit. 5 1/3.

Belgium, Rijksarchief, Bruges. Volkstelling 1815, no. 101.

Rijksarchief, Bruges. Gemeentearchief Lampernisse, no. 244 (1824), no. 245 (1826), no. 246 (1829).

Vlaamse Vereniging voor Familiekunde, afdeling Brugge, 1976–7. *Volkstelling 1814*, vols. I, III, V. Bruges.

Belletini, A., 1979. *See* Angeli and Belletini, 1979.

Benson, B. W., 1980. 'Mortality variation in the north of England, 1851–60 to 1901–10'. Unpublished Ph.D. thesis, Johns Hopkins University.

Berkner, L. K., 1972a. 'The stem family and the development cycle of the peasant household'. *American Historical Review*, 77, 2: 398–418.

1972b. 'Rural family organisation in Europe: a problem in comparative history'. *Peasant Studies Newsletter*, 1, 4: 145–56.

1973. 'Family, social structure and rural industry: a comparative study of the

Waldviertel and the Pays de Caux in the eighteenth century'. Unpublished Ph.D. thesis, Harvard University.

1975. 'The use and misuse of census data for the historical analysis of family structure'. *Journal of Interdisciplinary History*, 5, 4: 721–38.

1976. 'Inheritance, land tenure and peasant family structure: a German regional comparison'. In: Goody, Thirsk, and Thompson (eds.), 1976.

Berkner, L. K., and Mendels, F., 1978. 'Inheritance system, family structure and demographic patterns in western Europe, 1700–1900'. In: C. Tilly (ed.), 1978.

Berkner, L. K., and Shaffer, J. W., 1978. 'The joint family in the Nivernais'. *Journal of Family History*, 3, 2: 150–62.

Bielenstein, A., 1897. 'Art und Geschichte lettischen Siedlung'. *Baltische Monatsschrift*, 44. Reval.

Bitterauf, Th. (ed.), 1905–9. *Die Traditionen des Hochstifts Freising.* (Quellen und Erörterungen zur bayerischen Geschichte, n.s., 4 and 5.) 2 vols. Munich.

Blomkvist, E. E., and Gantskaia, O. A., 1967. 'Tipy russkogo krestianskogo zhilishcha serediny XIX – nachala XX v.'. In: Aleksandrov (ed.), 1967.

Blum, J., 1978. *The end of the old order in rural Europe.* Princeton.

Blumfeldt, E., 1931. 'Jooni taaniaegse Saaremaa agraarajaloost'. *Ajalooline Ajakiri*, 10, 1: 15–30; 2: 78–100.

Bobińska, C. (ed.), 1957. *Studia z dziejów wsi małopolskiej w drugiej połowie XVIII w.* [Studies in the history of the countryside of Little Poland during the second half of the eighteenth century]. Warsaw.

Boretius, A. (ed.), 1883. 'Brevium exempla ad describendas res ecclesiasticas et fiscales'. In: *Monumenta Germaniae historica: capitularia regum Francorum*, 1, no. 128. Hanover.

Bosl, K., 1975. 'Die "familia" als Grundstruktur der mittelalterlichen Gesellschaft'. *Zeitschrift für Bayerische Landesgeschichte*, 38: 403–24.

Boutruche, R., 1968. *Seigneurie et féodalité*, vol. I. Paris.

Braun, R., 1978. 'Early industrialization and demographic change in the Canton of Zürich'. In: C. Tilly (ed.), 1978.

Bresslau, H. (ed.), 1934. 'Annales s. Emmerammi maiores'. In: *Monumenta Germaniae historica: scriptores*, 30, pt 2. Leipzig.

Briavoinne, N., 1839. *De l'industrie en Belgique: causes de décadence et de prospérité*, vol. II. Brussels.

Brodsky-Elliot, V., 1978. 'Mobility and marriage in pre-industrial England'. Unpublished Ph.D. thesis, Cambridge University.

Bruckner, A. (ed.), 1949. *Regesta Alsatiae aevi Merovingici et Karolini (496–918)*, vol. I. Strasbourg–Zürich.

Brunner, O., 1968. *Neue Wege der Verfassungs und Sozialgeschichte.* Göttingen.

Buck, J. L. (ed.), 1937. *Land utilization in China.* Nanking.

Burch, T. K., 1972. 'Some demographic determinants of average household size: an analytical approach'. In: P. Laslett and Wall (eds.), 1972.

Butlin, R. A. (ed.), 1978. *See* Dodgshon and Butlin (eds.), 1978.

Byrnes, R. F. (ed.), 1976. *See* Mosely, 1943 *and* 1954.

Caro, G., 1902. 'Zwei Elsässer Dörfer zur Zeit Karls des Grossen'. *Zeitschrift für Geschichte des Oberrheins*, n.s., 17: 450–79, 563–87.

Carter, A. T., 1981. 'Household histories'. Unpublished paper presented to the Wenner-Gren Foundation symposium 'Households: changing form and function', New York.

Cederlund, C. O., 1964. 'Undantagsinstitutionen i Mönsterås socken 1860–1960'. *Stranda härads hembygdsföreningsårsbok*: 19–48.

Census, national. See under respective countries.

Charpentier, A., 1895. *Om sytning*. Helsinki.

Chayanov, A. V., 1966. *The theory of peasant economy*, ed. D. Thorner, B. Kerblay, and R. E. F. Smith. Homewood, Ill.

Chernenkov, N. N., 1905. *Kharakteristika krestianskogo khoziaistva*. Moscow.

Christensen, J. T., 1928. 'De gamles forsørgelse i forrige aarhundrede aftaegtsforholdets ordning i landbohjemmene'. *Aarbok for historiske Samfund for Sorø Amt*, 16: 69–95.

Chudacoff, H. P., 1978. 'Newlyweds and family extension'. In: Hareven and Vinovskis (eds.), 1978.

Clark, A., 1919. *The working life of women in the seventeenth century*. London.

Clarke, M., 1972. See P. Laslett and Clarke, 1972.

Coale, A. J., 1976. See Barclay et al., 1976.

    1979. See Goldman, Coale, and Weinstein, 1979.

Coale, A. J. et al. (eds.), 1965. See Levy, 1965.

Cole, J. W., and Wolf, E. R., 1974. *The hidden frontier*. New York.

Conze, W. (ed.), 1976. See Medick, 1976a *and* Mitterauer, 1976.

Corsica, Observatoire Economique d'Ajaccio, 1979. *Economie corse*. Ajaccio.

Costenoble, E., 1978. 'De bevolking van Adinkerke in de 19de eeuw'. *Handelingen van het Genootschup voor Geschiedenis te Brugge*, 115: 103–45.

Cuisenier, J. (ed.), 1977. *The family life cycle in European societies*. Paris.

Curschmann, F., 1900. *Hungersnöte im Mittelalter: ein Beitrag zur deutschen Wirtschaftsgeschichte des 8. bis 13. Jahrhunderts*. (Leipziger Studien aus dem Gebiet der Geschichte, 6, no. 1.) Leipzig.

Ćwiek, Z., 1966. *Z dziejów wsi koronnej XVII w.* [From the history of the royal estates of the seventeenth century]. Warsaw.

Czap, P., 1978. 'Marriage and the peasant joint family in Russia'. In: Ransel (ed.), 1978.

    1982. 'The perennial multiple family household, Mishino, Russia, 1782–1858'. *Journal of Family History*, 7, 1: 5–26.

Dal, V., 1956. *Tolkovyi slovar*. 4 vols. Moscow.

Dale, T. C., 1931. *The inhabitants of London in 1638*. London.

Dalle, D., 1964. 'De bevolking van de stad en van de Kasselrij Veurne in 1796'. In: *1964 Album Archivaris Jas de Smet*. Bruges.

Dandekar, K., and Unde, D. B., n.d. 'Size and composition of households'. *Census of India 1961*, I, monograph no. 9. New Delhi.

Dandekar, V. M., and Pethe, V., 1960. 'Size and composition of rural families'. *Artha Vijñana*, 2, 3: 189–99.

Dannenbauer, H., 1958. *Grundlagen der mittelalterlichen Welt*. Stuttgart.

Dannheimer, H., 1974. 'Aus der Siedlungsarchäologie des frühen Mittelalters in Bayern'. In: *Studien zur Vor- und Frühgeschichtlichen Archäologie: Festschrift für Joachim Werner*, 2. Munich.

Dányi, D., 1965. 'Városi háztartások és családok a. 18 század végén, Győr, 1787' [Urban families and households at the end of the eighteenth century]. In: *Történeti Statisztikai Évkönyv 1963–1964*: 73–109. Budapest.

1977. 'Háztartás és család nagysága és strukturája az iparosodás előtt Magyarországon' [Size and structure of family and household in pre-industrial Hungary]. *Történeti Statisztikai Tanulmányok*, 3: 5–104.

Dávid, Z., 1973. *A családok nagysága és összetétele a veszprémi püspökség területén 1747–1748* [Size and composition of families in the diocese of Veszprém 1747–1748]. Budapest.

Davies, D., 1795. *The case of the labourers in husbandry stated and considered*. Bath.

Davis, J., 1977. *People of the Mediterranean*. London.

Davis, K., 1955. 'Institutional patterns favouring high fertility in under-developed areas'. *Eugenics Quarterly*, 2: 33–9.

Demonet, M., 1972. *See* Klapisch and Demonet, 1972.

Den, V. E., 1902. *Naselenie Rossii po piatoi revizii*. 2 vols. Moscow.

Desportes, P., 1966. 'La population de Reims au XVe siècle'. *Le Moyen Age*, 21: 463–509.

Diderot, D., 1765. *L'encyclopédie ou dictionnaire raisonné des sciences, des arts et des métiers*. 17 vols. Paris.

Diepolder, G. (ed.), 1969. *Bayerischer Geschichtsatlas*. Munich.

Dobrowolski, K., 1933. *Włościańskie rozporządzenia ostatniej woli na Podhalu w XVII i XVIII w.* [Peasants' wills in the Podhale region during the seventeenth and eighteenth centuries]. Cracow.

Dodgshon, R. A., and Butlin, R. A. (eds.), 1978. *An historical geography of England and Wales*. London–New York.

Dollinger, P., 1949. *L'évolution des classes rurales en Bavière depuis la fin de l'époque carolingienne jusqu'au milieu du XIIIe siecle*. (Publications de la Faculté des Lettres de l'Université de Strasbourg, 112.) Paris.

Drake, M., 1969. *Population and society in Norway*. Cambridge.

Drake, M., and Barker, T. C. (eds.), 1982. *Population and society in Britain 1850–1950*. London.

Dronke, E. F. J. (ed.), 1844. *Traditiones et antiquitates Fuldenses*. Fulda.

Duby, G., 1968. *Rural economy and country life in the medieval West*. London.

Duceptiaux, E., 1855. 'Budgets économiques des classes ouvrières en Belgique'. *Bulletin de la Commission Centrale de Statistique*, 6: 201–438, 441–595.

Duclos, A., 1910. *Bruges: histoire et souvenirs*. Bruges.

Dunsdorfs, E., 1950. 'Der grosse schwedische Kataster in Livland 1681–1710'. *Kunglig Vitterhets- Historie- och Antikvitets-Akademiens Handlingar*, 72.

Dupâquier, J., 1979. *La population rurale du bassin parisien à l'époque de Louis XIV*. Lille.

Ebery, M., and Preston, B., 1976. *Domestic service in late Victorian and Edwardian England*. (Reading University Department of Geography, Geographical Papers, 42.)

Eden, Sir Frederick, 1797. *State of the poor.* 3 vols. London.

Efimenko, A. Ia., 1884. *Issledovaniia narodnoi zhizni.* Moscow.

Elklit, J., 1978. 'Household structure in Denmark 1769 – *ca.* 1890'. In: Akerman, Johansen, and Gaunt (eds.), 1978.

Epstein, A. L. (ed.), 1967. *See* J. A. Barnes, 1967.

Estonian Soviet Socialist Republic, Central Historical State Archive (ENSV RAKA), Tartu. Fond 1864, list 2, file IV–9; st. u. V–64.

Eversley, D. E. C. (ed.), 1965. *See* Glass and Eversley (eds.), 1965.

Falniowska-Gradowska, A., and Rychlikowa, I. (eds.), 1962–3. *Lustracje województwa krakowskiego, 1789* [The inventory of royal estates of Cracow Province of 1789]. Warsaw–Cracow.

Faragó, T., 1975. 'Household structure of Nagykovácsi in the eighteenth century'. Unpublished manuscript.

1976. 'Household structure and rural society in pre-industrial Hungary'. Paper presented at the colloquium on agrarian structure and regional development in the XIXth century, Gödöllö.

1977. 'Háztartásszerkezet és falusi társadalom-fejlődés Magyarországon 1787–1828' [Structure of households and development of rural society in Hungary 1787–1828]. *Történeti Statisztikai Tanulmányok,* 3: 105–214.

Fastlinger, M., 1902. *Die wirthschaftliche Bedeutung der bayerischen Klöster in der Zeit der Agilulfinger.* Freiburg i. B.

Fauve-Chamoux, A. (*née* Chamoux), 1972. 'La reconstitution des familles: espoirs et réalités'. *Annales: Economies, Sociétés, Civilisations,* 27, 4–5: 1083–90.

1973. 'L'enfance abandonée à Rheims'. *Annales de Démographie Historique,* 263–85.

1974. 'Town and child in eighteenth century Rheims'. *Local Population Studies,* 13: 45–6.

Feigl, H., 1967. 'Bäuerliches Erbrecht und Erbgewohnheiten in Niederösterreich'. *Jahrbuch für Landeskunde von Niederösterreich,* n.s., 37: 161–83.

Fél, E., 1944. *A nagycsalád és jogszokásai a Komárom megyei Martoson.* Budapest.

1948. *A magyar népi társadalom életének kutatása* [The study of the life of Hungarian peasant society]. Budapest.

Fél, E., and Hofer, T., 1967. *Arányok és mértékek az átányi gazdálkodásban és háztartásban* [Proportions and measures in the production and households of Átány]. Budapest.

1969. *Proper peasants.* Chicago.

Fenomenov, M. Ia., 1925. *Sovremennaia derevnia.* 2 vols. Leningrad–Moscow.

Fick, L., 1895. *Die bäuerliche Erbfolge im rechtsrheinischen Bayern* (Münchener volkswirtschaftlichen Studien, 8). Stuttgart.

Findl, P., and Helczmanovszki, H., 1977. *The population of Austria.* Vienna.

Finlands Allmänna Tidning, 1850. 'Om sytning och dess betydelse inom Finlands gällande kreditlagstiftningen'. In: nos. 40–2.

Flandrin, J.-L., 1976. *Familles: parenté, maison, sexualité dans l'ancienne société.* Paris. Translated as Flandrin 1979.

1979. *Families in former times: kinship, household and sexuality.* Cambridge.

Forsell, T., 1887. *Uudenmaan läänin itäinen puoli.* Helsinki.

Fortes, M., 1958. 'Introduction'. In: Goody (ed.), 1958.

France, Institut National de la Statistique et des Etudes Economiques. *Census of France, 1975.* Regional volumes. Paris. *See also* Corsica.

Freedman, M. (ed.), 1970. *See* Taeuber, 1970.

Fuchs, V. R., 1980. *See* Michael, Fuchs, and Scott, 1980.

Ganshof, F. L., 1949. 'Manorial organization in the Low Countries in the seventh, eighth and ninth centuries'. *Transactions of the Royal Historical Society,* 4th ser., 31: 29–59.

Gantskaia, O. A., 1967. *See* Blomkvist and Gantskaia, 1967.

Gaunt, D., 1977. 'I slottets skugga: om frälsebönders sociala problem i Borgeby och Löddeköpinge under 1700–talet'. *Ale,* 15–30.

Gaunt, D. (ed.), 1978. *See* Åkerman, Johansen, and Gaunt (eds.), 1978.

Gebhard, T., 1962. 'Zur Frage der frühen dörflichen Siedlungen in Bayern'. In: *Aus Bayerns Frühzeit: Friedrich Wagner zum 75. Geburtstag.* (Schriftenreihe zur bayerischen Landesgeschichte, 62.) Munich.

German Democratic Republic, 1974. *Statistisches Jahrbuch 1974 der Deutschen Demokratischen Republik.* Berlin.

Gieysztorowa, I., 1976. *Wstęp do demografii staropolskiej* [Introduction to Polish historical demography]. Warsaw.

Glass, D. V., and Eversley, D. E. C. (eds.), 1965. *Population in history: essays in historical demography.* London.

Goldman, N., Coale, A. J., and Weinstein, M., 1979. 'The quality of data in the Nepal fertility survey'. *World Fertility Survey Scientific Reports,* 6.

Goldschmidt, W., and Kunkel, E., 1971. 'The structure of the peasant family'. *American Anthropologist,* 73: 1058–76.

Gomme, G. L., 1890. 'A Highland folk-talc'. *Folklore:* p. 197.

Goody, J., 1976. *Production and reproduction.* Cambridge.

Goody, J. (ed.), 1958. *The developmental cycle in domestic groups.* Cambridge.

Goody, J., Thirsk, J., and Thompson, E. P. (eds.), 1976. *Family and inheritance: rural society in western Europe, 1200–1800.* Cambridge.

Götz, W., 1895. *Geographisch-historisches Handbuch von Bayern,* vol. I. Munich.

Granberg, G., 1934. 'Släktklubban'. *Budkavlan,* 13: 1–13.

Graunt, J., 1662. *Natural and political observations upon the Bills of Mortality.* Repr. in P. Laslett (ed.), 1973.

Gray, P. G., 1947. 'The British household: based on an enquiry carried out in April 1947'. Held by Cambridge University Library, OP 1100 92 02(B).

Great Britain. *See* United Kingdom.

Gutmann, F., 1906. *Die soziale Gliederung der Bayern zur Zeit des Volksrechtes.* (Abhandlungen aus dem staatswissenschaftlichen Seminar zu Strassburg i. E., 20.) Strasbourg.

Habermann, G., 1908. 'Das bäuerliche Ausgedinge und sein Ersatz'. *Zeitschrift für Volkswirtschaft, Sozialpolitik und Verwaltung,* 17: 617–36.

Haegen, H. van de, 1979. 'Bronnen voor de reconstructie van de agrarische struktuur: landschap, bedrijuen, huur – en eigendomsverhaudingen in

Vlaanderen'. In: *Bronnen voor de historische geografie van Belgie*. Transactions of the Brussels colloquium 25–7 April 1979.

Hajnal, J., 1953. 'Age at marriage and proportions marrying'. *Population Studies*, 7, 2: 111–36.

1965. 'European marriage patterns in perspective'. In: Glass and Eversley (eds.), 1965.

Halpern, J., 1972. 'Town and countryside in Serbia in the nineteenth century'. In: P. Laslett and Wall (eds.), 1972.

Halpern, J., and Halpern, B. K., 1972. *A Serbian village in historical perspective*. New York.

Hammel, E. A., 1972. 'The zadruga as process'. In: P. Laslett and Wall (eds.), 1972.

1978. *See* Wachter, Hammel, and Laslett, 1978.

1980. 'Household structure in fourteenth-century Macedonia'. *Journal of Family History*, 5, 3: 242–73.

1981. 'On the XX of investigating household functions'. Unpublished paper presented to the Wenner-Gren Foundation symposium 'Households: changing form and function', New York.

Hammel, E. A., and Laslett, P., 1974. 'Comparing household structure over time and between cultures'. *Comparative Studies in Society and History*, 16: 73–103.

Hanley, S. B., and Yamamura, K., 1977. *Economic and demographic change in pre-industrial Japan, 1600–1868*. Princeton.

Hansen, H. O., 1975. *Population census 1729 in three counties*. (Statistics of Iceland, II, 59.) Reykjavík.

Hareven, T. K., 1977. 'Family time and historical time'. *Daedalus*, Spring: 57–70.

1978a. 'Cycles, courses and cohorts: reflections on theoretical and methodological approaches to the historical study of family development'. *Journal of Social History*, 12: 97–109.

1978b. 'The search for generational memory: tribal rites in industrial society'. *Daedalus*, 107: 137–49.

Hareven, T. K. (ed.), 1977. *Family and kin in urban communities, 1700–1930*. New York.

Hareven, T. K., and Vinovskis, M. (eds.), 1978. *Family and population in nineteenth century America*. Princeton.

Harris, C. (ed.), 1979. *See* R. M. Smith, 1979a.

Harrison, S., 1977. *See* Macfarlane with Harrison and Jardine, 1977.

Hasselberg, G., 1955–76. 'Flatföring'. In: *Kulturhistorisk lexikon för nordisk medeltid*, vol. IV. Malmö.

Hausen, R. (ed.), 1881. *Dombok för sydvästra Tavastland 1506–1510*. (Bidrag till Finlands historia.) Helsinki.

Hauthaler, W. (ed.), 1910–16. *Salzburger Urkundenbuch*, vols. I–II. Salzburg.

Haxthausen, A. von, 1972. *Studies on the interior of Russia*, ed. S. Frederick Starr. Chicago.

Heers, J., 1974. *Le clan familial au moyen age*. Paris.

Heinzelmann, M., 1977. 'Beobachtungen zur Bevölkerungsstruktur einiger grundherrschaftlicher Siedlungen im karolingischen Bayern'. *Frühmittelalterliche Studien*, 11: 202–17.

Helczmanovszki, H., 1977. *See* Findl and Helczmanovszki, 1977.

Helczmanovszki, H. (ed.), 1973. *See* Mitterauer, 1973.

Hélin, E., 1970. 'Les codes socio-professionnels comme instruments d'analyse des populations antérieures à la révolution industrielle'. *Annales du XLI Congrès de la Féderation Archaeologique et Historique de Belgique*, 357–66. Malines.

1979. 'Profession et statut social'. In: M. L. Marcilio and H. Charbonneau (eds.), *Démographie historique*. Paris.

Helland-Hansen, K., 1955–76. 'Kår'. In: *Kulturhistorisk lexikon för nordisk medeltid*, vol. X. Malmö.

Hemmer, R., 1932. 'Vad förstår Östgötalagen med en gävträl?' *Tidskrift utgiven av Juridiska Föreningen i Finland*, 68: 229–37.

Herbst, S. (ed.), 1974. *Społeczenstwo gospordarka, kultura: studia ofiarowane M. Małowistowi w czterdziestolenci: pracy naukowej*. Warsaw.

Herlihy, D., 1978. 'Medieval children'. In: *Essays on Medieval Civilization* (The Walter Prescott Webb Memorial Lectures), XII: 109–41. Austin.

Herlihy, D., and Klapisch-Zuber, C., 1978. *Les Toscans et leurs familles: une étude du catasto florentin de 1427*. Paris.

Heuwieser, M. (ed.), 1930. *Die Traditionen des Hochstifts Passau*. (Quellen und Erörterungen zur bayerischen Geschichte, n.s., 6.) Munich.

Hilton, R., 1974. 'Some social and economic evidence in late medieval English tax returns'. In: Herbst (ed.), 1974.

Hobcraft, J., and Rees, P. (eds.), 1977. *Regional demographic development*. London.

Hofer, T., 1967. *See* Fél and Hofer, 1967.

1969. *See* Fél and Hofer, 1969.

Högnäs, H., 1938. *Sytning och arvslösen i den folkliga sedvänjan uti Pedersöre- och Nykarlebybygden 1810–1914*. Turku.

Hole, W. V., and Pountney, M. T., 1971. *Trends in population, housing and occupancy rates 1861–1961*. London, H.M.S.O.

Hollander, A. N. J. den, 1960–1. 'The great Hungarian plain: a European frontier'. *Comparative Studies in Society and History*, 3: 74–88, 155–67.

Holmes, S. S., 1976. 'Gregory King and the social structure of pre-industrial England'. *Transactions of the Royal Historical Society*: 41–68.

Homans, G., 1941. *English villagers of the thirteenth century*. Cambridge, Mass.

Horáček, C., 1904. *Das Ausgedinge, eine agrarpolitische Studie mit besonderer Berücksichtigung der böhmischen Länder* (Wiener staatswissenschaftliche Studien, V: 1). Vienna.

Houlte, J. van, 1977. *An economic history of the Low Countries, 800–1800*. New York.

Houtte, H. van, 1920. *Histoire économique de la Belgique à la fin de l'Ancien Régime*. Ghent.

Hovdhaugen, E., 1962. 'Frå det gamle bondesamfunnet i Gudbrandsdalen, den gamle føderådsskipnaden'. *Norveg*, 9: 1–71.

Hovstad, J., 1943. *Mannen og samfunnet: studiar i norrøn etikk*. Oslo.

574   *References*

Hufton, O., 1982. 'Women, work and marriage in eighteenth-century France'. In: Outhwaite (ed.), 1981.

Hülphers, A., 1793. *Samlingar til en Beskrifning öfwer Norrland och Gefleborgs lan, första afdelning: Gestrikland.* Västerås.

Hume, D., 1875. 'Of the populousness of ancient nations'. In: Hume, *Essays: moral, political and literary,* vol. I, ed. T. H. Green and T. H. Grose. London.

Hungary, Library of the Central Statistical Office and Archives Section of the Education Ministry, 1960. *Az első magyarországi népszámlálás (1784–1787)* [The first Hungarian census 1784–1787]. Budapest.

Iceland, Statistical Bureau of Iceland, 1960. *Manntalid 1703.* Reykjavík.

Statistics of Iceland, 1975. *See* Hansen, 1975.

Ilvonen, J. H., 1888. *Maataloudellisista oloista Kuopion läänin Karjalan osassa paitsi Kaavin pitäjää.* Helsinki.

Inama von Sternegg, K. T., 1879. *Deutsche Wirthschaftsgeschichte bis zum Schluss der Karolingerperiode,* vol. I. Leipzig.

India, 1951. *Census of India,* vol. I: *India.* New Delhi.

Jardine, C., 1977. *See* Macfarlane with Harrison and Jardine, 1977.

Johansen, H. C., 1975. *Befolkningsudvikling og familiestruktur i det 18 århundrede.* Odense.

Johansen, H. C. (ed.), 1978. *See* Åkerman, Johansen, and Gaunt (eds.), 1978.

Johansen, P., 1925. 'Siedlung und Agrarwesen der Esten im Mittelalter'. *Verhandlungen der Gelehrten Estnischen Gesellschaft,* 23. Dorpat.

1937. *Eesti majandusajalugu,* vol. I. Tartu.

Jones, E. L. (ed.), 1975. *See* Parker and Jones (eds.), 1975.

Jutikkala, E., 1942. *Suomen talonpojan historia.* Porvoo–Helsinki.

1963. *Bonden i Finland genom tiderna.* Stockholm.

Juul, S., 1940. *Faellig og hovedlod: studier over formueforholdet mellem Aegtefaeller i tiden før Christian V's Danske lov.* Copenhagen.

1955–76. 'Fledføring'. In: *Kulturhistorisk lexikon för nordisk medeltid,* vol. IV. Malmö.

Kabir, M., 1980. *The demographic characteristics of household populations.* (World Fertility Survey, Comparative Studies, 6.)

Kabuzan, V. M., 1959. 'Materialy revizii kak istochnik po istorii naseleniia Rossii XVIII-pervoi poloviny XIX v. 1718–1858 gg.' *Istoriia SSSR,* 5: 128–40.

1963. *Narodonaselenie Rossii v XVII-pervoi polovine XIX vv. (po materialam revizii).* Moscow.

Kakhk, Iu. Iu., and Uibu, Kh. E., 1977. 'K voprosu o sotsialnoi strukture semi i mobilnosti krestianstva v Estonii vo vtoroi chetverti XIX v.' In: *Problemy Istoricheskoi Demografii SSSR:* 148–55. Tallinn.

Keckowa, A., and Pałucki, W. (eds.), 1955–7. *Księgi Referendarii Koronnej z drugiej połowy XVIII wieku* [Records of the Royal Court of royal estates of the second half of the eighteenth century]. 2 vols. Warsaw.

Kent, F. W., 1977. *Household and lineage in Renaissance Florence.* Princeton.

Kerblay, B. (ed.), 1966. *See* Chayanov, 1966.

Keyserling, P. E. von, 1805. *Beschreibung der Provinz Kurland.* Mitau.

King, G. *See* P. Laslett (ed.), 1973.

Kiviahlo, K., 1927. *Maatalouskiinteistöjen omistajanvaihdokset ja hinnanmuodostus Halikon tuomiokunnassa 1851–1910*. Helsinki.

Kjellberg, S. T. (ed.), 1923. 'A. G. Barchaei resa 1772'. *Västmanlands Fornminnesforenings Årskrift*, 13: 11–110.

Klapisch, C., and Demonet, M., 1972. '"A uno vino e uno pane": la famille rurale toscane au début du XVᵉ siècle'. *Annales: Economies, Sociétés, Civilisations*, 27, 4–5: 873–901.

Klapisch-Zuber, C., 1978. *See* Herlihy and Klapisch-Zuber, 1978.

Klingsporn, A., 1965. *Beobachtungen zur Frage der bayerisch-fränkischen Beziehungen im 8. Jahrhundert*. Freiburg in Breisgau.

Knodel, J., and Maynes, M. J., 1976. 'Urban and rural marriage patterns in imperial Germany'. *Journal of Family History*, 1, 2: 129–61.

Kock, E., 1924. *Om hemföljd (förtida arv): svensk rätt tom 1734 års lag*. Lund.

König, R., 1969. 'Soziologie der Familie'. In: R. König (ed.), *Handbuch zur empirischen Sozialforschung*, 7. Stuttgart.

Kosáry, D., 1963. 'A paraszti familia kérdéséhez a 18. század elején' [On the question of the peasant family]. *Agrártörténeti Szemle*, 5, 1: 120–32.

Koskikallio, O., 1927. *Maatalouskiinteistöjen eläkerasituksesta Pirkkalan ja Ruoveden tuomiokunnissa vuosina 1800–1913*. Helsinki.

Kosven, M. O., 1963. *Semeinaia obschchina i patronimiia*. Moscow.

Kovalchenko, I. D., 1959. *Krestiane i krepostnoe khoziaistvo Riazanskoi i Tambovskoi gubernii v pervoi polovine xix veka*. Moscow.

Kramer, K. S., 1957. *Bauern und Bürger im nachmittelalterlichen Unterfranchen*. Würzburg.

Kriedte, P., Medick, H., and Schlumbohm, J., 1977. *Industrialisierung vor der Industrialisierung*. Göttingen. Trans. as *Industrialization before industrialization*. Cambridge, 1981.

Kuczynski, R. R., 1931. *The balance of births and deaths*. 2 vols. Washington, D.C.

Kula, W., 1956. *Szkice o manufakturach* [Essays on manufactures]. Warsaw.

1972. 'La seigneurie et la famille paysanne en Pologne au XVIIIᵉ siècle'. *Annales: Economies, Sociétés, Civilisations*, juillet–octobre: 949–58.

1976. *An economic theory of the feudal system: towards a model of the Polish economy, 1500–1800*. London.

Kunkel, E., 1971. *See* Goldschmidt and Kunkel, 1971.

Kurze, F. (ed.), 1895. 'Annales regni Francorum'. In: *Monumenta Germaniae historica: scriptores rerum Germanicarum in usum scholarium*, 6. Hanover.

Kussmaul, A., 1981. *Servants in husbandry in early-modern England*. Cambridge.

Lang, R. G., 1974. 'Social origins and social aspirations of Jacobean London merchants'. *Economic History Review*, 2nd ser., 27, 1: 28–47.

Lárusson, M. M., 1955–76a. 'Hreppr'. In: *Kulturhistorisk lexikon för nordisk medeltid*, vol. VII. Malmö.

1955–76b. 'Umagi'. In: *Kulturhistorisk lexikon för nordisk medeltid*, vol. XVII. Malmö.

Laslett, B., 1978. 'Family membership, past and present'. *Social Problems*, 25, 5: 476–90.

Laslett, P., 1969. 'Size and structure of the household in England over three centuries'. *Population Studies*, 23: 199–223.

1971. *The world we have lost*. London. Repr. 1979.

1972a. 'La famille et le ménage: approches historiques'. *Annales: Economies, Sociétés, Civilisations*, juillet–octobre: 847–72.

1972b. 'Introduction: the history of the family'. In: P. Laslett and Wall (eds.), 1972.

1972c. 'Mean household size in England since the sixteenth century'. In: P. Laslett and Wall (eds.), 1972.

1974. *See* Hammel and Laslett, 1974.

1977a. *Family life and illicit love in earlier generations*. Cambridge.

1977b. 'Characteristics of the Western family considered over time'. *Journal of Family History*, 2, 2: 89–115.

1978a. 'The stem-family hypothesis and its privileged position'. In: Wachter with Hammel and Laslett, 1978.

1978b. 'Le rôle des femmes dans l'histoire de la famille occidentale'. In: Sullerot (ed.), 1978.

1978c. *See* Wachter with Hammel and Laslett, 1978.

Laslett, P. (ed.), 1973. *The earliest classics: works by J. Graunt and G. King*. Farnborough.

Laslett, P., and Clarke, M., 1972. 'Houseful and household in an eighteenth-century Balkan city'. In: P. Laslett and Wall (eds.), 1972.

Laslett, P., Oosterveen, K., and Smith, R. M. (eds.), 1980. *Bastardy and its comparative history*. London.

Laslett, P., and Wall, R. (eds.), 1972. *Household and family in past time*. Cambridge.

Laszczenko, P. I., 1954. *Historia gospodarcza ZSRR* [An economic history of the USSR]. Trans. from the Russian 2nd edn. Warsaw.

Law, C., and Warnes, A. M., 1976. 'The changing geography of the elderly in England and Wales'. *Transactions of the Institute of British Geographers*, n.s., 1, 4: 53–71.

Le Bras, H., 1979. *Child and family: demographic developments in the OECD countries*. Paris, OECD.

Le Bras, H., and Todd, E., 1981. *L'invention de la France*. Paris.

Lehmann, H., 1965. 'Bemerkungen zur Sklaverei im frühmittelalterlichen Bayern und zu den Forschungsmethoden auf dem Gebiet germanischer Sozialgeschichte'. *Zeitschrift für Geschichtswissenschaft*, 13: 1378–87.

Lemche, J., 1940. 'Kan aftaegtskontrakter tjene til belysning af ernaerings-problemer?' *Ugeskrifter for Loger*, 102: 791–2.

Le Play, P. G. F., 1855. *Les ouvriers Européens: l'organisation des familles*. Paris. 1877–9. *Les ouvriers Européens: l'organisation des familles*. 6 vols. Tours.

Le Roy Ladurie, E., 1976. 'Family and inheritance customs in sixteenth century France'. In: Goody, Thirsk, and Thompson (eds.), 1976.

Leskiewiczowa, J., and Michalski, J. (eds.), 1954. *Supliki chłopskie XVIII w. z archiwum prymasa Michała Poniatowskiego* [Petitions of peasants of the eighteenth century from the archives of Primate Michał Poniatowski]. Warsaw.

Levine, D., 1977. *Family formation in an age of nascent capitalism*. London.

Levine, D., and Wrightson, K., 1979. *Poverty and piety in an English village –
Terling 1525–1700.* New York–London.

Levy, M. J., Jr, 1965. 'Aspects of the analysis of family structure'. In: A. J. Coale *et
al.* (eds.), *Aspects of the analysis of family structure.* Princeton.

Ligi, H., 1961. *Eesti talurahva olukord ja klassivõitlus Liivi sõja algul (1558–1561).*
Tallinn.

Lindert, P., and Williamson, J., 1980. 'English workers' living standards during
the industrial revolution: a new look'. (Department of Economics, University of California, Working Paper Series, 156.)

Linnus, J., 1975. *Maakäsitöölised Eestis 18. sajandil ja 19, sajandi algul.* Tallinn.

Lyashchenko, P. I., 1949. *History of the national economy of Russia to the 1917
Revolution.* Trans. from the Russian 1st edn. New York.

Łysiak, L. (ed.), 1965. *Księga sadowa kresu klimkowskiego, 1600–1762* [Records of
the village court of Kres Klimkowski, 1600–1762]. Warsaw.

McBride, T. M., 1976. *The domestic revolution.* London.

Macfarlane, A., 1970. *The family life of Ralph Josselin.* Cambridge.

1978. *The origins of English individualism.* Oxford.

1981. 'Demographic structures and cultural regions in Europe'. *Cambridge
Anthropology,* 6, 1: 1–17.

Macfarlane, A., with Harrison, S., and Jardine, C., 1977. *Reconstructing historical
communities.* Cambridge.

Mackeprang, E. P., 1907. 'Et brudstykke af en folketelling fra 1645' [A fragment of a census of 1645]. *Nationalokonomisk Tidskrift,* 3rd ser., 15, 3: 248–
70.

Maelen, P. H. van der, 1836. *Dictionnaire geographique de la Flandre occidentale.*
Brussels.

Mai, P., 1966. 'Der St. Emmeramer Rotulus des Güterverzeichnisses von 1031'.
Verhandlungen des Historischen Vereins von Oberpfalz und Regensburg, 106:
87–101.

Mándoki, L., 1971. 'A kölkedi népszámlálás 1816' [The conscription of Kölked
in 1816]. *Janus Pannonius Muzeum Evkönyve,* 13: 215–24.

Maynes, M. J., 1976. *See* Knodel and Maynes, 1976.

Medick, H., 1976a. 'Zur strukturellen Funktion von Haushalt und Familie im
Übergang von der traditionellen Agrargesellschaft zum industriellen Kapi-
talismus: die proto-industrielle Familienwirtschaft'. In: W. Conze (ed.),
Sozialgeschichte der Familie in der Neuzeit Europas. Stuttgart.

1976b. 'The proto-industrial family economy: the structural function of
household and family during the transition from peasant society to industrial capitalism'. *Social History,* 3: 291–315.

1977. *See* Kriedte, Medick, and Schlumbohm, 1977.

Mendels, F., 1975. 'Agriculture and peasant industry in eighteenth century
Flanders'. In: Parker and Jones (eds.), 1975.

1978a. 'La composition du ménage paysan en France au XIXe siècle: une
analyse économique du mode de production domestique'. *Annales: Economies, Sociétés, Civilisations,* 4: 780–802.

1978b. *See* Berkner and Mendels, 1978.

Miaskowski, A. von, 1884. *Das Erbrecht und die Grundeigenthumsvertheilung in Deutschen Reiche*, II: *Das Familienfideicommiss, das landwirtschaftliche Erbgut und das Anerbenrecht.* (Schriften des Vereins für Sozialpolitik, 25.) Leipzig.

1909. 'Altenteil, Altenteilsverträge'. In: *Handwörterbuch der Staatswissenschaften*, 3rd edn, vol. I. Jena.

Michael, R. T., Fuchs, V. R., and Scott, S. R., 1980. 'Changes in the propensity to live alone: 1950–1976'. *Demography*, 17, 1: 39–56.

Michalski, J. (ed.), 1954. *See* Leskiewiczowa and Michalski (eds.), 1954.

Michalski, J., Woliński, J., and Rostworowski, E. (eds.), 1955–69. *Materiały do dziejów Sejmu Czteroletniego* [Sources for the history of the Four Years Diet]. 6 vols. Warsaw.

Minenko, N. A., 1971. 'Russkaia semia na Obskom Severe v. XVIII-pervoi polovine XIX veke'. *Sovietskaia Etnografiia*, 6: 119–27.

1977. 'Gorodskaia semia Zapadnoi Sibiri na rubezhe XVII–XVIII vv.' In: *Istoriia gorodov Sibiri dosovetskago perioda (XVII–nachalo XX v.)*: 175–95. Novosibirsk.

Mironov, B. N., 1977. 'Traditsionnoe demograficheskoe povedenie krestian v XIX–nachale XX'. In: A. G. Vishnevskii (ed.), *Brachnost, rozhdaenost, smertnost v Rossii i v SSSR*: 83–104. Moscow.

Mitterauer, M., 1973. 'Zur Familienstruktur in ländlichen Gebieten Österreichs im 17. Jahrhundert'. In: H. Helczmanovszki (ed.), *Beiträge zur Bevölkerungs- und Sozialgeschichte Österreichs.* Vienna.

1975a. 'Familiengrösse – Familientypen – Familienzyklus: Probleme quantitativer Auswertung von österreichischem Quellenmaterial'. *Geschichte und Gesellschaft*, 1: 226–55. Vienna.

1975b. 'Vorindustrielle Familienformen: zur Funktionsentlastung des "ganzen Hauses" im 17. und 18. Jahrhundert'. *Wiener Beiträge zur Geschichte der Neuzeit*, 2: 123ff.

1976. 'Auswirkungen von Urbanisierung und Frühindustrialisierung auf die Familienverfassung an Beispielen des österreichischen Raumes'. In: W. Conze (ed.), *Sozialgeschichte der Familie in der Neuzeit Europas.* Stuttgart.

1979. *Grundtypen alteuropäischer Sozialformen: Haus und Gemeinde in vorindustriellen Gesellschaften.* Stuttgart.

Mitterauer, M., and Kagan, A., 1982. 'Russian family structures from a central European point of view'. *Journal of Family History*, 7, 1: 103–31.

Mitterauer, M., and Sieder, R., 1977. *Vom Patriarchat zur Partnerschaft: zum Strukturwandel der Familie.* Munich. 2nd edn, 1982. Trans. as *The European Family.* Oxford, 1980.

1979. 'The developmental process of domestic groups: problems of reconstruction and possibilities of interpretation'. *Journal of Family History*, Fall: 257–84.

Mols, R., 1954–6. *Introduction à la démographie historique des villes d'Europe du XIVᵉ siècle au XVIIIᵉ siècle.* 3 vols. Louvain.

Morassi, L., 1979. 'Strutture familiari in un comune dell'Italia settentrionale alla fine del secolo XIX'. *Genus*, 35, 1–2: 197–217.

Morvay, J., 1956. *Asszonyok a nagycsaládban* [Women in large families]. Budapest.

— 1965. 'The joint family in Hungary'. In: Gy. Ortutay and T. Bodrogi (eds.), *Europa et Hungaria*. Budapest.

Mosely, P. E., 1943. 'Adaptation for survival: the Varzic zadruga'. Repr. in R. F. Byrnes (ed.), *Communal families in the Balkans: the zadruga*. Notre Dame, Ind., 1976.

— 1954. 'The distribution of the zadruga within southeastern Europe'. Repr. in R. F. Byrnes (ed.), *Communal families in the Balkans: the zadruga*. Notre Dame, Ind., 1976.

Murdock, P., 1949. *Social structure*. New York.

Öller, J. J., 1800. *Beskrifning öfwer Jemshögs Sochn i Blekinge*. Wexiö.

Onitskanskii, M. S., 1911. *O rasprostranenii kholery v Rossii*. St Petersburg.

Oosterveen, K. (ed.), 1980. *See* P. Laslett, Oosterveen, and Smith (eds.), 1980.

Ortutay, Gy., and Bodrogi, T. (eds.), 1965. *See* Morvay, 1965.

Outhwaite, R. B. (ed.), 1981. *Marriage and society: studies in the history of marriage*. London.

Ouvriers des deux mondes, 1st ser., 1–5 (1857–85); 2nd ser., 1–5 (1885–99). (Société internationale des études pratiques d'économique sociale.)

Palli, H., 1971. 'Historical demography of Estonia in the 17th–18th centuries and computers'. In: *Studia historica in honorem Hans Kruus*. Tallinn.

— 1974. 'Perede struktuurist ja selle uurimisest. Vändra kihelkonna taluperede struktuur aastal 1683'. *Eesti NSV Teaduste Akadeemia Toimetised*, 23, 1: 64–76.

Pałucki, W. (ed.), 1955–7. *See* Keckowa and Pałucki (eds.), 1955–7.

Parish, W. L., and Schwartz, M., 1972. 'Household complexity in nineteenth century France'. *American Sociological Review*, 37: 154–73.

Parker, W. N., and Jones, E. L. (eds.), 1975. *European peasants and their markets: essays in agrarian economic history*. Princeton.

Pawlik, J. (ed.), 1915. *Polskie instruktarze ekonomiczne z końca XVII i XVIII w.* [Polish economic instruction from the end of the seventeenth and the eighteenth century]. Cracow.

Perkovskii, A. L., 1977. 'Krizis demograficheskogo vosproizvodstva krepostnogo krestianstva Rossii v pervoi polovine XIX stoletiia'. In: A. G. Vishnevskii (ed.), *Brachnost, rozhdaemost, smertnost v Rossii i v SSSR*. Moscow.

Perrenoud, A., 1979. *La population Genève du sixième au début du dix-neuvième siècle*. Geneva.

Pethe, V., 1960. *See* V. M. Dandekar and Pethe, 1960.

Phillips, R., 1981. *Family breakdown in late eighteenth century France: divorces in Rouen, 1792–1803*. Oxford.

Phythian-Adams, C., 1979. *Desolation of a city: Coventry and the urban crisis of the late Middle Ages*. Cambridge.

Piepenbrock, J., 1926. *Die Entwicklung des Altenteils oder Leibzucht unter besonderer Berücksichtigung von Westfalen*. Münster.

Plakans, A., 1975a. 'Peasant farmsteads and households in the Baltic littoral, 1797'. *Comparative Studies in Society and History*, 17, 1: 2–35.

1975b. 'Seigneurial authority and peasant family life: the Baltic area in the eighteenth century'. *Journal of Interdisciplinary History*, 4: 629–54.

1977. 'Identifying kinfolk beyond the household'. *Journal of Family History*, 2, 1: 3–27.

1978a. 'Parentless children in the soul revisions: a study of methodology and social fact'. In: Ransel (ed.), 1978.

1978b. 'Population turnover in a serf estate: Autzenbach 1797–1811'. Paper, Conference on Marriage and the Family in Historical Perspective, Brigham Young University.

Pokrovsky, B., 1899. 'Influence des récoltes et des prix du blé sur le mouvement naturel de la population de la Russie'. *Bulletin de l'Institut International de Statistique*, 11, 1, II: 176–89.

Poni, C., 1978. 'Family and *podere* in Emilia Romagna'. *Journal of Italian History*, 1, 2: 201–34.

Pountney, M. T., 1971. See Hole and Pountney, 1971.

Power, E., 1924. *Medieval people*. London.

Preston, B., 1976. See Ebery and Preston, 1976.

Ransel, D. (ed.), 1978. *The family in Imperial Russia*. Urbana.

Rauscher, H., 1926. 'Volkskunde des Waldviertels'. In: E. Stepan (ed.), *Das Waldviertel*, vol. III. Vienna.

Razi, Z., 1981. 'Family, land and the village community in later medieval England'. *Past and Present*, 93: 3–36.

Rees, P. (ed.), 1977. See Hobcraft and Rees (eds.), 1977.

Revesz, L., 1976. *Der osteuropäische Bauer: seine Rechtslage im 17. und 18. Jahrhundert*. Berne.

Riche, P., 1966. 'Problèmes de démographie historique du haut moyen âge (Vᵉ–VIIIᵉ siècles)'. *Annales de Démographie Historique*: 37–55.

Richter, S., 1891. *Das bäuerliche Ausgedinge*. Prague.

Riehl, W., 1855. *Die Naturgeschichte des Volkes als Grundlage einer deutschen Sozial-Politik*, vol. II. Stuttgart.

Ring, R., 1979. 'Early medieval peasant households in central Italy'. *Journal of Family History*, 4: 2–21.

Robberstad, K., 1948. 'Litt meir um gravgangsmennene'. *Historisk Tidsskrift*: 609–12.

Robin, J., 1980. *Elmdon: continuity and change in a north-west Essex village 1861–1964*. Cambridge.

Robinson, G. T., 1967. *Rural Russia under the old regime*. Berkeley.

Rostworowski, E. (ed.), 1955–69. See Michalski, Woliński, and Rostworowski (eds.), 1955–69.

Rowntree, B. S., 1902. *Poverty: a study of town life*. London.

Runde, C. L., 1805. *Die Rechtslehre von Leibzucht oder dem Altenteile auf deutschen Bauerngütern nach gemeinen und besonderen Rechten*, vol. I. Oldenburg.

Russell, J. C., 1972. 'Population in Europe, 500–1500'. In: *Fontana Economic History of Europe*, I: 25–70. London.

Russia, Central Statistical Committee, 1862, 1863, 1865, 1871, 1877. *Spiski naselennykh mest Rossiiskoi imperii, sostavlennye i izdavaemye Tsentralnym statis-*

ticheskim komitetom Ministerstva vnutrennikh del. Riazanskaia guberniia. St Petersburg.
See also Union of Soviet Socialist Republics.

Rutkowski, J., 1956. *Studia z dziejów wsi polskiej XVI–XVIII w.* [Studies in the history of the Polish countryside from the sixteenth to the eighteenth century]. Warsaw.

Rychlikowa, I. (ed.), 1962–3. *See* Falniowska-Gradowska and Rychlikowa (eds.), 1962–3.

Sabean, D., 1976. 'Aspects of kinship behaviour and property in rural western Europe'. In: Goody, Thirsk, and Thompson (eds.), 1976.

Saito, O., 1979. 'Who worked when: life-time profiles of labour force participation in Cardington and Corfe Castle in the late eighteenth and mid-nineteenth centuries'. *Local Population Studies*, 22: 14–29.

Schlumbohm, J., 1977. *See* Kriedte, Medick, and Schlumbohm, 1977.

Schmidt, K., 1920. *Gutsübergabe und Ausgedinge: eine agrarpolitische Untersuchung mit besonderer Berücksichtigung der Alpen- und Sudentenländer.* Vienna–Leipzig.

Schmidtbauer, P., 1977. 'Daten zur historischen Demographie und Familienstruktur'. Unpublished manuscript in the library of the SSRC Cambridge Group.

1978a. 'Modell einer lokalen Krise: zur Sozialgeschichte einer Innviertler Gemeinde'. *Zeitschrift für Bayerische Landesgeschichte*, 41, 1: 219–40.

1978b. 'Zur Sozialen Wirklichkeit der Wiener Juden'. *Studia Judaica Austriaca*, 6: 57ff.

1980. 'Households and household forms of Viennese Jews in 1857'. *Journal of Family History*, 5, 4: 375–89.

Schnyder, W., 1925. *Die Bevölkerung der Stadt und Landschaft Zürich vom 14.–17. Jahrhundert.* (Schweizer Studien zur Geschichtswissenschaft, 14, 1.) Zürich.

Schofield, R., 1981. *See* Wrigley and Schofield, 1981.

Schultze, A., 1931. 'Die Rechtslage des alternden Bauers nach den altnordischen Rechten'. *Zeitschrift der Savigny Stiftung für Rechtsgeschichte, Germ. Abt.*, 51: 258–317.

Schwind, F., 1977. *Das Dorf der Eisenzeit und des frühen Mittelalters.* (Abhandlungen der Akademie der Wissenschaften in Göttingen, Phil-hist. kl., 3rd ser., 101.) Göttingen.

Scott, J., 1978. *See* L. Tilly and Scott, 1978.

Scott, S. R., 1980. *See* Michael, Fuchs, and Scott, 1980.

Semenov, P. P., 1902. *Rossiia: polnoe geograficheskoe opisanie nashogo otechestva.* 5 vols. St Petersburg.

Semevskii, V. I., 1903. *Krestiane v tsarstvovanie Imperatritsy Ekateriny II.* 2 vols. St Petersburg.

Sering, M., 1908. *Erbrecht und Agrarverfassung in Schleswig-Holstein.* Berlin.

Shanin, T., 1972. *The awkward class.* Oxford.

Sieder, R., 1977. 'Probleme des Alterns im Strukturwandel der Familie'. In: Mitterauer and Sieder, 1977.

1978. 'Strukturprobleme der ländlichen Familie im 19. Jahrhundert'. *Zeitschrift für Bayerische Landesgeschichte*, 41, 1: 173–217.

1979. *See* Mitterauer and Sieder, 1979.

Siggaard, N., 1944. 'Aftaegtskontrakter og deras Aendringer gennem Tidene'. *Ugeskrift for Landmaend*, 89: 66–9.

Skrubbeltrang, F., 1961. 'Faestegården som forsørger: aftaegt og anden forsorg i det 18. århundrede'. *Jyske Samlinger*, n.s., 5: 237–74.

Skvortsov, P., 1892. 'Itogi krestianskogo khoziaistva po zemskim statisticheskim issledovaniiam'. *Iuridicheskii Vestnik*, 29, 5: 73–83.

Smith, R. E. F., 1977. *Peasant farming in Muscovy*. Cambridge.

Smith, R. E. F. (ed.), 1966. *See* Chayanov, 1966.

Smith, R. J., 1978. 'The domestic cycle in selected commoner families in urban Japan: 1757–1858'. *Journal of Family History*, 3, 3: 219–35.

Smith, R. M., 1978. 'Population and its geography in England 1500–1730'. In: Dodgshon and Butlin (eds.), 1978.

1979a. 'Some reflections on the evidence for the origins of the "European marriage pattern" in England'. In: C. Harris (ed.), *The sociology of the family*. Keele.

1979b. 'Kin and neighbours in a thirteenth century Suffolk community'. *Journal of Family History*, 4, 3: 219–56.

1981a. 'The people of Tuscany and their families in the fifteenth century: medieval or Mediterranean?' *Journal of Family History*, 6, 1: 107–28.

1981b. 'Fertility, economy and household formation in England over three centuries'. *Population and Development Review*, 7, 4: 595–622.

1982. 'The peasant family labour farm and English medievalists'. In: R. M. Smith (ed.), 1982.

Smith, R. M. (ed.), 1980. *See* Laslett, Oosterveen, and Smith (eds.), 1980.

1982. *Land, kinship and life-cycle*. London.

Smith, T. C., 1969. 'Farm family bye-employments in pre-industrial Japan'. *Journal of Economic History*, 29, 4: 687–715.

1977. *Nakahara: family and population in a Japanese village, 1717–1830*. Stanford, Calif.

Snell, K. D. M., 1980. 'The standard of living, social relations, the family and labour mobility in south-eastern and western countries, 1700–1860'. Unpublished Ph.D. thesis, Cambridge University.

Sobczak, T. (ed.), 1958–63. *See* Baranowski, Bartyś, and Sobczak (eds.), 1958–1963.

Sogner, S., 1979. *Folkevekst og flytting*. Oslo.

Spindler, M. (ed.), 1968. *Handbuch der bayerischen Geschichte*, vol. I. Munich.

Spufford, M., 1976. 'Peasant inheritance customs and land distribution in Cambridgeshire from the sixteenth to the eighteenth centuries'. In: Goody, Thirsk, and Thompson (eds.), 1976.

Staab, F., 1975. *Untersuchungen zur Gesellschaft am Mittelrhein in der Karolingerzeit*. (Geschichtliche Landeskunde, 11.) Wiesbaden.

Starr, S. Frederick (ed.), 1972. *See* Haxthausen, 1972.

Stengel, E. E. (ed.), 1958. *Urkundenbuch des Klosters Fulda*, vol. I. (Veröffentlichungen der Historischen Kommission für Hessen und Waldeck, 10, pt 1.) Marburg.

Stepan, E. (ed.), 1926. *See* Rauscher, 1926.

Störmer, W., 1973. *Früher Adel: Studien zur politischen Führungsschicht im fränkisch-deutschen Reich vom 8. bis 11. Jahrhundert.* (Monographien zur Geschichte des Mittelalters, 6.) Stuttgart.

Stoto, M. A., 1976. *See* Barclay *et al.*, 1976.

Strods, H., 1972. *Lauksaimiecība Latvijā pārejas periodā no feodalisma uz kapitalismu.* Riga.

Struve, P., 1913. *Krepostnoe khoziaistvo.* St Petersburg.

Sturm, J., 1955. 'Romanische Personennamen in den Freisinger Traditionen'. *Zeitschrift für bayerische Landesgeschichte,* 18: 61–80.

Styś, W., 1959. *Współzależność rozwoju rodziny chłopskiej i jej gospodarstwa* [Interdependence in the development of the peasant family and its farm]. Warsaw.

Sullerot, E. (ed.), 1978. *Le fait féminin: qu'est-ce qu'une Femme?* Paris.

Švābe, A., 1965. 'Latviešu dzimta un lielğimene'. *Straumes un avoti,* 3. Lincoln, Nebr.

Svanborg, A., 1977. 'Seventy-year-old people in Gothenburg'. *Acta Medica Scandinavica,* suppl.: 5–37.

Svedberg, A., 1868. *Om de förderfliga följderna af jordbrukets betungande med sytningar.* (Folkskrifter utgifna af K. Finska hushållningssällskapet.) Turku.

Szabó, L., 1968. *Munkaszervezet és termelékenység a magyar parasztságnál a 19–20. században* [Organization of work and productivity of Hungarian peasants in the nineteenth and twentieth centuries]. Szolnok.

Szakály, F., 1970. 'Sziget mezőváros (Somogy megye) lakosságának "connumeratiója" 1551-ben' [The enumeration of the inhabitants of the market-town Sziget in Somogy county in 1551]. In: *Történeti Statisztikai Évkönyv 1967–68*: 61–133. Budapest.

Szemberg, H., 1966. *Przemiany struktury agrarnej gospodarstw chłopskich* [Changes in agrarian structure of peasant family farms]. Warsaw.

Taba, I., 1962. 'Baranya megye család és lélekszáma 1696-ban' [The number of inhabitants and families in Baranya county in 1696]. In: *Történeti Statisztikai Évkönyv 1961–1962*: 131–58. Budapest.

Taeuber, I. B., 1970. 'The families of Chinese farmers'. In: M. Freedman (ed.), *Family and kinship in Chinese society.* Stanford, Calif.

Tamásy, J., 1963. 'Az 1784–1787. évi első magyarországi népszámlálás család-és háztartásstatisztikai vonatkozásai' [Family and household – statistical results of the first census in Hungary 1784–1787]. *Demográfia,* 6, 4: 526–38.

Tarvel, E., 1964a. *Adratalupoegade olukorrast Lõuna-Eestis XVI sajandi lõpul ja XVII sajandi algul.* Tallinn.

1964b. *Folvark, pan i poddannyi: agrarnye otnosheniia v polskikh vladeniiakh na territorii iuzhnoi Estonii v konetse XVI – nachale XVII veka.* Tallinn.

1972. *Adramaa: Eesti talurahva maakasutuse ja maksustuse alused 13.–19. sajandil.* Tallinn.

Tengström, J., and Wallenius, J. F., 1819. 'Underdånig hemställan angående åtskilliga utvägar att minska missbruket med sytningar och om medel att befrämja hemmansklyvningar'. *Finska Hushållningssällskapets Handlingar,* 3: 39ff.

Thirring, G., 1935a. 'Jászberény népessége és társadalmi viszonyai II. József korában' [Population and society of Jászberény in the period of Joseph II]. *Magyar Statisztikai Szemle,* 13, 1: 1–11.

   1935b. 'Kecskemét népessége és társadalmi viszonyai II. József korában' [Population and society of Kecskemét in the period of Joseph II]. *Magyar Statisztikai Szemle,* 13, 5: 369–81.

   1935c. 'Egy alföldi falu népességi viszonyai II. József korában, Magyarcsanád' [Population and society of Magyarcsanád, a village in the Great Plain, in the period of Joseph II]. *Magyar Statisztikai Szemle,* 13, 9: 753–60.

Thirsk, J. (ed.), 1976. *See* Goody, Thirsk, and Thompson (eds.), 1976.

Thompson, E. P. (ed.), 1976. *See* Goody, Thirsk, and Thompson (eds.), 1976.

Thomson, D. W., 1980. 'Provision for the elderly in England 1830–1908'. Unpublished Ph.D. thesis, Cambridge University.

Thorner, Kerblay, and Smith (eds.), 1966. *See* Chayanov, 1966.

Thrupp, S., 1948. *The merchant class of medieval London: 1300–1500.* Chicago.

Tilly, C. (ed.), 1978. *Historical studies of changing fertility.* Princeton.

Tilly, L., and Scott, J., 1978. *Women, work, and family.* New York.

Troinitskii, A. G., 1861. *Krepostnoe naselenie v Rossii po 10-i narodnoi perepisi.* St Petersburg.

Trolle-Bonde, C., 1906. *Trolleholm förr och nu,* vol. III. Lund.

Trotzig, D., 1938. 'Ätteklubban'. *Folkminnen och folktankar,* 25: 64–9.

Trussel, T. J., 1976. *See* Barclay *et al.,* 1976.

Uibu, Kh. E., 1977. *See* Kakhk and Uibu, 1977.

Unde, D. B., n.d. *See* K. Dandekar and Unde, n.d.

Union of Soviet Socialist Republics, Gosudarstvennyi Arkhiv Riazanskoi Oblasti (GARO), Riazan. Fond 129.

   Gosudarstvennaia Biblioteka SSSR im. V. I. Lenina, Moscow, Rukopisnyi Otdel. Fond 123.

   Tsentralyni Gosudarstvennyi Arkhiv Drevnikh Aktov (TsGada), Moscow. Fond 1262, Gagarina.

   See also Russia.

United Kingdom, Office of Population Censuses and Surveys, 1975. *Census of England and Wales 1971: household composition tables,* vol. III. London.

   Parliamentary Papers, Censuses, 1852–3. (1631) LXXXV *Census of Great Britain 1851: population tables,* pt I: *Numbers of inhabitants in the years 1801, 1811, 1821, 1831, 1841 and 1851.* London.

   Parliamentary Papers, Censuses, 1863. (3221) LIII, pt I: *Census of Great Britain 1861: general report.* London.

United Nations Organization, 1973. *The determinants and consequences of population trends,* I: 347–52. New York.

1977. *United Nations demographic yearbook 1976.* New York.

United States of America, Bureau of the Census, 1977. *Current population reports,* ser. P–20. Washington, D.C.

Utterström, G., 1965. 'Two essays on population in eighteenth century Scandinavia'. In: Glass and Eversley (eds.), 1965.

Vahtre, S., 1973. *Eestimaa talurahvas hingeloenduste andmeil 1782–1858.* Tallinn.

Van't Klooster-van Wingerden, C. M., 1979. *Huishoudenssamenstelling en Samenlevingsvormen.* (Monografieen Volkstelling 1971, 11.) The Hague.

Vaughan, M., 1981. 'Which family? The problems of the reconstruction of the history of the family as an economic and cultural unit'. Unpublished paper presented to a conference at the School of Oriental and African Studies, London.

Veletskii, S. N., 1899. *Zemskaia statistika.* 2 vols. Moscow.

Verdon, M., 1979. 'Sleeping together: the dynamics of residence among the Abutia Ewe'. *Journal of Anthropological Research,* 35, 4: 401–25.

Verein für Sozialpolitik, 1883. *Bäuerliche Zustände in Deutschland.* (Schriften des Vereins für Sozialpolitik, 22–4.) Leipzig.

Veress, É., 1958. 'A jobbágycsalád szervezete a sárospataki uradalom falvaiban a 17. század közepén' [Organization of the serf family in the villages of the domain of Sárospatak in the middle of the seventeenth century]. *Történelmi Szemle,* 1, 3–4: 379–429.

1966. 'Háztartás, telek és termelés viszonya hegyaljai és bodrogközi jobbágyfalvakban a XVI. század derekán' [Relation of household, plot and production in serf villages of Hegyalja and of Bodrogköz in the middle of the sixteenth century]. In: L. Makkai (ed.), *Jobbágytelek és parasztság az örökös jobbágyság kialakulásának korszakában.* Budapest.

Vetulani, A. (ed.), 1957. *Księga sadowa Uszwi dla wsi Zawady, 1690–1788* [Records of the village court of Uszew-Zawady]. Warsaw.

1962–3. *Księgi sadowe klucza łackiego, 1526–1811* [Records of the village court of the Klucz łacki, 1526–1811]. 2 vols. Warsaw.

Vinovskis, M. (ed.), 1978. *See* Hareven and Vinovskis (eds.), 1978.

Vishnevskii, A. G. (ed.), 1977. *See* Perkovskii, 1977 *and* Mironov, 1977.

Volckamer, V. von, 1963. *Das Landgericht Pfaffenhofen und das Pfleggericht Wolnzach.* (Historischer Atlas von Bayern, Teil Altbayern, 14.) Munich.

Vyšniauskaite, A. J., 1964. 'The development of the Lithuanian peasant family'. In: *VII International Congress of Anthropological and Ethnological Sciences.* Moscow.

Wachter, K. W., with Hammel, E. A., and Laslett, P., 1978. *Statistical studies of historical social structure.* New York.

Wall, R., 1972. 'Mean household size in England from printed sources'. In: P. Laslett and Wall (eds.), 1972.

1977. 'Regional and temporal variations in English household structure from 1650'. In: Hobcraft and Rees (eds.), 1977.

1978. 'The age at leaving home'. *Journal of Family History,* 3, 2: 181–202.

1981. 'Woman alone in English society'. *Annales de Démographie Historique.*

1982a. 'Regional and temporal variation in the structure of the British household since 1851'. In: Drake and Barker (eds.), 1982.

1982b. 'Real property, marriage and children: the evidence from four pre-industrial communities'. In: R. M. Smith (ed.), 1982.

Wall, R. (ed.), 1972. *See* P. Laslett and Wall (eds.), 1972.

Walle, E. van de, 1976. 'Household dynamics in a Belgian village 1847–1866'. *Journal of Family History*, 1, 1: 80–94.

Wallenius, J. F., 1819. *See* Tengström and Wallenius, 1819.

Warnes, A. M., 1976. *See* Law and Warnes, 1976.

Wartmann, H. (ed.), 1863. *Urkundenbuch der Abtei Sanct Gallen*, vol. I. Zürich.

Watson, J. L., 1980. 'Transactions in people: the Chinese market in slaves, servants and heirs'. In: J. L. Watson (ed.), *Asian and African systems of slavery*. Oxford.

Weber, H., 1941. *Der deutsche bäuerliche Uebergabevertrag als vorweggenommene Erbfolge in den Hof: ein Beitrag zur Geschichte der bäuerlichen Hofübergabe.* Berlin.

Weiland, H. G., 1939. *Die geschichtliche Entwicklung des bäuerlichen Altenteils und seine Regelung nach dem Reichserbhofgesetz.* Emsdetten.

Weinberger, S., 1973. 'Peasant households in Provence ca. 800–1100'. *Speculum*, 48: 247–57.

Weinstein, M., 1979. *See* Goldman, Coale, and Weinstein, 1979.

Weizsäcker, W., 1951. 'Die Familia des Klosters St Emmeram in Regensburg'. *Verhandlungen des Historischen Vereins von Oberpfalz und Regensburg*, 92: 5–48.

Werner-Hasselbach, T., 1942. *Die älteren Güterverzeichnisse der Reichsabtei Fulda.* (Marburger Studien zur älteren deutschen Geschichte, 2nd ser., 7.) Marburg.

Wheaton, R. B., 1973. 'Bordeaux before the Fronde'. Unpublished Ph.D. thesis, Harvard University.

1975. 'Family and kinship in Western Europe'. *Journal of Interdisciplinary History*, 5, 4: 601–28.

Widemann, J. (ed.), 1943. *Die Traditionen des Hochstifts Regensburg und des Klosters S. Emmeram.* (Quellen und Erörterungen zur bayerischen Geschichte, n.s., 8). Munich.

Wierzbicka-Michalska, K., 1959. 'Małżeństwa wśród chłopów w drugiej połowie XVIII w.' [Marriages among peasants in the second half of the eighteenth century]. *Kultura i Społeczeństwo*, 3, 1: 153–74.

Williamson, J., 1980. *See* Lindert and Williamson, 1980.

Wohlin, N. R., 1910. *Faran af bondeklassens undergräfvande i sammanhang med de gamla arfvejordåskådningarnas upplösning, emigrationen och bondejordens mobilisering.* Stockholm.

Wolf, E. R., 1974. *See* Cole and Wolf, 1974.

Woliński, J. (ed.), 1955–69. *See* Michalski, Woliński, and Rostworowski (eds.), 1955–69.

Woude, A. M. van der, 1972. 'Variations in the size and structure of the household in the Netherlands'. In: P. Laslett and Wall (eds.), 1972.

Wrightson, K., 1979. *See* Levine and Wrightson, 1979.

Wrigley, E. A., 1966. 'Family limitation in pre-industrial England'. *Economic History Review*, 19: 82–109.

    1978. 'Fertility strategy for the individual and the group'. In: C. Tilly (ed.), 1978.

    1981. 'Marriage, fertility and population growth in eighteenth-century England'. In: Outhwaite (ed.), 1981.

Wrigley, E. A., and Schofield, R., 1981. *The population history of England 1541–1871: a reconstruction*. London.

Yamamura, K., 1977. *See* Hanley and Yamamu'77.

Young, C. M., 1974. 'Ages, reasons and sex differences for children leaving home: observations from survey data for Australia'. *Journal of Marriage and the Family*: 769–77.

    1975. 'Factors associated with the timing and duration of the leaving home stage of the family life cycle'. *Population Studies*, 29: 61–73.

Yver, J., 1953–4. 'Les deux groupes de coutumes du Nord'. Pts I and II. *Revue du Nord*, 35, 140: 197–220; 36, 141: 5–36.

    1966. *Egalité entre héritiers et exclusion des enfants dotés: essai de géographie coutumière*. (Société d'histoire du droit Publications.) Sirey.

Zimányi, V., 1968. *A rohonc-szalonaki uradalom és jobbágysága a XVI–XVII. században* [The domain of Rohonc-Szalonak and its serfs in the sixteenth and seventeenth centuries). Budapest.

Index

children (*cont.*)
  conjugal family units, distribution in,
    187
  definition, 74, 75n, 93, 236n, 237–8,
    369, 383n, 424, 496n
  employed, 540, 544, 546
  foster, 34, 178, 237, 322–4, 328–9,
    332–3, 335, 369
  households, distribution in, 75–6, 83,
    90, 158–9, 296–9, 355
  households with, 50n, 102, 369–70
  independent, 178, 181
  industrialization and, 370, 373
  kin groups, distribution in, 187, 201
  kinsfolk of, 194–5
  leaving household, 16, 95–7, 158–9,
    163, 178, 192, 236, 246, 326, 335–6,
    340, 342, 369, 373, 411, 422, 453,
    480, 484–5, 493, 506; occupation
    and, 239, 381, 389, 398–400, 402–6
  married (*see also* generational conflict),
    285; aid, mutual, 17–18, 22–8, 60,
    250–3, 256; co-resident with
    parents, 33, 132, 170, 281, 299,
    366–7, 487, 532; dependent, 18, 23,
    69–70; household systems and, 69,
    83
  mean age, 369–71
  of inmates, 350–2
  of servants, 178, 354, 362
  role, 178, 339, 348
  sex ratio, 75, 79, 83, 89n, 90, 237, 409
  step, 46, 74, 140, 210, 328–9, 342,
    369, 381, 397n, 466n, 477
China, 21, 24, 31, 65, 81–3, 98
church, 58, 103, 218–19, 254–5
Clayworth, 42, 198
clothiers, 537
co-farmers, 207, 210, 214–16
Cogenhoe, 198
co-heirs, 256, 267–8, 272, 274, 277
cohorts (*see also* cross-sectional analysis;
    life cycle), 4, 69n, 73, 172, 194, 197,
    203, 397n, 463n
Cole, J. W., 313n
Colorno, 37, 40
Colyton, 15
commercial employment, *see*
    employment
communal obligations, 22, 62–3
commune, see *mir*
compagnons, 477, 488–9
conjugal family units (*see also* family,
    nuclear), 89n, 124, 145, 177–8, 187,
    239–42, 245, 289, 295–8
conscription, *see* men, recruitment of

consumers/workers ratio, 154, 156–8,
    268–70
consumption (*see also* pensions), 268–70
  unit, *see* household, definition
Corfe Castle, 391n, 494, 546
corvée, *see* serfs, labour services
cottagers, 17, 210, 311, 314–16, 325,
    327, 527, 540
cotters, 9, 211–15, 282, 301, 349
  conjugal family units: mean size, 295
  definitions, 207, 286, 294
  households: composition, 295–6, 351,
    364, 367; size of, 289–90, 295
cousins, 90, 130, 134, 195
Coventry, 539–44, 547, 549
crafts, 67, 93, 97, 546
craftsmen (*see also* artisans), 14, 27, 29,
    31, 62, 109, 156–61, 509, 540
cripples, 155, 157, 416n
Croatia (*see also* Hungary), 91–2, 101,
    281–2, 301–2
crofters, 61
cross-sectional analysis (*see also* cohorts;
    life cycle)
  life cycle and, 397n, 463n, 472, 535
Cuesenier, J., 33
cultural factors, *see* norms
Czap, P., 2, 16, 61n, 88, 89n, 90–2, 98,
    105–51, 179, 281, 516, 532, 549
Czechoslovakia, 21, 48, 169, 251n,
    264–5, 268, 271, 557

Dalle, D., 409
Danhieux, L., 4, 32, 380n, 409–20,
    421n
Daudzeva, 216
daughters (*see also* children; offspring),
    11, 23, 32, 34, 208, 246, 319,
    353–6, 391, 416
  adult, 44, 389, 400, 411
  age groups, 393, 398–400, 402–5,
    456–9, 461, 482, 485
  aid, mutual, 12, 25
  in-law, 52–3, 79, 89n, 134–5, 191,
    193–4, 260–1, 341n, 499–501
  leaving household, 398–400, 402–6,
    422, 485
  married, 198, 261, 405n
Davis, J., 12, 33, 60n, 407n
day labourers, *see* labourers
death rate (*see also* mortality), 82, 305
deaths, 47, 135, 138, 142, 165, 170, 337,
    340, 477
demographic factors
  family farm and, 154
  holdings, size of, and, 154, 164–5